Medical Care Law

Edward P. Richards III, JD, MPH
Professor of Law
University of Missouri Kansas City
School of Law
Kansas City, Missouri

Katharine C. Rathbun, MD, MPH
Preventive Medicine
Kansas City, Missouri

AN ASPEN PUBLICATION®
Aspen Publishers, Inc.
Gaithersburg, Maryland
1999

Library of Congress Cataloging-in-Publication Data

Richards, Edward P.
Medical care law / Edward P. Richards III, Katharine C. Rathbun.
p. cm.
Includes bibliographical references and index.
ISBN 0-8342-1603-5
1. Medical laws and legislation—United States. I. Rathbun,
Katharine C. II. Title.
KF3821.R53 1999
344.73′041—dc21
99-22815
CIP

About Aspen Publishers • For more than 35 years, Aspen has been a leading professional publisher in a variety of disciplines. Aspen's vast information resources are available in both print and electronic formats. We are committed to providing the highest quality information available in the most appropriate format for our customers. Visit Aspen's Internet site for more information resources, directories, articles, and a searchable version of Aspen's full catalog, including the most recent publications: **http://www.aspenpublishers.com**
Aspen Publishers, Inc. • The hallmark of quality in publishing
Member of the worldwide Wolters Kluwer group.

Editorial Services: Denise Hawkins Coursey
Library of Congress Catalog Card Number: 99-22815
ISBN: 0-8342-1603-5

Printed in the United States of America

1 2 3 4 5

Table of Contents

Preface ix

Chapter 1—Organization of the U.S. Legal System 1
    Introduction 1
    Federalism 1
    Checks and Balances 2
    State versus Federal Powers. 3
    The Adversarial System. 6
    The Role of Judges. 7
    Private Alternatives to the Courts—Alternative Dispute Resolution (ADR) 9

Chapter 2—Civil Claims and Monetary Damages. 12
    Introduction 12
    Types of Claims 12
    Procedural Aspects of Civil Actions 14
    Proving Medical Malpractice. 15
    Establishing the Standard of Care 19
    Nonmonetary Remedies. 22
    Monetary Damages 23
    Products Liability. 30
    Defensive Medicine 34

Chapter 3—Criminal Law Rights and Violations 38
    Introduction 38
    Commonalities in Criminal and Administrative Law 38
    The Constitutional Basis for Criminal Law. 39
    Applying the Constitutional Protections 41
    Investigation of the Criminal Case 44
    Federal Fraud Prosecutions 45
    Antitrust Laws 52
    Technical Fraud: RICO Violations 54
    The Federal Sentencing Guidelines and Compliance 57
    Appendix 3–A: Responding to Government Investigations 63

Chapter 4—Administrative Law and Violations...................................... **66**
    Introduction... 66
    Establishing Agencies... 66
    Agency Procedure... 69
    Judicial Review of Agency Actions 74
    Emergency Care and EMTALA 76
    Appendix 4–A: 42 U.S.C.A. sec 1395dd Examination and Treatment
       for Emergency Medical Conditions and Women in Labor................. 78
    Appendix 4–B: 42 CFR sec 489.24 Special Responsibilities of
       Medicare Hospitals in Emergency Cases 82
    Appendix 4–C: Interpretive Guidelines—Responsibilities of Medicare
       Participating Hospitals in Emergency Cases....................... 87

Chapter 5—Civil and Criminal Litigation.. **108**
    Introduction... 108
    Prefiling... 108
    Pretrial.. 112
    Which Cases Go To Trial? 118
    Admitting Evidence 119
    Posttrial.. 126
    The Cost of Litigation... 126
    Emotional Risks of a Trial 129
    Appendix 5–A: Guidelines for Expert Witness Testimony in Medical
       Liability Cases... 133

Chapter 6—The Law and Lawyers.. **137**
    Introduction... 137
    Legal Relationships... 137
    Working with Lawyers 139
    Clash of Cultures... 140
    Legal Education 141
    How To Approach the Law and Lawyers......................... 143
    Conflicts of Interest.. 144
    Paying for Legal Services 146
    Being an Effective Client 149
    Preventive Law and Compliance 150
    Confidentiality and Legal Privilege 151
    Conclusions... 155

Chapter 7—Medical Records **157**
    Introduction... 157
    A Historical Perspective 157
    Legal Uses of Medical Records 158
    Medical Office and Clinic Records.............................. 161
    Pediatric Records 168
    Hospital Medical Records...................................... 170
    Electronic Medical Records 170

Chapter 8—The Physician–Patient Relationship **173**
    Introduction 173
    Managed Care and the Professional Relationship 173
    Establishing the Relationship 174
    Referral and Consultation 180
    Limited Duty Relationships 190
    Contractual and Statutory Duties To Treat 192
    Expectation of Continued Treatment 194
    Terminating the Relationship 194
    Documenting the Termination 197
    Telemedicine and Internet Medicine 197

Chapter 9—Consent to Medical Treatment **205**
    Introduction 205
    Battery—No Consent 205
    Exceptions to the Requirement of Consent 206
    Informed Consent 209
    Conflicts of Interest and Informed Consent 217
    Consent for Minors 219
    Consent for Medical Research 223
    Documenting Consent 228
    Proxy Consent 230
    Guardianships 232
    Refusal of Care and Termination of Life Support 234
    Assisted Suicide 245

Chapter 10—Team Care and Managed Care **253**
    Introduction 253
    The Changing Nature of Physicians' Practices 254
    Fiduciary Duty 257
    ERISA Health Plans 260
    Team Care Issues 263
    Supervising NPPs 268
    Supervising Medical Students and Residents 274
    Medical Director's Liability 281
    Business Risks in Dealing with MCOs 282
    Appendix 10–A: Disease-Specific Protocols 290

Chapter 11—Peer Review and Deselection **291**
    Introduction 291
    Peer Review 291
    Legal Climate for Peer Review 293
    The Federal Peer Review Law 296
    Good Faith or Objective Standard? 302
    Documenting the Peer Review Process 305
    Deselection 305

Chapter 12—Public Health and Communicable Disease Control **309**
   Introduction... 309
   The History of Public Health Authority 310
   Legal Standards for Public Health Authority 311
   Disease Control... 312
   Immunizations... 320
   Food Sanitation... 324
   Environmental Health 325
   HIV/AIDS 325
   Vital Statistics... 327
   Law Enforcement Reporting 331
   Appendix 12–A: National Vaccine Injury Compensation Program Vaccine
     Injury Table... 340

Chapter 13—Family Planning, Adoption, and Surrogacy **345**
   Introduction... 345
   Ethical Dilemmas in Family Planning 345
   Taking a Sexual History 348
   Contraception 349
   Sterilization... 353
   Abortion 357
   Adoption and Parental Rights 361
   Surrogate Parenthood 368

Chapter 14—Obstetrics **378**
   Introduction... 378
   Genetic Counseling... 378
   Fertility Treatment 384
   A Structured Approach to Obstetric Care 389
   The Birth Plan... 392
   Evaluating the Mother's Medical Condition 394
   Medical Interventions 396
   Home Deliveries 398
   Working with Midwives 399
   Behavioral Risks in Pregnancy 401
   Obstetrics Risk Management 403

Chapter 15—Occupational Medicine and Disability Law **411**
   Introduction... 411
   Legal and Ethical Problems in Occupational Medicine 412
   Workers' Compensation 415
   Records 417
   Dealing with OSHA 417
   Drug Testing 428
   Occupational Medicine for Health Care Organizations 429
   The Americans with Disabilities Act 430
   ADA-Defined Disability... 432

Preemployment Medical Examinations 434
The Legal Risks of the ADA 437
Disability Insurance Evaluations 439
Determining Disability: Workers' Compensation versus ADA 443
Communicable Diseases in the Workplace 444
The Elements of a Communicable Disease Policy 448

Chapter 16—Institutional Medicine **459**
Introduction 459
The Prison Doctor 459
The Team Doctor 464
Screening for Participation 467
The School Doctor 467

Appendix A—Glossary **474**

Table of Cases **494**

Index **499**

Preface

Medical Care Law is written for health care practitioners, executive personnel who oversee patient care, and attorneys who work with health care clients and need guidance in areas outside their expertise. The authors are a unique team of a practicing physician with extensive experience in medical administration and a law professor with a background in medical education and law practice. The result is a book written in plain language that addresses the theoretical and practical legal issues facing health care practitioners.

The book discusses both legal theory and practical strategies for recognizing and avoiding legal problems. While *Medical Care Law* discusses the traditional medical legal problems such as malpractice litigation, it stresses the changes in the legal and medical landscapes that pose new risks to health care practitioners. The most important medical change is the shift from health care practitioners working for small, physician-controlled businesses or hospitals to practitioners working for large corporations, either as direct employees or as contractors who are tightly tied to the corporations. The major legal change is the shift in the primary legal concern from medical malpractice to a broad range of legal issues, including antidiscrimination laws and federal administrative and criminal law. Many health care providers, administrators, and even their lawyers have been prosecuted for health care–related crimes. More than a billion dollars in fines have been paid, health care businesses have

been closed, and several physicians and health care administrators have gone to jail.

The primary goals of *Medical Care Law* are to improve health care practitioners' peace of mind about the law and to encourage better medical-legal decision making. Many people involved in health care, including some attorneys, have begun to see the law as a random force that punishes without reason. This fosters anxiety and leads to practices that increase legal risks, rather than decreasing them. Most troubling, this anxiety can poison the relationship between health care practitioners and their patients, thereby impairing the quality of care. The authors believe that a better knowledge of the law will make health care practitioners more comfortable with their legal duties and help them avoid legal problems, while better serving patients. Even in areas where the law is not always fair, understanding the process can make a stressful experience more bearable.

Medical Care Law is extensively indexed and cross-referenced to allow it to be used as a reference. However, the book will be most valuable when it is read as a whole, starting at the beginning. Many concepts that are introduced in the early chapters on the law are developed in more detail later for specific practice areas. Most important, reading the entire book will give health care practitioners a comprehensive picture of the law and of how it is applied by lawyers and the courts. This is important because lawyering and the legal process are very different from providing medical care and working with health care institutions. Many conflicts and misunderstandings between health care practitioners and lawyers are due to these different ways of approaching problems. *Medical Care Law* explains the basis for these differences and illustrates them with examples drawn from real situations.

Medical Care Law is not a self-help legal guide or a substitute for an attorney's advice when health care practitioners face specific legal problems. However, health care practitioners must learn basic legal principles themselves. They cannot rely exclusively on attorneys to guide them, in the same way that it is now recognized that patients must learn about their own medical conditions and take personal responsibility for decisions about their health. This has been emphasized in recent criminal prosecutions where defendants have been convicted despite the defense that they were following an attorney's advice. The final responsibility for complying with these laws always rests with the health care practitioner. The book's objective is to help health care practitioners develop legal common sense and the ability to understand when they can safely act on their own knowledge and when they must get expert help. The basic lesson of *Medical Care Law* is that it is better to get help before you are in legal trouble. While this has always been true, it takes on special significance now that trouble means more than being a defendant in a medical malpractice lawsuit and includes possible criminal prosecution and imprisonment.

No work of manageable length can claim to be comprehensive on a subject as broad as medical law. *Medical Care Law* provides a general introduction to the subject and extensive annotations and bibliographies for readers who want to explore given areas in more depth. Since *Medical Care Law* is an interdisciplinary work, these references include both medical and legal sources, including health care practice materials. *Medical Care Law* does not provide guidance on specific state law issues. While much of the law that governs health care is federal, and thus applies uniformly in all states, there are significant variations between states on matters such as the standards for negligence, materials protected from discovery in court proceedings, and laws on the delegation and scope of medical practice. In some areas, such as drug laws, states differ so much that behavior that is encouraged in one state may be illegal in another. *Medical Care Law* identifies many situations where health care practitioners must seek specific state law advice.

CHAPTER 1

Organization of the U.S. Legal System

HIGHLIGHTS

- The United States divides legal powers between the state and federal governments.
- Medical care is regulated by both federal and state laws.
- State laws on medical care vary greatly and are sometimes contradictory between states.
- Health care practitioners must know the laws of the states where they practice.

INTRODUCTION

From the perspective of a health care practitioner, it is misleading to refer to the U.S. legal system as if it were one seamless entity. The United States has 50 state legal systems and one federal legal system, and each system has three major subdivisions. Individual health care practitioners have to be aware of the laws of the state they practice in and the federal laws applicable to their practice. A national corporate health care provider must deal with the federal rules and with the laws of every state it does business in. What is most surprising to a layperson is that these state laws can be dramatically different, with some states criminalizing what other states encourage.

The purpose of this chapter is to review the basic organization of the U.S. legal systems and to explain how they interrelate. This will help the reader in subsequent chapters, which discuss different parts of the system in detail. The key point

to remember from this chapter is that health care practitioners face multiple sources of law. The legislatures and agencies promulgating these laws and regulations do not necessarily coordinate or communicate with each other and, in some circumstances, they have conflicting expectations.

FEDERALISM

The American legal system was shaped during the period when the colonies were governed by England. Each of the original 13 colonies had its own government and colonial governor and answered independently to the Crown. With the Declaration of Independence, they became separate nations with complete control over their legal affairs. They first joined together under the Articles of Confederation to fight the Revolutionary War. This was a very weak federation because the colonies did not want to give up any of their powers. They came close to losing the war because the

---

Source: Reprinted with permission from E.P. Richards, Overview of U.S. Legal System, in *A Practical Guide to Food and Drug Law and Regulation*, K. Pina and W. Pines, eds., © 1998, FDLI.

central government could not force the individual colonies to provide troops and supplies. This experience caused the colonies to realize that they could not stand against the European powers without a stronger central government. The result was the U.S. Constitution, in which the federal government was given the power to deal with foreign governments and to resolve disputes between the states. The states retained many powers, including the right to run their state governments with only limited interference from the federal government. Although the federal government has inexorably increased its power at the expense of the states, the states still retain substantial power, especially in regard to health care delivery.

CHECKS AND BALANCES

The founders were very concerned that the president not become a king. To prevent this, they divided the federal government into three branches with overlapping authority. Their intention was that each branch would need to cooperate with the others, and that a single branch could not become too powerful because the other branches would check its grab for power. These three branches are the legislative branch (Congress), the executive branch (President), and the judicial branch (Supreme Court). The state governments generally have the same organizational structure, although some states make one branch of the government much stronger than the others. Whereas this chapter focuses on the federal system, the same principles apply to the states.

The Legislative Branch

Congress has two houses: the Senate and the House of Representatives. These houses have different procedural rules, and their members serve terms of different lengths. Senators were originally chosen by state legislatures, but now both senators and representatives are popularly elected. Reflecting the original compromise between the large states and the small states, each state has two senators, at least one representative, and each

state has as many more representatives as its share of the national population, for a total of 435 representatives. Senators are elected from the entire state, and representatives are elected by districts, if the state has more than one representative. The districts for representatives are redrawn every 10 years after the national census.

Congress is the only branch of government that can authorize the spending of government funds and the imposition of taxes. Each proposed law (bill) must be passed by both houses of Congress. The president can veto legislation he or she does not like, and Congress can override a presidential veto only by a two-thirds majority vote of both houses. The president also can propose legislation and does so each year when he or she presents the proposed budget. Ultimately, however, it is Congress that passes laws. To keep Congress from becoming too powerful, the Constitution gave the power to enforce the laws to the president.

The Executive Branch

The President is head of the executive branch and is charged with enforcing the laws passed by Congress. In the modern federal government, the president acts through the agencies that make up the executive branch. These include the Department of Health and Human Services (DHHS), the Department of Justice (DOJ), the Department of Labor, the Department of Commerce, and several others. The heads of these departments are members of the president's cabinet. They are political appointees that the president may remove at will, but the Senate must confirm the president's appointments to the cabinet. Many important health care agencies, including the Food and Drug Administration (FDA), the Health Care Financing Administration, and the Office of the Inspector General (OIG), which investigates Medicare/Medicaid fraud, are part of DHHS. The heads of these units are also political appointees who are selected by the Secretary of DHHS.

These cabinet-level agencies are created by Congress, and their powers are limited to those given by Congress in the laws that empower the agency to act. There are also independent agencies, such as the Securities and Exchange Commission (SEC) and the Federal Trade Commission (FTC), which are governed by appointed boards whose members have staggered terms. The president can replace board members only when their terms expire. These agencies typically are charged with politically sensitive enforcement.

The Judicial Branch

The federal court system has three levels. The first level is the federal district courts. Most lawsuits brought in the federal system start in the district court (although some go directly from state courts to the U.S. Supreme Court). There are several hundred district courts spread among 94 districts. In general, the case must be brought in the district court that is geographically related to the defendant or where the incident occurred. The choice of court is not a neutral decision. Districts differ in the way the judges apply the law and the willingness of their juries to award damages.

The second level is the federal courts of appeals. As the name suggests, those who believe that the district court has misapplied the law or abused its discretion in the handling of their case appeal to these courts. District courts are grouped together into 13 circuits, each with several judges who sit in panels of three, or *en banc* (all together) to hear the cases appealed from the district courts within the circuit. The appeals courts within a circuit attempt to apply the law consistently within their circuit. Although they try to maintain consistency with the other circuits, they are bound only by the Congress and by the U.S. Supreme Court, not the holding of the other circuits.

The third level is the U.S. Supreme Court. Some types of cases may be brought directly in the Supreme Court, but most travel from the federal district court through a circuit court of appeals, to the Supreme Court or from a state supreme court to the U.S. Supreme Court. The Supreme Court has four primary roles: determining if acts of the U.S. Congress are constitutional; reviewing state laws and court decisions for conflicts with the Constitution and acts of Congress; adjudicating conflicts between the states; and re-

solving conflicts between the federal circuit courts of appeals. The Supreme Court reviews only laws or court decisions that are contested in a court. It does not provide advisory opinions on the constitutionality of proposed state or federal laws. Even with this limited scope of review, the Supreme Court can decide only a small percentage of the cases that are presented to it each year. Its decision not to review a case, which allows the lower court's decision to stand, influences precedent nearly as much as the cases in which it issues an opinion. For this reason, the Supreme Court devotes substantial resources to sorting through the thousands of appeals cases presented each year.

Not every case may be brought in federal court. The case must involve federal statutes or regulations, constitutional rights, suits between states, or suits between citizens of different states. Medical malpractice cases are usually tried in state court unless one of the defendants is an employee of the federal government or the parties live in different states. Cases involving constitutional issues such as the right of privacy are brought in the federal courts. Cases involving antitrust law, racketeering law, and Medicare/Medicaid laws are brought in the federal courts because these are federal laws. A case originally brought in federal court may be sent back to the state court if the judge determines that it does not involve a federal issue. Alternatively, a case filed in state court may be sent (removed) to federal court if substantial federal questions arise as the case proceeds.

STATE VERSUS FEDERAL POWERS

Determining whether state or federal law takes precedence in a given situation was a central debate among the drafters of the U.S. Constitution, and it continues to be a critical legal issue. Some powers are reserved to the states, in other areas the Congress can overrule state law, and in some areas neither the states nor the Congress may freely make law. The Constitution determines which sovereign, if any, may make laws on a topic. The problem is that the Constitution is a general document, drafted over 200 years ago. Fortunately, the Constitution created the U.S. Supreme Court as a referee between the Congress and the states. Shortly after its creation, the Supreme Court reserved to itself the right to determine the meaning of the Constitution. It is through this power of interpretation that the Court can declare that a law is unconstitutional—that is, that it violates the protections that are part of the Constitution.

Consistent with the states' desire for the federal government to deal with foreign powers and to control disputes between the states, the Constitution gives the federal government sole authority over the regulation of interstate commerce, foreign affairs, and the power to declare war. Amendments adopted after the Civil War gave the federal government additional powers to protect individual rights. The remaining powers are either shared with, or retained solely by the states. In some areas this sharing of power can result in a health care practitioner facing both state and federal sanctions for a given activity. For example, the federal law criminalizes kickbacks to affect the referral of Medicare patients. Some states also criminalize these same violations. A health care practitioner who paid such kickbacks could be prosecuted by both the federal and state governments for the same transactions (see Chapter 3). Health law issues usually involve the federal power to regulate interstate commerce, and the important shared power is the police power to protect the public health and safety.

Regulation of Commerce

Most of the laws passed by the modern Congress are rooted in the Commerce Clause of the Constitution. The Supreme Court has ruled that the constitutional definition of interstate commerce is very broad: anything that moves between the states, or any business that uses raw materials that come from out of state are considered interstate commerce. For example, a barbecue restaurant whose only customers were local instate residents was found to be involved in interstate commerce because it bought food and condiments that originated outside the state. Although the delivery of medical services to individual patients is a local activity, everything that health care practi-

tioners use, from drugs to bandages to the paper that the medical records are written on, comes from other states. The courts have repeatedly found health care businesses to be subject to regulation as interstate commerce.

Although the states have ceded the power to regulate interstate commerce to the federal government, they retained, via their police powers, the right to regulate any activity that poses a threat to the public health or safety of their citizens. Thus, state laws that seek to ban the import of milk from outside the state to protect local dairies are an unconstitutional attempt to control trade. In contrast, state laws that focus on consumer protection, such as requiring the sanitary inspection of imported milk and banning the import of contaminated milk, are constitutional, provided they also apply to milk produced within the state. This distinction between laws affecting commerce and laws affecting health and safety is important to health care practitioners because the regulation of the practice of medicine is considered a health and safety issue and thus reserved to the states as a police power.

The Police Power

Police power is the right to protect the country and its population from threats to the public health and safety. The term "police power" predates the development of organized police forces, which did not develop until the postcolonial period. In the colonial period, police power was used to control nuisances, such as tanneries that fouled the air and water in towns, to prevent the sale of bad food, and to quarantine persons who were infected with communicable diseases. Many of the colonies had active boards of health to administer the police power. This was one of the main governmental functions in the colonial period.

Under the Constitution, the states retained much of their police power but share the right to regulate health and safety issues with the federal government. Examples of the federal use of the police power are food and drug regulations, environmental preservation laws, and workplace safety laws. The states have companion laws in most of these areas, plus local public health enforcement such as restaurant inspections, communicable disease control, and drinking water sanitation. In most cases, the states share jurisdiction with the federal government and the courts will enforce whichever is the more strict law. As discussed in Chapter 12, state and local public health laws are exercises of the police power.

Federal Preemption

Given the broad sweep of federal legislation and the activities of 50 state legislatures, it is inevitable that there will be conflicts between state and federal law. If there is a conflict, the Constitution provides that federal law preempts the conflicting state law unless it is an area specifically reserved to the states. These conflicts arise in two ways: explicit or implicit preemption. Explicit preemption occurs when Congress passes a law that explicitly reserves a given area of legislation to the federal government. There are several important areas of explicit federal preemption in health care. One example is the federal law that specifies the necessary labeling for medical devices and limits what additional requirements a state may impose without FDA permission. When Massachusetts passed a law requiring more information on hearing aid labels, a federal court barred enforcement of the law. Perhaps the most controversial is the Employment Retirement Income Security Act (ERISA), which preempts state regulation of many types of employer-provided health insurance plans.

Federal law implicitly preempts a state's right to regulate if the federal government so completely controls the area that there is no room for state regulation. Federal regulation of television and radio, both intrinsically interstate activities because of the potential for their signals to cross state lines, leaves no room for state laws governing electronic communications. The FDA regulations on the approval, manufacture, labeling, and promotion of prescription drugs are so comprehensive as to leave little room for state regulation.

In some cases, federal law also preempts private lawsuits brought under state law. The Cigarette Labeling Act provided that states cannot require more or different health warnings on a cigarette package than those required by federal law. The Supreme Court found that this preempted state court lawsuits by smokers who claimed that the cigarettes were defective because the packages did not carry adequate warnings (the tobacco litigation has been based on fraudulently concealing the risks of smoking). As discussed in Chapter 12, federal law also preempts certain lawsuits alleging vaccine-related injuries and substitutes an administrative compensation fund for possible state tort recoveries.

Limits to Federal Power

Federal power is limited. If there is no interstate commerce involved and the matter does not involve individual rights under the Constitution, the states have the right to control their affairs. The federal government also has very limited authority to commandeer state personnel to enforce federal law. If the federal government wants to regulate an area that is reserved to the states, or does not have the funds to take a specific action with a federal agency, it can provide the states with a financial incentive to encourage them to follow federal guidelines. When Congress wanted the states to pass laws requiring people in cars to wear seatbelts, it told the states to pass seatbelt laws or lose some of their federal highway construction money. The Medicaid program is a state–federal partnership in which the federal government controls actions of state personnel through restrictions on the federal matching money.

The State Court System

The state legal systems are quite diverse. Many predate the formation of the United States. The East Coast states derive their law from the English common law, many of the western states were influenced by the Spanish civil law, Louisiana follows the French civil law, and Texas entered the Union as an independent nation with a strong Spanish and Mexican heritage.

Despite the diverse backgrounds, the state court systems tend to follow the three levels of the federal courts. The levels have different names, but the process of starting in a trial court, progressing to an appeals court, and ending up in a state supreme court is common to most of the states. In some cases that involve federal laws or constitutional rights, it is possible to appeal the state supreme court decision directly to the U.S. Supreme Court.

With these exceptions, most litigation is brought directly in the state courts. Even in medical malpractice cases brought in the federal courts, the federal court will apply state law unless the case involves a specific federal statute or a constitutional right. For example, if a Veterans Administration physician working in Maryland is sued for medical malpractice, the case would be brought in federal court because the physician is an employee of the government. The federal court would then apply Maryland's law to determine if the physician was negligent.

One of the difficulties in this book is that the laws vary greatly among the states. This is most pronounced in laws that govern financial matters and tax, but it extends to some of the laws that affect medical practice. For example, in some states, hypodermic syringes are a prescription item. Possessing them without the requisite prescription violates the state's drug paraphernalia law. In other states, these same syringes are legal to buy without a prescription and may be possessed without violating the law.

THE ADVERSARIAL SYSTEM

The United States uses two different approaches to finding the facts in legal proceedings. The courts use an adversarial approach, and administrative law systems (state and federal agencies) use an inquisitorial approach. Several other countries use the inquisitorial approach in their courts. In both systems the opposing attorneys are charged with fighting for their clients; the difference is in the role of the judge.

The United States uses the adversarial system in its courts. The opposing attorneys have primary responsibility for controlling the development and presentation of the lawsuit. The attorneys may not lie but have no duty to volunteer facts that do not support their client's case. The judge acts as a referee, seeing that the rules of civil procedure are followed, especially the rules of evidence that concern the information that the jury is allowed to see. Neither the judge nor the jury is expected to have any special knowledge of the matters before the court. They are to base their judgment only on the materials presented by the attorneys. In many cases the attorneys will ask that persons with knowledge of the matter before the court be struck from the jury panel for fear of bias. The premise of the adversarial system is that each attorney, through discovery and courtroom confrontation, will flush out the facts concealed by the opposing side. The judge's role is to exclude questionable information, but the judge has little power to bring out information that both sides' attorneys choose to conceal.

In an inquisitorial system, the judge may question witnesses and inquire into the presentation of the case and its underlying facts. The judge may be an expert in the subject matter and may also have independent staff to investigate the case. There is less emphasis on excluding evidence, but the judge will tell the jury (if there is one) which evidence to ignore and which to give special credence. This gives the judge the ability to control the case and to ensure that justice (in a societal rather than a personal sense) is done. The attorneys in an inquisitorial system still endeavor to present the facts of a case in the light most favorable to their clients, but they are not permitted to withhold facts that are material to a case.

Supporters of the adversarial system argue that the competition between the opposing attorneys is a better guarantee of truth than inquiries by an impartial judge. This ideal is seldom achieved. In many cases, particularly those that involve complex or technological or scientific issues, truth becomes secondary to the theater presented by an effective, well-financed advocate. This is an especially difficult problem in criminal law. Most criminal defendants are poor and cannot afford expensive trial preparation. Even when the state provides an attorney to an indigent defendant, that attorney is usually not provided with enough money to hire experts and to properly prepare the case. It is only in the high profile cases such as the Oklahoma bombing case that the state really pays enough to the appointed counsel to allow the level of preparation and presentation afforded to wealthy defendants.

The greatest weakness of the adversarial system is in the resolution of complex disputes involving scientific or statistical evidence. The evidence in such disputes cannot be effectively evaluated by a judge and jury with no knowledge of the underlying subject matter or scientific analysis in general. This makes the litigation of medical malpractice and other technical health care cases, such as allegations that drugs or biomaterials are toxic, very problematic. It is for this reason that federal regulatory agencies that deal with technical matters use an inquisitorial method with expert judges and staff.

THE ROLE OF JUDGES

A current debate in our society is whether judges make law, and, if they do, whether that is their proper role. There is an underlying assumption that making law is a new role for judges and reflects a liberal bias in the judiciary. Common law judges were said to interpret law implicit in the statutes or precedent cases. In this sense, they found law rather than made it. It was this process of interpretation that gave life to the common law. Most critically, in the colonial period England had no equivalent to the U.S. Supreme Court. Parliament and the king had final authority and could overrule the courts. In the U.S. constitutional system, the Supreme Court can overrule both the president and Congress. Judges in the United States today make law just as surely as do legislators.

The difference between finding and making law may seem inconsequential, but it has profound implications. The Constitution prohibits ex post facto laws—laws that punish past conduct that was allowed at the time. This means that if a state passes a law making it a criminal offense to prescribe amphetamines, that law cannot be applied to allow the prosecution of physicians who wrote prescriptions for amphetamines before the effective date of the law. However, if a judge finds a common law rule, such as an obligation to obtain informed consent from patients, then, in theory, this is just a new interpretation of the existing law. A physician who fails to obtain informed consent for a surgery performed before the first court decision on informed consent in the state could still be sued.

From the defendants' perspective, there is little comfort in knowing that the judge did not make the law that they are accused of violating. Since the criminal law demands that the law be specific, most criminal law decisions are not retroactive. Some courts apply this same principle in civil law by making the new standards prospective when they dramatically increase a defendant's legal duties. They warn potential defendants of the new standard of conduct without allowing them to be sued for past conduct. This poses a policy problem because it denies compensation to persons previously injured by the now proscribed conduct.

The Importance of Precedent

In a common law system, judges are obliged to make their rulings as consistent as reasonably possible with previous judicial decisions on the same subject. The Constitution accepted most of the English common law as the starting point for American law. Situations still arise that involve rules laid down in cases decided more than 200 years ago. Each case decided by a common law court becomes a precedent, or guideline, for subsequent decisions involving similar disputes. These decisions are not binding on the legislature, which can pass laws to overrule unpopular court decisions. Unless these laws are determined to be unconstitutional by the Supreme Court, they preempt the common law precedent cases. Judges deciding cases are bound by the new law, rather than the precedent cases.

To better understand how the common law works, assume that there is a hypothetical drug, Zoneout, that is a psychoactive drug with some medical uses but a high potential for abuse: It is addictive and users lose their interest in going to work.

If Congress writes the statute regulating Zoneout very clearly and specifically—a complete ban on prescribing or using Zoneout—then the court's role is limited; if the physician prescribes Zoneout, then the physician has violated the statute and is guilty of a crime. All the cases involving prescriptions for Zoneout will look the same and the law will not evolve. But assume the statute is vague: no prescriptions for dangerous drugs. Then the court will have to decide under which circumstances Zoneout is a dangerous drug and when it is permissible to use it.

Assume that the court decides that Zoneout is a dangerous drug for treating workplace stress. That decision is then published and made available to the public. When the next case of a prescription for Zoneout comes before the court, the judge would be expected to follow the previous decision (the precedent) or to explain why it did not apply. The next case involves a Zoneout prescription for a patient with severe anxiety secondary to cancer treatment. The judge rules that Zoneout is not a dangerous drug under these facts because the risk of addiction is outweighed by the benefits of suppressing the anxiety. As more judicial opinions are written on prescribing Zoneout, it will become clearer when it is legal to use it and when it is prohibited. These opinions are the common law precedent on the prescription of Zoneout. They tell a physician when it is permissible to use Zoneout.

The value of a common law system is that the law can be adapted to situations that were not contemplated by the legislature. There are two disadvantages. First, judges must follow the precedent cases. If they do not, then it is impossible to predict what the law is. The second is that with hundreds of cases being decided every day, it is hard to keep up with the relevant decision. It is not unusual for several courts to be deciding cases on the same subject at the same time, with no good way to coordinate their opinions. Frequently the courts will reach different conclusions about the law. The state court in San Francisco might ban the use of Zoneout in the workplace, but the court in Los Angeles might allow it. Until the California Supreme Court resolves the issue, health care providers in the two different regions are facing different laws. This type of split also happens between federal courts of appeal, sometimes with three or four parts of the country under different interpretations of a given federal law.

The alternative to the common law system is called a civil law system. In a civil law country, the legislatures pass very specific statutes, and these are applied by the courts. Each judge who decides a case looks to the statute, rather than the previous cases, for guidance. In theory, in ambiguous cases each judge is free to reinterpret the statute as necessary to fit the facts of the specific case. Although this interpretation need not draw on previous decisions by other judges, civil law judges do try to ensure some consistency in the application of the law by taking into consideration previous court decisions. Louisiana retains some of the civil law procedures that were in force before it joined the United States.

Weaknesses in the Common Law Process

The state and federal court systems have at least two levels of courts. At the first level are the trial courts. The higher levels review the decisions of the trial courts. Most of the written legal decisions come from these higher-level courts. This can distort the law because more than 90 percent of lawsuits are settled before trial, and many of those that are tried are settled before a final verdict. Among those that are tried, only a small number are reviewed by higher courts. Cases become the subject of higher court review because they represent a departure from accepted law, they involve peculiar facts, or counsel made an error preparing or presenting the case. Even when a case is reviewed, the higher court may choose to uphold the trial court without an opinion. The tendency is for courts to write detailed legal opinions only when they are modifying the law.

The appellate process is lengthy. In many urban jurisdictions, it takes years to get a case to trial and nearly as long to appeal the case to a higher court. Rarely is a legal issue reviewed by a higher court in less than 5 years. Eight to 10 years is much more likely, with complex cases often appearing to be immortal. Cases involving the internment of the Americans of Japanese ancestry were still on appeal after 40 years. When the federal or state Supreme Court finally rules, the opinion is often peripheral to the legal conflict that resulted in the litigation. This is especially common in medical jurisprudence. In the *Cruzan v. Director, Missouri Dept. of Health*[1] case, which dealt with a family's right to terminate a patient's life support, the court made a narrow ruling on the right of a state to set evidentiary standards (see Chapter 9). Many landmark civil rights cases turn on arcane questions about the procedure of determining whether federal or state law applies in a given case.

The Litigation Bias

These problems with the selection of the cases and facts that give rise to legal opinions make it difficult to evaluate legal problems prospectively. There is often little congruence between real-world problems and the law as found in legal opinions. For example, most legal opinions discussing the duty of a physician to obtain the patient's informed consent also involve proved malpractice. The opinions do not discuss the malpractice because it does not involve any new issues. An attorney reading the opinion may not properly appreciate the importance of the underlying malpractice and attach too much significance to the technical requirement for informed consent.

Taken in the long view, the common law tradition has been critical to the development of our democratic traditions. In late–twentieth-century America, reliance on the common law tradition of deriving law from judicial opinions has given false direction to legal teaching and practice. The fundamental problem with deriving legal rules from published legal opinions is that most law practice does not involve litigation. Focusing on litigation ignores the role of lawyer as negotiator, conciliator, and counselor, and it distorts the attorney's perspective on the management of nonadversary situations: "From the point of view of the

parties to a lawsuit, the costs are in vain; almost every litigated case is a mistake."[2] It ignores the issue of prospective planning to prevent legal problems.

PRIVATE ALTERNATIVES TO THE COURTS—ALTERNATIVE DISPUTE RESOLUTION (ADR)

Litigation is expensive, time consuming, and unpredictable. Juror sympathy can distort the fact-finding, especially in cases where the defendant is a corporation and the plaintiff is an injured child or other sympathetic individual. In litigation between corporations, the years it can take to get a trial can make the eventual verdict meaningless if the cost of the delay in resolving the dispute exceeds the possible verdict. For an individual plaintiff with a small claim, the court system is usually too expensive to make litigation a viable way to resolve the claim. These problems have fueled interest in alternatives to the court system, generally lumped together as ADR. These are contractual remedies, in that the parties must both agree to use the process and to be bound by the result. To the extent that the contract binding the parties is enforceable in court, then the result of the ADR technique will be enforced by the court.

ADR raises two difficult policy issues. The first is the extent that one party can force the other to agree to ADR. For example, should a managed care organization (MCO) be allowed to make accepting ADR a condition of enrollment as a subscriber, when the MCO might be the only health plan offered by the patient's employer? Should an employer be allowed to demand that all employees sign a binding ADR agreement to keep their jobs? The second issue is that ADR is generally secret, unlike litigation where the issues are aired publically. Should an MCO be able to keep its medical malpractice claims secret by keeping them out of court? Should an employer be able to keep workplace discrimination claims, perhaps racial or sexual harassment, secret by requiring that they be settled through ADR and that the results be kept secret?

ADR Techniques

Of the several ADR techniques, the best established is *arbitration*, an agreement to use a private individual to decide the dispute and determine the damages, if any. If a party refuses to comply with an arbitration order, it can be enforced as a contract in the courts. The American Arbitration Association (AAA) provides a uniform set of rules for arbitration and a roster of approved arbitrators. In the usual agreement, each side chooses one arbitrator and these two arbitrators choose a third. Because there is a requirement that arbitrators have legal training, these arbitrators are often attorneys or retired judges.

The other techniques do not impose a binding settlement but are intended to help the parties resolve the dispute themselves. In *mediation*, each party agrees to share information with an impartial person who seeks to find areas of agreement that might otherwise be overlooked. In the simplest situation, the parties actually have common objectives but do not realize it. For example, a plaintiff may be willing to settle a $300,000 claim for as little as $100,000. The defendant, who has offered only $10,000 to the plaintiff, may be willing to pay as much as $110,000. In a lawsuit, these parties might expend enormous resources on pretrial preparation before reaching a settlement. The mediator can help them resolve the dispute without this prolonged warfare.

Mini-trials allow the parties to see what their cases will look like to a jury. These are used most commonly in disputes between corporations, but they can be useful in medical business disputes. In a mini-trial, each side's attorneys and experts present a brief (usually only a few hours) synopsis of their case. This is presented to the parties themselves rather than an arbitrator. The value of a mini-trial is that it allows a party to see the case through the eyes of the opposing counsel. In litigation, parties are carefully isolated from the opposing counsel until the trial itself. This makes the parties dependent on their own attorneys for information about the case. The attorneys, however, may not know the other side's strategy. More fundamentally, it is difficult for attorneys to remain objective while zealously representing their clients. The mini-trial ends this isolation and gives both parties more information about the nature of their case.

Implementing ADR

The major benefit of ADR is not as an alternative to disputes that have already ripened to the point that a lawsuit is about to be filed. ADR should been seen as part of a general strategy of avoiding disputes rather than just a more expeditious method of resolving them. ADR is most effective when it is incorporated in all business transactions. Many *Fortune* 500 companies are putting ADR provisions in their contracts with suppliers and corporate customers. In addition to requiring ADR should a formal dispute arise, the unavailability of litigation encourages the quick, informal resolution of disputes.

All states allow ADR for medical business disputes, and most allow it for medical malpractice claims, but only if the choice of ADR is voluntary. For example, an MCO might require persons who choose to subscribe to agree to the binding arbitration of potential medical malpractice claims. Although most states would accept this, there is growing trend to require that the ADR agreement be signed after the patient is injured so that it is really a free choice. The courts would likely reject an agreement with a private physician who allowed a patient to schedule an appointment and arrive at the office, but then required the patient to agree to arbitration before treatment. ADR agreements are not allowed as a condition of emergency care or in other situations where the patient cannot exercise free choice.

In many cases, it is the malpractice insurance companies that resist ADR agreements because ADR has the potential to increase the overall payments to claimants. An efficient system for resolving disputes will allow patients with small claims to be compensated. Studies of the incidence of medical malpractice find that many more patients are injured by negligent medical care than file medical malpractice lawsuits.[3] Some of these patients do not realize that they were the victims of malpractice, some intentionally choose not to sue their medical care providers, but most are unable to secure representation because their claim is too small. If the cost of these small claims exceeds the savings in limiting large claims and attorney's fees, then ADR will only increase the cost of insurance.

REFERENCES

1. *Cruzan by Cruzan v. Director, Mo. Dept. of Health*, 497 U.S. 261 (1990).
2. Fisher R. He who pays the piper. *Harv Bus Rev*. Mar–April 1985;150–159.
3. *Compensation in New York*. Report of the Harvard Medical Malpractice Study to the State of New York. 1990.

SUGGESTED READINGS

Adelman SH. Alternative forms of dispute resolution—we must be clear on what we want. *Mich Med*. 1991;90:55–56.

Bachman J. Alternative dispute resolution: facilitating new dispute resolution systems. *Aspens Advis Nurse Exec*. 1997;12:1,4–7.

Barton HM. Alternative dispute resolution of medical-legal issues. *Tex Med*. 1991;87:58–61.

B-Lynch C, Coker A, Dua JA. A clinical analysis of 500 medico-legal claims evaluating the causes and assessing the potential benefit of alternative dispute resolution. *Br J Obstet Gynaecol*. 1996;103:1236–1242.

Delaney C. Alternative dispute resolution: mediate your way to a solution. *Okla Nurse*. 1996;41:4.

Fraser JJ Jr. Medical malpractice arbitration: a primer for Texas physicians. *Tex Med*. 1997;93:76–80.

Freudman L. Alternative dispute resolution (ADR) for dentists: a better way. *Ont Dent*. 1998;75:25–29.

Graddy B. A sane alternative: Alternative dispute resolution offers way to bypass the traditional legal system. *Tex Med*. 1994;90:45–46.

Grant A. Alternative dispute resolution. *Can Nurse*. 1995;91:53–54.

Guenin LM. Alternative dispute resolution and research misconduct. *Camb Q Healthc Ethics*. 1997;6:72–77.

Harvard Medical Practice Study. *Patients, doctors, and lawyers: Medical injury, malpractice litigation, and patient compensation in New York: The report of the Harvard Medical Practice Study to the State of New York*. Cambridge, MA: Harvard, 1990.

Kinney ED. Malpractice reform in the 1990s: past disappointments, future success? *J Health Polit Policy Law*. 1995;20:99–135.

Klein CA. Alternative dispute resolution in health care. *AORN J*. 1996;63:457–459.

Klein CA. Alternative dispute resolution—issues in health care. *Colo Nurse*. 1995;95:19.

Klein CA. Alternative dispute resolution—who cares?—you care! *Colo Nurse*. 1994;94:5.

LeFevre TL. The use of nurses in alternative dispute resolution. *Natl Med Leg J*. 1997;8:4,7.

Liang BA. Understanding and applying alternative dispute resolution methods in modern medical conflicts (In Process Citation). *J Leg Med*. 1998;19:397–430.

Miller HD Jr. There is an alternative to litigation. *J Miss State Med Assoc*. 1995;36:71–72.

Treacy W. Alternative dispute resolution of medical malpractice cases in Wisconsin. *Wis Med J*. 1993;92:144–147.

White WF. Alternative dispute resolution for medical malpractice actions: an efficient approach to the law and health care. *Leg Med*. 1995:227–239.

CHAPTER 2

Civil Claims and Monetary Damages

HIGHLIGHTS

- Most medical care law is civil law.
- Civil cases can be brought by the government or by private citizens.
- Civil cases cannot be used to imprison.
- Defendants have fewer rights in civil cases than in criminal cases.
- Civil cases can result in huge damage awards.
- Health care practitioners must understand the civil law standards for medical care to avoid medical malpractice litigation.

INTRODUCTION

The U.S. legal system uses three models for legal proceedings. In criminal law proceedings the government prosecutes individuals and corporations to punish them for previous actions. In administrative law proceedings the government seeks to compel individuals to comply with rules and regulations established by government agencies. Civil law proceedings, which are the focus for this chapter, are used to force compliance with either public laws or private contracts, and to establish the liability and amount of monetary compensation that must be paid to compensate for injuries. Civil law proceedings can be brought by private citizens, corporations, and the government. The key distinction between civil and criminal law is that civil law proceedings cannot result in imprisonment. Administrative law proceedings are either done in the agency or in special administrative law courts that follow different procedural rules.

The civil law is concerned with the peaceable resolution of disputes between individuals. Physicians often ignore the importance of this peace-keeping function. Being sued for medical malpractice is an unpleasant experience, but it is much preferable to being gunned down in the hospital corridor by an irate patient. This is an extreme example, but it has occurred. The civil courts are an imperfect but essential safety valve. It has even been argued that the delays and rituals of the process, which decrease its economic efficiency, increase its ability to cool passions and prevent violence.

TYPES OF CLAIMS

Civil claims fall into several categories, depending on the nature of the alleged injury or the requested remedy.

Personal Injury

Medical malpractice litigation is the classic civil lawsuit in health care. It is brought by a private party—the patient—against a private entity—the health care practitioner or hospital—and the object of the lawsuit is to force the defendant to pay the plaintiff money to compensate the plaintiff for an injury cased by the defendant's actions. In most cases the defendant has medical malpractice insurance and the insurance pays both the cost of hiring an attorney to defend the claim and the claim itself, if the case is settled or the court finds for the plaintiff. If the award is very large, it may exceed the limits of the insurance and the defendant will have to contribute from personal or corporate resources.

There are many other possible personal injury claims in health care. Individuals can be injured by dangerous conditions that are unrelated to health care delivery itself, such as slick floors or a malfunctioning elevator. There can also be intentional injuries, such as the rape of a patient by hospital employee or an assault by another patient. If the injury results from criminal activity, it may not be covered by insurance. The health care practitioner or institution will have to pay for both the defense of the claim and any jury verdict or settlement.

Contract and Property Claims

Health care businesses and practitioners enter into many contracts, including leases and other property transactions. A common example is a contract of employment between a managed care company and an individual health care practitioner. The employer promises to pay the employee a given amount and promises to employ the person for some period of time unless the employee performs unsatisfactorily. The employee agrees to provide certain services and often agrees to not work for other managed care companies in the area for some time after the termination of the employment agreement.

Civil litigation could be used for resolving disputes under this contact. Employees who claim to be improperly terminated can sue for reinstatement and lost pay. The employer can sue to enforce the contract and prevent the employee from working for a competitor. In this case the court might pay the employer a given sum of money to compensate it for the employee's violation of the anticompete agreement, or the court might prevent the employee from continuing in the job.

Many contract disputes that involve the sale of goods or other commercial transactions are governed by the Uniform Commercial Code (UCC), a set of uniform laws adopted by all the states that facilitate the quick resolution of simple business disputes. The UCC establishes the general terms of the agreements for covered transactions and the measure of damages if the agreement is not properly carried out. While patient care services are not subject to the UCC, many ancillary transactions are.

Divorce, Custody, and Incompetence

Divorce, child custody proceedings, and adoptions are civil actions. Couples bring divorce proceedings as private civil actions against each other, with the purpose of the proceeding to be the resolution of property and support claims and the custody of the children, if any. These are not purely private actions since all the states require the judge to consider the best interest of the children, which often means that the state social welfare department must review the custody agreements. Many states also specific the nature of the support agreements and whether alimony is available.

The involuntary treatment of the mentally ill, the treatment of minors against their parents' consent, and the treatment of temporarily incompetent patients without or against consent is done through civil proceedings. These are often initiated by a health care practitioner who believes the person needs treatment or care and wants the court to intervene. As discussed in Chapter 9, judges may allow individuals to be treated or hospitalized without their consent, or even against their consent. While it is proper to use involuntary commitment to protect the public from a dangerous individual, the court cannot confine a person as a punishment without giving the person the full rights of criminal proceedings (see Chapter 12).

Statutory Causes of Action

The state or federal government can create civil causes of action through legislation. The most sweeping creation of such civil remedies were the Civil Rights Acts. The first were passed immediately after the Civil War. These were dramatically strengthened by the Civil Rights Act of 1964. These acts allowed persons who were discriminated against because of race to sue both state governments and private businesses for compensation and to prevent further discrimination. These Acts were broadened to include discrimination based on sex, ethnic origin, and religion. The Americans with Disabilities Act included discrimination based on disability status.

Individuals and the government, through the Equal Employment Opportunity Commission, may bring civil actions to enforce the provisions of the Act. If the behavior affects more than one employee, it can be litigated as class action lawsuits where the court will craft a remedy that benefits all the members of the class. Such actions can result in multimillion-dollar settlements and sweeping changes in workplace rules.

Some statutory cases of action give the plaintiff an easier way to recover for injuries that are already covered by civil remedies such as medical malpractice litigation. The Emergency Medical Treatment and Active Labor Act (EMTALA) is an example that should be familiar to every health care practitioner involved with emergency medical care. While claims for improper transfer or failure to stabilize a person in need of emergency medical care may be brought as state law medical malpractice cases, EMTALA allows these to be brought in federal court and simplifies the case the plaintiff must prove.

Government agencies often use civil litigation to enforce regulatory rulings. The Food and Drug Administration (FDA) may seek an injunction or institute a seizure or embargo action to take possession or forbid the sale of potentially contaminated food or drugs. These are very powerful measures in the food and drug industry, where seized or embargoed inventory can go out of date faster than the defendant can get a trial to contest the court's order. The Office of the Inspector General often brings civil claims for reimbursement against health care providers who have submitted what it believes are false claims for Medicare/Medicaid reimbursement. These civil actions can be almost impossible for the defendants to win. In the FDA action, the agency has great leverage to negotiate a settlement if the defendant has 1000 tons of fresh fruit that cannot be moved off a ship until the claim is resolved. In the false claims lawsuit, the defendant risks complete financial ruin if the jury finds against it because the potential damages are so large. This makes a settlement necessary even if it costs several million dollars (see Chapter 3).

PROCEDURAL ASPECTS OF CIVIL ACTIONS

There are key procedural differences between civil, criminal, and administrative actions. Criminal actions provide the greatest protections for the defendant's rights because they involve loss of liberty or even life if the defendant is convicted. Administrative actions provide the least protection for the regulated individual or industry because they are resolved outside the court system. Civil actions have the basic protections of the court system, but they have fewer protections for the defendant than do criminal actions because there is also a concern that the injured plaintiff be able to bring a case without undue hardship.

Discovery

The parties to a civil action—the plaintiff and the defendant—have great latitude to obtain information from each other and from persons not involved in the lawsuit (see Chapter 5). In a criminal proceeding, the Fifth Amendment of the Constitution gives the defendant the right to refuse to testify and the prosecutor may not even comment on the defendant's choice to not take the stand. In a civil proceeding, the defendant must testify and provide incriminating information or risk having the judge strike the defenses to the lawsuit, which nearly always ensures a victory for the plaintiff.

Standard of Proof

The courts use several different standards for proof, depending on the nature of the proceedings. In a criminal case, the state must prove the defendant's guilt beyond a reasonable doubt. This is the highest standard of proof and it recognizes the social policy that it is better to risk allowing a guilty person to go free than to wrongly convict an innocent person. The plaintiff in a civil lawsuit has to prove the case against the defendant by a preponderance of the evidence, which is taken to mean by more than 50%. This lower standard of proof is justified by the belief that the rights of the injured plaintiff must be accorded nearly as much respect as the rights of the defendant.

While the civil law may not be used to imprison a person as punishment, the involuntary commitment of the mentally ill to institutional care is considered a civil action, as are cases of commitment brought under the sexual predator laws passed by many states. These cases more resemble criminal than civil proceedings, ensuring more protections for the defendant. The usual standard of proof is raised to clear and convincing evidence that the defendant poses a danger to self or others.

Right to Counsel

The U.S. Supreme Court has determined that criminal defendants cannot effectively assert their rights without the assistance of counsel, and that these rights must be protected. As a result, the government must provide criminal defendants with an attorney if the defendant is unable to afford one. Generally, the right to counsel has not been extended to civil or administrative proceedings. If you are sued for medical malpractice and do not have insurance coverage or the money to pay an attorney, the state will not provide you with counsel and the plaintiff can continue the lawsuit even though you cannot protect your rights. This would be unlikely to happen, however, in a medical malpractice case because if you cannot pay an attorney you probably cannot pay a judgment.

There are certain civil proceedings, usually brought by governmental agencies, that so affect an individual's fundamental rights that the courts have found a limited right to counsel. These include proceedings to terminate parental rights, to take away custody of children, and to cancel certain public welfare benefits. There is also a right to counsel in civil commitment proceedings that may result in temporary or permanent confinement.

PROVING MEDICAL MALPRACTICE

A plaintiff initiates a lawsuit by filing papers with the court claiming that he or she was harmed by the defendant and is entitled to legal redress. These papers must set out the plaintiff's prima facie case: the statement of facts and legal theories that establish that the plaintiff has a legally enforceable claim against the defendant. There are four elements to a prima facie case of medical negligence:

1. Duty—a statement of the facts that establishes the legal relationship between the physician and the patient
2. Breach—a statement of facts that illustrate that the defendant breached the legal duties implied in the physician–patient relationship or duties generally imposed on members of society
3. Causation—that the breach of the defendant's duty caused the plaintiff's injuries
4. Damages—the monetary value of the plaintiff's injuries

Upon the filing of these claims, the defendant may ask the judge to dismiss the plaintiff's lawsuit for deficiencies in prima facie case. For the purpose of a motion to dismiss, the judge will assume that the facts presented by the plaintiff are correct. If, despite this assumption, the plaintiff's prima facie case is incomplete or legally unfounded, it may be dismissed, or the plaintiff may be given an opportunity to amend it to satisfy the defense's objections. During the pretrial phase of the lawsuit, the plaintiff must present legally sufficient evidence to support the allegations in the prima facie case.

Duty

A basic rule of Anglo-American law is that an individual has no duty to another person unless there is a legally recognized relationship with that person. Physicians have many legal relationships, all of which have accompanying duties that might form the basis of a lawsuit. In some cases, the defendant will deny that there was a legally recognized relationship with the plaintiff. If the plaintiff's claim is based on medical malpractice, the plaintiff must allege facts to support the existence of a physician–patient relationship. If the patient does not make the factual allegations necessary for the court to find a physician–patient relationship, the plaintiff's lawsuit will be dismissed. This often happens if a patient sues several physicians and includes one who did not treat the patient and had no legal relationships with the physicians who did treat the patient.

Standard of Care

Once the plaintiff has established that there was a legal relationship with the physician defendant, the plaintiff must establish the appropriate standard of care. In theory, establishing the standard of care and establishing the breach of that standard are legally separate. In reality, unless there is a factual question about what the defendant did, the proof of the standard of care also proves the defendant's breach. For example, assume that the defendant admits that she did not counsel the patient about prenatal testing for a genetic disease. If the patient can establish that the standard of care was to offer this testing, the defendant breached the standard. If, however, the physician claims to have done the counseling, the patient will have to prove both that counseling was the standard of care and that the physician did not do the counseling.

The most common legal definition of standard of care is how similarly qualified practitioners would have managed the patient's care under the same or similar circumstances. This is not simply what the majority of practitioners would have done. The courts recognize the *respectable minority rule.* This rule allows the practitioner to show that although the course of therapy followed was not the same as other practitioners would have followed, it is one that is accepted by a respectable minority of practitioners (*respectable* is used in both senses). The jury is not bound to accept the majority standard of care. Jurors may decide that a minority standard is the proper standard and that a physician following the majority standard was negligent.

In most medical malpractice cases, both the standard of care and its breach are established through the testimony of expert witnesses. There are situations in which the plaintiff may be able to establish the standard of care and breach without an expert witness.

Res Ipsa Loquitur

Res ipsa loquitur means, roughly, "the thing speaks for itself." Courts developed the concept of res ipsa loquitur to deal with cases in which the actual negligent act cannot be proved, but it is clear that the injury was caused by negligence. This doctrine was first recognized in the case of a man who was struck and severely injured by a barrel that rolled out of the second-story window of a warehouse. In the trial of the case, the defense attorney argued that the plaintiff did not know what events preceded the barrel rolling out of the window and thus could not prove that a warehouse employee was negligent. The plaintiff's attorney countered that barrels do not normally roll out of warehouse windows. The mere fact that a barrel fell from the window was res ipsa loquitur; "it spoke for itself," and it said that someone must have been negligent.

Most law students learn about res ipsa loquitur by reading a case about an airplane that disappears without a trace. There is no evidence of negligence, but there is a strong presumption that airplanes do not disappear without some negligence. In medical negligence cases, res ipsa loquitur can be invoked only when: (1) the patient suffers an injury that is not an expected complication of medical care; (2) the injury does not normally occur unless someone has been negligent; and (3) the defendant was responsible for the patient's well-being at the time of the injury. For example, assume that a portable X ray is ordered in an intensive care unit on a young, otherwise healthy patient recovering from peritonitis. After the technician leaves, it is found that the patient has a dislocated shoulder. This is not an expected complication of an X ray; there are no explanations for the injury other than mishandling or failing to restrain the patient properly, and the defendant was responsible for the patient's well-being at the time the injury occurred.

The strategic value of a res ipsa loquitur claim is that it does not require an expert to testify as to the proper standard of care. This has led plaintiffs to try to make res ipsa loquitur claims whenever they are unable to secure expert testimony to support their cases. Many states have limited the use of res ipsa loquitur in medical malpractice litigation, usually to claims such as a surgeon's leaving a foreign body in the patient or operating on the wrong patient. In all other cases, the plaintiff must present expert testimony as to standard of care and its breach.

Negligence Per Se

Negligence per se lawsuits are brought by private plaintiffs but are based on the defendant's violation of a law. In these cases the appropriate standard of care is defined by the law that was violated. For the court to accept a negligence per se claim, the plaintiff must show that a law was violated, that the law was intended to prevent the type of injury that occurred, and that the plaintiff was in the class of persons intended to be protected by the law. The plaintiff may claim negligence per se even if the defendant has not been convicted or administratively sanctioned under the law in question. In such cases, the plaintiff must prove that the defendant has violated the law. The plaintiff

does not need to prove independently the violation if the defendant has been convicted or had pleaded guilty. (The plaintiff may not rely on a plea of *nolo contendere*; that is, not contesting the charges but not admitting guilt.)

Traffic violations are a common instance of negligence per se. Assume that a driver hits a child while driving at night without headlights. This behavior is illegal; it is prohibited to prevent this type of accident, and the plaintiff is in the class of persons who were intended to be protected. The driver could be found negligent based on the violation of the statute. Conversely, assume that a physician injures a patient while practicing without a current medical license. This alone will not support a negligence per se claim because medical licensing laws are not intended to protect specific patients from medical malpractice.

The most common prosecutions of physicians for practice-related crimes involve tax and other economic fraud laws. These will not support negligence per se claims in medical malpractice cases because the laws are not intended to prevent patient injuries (as discussed in Chapter 10, such violation can support other causes of action against the physician). Negligence per se claims are a threat to physicians who disregard laws intended to protect patients, such as the federal provisions on patient dumping (discussed in Chapter 4) and state laws requiring physicians to provide emergency care. Since these laws make it illegal to deny a person necessary emergency medical care, a person refused emergency care suffers the injury the law was intended to prevent. Negligence per se claims also could be brought against physicians who do not obey disease control regulations and laws requiring the reporting of dangerous individuals.

Intentional Torts

Intentional torts are intentional actions that result in harm to the plaintiff. The harm need not be intended, but the act must be intentional, not merely careless or reckless. Most intentional torts are also crimes. The classic intentional tort in medical practice is forcing unwanted medical care on a patient. The care may benefit the patient, but if it was refused and the physician has no state mandate to force care on the patient, the patient may sue for the intentional tort of battery (see Chapter 9).

The most common intentional tort is battery. The legal standard for a battery is "an intentional, unconsented harmful or offensive touching." (Batteries such as shootings, stabbings, and beatings are also criminal law violations.) Although battery is commonly linked with assault, an assault is the act of putting a person in fear of bodily harm. Battery occurs only if there is an actual physical contact. The law of battery has been tailored to the problems of living in a crowded society. Not every unconsented touching is a battery—only those that are intended. Even among intentional unconsented touchings, the courts will allow recovery only for those that a reasonable person would find offensive. Thus, neither bumping into a person on a bus nor grabbing a person to prevent him or her from falling is a battery. In contrast, an unwanted kiss is a battery, though it does not cause any physical injury.

Most battery claims against health care providers are based on real attacks, not technical violations of informed consent rules. One case involved a patient who became pregnant while having an affair with her physician.[1] When she allowed the physician to examine her to confirm the pregnancy, he repeatedly forced a metal instrument into her uterus, triggering a miscarriage. The court found this constituted a battery, allowing the patient to claim for wrongful abortion.

Sexual Assault

One particularly troubling, and legally dangerous, class of batteries is sexual assault. It is difficult to determine the true number of sexual assault claims against physicians. When a claim is made public, it receives extensive publicity, creating the impression that sexual assaults are a common problem. In other cases, sexual assault claims are paid off by the physician's malpractice insurance company with the patient's silence a condition of the settlement. While all medical malpractice insurance policies exclude coverage for criminal activity, plaintiffs' attorneys include an allegation that the assault was a breach of medical standards as well as a criminal act. This creates a dilemma for the insurance company.

If the insurance company pays the claim, it forces its other insureds to subsidize illegal conduct. If it refuses to pay the claim, the plaintiff's attorney can make a deal with the defendant physician. In return for the physician's agreeing to confess to negligent (and covered) behavior, the plaintiff's attorney will agree to settle both claims for whatever can be extracted from the insurance company. If the insurance company refuses to settle the case, the plaintiff's attorney may offer to represent the physician defendant in a claim of bad faith against the insurance company. The defendant, now represented by the plaintiff's attorney, sues the insurance company on a breach of contract theory for failing to pay the claim. If the plaintiff's attorney wins the lawsuit, the defendant collects from the insurance company and then passes the money to the plaintiff.

Sexual assault claims are increasing because of the heightened societal concern with sex crimes and child sexual abuse. A sexual assault claim stigmatizes the physician and gives the plaintiff a strategic advantage in what might otherwise be a weak medical malpractice case. Ethical attorneys will not make such a claim if they know it to be false. However, if the attorney's client insists that she or he has been assaulted, the attorney can only judge the assertion based on the circumstances of the medical treatment. The legal standard of care is that male health care providers do not examine female patients without a female attendant present. This standard is frequently ignored, however. A physician who violates this norm or allows a male nurse or physician's assistant to examine a female patient unattended will find it very difficult to defend a sexual assault claim. An attorney representing such a patient will accept the patient's claims as credible because allowing an unattended examination of a female patient is concrete evidence that, at the least, the physician has bad judgment.

Causation

Merely breaching established standards is not enough to support a medical malpractice lawsuit.

Once a breach of standards has been established by expert testimony, the plaintiff must establish that the breach was the proximate cause of the injury. For example, assume that the patient is brought to the emergency room with severe injuries from a motorcycle accident. After a prolonged stay in the intensive care unit (ICU), the patient ultimately loses his leg. Upon discharge from the hospital, the patient has an attorney investigate the care he received in the ICU. The attorney finds that the patient was repeatedly given the wrong dosage of his antihypertensive medication, and, as a result, his blood pressure was out of control. Although this is a clear breach of the standard of care, the attorney also must prove, by expert testimony, that the incorrect dosage of medication caused the loss of the leg. Showing that the standard of care was breached and that the patient has an injury is not enough. The attorney must demonstrate that but for the incorrect dosage of medicine, the patient would still have his leg.

Causation is a problematic defense. Juries are not sympathetic to a physician who acts negligently and then claims that the patient's injuries are not due to the substandard care. Since there is usually an element of punishment in a verdict against a physician, jurors tend to focus on the negligent behavior and ignore whether the negligence actually caused the injury. They believe the physician should not escape punishment because the patient was lucky enough to escape injury. Causation defenses work best when the physician's behavior is below the acceptable standard but is not obviously dangerous. A physician who misses a shadow on a lung film may successfully argue that the tumor was too far advanced for an earlier diagnosis to matter. A physician who refuses to continue caring for a pregnant woman because her insurance lapses at 34 weeks will have difficulty convincing a jury that this was unrelated to her baby's brain injury.

ESTABLISHING THE STANDARD OF CARE

The courts have delegated the setting of professional standards to members of the various professions. This is in contrast to the standards for non-professional skills, such as driving a car. The legislature establishes the rules of the road, and a lay juror is deemed capable of determining when they have been violated. In contrast, legislatures do not adopt detailed standards for professional practice. Medical practice standards are drawn from the customs and behavior of the members of the profession. If the profession has developed documents that reflect a consensus on how the profession is to be practiced, these documents will set the standard for judging individual transgressions.

The Expert's Role

An expert witness must establish a standard for medical care and give an opinion on whether the defendant's conduct met this standard. The standard must at once be general to all practitioners and specific to the individual plaintiff's circumstances. Ideally, it should be supported by uncontroverted scholarly literature. While it need not prescribe a single course of action, it must either (for the plaintiff) proscribe the defendant's conduct or (for the defense) endorse the defendant's conduct as an acceptable alternative.

These standards ignore the conflict between actual medical practice and legal expectations. The courts expect that medicine, as a learned, science-based discipline, will have articulated standards for practice. While recognizing the art in medicine, the law assumes that the science of medicine will be sufficiently formalized that the regions of art will be readily identifiable. Rather than face the core problem of inadequately defined practice standards, the courts allow experts to step into this void with standards tailored to serve the desired ends of the lawyer engaging the expert.

Schools of Practice

Obtaining expert testimony has always been the most difficult part of medical malpractice litigation. Historically, there have been two competing interests: members of a professional group did not want to testify against their colleagues, but they did want to run their competitors out of business. Allopathic physicians were happy to label homeopathic physicians as incompetent, and any physician would dispute the competence of a chiropractor. These rivalries led the courts to use the legal doctrines of the school of practice and the locality rule as the basis for qualifying a person as an expert witness.

The school of practice distinctions also predated modern medical training and certification. At one time medical practitioners were divided into chiropractors, homeopaths, allopaths, osteopaths, and several other schools based on different philosophical and psychological beliefs. Since state legislatures did not discriminate among these different schools of healing, judges were reluctant to allow litigation to be used to attack an approved school. Except for chiropractors, allopathic practices (and osteopaths using primarily allopathic methods) have driven out the other schools of medical practice. The courts retain the traditional school of practice rule when they refuse to allow physician experts to question chiropractic care or chiropractors to testify in cases with physician defendants.

While not as rigidly enforced as the school of practice rule, differentiation of physicians into self-designated specialties is also taken into account. (Self-designated because few state licensing boards recognize specialties or limit physicians' right to practice the specialties in which they have been trained.) The relevance of the specialty qualifications of an expert witness depend on whether the case concerns procedures and expertise that are intrinsic to the specialty or general medical knowledge and techniques that are common to all physicians. This dichotomy is reflected in strategies for expert testimony. Whether the parties to the lawsuit will stress the specialty or general knowledge depends on the qualifications of the expert that each has retained.

The Locality Rule

The locality rule is the progenitor of the debates over the proper specialty qualifications for an expert witness. The locality rule evolved before the standardization of medical training and certification. During this period, there was a tremendous gulf between the skills and abilities of university-trained physicians and the graduates of the unregulated diploma mills. In many parts of the country, parochialism and necessity combined to create the rule that a physician's competence would be determined by comparison with the other physicians in the community, or at least in similar neighboring communities. The strictest form of the locality rule required the expert to be from the same or a similar community. This made it nearly impossible for injured patients to find experts to support their cases, effectively preventing most medical malpractice litigation.

The underpinnings of the locality rule are diametrically opposed to contemporary specialty training and certification. There is no longer a justification for a rule that shelters substandard medical decision making on the sole excuse that it is the norm for a given community. Many states have explicitly abolished the locality rule for physicians who hold themselves out as certified specialists. Unfortunately, the locality rule is being reinvigorated in some states as a tort reform measure. This resurgence is driven by the problem of access to care and facilities in rural areas.

Proponents of the locality rule often confuse access to facilities with physician competence. A national standard of care implies that the rural physician will have the same training and exercise the same level of judgment and diligence as an urban practitioner. It does not require that the rural physician have the same medical facilities available. If the community does not have facilities for an emergency Cesarean section, the physician cannot be found negligent for failing to do this surgery within the 15 minutes that might be the standard in a well-equipped urban hospital.

Under a national standard, however, the physician must inform the patient of the limitations of the available facilities and recommend prompt transfer if indicated. This allows patients to balance the convenience of local care against the risks of inadequate facilities. The protection of a national standard is especially important as rural hospitals attempt to market or retain lucrative medical services that their facilities are not properly equipped to handle.

The Importance of Setting Objective Standards

There have been many suggested solutions to the expert witness problem. Most of these are defensive strategies that seek to reduce the availability of plaintiff's experts; they do not address the root problem of ambiguous medical practice standards.

The best approach is to reduce the ambiguity in practice standards. While courts will still require expert testimony, both judges and juries are very deferential toward explicit standards of practice that are promulgated by credible professional organizations. Since plaintiffs' attorneys are aware of the increased difficulty in proving a case against a physician who has followed approved standards, standards lead to reduced litigation.

Most important, standards allow effective quality assurance review. This reduces the legal risk to peer reviewers and improves the quality of care. Standards are also critical in medical cost containment. Most standard-setting efforts in the financial context have been directed at reducing unnecessary care. As the pressure to reduce medical care costs increases, well-articulated practice standards will be critical in ensuring that cost-containment efforts do not deny patients necessary care. Without standards to back their decisions, individual practitioners will not be able to resist third-party payer pressures to reduce medically indicated care.

There are three impediments to standard setting in medical practice. The first is the belief that setting a standard will inhibit innovation. While this may be relevant in a medical research setting, innovation is much less significant in routine medical care. Even in a research setting, rigid adherence to standard protocols is fundamental to the controlled trials that advance medical science. The second is resistance by medical malpractice defense lawyers. Defense lawyers assert, correctly, that it is much more difficult to defend a physician who violates an explicit practice stan-

dard. This ignores the reduced litigation against physicians who do comply. It also ignores the long-term reduction of negligent practice as the peer review process urges practitioners to follow appropriate practice standards.

The third, and most important, impediment to standard setting is the Federal Trade Commission (FTC). In its efforts to reduce anticompetitive practices in medical care delivery, the FTC has discouraged professional standard setting. While correctly recognizing that many professional standards are anticompetitive, the FTC does not seem to recognize that this is the price of professional self-regulation. Any rule that restricts marginal practitioners will reduce competition. The fear of FTC enforcement actions has discouraged professional societies from setting standards for practice. This has been most evident in the reluctance to address entrepreneurial practices that encourage patients to undergo unnecessary and vanity procedures. The FTC has focused on reducing prices through competition, ignoring the problem of physicians' and hospitals' using the classic advertising technique of creating a demand for unnecessary or inappropriate services.

Malpractice Considerations in Pediatrics

For the most part, malpractice cases involving children are handled the same as cases that involve adults. Discovery, standards, and expert testimony are not substantially different; however, there are some differences that are important to anyone who cares for children. The most fundamental of these is that juries like children. The child may have been injured by the parents' neglect and refusal to follow the physician's orders, but the jury gives the money to the child. If the physician is concerned about liability secondary to parental neglect, then the proper course of action is to contact child protection services.

Acute Medical Care

Physicians have an obligation to ensure that children are not deprived of medical care for financial reasons. Ethically, children are entitled to special consideration because of their dependent status. Legally, it is risky to turn away a child in need of care because of the volatility of childhood diseases. A simple case of diarrhea can prove fatal quickly in an infant. The delay that is attendant upon being refused care without a proper referral to a physician willing to care for the child may prove fatal. A physician must never allow a child to be turned away from a hospital or emergency room because the parents do not have money or insurance. If there is an ongoing physician–patient relationship, the physician must be the child's advocate and demand care. Payment issues between the parents and the hospital should not be allowed to interfere with medical care. A physician who is not willing to insist on proper hospital care may violate federal laws governing the provision of emergency medical care.

Long Statutes of Limitation

The period of time that a physician may be sued for malpractice by or for a child is much longer than it is for an adult. Most states have a statute of limitations that starts when the injury occurs or when it is discovered by the patient. It is common practice to toll the statute of limitations on children until the child reaches the age of majority. For instance, an adult patient might have 2 years to bring suit. A 3-year-old child may have until age 18 plus 2 more years to bring a malpractice suit, a total of 17 years. This prevents the child's rights from being compromised if the parents fail to pursue the action.

The functional statute of limitations may also be quite long if the statutory period does not begin to run until the injury is discovered. Assume that the uterus of a 5-year-old child is negligently damaged during bladder surgery. As the child grows, her sexual development is normal, and no problem is suspected. The girl reaches adulthood, marries, and uses contraceptives to postpone childbearing until she is ready for children. At age 30, she attempts to conceive and is unable to do so. After 2 years of infertility, she has a surgical procedure that reveals that the damage from the first surgery is the reason for her infertility. If the statute of limitations runs until 2 years after the injury is discovered, this patient may be age 34

when she sues the surgeon for an operation done 29 years before.

Despite the long-term potential liability and the uncertainty it generates in malpractice insurance rate setting, general pediatricians still pay relatively low rates. Nonetheless, all physicians who care for children should be careful to preserve medical records until at least a few years past the child's maturity. As with other medical records, the physician should attempt to provide the patient with a copy before destroying the old record (see Chapter 7). While this is difficult with records of now-adult pediatric patients, these records can be especially valuable. Unlike adults who are informed of the nature of their illness at the time the care is rendered, pediatric patients have no personal memory of their early medical history. This history can be important for their adult medical care and for determining the presence of inherited conditions that may afflict their own children.

NONMONETARY REMEDIES

The most important nonmonetary civil remedy is the injunction. In certain situations, the court has the right to order that a person be prevented from or, more rarely, required to do something. This order is called an *injunction.* To obtain a temporary injunction, the plaintiff must show that the defendant's actions would cause irreparable harm and that the plaintiff has a substantial chance of prevailing in a trial. The key issue in an injunction is convincing the court that the harm cannot be cured by just paying the plaintiff money later. In a medical context, a surgeon might try to get an injunction to prevent a hospital from a summary termination of his or her medical staff privileges. The surgeon's argument would be that his or her career and reputation would be permanently damaged and that his or her patients would be put at risk. The judge might grant such an injunction unless the hospital could show that the risk to patients was greater if the surgeon were allowed to continue to practice while the hospital conducted hearings on the termination of privileges.

When a temporary injunction is granted, the plaintiff must post a bond that is sufficient to compensate the defendant if the plaintiff does not prevail in the case. If the plaintiff does prevail, the bond is refunded, and the court may enter a permanent injunction to prevent the complained-of conduct. If the defendant prevails, the bond will be used to pay any damages that the defendant can prove were caused by the injunction. Since an injunction is a court order, violating an injunction is contempt of court and may be punished by a fine or imprisonment.

Injunctions are often requested in cases such as medical staff disputes, withdrawal of life support cases, and cases involving the treatment of children. In these cases, the complaining party attempts to convince the court that since human lives are at stake, the court must step in. In some cases, courts have tried to order pregnant women not to have abortions, or to submit to certain types of medical care ordered by their physicians. These are controversial actions and will be discussed in greater detail in subsequent chapters. In some cases these are resolved by injunctions, but in most cases they require the appointment of a guardian who will determine what is in the best interest of the patient.

The courts are generally unwilling to use injunctions to enforce personal service contracts, such as research contracts or employment contracts. As an example, assume that you sign a contract to perform a study for the Dreck drug company but never complete the study. Dreck is furious and sues to force you to complete the study. You offer to return the money you have been paid, but Dreck refuses, claiming that you must complete the study so approval of its drug will not be delayed. Since you have a detailed agreement as to how the study is to be conducted, why shouldn't the court force you to comply with the agreement?

The problem with ordering the performance of a personal services contract is that courts want to make rulings that end disputes. If the court orders you to complete the study, it will be faced with determining whether you are working fast enough, if your work is of acceptable quality, and

other issues as to the performance of the contract. The court's ruling would only create new disputes. This pragmatism, combined with a reluctance to interfere in individual behavior, results in the policy of refusing to enforce personal services contracts. The court may award the plaintiff (Dreck) monetary damages for any extra costs entailed in having someone else complete the study.

An increasingly common problem is the reverse of this situation: the health care practitioner has signed a contract that has a noncompete agreement. This might say that the signer agrees not to work for competing managed care plan for a year, or that the practitioner will not practice within three miles of the previous employer for two years. If the practitioner violates the terms of these contracts, the courts are often willing to grant an injunction to force the practitioner to quit the noncomplying job. Unlike an order to do a job, which can require ongoing supervision, an order to not do a job is simple to enforce.

MONETARY DAMAGES

Most civil litigation is about compensating injured individuals or corporations, or preventing future harm through injunctive relief. The exceptions are those cases where government agencies use civil proceedings to collect money or enforce regulations, and divorce cases. In compensation cases, the monetary damages—the amount of money necessary to "make the plaintiff whole"— are the engine that drives civil litigation. If the plaintiff is personally wealthy or backed by a litigation advocacy group such as the American Civil Liberties Union, the decision to proceed with the case may be made on moral principle. Otherwise, without adequate damages to pay the plaintiff's attorney's contingent fee and provide reasonable compensation for the client, most plaintiffs will be unable to obtain representation.

Direct Economic Damages

Direct damages are the money that plaintiffs will not get or will pay out as a consequence of their injuries. There are two classes of direct economic losses: those that have already matured as of the time of trial and those that will mature in the future. Although there may be disagreement over whether a past loss was proximately caused by the injury, the amount of these matured losses may be determined with reasonable certainty. Future losses are much more difficult to analyze. In addition to factors unique to each type of future loss, all financial prognostications are subject to the vagaries of the economy. Interest rates rise and fall, wages fluctuate, and, most important, future expenses such as medical care are difficult to estimate. Future losses also depend on projections of the plaintiff's future behavior. Every plaintiff's attorney will argue that the client would have had a meteoric rise in his or her chosen field. Every defense lawyer will argue that the plaintiff was on an inexorable slide to financial ruin. The truth usually lies between these extremes, giving the jury considerable latitude in arriving at an award. In medical malpractice litigation, direct damages usually consist of lost earnings, medical expenses, and rehabilitation and accommodation expenses.

Lost Earnings

Lost earnings are calculated by comparing the plaintiff's expected income with actual income. For past losses (those that occurred prior to trial), this calculation is usually based on the assumption that the plaintiff's earnings would have been in equilibrium. Plaintiff's expected income is assumed to include cost-of-living adjustments and scheduled promotions and raises but does not include factors such as claims that the plaintiff was about to change to a more lucrative occupation. This calculation is simple for employees and persons in stable businesses. It becomes more difficult when it involves a plaintiff in a transitory state. For example, assume that the plaintiff is just starting a private medical practice. He has been in business six months when he is severely injured in an automobile accident and he is unable to return to work. If it takes four years for his case to go to trial, he will be entitled to the earnings he lost during that period. His income during the first six months of practice probably will not be represen-

tative of what his earnings would have been when the practice was fully established. In this case, the plaintiff's counsel will need to present projections of his client's potential earnings capacity.

Future earning capacity is what the plaintiff might have earned had the injury not occurred. The damages would be this earning capacity minus projected earnings in the injured condition. This is not always a positive number. If, because of injuries, the plaintiff was retrained for a higher paying job, he or she may have no damages attributable to lost earning capacity. If the plaintiff is well along in life in a dead-end job, then his or her future earning capacity may simply equal present wage plus cost-of-living adjustments.

The difficult cases involve plaintiffs starting their careers. These cases require a balancing of the plaintiff's goals against the probability of his or her achieving those goals.

Assume that the plaintiff has suffered a head injury that makes it impossible to do any job more demanding than manual labor. If the plaintiff is a successful surgeon, then his future earning capacity is fairly certain, as is his potential professional lifetime. Assuming a net income of $200,000 per year and 25 years until retirement, minus a potential income of $5,000 per year as a laborer, a first-level approximation of lost earning capacity would be ($200,000–$5,000) × 25, or $4,875,000. If he is a first-year medical student, it is fairly certain that he would have become a physician, but his level of future financial success is much less certain. In this situation, the plaintiff's future earning capacity may be limited to the average income for physicians in general. If the plaintiff is a freshman in college, then the probability of his becoming a surgeon is further reduced, as is his ability to establish a high future earning capacity.

These assumptions about the uncertainty of the plaintiff's future may cause the jury to award him less money for lost future earning capacity, but they do not prevent the plaintiff from putting on evidence to reduce the assumption of uncertainty. If the college freshman is an honor student at Yale whose mother is a prominent surgeon and there is evidence that he intended to join her practice, the jury might assume that he had a high probability of achieving his goals. Information that tends to convince a jury that the plaintiff's goals were both reasonable and personally achievable is key to a successful claim for a large award for loss of future earning capacity.

Medical Expenses

Plaintiffs are entitled to be reimbursed for all of the medical expenses attributable to their injuries. They must first prove that the expenses were due to the defendant's conduct rather than a preexisting or coincidental condition. They must then prove that the expenses were reasonable and necessary. Finally, they must project the cost of future medical care necessitated by the injury. Each of these issues requires expert testimony, usually available from the plaintiff's treating physician. (This is true even in medical malpractice cases because it does not require questioning the competence of a fellow physician.) The defendant must then contest the plaintiff's need for medical care. This is complicated by the general assumption that a plaintiff has no incentive to submit to unnecessary medical care. Unfortunately for the defense, medical expenses have great strategic value.

Unlike medical malpractice litigation, most personal injury cases begin with a plaintiff who was in good health and suffered an acute injury. In an automobile accident case, the plaintiff must prove that the accident was due to the defendant's negligence. The plaintiff also must put on evidence that the accident caused the injuries in question. This is usually a perfunctory matter because the link between the accident and the plaintiff's injuries is obvious. The only question is whether some of the medical expenses are attributable to a preexisting condition and would have been incurred without the accident. Even if the plaintiff has chronic back pain, she may still claim that the accident aggravated her problems. The defendant will be liable for the additional expense of treating the now-worsened back pain. Determining the extent that a defendant's conduct aggravated a plaintiff's preexisting condition is difficult even in simple automobile accidents. It is frequently the pivotal issue in medical malpractice litigation.

Preexisting Illness

Unlike automobile accidents, most medical malpractice litigation involves plaintiffs with substantial preexisting illness. These cases require expert testimony on the issue of causation—the extent that the defendant's negligence increased the patient's medical costs. If the patient has a serious chronic disease, it may be impossible to prove that the physician's negligence increased the cost of the patient's care. This fact, combined with the patient's limited earning capacity, makes it very difficult to establish sufficient damages to justify bringing a medical malpractice lawsuit on behalf of an elderly, chronically ill patient.

There are two classes of cases in which the defendant causes an injury independent of the patient's preexisting illness or condition. A small number are pure accidents, unrelated to questions about medical judgment. Typical of these are slips and falls in the hospital, burns from improperly grounded electrosurgical devices, and the patient's receiving medications and procedures meant for a different patient. It is usually easy to separate the medical costs of these mishaps from the patient's overall medical care. The more difficult cases are those in which the patient has a self-limited or curable medical condition and suffers a severe injury from medical treatment—for example, birth trauma cases and anesthesia-related injuries in otherwise healthy persons undergoing elective procedures such as orthopaedic surgery. The plaintiff may have difficulty in proving that the defendant was negligent, but once negligence has been established, the excess medical costs are obvious.

Future Medical Costs

The uncertainty of future medical expenses makes them controversial. Projecting future medical costs requires a long-term prognosis for both the plaintiff and the economy. Given the recent inflation rate for health care, any projection of the cost of care 30 years in the future will result in an astronomical number. The plaintiff's most certain evidence of future medical needs is the current cost of the needed medical care. If the plaintiff requires constant care, the jury's starting point is the current cost of these services. To attack the plaintiff's projections successfully, the defendant must convince the jury that the plaintiff's condition will improve. Conversely, the defendant's position is strongest when the plaintiff is not currently in need of medical care.

Awards for future medical expenses underlie many large jury verdicts. The largest awards are for persons who will require long-term skilled nursing care, augmented with acute medical services. Central nervous system injuries are perhaps the most expensive, especially given the legal assumption that the patient will have the same life span as an uninjured person of the same age. Although respiratory and other complications greatly decrease the average survival of severely brain-injured patients or those with high spinal cord injuries, the law is concerned with the theoretical possibility of a long life, not its statistical probability. It is the cost of future medical rehabilitative services that makes birth injury cases so expensive.

Rehabilitation and Accommodation

The plaintiff is entitled to rehabilitation and retraining expenses. These are also to the defendant's benefit if they increase the plaintiff's earning capacity or reduce his or her need for custodial care. They are detrimental to the plaintiff's case if they create the impression that the plaintiff may recover from the injuries. Plaintiff's attorneys do not stress the extent to which their clients might be rehabilitated. Insurance companies exacerbate this problem by not offering the plaintiff money for rehabilitation expenses immediately. The ideal situation for the plaintiff's attorney is to convince the jury that the client might have been rehabilitated but for the callous refusal of the defendant to pay the claim, but now it is too late.

A plaintiff who has been disabled or requires special care is entitled to the cost of any housing modifications necessary to facilitate his or her care. These may be as simple as installing wheelchair ramps or as costly as buying the plaintiff a house to ensure that his or her medical needs will be met. The plaintiff is also entitled to the value of any property damaged as a result of the defendant's conduct. This is usually an automobile, but it may be a house (plane crash cases), a horse, or any other property involved in the accident.

The Strategic Value of Medical Expenses

Medical expenses and lost wages are the most concrete elements of the plaintiff's damages. The plaintiff's personal characteristics often undermine his or her lost wage claims, but medical expense claims do not depend on the personal worth of the plaintiff. In many medical malpractice cases, the medical expenses are the bulk of the plaintiff's damages, driving the enormous awards in cases involving brain-damaged infants. Juries are not reticent about giving the plaintiff money to pay for medical care. From their perspective, it is not a choice between the plaintiff's or the physician's bearing the costs; it is a choice between the physician and society. The jury may assume that if they do not give the plaintiff money to pay for medical care, he or she is likely to become a ward of the state.

Medical expenses provide the most psychologically convincing evidence of personal injuries. A long stay in the hospital and a projection of substantial future medical needs add credibility to all of the other elements of the plaintiff's case. There is a rule of thumb in automobile accident cases that the cases should settle for a multiple of the sum of the medical expenses and the plaintiff's lost wages (usually three to five times the sum).

Indirect Economic Damages

Indirect economic damages are those that do not have a ready monetary equivalent. They fall into two classes: those that represent services that the injured person might have provided to his or her family, and those that represent various aspects of mental or physical suffering by the injured person or his or her family. Services include home repairs, household services, and special services that the plaintiff might have provided. The value of sexual services in a marriage are an important component in these damages, but they are lumped with loss of companionship to form consortium. This avoids the problem of presenting expert testimony on the value of sexual services.

Defending against these noneconomic claims has pitfalls. If the defense disputes the plaintiff's pain but that pain is credible to the jury, the defendant will be seen as cruel. Establishing that the plaintiff was a shiftless wife beater is unlikely to defuse the testimony of a small child that he misses his daddy. The high ground in defending these claims is to sympathize but to question the propriety of replacing daddy with money. Inevitably, the award of indirect economic damages depends on the jury's balancing their sympathy for the plaintiff with their sympathy for the defendant.

Juries may use noneconomic damages as a way of compensating plaintiffs for items that are not directly compensable. For example, juries know that attorneys do not work for free, and they also recognize that the list of compensable items that plaintiff's counsel presents does not contain an entry for legal fees. It is widely believed, but untested, that jurors put money for attorney's fees in soft categories, such as pain and emotional distress.

Pain and Emotional Distress

One of the most controversial damage elements is compensation for pain and suffering. Pain is difficult to measure, and money does not reduce the pain, so the rationale of making the plaintiff whole falls apart. Conversely, pain profoundly disrupts the plaintiff's life, and it would seem to be an injustice to deny any recovery for it. Currently, all states allow compensation for pain, although some have established monetary ceilings for allowable recoveries for pain.

Pain and suffering may be emotional or physical. Valuing these states of mind is a speculative process. The jurors are asked to determine how much money they would need to be paid to endure the suffering that the plaintiff must live with. More specifically, they are asked to determine this sum with a short time unit, say, a few dollars an hour. The objective is to have the juror accept that the plaintiff's pain is worth a certain small amount of money per hour or per day. It is a simple exercise to multiply this small number by the number of units in the rest of the plaintiff's life and arrive at a large dollar value. (Some courts bar this approach as prejudicial.)

Pain is highly idiosyncratic. Some medical conditions are always associated with severe pain (burns, tic douloureux), but for most conditions, the presence and intensity of pain are a function of the individual. Experts may testify that the plaintiff's condition is not usually painful, but they cannot objectively establish that the plaintiff does not feel pain. The jurors weigh the plaintiff's credibility, the nature of the injury, and the medical testimony on the plaintiff's condition and prognosis. If the injury was not severe and there is no credible medical testimony that there is a physiologic basis for severe pain, typically they will award little or nothing for pain. In a medical malpractice case that involves the treatment of an inherently painful condition, the defendant may argue that the plaintiff is entitled to compensation only for increased pain.

As with pain, compensation for emotional distress is not readily reduced to a monetary value. The old rule for emotional distress limited recovery to plaintiffs who were personally in the zone of danger related to the accident. If a mother was in the street next to her child when the child was struck by a car, the mother could recover. If she was not threatened or injured herself, but only witnessed the accident, she could not recover. This harsh rule has been relaxed in most states to allow recovery in cases in which the plaintiff was not personally threatened. Recovery is still limited to close relatives. Friends and cohabitants cannot recover for emotional distress occasioned by injury to another. Most medical malpractice cases do not give rise to injury-related claims for emotional distress. It is an issue in cases that involve intentional actions, such as refusing treatment, or engaging in outrageous activities, such as sexually assaulting a patient.

Consortium

Consortium is a relatively new damage element that arose from the acceptance that the services performed by a homemaker have economic value. It has evolved to cover either spouse, and in some states it can include claims by children. Consortium is the economic value of the services that the injured person would have provided to the family but for the injury: cooking, cleaning, shopping, helping with school work, fixing the roof, and other domestic services that could conceivably be purchased from a third party. Consortium also includes elements that are unique to the injured individual: advice and counseling, companionship, and sexual services. These not readily reducible to a monetary value but are compensable in the same way as pain and emotional distress.

Consortium claims are important in cases in which there is no significant wage loss or when loss of sexual services includes the loss of reproductive potential. If the couple has not completed their family and the accident makes procreation impossible or improbable, they are entitled to compensation. They are not required to mitigate their damages through fertility technologies, and the courts do not regard adoption as a substitute for personally bearing children.

Punitive Damages

The primary role of the tort system is to compensate injured persons. A secondary role is the deterrence of socially unacceptable behavior. Making defendants pay for the harm they cause does have a deterrent effect, but in some situations the outrageous nature of a defendant's actions is out of proportion to the cost of compensating the plaintiff. In these cases, the jury is allowed to award *punitive* (also called *exemplary*) *damages* to punish the defendant:

> It is a well-established principle of the common law, that ... a jury may inflict what are called exemplary, punitive or vindictive damages upon a defendant, having in view the enormity of his offense rather than the measure of compensation to the plaintiff. ... By the common as well as by statute law, men are often punished for aggravated misconduct or lawless acts, by means of civil action, and the damages, inflicted by way of penalty or punishment, given to the party injured.[2]

Punitive damages may not be awarded for merely negligent behavior. The conduct must be intentionally harmful or grossly negligent:

> The penal aspect and public policy considerations which justify the imposition of punitive damages require that they be imposed only after a close examination of whether the defendant's conduct is "outrageous," because of "evil motive" or "reckless indifference to the rights of others." Mere inadvertence, mistake or errors of judgment which constitute mere negligence will not suffice. It is not enough that a decision be wrong. It must result from a conscious indifference to the decision's foreseeable effect. ... We prefer the term "reckless indifference" to the term "wanton," which has statutory roots now largely extinct. Wantonness is no more a form or degree of negligence than is willfulness. Willfulness and wantonness involve an awareness, either actual or constructive, of one's conduct and a realization of its probable consequences, while negligence lacks any intent, actual or constructive.[3]

Punitive damages are seldom at issue in medical malpractice litigation that arises from traditional treatment situations. In the medical treatment context, the plaintiff would need to show that the physician engaged in outrageous conduct—medical (a drunk surgeon), social (sexual abuse), or financial (fraudulently inducing the patient to undergo medically unnecessary treatment)—before a court would allow the awarding of punitive damages. They are a more significant problem for medical device manufacturers. Even in these cases, the plaintiff must usually show that the defendant knew that the product was dangerous, continued to market the product, and covered up the product defect.

The Collateral Source Rule

The United States has a tradition of favoring private insurance for compensation. One strategy to encourage the purchase of private insurance is to allow plaintiffs to recover from defendants irrespective of their own insurance coverage. This is called the *collateral source rule.* The rationale for this rule is that the defendant should not benefit from the plaintiff's foresight in paying insurance premiums. This allows insured plaintiffs to get a double recovery, to the extent that their medical bills and lost wage claims have already been paid by their insurance carrier. The traditional collateral source rule also prevented the defendant from informing the jury that the plaintiff had already been compensated by private insurance.

If the insurance company wishes to be reimbursed, this may be made part of the insurance contract. This is called a *subrogation agreement.* Workers' compensation insurance usually contains a subrogation provision, and many group health insurance policies are adding subrogation clauses, which require plaintiffs to repay their own insurance company. A subrogation agreement reduces the value of a plaintiff's case, often dramatically. If the insurer insists on full reimbursement, the plaintiff will not be able to find representation. Although the subrogation agreement allows the insurance company to litigate the claim on behalf of the plaintiff, there is no incentive for plaintiffs to cooperate if they will not receive the award. Some insurers agree to a discounted reimbursement to make it attractive for the plaintiff to sue for compensation. Others refuse to compromise their claims, forcing the plaintiff to omit medical costs from the lawsuit.

Some states have moved to modify or abolish the collateral source rule. They may allow the judge to reduce the plaintiff's award by the amount of already paid expenses, allow the defense to tell the jury that the plaintiff has been compensated, or prevent the plaintiff from claiming for reimbursed injuries. It is not clear how these rules affect claims for future medical expenses since their payment is contingent on the plaintiff's maintaining his or her insurance.

Strategies for Paying Damages

The central problem in determining the proper compensation for an injury is the speculative nature of the claimant's future medical and economic needs. Traditional insurance schemes pay medical costs as they are incurred. If the claimant requires treatment five years after the injury, that claim is paid by the insurer at the time the care is rendered. This creates an open-ended obligation, but it obviates the need to speculate on the future needs of the claimant when evaluating the claim.

Lump Sum Payments

Courts do not like open-ended obligations. When the court enters a judgment, it wants to be rid of the case. If the defendant is found not liable, the plaintiff may not bring another lawsuit on the same facts. If the defendant is found liable, he or she must pay the plaintiff a sum that will compensate the plaintiff for both existing losses and all the future losses related to the injury. The plaintiff cannot come back to the court and ask for money for unforeseen consequences of the injury, and the defendant cannot come back to court and request a refund of the money if the plaintiff does not need all of it. This finality creates an incentive on both sides to put an unrealistic value on the plaintiff's injuries: plaintiffs demand too high a figure, and defendants offer too little. If the plaintiff prevails with the high value, the defendant must pay more than is appropriate. If the defendant prevails, the plaintiff may become a ward of the state for unpaid medical expenses.

The lump sum payment in a lawsuit is intended to last for the duration of the effects of the injury. For many cases, this means the rest of the plaintiff's life. These judgments may be $1 million cash, tax free. (Personal injury settlements and court awards are tax free.) Managing a sum of this magnitude so that it provides current income and future security is a difficult task. In many, perhaps most, cases, the money will be gone in a few years, and the plaintiff is left in debt, sometimes from failed investment schemes. This is undesirable social policy because plaintiffs or their dependents often become wards of the state after the lump sum has been dissipated.

Structured Settlements

The most desirable situation is to provide a way of paying the plaintiff's expenses as they arise, with offsets for both increased and reduced needs. This is incompatible with having lawsuits result in fixed obligations.

The remaining alternative is to retain the lump sum determination but to pay out the lump sum only as it is needed by the plaintiff. This is termed a *structured settlement* and is available only in a structured manner. Structured settlements may be agreed to as part of the overall judgment in a case or required by the court if the plaintiff is a minor or the state has a specific statute requiring that certain awards be structured.

Plaintiff's attorneys have an ethical obligation to inform the client fully of the value of entering into a structured settlement. Many attorneys will even reduce their fees to provide an incentive for the client to waive a right to the lump sum.

There have been many proposals to require that all large settlements and verdicts be paid on a structured or periodic payment basis. The intent is to ensure that money is available to meet the plaintiff's needs and to allow the defendant to recoup any unused money. This can happen when a plaintiff does not live long enough to use up the projected nursing and medical care allowances. In one extreme instance, a quadriplegic plaintiff was awarded more than $1 million for future medical needs. The plaintiff died shortly after the settlement papers were signed, and the money went into the plaintiff's estate. In this case, a periodic payment law would have led to a more just result.

There are problems with structured settlements. Most periodic payment proposals are not symmetric; the defendant's contribution is reduced if the plaintiff's needs diminish, but it is not increased if the plaintiff's needs were underestimated. A second problem is that they make the calculation and awarding of attorney's fees difficult. The value of the award must be reduced to net present value and fees calculated and paid as a lump sum in addition to the periodic payments. The most serious problem is ensuring that the defendant will be solvent during the period over which the award must be paid out. The usual way to handle this is to require the defendant to buy an annuity from a third-party financial institution. The defendant will want to buy the least expensive annuity that will provide the necessary payments to the plaintiff. Since the stability of the financial institution is a factor in the pricing of annuities, the least expensive annuity may be backed by the least stable institution. If the institution fails, the plaintiff will receive no compensation.

PRODUCTS LIABILITY

Physicians become involved in products liability litigation as witnesses and defendants. When medical devices fail, injured patients usually sue the physician using or prescribing the device, as well as suing the device manufacturer. Lawsuits involving products are brought under the legal theory of strict liability because they use a less rigorous standard of proof than a negligence lawsuit. The general form of this standard is found in the Restatement of Torts, Second, section 402a. (The Restatement is a compilation of legal principles. It is not a statute and does not have legal force unless adopted by a state's courts or legislature.)

Sec. 402A. Special Liability of Seller of Product for Physical Harm to User or Consumer

(1) One who sells any product in a defective condition unreasonably dangerous to the user or consumer or to his property is subject to liability for physical harm thereby caused to the ultimate user or consumer, or to his property, if
   (a) the seller is engaged in the business of selling such a product, and
   (b) it is expected to and does reach the user or consumer without substantial change in the condition in which it is sold.

(2) The rule stated in Subsection (1) applies although
   (a) the seller has exercised all possible care in the preparation and sale of his product, and
   (b) the user or consumer has not bought the product from or entered into any contractual relation with the seller.

It is section 1 that creates the strict liability. It allows the injured person to recover if the product was defective and unreasonably dangerous but does not require that the defect be caused by negligence of the defendant. Some states also reduce the plaintiff's burden of proving causation in products cases. For example, assume the respirator hose connector breaks on a patient dependent upon the respirator. An ICU nurse notices that the patient has suddenly developed an arrhythmia but does not check the patient for 20 minutes. When the nurse finally checks the patient, the broken connector is found, and so is a severely hypoxic patient.

The nurse was clearly negligent in not checking on the patient. This is the proximate cause of the injury and would support an independent negligence action against the nurse and his or her employer. While the respirator connector was defective, the injury would not have occurred if the nurse had attended to the patient properly. In a pure negligence case, the product manufacturer might successfully argue that the nurse's intervening negligence cut off its liability. This is a strong argument in the ICU because part of the nurse's job is to be alert to failing equipment. In most states, however, the device manufacturer will be held strictly liable for the injury, irrespective of the nurse's negligence. Both the connector manufacturer and the nurse (hospital) would be liable for the injury.

Physicians are often drawn into products liability litigation. The plaintiff sues the physician in hopes of a potential second recovery or help in pinning the liability on the product manufacturer. The manufacturer may force the physician to be joined as a codefendant by alleging that the injury was caused by misuse of the device rather than by a defect. This is common when the alleged defect is in design, not manufacture. One series of cases involved an anesthesia machine whose connectors could be reversed, with fatal consequences. The manufacturer alleged that the machine was designed for an expert user who had the responsibility for ensuring that the device was properly assembled. The anesthesiologist claimed that the machine should have been designed to prevent misassembly. The manufacturer lost because the jury determined that the manufacturer could not rely on the anesthesiologist to know how to properly assemble the anesthesia machine.[4]

The Legal Risks of Safety Devices*

Paradoxically, medical instrumentation poses the greatest challenges in critical care units (CCUs) but generates the most litigation in areas such as obstetrics and anesthesia. CCUs are the subject of legal debate far in excess of the medical malpractice cases they spawn. Most of the legal attention has been focused on the right of patients to refuse life support rather than on medical malpractice issues. As financial considerations reduce the availability of CCU care, it is expected that the legal controversies will shift from refusal of care to denial of care and conventional malpractice claims. Before discussing the expected increase in CCU-related litigation, it is important to understand why a relatively simple problem such as obstetric monitoring has generated much more litigation than the difficult problem of CCU monitoring.

When physicians think of medical device litigation, it usually brings to mind products liability claims against the device's manufacturer. Such primary litigation is a problem for device manufacturers but not a direct threat to physicians using the devices. The problem for physicians is secondary litigation. Secondary litigation arises from medical devices that perform properly but increase litigation against the physicians who use them. Safety devices such as monitors have generated most secondary litigation, although it can occur with life-supporting devices as well. The best-documented example of secondary litigation is that due to obstetric fetal monitors. The problems that arose from fetal monitors have implications for selection of new technologies by physicians and hospitals.

Electronic fetal heart monitors and pulse oximeters illustrate a continuum from devices that increase secondary litigation to those that decrease it. The widespread use of fetal heart moni-

Source: This section adapted from E.P. Richards, Living with Uncertainty: Information Theory and Critical Care Decision Making, *Journal of Intensive Care Medicine*, Vol. 5, pp. 91–92, © 1990 E.P. Richards and E.P. Richards and C.W. Walter, How Effective Safety Devices Lead to Secondary Litigation, *IEEE Engineering in Medicine and Biology*, Vol. 10, No. 2, pp. 66–68, © 1991 E.P. Richards.

tors was accompanied by a dramatic increase in obstetric malpractice litigation. It is certain that factors other than fetal heart monitors were primarily responsible for this increase. It is also certain, however, that the use of these monitors did not decrease litigation and, in the cases where fetal heart monitor records are available, these records increase the probability of litigation when an infant is born damaged. Conversely, the widespread adoption of pulse oximetry in the operating room was accompanied by a dramatic reduction in malpractice claims against anesthesiologists. These monitors appear to be among the primary causes of this reduction in claims. They clearly are not being used against anesthesiologists in the way that fetal heart monitors have been used against obstetricians.

Secondary litigation does not imply a defectively designed product, at least not in the traditional sense. Fetal heart monitors perform accurately and reliably within the constraints of what they measure. Devices that are unreliable or otherwise directly dangerous to patients will be the target of primary litigation against the device manufacturer. Pure secondary liability is an issue for otherwise safe and well-engineered devices. Secondary liability becomes a problem when the device in question documents previously undocumented behavior indicating negligence on the part of the medical care providers, records data with ambiguous interpretations, and/or inappropriately leads to changes in medical care supervision, staffing, or patient contact because of reliance on the device.

Filtering Data

The first problem, documentation of previously undocumented behavior, is common to all recording instruments. Medical record systems that depend on people to record events, either on paper or computer, are highly filtered. Sometimes this filtering is conscious and intentional, as when personnel attempt to cover up an error by not entering incriminating information into the medical chart. In the worst case, there may even be attempts to change previous entries. This intentional distortion of data, however, is assumed to be relatively infrequent. Most commonly the filtering is unconscious and unintentional. It may occur because the recorder's memory fades between rendering the care or making the observations and recording them in the medical record. In many situations, it occurs because the nurses do not make their primary entries into the medical record.

While generally discouraged by protocols on medical records management, off-chart records are commonly used by nurses to keep track of things to do, medications given, and patient observations. These temporary records allow the nurses to batch-enter data into medical records rather than keep contemporaneous records. This allows two stages of filtering: first the information is compressed into a minimal temporary record, and then that minimal record is expanded into the permanent chart record. Such filtering makes it easy to transform an item accidentally from the to-do list to the done list without the task's actually being performed. It also gives the filter an extra chance to remove nonconforming information.

Filters are defined by what they exclude. Human clinical filters tend to exclude things that do not easily fit into the expectations associated with the care of a given patient. This should not be seen as an act of deception or even of carelessness. It is more a smoothing of data that tends to obscure anomalies. The smoothing is aided by the limited amount of information that can be recorded by periodic observations recorded in essentially narrative format. The end result of this process of smoothing and filtering is a medical record that is more often characterized by what it does not contain than by what it does document. This is borne out in litigation where records are usually incriminating because they fail to record what was allegedly done.

Fetal Monitors

When a real-time recording technology is introduced into a situation that previously depended on manual records, the amount of data recorded increases dramatically. A record that displayed fetal heart rates taken at 15- to 30-minute intervals and recorded at some later time by a nurse is suddenly displaced with a fetal heart monitor that generates a paper tape with a continuously recorded fetal rate. Previously unnoted short-term irregularities are now carefully preserved. Whenever an injured child is born, the fetal heart rate record will be scanned by plaintiff's counsel in the hopes of finding some deviation from normal that can be used to build a case against the delivering physician. This search is seldom in vain because of the second problem that leads to secondary liability: data with ambiguous interpretations.

Fetal heart rate is monitored in women in labor to determine if the fetus's well-being is compromised. If the fetus is in trouble, the usual response is an emergency Cesarean section. Fetal heart monitors provide a reasonably accurate record of fetal heart rate. The problem is in interpreting these records. Dramatic, prolonged slowing of the fetal heart rate clearly means trouble. But many other patterns of fetal heart rate irregularities do not so clearly point to trouble that they unambiguously call for an emergency Cesarean section with its attendant risks and costs. On the other hand, if the infant is born damaged, such irregularities will seem very important in hindsight. In a strict sense, much of what a fetal heart monitor records is not information: it does not reduce the physician's uncertainty over the selection and timing of Cesarean sections.

In retrospect, the major factor in secondary litigation from fetal heart monitors may be the third factor: the shift in patient care patterns that accompanied the routine use of the devices. The traditional method of determining fetal fitness was to auscultate the fetal heart with a stethoscope. This requires that someone closely observe the laboring woman at frequent intervals. The premise of electronic fetal monitoring was that the heart rate itself was the critical parameter in this evaluation. It may be that other observations that accompanied this direct and intimate contact with the patient provided a necessary context for interpreting the significance of changes in the heart rate. As physicians and nurses came to rely on fetal heart monitors, they could evaluate the fetus by looking at the monitor strip and ignore the patient entirely. It is also likely that these cursory evaluations decreased in frequency because the monitor allowed

the retrospective review of the heart rate. While it is difficult to sort out the causal factors, the most recent research indicates that the use of fetal monitors increases the probability of adverse fetal outcomes.

Pulse Oximeters

Pulse oximetry is a relatively simple technology that measures arterial oxygen saturation in real time. The oximeters that are routinely used in clinical care are display-only instruments; they do not produce a continuous historical record of oxygen saturation. When saturation falls below a certain threshold, an alarm is sounded, unambiguously signaling that the patient needs more oxygen or that the instrument has become detached or dysfunctional. In either case, definitive action can be taken at once. These factors make oximetry an ideal safety technology. It helps prevent injuries while not otherwise affecting record-keeping or staffing practices. This is not entirely due to special virtues of oximetry.

It is rare that the patient is left completely alone in the operating room. The genius of oximetry is that it is an easily understandable monitor. When the alarm goes off, the surgeon can call for help if the anesthesiologist has drifted away. It can be assumed that oximetry used as a remote-sensing, continuous-recording technology will pose the same documentation and staffing problems as fetal heart monitors. These may be outweighed by the clear intervention signal provided by oximetry. If, however, hospitals use recording-remote oximeters in situations where this clear signal is ignored, they will suddenly find oximetry to be a fertile source of litigation.

Lessons for Technology Assessment

Continuous-recording instruments are invaluable research tools. If there is a central criticism of fetal heart monitor usage, it is that the monitors were adopted for routine use without the research background necessary to understand their limitations. Fetal heart monitors illustrate that data, as opposed to information, increase the risk of litigation. This happens because plaintiffs' attorneys thrive on ambiguity. If a patient is injured, the plaintiff's attorney will comb the records for anything that cannot be clearly explained to portray as the cause of the injury. This is countered to some extent by the highly filtered nature of traditional medical records. Continuously recorded streams of ambiguous instrument output, in contrast, provide a gold mine of exploitable ambiguity.

It is critical that new instruments be evaluated for the reliability of their intrinsic measurements and for the clinical significance of those measurements. Do the data resolve clinical questions or merely complicate them? This question becomes more interesting as hospitals purchase clinical information systems that feed the outputs of various monitors into a computer-based continuous-recording system. The assumption is that since these instruments are already in place, their output must be useful. It is possible, however, that many existing measurements are useful only in the larger context of patient care. Like a fetal heart rate observed without the context of the mother, their readings may be much less valuable as retrospective records. Given that efficacy testing is a recent innovation for medical devices, it is also possible that some existing measurements are clinically irrelevant. This means that their outputs will be randomly related to the patient's condition, creating that ambiguity so valuable to plaintiffs' attorneys.

Clinical instruments provide data, not necessarily information that aids in clinical decision making. The data create noise that can obscure significant clinical information while providing clear hindsight to those who would second-guess the physician's actions. Real-time clinical information systems take this to the extreme. Some of these systems carefully log the output of every monitor in the CCU, allow free-text comments by CCU personnel who have not necessarily seen all the recorded data, and create the expectation that all data will be recorded. This last expectation may be the most damaging, given the traditional presumption that missing information is assumed to support the plaintiff's case. Unless these systems are carefully thought through and tested, it may be that the connector that is used to connect most real-time recording systems will someday be renamed the plaintiff's best friend.

DEFENSIVE MEDICINE

Defensive medicine is aptly named. The term implies both actions to prevent litigation and an untrusting attitude toward patients. Defensive medicine is based on three assumptions: that making more accurate diagnoses will reduce malpractice claims; that tests and procedures improve the probability of a correct diagnosis; and that the use of more technology implies better medical care.[5] These assumptions come from a physician-oriented view of medical care. The problem is that patients, not physicians, bring malpractice lawsuits. Patients are primarily concerned with the outcome and the humanistic aspects of their treatment. It is physicians who care about diagnoses. Patients want to be treated well and successfully. Defensive medicine generates anger and expense, both of which increase the probability that an injured patient will seek legal counsel.

Defensive medicine directly increases the probability of injury when it involves dangerous tests or procedures. For example, intravenous pyelograms (IVPs) pose a significant risk of complications. If an IVP is ordered as a necessary diagnostic test, the risk of the procedure is balanced by the benefit of the diagnostic information that it produces. If an IVP is ordered as a defensive measure, there is no benefit to the patient to offset the risk. Since a defensive test or procedure is, by definition, one that does not have a favorable risk or cost benefit ratio for the patient, the patient may be expected to sue successfully for any major complications of a defensive test or procedure.

Technology-Oriented Medicine

The last 30 years of technology-oriented medicine have shifted patients' perception of the role of the physician. Before the explosion of technological medicine, the role of the physician was to cure, if possible, and to comfort. It was accepted that in many cases the physician would not be able to cure the disease. This was not a failing of the physician but a recognition that illness and death are an integral part of life. The shift to technology-oriented medicine helped to drive the growth of procedure-oriented specialty medical practice. This view of the physician as a skilled mechanic leads to an expectation of cure and to irreconcilable conflicts.

If the technological interventions offered fail, the physician fails because the supplementary role of comforter has been lost. Defensive medicine must perceptibly improve the outcome of care if it is to be an effective strategy. If it does not improve the patient's perception of the outcome of the care, its negative impact on the humanistic aspects of care will engender patient dissatisfaction and hostility, resulting in an increase in litigation. In the worst case, it interferes with providing quality medical care: angering the patient and providing the grounds for a lawsuit.

Diagnosis and Testing

Arriving at a diagnosis is the intellectual end point of defensive medicine. Defensive medicine is directed at finding the definitive test to establish the diagnosis or doing enough tests to rule out other possible diagnoses. This ruling out is considered an important legal protection should someone later determine the patient's actual problem.

The ruling out of alternative diagnostic hypotheses is a valid strategy if the universe of possible alternatives is sufficiently large. But it is a dangerous strategy if the initial diagnostic assumptions constrain subsequent data collection and hypothesis generation. The physician must guard against ignoring the patient's stated problem in favor of a diagnostically tidier problem. For example, if the patient has trouble walking because of a plantar wart, the physician should not attempt to repair the patient's asymptomatic slipped disk as a substitute for removing the plantar wart.

This emphasis on diagnosis leads to laboratory diagnosis as the ideal of technological medicine.[6] Clinical laboratory tests are seen as objective, while taking a history and physical is subjective. Laboratory tests are easy to replicate, may be dis-

cussed without reference to the context of the specific patient, and, at least superficially, are easy to interpret. Tests with numerical results lend an air of science to medical practice.

Before the advent of digital electronic calculators, calculations were worked out with slide rules. When digital calculators became cheap enough for general use in the classroom, many teachers opposed their use. There was a philosophical concern with the false rigor that electronic calculators created. The slide rule was accurate to only two or three digits; thus, using a slide rule constantly reminded the student of the approximate nature of the underlying data. Digital calculators and digital reading instruments display many digits—but most medical data are approximate, usually to only two digits of accuracy and sometimes less. Manipulations of these data that do not take into account their limited accuracy lead to spurious results, but results that appear to be scientific because they are numerical.

This problem of false rigor is exacerbated by the use of multiple test panels. These panels include large numbers of tests that measure mostly unrelated parameters. The test results are expressed numerically, but the evaluation of the results depends on the comparison of these numerical values with normal values. Normal values are determined by statistical techniques. They are usually set such that 5% or 10% of healthy people given the test will have values outside the normal range.

When a patient is given a panel with 20 independent tests, each with a normal value defined by the 95th percentile, then the probability is high that at least one test will be falsely normal or abnormal. The noise from the false test results makes it more difficult to evaluate the diagnostic content of the test panel and increases the chance that important information will be lost in the mass of data. The tests may also document important problems that the physician missed. When an injured patient seeks the advice of an attorney, the attorney has the luxury of working backward from the injury. If the physician did not order the proper tests, then all the other tests that were ordered become irrelevant. And if the proper test was ordered but the results were overlooked or ignored, the emphasis on ordering tests accentuates the error in not acting on the relevant test results.

Specialty Blinders

Many specialists believe that the best way to avoid litigation is to ignore all problems that are not part of their specialty. But many patients have multispecialty problems that require one physician to take overall responsibility for their care. This problem is exacerbated if the specialist is at the end of a long referral chain. In this situation, the specialist is prone to assume that someone else has ruled out all diagnoses other than those that would be appropriate to his or her special field of practice.

One case that settled prior to trial involved a woman in her mid-50s who presented to her physician with abdominal pain. Initial evaluation did not uncover an explanation, and she eventually sought care at a hospital emergency room. The emergency room physician did a general evaluation and wrote a differential diagnosis that included abdominal aortic aneurysm. She was admitted to the hospital under the care of a gynecologist and given an ultrasound and a pelvic examination. A mass was noted in her abdomen, and the pelvic examination discovered cervical cancer. She was then transferred to the regional cancer center for definitive treatment. Once in the cancer center on the gynecology service, she was treated for the cancer.

Over the next couple of weeks, she continued to complain of pain that was inappropriate for the extent of her cancer. Her treating physicians assumed that this pain was partially psychogenic, and they had her evaluated by a psychiatrist. The pain suddenly became much worse, and she was given a tranquilizer for anxiety. When she was finally examined three hours later, there was no blood supply to her legs; she had clotted off an abdominal aortic aneurysm. This diagnosis had been hinted at early in her evaluation, but once she was on a subspecialty gynecology cancer service, all diagnostic considerations were limited to gynecologic cancer and its complications.

REFERENCES

1. *Collins v. Thakkart*, 552 N.E.2d 507 (1990).
2. *Day v. Woodworth*, 54 U.S. (13 How) 363, 371, 14 L. Ed. 181 (1851).
3. *Jardel Co. v. Kathleen Hughes*, 523 A.2d 518, 529–530 (1987).
4. Richards EP, Walter CW. How is an anesthesia machine like a lawnmower?—the problem of the learned intermediary. *IEEE Eng Med Biol Mag*. 1989;8:55.
5. Harris JE. Defensive medicine: it costs, but does it work? *JAMA*. 1987;257:2801–2802.
6. Fortess EE, Kapp MB. Medical uncertainty, diagnostic testing, and legal liability. *Law Med Health Care*. 1985;13:213–218.

SUGGESTED READINGS

Annas GJ. Breast cancer screening in older women: Law and patient rights. *J Gerontol*. 1992;47 (special issue):121–125.

Baldwin LM, Hart LG, Lloyd M, Fordyce M, Rosenblatt RA. Defensive medicine and obstetrics. *JAMA*. 1995;274:1606–1610.

Berlin L. Standard of care. *AJR*. 1998;170:275–278.

Bovbjerg RR, Dubay LC, Kenney GM, Norton SA. Defensive medicine and tort reform: new evidence in an old bottle. *J Health Polit Policy Law*. 1996;21:267–288.

Burroughs CE. The use of practice guidelines in Wisconsin for liability protection. *Wis Med J*. 1994;93:69–75.

Cantrill SV. Clinical standards. *Emerg Med Clin North Am*. 1992;10:507–522.

Corrigan J, Wagner J, Wolfe L, Klingman D, Polishuk P. Medical malpractice reform and defensive medicine. *Cancer Invest*. 1996;14:277–284.

Daly M. Attacking defensive medicine through the utilization of practice parameters: panacea or placebo for the health care reform movement? *J Leg Med*. 1995;16:101–132.

Fish R, Ehrhardt M. The standard of care. *J Emerg Med*. 1994;12:545–552.

Ginsburg WH Jr. When does a guideline become a standard?

The New American Society of Anesthesiologists guidelines give us a clue. *Ann Emerg Med*. 1993;22:1891–1896.

Hirshfeld EB. From the Office of the General Counsel: should practice parameters be the standard of care in malpractice litigation? *JAMA*. 1991;266:2886–2891.

Jacobson PD, Rosenquist CJ. The use of low-osmolar contrast agents: technological change and defensive medicine. *J Health Polit Policy Law*. 1996;21:243–266.

Jerrold L. Litigation, legislation, and ethics: errors of judgment and the standard of care. *Am J Orthod Dentofacial Orthop*. 1997;112:694–695.

Kapp MB. Informed consent to defensive medicine: letting the patient decide. *Pharos*. 1993;56:12–14.

King JY. Practice guidelines & medical malpractice litigation. *Med Law*. 1997;16:29–39.

Kinney ED. Malpractice reform in the 1990s: past disappointments, future success? *J Health Polit Policy Law*. 1995;20:99–135.

Klingman D, Localio AR, Sugarman J, et al. Measuring defensive medicine using clinical scenario surveys. *J Health Polit Policy Law*. 1996;21:185–217.

Kravitz RL, Rolph JE, Petersen L. Omission-related malpractice claims and the limits of defensive medicine. *Med Care Res Rev*. 1997;54:456–471.

Meadow W, Lantos J. A proactive, data-based determination of the standard of medical care in pediatrics. *Pediatrics*. 1998;101:E6.

Meadow W, Lantos JD. Expert testimony, legal reasoning, and justice: the case for adopting a data-based standard of care in allegations of medical negligence in the NICU. *Clin Perinatol*. 1996;23:583–595.

Meadow WL, Lantos J, Tanz RR, Mendez D, Unger R, Wallskog P. Ought 'standard care' be the 'standard of care'? A study of the time to administration of antibiotics in children with meningitis. *Am J Dis Child*. 1993;147:40–44.

Miller FH. The legal ramifications of the NCCN practice guidelines. *Oncology (Huntingt)*. 1996;10(suppl 11):35–39.

Murphy RN. Legal and practical impact of clinical practice guidelines on nursing and medical practice. *Nurse Pract*. 1997;22:138, 147–148.

Murphy RN. Legal and practical impact of clinical practice guidelines on nursing and medical practice. *Adv Wound Care*. 1996;9:31–34.

Noble A, Brennan TA, Hyams AL. Snyder v. American Association of Blood Banks: a re-examination of liability for medical practice guideline promulgators. *J Eval Clin Pract*. 1998;4:49–62.

Pauker SG, Pauker SP. Expected-utility perspectives on defensive testing: torts, tradeoffs, and thresholds—is defensive medicine defensible? *Med Decis Making*. 1998;18:29–31.

Summerton N. Positive and negative factors in defensive medicine: a questionnaire study of general practitioners. *BMJ*. 1995;310(6971):27–29.

Taragin MI, Willett LR, Wilczek AP, Trout R, Carson JL. The influence of standard of care and severity of injury on the resolution of medical malpractice claims. *Ann Intern Med*. 1992;117:780–784.

Tingle J. Legal implications of standard setting in nursing. *Br J Nurs*. 1992;1:728–731.

Tussing AD, Wojtowycz MA. Malpractice, defensive medicine, and obstetric behavior. *Med Care*. 1997;35:172–191.

CHAPTER 3

Criminal Law Rights and Violations

HIGHLIGHTS

- The government routinely prosecutes health care practitioners for criminal law violations.
- Criminal cases can result in imprisonment, large fines, and expensive defense costs, which are not paid by medical malpractice insurance.
- Criminal defendants have substantial constitutional protections.
- Health care practitioners must know the special criminal laws that apply to medical care.
- Health care practitioners must know how to protect their rights in criminal investigations.

INTRODUCTION

Ten years ago, in the late 1980s, health care practitioners were mostly concerned with civil litigation, especially medical malpractice litigation. They were constantly involved with administrative proceedings through Medicare/Medicaid reimbursement and other federal pay programs, but this was a billing office matter, not a source of personal constant concern for the physicians and nurses. There were occasional criminal actions against physicians who sold prescriptions for controlled substances and against "Medicaid mills," but "nice" physicians and hospitals did not worry about criminal prosecution. Suggestions that physicians might face criminal prosecution for what were considered routine business practices were dismissed by most health care attorneys.[1]

Now, prominent hospitals and medical schools have paid hundreds of millions of dollars in administrative and criminal fines, health care practitioners and administrators have gone to jail, and all hospitals are working on plans to demonstrate

compliance with federal law so that they can claim mitigation under the Federal Sentencing Guidelines if they are accused of criminal behavior. Although medical malpractice litigation continues at about the same pace, it has faded into the background as a concern in the face of jail time or the administrative law death penalty: banishment from all federal programs and any facilities that deal with federal programs. It is critical that health care practitioners understand the special characteristics of the criminal law system and how to protect themselves from liability.

COMMONALITIES IN CRIMINAL AND ADMINISTRATIVE LAW

Whereas this chapter deals with criminal law, it is important to understand the parallels between criminal and administrative law, especially because in health law most of the criminal prosecutions arise from administrative law problems. Both are related in that both are actions between the state and an individual or corporation. In criminal law, the state brings and prosecutes the case in the name of the people against the defendant. (A few states still allow private individuals to bring criminal prosecutions, but these are very infrequent and involve unusual facts.) Only criminal law proceedings can result in imprisonment as a punishment for crime. Administrative law proceedings may be initiated by the state or by an individual. An example would be a hospital petitioning a local zoning board for permission to rezone land so that it could be used for a clinic. Administrative proceeding can result in fines, various remedies such as injunctions, but cannot result in imprisonment. If an administrative agency such as the Health Care Financing Administration uncovers criminal behavior, it must take it to a prosecutor who will determine whether a criminal action will be brought.

At the federal level, criminal prosecutions are brought by the Department of Justice (DOJ). Structurally, DOJ is an executive branch agency no different from the Department of Health and Human Services (DHHS) or the other cabinet-level departments. It is headed by the Attorney General, who is a political appointee of the president, confirmed by the Senate. It is subject to the same political pressures as other agencies and it shifts its enforcement priorities with the political winds. Except for its unique powers to bring criminal charges, it operates much as DHHS, and the two interact as independent agencies. DHHS brings its own civil investigations through the Office of the Inspector General (OIG) and can demand millions of dollars in reimbursement if it finds improper claims practices. It can also refer the matter to DOJ for further investigation as a criminal matter. DOJ can bring its own investigation of the same matters, either involving OIG or not. From the perspective of a health care practitioner, these federal investigations seem to be a seamless blend of administrative and criminal proceedings.

At the state level, criminal justice is much more fragmented. Each state has an Office of the Attorney General, which functions much like DOJ, except in many states the Attorney General is an independently elected office that is not under the control of the governor. In addition, counties have district attorneys and courts and cities have municipal courts, all of which, depending on the jurisdiction, can bring criminal charges. State administrative agencies are similarly fragmented. Some health functions, such as licensing professionals, are reserved to a state agency. Others, such as public health matters, may be divided between a state Department of Health, and city and county health agencies. There is usually limited effective cooperation between the state and the local agencies, and between the local agencies, whether administrative or criminal. In some situations, such as Medicaid—a state-administered program with substantial federal funding and oversight—investigations will involve both state, local, and federal authorities.

THE CONSTITUTIONAL BASIS FOR CRIMINAL LAW

The criminal law is part of the police power— the power to protect the public health and safety— that was shared between the states and the federal government. Historically, federal criminal law dealt with uniquely federal issues such as antitrust activities by interstate corporations, income tax evasion, treason, and specific crimes such as federal civil rights violations that did not exist under state law. The last several decades have seen the expansion of federal criminal law into areas such as narcotics dealing that are also prosecuted by the states and development of state parallels with federal civil rights laws. The result is that state and federal powers now overlap to such an extent that many crimes can be prosecuted by either authority, and sometimes both.

Criminal law is used to protect individuals both for their own good and to protect the social order that makes it possible to govern. Criminal prosecution redresses the injury to the state by punishing the defendant and deters future criminal activity by the example of the defendant and by the practical expedient of keeping defendants in prison where they cannot commit new crimes against society. Individuals who are injured by crimes can bring civil (tort) litigation against the criminal for compensation. Except in the rarest of circumstances, the individual cannot bring a criminal prosecution but must persuade the police or the state's attorney to bring the prosecution. The state may choose to not prosecute despite the victim's evidence and the state may choose to prosecute even if the victim does not want the defendant prosecuted. Unlike in civil litigation, these choices are reserved to the state because the criminal prosecution is ultimately about protecting the state, rather than individuals. Criminal laws are enforced by the government in its own name: *United States v. Salerno*, or *Texas v. Powell*.

Punishment versus Prevention

The key distinction between criminal law and civil or administrative law is that only criminal laws can punish a person with imprisonment or execution. This distinction is critically important because an individual charged with a crime is entitled to several legal protections that are not available in civil or administrative proceedings. Sometimes the distinction is difficult to understand because the nature of the confinement may be the same as one that would usually be imposed by a criminal law. Thus disease control laws that use the jail for quarantine were found to not be criminal laws, nor are mental health laws that allow persons to be confined for life because they were dangerous to self or others. Even laws designed to prevent witnesses from fleeing by confining them in prison and treating them as prisoners were not found to be criminal laws.[2]

The courts reviewing these laws to determine whether defendants were entitled to criminal law protections looked to the purpose of the law, not the ultimate confinement. If the imprisonment is to punish for past actions, it is a criminal law. If it is to prevent some type of future harm—spreading a communicable disease, endangering others because of mental illness, or leaving the jurisdiction before testifying at trial—then it is a civil law and the defendant is not entitled to full criminal law due process protections. Although the courts tend to make this determination on the stated intent of the law as passed by the legislature, they are sen-

sitive to claims that the legislature is using a civil law to punish without proper safeguards.

Constitutional Protections

Most health care practitioners' experience with litigation is limited to civil litigation. Although most health care practitioners have not been personally sued for medical malpractice, all know someone who has been. Traumatic as this litigation can be for a health care practitioner, criminal prosecution is much worse. The first shock is that health care practitioners are not insured against criminal prosecution and must pay all defense costs and any bail from their own pockets. This can amount to tens to hundreds of thousands of dollars, much of which must be paid up front. Although a truly indigent defendant is entitled to a court-appointed attorney, few health care practitioners fall into this category. Unfortunately, the chances of successfully defending a criminal case is closely related to how much money the defendant can put into the case. If the defendant is found not guilty, there is only an extremely limited right to reimbursement for the defense costs. As one criminal law professor aptly put it, "You can beat the rap, but you cannot beat the ride."

The publicity can be devastating to a legitimate business or a professional, even if the jury finds them not guilty. For health care practitioners and other providers, conviction of a crime related to a federal health program means that the defendant cannot participate in federal programs such as Medicare and cannot work for an entity that does participate. This will put a hospital out of business and can make it almost impossible for practitioners to find work, even if they do not lose their professional licenses as a result of the conviction. In the worst case scenario, the defendant can go to prison. The potential sanctions from criminal prosecution and conviction are so devastating that the Constitution provides several unique safeguards for criminal defendants.

Habeas Corpus

"The privilege of the writ of habeas corpus shall not be suspended, unless when in cases of rebellion or invasion the public safety may require it."[3]

Bill of Attainder—Ex Post Facto Laws

"No Bill of Attainder or ex post facto Law shall be passed."[4]

Trial by Jury

"The Trial of all Crimes, except in Cases of Impeachment, shall be by Jury; and such Trial shall be held in the State where the said Crimes shall have been committed; but when not committed within any State, the Trial shall be at such Place or Places as the Congress may by Law have directed."[5]

Unreasonable Searches and Seizures

"The right of the people to be secure in their persons, houses, papers, and effects, against unreasonable searches and seizures, shall not be violated, and no Warrants shall issue, but upon probable cause, supported by Oath or affirmation, and particularly describing the place to be searched, and the persons or things to be seized."[6]

Criminal Actions—Provisions Concerning—Due Process of Law and Just Compensation Clauses

"No person shall be held to answer for a capital, or otherwise infamous crime, unless on a presentment or indictment of a Grand Jury, except in cases arising in the land or naval forces, or in the Militia, when in actual service in time of War or public danger; nor shall any person be subject for the same offence to be twice put in jeopardy of life or limb; nor shall be compelled in any criminal case to be a witness against himself, nor be deprived of life, liberty, or property, without due process of law; nor shall private property be taken for public use, without just compensation."[7]

Rights of the Accused

"In all criminal prosecutions, the accused shall enjoy the right to a speedy and public trial, by an impartial jury of the State and district wherein the crime shall have been committed, which district shall have been previously ascertained by law,

and to be informed of the nature and cause of the accusation; to be confronted with the witnesses against him; to have compulsory process for obtaining witnesses in his favor, and to have the Assistance of Counsel for his defense."[8]

Bail-Punishment

"Excessive bail shall not be required, nor excessive fines imposed, nor cruel and unusual punishments inflicted."[9]

APPLYING THE CONSTITUTIONAL PROTECTIONS

Although most criminal law prosecutions are done by the states or their political subdivisions, under state and local laws, these are conducted under rules established through interpretations of the Constitution by the U.S. Supreme Court. What constitutes a crime varies between states, but the constitutional rights of the accused criminal apply uniformly across the states.

Specificity Requirements

One of the great complaints about the civil law system is that you can sue over anything. Although this is not strictly true, the civil law system is designed to be very flexible and to provide remedies for new problems that have not yet been anticipated by the courts or the legislatures. The administrative law system also has very broad authority to deal with new problems, or to apply new solutions to old problems, much to the chagrin of a regulated industry, as anyone who tries to keep up with Medicare/Medicaid rules can attest. In contrast, the common law tradition and the Constitution require that a person be given specific notice of what constitutes a crime. For example, the Constitution bans ex post facto laws—those that are passed to criminalize behavior that has already occurred—and bills of attainder—laws passed to punish specific individuals without trial or other due process protections.[10]

More generally, a defendant may attack a criminal law as vague or overbroad, meaning that it does not define the crime or the elements of the crime in such a way that a reasonable person would know what was illegal. If the court agrees, it will declare the law unconstitutional, preventing the prosecution of the defendant. As a result of this constitutional requirement, criminal statutes are very specific, spelling out the required details of the crime. This is most true when the crime is a conventional crime against another person, such as rape, murder, assault, or fraud. The standards for business-related crimes, such as antitrust or Medicare fraud, are much less specific, sometimes saying little more than that submitting a false claim is a crime. Although such laws have been attacked for vagueness and overbreadth, these challenges have been unsuccessful.

Right to Counsel

It is almost impossible for a nonlawyer to present a case successfully in the U.S. legal system. Lack of representation so compromises a criminal defendant's rights that the U.S Supreme Court requires all criminal defendants to have appointed counsel at government expense, if the defendant is unable to pay a lawyer.[11] This means that the defendant has to be informed of the right to have counsel, that if he says anything before counsel arrives it can be used against him at trial, and that if he cannot afford a lawyer, one will be appointed for him—his *Miranda* rights.[12] This does not mean that unless the defendant can afford the O.J. defense team that the state will pay for his defense. The state is required only to pay the defense lawyer for the minimum defense necessary to preserve the client's constitutional rights, not to win the client's case. Other than cases involving the death penalty, the state is usually unwilling to pay for expert testimony, the evaluation of forensic evidence, investigators, or the other basic requirements for properly defending complex criminal cases.

The police have to inform a potential defendant of his rights when it is probable that he will be charged. They do not have to inform witnesses of their Miranda rights during the routine investigation of case. If an investigator starts reading the Miranda rights to you, you are in trouble and need to get an attorney before you say anything else.

Privilege against Self-Incrimination

The Fifth Amendment of the Constitution establishes the privilege against self-incrimination. This prevents the government from forcing a person to testify against himself. Although the founders were particularly concerned about persons being tortured into incriminating themselves, the courts have extended the privilege to any forced testimony. The result of the privilege against self-incrimination is that the state must prove its case without the help of the defendant. If the defendant stands silent, he wins unless the state can produce sufficient evidence of his guilt. At trial, the defendant can refuse to take the stand and testify, and the prosecutor may not comment on the defendant's silence; that is, no remarks about why the defendant will not take the stand and explain what really happened.

The privilege against self-incrimination also applies to the investigation of a case. A defendant can refuse to talk to the police, but cannot refuse to appear before the grand jury. The defendant can refuse to answer questions that he believes will incriminate him, which is called "taking the Fifth." The privilege applies to any crime, state or federal, so the defendant can take the Fifth when he is being investigated by the state because he is concerned about implicating himself for a federal crime. Witnesses, however, who are not defendants or potential defendants, cannot refuse to testify, and may even be imprisoned for contempt of court if they refuse. In some circumstances the prosecution can get around the defendant's privilege against self-incrimination by offering the defendant immunity for the crimes he might mention in testifying. Once immunized against the possibility of prosecution, the witness can no longer refuse to testify by invoking the privilege against self-incrimination.

The privilege against self-incrimination is limited to testimony. Defendants can be forced to give hair samples, blood samples, and other bodily fluids. They can be forced to produce writing samples, and in some cases to give over information such as combinations to safes or the location of bank accounts. These are governed by the rules on searchs and seizures, rather than those governing self-incrimination.

Searches and Seizures

The Fourth Amendment provides two interrelated protections for persons subjected to searches and seizures: (1) they must be reasonable; and (2) there must be some proper basis for warrants to authorize searches and seizures. These provisions are related in that the reasonability of a search or seizure is usually defined by reference to whether it was performed with a proper warrant. Warrants are issued by a judge who reviews the evidence presented by the police or prosecutor on the basis for the probable cause that the warrant will lead to evidence and what that evidence is. Probable cause can be an informant's tip, the statement of a witness, or leads developed by the police or others who are investigating the case.

The courts have carved out some exceptions to the requirement of a warrant. One deals with searches of the immediate vicinity of the suspect made for the purpose of finding weapons that might endanger the officers or others. Another is plain view exception: the police do not need a warrant for evidence that is in plain view. This can be on the car seat next to the driver, assuming that the car was stopped for a proper reason. It can be in a house if the officer is otherwise properly in the house. (The difficult cases for the plain view exception are those that involve technological aids such as telescopes, satellite cameras, infrared sensors, and other techniques that extend surveillance beyond the unaided eye.) Chapter 12 discusses the exception for routine health and safety inspections. Although these can be done without a warrant, they are restricted to the public health purpose of the inspection—if the rat inspector finds a stash of cocaine, it cannot be used as evidence in a criminal prosecution.[13]

Search and seizure protections extend to everything that is not testimony. Blood samples, writing samples, records, phone taps, email, and every other form of physical evidence is protected by the Fourth Amendment. With a proper warrant, even confidential information such as patient records is subject to search and seizure. The seizure is literal: the police will physically take away any evidence that they find, with little regard for the impact on the defendant's business. Medical records, business records, even computers that contain records are subject to seizure. In some Medicare fraud investigations, the government has gone into hospitals and practices with moving vans to haul away evidence.

The remedy for an improper search is the exclusion of the evidence from the trial. This exclusionary rule extends to all evidence that was found because of the original improperly obtained evidence—the "fruit of the poisoned tree" doctrine. The rationale for the exclusionary rule is that there is no other appropriate remedy because it is impossible to mitigate the damage that the evidence might do to the defendant's case. In a sense it punishes the police for failing to get proper warrants or for not sticking to the terms of their warrants.

Evidentiary issues are complex in health care because there are overlapping claims on who controls medical information. For example, a physician may own the paper that a medical chart is written on or the computer it is stored in, but patients also have a right to the information in their medical records. Patients can give permission for the police to have access to their medical records, even if those records will incriminate their physician. When health care practitioners participate in Medicare or Medicaid, the terms of participation give the government inspectors access to the records that the claims are based on. The OIG can get these records without a warrant and refer any wrongdoing it finds to the DOJ for prosecution. Health care practitioners should not expect to be able to protect any medical or business records from search and seizure in a criminal investigation. The best they can hope is to convince the judge to limit access to confidential information such as individual medical records.

If police or the FBI want to search a medical business, it is critical that all efforts be made to not give up any legal privilege or right of confidentially. If they do not have a search warrant, then they should not be allowed to enter the premises without your attorney present. If they push their way in, do not attempt to interfere with their actions, but stress that they are there without your permission. If they do have a search warrant, ask them to wait until you can talk to your attorney. They will probably not wait, but you must ask. Once the search is started, you should carefully monitor it. For an example of a protocol for monitoring a search, see Appendix 3–A.

Standard of Proof

One of the unique protections in criminal law is standard of proof. Crimes must be proved *beyond a reasonable doubt.* Torts and other civil wrongs must be proved by a *preponderance of the evidence.* "Preponderance" is taken to mean a majority, 51%, or other equivalent measures that imply that the defendant more likely than not committed the act. "Beyond a reasonable doubt" is a more difficult standard to define, but it clearly requires a much higher level of certainty than does preponderance of the evidence. Sometimes these are applied to the same facts: in the O.J. Simpson case, the jury in the criminal trial found him not guilty because they were not convinced beyond a reasonable doubt that he killed Nicole Brown Simpson and Ronald Goldman. The jury in the civil case seeking compensation for the same actions found that the proof did meet the preponderance of the evidence standard and they found him liable for the killing.

The role of the defense attorney in a criminal case is to identify weaknesses in the prosecution's case and convince the jury that these raise a reasonable doubt about the defendant's guilt. This strategy is most successful in complex crimes that require proof of a guilty mind (the defendant intended to commit the crime). Most of the crimes discussed in this book involve fraud and do not require the same type of intent as a traditional violent crime. This makes these much more difficult to defend. The health care practitioner does not need to intend to defraud the government, only to intend to file the improper claim. The only instances where we will deal with the traditional criminal law issue of a guilty mind involve withdrawal of life support. In these cases, the state may raise the issue of whether the physician intended to commit active euthanasia.

Double Jeopardy

The Constitution prevents a person from being tried more than once for the same crime. Jeopardy does not attach until there is a jury verdict or a dismissal with prejudice by the judge. If there is a mistrial because of attorney misconduct or because the jury cannot reach a verdict, then there is no final ruling and the prosecutor may retry the case. Generally, the prosecutor may only try the defendant once on a given set of facts. If the defendant is found innocent of murder, he or she cannot be retried on the same facts for a lesser included offense such as manslaughter.

Double jeopardy only applies to one level of government. If the state tries a person for murder and the defendant is acquitted, the federal government can retry the person on the same facts, perhaps for civil rights violations. This is a significant problem in health care because many of the prohibited activities, especially fraudulent transactions, violate both state and federal law.

INVESTIGATION OF THE CRIMINAL CASE

Prosecutorial Discretion

Depending on the nature of the crime, the initial investigation will be carried out by the police, the prosecutor's office, or the grand jury. The ultimate decision to prosecute is reserved to the prosecutor. This is an important safeguard to prevent aggrieved victims or political enemies from forcing the prosecution of innocent individuals. Prosecutors have a unique role in the legal system in that their duty is to see that justice is done, not just to prosecute every case they think they can win. The prosecutor should not file a case unless he or she believes that the defendant is guilty. Although this is certainly abused in some circumstances, most prosecutors take the duty seriously. This is very different from the defense attorney, who should not be concerned with the guilt or innocence of the defendant, but only with poking holes in the prosecutor's case. The victim does not prosecute the criminal case and does not have the right to determine if the state will prosecute.

The Citizen's Duty

In general, a person is required to report criminal activity and to appear and testify as a witness if requested by the defendant or the state. As long as the report is made in good faith, the law protects persons who report crimes from being sued for defamation by the person they report.

This creates a conflict of interest with a patient's expectation that a physician will preserve the confidences of the physician–patient relationship. This conflict is most acute for psychiatrists: their physician–patient relationships are critically dependent on trust, and their patients are much more likely to discuss matters such as criminal activity with them. As discussed in Chapter 2, the general duty of a health care practitioner is limited to the reporting of possible future criminal activity, not to turn in their patients for past acts that come out in during medical treatment or consultation.

The health care practitioner's duties are much more rigorous when dealing with crimes related to health care business practices.

Protecting Your Rights

Although it is a good policy to cooperate with the police and with government investigators when you are innocent of wrongdoing, health care providers should be wary of answering questions about health care–related crimes that they might be involved with, say Medicare false claims, without getting the advice of a lawyer just to make sure they are not compromising their rights. Even when just answering questions as a witness or for background, it is important to keep notes of what you were asked and what information you gave

the investigator. If you have any reason to believe that you are target of a criminal investigation, or if any of your business partners are a target, you should discuss the matter with a criminal defense lawyer before you talk to any investigators.

FEDERAL FRAUD PROSECUTIONS

The greatest legal threat facing health care practitioners, hospitals, and managed care organizations (MCOs) is prosecution for fraud under the Medicare-Medicaid self-referral laws,[14] the False Claims Act (FCA),[15] or the Kassebaum-Kennedy bill.[16] These acts include substantial civil penalties, which have resulted in total settlements in excess of a billion dollars, so far, and the imprisonment of many health care practitioners and administrators. Many health care practitioners are unaware of the reach of these laws. This confusion arises because these laws criminalize conduct that is not generally illegal when it only involves private pay patients. For example, assume that a hospital has an incentive program for the medical staff to encourage hospital admissions. The three physicians with the highest total of patient admission days get a free trip to Jamaica. If the hospital only treats private pay patients, then this program is legal, assuming that it does not violate any contractual agreements with the patient's insurance plans, or any specific state laws. If the hospital treats any Medicare patients, then the incentive program is a prohibited kick-back.[17]

The Prohibited Transactions[18]

These are the prohibited acts under the Medicare/Medicaid laws. These are only the broad prohibitions. There are some exceptions, but more important, there are many more statutes and regulations that anyone working in this area should be familiar with.

(a) Making or causing to be made false statements or representations

Whoever—

(1) knowingly and willfully makes or causes to be made any false statement or representa-

tion of a material fact in any application for any benefit or payment under a Federal health care program (as defined in subsection (f) of this section),

(2)   at any time knowingly and willfully makes or causes to be made any false statement or representation of a material fact for use in determining rights to such benefit or payment,

(3)   having knowledge of the occurrence of any event affecting (a) his initial or continued right to any such benefit or payment, or (b) the initial or continued right to any such benefit or payment of any other individual in whose behalf he has applied for or is receiving such benefit or payment, conceals or fails to disclose such event with an intent fraudulently to secure such benefit or payment either in a greater amount or quantity than is due or when no such benefit or payment is authorized,

(4)   having made application to receive any such benefit or payment for the use and benefit of another and having received it, knowingly and willfully converts such benefit or payment or any part thereof to a use other than for the use and benefit of such other person,

(5)   presents or causes to be presented a claim for a physician's service for which payment may be made under a Federal health care program and knows that the individual who furnished the service was not licensed as a physician, or

(6)   for a fee knowingly and willfully counsels or assists an individual to dispose of assets (including by any transfer in trust) in order for the individual to become eligible for medical assistance under a State plan under subchapter XIX of this chapter, if disposing of the assets results in the imposition of a period of ineligibility for such assistance under section 1396p(c) of this title,

shall (i) in the case of such a statement, representation, concealment, failure, or conversion by any person in connection with the furnishing (by that person) of items or services for which payment is or may be made under the program, be guilty of a felony and upon conviction thereof fined not more than $25,000 or imprisoned for not more than five years or both, or (ii) in the case of such a statement, representation, concealment, failure, conversion, or provision of counsel or assistance by any other person, be guilty of a misdemeanor and upon conviction thereof fined not more than $10,000 or imprisoned for not more than one year, or both. In addition, in any case where an individual who is otherwise eligible for assistance under a Federal health care program is convicted of an offense under the preceding provisions of this subsection, the administrator of such program may at its option (notwithstanding any other provision of such program) limit, restrict, or suspend the eligibility of that individual for such period (not exceeding one year) as it deems appropriate; but the imposition of a limitation, restriction, or suspension with respect to the eligibility of any individual under this sentence shall not affect the eligibility of any other person for assistance under the plan, regardless of the relationship between that individual and such other person.

(b) Illegal remunerations

(1)   whoever knowingly and willfully solicits or receives any remuneration (including any kickback, bribe, or rebate) directly or indirectly, overtly or covertly, in cash or in kind—

(A)   in return for referring an individual to a person for the furnishing or arranging for the furnishing of any item or service for which payment may be made in whole or in part under a Federal health care program, or

(B)   in return for purchasing, leasing, ordering, or arranging for or recommending purchasing, leasing, or ordering any good, facility, service, or item for which payment may be made in whole or in part under a Federal health care program,

shall be guilty of a felony and upon conviction thereof, shall be fined not more than $25,000 or imprisoned for not more than five years, or both.

(2)   whoever knowingly and willfully offers or pays any remuneration (including any kickback, bribe, or rebate) directly or indirectly, overtly or covertly, in cash or in kind to any person to induce such person

(A)   to refer an individual to a person for the furnishing or arranging for the furnishing of any item or service for which payment may be made in whole or in part under a Federal health care program, or

(B) to purchase, lease, order, or arrange for or recommend purchasing, leasing, or ordering any good, facility, service, or item for which payment may be made in whole or in part under a Federal health care program,

shall be guilty of a felony and upon conviction thereof, shall be fined not more than $25,000 or imprisoned for not more than five years, or both.

(c) False statements or representations with respect to condition or operation of institutions

Whoever knowingly and willfully makes or causes to be made, or induces or seeks to induce the making of, any false statement or representation of a material fact with respect to the conditions or operation of any institution, facility, or entity in order that such institution, facility, or entity may qualify (either upon initial certification or upon recertification) as a hospital, critical access hospital, skilled nursing facility, nursing facility, intermediate care facility for the mentally retarded, home health agency, or other entity (including an eligible organization under section 1395mm(b) of this title) for which certification is required under subchapter XVIII of this chapter or a State health care program (as defined in section 1320a-7(h) of this title), or with respect to information required to be provided under section 1320a-3a of this title, shall be guilty of a felony and upon conviction thereof shall be fined not more than $25,000 or imprisoned for not more than five years, or both.

(d) Illegal patient admittance and retention practices

Whoever knowingly and willfully—

(1) charges, for any service provided to a patient under a State plan approved under subchapter XIX of this chapter, money or other consideration at a rate in excess of the rates established by the State (or, in the case of services provided to an individual enrolled with a medicaid managed care organization under subchapter XIX of this chapter under a contract under section 1396b(m) of this title or under a contractual, referral, or other arrangement under such contract, at a rate in excess of the rate permitted under such contract), or

(2) charges, solicits, accepts, or receives, in addition to any amount otherwise required to be paid under a State plan approved under subchapter XIX of this chapter, any gift, money, donation, or other consideration (other than a charitable, religious, or philanthropic contribution from an organization or from a person unrelated to the patient)

(A) as a precondition of admitting a patient to a hospital, nursing facility, or intermediate care facility for the mentally retarded, or

(B) as a requirement for the patient's continued stay in such a facility, when the cost of the services provided therein to the patient is paid for (in whole or in part) under the State plan,

shall be guilty of a felony and upon conviction thereof shall be fined not more than $25,000 or imprisoned for not more than five years, or both.

(e) Violation of assignment terms

Whoever accepts assignments described in section 1395u(b)(3)(B)(ii) of this title or agrees to be a participating physician or supplier under section 1395u(h)(1) of this title and knowingly, willfully, and repeatedly violates the term of such assignments or agreement, shall be guilty of a misdemeanor and upon conviction thereof shall be fined not more than $2,000 or imprisoned for not more than six months, or both.

(f) "Federal health care program" defined

For purposes of this section, the term "Federal health care program" means

(1) any plan or program that provides health benefits, whether directly, through insurance, or otherwise, which is funded directly, in whole or in part, by the U.S. Government (other than the health insurance program under chapter 89 of Title 5); or

(2) any State health care program, as defined in section 1320a-7(h) of this title.

The History of Enforcement

These are not new laws, having been on the books in essentially the same form for more than 20 years. Yet government inspectors have recently found billions of dollars of fraud in business arrangements that violate these laws, and many shocked health care practitioners have found themselves the subjects of criminal investigation. The reality is that health care practitioners and institutions have been in denial about the importance of the laws, a denial made possible because the federal government did little enforcement of the laws until about 1994. For comparison, consider the imaginative tax schemes that business would engage in if the Internal Revenue Service stopped enforcing the tax laws for 20 years.

The Constitutionality of the Laws

There were no cases under these laws for some years, so many health care attorneys assumed that they were unconstitutionally vague, if they really prohibited everything they seemed to prohibit. There were several court challenges to the constitutionality of these laws on the legal basis that they are too broad and too vague to put the defendant on clear notice of that what is prohibited. The real challenge was that these laws ban business as usual and that cannot be what Congress meant to do. One of the first cases dealt with the owner of a laboratory service, Greber, that provided Holter monitors.[19] These monitors were ordered by cardiologists. Greber's business fitted them to the patient, collected the data, and prepared the data for reading by the ordering cardiologist. The ordering cardiologist was paid a consultant's fee for analyzing a patient's Holter monitor data. In the defendant's criminal prosecution for fraud, the government asserted that this fee was an illegal inducement to persuade physicians to use Greber's services.

Greber argued that these were not illegal inducements to refer patients but legitimate fees for evaluating the Holter monitor data. The court's record does not indicate that these consultants' fees were higher than the fee that would have been paid to a cardiologist who was retained to analyze the data but who had not ordered a Holter monitor. There was evidence, however, that some physicians received consulting fees when Greber had already evaluated the Holter monitor data. Per-

haps most telling for the government's case was Greber's own testimony in a related civil case: "In that case, he had testified that ... if the doctor didn't get his consulting fee, he wouldn't be using our service. So the doctor got a consulting fee."

The Court found that "if the payments were intended to induce the physician to use Cardio-Med's services, the statute was violated, even if the payments were also intended to compensate for professional services." This interpretation was upheld in a subsequent case in which the Court found that "the jury could convict unless it found the payment 'wholly and not incidentally attributable to the delivery of goods or services.'"[20] This ruling made it clear that the prohibited conduct was any payment that accompanied a referral, irrespective of whether the physician receiving the payment provided some goods or services in return.

A case involving payments allegedly intended to influence a decision to award an ambulance contract approved of the *Greber* decision and extended it to cover subsequent modifications that had been made in the law.[21] This case directly considered the constitutionality of the Medicare fraud and abuse law: "Defendants next claim that, if we read the Medicare Fraud statute to criminalize, under certain circumstances, reasonable payment for services rendered, the statute becomes unconstitutionally vague."[22] The Court rejected this reasoning, finding that Congress's broad power to regulate commerce included the power to prohibit practices that might induce referrals, even if they had other, proper, motives.[23] All subsequent cases have upheld these decisions.

The Everyone-Does-It Defense

Despite the decision in *Greber* and clear wording of the law, health care attorneys and their clients continued to structure deals in violation of the laws. As one attorney put it, "the standard set in the *United States v. Greber* case is clear: If one purpose of payment is to induce future referrals, the Medicare statute has been violated." But, he adds, it is not followed absolutely. "You've got this case law that says everybody goes to jail and you know that can't be right." The question then becomes which of the transactions is more likely to stimulate the interest of a prosecutor, he says.[24]

As late as 1993, the authors of this book wrote:

> For unstated reasons, the Justice Department has not enforced the fraud and abuse law in any meaningful way, leaving physicians and their attorneys in an ethical quandary. If physicians follow the law and the cases interpreting the law, they will be at a tremendous competitive disadvantage. Under the plain language of the law, its interpretation by the courts, and the administrative agency regulations, attorneys are compelled to recommend against many common medical care business practices. If attorneys do so, their clients will seek counsel who are more realistic.

Since that was written, the DOJ and the OIG have "discovered" fraud and abuse prosecutions and have sanctioned many health care providers for their illegal deals. In the latest enforcement actions, the government has started to indict the attorneys who advised on abusive deals.

False Claims Act

The FCA was passed during the Civil War to fight corruption among the contractors who supplied the Union Army. It is a qui tam law, which allows a private litigant to sue on behalf of the government.[25] The government may take over the lawsuit, ask that it be dismissed, or allow the private litigant to prosecute the lawsuit for a civil remedy. If the government prosecutes the lawsuit, then the private litigant is entitled to between 15% and 25% of the recovery,[26] and between 25% and 30% if the government does not intervene.[27] The attraction of these actions in health care is the statutory penalty—$5,000 to $10,000 per false claim submitted.[28] The court does not have the authority to reduce this penalty.[29]

If the government does intervene, then it has the additional power to bring associated criminal charges under the FCA, for mail and wire fraud, depending on how the claims were submitted, and under other criminal conspiracy laws, such as RICO (Racketeering Influenced Corrupt Organizations Act). The usual pattern is for the government to investigate the claim, then to propose a settlement for some fraction of the potential false claims.[30] This is attractive because very few health care providers have defended a false claims action successfully. The government often will agree to settle any potential criminal liability claims as part of the financial settlement, which usually makes the offer irresistible.[31]

Risk Management Issues

These federal fraud prosecutions have become a major legal threat for several reasons. First, they are politically attractive as a way to save wasted federal dollars.[32] Second, there are a lot of talented financial fraud investigators available as the Resolution Trust Corporation wound down. Third, there is a lot of fraud. The government estimates about $23 returned for each dollar invested in fraud investigations. Fourth, there is great deterrent value in these prosecutions and settlements. The large settlements against three medical schools[33] have other medical schools scrambling to ensure that they are complying with billings laws, in some cases with dramatic reductions in billing to Medicare and Medicaid. There also have been settlements in excess of $100 million with a hospital chain and with a laboratory, putting both industries on notice of substantial potential liability.

The risk is dramatically increasing for physicians in MCOs because the federal government and the states are pushing Medicare and Medicaid patients into MCOs. Plan terms and physician practices that are standard for private pay patients may become illegal when a government pay patient enters the plan. Many plans and most physicians do not appreciate this fact and fail to change their practices accordingly. The Kassebaum-Kennedy bill extends the jurisdiction of the federal government to private health plans, allowing the criminal prosecution of physicians for fraud against private plans and beneficiaries.

Physicians in MCOs must be alert to these dangers. If there is any potential criminal activity, then the physician must seek private counsel at once to ensure that his or her rights are protected. Although the attorney for the MCO can protect the MCO's interests, those interests may be adverse to those of the physician. This is especially important as the plan conducts compliance audits because the physician cannot automatically invoke attorney–client privilege for communications to the plan's attorney.

Waiving Deductibles and Copays as Fraud[34]

Professional courtesy—taking care of the families of other physicians without charge—is a tradition that dates back to Hippocrates. The practice served to build bonds between physicians, and to reduce the incentive for physicians to treat their own families. Although the authors believe that, on balance, professional courtesy is good for the medical profession, the Congress and private insurance companies have greatly reduced the permissible scope for reducing charges for medical care. Since the penalties for violating these restrictions include denial of the claim, deselection from the plan, fines, and imprisonment, health care practitioners must review their practices to ensure that they are in compliance.

Private insurers and the federal government have basic restrictions on how you charge patients for medical care. Neither creates an exception for professional courtesy: in general, if you cannot reduce the cost of care for anyone else in your practice, you cannot reduce it for other health care practitioners. There are even situations where it is permissible to reduce the cost of care for everyone except physicians.

Waiving Copays

The most common ways physicians reduce the cost of care for patients are waiving the copay ("insurance only") and giving the patient a discount on the care. In most situations, both private insurers and the federal government ban waiving the copay. (Medicare has some provisions allowing the copay to be waived for documented indigency.) They do this because the copay is meant to discourage casual trips to the physician. The theory is that making the patient share the cost of treatment will make the patient a more sophisticated health care consumer. The reality is that the copay limits access to care for many people. The less care the patient seeks, the less money the health plan has to pay to physicians and hospitals for that care. Both private insurers and Medicare require the physician to make reasonable efforts to collect copays that are billed to the patient.

Discounts

A discount is a reduction in the normal charge based on a specific amount of money or a percentage of the charge. Just as the hardware store can give you $5 off on all tools or a 10% discount on your total purchase, a physician may take $5 off or 10% off of the bill for an office visit or a surgery. However, there are things that the physician must beware of in doing this. The discount must apply to the total bill, not just the part that is paid by the patient. If the patient owes a 20% copay on a $25 charge ($5) and you are giving a discount of $5, then the patient pays $4 and the insurance company pays $16. If the patient owes a $5 copay regardless of the amount of the charge, then the patient must pay $5 and the insurance company pays $15. In this situation, the discount would only benefit the insurance company.

Discounts raise the issue of the physician's customary charges for a procedure. Many private insurance plans and some federal programs have a "most favored nation" clause in the contract with the physician. This entitles the plan to pay the lowest charge the physician bills to anyone. Any systematic pattern of discounts could trigger a reduction in the physician's allowable reimbursement schedule to the discounted price.

"No Charge"

As far as the authors have determined, none of the private insurers bans waiving the entire charge for the care. You may also charge for some visits and not for others. Many pediatricians do not charge for the first follow-up visit for otitis media. This increases the likelihood that the child will be brought back for the recheck. The insurance company is also getting a free visit, but at least the patient is getting the care.

"No charge" visits are prohibited if they are part of a fraudulent scheme. For example, a no charge visit is still a patient care encounter and must be fully documented. Assume that a patient has severe asthma and is waiting out a one year preexisting illness exclusion in a health insurance policy. If that patient requires treatment a month before the end of the year waiting period, you have to fully document the treatment even if you do not charge the insurance company for it. You cannot use "no charge" to hide medical information.

You may also deliver nonreimbursable care as part of an otherwise justified office visit and bill the company for the authorized part of the visit. For example, if the insurance doesn't cover immunizations, then you could do the immunizations at the time you do an authorized well-child checkup, or when the child is in for some other medical condition that is not a contraindication for immunizations. You cannot, however, bill for an office visit when the only reason the patient is being seen is to deliver care that is not authorized under the policy. It would also be improper to "no charge" as a way to waive a copay in order to generate ancillary business for the physician's office lab or other health services business. In other words, you cannot no charge for the visit and bill the insurance company for $100 worth of lab work that it would not have approved as part of a reimbursed visit.

"Kickbacks" and Inducements To Refer Patients

The Federal government, and several of the states, have specific laws governing financial transactions between health care providers. These laws include the Medicare Fraud and Abuse laws and the Stark I and Stark II, which apply to care paid for in whole or in part by the Federal government.

These laws can prohibit otherwise permissible discounts or "no charges." For example, a surgeon who only gave professional courtesy to physicians who referred her business would clearly violate the law. Professional courtesy based on being on the same hospital staff would raise the same issues, although the link to referrals is more tenuous. Giving professional courtesy to all physicians without conditions would be more

defensible, but if the government could show that a disproportionate number of physicians receiving the courtesy were also referring physicians, the court would probably rule that this was a prohibited inducement.

Penalties

Traditionally, if physicians violated the terms of their contracts with private insurers, the insurer could refuse to pay the claim and/or deselect the physician from the plan. The insurer could also sue the physician for fraud. In extreme cases, the local district attorney or U.S. Attorney could prosecute the physician for mail and wire fraud for using the mail and electronic communications to file the fraudulent claims. The Health Insurance Portability and Accountability Act of 1996 (HIPAA), better known as the Kassebaum-Kennedy bill, now makes it a federal crime to defraud private insurance companies. Violations of the contracts with a private insurer are criminal fraud under HIPAA and could result in fines and criminal prosecution.

To date, there have been no reported cases, prosecutions, or settlements solely based on professional courtesy to health care providers. Looking at general patient care, rather than just professional courtesy, there have been private insurance fraud actions based on illegally waiving copays and/or providing discounts that were not passed on to the insurer. There have been federal actions for the same violations, as well as for using waivers and discounts to induce Medicare patients to use other health care services.

Professional courtesy means making no charge to anyone, patient or insurance, for medical care. There are no special exceptions in the law that allow professional courtesy to physicians in situations where the same courtesy could not be extended to all patients. Conversely, there are some situations where such courtesy can be extended to all patients except physicians and other health care providers. Health care providers must examine their professional courtesy policies to ensure that they do not violate either the contractual terms in private insurance policies or the Medicare/Medicaid laws and regulations. Although there may be situations where it is defensible to "no charge" for services to health care professionals, the physician should ensure that this professional courtesy is not linked to referrals, either in reality or in appearance.

ANTITRUST LAWS

The federal antitrust laws, embodied in the Sherman and Clayton acts, are intended to protect competition that affects interstate commerce. These laws apply to all medical practice activities because of the court's broad definition of interstate commerce. Antitrust laws have three attractions to physicians attacking peer review proceedings. As federal laws, they obviate state law peer review protections. In other business contexts, they are used to attack exclusionary agreements that have a surface resemblance to medical staff contracts. Finally, prevailing plaintiffs can recover three times the proved damages plus their attorney's fees.

The antitrust laws do not condemn bigness in itself, but they prevent a business from using its size or control of the market (monopoly power) against its competitors. The antitrust laws also prevent competitors from reaching agreements to divide markets (horizontal restraints) or otherwise reduce competition. The policy of the antitrust laws is to protect competition, not competitors. There are certain actions, such as price fixing, that are illegal without reference to their effect on the market. These are called *per se violations;* they are illegal irrespective of the market power of the offenders. For all other violations, the plaintiff must prove that the business, or businesses, involved in the alleged violation have a dominant market position.

Market Share

The effect of the market share requirement is that unless the hospital is the major provider in a small community or is possessed of a unique community resource (say, the only federally funded level 3 nursery in the community), then the court will reject antitrust claims against it if these claims depend on monopoly power. Even if a hospital has sufficient market share, the court is concerned with the impact of the practices on the consumer, not on the competitors. The court will not be concerned if the hospital uses its market power in a way that injures an individual physician, as long as it does not injure consumers. This was the heart of the *Jefferson Parish Hospital District No. 2 v. Hyde* case,[35] which is taken as sanctioning exclusive contracts with medical staff members.

In this case the plaintiff was an anesthesiologist. He applied for medical staff privileges at Jefferson Parish Hospital and was rejected because the hospital had an exclusive contract with a group of anesthesiologists. Hyde sued, alleging that this exclusive contract was a violation of the antitrust laws in that it interfered with his right to practice in the hospital.

Although there were several other issues in the case, the heart of the U.S. Supreme Court's ruling was that Hyde only wanted to join the conspiracy. He did not claim that he would compete with the existing group and thus benefit the public through lower prices or better service. He just complained that he was denied the opportunity to profit from the price fixing and work allocation aspects of the exclusive contract granted to the existing anesthesia group. Finding that this would be of no benefit to the community, the Court rejected Hyde's claim. Rather than an endorsement of exclusive contracts as a way to allocate medical staff privileges, this case should be seen as the Court's lack of sympathy for would-be conspirators who are left out. The Court did not rule on the fate of exclusive contracts in the face of an attack by a physician who offered a competitive alternative in the delivery of services.

State Action Immunity

There is an exemption to the federal antitrust laws for actions taken by states. This is called the *Parker v. Brown* immunity, after a famous 1943 case upholding the right of California to enforce agreements to protect raisin growers.[36] The agreements at issue in the "raisin case" allocated market share to the various growers. This guaranteed a profit to the growers in the scheme, artificially raised the prices for raisins, and excluded new growers. Although it would have been illegal for the growers themselves to have entered into these agreements, the Court found that a state may proscribe competition among its own citizens. Several courts tried to use this principle to block peer review lawsuits in states where the board of medical examiners had some role in reviewing peer review decisions.

This state action immunity was at issue in the much publicized case of *Patrick v. Burget*,[37] which involved the sole hospital in a small community. Because of geographic isolation, this hospital had monopoly power in the local market. As a result of a business disagreement, the other members of the medical staff conspired to terminate Dr. Patrick's staff privileges. This was a blatant conspiracy that included even attempts to manipulate the state board of medical examiners. Dr. Patrick won a multimillion-dollar verdict at trial, and the case was appealed to the federal circuit court. Several medical groups filed briefs urging the court to overturn the verdict, while acknowledging that the review itself was grossly unfair. The appeals court found that the termination of Dr. Patrick's staff privileges did violate the antitrust laws. The court also found that the peer review process in Oregon was not an independent activity conducted by private individuals but an extension of state power and thus subject to active supervision by the state. Based on this regulation by the state, which, on paper at least, is quite detailed, the court found that the defendant's conduct was immune from legal challenge.

Dr. Patrick appealed the circuit court's decision to the U.S. Supreme Court, with his request for review supported by the Federal Trade Commission (FTC). The FTC argued that there was insufficient state involvement to justify state action immunity. The Supreme Court found:

> Because we conclude that no state actor in Oregon actively supervises hospital peer-review decisions, we hold that the state action doctrine does not protect the peer-review activities challenged in this case from application of the federal antitrust laws. In so holding, we are not unmindful of

the policy argument that respondents and their Amici have advanced for reaching the opposite conclusion. They contend that effective peer review is essential to the provision of quality medical care and that any threat of antitrust liability will prevent physicians from participating openly and actively in peer-review proceedings. This argument, however, essentially challenges the wisdom of applying the antitrust laws to the sphere of medical care, and as such is properly directed to the legislative branch.[38]

The *Patrick* case may be a classic example of the cliché that hard cases make bad law. The egregious facts in the case made it unlikely that the Supreme Court would find that Oregon supervised the review of Dr. Patrick's competence. To have accepted that the *Patrick* case was a valid exercise of state oversight would have only shifted the issue to a due process claim based on improper state action. Although many physicians were concerned that the *Patrick* holding would cripple peer review, the Health Care Quality Improvement Act immunizes properly conducted peer review irrespective of state action.

The Federal Trade Commission

The next assault on the self-regulation of the professions came in the 1970s from the concern of the courts and the FTC about anticompetitive practices. This was not the first time the FTC had entered medical society politics. As early as the 1930s, it had brought legal action against certain medical societies for blacklisting physicians who participated in prepaid medical plans. These antitrust efforts died out during World War II and were not resumed in earnest until the 1970s.

The case that finally reached the Supreme Court involved attempts by a bar association to fix fees. In *Goldfarb v. Virginia State Bar*,[39] the U.S. Supreme Court held that the delegation of authority to professional societies to conduct peer review did not encompass a grant of authority to engage in price fixing. This decision was followed by a ruling against an engineering society that held that attempts to manipulate technical standards to benefit one competitor over another, hidden in the guise of standards to protect the public, would not be allowed.[40] The result of these rulings has been an effort by the FTC and private litigants to force professional societies to refrain from anticompetitive actions.

The effect of FTC enforcement actions and private litigation has been perverse at times. Exemplary attempts to establish objective standards for medical practice (such as the Academy of Pediatrics' "Blue Book") have been thwarted because of the fear of litigation. Simultaneously, some practitioners have used threats of antitrust litigation to suppress criticism of questionable procedures or marketing practices. A cynical observer might say that the FTC has removed curbs on unprofessional practices, which has increased the cost of medical care by increasing the marketing of dubious procedures. Except for the certification activities of the large professional societies, the control of medical staff privileges has passed from local medical societies to hospital and other corporate committees.

TECHNICAL FRAUD: RICO VIOLATIONS

The Medicare fraud and abuse law is not the only restriction on physician business practices. The greatest threat is that physicians will violate the federal RICO. Losing defendants in a RICO action are subject to treble damages: the payment of the plaintiff's attorney's fees, confiscation of their assets, and incarceration. The implications of these potential damages are illustrated in the medical care RICO case that resulted in a judgment for $100 million.[41] As with the Medicare fraud and abuse provisions, physicians may commit RICO violations without engaging in what is traditionally thought of as illegal activities.

It is controversial to discuss routine medical practices as potential RICO violations. As with the fraud and abuse laws, there have been few RICO lawsuits or prosecutions against physicians. This lack of litigation, combined with a belief that RICO applies only to criminals, has led most lawyers to reject RICO as a problem for physicians and medical care businesses. Few physicians have been counseled about the risks of RICO yet, but many unknowingly engage in practices that could subject them to RICO liability. Understanding how this might happen requires an understanding of the RICO law.

Understanding RICO

RICO is a conspiracy law. Congress's intent in passing it is unclear. Many businesspersons assert that it was intended only to apply to gangsters, but one of the drafters of RICO counters that it was intended to be a sort of national deceptive business practices act. Irrespective of congressional intent, the U.S. Supreme Court has ruled that RICO is not restricted to organized crime enforcement. This is consistent with the plain language of RICO. It is also more reasonable to assume that a plaintiff would be inclined to sue a business person rather than a gangster.

A person violates RICO by engaging in a conspiracy—a joint effort with at least one or more individuals or organizations—to break any of a lengthy list of specific state and federal laws. Violating one of the listed laws is called a *predicate act*. Physicians are at risk because breaching their fiduciary duty to patients, or violating other technical laws such as the Medicare fraud and abuse provisions, can support fraud allegations that are predicate acts under RICO.

Mail and Wire Fraud

Most RICO cases are based on violations of the federal mail and wire fraud statutes. Any fraudulent conduct that directly or indirectly uses the mails or telephone is a violation of the federal mail and wire fraud laws. The courts use a spacious definition of fraud in mail and wire fraud cases: "It is a reflection of moral uprightness, of fundamental honesty, fair play and right dealing in the general and business life of members of society.... As Judge Holmes so colorfully put it '[t]he law does not define fraud; it needs no definition; it is as old as falsehood and as versatile as human ingenuity.'"[42]

The Supreme Court reiterated the expansive reach of mail and wire fraud in the 1987 case of *Carpenter v. United States*. It affirmed the mail fraud conviction of a *Wall Street Journal* reporter who used the paper's confidential information in an insider trading scheme. The reporter was held to have violated his fiduciary obligation to protect his employer's confidential information:

> We cannot accept petitioners' further argument that Winans' conduct in revealing pre-publication information was no more than a violation of workplace rules and did not amount to fraudulent activity that is proscribed by the mail fraud statute. [The statutes ... reach any scheme to deprive another of money or property by means of false or fraudulent pretenses, representations, or promises.... [T]he words 'to defraud' in the mail fraud statute have the 'common understanding' of 'wronging one in his property rights by dishonest methods or schemes,' and 'usually signify the deprivation of something of value by trick, deceit, chicane or overreaching.'[43]

The duty of fidelity between the employer and employee that was at issue in this case is precisely the same type of common law fiduciary duty as that between physician and patient. Providing incentives to physicians to change the medical care offered their patients is a breach of fiduciary duty. The nature of the motive behind such incentives is judged from the patient's perspective, not the persons offering the incentives. For example, it is common for managed care plans to give physicians an incentive to reduce specialty referrals in an effort to control medical care costs. Although this might be seen as a laudatory action on the part of the managed care plan, the individual patient denied a referral will probably see it as an improper interference with the physician–patient relationship. Irrespective of the payers' motive, these incentives are legally indistinguishable from giving bribes to employees to violate their duty to their employers.

Incentives and Commercial Bribery

In most states health maintenance organizations (HMOs), preferred provider organizations (PPOs), and other managed care plans do not directly employ and supervise physicians. The phy-

sicians are either employed by physician's associations that contract with the plan or independent practitioners who contract directly with the plan. These contracts contain provisions that are intended to encourage the physicians to change the medical care decisions that they would have made in the absence of the plan.

Some of these provisions, such as those governing the submission of bills and discount schedules for prompt payment, have no effect on medical care decision making. Others have profound effects on physician decision making. The most benign of these incentives are disallowing or heavily discounting procedures that the plan wants to discourage. This gives physicians the option to offer the care and absorb the reduced reimbursement. These become more troubling when they are coupled with provisions that prevent discounting care. This prevents physicians from providing the treatment at cost to help needy patients. The most ethically and legally problematic provisions are those that prohibit the physician from rendering the necessary care. Some plans attempted to have physicians contractually agree not to provide routine ultrasound to pregnant women and not to inform the women that routine ultrasound was available. By preventing women from knowing about the procedure, the plans hoped to avoid complaints from women who wanted ultrasound.

As discussed in Chapter 10, these practices violate the physician's fiduciary duty to the patient, and may violate state criminal laws, such as commercial bribery laws. Such violations would be mail and wire fraud, if they involved the telephone or mails, and may be predicate acts on their own, depending on the wording of the state statute. Violating a state commercial bribery statute is a predicate act for RICO if the statute provides for imprisonment for greater than one year. Several states specifically prohibit physician incentives under their commercial bribery laws and provide for imprisonment for more than a year. In these states, physician incentive plans are clearly predicate acts for RICO. Some states do not specifically mention physicians in their commercial bribery statutes but prohibit bribing physicians. These states have case law that defines a physician as fiduciary. Even in states that do not directly criminalize physician incentives under a commercial bribery statute, a plaintiff can argue that the model penal code prohibitions on bribing physicians are evidence that incentive plans violate the physician's common law fiduciary duty. These breaches of the physician's fiduciary duty can be the basis for mail and wire fraud, which are predicate acts for RICO.

The Pattern of Racketeering

Engaging in one predicate act, such as accepting a bribe, is not enough to trigger RICO. The defendant must engage in a pattern of racketeering. The risk of physicians' being charged with RICO violations was increased by the 1989 ruling in *H. J. Inc. v. Northwestern Bell Telephone Company*,[44] in which the Supreme Court completed the expansion of RICO that began with the 1985 decision in *Sedima, S.P.R.L. v. Imrex Co.*[45] In *Sedima,* the Court held that RICO defendants need not be convicted of the underlying predicate acts that were used to charge a pattern of racketeering. This ruling greatly simplified criminal prosecutions and private civil actions brought under RICO because the prosecutors or plaintiffs were no longer compelled to wait until the defendants were tried for the underlying predicate acts. The *Sedima* ruling left open the definition of a pattern of racketeering, allowing some courts to limit the application of RICO by defining a pattern of racketeering as sustained criminal activity involving many, even hundreds, of predicate acts.

The Supreme Court in *Northwestern Bell* held that the RICO pattern requirements were meant to have a broad reach. In particular, the Court stressed that RICO was meant to apply to situations "in which persons engaged in long-term criminal activity often operate wholly within legitimate enterprises." The Court also reiterated that a pattern might be as few as three predicate acts. This ruling makes clear that a legitimate business, such as a medical care enterprise, that commits three or more predicate acts can be charged with the requisite pattern of racketeering for a RICO action.

Prosecuting a RICO Claim

RICO is a criminal law prosecuted by the Justice Department. The Justice Department has sued physicians under RICO for submitting false insurance claims using the mails and telephone.[46] RICO also has a private attorney general provision; this allows individuals who have been harmed by the RICO violations to sue for treble damages and attorney's fees. Their damages are trebled to punish the defendant. As with the antitrust laws, RICO is intended to compensate only for economic injuries. RICO cannot be used in place of a medical malpractice lawsuit by an injured patient.

The most likely RICO plaintiffs will be other physicians or health care business.[47] Plaintiffs do not need to be a direct target of the illegal activity to recover under RICO. They need only be injured through the pattern of racketeering. For example, assume that a managed care plan provides illegal incentives to participating physicians. Some physicians in the community are injured because they refuse to participate in a plan that requires them to compromise their medical care decision making. If this plan has enough market share, these physicians will lose business. If the insurance company insures a substantial percentage of the community, the nonparticipating physicians may be driven out of business. The nonparticipating physicians could sue the insurance company and the physicians who "stole" their patients by participating in the plan.

Peer review actions could be fertile ground for RICO litigation. Any physician participating in a peer review action who also receives illegal incentives is at risk for a RICO lawsuit. The plaintiff might be a physician who is being reviewed by a peer review committee for a PPO that provides incentives to encourage physicians to reduce hospitalization. Assume that the physician is being reviewed because she keeps patients in the hospital too long and orders too many tests. There is no evidence that she harms the patients, but she does cost the PPO a lot of money. If the peer review committee sanctions the physician, she could sue independent contractor physicians and the PPO for conspiring to sanction physicians who did not support the scheme to reduce hospitalizations.

The physician would argue that the peer review committee members were given financial incentives to put financial considerations above their fiduciary obligations to the patient. Since the federal law protecting peer review activities (see Chapter 11) does not protect actions taken in bad faith, this physician could get to the jury because the illegal incentive plan would be evidence of bad faith.

Failing medical businesses will also generate RICO claims as creditors and debtors look for solvent parties to share the costs. A hypothetical example might be Doctors' Hospital, which begins providing incentives to physicians to admit insured patients to its facility. These physicians begin to divert to Doctors' Hospital insured patients who otherwise would have been admitted to Holy Name Hospital. The patient mix at Holy Name Hospital shifts to medically indigent patients, and the hospital goes bankrupt. Holy Name Hospital was injured by the incentives provided by Doctors' Hospital. If Holy Name Hospital can establish that these incentives were predicate acts under the definition in RICO, it can sue Doctors' Hospital and the individual members of its medical staff under RICO. The damages in such a lawsuit could easily exceed $100 million. The individual physicians would share responsibility for paying the verdict.

THE FEDERAL SENTENCING GUIDELINES AND COMPLIANCE

Historically, judges were given great discretion in setting the sentences for crimes. This lead to great disparities among sentences for the same crimes, with some judges giving life sentences in situations where others would give short prison terms. There also seemed to be a bias against the poor and minorities. As a result, Congress passed a law establishing the U.S. Sentencing Commission. The liberal supporters of the bill hoped that it would reduce the harsh sentences given by some judges and would reduce the disparity between sentences for street crime and white-collar crime. The resulting Sentencing Guidelines did reduce the disparities, but tended to raise shorter sentences, rather than lower high ones.

Sentencing Implications for Health Care Practitioners

The Sentencing Guidelines establish standards for three aspects of sentencing: (1) they set base sentences for each type of crime charged; (2) they establish how sentences will be combined when the defendant is guilty of more than one crime; and (3) they establish how the specific facts in a given case affect the sentence. The result of these guidelines has been to dramatically change the sentencing prospects for health care providers, especially physicians and hospitals. The first change was to increase the sentences for white-collar crimes and require that nearly every defendant who is convicted of a white-collar crime goes to jail for some period of time. A health care practitioner convicted of health care fraud or antitrust violations now can expect to spend time in jail, which, in most states, ensure that the practitioner will lose his or her license and not be able to practice when the sentence has been served.

The sentencing guidelines also contain a provision that requires the sentence to be increased whenever the crime involves abuse of a professional relationship.

Abuse of Position of Trust or Use of Special Skill

"If the defendant abused a position of public or private trust, or used a special skill, in a manner that significantly facilitated the commission or concealment of the offense, increase [the sentence] by 2 levels."[48]

Commentary

"For this adjustment to apply, the position of public or private trust must have contributed in

some significant way to facilitating the commission or concealment of the offense (e.g., by making the detection of the offense or the defendant's responsibility for the offense more difficult). This adjustment, for example, applies in the case of ... the criminal sexual abuse of a patient by a physician under the guise of an examination."[49]

Although the example is that of a violent crime, this provision would also increase the sentence of a health care practitioner who is convicted of a financial crime that was related to the practitioner–patient relationship, such as billing fraud.

Compliance Plans

The Federal Sentencing Guidelines apply to institutions as well as individuals. If an institution such as a hospital or clinic is run in a criminal manner, the individual employees and officers of the institution can be sentenced to prison and fined as individuals and the institution itself can be fined. The fines can be statutory fines designed to punish the institution or they can be based on the value of the illegal benefits with the intent of depriving the institution of ill-gotten gains. If the government finds that the institution was run as a criminal enterprise—if the reason for the existence of the enterprise is its criminal activity—the fines will be set high enough to destroy the institution. The level of the fines and, indirectly, the culpability of the officers of the institution depend on its ability to show that it tried to obey the law and was the victim of unpreventable fraud by certain employees. The Federal Sentencing Guidelines have set standards for evaluating the intent of the institution. These are important to health care practitioners because the OIG now requires all hospitals and many other health care institutions to have plans to ensure that the institutions comply with the relevant federal laws. These are generically known as "compliance plans." The OIG requirements are based on the standards of the Federal Sentencing Guidelines. Health care practitioners will have to implement these plans as administrators and will have to abide by them as practitioners. Failure to do so can be considered evidence of criminal intent.

Sentencing Guideline Standards for Compliance[50]

An 'effective program to prevent and detect violations of law' means a program that has been reasonably designed, implemented, and enforced so that it generally will be effective in preventing and detecting criminal conduct. Failure to prevent or detect the instant offense, by itself, does not mean that the program was not effective. The hallmark of an effective program to prevent and detect violations of law is that the organization exercised due diligence in seeking to prevent and detect criminal conduct by its employees and other agents. Due diligence requires at a minimum that the organization must have taken the following types of steps:

(1) The organization must have established compliance standards and procedures to be followed by its employees and other agents that are reasonably capable of reducing the prospect of criminal conduct.

(2) Specific individual(s) within high-level personnel of the organization must have been assigned overall responsibility to oversee compliance with such standards and procedures.

(3) The organization must have used due care not to delegate substantial discretionary authority to individuals whom the organization knew, or should have known through the exercise of due diligence, had a propensity to engage in illegal activities.

(4) The organization must have taken steps to communicate effectively its standards and procedures to all employees and other agents, e.g., by requiring participation in training programs or by disseminating publications that explain in a practical manner what is required.

(5) The organization must have taken reasonable steps to achieve compliance with its standards, e.g., by utilizing monitoring and auditing systems reasonably designed to detect criminal conduct by its employees and other agents and by having in place and publicizing a reporting system whereby em-

ployees and other agents could report criminal conduct by others within the organization without fear of retribution.

(6) The standards must have been consistently enforced through appropriate disciplinary mechanisms, including, as appropriate, discipline of individuals responsible for the failure to detect an offense. Adequate discipline of individuals responsible for an offense is a necessary component of enforcement; however, the form of discipline that will be appropriate will be case specific.

(7) After an offense has been detected, the organization must have taken all reasonable steps to respond appropriately to the offense and to prevent further similar offenses—including any necessary modifications to its program to prevent and detect violations of law.

Special Characteristics of the Organization[51]

The precise actions necessary for an effective program to prevent and detect violations of law will depend upon a number of factors. Among the relevant factors are:

(i) Size of the organization: The requisite degree of formality of a program to prevent and detect violations of law will vary with the size of the organization: the larger the organization, the more formal the program typically should be. A larger organization generally should have established written policies defining the standards and procedures to be followed by its employees and other agents.

(ii) Likelihood that certain offenses may occur because of the nature of its business: If because of the nature of an organization's business there is a substantial risk that certain types of offenses may occur, management must have taken steps to prevent and detect those types of offenses. For example, if an organization handles toxic substances, it must have established standards and procedures designed to ensure that those substances are properly handled at all times. If an organization employs sales personnel who have flexibility in setting prices, it must have established standards and procedures designed to prevent and detect price-fixing. If an organization employs sales personnel who have flexibility to represent the material characteristics of a product, it must have established standards and procedures designed to prevent fraud.

(iii) Prior history of the organization: An organization's prior history may indicate types of offenses that it should have taken actions to prevent. Recurrence of misconduct similar to that which an organization has previously committed casts doubt on whether it took all reasonable steps to prevent such misconduct.

An organization's failure to incorporate and follow applicable industry practice or the standards called for by any applicable governmental regulation weighs against a finding of an effective program to prevent and detect violations of law.

Considerations for Physicians

Physicians must determine if any of their business practices breach their fiduciary duty to their patients or are otherwise legally improper:

1. All physicians must personally read the safe harbor regulations and the accompanying preface by the OIG.

2. They must determine their state's laws on physicians as fiduciaries. This includes commercial bribery laws and cases holding that the physician is a fiduciary.

3. If the attorney who drafted or reviewed their medical business arrangements did not provide full information about the potential risks of these arrangements, they must request this information.

4. If they did receive a disclosure of risks, they must ask their attorney if the safe harbor regulations have modified these risks.

5. If they are in a noncomplying deal, a written opinion on the specific problems and how they might be remedied is needed.

6. If they feel they were not properly advised of the risks when entering into the arrangement, they should consider getting a second opinion from an attorney who was not involved with the original attorney or the original deal.

Physicians must educate themselves about the problems of financial conflicts of interest with their patients. Conflicts should be avoided when possible and disclosed when they cannot be avoided. In some cases, such as the disclosure of the selection criteria for physician referral services, disclosure is legally required. In all cases, there is an ethical duty to disclose interests in medical care businesses and other potential conflicts of interest.

The nature of the fiduciary relationship is such that disclosure does not cure conflicts of interest. The physician–patient relationship is a fiduciary relationship precisely because patients must rely on their physician's integrity. Disclosing a conflict of interest does not help the patient avoid the effects of the conflict. Disclosure can show good faith but will not make an improper activity legally acceptable.

Managing conflicts of interest poses a profound ethical problem for physicians and for the rest of society. They underlie questions about appropriate termination of life support, access to care for indigents, and many other critical medical care problems. If physicians and their attorneys continue to ignore the significance of financial conflicts of interest, they should not be surprised by ever more Draconian laws regulating medical business practices.

Implications for Health Care Practitioners

The most important implication of the Federal Sentencing Guidelines is that they erase the traditional deference toward professionals who are accused of "technical" crimes such as Medicare fraud. Health care practitioners who are accused of crimes can expect to be held to higher standards because of their special skills and relationship with the patients. This reflects the importance the courts attach to the fiduciary aspects of the provider patient relationship, as discussed in Chapter 8. In their role as caregivers, providers must be careful to follow the applicable federal and state laws regarding their relationship with the patients and other providers.

As managers and supervisors, health care practitioners must ensure that their institution has a compliance plan that meets all the criteria of the Federal Sentencing Guidelines. More important, the plan must actually work and deal with the problems of the institution. The existence of the plan is not a defense to criminal prosecution, it is only a mitigating factor in the punishment for the violations. A successful compliance plan must prevent the violations if it is to protect the institution and the providers involved with the regulated activity. A health care practitioner can be found liable for the actions of others whom the provider relies on: if your billing service is submitting fraudulent bills to Medicare for your services, you are on the hook because you have a nondelegable duty to ensure that every claim you submit is proper. If you believe the compliance plan is not working, but do nothing to report or change it, you can be liable for failing to prevent the criminal activity of those under your supervision.

REFERENCES

1. Richards EP, Deters DJ, Gray RJ. Physicians and their profession: do racketeering rules apply? *Nat Law J.* 1989;38.
2. *Bell v. Wolfish*, 441 U.S. 520 (1979).
3. U.S.C.S. CONST. art. I, § 9, cl. 2 (1998).
4. U.S.C.S. CONST. art. I, § 9, cl. 3 (1998).
5. U.S.C.S. CONST. art. III, § 2, cl. 3 (1998).
6. U.S.C.S. CONST. amend. IV (1998).
7. U.S.C.S. CONST. amend. V (1998).
8. U.S.C.S. CONST. amend. VI (1998).
9. U.S.C.S. CONST. amend. VIII (1998).
10. *Fletcher v. Peck*, 6 Cranch 87 (1810).
11. *Gideon v. Wainwright*, 372 U.S. 335 (1963).
12. *Miranda v. Arizona*, 384 U.S. 436, 16 L. Ed. 2d 694, 86 S. Ct. 1602 (1966).
13. *Camara v. Municipal Ct. of San Francisco*, 387 U.S. 523 (1967).
14. 42 U.S.C. § 1395nn. This section prohibits any arrange-

ments that encourage the referral of patients to a specific medical facility:

"...if a physician...has a financial relationship with an entity...then—(A) the physician may not make a referral to the entity for the furnishing of designated health services for which payment otherwise may be made under this subchapter, and(B) the entity may not present or cause to be presented a claim under this subchapter or bill to any individual, third party payor, or other entity for designated health services furnished pursuant to a referral prohibited under subparagraph (A)."

15. 31 U.S.C. §§ 3729, et seq. (1997).
16. Health Insurance Portability and Accountability Act of 1996, Pub. L. 104-191, 110 Stat. 1936 (1996).
17. *United States v. Greber*, 760 F.2d 68 (3d Cir. 1985).
18. 42 U.S.C.A. § 1320a-7b (1998).
19. *Greber*, 760 F.2d 68.
20. *United States v. Kats*, 871 F.2d 105 (9th Cir. 1989).
21. *United States v. Bay State Ambulance & Hosp. Rental Serv., Inc.*, 874 F.2d 20 (1st Cir. 1989).
22. *Id.* at 32.
23. Holthaus D. Courts broadly interpret antikickback laws. *Hospitals.* 1989;63:44.
24. Hudson T. Fraud and abuse rules: enforcement questions persist. *Hospitals.* 1990;64:36.
25. This is a very old legal tool, dating to the pre-colonial period. *See e.g., Shoemaker v. Shirtliffe*, 1 U.S. 127 (1785) and *Purvance v. Angus*, 1 U.S. 180 (1786).
26. 31 U.S.C. § 3730(d)(1).
27. *Id.* § 3730(d)(2).
28. *United States v. Bornstein*, 423 U.S. 303 (1976).
29. *United States v. Lorenzo*, 768 F. Supp. 1127 (E.D. Pa. 1991). In this case, a dentist presented 3,683 false claims, worth approximately $140,000. The court found that it had no authority to reduce the penalty below the $5,000 minimum and awarded the government $18,415,000.
30. In a settlement, the government is not bound by the $5,000 minimum penalty.
31. Because of the importance of reputation, health care providers can have their practice destroyed by the publicity of a major fraud prosecution, even if they ultimately prevail.
Because criminal defense is not covered by insurance, settling a case may result in personal savings of more than $100,000 in legal fees.
32. The Health Care Financing Administration has launched a program called "Operation Restore Trust" to coordinate fraud prosecutions and to maximize the visibility of these actions.
33. $30 million settlement against the University of Pennsylvania, $15 million against New York University, and $12 million against Thomas Jefferson.
34. This section adapted from Richards EP, Rathbun KC. Professional Courtesy. *Mo. Med.* January 1998;95:18–20.
35. *Jefferson Parish Hosp. Dist. No. 2 v. Hyde,* 466 U.S. 2 (1984).
36. *Parker v. Brown,* 317 U.S. 341 (1943).
37. *Patrick v. Burget,* 486 U.S. 94 (1988).
38. *Id.* at 105
39. *Goldfarb v. Virginia State Bar,* 421 U.S. 733 (1975).
40. *American Soc'y of Mechanical Eng'rs v. Hydrolevel,* 456 U.S. 556 (1982).
41. BNA. Court approves settlement in physicians' suit against HMO. *Sec Reg Law Rep.* February 24, 1989; 21:313.
42. *Gregory v. United States,* 253 F.2d 104, 109 (5th Cir 1958).
43. *Carpenter v. United States,* 484 U.S. 19 (1987).
44. *H.J. Inc. v. Northwestern Bell Tel. Co.,* 492 U.S. 229 (1989).
45. *Sedima, S.P.R.L. v. Imrex Co.,* 473 U.S. 479 (1985).
46. *United States v. Bachynsky,* 934 F.2d 1349 (5th Cir. 1991).
47. *Hinsdale Women's Clinic, S.C. v. Women's Health Care of Hinsdale,* 690 F. Supp. 658 (N.D. Ill. Jun. 20, 1988).
48. United States Sentencing Guidelines § 3B1.3 (1998).
49. Official Commentary and Application Notes to United States Sentencing Guidelines § 3B1.3 (1998).
50. Official Commentary and Application Notes to United States Sentencing Guidelines § 8A1.2, subsection 3 (k).(1–7) (1998).
51. Official Commentary and Application Notes to United States Sentencing Guidelines §8A1.2, subsection 3 (k).(7)(i–iii) (1998).

SUGGESTED READINGS

Aussprung L. Fraud and abuse: federal civil health care litigation and settlement. *J Leg Med.* 1998;19:1–62.
Bennett T, Gerber RS, Mueller DG Jr. Making sense of antitrust policy: its application to physician directed networks. *Mo Med.* 1997;94:180–184.
Bloche MG. Cutting waste and keeping faith. *Ann Intern Med.* 1998;128:688–689.
Boyd W III. Combating fraud and abuse: anti-kickback statute. *Iowa Med.* 1997;87:23–24.
Boyer MM. Fraud and abuse gaining attention amid national E&M guideline controversy. *Pa Med.* 1998;101:12.
Cook DA. Fraud, abuse, and beyond: costly pitfalls for physicians who serve Medicare and Medicaid patients. *J Med Assoc Ga.* 1997;86:321–324.
Cook DA. New antitrust rules ease restrictions on physician networks. *J Med Assoc Ga.* 1996;85:257–259.
DeWitt AL. The citizen attorney general and Medicare fraud. *Mo Med.* 1996;93:688–689.

Dranove D, White WD. Emerging issues in the antitrust definition of healthcare markets. *Health Econ.* 1998;7:167–170.

Farrell MG. ERISA preemption and regulation of managed health care: the case for managed federalism. *Am J Law Med.* 1997;23:251–289.

Feldman R, Given RS. HMO mergers and Medicare: the antitrust issues. *Health Econ.* 1998;7:171–174.

Fifer WR. Compliance...or else! *Minn Med.* 1998;81:46–48.

Forgione DA. Corporate compliance plans in health care organizations: a top-down perspective. *J Health Care Finance.* 1998;24:87–92.

Frech HE III, Danger KL. Exclusive contracts between hospitals and physicians: the antitrust issues. *Health Econ.* 1998;7:175–178.

Glaser D. 500 FBI agents. *Iowa Med.* 1996;86:110–112.

Glaser D. What to do if an investigator is at your office door. *Iowa Med.* 1996;86:113–114.

Glaser DM. Health care audits and investigations: act now to avoid trouble later. *Minn Med.* 1996;79:43–46.

Greaney TL. Night landings on an aircraft carrier: hospital mergers and antitrust law. *Am J Law Med.* 1997;23:191–220.

Hebert DE, Ogaitis JM. Revised antitrust policy statements on healthcare. *AANA J.* 1996;64:512–514.

Hirshfeld EB. Provider sponsored organizations and provider service networks—rationale and regulation. *Am J Law Med.* 1996;22:263–300.

Hoffman DR. The federal effort to eliminate fraud and ensure quality care. *Adv Wound Care.* 1997;10:36–38.

Iglehart JK. Pursuing health care fraud and abuse. *Health Aff (Millwood).* 1998;17:6.

Jost TS, Davies S. The fraud and abuse statute: rationalizing or rationalization? *Health Aff (Millwood).* 1996;15:129–131.

Kleinke JD. Deconstructing the Columbia/HCA investigation. *Health Aff (Millwood).* 1998;17:7–26.

Kurlander SS, Scherb E. Liability under the False Claims Act for inadequate care of nursing facility residents. *Adv Wound Care.* 1997;10:47–49.

Kuttner R. Physician-operated networks and the new antitrust guidelines. *N Engl J Med.* 1997;336:386–391.

Lawton SE, Leibenluft RF, Loeb LE. Antitrust implications of physicians' responses to managed care. *Clin Infect Dis.* 1995;20:1354–1360.

Liggett N. New law adds significant penalties for the waiver of copayments. *Tenn Med.* 1997;90:354–355.

Luce GM, Graham JJ. Responding to a health care fraud investigation: a practice guide. *Va Med Q.* 1996;123:9–13.

Lundquist JW, Glaser DM. Fraud investigations: the heat is on. *Minn Med.* 1998;81:49–51.

Mason C. Who carries the risk? Networks, antitrust, and carve-outs. *Acad Radiol.* 1996;3:S150–S153.

McCampbell RG. Fraud and abuse provisions in the Health Insurance Portability and Accountability Act: a guide to the new act for physicians. *J Okla State Med Assoc.* 1997;90:139–141.

McMenamin JP, Scoggins GA. Developing a compliance program to identify and prevent inaccurate or improper Medicare billing practices. *Va Med Q.* 1998;125:12–14.

Meyer A. The Health Insurance Portability and Accountability Act. *Tenn Med.* 1997;90:86–89.

Miale PA. Wake-up call: can you protect yourself and your nuclear medicine practice from fraud and abuse? *J Nucl Med.* 1998;39:21N–22N.

Minarik PA. Opposition to antitrust legislation: support for Medicaid and Medicare reimbursement. *Clin Nurse Spec.* 1997;11:139–140.

Murphy LS. How much should physicians worry about antitrust? *Del Med J.* 1997;69:305–309.

Nordenberg T. Selling drug samples lands doctor in prison. *FDA Consum.* 1998;32:39.

Ortolon K. Medicare rerun: congress tinkers with but does not fix Medicare solvency. *Tex Med.* 1997;93:28–32.

Parmley WW. Public enemy number 2: academic medicine under the Federal spotlight. *J Am Coll Cardiol.* 1997;29:11–17.

Phillips JR. Qui tam litigation: a new forum for prosecuting false claims against the government. *J Leg Med.* 1993;14:267–277.

Polston MD. Reporting fraud. *Am J Nurs.* 1998;98:78.

Pristave RJ, Riley JB Jr. OIG on the warpath, II: when the OIG knocks on your door. *Nephrol News Issues.* 1996;10:45–46.

Russell LS. Fraud, abuse, and IDSs. *J Law Med Ethics.* 1996;24:162–166.

Sage WM. Judge Posner's RFP: antitrust law and managed care. *Health Aff (Millwood).* 1997;16:44–61.

Shepherd SR. The rewards of exposing fraud against the government. *J Pract Nurs.* 1997;47:4–7.

Smith JJ, Gay SB. Reducing the number of radiology residents: antitrust and action by the Accreditation Council for Graduate Medical Education. *Acad Radiol.* 1996;3:766–769.

Spear SL. On the importance of being honest. *Plast Reconstr Surg.* 1998;102:899.

Stahl DA. Consolidated billing and compliance program—Part 1. *Nurs Manage.* 1998;29:16–18.

Stahl DA. Consolidated billing and compliance program—Part 2. *Nurs Manage.* 1998;29:12–15.

Ward RD. Medicare fraud and abuse. *Mich Med.* 1998;98:24–31.

APPENDIX 3–A

Responding to Government Investigations

PURPOSE

Government investigators may arrive unannounced at _____ or the homes of present or former employees and seek interviews and documentation. The purpose of this policy is to establish a mechanism for the orderly response to government investigations to enable _____ to protect its interests as well as appropriately cooperate with the investigation.

POLICY

_____ will cooperate with any appropriately authorized government investigation or audit; however, _____ will assert all protections afforded it by law in any such investigation or audit.

PROCEDURE

Request for Interview

1. When government investigators request an interview, there is no obligation to consent to an interview although anyone may volunteer to do so. One may require the interview be conducted during normal business hours, at _____ or another location.
2. The staff member should always be polite and should obtain the following information:

Courtesy of von Briesen, Purtell & Roper, s.c., Milwaukee, Wisconsin.

a. The name, agency affiliation, business telephone number and address of all investigators
b. The reason for the visit.
3. When the investigator arrives, ask if there is a subpoena or warrant to be served and request a copy of the subpoena or warrant.
4. The interview may be stopped at any time, with a request that the investigator return when counsel can be present. _____ will be represented by its corporate counsel; employees have the right to their own individual legal counsel. Local counsel should be present for interviews whenever possible.
5. If an employee chooses not to respond to the investigator's questions, the investigator has the authority to subpoena the employee to appear before a grand jury.
6. Any staff member contacted by an investigator should immediately notify his or her supervisor. Provide this individual with as much information and documentation about the investigation that is known. Ultimately the request should be reported to the Chief Financial Officer and the Corporate Compliance Officer.

The Search

1. Request an investigator on _____ premises to wait until either the Corporate Compliance Officer, counsel, the Administrator on-call, or the Chief Financial Officer

arrives (each referred to as "the employee in charge").

2. _____ employees must not alter, remove, or destroy permanent documents or records of _____. All records are subject to state or nationally recognized retention guidelines and may be disposed of only in accordance with these guidelines. Once there has been notice of an investigation, the destruction portion of any policy on record retention is suspended.

3. If the investigators present a search warrant or warrant, the investigators have the authority to enter private premises, search for evidence of criminal activity, and seize those documents listed in the warrant. No staff member has to speak to the investigators, but must provide the documents requested in the warrant.

4. Request copies of the warrant and the affidavit providing reasons for the issuance of the warrant.

5. All staff members should request an opportunity to consult with _____'s counsel before the search commences. Provide counsel with a copy of the warrant immediately. If counsel can be reached by phone, put counsel directly in touch with the lead investigator.

6. Cooperate with the investigators, but do not consent to the search.
   a. The employee in charge should instruct the lead investigator that:
      i. _____ objects to the search;
      ii. The search is unjustified because _____ is willing to voluntarily cooperate with the government; and
      iii. The search will violate the rights of _____ and its employees.
   b. Under no circumstances should staff obstruct or interfere with the search. Although they should cooperate, any staff member should clearly state that this does not constitute consent to the search.
   c. Whenever possible, keep track of all documents and what information the

documents contain given to the investigators.

7. If local counsel is not available, the employee in charge should contact the prosecutor immediately and request that the search be stopped. One can negotiate alternatives to the search and seizure, including provisions to ensure that all existing evidence will be preserved undisturbed. If the prosecutor refuses to stop the search, request agreement to delay the search to enable _____ to obtain a hearing on the warrant.

8. The employee in charge should attempt to negotiate an acceptable methodology with the investigators to minimize disruptions and keep track of the process. Considerations include the sequence of the search; whether investigators are willing to accept copies in place of originals; and if so, who will make the copies and how; whether _____ will be permitted to make its own set of copies; and arrangements for access to records seized.

9. The employee in charge should point out limitations on the premises to be searched and on the property to be seized.
   a. Avoid expansion beyond the proper scope of the search from confusion or overreaching.
   b. Never consent to an expansion of the search.
   c. Disputes regarding the scope must be brought to the attention of the prosecutor or the court to be settled. _____ staff should not prevent the investigators from searching areas they claim to have the right to search.
   d. Investigators generally have the right to seize evidence of crimes that is in their "plain view" during a search regardless of whether such evidence is described in the warrant.

10. The employee in charge should take appropriate steps to protect other _____ staff members.

a. _____ should send all, but essential personnel home, or temporarily reassign them to other areas when a warrant is served.

b. Selected employees should remain along with the employee in charge and/or _____ counsel to monitor the search.

c. Investigators should never be left alone on _____'s premises, and no employee should be left alone with the investigators.

11. Object to any search of privileged documents.

a. If there is any possibility that the search will compromise privileged information, _____ should object on that basis, and raise the issue with the court if necessary.

b. Negotiate a methodology to protect the confidentiality of any privileged information pending a resolution of these objections. For example, segregate the privileged documents from other files and investigators will not read the documents until the court had made a decision or the investigators will seize the documents, but place them unread in sealed envelopes until the matter is resolved.

12. The employee is charge should keep a record regarding the search.

a. Ask each investigator for proper identification, including their business cards.

b. List the names and positions of all the investigators with the date and time. Verify the list with the lead agent and request he or she sign it.

c. Monitor and record the manner in which the search is conducted. Note in detail the precise areas and files searched, the time periods when each of them was searched, the manner in which the search was conducted, the agents who participated, and which files were seized.

d. Several individuals will be probably be needed to monitor the different areas being searched simultaneously.

e. If the monitor is ordered to leave, contact the lead investigator. A person should only be ordered to move if they are in the way, not to avoid being observed. Never provoke a confrontation with an agent.

13. If possible, do not release a document to the investigators unless it has been reviewed by counsel. This is not possible under a search warrant.

14. Keep all privileged and confidential documents separate and labeled accordingly. If seized, the documents should be protected from disclosure if labeled properly.

15. If possible, the employee in charge should make a record and a copy of all records seized.

a. If this is not possible, before the agents leave _____'s premises, request an inventory of the documents seized.

b. Request the lead agent to note the date and time the search was completed as well as sign the inventory with the agent's full title, address, and telephone number.

c. When documents are seized, the investigators are required to give the occupant a copy of the warrant.

d. Copies of the seized documents should be requested as well, especially medical records, as this is the most efficient way to inventory the documents seized.

e. Create a parallel inventory of the documents seized.

f. Download copies of files from hard drives of computers, and copy diskettes, especially if the material is essential to the ongoing operations of _____.

16. If possible, videotape the search.

a. A videotape may provide evidence of undue disruption or misconduct on the part of the investigators.

b. If the investigators claim the taping interferes with the search, the employee in charge should make a record of the refusal. Do not persist if the agents have warned that they regard the taping as an interference.

CHAPTER 4

Administrative Law and Violations

HIGHLIGHTS

- Administrative law deals with regulation by state and federal agencies.
- Participation in Medicare, Medicaid, and other governmental programs subjects health care practitioners to broad administrative regulations.
- Violation of administrative regulations can result in fines and imprisonment.
- Administrative agencies have almost unlimited access to health care practitioners' records and offices.
- Health care practitioners must understand agency procedures as a first step to compliance.

INTRODUCTION

Most of the day-to-day legal issues faced by health care practitioners are related to administrative agencies. The Health Care Financing Administration (HCFA) enforces Medicare/Medicaid regulations, the Food and Drug Administration (FDA) determines what drugs and medical devices are available and what information about them must be provided by the manufacturer, the Office of the Inspector General (OIG) investigates possible false claims, state licensing boards determine if the practitioner may practice at all, the local fire department will check the clinic for fire hazards, and, if you do not comply with the rules of the other agencies, the Department of Justice (DOJ) may prosecute for criminal misconduct. Health care practitioners must understand how administrative law differs from criminal law and from private civil litigation. Although agencies (other than DOJ or other prosecutors) cannot put you in jail, they can take away your livelihood,

and they do not have to give you all the constitutional protections that the criminal law system provides.

This chapter discusses basic administrative law, then uses the agency regulations on enforcement of the Emergency Medical Treatment and Active Labor Act (EMTALA) as an example of agency action.

ESTABLISHING AGENCIES

For its first century, the United States was governed with a very small federal government. The balance of governmental functions were carried out locally and at the state level. This began to shift as the United States gained its overseas empire and as President Theodore Roosevelt started his trust-busting. The government continued to grow, albeit slowly, during the Depression. The major change came with World War II, when the federal government took on extraordinary powers to coordinate the nation's fighting of the war.

These powers were exercised by executive branch agencies, created by Congress and overseen by the president. The federal government never really demobilized after World War II, creating the large and powerful central government that has characterized modern U.S. politics. Outside of the military, almost all the growth in government has been the growth of administrative agencies.

Agencies must be established by the legislature, either Congress or the state legislature. (This chapter mostly discusses federal agencies, but state law closely follows the federal law.) Congress starts agencies and expands them to deal with public relations problems. For example, the original agency regulating food and drugs was formed in response to Upton Sinclair's novel, *The Jungle*. This was meant to be an exposé of the horrible working conditions in the Chicago food processing industries. Unfortunately for the author, the general public was a lot more horrified by what the book told them about the contents of their food than by the suffering of the workers. Congress was pressured to deal with the problem and formed the predecessor to the FDA. In the 1930s there was a scandal involving a pediatric elixir that was prepared with ethylene glycol—a pleasant tasting but deadly solvent. The result was the modern food and drug regulation acts. In the 1970s there was great concern with the growing medical devices industry and congressional hearing about the dangers of some of the medical devices. Soon after, the FDA was given the right to regulate medical devices. (This works both ways—concentrated lobbying by the "health" foods industry caused Congress to take away the FDA's right to regulate food supplements, leaving the public with few protections in this area.)

The Delegation Problem

The Constitution demands that the branches of government be separate so each can provide checks and balances on the other two's powers. The main power of Congress is passing laws: "To make all laws which shall be necessary and proper."[1] An agency can only exercise the power that Congress gives it. The early Supreme Court decisions saw this as a problem to the extent that the agency transferred the power of Congress to make laws to the executive branch. The court required that the enabling legislation—the law establishing the agency—be sufficiently specific to limit the agency's discretion. Since early agencies were small and exercised few powers, the courts were content to find that they did not usurp the law-making function.

As federal agencies grew in power, the courts again became concerned with the delegation issue. One of their concerns was that agencies could make rules with the force of law behind closed doors without any citizen participation. Congress addressed this with two laws. The Administrative Procedures Act established rules for agency proceedings, including requiring agencies to give the public notice of proposed rules and a chance to comment on the rules. Congress also passed the Federal Freedom of Information Act, which requires agencies to provide information to persons who request it, assuming that the request is sufficiently specific and does not involve certain classes of confidential information. These rules made agency proceedings more democratic and allayed some of the court's objections. Although the courts are still concerned with delegation of congressional power, they have generally accepted the broad modern role of agencies.

Enabling Legislation

The primary control over an agency is the enabling legislation that the legislature passes to establish the agency. Some enabling legislation is very general. It is not unusual to see state public health laws, at least older ones, say only that the public health department should protect the public's health in whatever ways are appropriate. This is sufficient for civil enforcement, although it would probably be seen as too vague to support criminal prosecution. Congress seldom passes any simple laws, but there is still great variation in the detail in the legislation for various agency functions and civil law enforcement. In some cases, the law sets out the policy that Congress wants implemented and the basic nature of the enforcement mechanisms, and the agency is given the power to flesh out the details with administrative rules. At least theoretically, Congress leaves more details to the agency when the regulated matter involves scientific or technical decision making. An example would be the decisions on research funding by the National Institutes of Health (NIH). NIH is generally allowed broad discretion to distribute research funds based on peer reviewed grant proposals. In some cases, however, influential congresspersons get laws bypassing NIH review and giving research money directly to institutions in their states.

The Americans with Disabilities Act is an example of a very specific, detailed law that leaves the agency little latitude for regulatory discretion. Many provisions of this law were very controversial and the final statute represents detailed compromises worked out between various interest groups. Little was left to the agencies to flesh out because businesses and others needed certain and consistent interpretation of the law if they were to make fundamental changes in the way they dealt with persons with disabilities. The details of enforcement and ambiguities in the law have to be worked out by the courts, rather than by the agency, resulting in a high volume of litigation.

Political Control over Agencies

The main control over agency action is political. At the federal level, this is exercised by the president and Congress. Such control can be explicit and legally proper, or it can be *sub rosa* and abusive. Political control is most problematic at the state and local level because the employees and agency executive personnel do not have the protections provided by the federal civil service system.

Executive Branch Supervision

The major control over agency power is political. Most agencies are under the direct control of the president, who can replace their directors with the consent of Congress and these directors can replace their employees who are in high-level policy-making positions. For example, when Presi-

dent Clinton assumed office, his attorney general took the unprecedented action of asking for the resignation of the hundreds of U.S. Attorneys around the United States so they could be replaced with more politically compatible appointees. (Lower-level employees are protected by the civil service laws so that they cannot be fired and replaced with political cronies of the newly elected administration.) The president can issue Executive Orders to tell agencies to change what they are doing, as long as the order is consistent with the agency's enabling legislation. If Congress objects, then it can change the enabling legislation. The president also has the power to reorganize agency functions while seeking approval from Congress.

There are independent agencies that are not under the direct control of the president, although they are still considered part of the executive branch. One example is the Securities and Exchange Commission, which is charged with enforcing the laws governing stocks and securities. Another is the Federal Reserve Bank. It is critical to the economy that these agencies be seen as honest and impartial, rather than just doing the political bidding of Congress or the president. They are governed by boards whose members serve staggered terms whose duration is not contiguous with the president's term. Although presidents may fill vacancies as they arise, the president cannot remove board members, absent extraordinary circumstances. The Independent Counsel's office is the most legally unusual of these independent agencies because the counsels are appointed by judges and exercise the prosecutorial power generally reserved to the DOJ. The Supreme Court found this arrangement constitutional only because the Attorney General has the right, if not the political power, to remove an Independent Counsel.

Congressional Supervision

The most problematic political control is by Congress. Congress may properly control agencies by changing the laws that govern the agencies. This requires that both houses of Congress pass the law and that it be signed by the president. Congress also directs agencies through the appropriations power. Each year Congress passes a budget that authorizes federal spending. The budget is specific and the president has only limited power to reallocate appropriations. Agencies only get the money Congress gives them, and Congress can specify the funds down to the level of departments and programs within the agency. These agency budgets are set by congressional subcommittees and they are usually adopted by the rest of the Congress without further review. This gives a subcommittee the power to influence agency policy by cutting the funding for programs it does not like.

This power over agencies is proper because the agency's power is derived from the delegation of congressional power. Members of Congress should take an interest in agency activities and provide a useful ombudsman function to ensure that constituents in their district are treated properly by an agency. This congressional casework might involve asking an agency to review a Social Security disability claimant's file more expeditiously, or to look into a matter that has been lost in the agency bureaucracy. Congressional casework becomes improper interference when the member of Congress tries to force the agency to make a decision that is against agency policy. This becomes a particular problem when the casework is being done by the members or chairperson of the subcommittee that governs the agency's budget. The subcommittee can threaten the agency's future funding if it does not change its policies to please the chairman or members of its appropriations committee. The subcommittee can also call the agency director or other personnel before it in congressional hearings and cross-examine them about agency policy. Since adverse publicity in congressional hearing can end the career of agency professionals, this gives the subcommittee considerable leverage over individuals. This informal manipulation of agency policy violates the separate of powers, but has, so far, been impossible to attack in the courts.

State and Local Control

In 1988 the Institute of Medicine published a study of public health in the United States.[2] The report was scathing in its review of quality of state and local public health agencies, describing them as "… a hodgepodge of agencies, and well-intended but unbalanced appropriations—without coherent direction by well-qualified professionals." The lack of direction by well-qualified professionals is because of the intense political pressure on state and local agency personnel, especially directors of agencies. In many states and localities, agency salaries are set well below market rates, and agency directors can be dismissed without notice and with no severance pay. Thus a local health director who closes the mayor's brother's restaurant for health code violations, or who objects to the misuse of agency funds by the city administration, will be fired with no recourse. This ensures that local agency personnel are selected for their willingness to accommodate political pressure, rather than their expertise or commitment to the public welfare. Although there are many dedicated professionals in state and local agencies, they have only limited ability to resist improper political pressures.

AGENCY PROCEDURE

Agencies provide an alternative to the courts for the resolution of disputes and the enforcement of laws. The key values in administrative law are accuracy, fairness, efficiency, and acceptability. In the court system, the judge is a referee and the jurors are selected for impartiality, which usually includes not knowing anything about the dispute before the court. The lawyers put on their cases and, to some extent, the outcome is determined by the lawyer's skill, the money available to litigate the case, and the sympathy of the jury. All too often, juries come in with verdicts that conflict with the best medical or scientific knowledge.

Court proceedings are also very time consuming. Some problems, such as a food-borne illness outbreak, must be addressed quickly. Agencies are empowered to take action without preceding court hearings, and to take novel actions if needed to protect the public. Since agencies do not have the power to imprison, they are not bound by the Constitutional protections provided to criminal law defendants. Without such powers, the government would be paralyzed because the only way to respond to new problems would be to pass specific legislation addressing the problem. The obverse of this power is potential tyranny by a powerful agency. To combat this, the states and the federal government have passed laws establishing the bounds on agency power, and establishing procedural guidelines for agencies.

Agency Expertise

The first administrative agencies were the local boards of health and citizens commissions in the colonies. They dealt with quarantine and nuisance and any other threats to the public health and welfare. Although the members were volunteers, rather than governmental employees, they tried to get citizen members who had expertise in the matters at hand, which usually included a physician to advise on health issues. These boards were preserved in the early post-Constitutional period, becoming the first agencies of the new state governments. At this period, the federal government was very small and its first agency functions were also health related—the formation of the public health hospital system to treat sailors. Although these hospitals treated the full range of naval injuries, they were termed public health hospitals because sailors were a major source of contagion brought in from foreign voyages.

This early history shaped the legal conception of agencies as bodies with expertise in the area that they regulated, exercising governmental power to remedy threats to the public health. They might be made up of private citizens or of government employees, or, commonly, a citizen board including experts such as physicians and engineers overseeing governmental employees. They were not a police force, in that their legal authority extended only to controlling threats to the public health and safety, not punishing the persons who caused the threats. The distinction between punishment and prevention is critical: whenever there is threat of imprisonment, the government must provide full criminal law due process provisions. Since such protections include pervasive limits on

searches, the necessity of court hearings before many actions can be taken, and the right of the defendant to have counsel and to contest most stages of the proceeding, they make it impossible to act quickly or flexibly. In a classic case, the owners of a freezer plant attacked the right of a public health agency to seize and destroy thousands of pounds of chickens that had thawed when the refrigeration failed. The court ruled that the agency was justified in seizing and destroying the chicken without having a court hearing first because of the potential threat to the public.[3]

Inquisitorial versus Adversarial

If agencies are going to act without the prior approval of the courts, there must be some way to ensure that their actions are proper. The court system operates on adversarial principles, depending on the parties before it to bring out the facts through their own arguments. The judge is a referee to ensure fairness and consistent procedure. The judge is not an expert in the matters before the court, nor is the judge expected (or even permitted in some courts) to question the witnesses and comment on the evidence presented by the parties before the court. The credibility of the evidence is judged by a jury, selected to be impartial, not to be knowledgeable about the subject matter. If one side is poorly represented, or not represented at all, then that party's evidence will not be presented and the case will be decided on the evidence presented by the opposing party. This will generally ensure that the unrepresented party loses, thus the courts have ruled that the state must provide counsel to all defendants or their rights will be so compromised as to constitute a constitutional violation. Agency law is based on a different model, the inquisitorial system. The agency is charged with finding the best solution to a problem, based on using its own expertise and that of outside experts. Unlike a prosecutor or private litigant, the agency is expected to consider and present both sides of a controversy.

Formal Agency Action

In the federal court, civil trials are conducted according the Federal Rules of Civil Procedure, and criminal trials must abide by the Federal Rules of Criminal Procedure. There are also rules governing the presentation of evidence. The states have either adopted the federal rules, with their own modifications, or have developed their own rules for civil and criminal procedure. These rules do not apply to agency proceedings. Instead, federal agencies are governed by the Administrative Procedure Act (APA), and each state has a comparable set of rules for its agencies. The APA sets out how administrative hearings are conducted, and how the agencies make regulations.

These hearings are presided over by an administrative law judge (ALJ). These are generally much more informal than trials. Agencies usually allow regulated parties to talk directly to the staff, who may help the regulated party prepare its case or comply with the regulation. Unlike a judge in an adversary civil or criminal case, the ALJ is often an expert in the area, either because of special training or through years of reviewing cases on the same issues. Agency hearings do not have juries. Although live witness testimony is permitted, agencies generally prefer written reports from experts because they are easier to evaluate than live testimony.

The Goldberg Rights

Persons whose rights are at issue in an administrative proceeding do have due process protections, depending on the rights at issue. The leading case involved welfare beneficiaries whose benefits under the Aid to Families with Dependent Children program were terminated. The U.S. Supreme Court held that they were entitled to a hearing and certain due process rights:

1. the right to present an oral case
2. the right to confront witnesses
3. the right to be represented by an attorney, although the court did not create a right to appointed counsel
4. the right to have the decision based on the record before the ALJ

These are known as the Goldberg rights, after the case that established them.[4] The availability of the Goldberg rights depends on the nature of the private interest that is threatened, the probability of an erroneous decision, the potential value of the evidence, and the cost to the government. These are important to health care practitioners in proceedings such as license revocation hearings and other proceedings where the practitioner's livelihood is at issue.

The ALJ's Decision

The ALJ questions witnesses, the agency staff, and the outside parties. The ALJ role is to ensure that a full and balanced record is developed to aid in making his or her decision, and for the agency to use in the review of the ALJ's decision. When the proceeding is completed, the ALJ makes a decision and that becomes part of the record. Unlike the decision of a judge in a court proceeding, the ALJ's decision is not final. It is legally only a recommendation to the agency director as to the best way to proceed. In most cases the agency will adopt the ALJ's recommendation, but it is not bound to. In federal agencies, the head of the agency is free to come to a different conclusion, based on the record, and to make a final agency rule that is different from that of the ALJ. In some circumstances the agency provides an internal appeal procedure for ALJ determinations. In some states the administrative hearing process is done outside of the agency and the ALJ's decision is final. There are procedures for appealing agency decisions in the courts.

Informal Agency Action

The vast majority of agency actions are done informally. For example, every claim for payment for medical treatment rendered to a Medicare patient requires agency action. There must be a determination that the care was rendered by a provider entitled to payment, that the care was necessary and proper, and the amount that should be reimbursed for the care. These must be resolved in a more efficient way than an agency hearing, or the system cannot function. Medicare does this by setting out specific objective criteria for payment, many of which are set out in the Conditions of Participation, and they contract with private companies to check claims against the criteria. Many of the requirements are assumed to be met, such the requirements for medical record keeping to support the claims. Although these are not checked on an ongoing basis, they are subject to audit. If the auditor finds that there is not appropriate documentation, then past claims can be disallowed and the provider required to provide a full medical record with every claim.

Agencies may also use what are termed "grid" or "matrix" regulations, meaning that there is set of criteria, often set out in the table—hence the name—for eligibility for a particular government benefit, such as a disability claim. The claims examiner just checks off the information in the application for benefits to see if it meets the criteria. If the application is denied, the agency provides an appeal process, which usually culminates in a hearing before an ALJ. This gives the applicant the opportunity to provide additional information or to argue that the grid regulations are inappropriate in the specific case.

Rule Making

A federal agency can do only what Congress gives it the power to do in its enabling legislation. In many cases, however, that enabling legislation is broad and general. This gives the agencies flexibility, but can make it difficult to understand what is required to comply with agency regulations. Agencies write regulations to provide industries and individuals with more detailed and specific information than the enabling legislation does.

Notice-and-Comment Rule Making

The APA and an agency's enabling legislation provide a formal process for promulgation regulations to ensure that there is public notice of proposed regulations and a chance for public comment before the regulation is finalized (notice-and-comment rule making). Properly promulgated regulations have the same force as a law passed by Congress. For example, its enabling legislation may direct the FDA to prevent the sale of food packed under insanitary conditions. The agency must define insanitary in such a way as to carry out the wishes of Congress, while recognizing the realities of food production and handling.

One such rule could define how many insect parts are allowed in a pound of butter. The FDA must first publish its proposed regulation in the *Federal Register*, which is a compilation of the federal notices and proposed and final rules by agencies. This notice could exceed 100 pages. All interested persons, which might include butter and cookie makers, are given a period to comment on the rule. If the proposed rule allows three insect parts per pound, the butter industry might complain that reducing insect parts to less than twenty per pound would increase the cost of butter. A public interest group might comment that there should be no insect parts in butter and, if there are, they should appear on the label so consumers know what they are buying.

The FDA must the review the responses to the proposed regulation, and in some cases must hold public hearings to get more input. It then decides whether it wants to change the standard. In this case, assume it decides to raise the level to five parts per pound. It then publishes in the *Federal Register* a final rule with this standard. The final rule will include a summary of the comments the FDA received and explanations why it did or did not follow them. In this case it would say that it was persuaded that three would be too expensive, but that twenty was too many and indicated filthy conditions. It also would say that it is too expensive to ban insect parts, and because they do not carry disease, putting insect parts on the label would give consumers the wrong impression that the butter was unsafe.

When the final rule goes into effect, it is published as part of a series of books called the *Code of Federal Regulations* (CFR). A food manufacturer who wants to start producing butter could look in the Title 21 of the CFR, where the FDA regulations are codified. Agencies also can publish informal guides for the industries they regulate. Although these do not have same legal standing as regulations that were subject to notice-and-comment in the *Federal Register*, they are very useful guides to agency practice. The FDA publishes both formal regulations and more informal guidelines to help industry comply with its requirements.

Informal Rule Making

Notice and comment rule making is very time consuming and expensive. It is not unusual for years to elapse between the initial proposed rule and the final rule. Agencies are empowered to issue guidelines and other documents to help regulated entities. These do not have the same legal force as formal rules, but they can be done quickly and cheaply. The Equal Employment Opportunity Commission and the DOJ have issued several documents clarifying the Americans with Disabilities Act. HCFA and its OIG have issued documents such as the Compliance Plan for Hospitals that provide guidance on how the agency views the law and what an entity will need to do to show compliance with the law.

Some agencies will give advice on specific problems posed by a regulated entity. The Internal Revenue Service (IRS) has the most extensive program through its letter rulings. These are rulings that are binding for the specific persons and transactions addressed in the ruling, but are not legally binding precedents for other transactions. For example, a not-for-profit hospital wants to partner with a physician group and start an ambulatory surgical center. The hospital is concerned that this might jeopardize its not-for-profit status. It can request a letter ruling from the IRS based on a detailed description of the transaction. The IRS will advise it on the potential tax issues and how the IRS will view them.

Given the complex regulations in health care, and the Draconian consequences of noncompliance, this process is very important for health care practitioners. In addition to the IRS, the DOJ will give advisory opinions on potential antitrust problems, and the HCFA OIG now provides advisory opinions on potential fraud and abuse issues and other HCFA regulatory matters (see Chapter 3). These are not binding in the way that IRS letter rulings are, but they are very strong evidence of the views of the agency. It would be surprising if the agency were to take enforcement action against an entity that had a clean bill of health in an advisory ruling.

The most important consideration in requesting agency advice is the timing: you should do it before you enter into the transaction. The agencies make it clear that this is not a mechanism for immunizing past violations. They are free to investigate any existing transaction they learn about through the request for an advisory ruling. Since the request for advice does show good faith in trying to determine how to comply with the law, it is probably better to request an opinion on a questionable practice than to continue it and hope it is not discovered. These opinions should never be requested without the assistance of counsel who can ensure that the issues are properly framed so the agency will address all of them. If an issue is not directly addressed by the advisory opinion, the requester cannot rely on the opinion in planning the transaction.

Enforcement

A key value of administrative agencies is that they have many more enforcement tools than do private litigants or law enforcement agencies. In addition, if provided for in their enabling legislation, an agency can refer a matter to the DOJ or to state and local prosecutors for criminal prosecution. In health care, regulatory agencies are especially powerful because they control access to payment and to the licenses that allow health care practitioners and facilities to provide medical services (see Chapter 12 for more information on enforcement strategies).

Permits, Licenses, and Registrations

As a regulated industry, health care practitioners and facilities are dependent on licenses, permits, and registrations controlled by the regulatory agencies. With limited exceptions under the Constitution for religious healers, no one can provide health care services without a license from the state. Physicians also need a registration with the Drug Enforcement Administration to prescribe certain controlled substances. Hospitals will generally have a license from the state to operate as a hospital, as well a local fire-safety permit as a commercial building, and a food-handling permit to operate a cafeteria and to provide food to the patients. In many jurisdictions, private clinics must be licensed as health care facilities, and all of them must meet the standards for commercial buildings open to the public.

Permits, licenses, and registrations are not legal rights or entitlements. They are privileges awarded by the state to persons or entities who meet the applicable standards and who agree to compliance with various laws and regulations as a condition of maintaining the state-granted privilege. For example, as a condition of licensure, a health care practitioner will agree to forgo certain behaviors, that, whereas not illegal, are considered unprofessional. A hospital agrees to allow the state hospital inspectors access to hospital facilities whenever they want, without a warrant or prior notice. An health care practitioner or facility that accepts payment for Medicare patients agrees to abide by all the terms of the Conditions of Participation, even though many have no detailed knowledge of what they have agreed to abide by. The Conditions of Participation give the federal auditors access to the participant's offices, medical records, and any other information related to compliance with the regulations.

Permits, licenses, and registrations give the agency tremendous power because they can be suspended if the regulated person or entity does not cooperate with the agency. If a hospital refuses access to the state inspectors, it can lose its operating license. Refusal to cooperate with federal auditors can result in termination of the provider's right to receive federal payments, and can require that past payments be refunded. Health care practitioners who violate the restrictions on their license can lose their license and livelihood.

Administrative Orders and Civil Penalties

License revocations or termination of participation in federal programs is the administrative death penalty. Agencies use these as a last resort. In most cases, the agency will enter an administrative order specifying what must be done to elimi-

nate the violation. This may be to clean up the refrigerator in the hospital kitchen, to build fire escapes, or to stop billing for work that the health care practitioner is not personally supervising. Many agencies may also assess fines or other civil penalties, such as reimbursement for improper payments. These penalties can run to tens of millions of dollars if they involve systematic improper billing to the federal government. A hospital would have little choice but to pay the penalty because termination of its participation in federal programs will put it out of business.

Injunctions and Seizures

Injunctions and seizures are widely used in FDA enforcement. These are court orders that require that an entity or person desist from some action, such as selling tainted food or manufacturing a drug or device that does not conform to FDA regulations. Because an FDA injunction can close a business by preventing the sale of its products, it is a very powerful enforcement tool. There are variations on injunctions, called embargoes or seizure orders, that allow specific products to be kept off the market. The product is locked down in the company warehouse, or it may be physically seized and impounded by the government. When a product is seized because it presents a threat to the public health or safety, the government does not have to pay compensation because dangerous property that is not fit for its intended use is treated as having no value. If the product has a short lifetime, such as fresh produce or a drug with a short expiration date, the business must comply with whatever restrictions the agency requests because the delay in fighting the order will render the product worthless.

JUDICIAL REVIEW OF AGENCY ACTIONS

If every agency action were reviewable in court, the cost of the proceedings and the delay involved would paralyze the administrative law system. The Congress and the courts have developed a strategy of limited review of agency actions that is intended to protect the rights of the regulated entities, while protecting the efficiency of agency practice.

Exhaustion of Remedies

The first principle of agency law is that you have to exhaust the procedures provided by the agency before you can go to court. This preserves an orderly review process, allows the agency to resolve the problem, and, if the court eventually does review the action, gives the agency a chance to develop a record that will aid the court in its deliberations. In most cases, if a court action is filed before all the agency remedies have been tried, the court will dismiss the case. Even if the court hears the case, it may find that the regulated entity waived critical rights by not presenting evidence at the agency level. The courts will consider an action against an agency without first exhausting the agency remedies if the claim is that the agency is exceeding its legal powers, if action raises only questions of law, rather than agency expertise, or if the agency proceedings do not provide an adequate remedy.

Standard of Review

The courts use the term "standard of review" as a broad defined notion of how they judge a case. There are many levels of review, and the selection of the level often determines the result in a case. In cases where the courts are determining if a law is constitutional, for example, there is a standard called strict scrutiny that is used if the courts believe that the law poses a substantial threat to fundamental rights. In reality, this is not really a standard of review because few laws are ever found constitutional when looked at with strict scrutiny. If, instead, the court chooses the "rational relationship" test, most laws pass as long as there is some relationship between the goals of the law and the method it prescribes to achieve those goals. Thus the determination of the proper standard of review usually predicts the results of that review.

Agency Interpretation of Law

All agencies have to interpret their enabling legislation to determine what they can legally do.

If the legislation is clear and detailed, the agency's role will be easy to determine and there will be little controversy over the interpretation of the law. In many cases, however, the enabling legislation is complex and ambiguous, and sometimes has internal contradictions. The agency must make its best guess as to the meaning of the law, and anticipate that it will be challenged in the courts. Even when the law is clear, the agency may have to respond to pressure from the president to or from Congress regulate in ways that are questionable under the law. Wherever an agency is operating beyond the clear limits of its enabling legislation, it can expect to have its actions challenged in court because such challenge does not require the litigant to exhaust the agency procedures and thus expose itself to agency sanction as the price of appeal.

The courts do not defer to agencies' interpretation of laws because that is the area of the courts' expertise. It is not unusual for a court to prohibit an agency from regulating an activity because Congress did not give the agency authority for the contested regulations. For example, when the FDA tried to restrict a physician's right to give patients his homemade drugs, the court found that the agency's enabling legislation did not give it the power to regulate medical practice. The courts will also intervene if the agency actions, even if authorized by the enabling legislation, violate constitutional protections, as in the Goldberg case on the rights of persons being denied government benefits.

Scientific or Technical Expertise

The U.S. Supreme Court has ruled that in reviewing the order of a public health agency, the courts should not second-guess the underlying scientific basis of the agency's decision. This is a well-established principle, extending back to a 1905 case involving smallpox immunizations. The litigant tried to argue that he should not be subjected to smallpox vaccination because it was dangerous.[5] The court ruled that it would not second-guess the expertise of the agency in requiring the vaccination. To successfully attack an agency's expert decision making, it must be shown that the agency acted "arbitrarily or capriciously," which means that the agency acted without a rational basis for its decision. To defeat such a challenge, the agency must present a proper record explaining the factual and legal basis for its actions. If the record documents a proper basis for the agency's decision, the regulated entity challenging the decision will not be permitted to bring in experts to dispute the agency's findings. If the agency presents a proper record, and stays within its statutory bounds, the courts are very reluctant to overturn agency actions.

Most cases challenging agency scientific decision making are brought because the agency took an action. In rare cases, an agency may be successfully sued for failing to act. In one case, the Secretary of the Department of Health and Human Services refused to promulgate a rule banning the interstate shipment of unpasteurized milk. A group of public interest groups, including the American Academy of Pediatrics, sued the agency, arguing that such a rule was necessary to protect the public's health. The agency record showed that FDA scientists had built an overwhelming record that unpasteurized milk posed a threat to the public health. The court found that the Secretary was acting arbitrarily and capriciously in refusing to promulgate the rule, and ordered her do so.[6]

EMERGENCY CARE AND EMTALA

The Emergency Medical Treatment and Active Labor Act (EMTALA), also known as COBRA to many health care providers because it was part of the Consolidated Omnibus Budget Reconciliation Act, is a classic administrative law. It was passed in response to a crisis: emergency rooms denying care to indigent patients and private emergency rooms dumping indigent patients onto already overburdened county hospitals. One of the stories that persuaded Congress to act was a nationally publicized effort to find care for a premature infant, including flying the infant around in an air ambulance with nowhere to land. Congress passed the law requiring all persons who presented in the emergency room to be screened and treated, if necessary, and not to be transferred unless it was in the patient's best interest. The law provides two enforcement mechanisms, private civil litigation (essentially federal law malpractice litigation) and enforcement by the HCFA as part of the Conditions of Participation for Hospitals. Although there has been significant private litigation under EMTALA, the primary enforcement has been by the HCFA. Health care practitioners must understand EMTALA enforcement because the agency can fine health care practitioners up to $50,000. Noncomplying hospitals can be fined and banned from participation in federal health care programs.

There are three appendixes to this chapter. Appendix 4–A is the EMTALA statute as passed and modified by Congress. Appendix 4–B are formal published regulations promulgated by the HCFA as guidance for hospitals. Appendix 4–C are the guidelines for governmental auditors who actually investigate hospitals to determine if they are in compliance with EMTALA. These documents illustrate the different steps in agency process, from enabling legislation to actual audit guidelines. Ultimately, as is evident from Appendix 4-C, it is only the audit guidelines that really provide the detailed information necessary to know if you are complying with the statute.

REFERENCES

1. U.S.C.S. CONST. art. 1, § 8, para. 18.
2. Institute of Medicine. *The Future of Public Health*. Washington, DC: National Academy Press; 1988.
3. *North Am. Cold Storage Co. v. City of Chicago*, 211 U.S. 306 (1908).
4. *Goldberg v. Kelly*, 397 U.S. 254 (1970).
5. *Jacobson v. Massachusetts,* 197 U.S. 11 (1905).
6. *Public Citizen v. Heckler*, 653 F. Supp. 1229 (D.D.C. Dec. 31, 1986).

SUGGESTED READINGS

Bishop DWD. Navigating the Board of Medical Examiners system. *Tex Med*. 1993;89:50–55.

Cardwell MS. Interhospital transfers of obstetric patients under the Emergency Medical Treatment and Active Labor Act. *J Leg Med*. 1995;16:357–372.

Cardwell MS. The Emergency Medical Treatment and Active Labor Act: reading between the lines.... *Obstet Gynecol Surv*. 1994;49:443–444.

Diekema DS. Unwinding the COBRA: new perspectives on EMTALA. *Pediatr Emerg Care*. 1995;11:243–248.

Diekema DS. What is left of futility? The convergence of anencephaly and the Emergency Medical Treatment and Active Labor Act. *Arch Pediatr Adolesc Med*. 1995;149:1156–1159.

Federgreen WR. Office of Inspector General U.S. Department of Health and Human Services: an overview. *J Fla Med Assoc*. 1993;80:236–240.

Furrow BR. An overview and analysis of the impact of the Emergency Medical Treatment and Active Labor Act. *J Leg Med*. 1995;16:325–355.

George JE, Quattrone MS, Goldstone M. Persons brought to the emergency department by police: are they patients? *J Emerg Nurs*. 1997;23:354–355.

Graber MA, Gjerde C, Bergus G, Ely J. The use of unofficial "problem patient" files and interinstitutional information transfer in emergency medicine in Iowa. *Am J Emerg Med*. 1995;13:509–511.

Grossman AR. Regulation by the Board of Medicine. *J Fla Med Assoc*. 1997;84:97–100.

Guertler AT. The clinical practice of emergency medicine. *Emerg Med Clin North Am*. 1997;15:303–313.

Gwynne A, Barber P, Tavener F. A review of 105 negligence claims against accident and emergency departments. *J Accid Emerg Med*. 1997;14:243–245.

Jain SC, Hoyt S. Patient dumping in the federal courts: expanding EMTALA without preempting state malpractice law. *Law Med Health Care*. 1992;20:249–252.

Johnson JA. Court limits board of medicine's ability to discipline. *J Law Med Ethics*. 1996;24:390–391.

Johnston ME. When the board comes a'callin'. *J Tenn Med Assoc*. 1996;89:54–55.

Kuettel AC. The changing role of receiving hospitals under the Emergency Medical Treatment and Active Labor Act. *J Leg Med*. 1998;19:351–376.

Levine RJ, Guisto JA, Meislin HW, Spaite DW. Analysis of federally imposed penalties for violations of the Consolidated Omnibus Reconciliation Act. *Ann Emerg Med*. 1996;28:45–50.

Ludwig H. Emergencies in obstetrics. *Ther Umsch*. 1996;53:477–496.

Michael KI, McMenamin JP. What you can't afford to ignore about EMTALA. *Va Med Q*. 1995;122:102–107, 111.

Morrison J, Wickersham P. Physicians disciplined by a state medical board. *JAMA*. 1998;279:1889–1893.

Parmley WW. Disciplinary actions: how often and why? *J Am Coll Cardiol*. 1994;23:278–279.

Selbst SM. Emergency Medical Treatment and Active Labor Act: legal concerns about private or managed care patients in the emergency department. *Curr Opin Pediatr*. 1997;9:465–469.

Stratas NE. The contrast between physicians seen by the medical board and those seen in private practice. *NC Med J*. 1996;57:218–222.

Tammelleo AD. Nurse's role in hospital compliance with EMTALA. *Regan Rep Nurs Law*. 1995;36:1.

Toreki W, Toreki P. Emergency Medical Treatment and Active Labor Act. *Trends Health Care Law Ethics*. 1992;7:58–60.

APPENDIX 4–A

42 U.S.C.A. sec 1395dd Examination and Treatment for Emergency Medical Conditions and Women in Labor

(a) Medical screening requirement

In the case of a hospital that has a hospital emergency department, if any individual (whether or not eligible for benefits under this subchapter) comes to the emergency department and a request is made on the individual's behalf for examination or treatment for a medical condition, the hospital must provide for an appropriate medical screening examination within the capability of the hospital's emergency department, including ancillary services routinely available to the emergency department, to determine whether or not an emergency medical condition (within the meaning of subsection (e)(1) of this section) exists.

(b) Necessary stabilizing treatment for emergency medical conditions and labor

(1) In general

If any individual (whether or not eligible for benefits under this subchapter) comes to a hospital and the hospital determines that the individual has an emergency medical condition, the hospital must provide either

(A) within the staff and facilities available at the hospital, for such further medical examination and such treatment as may be required to stabilize the medical condition, or

(B) for transfer of the individual to another medical facility in accordance with subsection (c) of this section.

(2) Refusal to consent to treatment

A hospital is deemed to meet the requirement of paragraph (1)(A) with respect to an individual if the hospital offers the individual the further medical examination and treatment described in that paragraph and informs the individual (or a person acting on the individual's behalf) of the risks and benefits to the individual of such examination and treatment, but the individual (or a person acting on the individual's behalf) refuses to consent to the examination and treatment. The hospital shall take all reasonable steps to secure the individual's (or person's) written informed consent to refuse such examination and treatment.

(3) Refusal to consent to transfer

A hospital is deemed to meet the requirement of paragraph (1) with respect to an individual if the hospital offers to transfer the individual to another medical facility in accordance with subsection (c) of this section and informs the individual (or a person acting on the individual's behalf) of the risks and benefits to the individual of such transfer, but the individual (or a person acting on the individual's behalf) refuses to consent to the transfer. The hospital shall take all reasonable steps to secure the individual's (or person's) written informed consent to refuse such transfer.

(c) Restricting transfers until individual stabilized

(1) Rule

If an individual at a hospital has an emergency medical condition that has not been stabilized

Source: Reprinted from 42 C.F.R., Section 1395dd, 1999.

(within the meaning of subsection (e)(3)(B) of this section), the hospital may not transfer the individual unless

(A)(i) the individual (or a legally responsible person acting on the individual's behalf) after being informed of the hospital's obligations under this section and of the risk of transfer, in writing requests transfer to another medical facility,

(ii) a physician (within the meaning of section 1395x(r)(1) of this title) has signed a certification that based upon the information available at the time of transfer, the medical benefits reasonably expected from the provision of appropriate medical treatment at another medical facility outweigh the increased risks to the individual and, in the case of labor, to the unborn child from effecting the transfer, or

(iii) if a physician is not physically present in the emergency department at the time an individual is transferred, a qualified medical person (as defined by the Secretary in regulations) has signed a certification described in clause (ii) after a physician (as defined in section 1395x(r)(1) of this title), in consultation with the person, has made the determination described in such clause, and subsequently countersigns the certification; and

(B) the transfer is an appropriate transfer (within the meaning of paragraph (2)) to that facility.

A certification described in clause (ii) or (iii) of subparagraph (A) shall include a summary of the risks and benefits upon which the certification is based.

(2) Appropriate transfer

An appropriate transfer to a medical facility is a transfer

(A) in which the transferring hospital provides the medical treatment within its capacity which minimizes the risks to the individual's health and, in the case of a woman in labor, the health of the unborn child;

(B) in which the receiving facility

(i) has available space and qualified personnel for the treatment of the individual, and

(ii) has agreed to accept transfer of the individual and to provide appropriate medical treatment;

(C) in which the transferring hospital sends to the receiving facility all medical records (or copies thereof), related to the emergency condition for which the individual has presented, available at the time of the transfer, including records related to the individual's emergency medical condition, observations of signs or symptoms, preliminary diagnosis, treatment provided, results of any tests and the informed written consent or certification (or copy thereof) provided under paragraph (1)(A), and the name and address of any on-call physician (described in subsection (d)(1)(C) of this section) who has refused or failed to appear within a reasonable time to provide necessary stabilizing treatment;

(D) in which the transfer is effected through qualified personnel and transportation equipment, as required including the use of necessary and medically appropriate life support measures during the transfer; and

(E) which meets such other requirements as the Secretary may find necessary in the interest of the health and safety of individuals transferred.

(d) Enforcement

(1) Civil money penalties

(A) A participating hospital that negligently violates a requirement of this section is subject to a civil money penalty of not more than $50,000 (or not more than $25,000 in the case of a hospital with less than 100 beds) for each such violation. The provisions of section 1320a-7a of this title (other than subsections (a) and (b)) shall apply to a civil money penalty under this subparagraph in the same manner as such provisions apply with respect to a penalty or proceeding under section 1320a-7a(a) of this title.

(B) Subject to subparagraph (C), any physician who is responsible for the examination, treatment, or transfer of an individual in a participating hospital, including a physician on-call for the care of such an individual, and who negligently violates a requirement of this section, including a physician who

(i) signs a certification under subsection (c)(1)(A) of this section that the medical benefits reasonably to be expected from a transfer to another facility outweigh the risks associated with the transfer, if the physician knew or should have known that the benefits did not outweigh the risks, or

(ii) misrepresents an individual's condition or other information, including a hospital's obligations under this section,

is subject to a civil money penalty of not more than $50,000 for each such violation and, if the violation is gross and flagrant or is repeated, to exclusion from participation in this subchapter and State health care programs. The provisions of section 1320a-7a of this title (other than the first and second sentences of subsection (a) and subsection (b)) shall apply to a civil money penalty and exclusion under this subparagraph in the same manner as such provisions apply with respect to a penalty, exclusion, or proceeding under section 1320a-7a(a) of this title.

(C) If, after an initial examination, a physician determines that the individual requires the services of a physician listed by the hospital on its list of on-call physicians (required to be maintained under section 1395cc(a)(1)(I) of this title) and notifies the on-call physician and the on-call physician fails or refuses to appear within a reasonable period of time, and the physician orders the transfer of the individual because the physician determines that without the services of the on-call physician the benefits of transfer outweigh the risks of transfer, the physician authorizing the transfer shall not be subject to a penalty under subparagraph (B). However, the previous sentence shall not apply to the hospital or to the on-call physician who failed or refused to appear.

(2) Civil enforcement

(A) Personal harm

Any individual who suffers personal harm as a direct result of a participating hospital's violation of a requirement of this section may, in a civil action against the participating hospital, obtain those damages available for personal injury under the law of the State in which the hospital is located, and such equitable relief as is appropriate.

(B) Financial loss to other medical facility

Any medical facility that suffers a financial loss as a direct result of a participating hospital's violation of a requirement of this section may, in a civil action against the participating hospital, obtain those damages available for financial loss, under the law of the State in which the hospital is located, and such equitable relief as is appropriate.

(C) Limitations on actions

No action may be brought under this paragraph more than two years after the date of the violation with respect to which the action is brought.

(3) Consultation with peer review organizations (PROs)

In considering allegations of violations of the requirements of this section in imposing sanctions under paragraph (1), the Secretary shall request the appropriate utilization and quality control PRO (with a contract under part B of subchapter XI of this chapter) to assess whether the individual involved had an emergency medical condition which had not been stabilized, and provide a report on its findings. Except in the case in which a delay would jeopardize the health or safety of individuals, the Secretary shall request such a review before effecting a sanction under paragraph (1) and shall provide a period of at least 60 days for such review.

(e) Definitions

In this section

(1) The term "emergency medical condition" means

(A) a medical condition manifesting itself by acute symptoms of sufficient severity (including severe pain) such that the absence of immediate medical attention could reasonably be expected to result in

(i) placing the health of the individual (or, with respect to a pregnant woman, the health of the woman or her unborn child) in serious jeopardy,

(ii) serious impairment to bodily functions, or

(iii) serious dysfunction of any bodily organ or part; or

(B) with respect to a pregnant women who is having contractions

(i) that there is inadequate time to effect a safe transfer to another hospital before delivery, or

(ii) that transfer may pose a threat to the health or safety of the woman or the unborn child.

(2) The term "participating hospital" means hospital that has entered into a provider agreement under section 1395cc of this title.

(3)(A) The term "to stabilize" means, with respect to an emergency medical condition described in paragraph (1)(A), to provide such medical treatment of the condition as may be necessary to assure, within reasonable medical probability, that no material deterioration of the condition is likely to result from or occur during the transfer of the individual from a facility, or, with respect to an emergency medical condition described in paragraph (1)(B), to deliver (including the placenta).

(B) The term "stabilized" means, with respect to an emergency medical condition described in paragraph (1)(A), that no material deterioration of the condition is likely, within reasonable medical probability, to result from or occur during the transfer of the individual from a facility, or, with respect to an emergency medical condition described in paragraph (1)(B), that the woman has delivered (including the placenta).

(4) The term "transfer" means the movement (including the discharge) of an individual outside a hospital's facilities at the direction of any person employed by (or affiliated or associated, directly or indirectly, with) the hospital, but does not include such a movement of an individual who (A) has been declared dead, or (B) leaves the facility without the permission of any such person.

(5) The term "hospital" includes a critical access hospital (as defined in section 1395x(mm)(1) of this title).

(f) Preemption

The provisions of this section do not preempt any State or local law requirement, except to the extent that the requirement directly conflicts with a requirement of this section.

(g) Nondiscrimination

A participating hospital that has specialized capabilities or facilities (such as burn units, shock-trauma units, neonatal intensive care units, or (with respect to rural areas) regional referral centers as identified by the Secretary in regulation) shall not refuse to accept an appropriate transfer of an individual who requires such specialized capabilities or facilities if the hospital has the capacity to treat the individual.

(h) No delay in examination or treatment

A participating hospital may not delay provision of an appropriate medical screening examination required under subsection (a) of this section or further medical examination and treatment required under subsection (b) of this section in order to inquire about the individual's method of payment or insurance status.

(i) Whistleblower protections

A participating hospital may not penalize or take adverse action against a qualified medical person described in subsection (c)(1)(A)(iii) or a physician because the person or physician refuses to authorize the transfer of an individual with an emergency medical condition that has not been stabilized or against any hospital employee because the employee reports a violation of a requirement of this section.

APPENDIX 4–B

42 CFR sec 489.24 Special Responsibilities of Medicare Hospitals in Emergency Cases

(a) General. In the case of a hospital that has an emergency department, if any individual (whether or not eligible for Medicare benefits and regardless of ability to pay) comes by him- or herself or with another person to the emergency department and a request is made on the individual's behalf for examination or treatment of a medical condition by qualified medical personnel (as determined by the hospital in its rules and regulations), the hospital must provide for an appropriate medical screening examination within the capability of the hospital's emergency department, including ancillary services routinely available to the emergency department, to determine whether or not an emergency medical condition exists. The examinations must be conducted by individuals determined qualified by hospital by-laws or rules and regulations and who meet the requirements of § 482.55 concerning emergency services personnel and direction.

(b) Definitions. As used in this subpart

Capacity means the ability of the hospital to accommodate the individual requesting examination or treatment of the transferred individual. Capacity encompasses such things as numbers and availability of qualified staff, beds and equipment and the hospital's past practices of accommodating additional patients in excess of its occupancy limits.

Comes to the emergency department means, with respect to an individual requesting examina-

tion or treatment, that the individual is on the hospital property (property includes ambulances owned and operated by the hospital, even if the ambulance is not on hospital grounds). An individual in a nonhospital-owned ambulance on hospital property is considered to have come to the hospital's emergency department. An individual in a nonhospital-owned ambulance off hospital property is not considered to have come to the hospital's emergency department, even if a member of the ambulance staff contacts the hospital by telephone or telemetry communications and informs the hospital that they want to transport the individual to the hospital for examination and treatment. In such situations, the hospital may deny access if it is in "diversionary status," that is, it does not have the staff or facilities to accept any additional emergency patients. If, however, the ambulance staff disregards the hospital's instructions and transports the individual onto hospital property, the individual is considered to have come to the emergency department.

Emergency medical condition means

(i) A medical condition manifesting itself by acute symptoms of sufficient severity (including severe pain, psychiatric disturbances and/or symptoms of substance abuse) such that the absence of immediate medical attention could reasonably be expected to result in

(A) Placing the health of the individual (or, with respect to a pregnant woman, the health of

---

Source: Reprinted from 42 C.F.R., Section 489.24, 1999.

the woman or her unborn child) in serious jeopardy;

(B) Serious impairment to bodily functions; or

(C) Serious dysfunction of any bodily organ or part; or

(ii) With respect to a pregnant woman who is having contractions

(A) That there is inadequate time to effect a safe transfer to another hospital before delivery; or

(B) That transfer may pose a threat to the health or safety of the woman or the unborn child.

Hospital includes a critical access hospital as defined in section 1861(mm)(1) of the Act.

Hospital with an emergency department means a hospital that offers services for emergency medical conditions (as defined in this paragraph) within its capability to do so.

Labor means the process of childbirth beginning with the latent or early phase of labor and continuing through the delivery of the placenta. A woman experiencing contractions is in true labor unless a physician certifies that, after a reasonable time of observation, the woman is in false labor.

Participating hospital means (i) a hospital or (ii) a critical access hospital as defined in section 1861(mm)(1) of the Act that has entered into a Medicare provider agreement under section 1866 of the Act.

Stabilized means, with respect to an "emergency medical condition" as defined in this section under paragraph (i) of that definition, that no material deterioration of the condition is likely, within reasonable medical probability, to result from or occur during the transfer of the individual from a facility or, with respect to an "emergency medical condition" as defined in this section under paragraph (ii) of that definition, that the woman has delivered the child and the placenta.

To stabilize means, with respect to an "emergency medical condition" as defined in this section under paragraph (i) of that definition, to provide such medical treatment of the condition necessary to assure, within reasonable medical probability, that no material deterioration of the condition is likely to result from or occur during the transfer of the individual from a facility or that, with respect to an "emergency medical condition" as defined in this section under paragraph (ii) of that definition, the woman has delivered the child and the placenta.

Transfer means the movement (including the discharge) of an individual outside a hospital's facilities at the direction of any person employed by (or affiliated or associated, directly or indirectly, with) the hospital, but does not include such a movement of an individual who (i) has been declared dead, or (ii) leaves the facility without the permission of any such person.

(c) Necessary stabilizing treatment for emergency medical conditions

(1) General. If any individual (whether or not eligible for Medicare benefits) comes to a hospital and the hospital determines that the individual has an emergency medical condition, the hospital must provide either

(i) Within the capabilities of the staff and facilities available at the hospital, for further medical examination and treatment as required to stabilize the medical condition; or

(ii) For transfer of the individual to another medical facility in accordance with paragraph (d) of this section.

(2) Refusal to consent to treatment. A hospital meets the requirements of paragraph (c)(1)(i) of this section with respect to an individual if the hospital offers the individual the further medical examination and treatment described in that paragraph and informs the individual (or a person acting on the individual's behalf) of the risks and benefits to the individual of the examination and treatment, but the individual (or a person acting on the individual's behalf) refuses to consent to the examination and treatment. The medical record must contain a description of the examination, treatment, or both if applicable, that was refused by or on behalf of the individual. The hospital must take all reasonable steps to secure the individual's written informed refusal (or that of the person acting on his or her behalf). The written document should indicate that the person has been informed of the risks and benefits of the examination or treatment, or both.

(3) Delay in examination or treatment. A participating hospital may not delay providing an ap-

propriate medical screening examination required under paragraph (a) of this section or further medical examination and treatment required under paragraph (c) in order to inquire about the individual's method of payment or insurance status.

(4) Refusal to consent to transfer. A hospital meets the requirements of paragraph (c)(1)(ii) of this section with respect to an individual if the hospital offers to transfer the individual to another medical facility in accordance with paragraph (d) of this section and informs the individual (or a person acting on his or her behalf) of the risks and benefits to the individual of the transfer, but the individual (or a person acting on the individual's behalf) refuses to consent to the transfer. The hospital must take all reasonable steps to secure the individual's written informed refusal (or that of a person acting on his or her behalf). The written document must indicate the person has been informed of the risks and benefits of the transfer and state the reasons for the individual's refusal. The medical record must contain a description of the proposed transfer that was refused by or on behalf of the individual.

(d) Restricting transfer until the individual is stabilized

(1) General. If an individual at a hospital has an emergency medical condition that has not been stabilized (as defined in paragraph (b) of this section), the hospital may not transfer the individual unless

(i) The transfer is an appropriate transfer (within the meaning of paragraph (d)(2) of this section); and

(ii)(A) The individual (or a legally responsible person acting on the individual's behalf) requests the transfer, after being informed of the hospital's obligations under this section and of the risk of transfer. The request must be in writing and indicate the reasons for the request as well as indicate that he or she is aware of the risks and benefits of the transfer;

(B) A physician (within the meaning of section 1861(r)(1) of the Act) has signed a certification that, based upon the information available at the time of transfer, the medical benefits reasonably expected from the provision of appropriate medi-

cal treatment at another medical facility outweigh the increased risks to the individual or, in the case of a woman in labor, to the woman or the unborn child, from being transferred. The certification must contain a summary of the risks and benefits upon which it is based; or

(C) If a physician is not physically present in the emergency department at the time an individual is transferred, a qualified medical person (as determined by the hospital in its by-laws or rules and regulations) has signed a certification described in paragraph (d)(1)(ii)(B) of this section after a physician (as defined in section 1861(r)(1) of the Act) in consultation with the qualified medical person, agrees with the certification and subsequently countersigns the certification. The certification must contain a summary of the risks and benefits upon which it is based.

(2) A transfer to another medical facility will be appropriate only in those cases in which

(i) The transferring hospital provides medical treatment within its capacity that minimizes the risks to the individual's health and, in the case of a woman in labor, the health of the unborn child;

(ii) The receiving facility

(A) Has available space and qualified personnel for the treatment of the individual; and

(B) Has agreed to accept transfer of the individual and to provide appropriate medical treatment;

(iii) The transferring hospital sends to the receiving facility all medical records (or copies thereof) related to the emergency condition which the individual has presented that are available at the time of the transfer, including available history, records related to the individual's emergency medical condition, observations of signs or symptoms, preliminary diagnosis, results of diagnostic studies or telephone reports of the studies, treatment provided, results of any tests and the informed written consent or certification (or copy thereof) required under paragraph (d)(1)(ii) of this section, and the name and address of any on-call physician (described in paragraph (f) of this section) who has refused or failed to appear within a reasonable time to provide necessary stabilizing treatment. Other records (e.g., test results not yet available or historical records not readily available from the hospital's files) must be sent as soon as practicable after transfer; and

(iv) The transfer is effected through qualified personnel and transportation equipment, as required, including the use of necessary and medically appropriate life support measures during the transfer.

(3) A participating hospital may not penalize or take adverse action against a physician or a qualified medical person described in paragraph (d)(1)(ii)(C) of this section because the physician or qualified medical person refuses to authorize the transfer of an individual with an emergency medical condition that has not been stabilized, or against any hospital employee because the employee reports a violation of a requirement of this section.

(e) Recipient hospital responsibilities. A participating hospital that has specialized capabilities or facilities (including, but not limited to, facilities such as burn units, shock-trauma units, neonatal intensive care units, or (with respect to rural areas) regional referral centers) may not refuse to accept from a referring hospital within the boundaries of the United States an appropriate transfer of an individual who requires such specialized capabilities or facilities if the receiving hospital has the capacity to treat the individual.

(f) Termination of provider agreement. If a hospital fails to meet the requirements of paragraph (a) through (e) of this section, HCFA may terminate the provider agreement in accordance with § 489.53.

(g) Consultation with PROs

(1) General. Except as provided in paragraph (g)(3) of this section, in cases where a medical opinion is necessary to determine a physician's or hospital's liability under section 1867(d)(1) of this Act, HCFA requests the appropriate PRO (with a contract under Part B of title XI of the Act) to review the alleged section 1867(d) violation and provide a report on its findings in accordance with paragraph (g)(2)(iv) and (v) of this section. HCFA provides to the PRO all information relevant to the case and within its possession or control. HCFA, in consultation with the OIG, also provides to the PRO a list of relevant ques-

tions to which the PRO must respond in its report.

(2) Notice of review and opportunity for discussion and additional information. The PRO shall provide the physician and hospital reasonable notice of its review, a reasonable opportunity for discussion, and an opportunity for the physician and hospital to submit additional information before issuing its report. When a PRO receives a request for consultation under paragraph (g)(1) of this section, the following provisions apply

(i) The PRO reviews the case before the 15th calendar day and makes its tentative findings.

(ii) Within 15 calendar days of receiving the case, the PRO gives written notice, sent by certified mail, return receipt requested, to the physician or the hospital (or both if applicable).

(iii)(A) The written notice must contain the following information:

(1) The name of each individual who may have been the subject of the alleged violation.

(2) The date on which each alleged violation occurred.

(3) An invitation to meet, either by telephone or in person, to discuss the case with the PRO, and to submit additional information to the PRO within 30 calendar days of receipt of the notice, and a statement that these rights will be waived if the invitation is not accepted. The PRO must receive the information and hold the meeting within the 30-day period.

(4) A copy of the regulations at 42 CFR 489.24.

(B) For purposes of paragraph (g)(2)(iii)(A) of this section, the date of receipt is presumed to be 5 days after the certified mail date on the notice, unless there is a reasonable showing to the contrary.

(iv) The physician or hospital (or both where applicable) may request a meeting with the PRO. This meeting is not designed to be a formal adversarial hearing or a mechanism for discovery by the physician or hospital. The meeting is intended to afford the physician and/or the hospital a full and fair opportunity to present the views of the physician and/or hospital regarding the case. The following provisions apply to that meeting:

(A) The physician and/or hospital has the right to have legal counsel present during that meeting. However, the PRO may control the scope, extent, and manner of any questioning or any other presentation by the attorney. The PRO may also have legal counsel present.

(B) The PRO makes arrangements so that, if requested by HCFA or the OIG, a verbatim transcript of the meeting may be generated. If HCFA or OIG requests a transcript, the affected physician and/or the affected hospital may request that HCFA provide a copy of the transcript.

(C) The PRO affords the physician and/or the hospital an opportunity to present, with the assistance of counsel, expert testimony in either oral or written form on the medical issues presented. However, the PRO may reasonably limit the number of witnesses and length of such testimony if such testimony is irrelevant or repetitive. The physician and/or hospital, directly or through counsel, may disclose patient records to potential expert witnesses without violating any nondisclosure requirements set forth in part 476 of this chapter.

(D) The PRO is not obligated to consider any additional information provided by the physician and/or the hospital after the meeting, unless, before the end of the meeting, the PRO requests that the physician and/or hospital submit additional information to support the claims. The PRO then allows the physician and/or the hospital an additional period of time, not to exceed 5 calendar days from the meeting, to submit the relevant information to the PRO.

(v) Within 60 calendar days of receiving the case, the PRO must submit to HCFA a report on the PRO's findings. HCFA provides copies to the OIG and to the affected physician and/or the af-

fected hospital. The report must contain the name of the physician and/or the hospital, the name of the individual, and the dates and times the individual arrived at and was transferred (or discharged) from the hospital. The report provides expert medical opinion regarding whether the individual involved had an emergency medical condition, whether the individual's emergency medical condition was stabilized, whether the individual was transferred appropriately, and whether there were any medical utilization or quality of care issues involved in the case.

(vi) The report required under paragraph (g)(2)(v) of this section should not state an opinion or conclusion as to whether section 1867 of the Act or § 489.24 has been violated.

(3) If a delay would jeopardize the health or safety of individuals or when there was no screening examination, the PRO review described in this section is not required before the OIG may impose civil monetary penalties or an exclusion in accordance with section 1867(d)(1) of the Act and 42 CFR part 1003 of this title.

(4) If the PRO determines after a preliminary review that there was an appropriate medical screening examination and the individual did not have an emergency medical condition, as defined by paragraph (b) of this section, then the PRO may, at its discretion, return the case to HCFA and not meet the requirements of paragraph (g) except for those in paragraph (g)(2)(v).

(h) Release of PRO assessments. Upon request, HCFA may release a PRO assessment to the physician and/or hospital, or the affected individual, or his or her representative. The PRO physician's identity is confidential unless he or she consents to its release (see §§ 476.132 and 476.133 of this chapter).

APPENDIX 4–C

Interpretive Guidelines—Responsibilities of Medicare Participating Hospitals in Emergency Cases

Tag Number	Regulation	Guidance to Surveyors
		INTERPRETIVE GUIDELINES: §489.20(I)
	§489.20 Basic Section 1866 commitments relevant to Section 1867 responsibilities. The provider agrees—	§489.20(I) requires the provider to comply with §489.24. However §1866(a)(1)(I)(i) of the Act requires providers to adopt and enforce a policy to ensure compliance with the requirements of §1867 (§489.24). Non-compliance is a violation of the provider's agreement with the Health Care Financing Administration (HCFA). Therefore, if the provider violates §489.24, cite a corresponding violation of §489.20(I); but if the provider does not adopt and enforce procedures and policies to ensure compliance with §489.24, cite a violation of §1866(a)(1)(I)(i).
A400	(I) In the case of a hospital as defined in §489.24(b), to comply with §489.24.	• Check the bylaws/rules and regulations of the medical staff to determine if they reflect the requirements of §489.24 and the related requirements at §489.20. • Review the emergency department policies and procedure manuals for procedures related to the requirements of §489.24 and the related requirements at §489.20. The term "hospital" is defined in §489.24(b) as including a rural primary care hospital as defined in §1861(mm)(1) of the Act.
		INTERPRETIVE GUIDELINES: §489.20(m)
A401	(m) In the case of a hospital as defined in §489.24(b), to report to HCFA or the State survey agency any time it has reason to believe it may have received an individual who has been transferred in an unstable emergency medical condition from another hospital in violation of the requirements of §489.24(d).	Look for evidence that the receiving (recipient) hospital knew or suspected the individual had been to a hospital prior to the receiving (recipient) hospital and had not been transferred in accordance with §489.24(d). (Evidence may be obtained in the medical record or through interviews with the patient, family members or staff.) However, termination of the receiving (recipient) hospital should be suspended pending confirmation of the suspected offense. Review the emergency department log and medical records of patients received as transfers. Look for evidence that: • The hospital had agreed in advance to accept the transfers; • The hospital had received appropriate medical records; • All transfers had been effected through qualified personnel, transportation equipment and medically appropriate life support measures; and • The hospital had available space and qualified personnel to treat the patients.

Source: Reprinted from *1999 Health Care Financing Administration Medicare State Operations Manual.*

Tag Number	Regulation	Guidance to Surveyors
A402	(q) In the case of a hospital as defined in §489.24(b)—	INTERPRETIVE GUIDELINES: §489.20(q)
		At a minimum:
	(1) To post conspicuously in any emergency department or in a place or places likely to be noticed by all individuals entering the emergency department, as well as those individuals waiting for examination and treatment in areas other than traditional emergency departments (that is, entrance, admitting area, waiting room, treatment area) a sign (in a form specified by the Secretary) specifying the rights of individuals under section 1867 of the Act with respect to examination and treatment for emergency medical conditions and women in labor; and	• The sign(s) must specify the rights of individuals with emergency conditions and women in labor who come to the emergency department for health care services; • It must indicate whether the facility participates in the Medicaid program; • The wording of the sign(s) must be clear and in simple terms and language that are understandable by the population served by the hospital; and • The sign(s) must be posted in a place or places likely to be noticed by all individuals entering the emergency department, as well as those individuals waiting for examination and treatment (e.g., entrance, admitting area, waiting room, treatment area).
	(2) To post conspicuously (in a form specified by the Secretary) information indicating whether or not the hospital or rural primary care hospital participates in the Medicaid program under a State plan approved under Title XIX;	
A403	(r) In the case of a hospital as defined in §489.24(b) (including both the transferring and receiving hospitals), to maintain—	INTERPRETIVE GUIDELINES: §489.20(r)(1)
		The medical records of individuals transferred to or from the hospital must be retained in their original or legally-reproduced form in hard copy, microfilm, microfiche, optical disks, computer disks, or computer memory.
	(1) Medical and other records related to individuals transferred to or from the hospital for a period of 5 years from the date of the transfer;	

Tag Number	Regulation	Guidance to Surveyors
A404	(2) A list of physicians who are on call for duty after the initial examination to provide further evaluation and/or treatment necessary to stabilize an individual with an emergency medical condition; and	INTERPRETIVE GUIDELINES: §489.20(r)(2) The purpose of the on-call list is to ensure that the emergency department is prospectively aware of which physicians, including specialists and subspecialists, are available to provide treatment necessary to stabilize individuals with emergency medical conditions. If a hospital offers a service to the public, the service should be available through on-call coverage of the emergency department. The medical staff by-laws or policies and procedures must define the responsibility of on-call physicians to respond, examine and treat patients with emergency medical conditions. Physicians, including specialists and subspecialists (e.g., neurologists) are not required to be on call at all times. The hospital must have policies and procedures to be followed when a particular specialty is not available or the on-call physician cannot respond because of situations beyond his or her control. Each hospital has the discretion to maintain the on-call list in a manner to best meet the needs of its patients. Physicians are not required to be on call in their specialty or subspecialty for emergencies whenever they are visiting their own patients in a hospital. Review the hospital's policy with respect to response time of the on-call physician. Hospitals are responsible for ensuring that on-call physicians respond within a reasonable period of time. Note the time of notification and the response (or transfer) time. If a staff physician is on-call to provide emergency services or to consult with an emergency room physician is in the area of his or her expertise, that physician would be considered to be available at the hospital. Where a physician is on-call in an office it is not acceptable to refer emergency cases to their offices for examination and treatment. The physician must come to the hospital to examine the patient unless the physician is a hospital-owned facility on contiguous land or on the hospital campus. If a physician demonstrates a pattern of not arriving at the hospital where that physician can treat the patient, this may be a violation.

Guidance to Surveyors

Tag Number   *Regulation*

A405

(3) A central log on each individual who "comes to the emergency department," as defined in §489.24(b), seeking assistance and whether he or she refused treatment, was refused treatment, or whether he or she was transferred, admitted and treated, stabilized and transferred, or discharged.

INTERPRETIVE GUIDELINES: §489.20(r)(3)

The purpose of the central log is to track the care provided to each individual who comes to the hospital seeking care for an emergency medical condition.

Each hospital has the discretion to maintain the central log in a form that best meets the needs of its patients. The central log includes, directly or by reference, patient logs from other areas of the hospital, such as pediatrics and labor and delivery where a patient might present for emergency services or receive a medical screening examination instead of in the emergency department. These additional logs must be available in a timely manner for surveyor review.

Review the emergency department log covering at least a six month period that contains information on all patients coming to the emergency department and check for completeness, gaps in entries or missing information.

Select a sample of records from the past six months from the log for review to determine compliance with the §489.24 requirements, according to the sample size methodology in Task 2. Select an older sample if the case to be investigated occurred longer than six months ago, or if you are concerned about a possible long-term pattern of dumping.

§489.24 Special responsibilities of Medicare hospitals in emergency cases.

The provisions of this regulation apply to all hospitals that participate in Medicare and provide emergency services.

Hospitals providing emergency services are required to provide for an appropriate medical screening examination; provide necessary stabilizing treatment for emergency medical conditions and labor; provide for an appropriate transfer of the patient if the hospital does not have the capability or capacity to provide the treatment necessary to stabilize the emergency medical condition; not delay examination and/or treatment in order to inquire about the patient's insurance or payment status; accept appropriate transfers of patients with emergency medical conditions if the hospital has the specialized capabilities not available at the transferring hospital and has the capacity to treat those individuals; if the patient refuses examination, treatment, or transfer to obtain or attempt to obtain written and informed refusal of examination, treatment or appropriate transfer; and not take adverse action against a physician or qualified medical personnel who refuses to transfer a patient with an emergency medical condition, or against an employee who reports a violation of these requirements.

Tag Number	Regulation	Guidance to Surveyors
A406	(a) General. In the case of a hospital that has an emergency department,	**INTERPRETIVE GUIDELINES §489.24(a)**

A "hospital with an emergency department" is defined in paragraph (b) of this section as one which offers services for emergency medical conditions within its capability to do so. Lack of an established emergency department is not an indication that emergency services are not provided. If a hospital offers emergency services for medical, psychiatric or substance abuse emergency conditions, it is required, within its capability and capacity, to comply with all the anti-dumping statutory requirements.

If a psychiatric hospital offers services for medical, psychiatric, or substance abuse emergency conditions, it is obligated to comply with all of the anti-dumping requirements of §§489.20 and 489.24.

Most psychiatric hospitals are accredited by the Joint Commission and have an emergency department which provides reasonable care in determining whether an emergency exists, renders life saving first aid, and makes appropriate referrals to the nearest organizations that are capable of providing needed services. The emergency department must have a mechanism for providing physician coverage at all times. |
| | If any individual (whether or not eligible for Medicare benefits and regardless of ability to pay) comes by him or herself or with another person to the emergency department and a request is made on the individual's behalf for examination or treatment of a medical condition by qualified medical personnel (as determined by the hospital in its rules and regulations), the hospital must provide for an appropriate MEDICAL SCREENING EXAMINATION within the capability of the hospital's emergency department, including ancillary services routinely available to the emergency department | Emergency services need not be provided in a location specifically identified as an emergency room or an emergency department. If an individual arrives at a hospital and is not technically in the emergency department, but is on the premises (including the parking lot, sidewalk and driveway) of the hospital and requests emergency care, he or she is entitled to a medical screening examination. For example, it may be the hospital's policy to direct all pregnant women to the labor and delivery area of the hospital. Hospitals may use areas to deliver emergency services which are also used for other inpatient or outpatient services. Medical screening examinations or stabilization may require ancillary services available only in areas or facilities of the hospital outside of the emergency department. As long as the patient is directed to a hospital-owned facility which is contiguous (i.e., any area within the hospital or a hospital-owned facility on land that touches land where a hospital's emergency department sits) or is part of the hospital "campus" and is owned by the hospital, and is operating under the hospital's provider number, the hospital is complying with §1867. Physicians' offices may be defined as such a facility, provided they are located in a hospital-owned building which is contiguous or located in a hospital-owned building which is "on hospital-campus." For example, a patient who presents to the emergency department could be sent to whatever hospital-owned contiguous or on-campus facility that the hospital deemed appropriate to conduct or complete the medical screening examination as long as (1) all persons with the same medical condition are moved to this location, regardless of their ability to pay for the treatment; (2) there is a bona fide medical reason to move the patient; and (3) qualified medical personnel accompany the patient. If the patient was initially screened in a facility outside of the emergency department, the patient could be moved to another hospital-owned contiguous or hospital-owned on-campus facility to receive additional screening or for stabilization without such movement |

Tag Number	Regulation	Guidance to Surveyors

A406

Guidance to Surveyors

being regarded as a transfer, as long as (1) all persons with the same medical condition are moved in such circumstances, regardless of their ability to pay for treatment; (2) there is a bona fide medical reason to move the patient; and (3) qualified medical personnel accompany the patient.

If a patient comes to any contiguous or on-campus facility of a hospital that has one or more hospital-owned non-contiguous or off-campus facilities (such as an urgent care center or satellite clinic), the medical screening examination must be performed within the contiguous or on-campus facilities of the hospital. The hospital should not move the patient to a non-contiguous or off-campus facility for the medical screening examination.

If a patient comes to a hospital-owned facility which is non-contiguous or off-campus and operates under the hospital's Medicare provider number, §1867 applies to that facility. The facility must therefore screen and stabilize the patient to the best of its ability or execute an appropriate transfer according to §1867 guidelines if necessary.

If an individual is not on hospital property, this regulation is not applicable.

Hospital property includes ambulances owned and operated by the hospital, even if the ambulance is not on hospital grounds. An individual in a nonhospital-owned ambulance which is on hospital property is considered to have come to the hospital's emergency department. An individual in a nonhospital-owned ambulance not on "Hospital A's" property is not considered to have come to "Hospital A's" emergency department when the ambulance personnel contact "Hospital A" by telephone or telemetry communications. A hospital may deny access to patients when it is in "diversionary" status because it does not have the staff or facilities to accept any additional emergency patients at that time. However, if the ambulance disregards the hospital's instructions and brings the individual on to hospital grounds, the individual has come to the hospital and the hospital cannot deny the individual access to hospital services.

Should a hospital which is not in diversionary status fail to accept a telephone or radio request for transfer or admission, the refusal could represent a violation of other Federal or State requirements (e.g., Hill-Burton). If you suspect a violation of related laws, refer the case to the responsible agency for investigation.

Hospitals are obligated to screen patients to determine if an emergency medical condition exists. It is not appropriate to merely "log in" a patient and not provide a medical screening examination.

Medicare participating hospitals that provide emergency services must provide a medical screening examination to any individual regardless of diagnosis (e.g., labor, AIDS), financial status (e.g., uninsured Medicaid), race, color, national origin (e.g., Hispanic or Native American surnames), handicap, etc.

Individuals coming to the emergency department must be provided a medical screening examination beyond initial triaging. Triage is not equivalent to a medical screening examination. Triage

Tag Number	Regulation	Guidance to Surveyors
A406		merely determines the "order" in which patients will be seen, not the presence or absence of an emergency medical condition.
		A hospital, regardless of size or patient mix, must provide screening and stabilizing treatment within the scope of its abilities, as needed, to the individuals with emergency medical conditions who come to the hospital for examination and treatment.
		The medical screening examination must be the same medical screening examination that the hospital would perform on any individual coming to the hospital's emergency department with those signs and symptoms, regardless of the individual's ability to pay for medical care. If the medical screening examination is appropriate and does not reveal an emergency medical condition, the hospital has no further obligations under 42 CFR 489.24. Regardless of a positive or negative patient outcome, a hospital would be in violation of the anti-dumping statute if it fails to meet any of the medical screening requirements under 42 CFR 489.24.
		A medical screening examination is the process required to reach with reasonable clinical confidence, the point at which it can be determined whether a medical emergency does or does not exist. If a hospital applies in a nondiscriminatory manner (i.e., a different level of care must not exist based on payment status, race, national origin) a screening process that is reasonably calculated to determine whether an emergency medical condition exists, it has met its obligations under the Emergency Medical Treatment and Labor Act (EMTALA).
		Depending on the patient's presenting symptoms, the medical screening examination represents a spectrum ranging from a simple process involving only a brief history and physical examination to a complex process that also involves performing ancillary studies and procedures such as (but not limited to) lumbar punctures, clinical laboratory tests, CT scans, and/or diagnostic tests and procedures.
		A medical screening examination is not an isolated event. It is an ongoing process. The record must reflect continued monitoring according to the patient's needs and must continue until he/she is stabilized or appropriately transferred. There should be evidence of this evaluation prior to discharge or transfer.
		The clinical outcome of an individual's condition is not a proper basis for determining whether an appropriate screening was provided or whether a person transferred was stabilized. However, it may be a "red flag" indicating a more thorough investigation is needed. Do not make decisions based on clinical information that was not available at the time of stabilization or transfer.
		If a misdiagnosis occurred, but the hospital utilized all of its resources, a violation of the screening requirement did not occur.
		A hospital may not refuse to screen an enrollee of a managed care plan because the plan refuses to authorize treatment or to pay for such screening and treatment. Likewise, the managed care plan

Tag Number	Regulation	Guidance to Surveyors
A406		cannot refuse to screen and treat or appropriately transfer individuals not enrolled in the plan who come to a plan hospital that participates in the Medicare program.

It is not appropriate for a hospital to request or a health plan to require prior authorization before the patient has received a medical screening exam to determine the presence or absence of an emergency medical condition or until an existing emergency medical condition has been stabilized. Once an emergency medical condition has been determined not to exist or the emergency medical condition has been stabilized, §1867 of the Act no longer applies and prior authorization for further services can be sought.

(NOTE: Background issue on payment:

Once a patient has presented to the hospital seeking emergency care, the determination of whether an emergency medical condition exists is made by the examining physician(s) or other qualified medical person actually caring for the patient at the treating facility, not the managed care plan. Beneficiaries have a right to emergency services if they have symptoms of sufficient severity (which may include severe pain) and sudden onset, and they are acting reasonably, given their knwoledge, experiences, and state of mind.)

Prearranged community or State plans which identify certain hospitals that will care for selected individuals (e.g., Medicaid patients, psychiatric patients, pregnant women; (see tag A407)) do not relieve other hospitals of the obligation to comply with the screening and treatment requirements of §489.24 before appropriately transferring the individual.

If a screening examination reveals an emergency medical condition and the individual is told to wait for treatment, but the individual leaves the hospital, the hospital did not "dump" the patient unless:

- The individual left the emergency department based on a "suggestion" by the hospital, and/or
- The individual's condition was emergent, but the hsopital was operating beyond its capacity and did not attempt to transfer the individual to another facility.

Hospital resources and staff available to inpatients at the hospital for emergency services must likewise be available to individuals coming to the hospital for examination and treatment of emergency medical conditions because these resources are within the capability of the hospital. For example, a women in labor who presents at a hospital providing obstetrical services must be treated with the resources available, whether or not the hospital normally provides unassigned emergency obstetrical services.

If a hospital chooses to meet its responsibility to provide adequate medical personnel to meet its anticipated emergecny needs by using on-call physicians either to staff or to augment its emergency department, then the capability of its emergency department includes the services of its on-call physicians.

Tag Number	Regulation	Guidance to Surveyors
A406	to determine whether or not an emergency medical condition exists.	"Emergency medical condition" means a medical condition manifesting itself by acute symptoms of sufficient severity (including severe pain, psychiatric disturbances, and/or symptoms of substance abuse) such athat the absence of immediate medical attention could reasonably be expected to result in:
		• Placing the health of the individual (or, with respect to a pregnant woman, the health of a woman or her unborn child) in serious jeopardy;
		• Serious impairment to any bodily functions;
		• Serious dysfunction of any bodily organ or part; or
		• With respect to a pregnant woman who is having contractions:
		—That there is inadequate time to effect a safe transfer to another hospital before delivery, or
		—That the transfer may pose a threat to the health or safety of the woman or the unborn child.
		Psychiatric hospitals that provide emergency services are obligated under these regulations to respond within the limits of their capabilities.
		Some intoxicated individuals may meet the definition of "emergency medical condition" because the absence of medical treatment may place their health in serious jeopardy, result in serious impairment of bodily functions, or serious dysfunction of a bodily organ. Further, it is not unusual for intoxicated individuals to have unrecognized trauma.
		Likewise, an individual expressing suicidal or homicidal thoughts or gestures, if determined dangerous to self or others, would be considered to have an emergency medical condition.
	The examinations must be conducted by individuals determined qualified by hospital bylaws or rules and regulations and who meet the requirements of §482.55 concerning emergency services personnel and direction.	This delegation should be set forth in a document approved by the governing body of the hospital. If the rules and regulations of the hospital are approved by the board of trustees or other governing body, those personnel qualified to perform these examinations may be set forth in the rules and regulations, instead of placing this information in the hospital by-laws. It is not acceptable for the hospital to allow informal personnel appointments that could frequently change.
	(c) Necessary stabilizing treatment for emergency medical conditions and labor—	"Labor", as defined in paragraph (b) of this section, means the process of childbirth beginning with the latent or early phase of labor and continuing through the delivery of the placenta. A woman is in true labor unless a physician or qualified individual certifies that, after a reasonable time of observation, the woman is in false labor.

Tag Number	Regulation	Guidance to Surveyors
A407	(1) General. If any individual (whether or not eligible for Medicare benefits) comes to a hospital and the hospital determines that the individual has an emergency medical condition, the hospital must provide either— (I) Within the capabilities of the staff and facilities available at the hospital,	INTERPRETIVE GUIDELINES: §489.24(c)(I) A managed health care plan (e.g., HMO, PPO) cannot deny a hospital permission to treat its enrollees. It may only state what it will or will not pay for. Regardless of whether a hospital will be paid, it is obligated to provide the services specified in the statute and this regulation. Capabilities of a medical facility means that there is physical space, equipment, supplies, and services that the hospital provides (e.g., surgery, psychiatry, obstetrics, intensive care, pediatrics, trauma care). Capabilities of the staff of a facility means the level of care that the personnel of the hospital can provide within the training and scope of their professional licenses. The capacity to render care is not reflected simply by the number of persons occupying a special- ized unit, the number of staff on duty, or the amount of equipment on the hospital's premises. Capacity includes whatever a hospital customarily does to accommodate patients in excess of its occupancy limits §489.24(b). If a hospital has customarily accommodated patients in excess of its occupancy limits by whatever means (e.g., moving patients to other units, calling in additional staff, borrowing equipment from other facilities) it has, in fact, demonstrated the ability to provide services to patients in excess of its occupancy limits. The by-laws, protocols and medical staff appoinmtents approved by the governing body should require that all individuals are screened and stabilized within the capability of the hospital and should specify which staff members (by position) are authoriz3ed to perform the treatment. A hospital may appropriately transfer an individual before the sending hospital has used and exhausted all of its resources available if the individual requests the transfer to another hospital for his or her treatment, and refuses treatment at the sending hospital. (See Tag A409.) If a community-wide plan exists for certain hospitals, to treat certain emergency medical condi- tions, then the individual should be screened, stabilized, or appropriately transferred to the community-plan hospital.
	for further medical examination and treatment as required to stabilize the medical condition; or	Compliance with the medical screening examination and stabilization requirements under §1867 mandate that all patients with similar medical conditions be treated consistently. In some cases, local, State, or regionally-approved emergency medical systems (EMS), point-of-entry, and/or system protocols are in place. Compliance with EMS protocols with respect to the transport of emergent patients is usually deemed to indicate compliance with §1867; however a copy of the protocol should be obtained and reviewed at the time of the survey. If a hospital complies with other regional authority or State or locally approved point-of-entry protocols for emergency care

Tag Number	Regulation	Guidance to Surveyors
A407		(e.g., for psychiatric emergencies or physical or sexual abuse) then the hospital is usually in compliance with §1867 of the Act, as long as the hospital ensures that the patient is stable for transfer.

If the individual seeking care is a member of an HMO or CMP, the hospital's obligation to comply with the requirements of §489.24 is not affected.

"To stabilize," as defined in paragraph (b) of this section means, with respect to an emergency medical condition, to either provide such medical treatment of the condition necessary to assure, within reasonable medical probability, that no material deterioration of the condition is likely to result from, or occur during, the transfer of the individual from a facility, or that the woman has delivered the child and the placenta. A patient will be deemed stabilized if the treating physician attending to the patient in the emergency department/hospital has determined, within reasonable clinical confidence, that the emergency medical condition been resolved. For patients whose emergency medical condition has not been resolved, the determination of whether they are stable "medically" may occur in one of the following two circumstances:

- For purposes of transferring a patient from one facility to a second facility "stable for transfer"; and
- For purposes of discharging a patient other than for the purpose of transfer from one facility to another facility "stable for discharge".

For transfer between facilities: a patient is stable for transfer if the patient is transferred from one facility to a second facility and the treating physician attending to the patient has determined, within reasonable clinical confidence, that the patient is expected to leave the hospital and be received at the second facility, with no material deterioration in his/her medical condition; and the treating physician reasonably believes the receiving facility has the capability to manage the patient's medical condition and any reasonably foreseeable complication of that condition.

If there is a disagreement between the treating physician and an off-site physician (e.g., a physician at the receiving facility or the patient's primary care physician if not physically present at the first facility) about whether a patient is stable for transfer, the medical judgment of the treating physician usually takes precedence over that of the off-site physician.

If a physician is not physically present at the time of transfer, then qualified personnel (as determined by hospital bylaws or other board-approved documents) in consultation with a physician can determine if a patient is stable for transfer.

The failure of a receiving facility to provide the care it maintained it could provide to the patient when the transfer was arranged, should not be construed to mean the patient's condition worsened as a result of the transfer.

A patient is considered stable for discharge (vs. for transfer from one facility to a second facility) when, within reasonable clinical confidence, it is determined that the patient has reached the point

Tag Number	Regulation	Guidance to Surveyors
A407		where his/her continued care, including diagnostic work-up and/or treatment, could be reasonable performed as an outpatient or later as an inpatient, provided the patient is given a plan for appropriate follow-up care with the discharge instructions.

For purposes of transferring a patient from one facility to a second facility, for pscyhhiatric conditions, the patient is considered to be stable when he/she is protected and prevented from injuring himself/herself or others. For purposes of discharging a patient (other than for the purpose of transfer from one facility to a second facility), for psychiatric conditions, the patient is considered to be stable when he/she is no longer considered to be a threat to him/herself or to others.

"Stable for transfer" or "Stable for discharge" does not require the final resolution of the emergency medical condition.

Hospitals may not circumvent the requirements in §489.24 by admitting individuals with emergency medical conditions to other departments of the hospital and then discharging them prior to stabilization. These requirements apply to all areas of the hospital.

"Transfer" as defined in paragraph (b) of this section, means the movement (including the discharge) of an individual outside a hospital's facilities at the direction of any person employed by (or affiliated or associated, directly or indirectly, with) the hospital, but does not include such a movement of an individual who has been declared dead or leaves the facility without the permission of any such person. If discharge would result in the reasonable medical probability of material deterioration of the patient, the emergency medical condition should not be considered to have been stabilized.

When a hospital has exhausted all of its capabilities in attempting to remove the emergency medical condition, it must effect an appropriate transfer of the individual. (See Tag A409.)

Emergency medical conditions must be stabilized. If a woman is in labor, the hospital must deliver the baby or transfer aporopriately. She may not be transferred unless she, or a legally responsible person acting on her behalf, requests a transfer or if a physician or other qualified medical personnel, in consultation with a physician, certifies that the benefits to the condition of the woman and/or the unborn child outweigh the risks associated with the transfer.

If the individual's condition requires immediate medical stabilizing treatment and the hospital is not able to attend to that individual because the emergency department is operating beyond its capacity, then the hospital should transfer the individual to a facility that has the capability and capacity to treat the individual's emergency medical condition, it possible. |
| | (ii) For transfer of the individual to another medical facility in accordance with paragraph (d) of this section. | |

Tag Number	Regulation	Guidance to Surveyors
A407	(2) Refusal to consent to treatment. A hospital meets the requirements of paragraph (c)(1)(i) of this section with respect to an individual if the hospital offers the individual further medical examination and treatment described in that paragraph and informs the individual (or a person acting on the individual's behalf) of the risks and benefits to the individual of the examination and treatment, but the individual (or a person acting on the individual's behalf) refuses to consent to the examination and treatment. The medical record must contain a description of the examination, treatment, or both if applicable, that was refused by or on behalf of the individual. The hospital must take all reasonable steps to secure the individual's written informed refusal (or that of a person acting in his or her behalf). The written document should indicate that the person has been informed of the risks and benefits of the examination or treatment, or both.	INTERPRETIVE GUIDELINES: §489.24(c)(2) The medical record should reflect that screening, further examination, and/or treatment was offered by the hospital prior to the individual's refusal. In the event an individual refuses to consent to further examination or treatment, the hospital must indicate in writing the risks/benefits of the examination and/or treatment; the reasons for refusal; a description of the examination or treatment that was refused; and the steps taken to try to secure the written, informed refusal if it was not secured. Hospitals may not attempt to coerce individuals into making judgments against their best interest by informing them that they will have to pay for their care if they remain, but that their care will be free or at low cost if they transfer to another hospital. A hospital cannot be left without recourse if an individual refuses treatment, refuses to sign a statement to that effect, and leaves against medical advice. Hospitals may document such refusals as they see fit. An individual may only refuse examination, treatment, or transfer on behalf of the patient if the patient is incapable of making an informed choice for him/herself.
A408	(3) Delay in examination or treatment. A participating hospital may not delay providing an appropriate medical screening examination required under paragraph (a) of this section or further medical examination and treatment required under paragraph (c) in order to inquire about the individual's method of payment or insurance status.	INTEREPRETIVE GUIDELINES: §489.24(c)(3) Hospitals should not delay in providing a medical screening examination or necessary stabilizing treatment by inquiring about an individual's ability to pay for care. All individuals who have an emergency medical condition must be served, regardless of the answers the individual may give to the insurance questions asked during the registration process. In addition, a hospital may not delay screening or treatment to any individual while it verifies the information provided. However, hospitals may continue to follow reasonable registration processes for individuals presenting with an emergency medical condition. Reasonable registration processes may include requesting information about insurance as long as these procedures do not delay screening or treatment. If a delay in screening was due to an unusual internal crisis whereby it was simply not within the capability of the hospital to provide an appropriate screening examination at the time the indi-

Tag Number	Regulation	Guidance to Surveyors
A408		vidual came to the hospital (e.g., mass casualty occupying all the hospital's resources for a time period), interviews with staff members should elicit this information.

This requirement applies equally to both the referring and the receiving (recipient) hospital. |
| A409 | (d) Restricting transfer until the individual is stabilized.—

(1) General.

If an individual at a hospital has an emergency medical condition that has not been stabilized (as defined in paragraph (b) of this section), the hospital may not transfer the individual unless—

(i) The transfer is an appropriate transfer within the meaning of paragraph (d)(2) of this section); and

(ii)(A) The individual (or a legally responsible person acting on the individual's behalf) requests the transfer after being informed of the hospital's obligations under this section and of the risk of transfer. The request must be in writing and indicate the reasons for the request as well as indicate that he or she is aware of the risks and benefits of the transfer; | INTERPRETIVE GUIDELINES: §489.24(d)(1)

(See the definition of "Stable for transfer" at Tag A407)

INTERPRETIVE GUIDELINES: §489.24(d)(1)(i)

There are 4 requirements of an "appropriate" transfer. These requirements are found in §§489.24(d)(2)(i), 489.24(d)(2)(ii), 489.24(d)(2)(iii), and 489.24(d)(2)(iv).

INTERPRETIVE GUIDELINES: §489.24(d)(1)(ii)(A)

The request must contain a brief statment of the hospital's obligations under the statute and the benefits and risks that were outlined to the person signing the request.

Any transfer of an individual with an emergency medical condition must be initiated by either a written request for transfer or a physician's certification. If both are provided (as is often the case), the individual must still be informed of the risks vs. benefits of the transfer.

The request must be made a part of the individual's medical record, and a copy of the request should be sent to the receiving (recipient) facility along with the individual transferred.

If an individual's request for transfer is obtained by coercion or by misrepresenting the hospital's obligations to provide a medical screening examination and treamtent for an emergency medical condition or labor, the request does not meet the hospital's obligations under these regulations. |

Tag Number	Regulation	Guidance to Surveyors
A409	(ii)(B) A physician (within the meaning of §1861(r)(1) of the Act) has signed a certification that, based upon the information available at the time of transfer, the medical benefits reasonably expected from the provision of appropriate medical treatment at another medical facility outweigh the increased risks to the individual or, in the case of a woman in labor, to the unborn child, from being transferred. The certification must contain a summary of the risks and benefits upon which it is based; or	INTERPRETIVE GUIDELINES: §489.24(d)(1)(ii)(B)

Section 1861(r) of the Act defines physicians as:

(i) A doctor of medicine or osteopathy. (This provision is not to be construed to limit the authority of a doctor of medicine or osteopathy to delegate tasks to other qualified health care personnel to the extent recognized under State law or a State's regulatory mechanism);

(ii) A doctor of dental surgery or dental medicine who is legally authorized to practice dentistry by the State and who is acting within the scope of his or her license;

(iii) A doctor of podiatric medicine, but only with respect to functions which he or she is legally authorized by the State to perform;

(iv) A doctor of optometry who is legally authorized to practice optometry by the State, but only with respect to services related to the condition of aphakia; or

(v) A chiropractor who is licensed by the State or legally authorized to perform the services of a chiropractor, but only with respect to treatment by means of manual manipulation of the spine to correct a subluxation demonstrated by X-ray to exist.

The regulation requires an express written certification. Physician certification cannot simply be implied from the findings in the medical record and the fact that the patient was transferred.

The certification must state the reason(s) for transfer. The narrative rationale need not be a lengthy discussion of the individual's medical condition reiterating facts already contained in the medical record, but it should give a complete picture of the benefits to be expected from appropriate care at the receiving (recipient) facility and the risks associated with the transfer, including the time away from an acute care setting necessary to effect the transfer.

This rationale may be on the certification form or in the medical record. In cases where the individual's medical record does not include a certification, give the hospital the opportunity to retrieve the certification. Certifications may not be backdated. Document the hospital's response.

Regardless of practices within a State, a woman in labor may be transferred only if she or her representative requests the transfer or if a physician or other qualified medical personnel signs a certification that the benefits outweigh the risks. If the hospital does not provide obstetrical services, the benefits of a transfer may outweigh the risks. A hospital cannot cite State law or practice as the basis for the transfer.

Hospitals that are not capable of handling high-risk deliveries or high-risk infants often have written transfer agreements with facilities capable of handling high-risk cases. The hospital must still meet the screening, treatment, and transfer requirements. |

Tag Number	Regulation	Guidance to Surveyors
A409		The certification that the benefits reasonably expected from the provision of appropriate medical treatment at another medical facility outweigh the risk of the transfer is not required for transfers of individuals who no longer have an emergency medical condition.
		The date and time of the physician certification should closely match the date and time of the transfer.
A409	(c) If a physician is not physically present in the emergency department at the time an individual is transferred, a qualified medical person (as determined by the hospital in its by-laws or rules and regulations) has signed a certification described in paragraph (d)(1)(ii)(B) of this section after a physician (as defined in section 1861(r)(1) of the Act), in consultation with the qualified medical person, agrees with the certification and subsequently countersigns the certification. The certification must contain a summary of the risks and benefits upon which it is based.	INTERPRETIVE GUIDELINES: §489.24(d)(1)(C)
		Individuals other than physicians may sign the cerrtification of benefits versus risks of a transfer. These individuals must be identified in hospital bylaws, rules and regulations, or another board-approved document.
		If a certification of benefits versus risks was signed by a qualified medical person, a physician's countersignature must be present. Hospital by-laws or policies and procedures will describe the maximum amount of time allowed to obtain physician countersignatures on hospital documents.
	(d)(2) A transfer to another medical facility will be appropriate only in those cases in which—	INTERPRETIVE GUIDELINES: §489.24(d)(2)(i)
	(i) The transferring hospital provides medical treatment within its capacity that minimizes the risks to the individual's health and, in the case of a woman in labor, the health of the unborn child;	This is the first requirement of an appropriate transfer.
		The provision of treatment to minimize the risks of transfer is merely one of the 4 requirements of an appropriate transfer. If the patient requires treatment, it must be sufficient so that no material deterioration is likely to occur or result from the transfer.
		NOTE: The 4 requirements of an "appropriate" transfer are applied only if the transfer is to another medical facility. In other words, the hospital has the alternative of either (1) providing treatment to stabilize the emergency medical condition and subsequently discharging or transferring the individual, or (2) appropriately transferring an unstabilized individual to another medical facility if the emergency medical condition still exists. There is no "third" option of simply "referring" the individual away after performing step one (treatment to minimize the risk of transfer) of the 4 transfer requirements of an appropriate transfer.

Tag Number	Regulation	Guidance to Surveyors
A409		If a patient is moved to another part of the hospital, the transfer requirements are not applicable because technically the patient has not been transferred.
		If an individual is moved to a diagnostic facility owned by another hospital with the intention of returning to the first hospital, an appropriate transfer (within the meaning of paragraph (d)(2) of this subsection) must still be effectuated. For example, when Hospital A shares a CT Scanner with Hospital B (Hospital B houses the CT Scanner), if Hospital A sends the individual to Hospital B for a CT scan as part of the appropriate medical screening examination to determine whether the individual has an emergency medical condition, the appropriate transfer requirements must be met.
		After the investigation of the transferring hospital, call or go to the receiving (recipient) facility and determine whether the receiving (recipient) facility verifies the transferring hospital's information. In cases of discrepancy, obtain the medical record from the transferring and receiving hospitals and the ambulance service for review. Review each hospital's information. If you determine that it is necessary to conduct a complaint investigation at the receiving (recipient) hospital, notify the RO to request an extension of the investigation timeframe.
		Review the transfer logs for the entire hospital, not merely the emergency department. Examine the following for appropriate transfers:
		• Transfers to off-site testing facilities and return; • Death or significant adverse outcomes; • Refusals of examination, treatment, or transfer; • Patients leaving against medical advice (AMA); • Returns to the emergency department within 48 hours; and • Emergency department visits where the patient is logged in for an unreasonable amount of time before the time indicated for commencement of the medical screening examination.
A409	(ii) The receiving facility — (A) Has available space and qualified personnel for the treatment of the individual; and (B) Has agreed to accept transfer of the individual and to provide appropriate medical treatment;	INTERPRETIVE GUIDELINES: §489.24(d)(2)(ii) This is the second requirement of an appropriate transfer. The transferring hospital must obtain permission from the receiving (recipient) hospital to transfer an individual. The transferring hospital should document its communication with the receiving (recipient) hospital, including the date and time of the transfer request and the name of the person accepting the transfer.

Tag Number	Regulation	Guidance to Surveyors
A409	(iii) The transferring hospital sends to the receiving facility all medical records (or copies thereof) related to the emergency condition which the individual has presented that are available at the time of the transfer, including available history, records related to the individual's emergency medical condition, observations of signs or symptoms, preliminary diagnosis, results of diagnostic studies or telephone reports of the studies, treatment provided, results of any tests and the informed written consent or certification (or copy thereof) required under paragraph (d)(1)(ii) of this section, and the name and address of any on-call physician (described in paragraph (f) of this section) who has refused or failed to appear within a reasonable time to provide necessary stabilizing treatment. Other records (e.g., test results not yet available or historical records not readily available from the hospital's files) must be sent as soon as practicable after transfer; and	INTERPRETIVE GUIDELINES: §489.24(d)(2)(iii)

This is the third requirement of an appropriate transfer.

Individuals being transferred to another hospital must be accompanied by necessary medical records.

To the extent that services are performed before transfer, those services should be reflected in the medical records transferred.

If transfer is in an individual's best interest, it should not be delayed until records are retrieved or test results come back from the laboratory. Whatever medical records are available at the time the individual is transferred should be sent to the receiving (recipient) hospital with the patient. Test results that become available after the individual is transferred should be telephoned to the receiving (recipient) hospital, and then mailed or sent via electronic transmission. |

Tag Number	Regulation	Guidance to Surveyors
A409	(iv) The transfer is effected through qualified personnel and transportation equipment, as required, including the use of necessary and medically appropriate life support measures during the transfer.	INTERPRETIVE GUIDELINES: §489.24(d)(2)(iv) This is the fourth requirement of an appropriate transfer. Emergency medical technicians may not always be "qualified personnel" for purposes of transferring an individual under these regulations. Depending on the individual's condition, there may be situations in which a physician's presence or some other specialist's presence might be mandatory. The physician at the sending hospital (and not the receiving hospital) has the responsibility to determine appropriate mode, equipment, and attendants for transfer. While the hospital is ultimately responsible for ensuring that the transfer is effected appropriately, the hospital may meet its obligations as it sees fit. These regulations do not require that a hospital operate an emergency medical transportation service.
	(4) Refusal to consent to transfer. A hospital meets the requirements of paragraph (c)(1)(ii) of this section with respect to an individual if the hospital offers to transfer the individual to another medical facility in accordance with paragraph (d) of this section and informs the individual (or a person acting on his or her behalf) of the risks and benefits to the individual of the transfer, but the individual (or a person acting on the individual's behalf) refuses to consent to the transfer. The hospital must take all reasonable steps to secure the individual's written informed refusal (or that of a person acting on his or her behalf). The written document must indicate the person has been informed of the risks and the benefits of the transfer and the reasons for the individual's refusal. The medical record must contain a description of the proposed transfer that was refused by or on behalf of the individual.	INTERPRETIVE GUIDELINES: §489.24(c)(4) A hospital cannot be left without recourse if an individual or the individual's representative refuses transfer and also refuses to sign a statement to that effect. Hospitals may document such refusals as they see fit.

Tag Number	Regulation	Guidance to Surveyors
A410	(3) A participating hospital may not penalize or take adverse action against a physician or a qualified medical person described in paragraph (d)(1)(ii)(C) of this section because the physician or qualified medical person refuses to authorize the transfer of an individual with an emergency medical condition that has not been stabilized, or against any hospital employee because the employee reports a violation of a requirement of this section.	INTERPRETIVE GUIDELINES: §489.24(d)(3) A "participating hospital" means a hospital that has entered into a provider agreement under §1866 of the Act.
A411	(e) Recipient hospital responsibilities. A participating hospital that has specialized capabilities or facilities (including, but not limited to such facilities as burn units, shock-trauma units, neonatal intensive care units, or (with respect to rural areas) regional referral centers) may not refuse to accept from a referring hospital within the boundaries of the United States, an appropriate transfer of an individual who requires such specialized capabilities or facilities if the receiving hospital has the capacity to treat the individual.	INTERPRETIVE GUIDELINES: §489.24(e) Recipient hospitals only have to accept the patient if the patient requires the specialized capabilities of the hospital in accordance with this section. If the transferring hospital wants to transfer a patient because it has no beds or is overcrowded, but the patient does not require any "specialized" capabilities, the receiving (recipient) hospital is not obligated to accept the patient. If the patient required the specialized capabilities of the intended receiving (recipient) hospital, and the hospital had the capability and capacity to accept the transfer but refused, this requirements has been violated. Lateral transfers, that is, transfers between facilities of comparable resources, are not sanctioned by §489.24 because they would not offer enhanced care benefits to the patient except where there is a mechanical failure of equipment, no ICU beds available, or similar situations. However, if the sending hospital has the capability but not the capacity, the individual would most likely benefit from the transfer. The number of patients that may be occupying a specialized unit, the number of staff on duty, or the amount of equipment on the hospital's premises do not in and of themselves reflect the capacity of the hospital to care for additional patients. If a hospital generally has accommodated additional patients by whatever means (e.g., moving patients to other units, calling in additional staff, borrowing equipment from other facilities), it has demonstrated the ability to provide services to patients in excess of its occupancy limit. For example, a hospital may be able to care for one or more severe burn patients without opening up a "burn unit." In this example, if the hospital has the capacity, the hospital would have a duty to accept an appropriate transfer of an

Tag Number	Regulation	Guidance to Surveyors
A411		individual requiring the hospital's capabilities, provided the transferring hospital lacked the specialized services to treat the individual.
		The provisions of this requirement are applicable only when the sending hospital is located within the boundaries of the United States. Medicare participating hospitals with specialized capabilities or facilities are not obligated to accept transfers from hospitals located outside of the boundaries of the United States.
		RURAL REGIONAL REFERRAL CENTERS
		The criteria for classifying hospitals as rural regional referral centers have been defined in 42 CFR 412.96 for the purpose of exemptions and adjustments of payment amounts under the Prospective Payment System. The criteria in 42 CFR 412.96 are applicable to the nondiscrimination provisions of §489.24. Check with the Division of Medicaid and State Operations in the appropriate HCFA RO for information as to whether the hospital is designated as a rural regional referral center. A designated rural regional referral center is obligated to accept appropriate transfers of individuals who require the hospital's specialized capabilities if the hospital has the capacity to treat the individual.

CHAPTER 5

Civil and Criminal Litigation

HIGHLIGHTS

- Criminal investigations are done before the defendants know they are targets.
- Civil investigations are usually done after the case is filed and the defendant is notified.
- Legal privilege for communications and records must be protected at all times—once lost, it cannot be regained.
- Courts and juries do not understand scientific evidence.
- Understanding how trials work can help health care practitioners cope with the stress of litigation.

INTRODUCTION

Only lawyers love litigation. For the parties, especially the defendant, it can be terrifying and incomprehensible. Understanding how civil litigation works can defuse some litigation anxiety and can help plaintiffs and defendants be better partners in their own cases. For defendants, this can save their life: several physicians have committed suicide as a result of depression over medical malpractice litigation. For plaintiffs, and health care practitioners are increasingly being forced to become plaintiffs to protect their own rights, it is critical to understand the limitations of litigation and the risks, both economic and psychological.

To the untutored observer, civil and criminal litigation seem very similar. In many jurisdictions, including the federal courts, they are tried in the same courtrooms by the same judges. They both have juries and the basic rules of procedure and evidence are similar. There are profound differences, however, that derive from the extra constitutional protections afforded criminal defendants. This chapter will use civil litigation as a model and will discuss the differences with criminal litigation as they arise.

Movies and television give the impression that trials move quickly and are interesting; the testimony of witnesses is fast-paced and stimulating; and, most deceptively, that the trial quickly follows the crime or accident precipitating it. In real life, trials are tedious, emotionally draining, and generally bewildering to plaintiffs and defendants alike. Health care practitioners should understand how trials are conducted and the basic standards for the admission of evidence. This will help them make decisions about when it is appropriate to go to trial. More important, by understanding how evidence is presented to the jury, health care practitioners can better avoid situations that lead to liability.

PREFILING

The biggest difference between civil and criminal litigation is in the investigations that are done before the case is filed. In a criminal case, most of the investigation is done before the case is brought against the defendant. The police and prosecutor's office have extensive legal powers to obtain information and deal with witnesses before a case is filed; the process is called discovery. A private civil litigant, such as a plaintiff in a medical malpractice case, has only limited access to legal process to assist discovery before a case is filed. Once the case is filed, however, both the plaintiff and defendant in civil cases have extensive powers to get information from each other and from witnesses and other persons who have information about the case. In contrast, the criminal defendant has only a very limited duty to provide any information to the prosecutor, and, although the prosecutor must provide the defendant with certain information, there is much less discovery between the parties than in a civil case.

Investigating the Criminal Case

The city police or other law enforcement personnel, such as the Drug Enforcement Administration (DEA) or the Federal Bureau of Investigation (FBI), do the initial investigation of crimes. They may begin with a citizen report of a crime, or they may carry out ongoing investigations of businesses such as importers to detect crimes such as smuggling that are unlikely to be reported.

Witness Statements

The government has the right to interrogate anyone with knowledge of the crime who is not protected by some legal privilege. For example, the police can interrogate a health care practitioner's employees, but cannot interrogate his wife because the wife is prevented from testifying by a legal rule that is intended to protect marital confidences. In most circumstances, the government would be barred from interrogating someone's lawyer or a priest who took the defendant's confession. If a witnesses refuses to cooperate with the investigation, the government can request that a judge hold the witness in contempt of court and punish the witness until he or she testifies.

These witness statements are usually written down, but are not usually provided to the defen-

dant. In federal court, the identities of the government's witnesses and the content of their statements is protected from discovery by the defendant. This is done to prevent witness tampering and intimidation. If the defendant can convince the judge that identities and statements of the witnesses are vital to the defense, and that there is likelihood of jury tampering, the judge may allow the defendant to know who the witnesses are and what their statements contain. Some prosecutors routinely disclose this information when there is no concern about jury tampering.

Search Warrants

If they have probable cause to believe that a crime has been committed or that there is evidence of criminal activity, offices can obtain a search warrant from a judge. The search warrant empowers them to enter onto private property, by force, if necessary. Once there, they can search for the items or individuals specified in the warrant, and seize them if found.

Search warrants can also be issued to obtain information from persons or institutions who are not participants in the crime. This information can include banking and phone records, medical records, or any other information that may provide evidence of a crime. In limited cases, phone taps and other methods of electronic surveillance may be used. These require close supervision by the courts because they also affect the rights of all the innocent persons with whom the suspect deals.

Investigating the Private Civil Case

Most private civil actions, such as medical malpractice claims, begin by the aggrieved person finding an attorney and asking for help. The attorney interviews the client to find out the facts and whether these will support a lawsuit with sufficient damages to pay for the attorney's time and to compensate the plaintiff. (In some situations, such as the breast implant litigation, the attorneys know the lawsuit they want to bring and advertise for persons with the appropriate injuries to be plaintiffs.) Once the attorney has determined that there may be a valid lawsuit, the attorney will sign a contract to establish the terms of the attorney–client relationship and to document the client's permission to proceed with further investigation of the case.

Preclaim Discovery

In contrast with the police or prosecutor, a private attorney has very limited access to court-ordered discovery before a case is filed. Even in the limited circumstances where process is available—certain situations where evidence will disappear or witnesses may die before trial—the potential defendants are entitled to notice and a chance to object. This will put them on notice of whatever the plaintiff is trying to investigate. Plaintiffs use informal techniques for pretrial investigation as much as possible because they do not put the defendant on notice and because they are much more flexible. The attorney may conduct the investigation personally, or hire a private investigator.

The first step is to check all public records. There are many legitimate vendors of information about individuals, information that is obtained from driver's license records, police records, property tax records, all the public information that is available if you just know where to look. Increasingly, this is all available online for anyone who pays the search fee. An unscrupulous investigator may also use contacts in various businesses to obtain private information, such as banking and phone records. The investigator will talk to potential witnesses, persons who know the defendant, employees of the defendant (unless forbidden by state law), and anyone who can provide information about the incident. If there are medical records involved, the attorney will request copies or will examine the original in person. The attorney may hire an expert to evaluate the information to determine if it supports the plaintiff's case.

Statute of Limitations

The plaintiff has a fixed period of time to file the claim in civil cases. This is called the statute of limitations. In many states, medical malpractice cases must be filed within 2 years. Perhaps the longest statutes of limitations are in certain types of conspiracy cases. Private cases brought under the Racketeering Influenced Corrupt Organizations Act (RICO) laws can involve incidents back 10 years. Any claim filed after the statute of limitations has run will be dismissed.

In many cases, the plaintiff does not know about the negligence at the time it occurs. For example, if a surgeon leaves a pair of forceps in the patient, the patient might not know about it for months or years. In other cases, the patient cannot know until some other condition occurs, such as Rh sensitization that might not show up until the patient is pregnant again. Toxic exposure cases pose the problem of whether the statute runs from when the victim was exposed, or when the disease occurs. To avoid injustice in these cases, the courts developed the discovery rule, holding that the statute of limitations would not run until the patient knew, or should have known, of the injury.[1] Many states, however, have abolished the discovery rule as part of tort reform. In one case under these tort reform rules, a gynecologist did a PAP smear on a patient and told her she would be informed if the test was abnormal. The test did come back abnormal, but the physician's office staff filed it without telling the physician. Four years later she had a pelvic examination and was found to have stage IIb cancer of the endocervix. The court ruled that the statute of limitations had run and the plaintiff's complaint must be dismissed, even though there was no way for the plaintiff to have known of the negligence.

Pretrial Settlements

Many cases are settled before any legal claim is filed or a trial is held. Settlements are driven by the strength of the plaintiff's or prosecutor's case, the potential cost of the litigation, the possible adverse publicity from a public airing of the dispute, the potential risk of loss in court, and each party's concern with resolving the dispute quickly. The terms of many settlements, both private and criminal, include confidentiality agreements that reduce or eliminate the defendant's public relations problem. This can be a powerful settlement tool if the defendant will suffer from the adverse publicity even if ultimately found innocent. As discussed in Chapter 6, there are financial incentives for defense lawyers to fight claims that are better settled, so defendants must be attentive to their own best interests.

Criminal Settlements

Since most of a criminal investigation is over before the defendant is charged, the defendant does not know what is being investigated, who the investigators are talking to, or what information they have developed. It is not unusual for criminal investigations to be carried out for a year or more. In some of the Medicare/Medicaid false claims cases that have been settled, the government investigated the case for 3 years before confronting the defendants. This allows the prosecutor or U.S. Attorney to put the defendant under tremendous pressure: the defendant, say a major hospital and its administrators, is threatened with civil and criminal prosecution, potential fines in the hundred-million-dollar range, and an offer to settle for $10,000,000 and a misdemeanor plea from the administrator. They have a day to decide. They know there are some problems, but have no idea what the government knows. The downside, even if they win, is huge attorney's fees (not paid by insurance) and months or years of adverse publicity. If they lose, it can be prison for a felony conviction and a mandatory fine that will cripple the institution.

In this situation, almost all corporate defendants settle the case and pay the fine. As long as the government sets the fine at a level that will not cripple the institution, few institutions are willing to take the risk of a jury trial. Although the institutions often accuse the government of extortion in such cases, the reality is that the government usually only goes after serious cases and only threatens to charge the defendants when it has substantial evidence. The government does not want to try most of the cases because it costs so much money and takes so much personnel time that it may draw critical resources from many other investigations.

The settlement decision is harder for individual defendants, especially physicians and other licensed health care practitioners. If they plead to a crime, they will usually lose their license to practice. If the crime involves fraud against a federal program, they will be barred from treating federal pay patients and from working for any entity that treats federal pay patients. This would include almost all hospitals and clinics. Even if they avoid prison, their career will be ruined. They have a strong incentive to fight the charges, at least long enough to see more of the government's case to make a more informed settlement decision.

Civil Settlements

In most civil cases, the plaintiff's attorney will contact the potential defendants and try to negotiate a settlement before filing a lawsuit. To encourage this informal resolution of claims, some states require that defendants in medical malpractice lawsuits be notified some period—perhaps 60 days—before a lawsuit is filed. Health care practitioners contacted by an attorney with a claim that is covered by the practitioner's insurance should notify their insurer at once and not talk to the attorney until discussing the claim with the insurer. If it is an uninsured claim, perhaps for defamation or antitrust, the defendant must contact his or her own attorney at once and have the attorney deal with the plaintiff's attorney.

If the plaintiff makes a settlement offer before a lawsuit is filled, that offer should always be evaluated. Outside of the malpractice area, many cases can be resolved much more satisfactorily before litigation hardens both sides' positions. In employment cases, for example, the defendant may be able to resolve the situation by a job transfer or some severance pay, whereas fighting the case could disrupt the workplace and risk a substantial jury verdict. For problems that affect more than one potential plaintiff, every additional case will have access to all the information produced in the first lawsuit, and the publicity will only encourage others to sue. Medical malpractice cases are much less likely to be settled because of the federal reporting requirements for the National Practitioner Databank (see Chapter 11).

PRETRIAL

The pretrial phase of a criminal trial begins when the defendant is indicted. The indictment states the crime the defendant is accused of in sufficient detail to put the defendant on notice of the charges. This is important because it allows the defendant to prepare a defense and it delineates the subject matter that the defendant cannot be prosecuted for in the future because of double jeopardy. The defendant can also ask for a "bill of particulars," which elaborates on the charges and states the facts that support the specific elements of offenses that the defendant is charged with. Although this will provide the defendant with additional information, the government can comply with the requirements of a bill of particulars without giving away much of its case.

The pretrial phase of a civil case begins when the plaintiff or a government agency files pleadings with the court that notify it that the plaintiff is commencing litigation against the defendant.

Pleadings

Pleading is the general term for the papers that set out the plaintiff's allegations and the defendant's defenses. These pleadings go by different names in different courts. In some courts, the plaintiff's pleading is called the *complaint* and the defendant's is the *answer.* In others they are *original petition* and *answer.*

It is this initial pleading that the plaintiff must have served on the defendant. The defendant has a certain amount of time (frequently 20 days) to file a reply to the initial pleading. If the defendant has been properly served and fails to file the reply on time, the plaintiff may ask the court to rule in his or her favor as a matter of law. In most cases, the court will allow the defendant to file after the deadline but frequently requires the payment of a fine to cover the cost of the delay to the plaintiff. Since the court is not required to accept late filings, it is imperative that the plaintiff's allegations be answered on time.

Service of Process

One distressing part of litigation is that someone comes to the defendant's office—a police officer or sheriff in uniform—and demands to hand the health care practitioner personally the documents alleging wrongdoing. This is called *service of process,* and it begins the timetable on the various parts of the lawsuit. The papers that begin the lawsuit, as well as papers that announce certain other critical events, are served personally to ensure that the party being sued is notified of the lawsuit. The ignominy of being served personally is preferable to missing a deadline that can irretrievably compromise a defendant's legal rights.

Defendants are always advised to accept service politely; process servers have no interest in the litigation, and there is no justification for vilifying them. There is also a risk to dodging service. Dodging service in the office may result in being served at church, the country club, or another acutely embarrassing situation.

A health care practitioner who is served legal papers should call his or her insurance company and attorney—*not* the plaintiff or the plaintiff's attorney. A copy of the papers should be retained, with the date and time of service carefully noted. Once the defendant's attorney has filed a reply to the plaintiff's allegations, most of the succeeding documents are sent to the defendant's attorney without the need for personal service.

The Plaintiff's Complaint

A plaintiff begins a lawsuit by formally alleging that the defendant violated a legal duty owed to the plaintiff. Historically, the common law rules for pleading a cause of action were very complex. These rules have been greatly simplified, but have a vestigial remnant in the form of the prima facie case that a plaintiff must plead in most states. A prima facie case is a formal statement of the facts that support the plaintiff's claim for compensation or other legal relief. For example, in a medical malpractice lawsuit, the plaintiff must allege that:

1. The defendant had a duty to treat the plaintiff in a proper manner.
2. The defendant breached this duty.
3. The breach of the defendant's duty proximately caused the plaintiff's injuries.
4. A certain sum of money paid to the plaintiff will compensate for the injuries.

These allegations must be supported with a recitation of facts surrounding the plaintiff's injuries, but the plaintiff need not present expert opinion to support the prima facie case.

The Defendant's Answer

The defendant must file an answer to the complaint within a certain period of time, usually 20 days or less. The answer tells the court in what ways the plaintiff's prima facie case is defective and asserts any affirmative defenses. This is also the time to object if the case has been brought in the wrong court. In some states, the defendant may file a denial of all of the plaintiff's allegations without addressing the specific issues raised by the plaintiff. This is called a *general denial*. The defendant may also deny the plaintiff's allegations specifically. The advantage of specifically addressing the plaintiff's allegations is that it personalizes the case for the judge. If the defendant is in the right, it is better for the judge to see the facts of the case. For example, assume that the defendant has been sued solely because his name appears on the plaintiff's medical records. If the defendant did not treat the patient and did not have any legal duties to the patient, then it is better to explain this than to file a general denial. It is frustrating for both the plaintiff's attorney and the defendant physician to fight a lawsuit for years, only to find at deposition that the plaintiff would have dismissed the case earlier if the defense attorney had explained the situation, rather than relying on a general denial.

Civil Discovery

Discovery is the process of finding (discovering) the relevant facts that must be presented to the court. Discovery by set rules is a modern innovation designed to further justice by giving both litigants access to the facts in the case. Discovery is termed a procedural rather than a substantive matter (an ironic use of language, since rules that affect the procedure of the law often have more profound effects than rules that affect the substance of the law). In most civil litigation, and especially in medical malpractice litigation, the majority of the time between the filing of the plaintiff's complaint and the point at which the case is ready for trial is taken up with discovery proceedings. These proceedings can be time consuming and expensive. A major argument for alternatives to litigation for resolving disputes is avoiding of the cost of discovery.

Discovery is meant to help the parties to find the truth and properly prepare their cases. Discovery rules are very liberal, allowing parties to obtain information that they may not be able to use in court, as long as there is a chance that it will lead to admissible evidence. This does not mean that all the information developed in discovery can be used at trial. The scope of pretrial discovery is much broader than the scope of allowable evidence as defined by the rules of evidence. After the information is obtained through discovery, the judge will make a separate determination on whether it will be allowed into evidence—presented to the jury—at trial.

Discovery may be carried out by directly asking a person questions (*oral depositions*), by sending a person written questions (*interrogatories* and *depositions on written questions*), and by requesting that the person provide documents (*motions for production, subpoenas duces tecum*). The person answering the questions must refuse to answer the questions or swear that the answers provided are correct to the best of his or her knowledge. If it is later determined that the person was lying, he or she may be fined or prosecuted for perjury. If a party to the lawsuit lies, the court has the authority to direct a verdict for the opposing party. Most judges conduct a discovery conference at some point in the pretrial preparation of a case to work out the remaining discovery issues so the case can proceed to trial. Federal judges usually enter discovery orders to control and hasten the discovery process.

Interrogatories

Interrogatories are written questions that may be sent to any person or legal entity who is a party to the lawsuit (plaintiff or defendant). They may not be sent to persons who are not parties to the litigation. Most jurisdictions limit the number of questions that can be asked and the number of sets of interrogatories that can be sent. The questions are directed to the party personally, but they are sent to the party's attorney and the attorneys representing all the other parties to the litigation. The attorney gives the questions to the client and either asks the client to prepare a set of draft answers or has a paralegal work with the client to prepare the draft.

Once the draft answers are prepared, the attorney edits this draft to prepare answers that are technically correct and provide the requested factual information, but provide as little speculation from the client as possible. If the question is even slightly ambiguous, the attorney will refuse to provide an answer until the ambiguities have been resolved. This process of disputing the interrogatories can take several months and one or more hearings before the judge. Interrogatories can be a cost-effective way of collecting information, but in practice they are often abused.

Requests for Admissions

Like interrogatories, these may be directed only at parties to the litigation. Unlike interrogatories, however, the questions do not allow for narrative answers. Each question is phrased so that it must be answered as "admitted" or "denied." Requests for admissions are used to delineate which facts are not in issue and may thus be agreed to before trial. A typical question might be, "Admit or deny that you treated plaintiff on 23 October 1985."

Once an item has been admitted or denied, the court is reticent about allowing the answer to be changed. The party requesting the right to amend a request for admissions has the burden of convincing the court that there is a good reason that the original answer is incorrect. Conversely, the party requesting the admissions must ask simple and unambiguous questions if he or she wants the answers to be effective in court.

Depositions by Written Questions

These written questions resemble interrogatories, but they may be addressed to any person or entity, not just persons who are party to the litigation. Before a deposition on written questions is sent to the deponent, it must be sent to the other parties in the lawsuit. Any other party may object to a question or request that additional (cross) questions be asked, serving the purpose of cross-examination. (Interrogatories do not require cross-questions because there will be other opportunities to cross-examine the party.) In a deposition by written questions, a third party, such as a notary public or process server, presents the questions to the deponent. The questions are answered in the presence of the third party, who also attests that the answers are properly sworn.

The most common use of depositions by written questions is to establish the authenticity of medical and other business records. Some states also allow depositions by written questions as proof that the charges to the patient were reasonable and customary. They must be answered by either the person who made the entry or by the custodian of the records. The custodian does not need to have personal knowledge of the entries in question to testify about the recordkeeping protocol. However, the custodian must be able to answer certain legal questions for the medical records to be admissible in the court.

In the following example, the required set of questions is directed to a witness who is the custodian of records for Dr. Mary Jones:

Sample Affidavit

1. State your full name, residence, and occupation.

2. Has John Doe been treated or examined by Dr. Mary Jones?

PROOF OF RECORDS

1. Has Dr. Jones made or caused to be made any notes, records, and/or reports of the examination and/or treatment of said patient?

2. Were the entries on these notes, records, and/or reports made at the time, or shortly after the time, of the transaction recorded by these entries?

3. Were these notes, records, and/or reports made or caused to be made by Dr. Jones in the regular course of business as a doctor or physician?

4. In the regular course of business at Dr. Jones's facility, did each of the persons who signed the reports contained in the record either have personal knowledge of the entries shown on the report or obtain information to make the entry from sources who had such personal knowledge?

5. Do you have such records as described above on John Doe?

6. Were these records kept as described above?

7. Please hand such records on John Doe to the notary public taking this deposition for photocopying and marking as exhibits to be attached to this deposition.

8. Have you done as requested in the preceding question? If not, why not?

PROOF OF CHARGES

1. Are you familiar with the charges usually and customarily made for the medical services reflected in the bills furnished as a part of the requested written records?

2. Please state the full amount of charges in the treatment of John Doe.

3. Please state whether such charges are reasonable and customary for like or similar services rendered in the vicinity in which they were incurred.

4. Were the services performed, as reflected in the records, necessary for the proper treatment of the patient in question?

Oral Depositions

A party may take the oral deposition of any person who has information relevant to the litigation. The person to be deposed may agree to appear at a certain time and place for the deposition, or the deposing party may ask the court to order the witness to appear. All of the parties to the litigation must be notified of the time and place for the deposition. Each party to the litigation has the right to be present and to question the witness, usually through attorneys.

At the beginning of the deposition, the witness must swear or affirm an oath to tell the truth. The deposition is recorded stenographically or electronically. Many depositions are now videotaped. This is useful if the witness does not appear at trial. If either a witness's or a party's testimony at trial is substantially different from their deposition, the videotape can be played at trial to impeach the testimony. After the deposition is completed, a transcript will be prepared so that the attorneys and the judge will be able to discuss the admissibility of each question and answer. This transcript can also be entered into evidence at trial to create a record of proof if the testimony changes between the deposition and the trial.

The attorney requesting the deposition asks the first questions. When this attorney completes the questioning, the attorneys for the other parties ask their questions (cross-examination). When all the parties' attorneys have had their turn, the requesting attorney may ask additional questions (redirect), starting the round robin again. This process of cross-examination makes depositions time consuming for the participants and expensive for the clients. It is not unusual for a deposition of a party in a simple case to last for a day. In complex matters, such as Medicare fraud cases, a party may be deposed for days.

Requests for Production

These are written orders that may be directed only to persons who are parties to a lawsuit. A request for production describes certain documents or classes of documents and requests that the party either provide copies or produce the document at a convenient time for inspection by the requesting attorney. These requests can be quite onerous. In business litigation, opposing counsel might request all of a company's business records for the last 10 years. In medical litigation involving allegations of systematic fraud, the physician may be required to produce the records of all patients treated during the period.

Motions for production are also used by defense attorneys to evaluate the plaintiff's case.

These defense motions may inquire into past tax returns, employment records, divorce decrees and settlements, and any other documents that may illuminate the value of the plaintiff's case. Motions for production can be a valuable way to develop evidence, or they may be used to harass and financially exhaust an opponent. Since they may be sent only to a party in a lawsuit, that party's attorney will review and contest unreasonable requests.

Once the items to be produced have been agreed upon, it is critical to comply fully with the request. Under no circumstances should records be destroyed after they have been requested. This can result in monetary fines. In extreme cases, when it is clear that the party intended to obstruct justice through the destruction of the documents, the judge may order that the opposing party wins the case.

Subpoenas

Subpoenas are written orders requiring that a person or documents be brought to a certain place at a certain time. Subpoenas are issued under the authority of the court, although in most situations they do not need to be approved by a judge. Subpoenas may be issued to any person; they are not restricted to the parties in the lawsuit. Subpoenas may be used to ensure the attendance of a person at a court hearing or a deposition. These subpoenas must specify the place the person is to appear and a time to appear. Subpoenas used at trials may require a person to appear at a set time, or they may request that the person be available to testify during the course of the trial. If the subpoena is not for a specified time, the judge usually makes arrangements to give the subpoenaed person adequate notice of the time when he or she is actually needed at the courthouse. In most cases, the judge will also accommodate the person's schedule as much as possible. The courts show particular deference to physicians who request a reasonable accommodation. Conversely, ignoring a subpoena, especially one to testify at a trial, can result in the refusing party's being taken into custody (arrested) and brought to the trial at the judge's convenience.

A health care practitioner who is not a party to a lawsuit and who receives an unexpected personal subpoena should talk to the attorney who sent it to find out what he or she is being summoned to and why the testimony is necessary. He or she should discuss rescheduling the appearance if it is unduly burdensome. If agreements are made, the attorney must be asked to reissue the subpoena in accordance with the changes. The attorney may also agree to withdraw the subpoena and reach an informal agreement as to the time and place of the physician's appearance. The health care practitioner should request that this informal agreement be confirmed in writing and sent to him or her at once.

Subpoena Duces Tecum

These are subpoenas for physical objects. In the context of personal injury litigation, they typically request the production of medical records, calendars, office diaries, X rays, and any other physical record that concerns the medical care of a specified person. Subpoenas for any relevant records are usually sent to persons who are scheduled to give depositions. The records are usually those of the plaintiff, but an attorney may issue a subpoena for the records of any person whose medical condition is at issue in the lawsuit. In some situations, such as toxic exposure litigation, the records of many patients may be subpoenaed. The attorney is not allowed to keep the subpoenaed records but may inspect them and make copies.

Attorneys usually do not issue a subpoena for records without first attempting to obtain them through informal means. Since subpoenas may be issued without the approval of the court, health care practitioners should ensure that they are valid before releasing records by calling the issuing attorney and determining the circumstances of the case. In most states now, a subpoena for medical records should include a signed release by the patient. If the attorney is requesting records for persons other than his or her client, the physician may want to ask his or her own attorney to investigate the validity of the request. In cases that involve records with special legal protection (such as patients in a substance abuse treatment program) it may be necessary to request that the court deny (quash) the subpoena or restrict access to the records. The court may order that all patient identifiers be removed, or that the records be given to the judge, rather than the requesting attorney.

Objecting to Civil Discovery

Health care practitioners frequently receive questionable discovery requests, especially subpoenas for medical records. These should not be honored unless they include a signed release from the patient. If there is no release, the health care practitioner should contact his or her attorney to review the request. In institutional settings, all discovery requests should be sent to the institution's attorney. If the subpoena is improper, the attorney can ask the judge to cancel it. The judge may quash it—rule that the request need not be complied with—or, more commonly, modify the request to limit the information that is provided. If the request is from a law enforcement agency, the health care practitioner should contact an attorney at once.

Since the latitude for discovery is very broad, judges will generally grant most requests that do not involve privileged information or unnecessary access to information about uninvolved third parties. The trial judge controls the discovery in a case through the discretion granted in the rules of procedure for the court's jurisdiction. In theory the judge should be involved in discovery only in the rare situation of a request for information that is not admissible and has no chance of leading to admissible information. Traditionally, defense attorneys would contest every discovery order to inconvenience the opposition and delay the trial. The federal courts and most states now try to limit this dilatory practice, but this has problems as well because it can be difficult to ensure that a case has been thoroughly investigated when the judge is pushing the case to trial.

Criminal Discovery

The allowable scope of discovery by defendants is much more limited in criminal cases. This is rationalized by the high burden of proof that the prosecutor must meet: even if defendants do nothing in their defense, the state will still lose unless it convinces the jury of the defendant's guilt beyond a reasonable doubt. Under federal law, the defendant need not provide any testimony to the prosecutor unless the defendant wants to raise a defense of mental incapacity, alibi, or governmental authority. The courts and legislatures are also concerned with the reluctance of witnesses to testify if they fear retaliation. There is also the possibility that if defendants in some cases know before about adverse testimony before trial, they would attempt to suborn perjury—get the witnesses to lie or find other persons to lie to contradict them. In extreme cases, the federal law provides for preventive detention of the defendant or of the witnesses to prevent witness intimidation or murder.[2]

Although the defendant does not have a right to all the information that the government holds, the defendant does have a constitutional right to favorable evidence that the government holds.[3] The difficulty is for the defendant to figure out how to ask for specific evidence that meets this test when the defendant does not know what evidence the government is holding. The defendant's attorney must craft a "Brady request" that forces the government to either turn over the evidence or risk having their case reversed on appeal if the evidence comes out at trial or even posttrial. For reversal, the defendant must show that he or she did not have other notice of the information. There is no violation "where a defendant knew or should have known the essential facts permitting him to take advantage of any exculpatory information, or where the evidence is available from another source."[4] The defendant must also show that the evidence that was withheld is "material," in that there is a reasonable probability that it would have affected the result of the trial.[5]

The defendant is entitled to the records of certain of his or her own statements made to the police and to recorded statements made by witnesses who testify. These are generally not provided before the trial, but only at the time the witnesses testify. The government is permitted to give the defendant more information, and the defendant may petition the judge to order the government to produce other information. The government has an incentive to provide additional information because it reduces the defendant's grounds for appeal based on withholding exculpatory evidence. This is most important in cases involving the death penalty where the postconviction review is the most thorough and the defendant gets the greatest benefit of the doubt as to the importance of the evidence.

WHICH CASES GO TO TRIAL?

Most civil and criminal cases settle before trial. The plaintiff and the defendant in civil cases work out a settlement based on information obtained during discovery. Criminal cases end with a plea bargain, especially if the defendant is not wealthy enough to mount a substantial private defense.

Why Settle before Trial?

The uncertainty inherent in the jury system encourages these settlements because both sides realize that although they may win more than the settlement provides, they can also lose everything. In some cases, innocent defendants, both civil and criminal, settle or accept a plea bargain because they believe that jury prejudice will make it impossible to get a fair trial. This happens both to poor members of disadvantaged groups who fear racial or ethnic prejudice, and to large corporations that fear that juries will disregard scientific evidence in favor of emotion, especially in cases that involve difficult issues of statistical proof, such as the breast implant cases or environmental toxin cases.

Cases go to trial when either or both parties would rather risk a loss than take a settlement on the terms available. Physicians accused of criminal Medicare fraud often fight, even when their chances of winning are very low, because a plea will cost them their medical license and the right to work in health care. Conversely, institutions charged with Medicare fraud usually settle because the government sets the fine they must pay low enough so they will not go out of business, but

the mandatory fines that accompany a guilty verdict will bankrupt them. The reporting requirements of the National Practitioner Databank discourage settlements in medical malpractice cases because the settlements cannot be made confidential (see Chapter 11).

Incentives against Settlement

A candid defense attorney once described a medical malpractice case as an annuity, bearing interest above the prevailing rate. The longer a file is open, the longer the law firm can draw that interest. Every few months additional court papers can be filed. Client reports need to be done on a regular basis. Each piece of paper and court appearance that the defense attorney can generate, or force the plaintiff's attorney to generate, results in substantial fees. This approach is usually described as being "tough" on the plaintiff. Being tough usually means forcing court appearances and motion practice rather than coming to agreement.

Most malpractice lawsuits settle before a final jury verdict. Unlike attorneys who defend criminals, malpractice defense attorneys have an incentive not to cooperate with the plaintiff's attorney in reaching a settlement. Cases are often settled at the courthouse door because that is the longest the defense can delay before running the risk of a trial. Defense attorneys are risk adverse; they would rather settle a case than run any substantial chance of losing the case. This is related to the public relations aspects of litigation. A successful defense of a malpractice lawsuit is not news, but a $1 million verdict will attract publicity. A case that is settled is not lost and usually does not generate adverse publicity. From an earnings perspective, the ideal defense case is one in which the defendant was negligent enough to justify settling the case but careful enough to justify delaying that settlement to the bitter end.

Delays in Getting to Trial

Most of the delay in criminal cases takes place before the indictment. The government may investigate a case for years before bringing the indictment, but once the indictment is brought, there are limits on how much time the government may delay the trial of the case. Although the defendant has some latitude in obtaining additional time for preparation, the limits on the discovery in criminal trials mean that there is less reason for delay than in civil trials. Once the defense is ready, the case is set for trial and takes precedence over pending civil cases.

Civil discovery is much more complicated and time consuming. In most jurisdictions, the discovery proceedings must be substantially complete before the attorneys can ask for a trial date. Once a trial date has been requested, the case is put in a queue with every other case set for trial. This queue is often six months to a year long. In some urban courts, it may take two or more years to go to trial after discovery is complete. The delay can be longer in jurisdictions where there are a lot of pending criminal cases because these bump civil trials, irrespective of how long the civil trial has been pending.

It is the uncertainty of the process, not the delay itself, that is the most difficult aspect of the trial-setting queue. It is difficult to predict how long a trial will last, so to increase their efficiency, many courts schedule several cases for each trial date. This ensures that the court will have work to do, even if several of the cases settle right before trial. This also means that several of the cases that are set on a given date will not be tried as scheduled. The attorneys cannot be sure whether their case will be reached. To be prepared to try the case on the specified date, they must contact witnesses, prepare trial documents, and review the case with their client—time-consuming, and thus expensive, work. It is not unusual for a case to be set for trial and then be postponed several times.

ADMITTING EVIDENCE

The rules of civil procedure allow the attorneys to discover any information that may lead to admissible evidence. Some time before, or at the start of trial, the court will begin the process of reviewing the evidence that the attorneys plan to submit and determining, what, if any, of it is admissible. The rules for admissibility are much stricter for evidence in criminal cases because of the constitutional protections for the defendant. The outcome of many criminal cases is decided by the judge's rulings on which evidence is admissible. For example, the judge may exclude a confession or a murder weapon because it was obtained improperly. Although the constitutional issues of improper search and self-incrimination are not a problem in civil trials, witnesses and other evidence may still be excluded if it is unduly prejudicial or if it does not meet the legal standards for credibility. Once evidence has been admitted, it is subject to cross-examination.

Protecting the Jury

The legal preliminaries necessary to establish the qualifications of a witness are long and tedious. If the opposing attorney takes issue with the witness's qualifications or testimony, these objections will usually be discussed outside of the presence of the jury. First, the jury will be removed from the courtroom. Then the lawyers and judge spend several minutes discussing the legal issues involved, and finally the jury is brought back into the courtroom. The effect is to break up the flow of trial, making the proceedings confusing and frequently tense. In a hotly contested case, there can be days of hearings on evidence before the jury is impaneled and, once it is sitting, the jury may be out of the room for more than half of the trial.

Invoking the "Rule"

The procedure known as "invoking the rule"— a rule of civil procedure that allows a party to request that a witness be prevented from hearing the testimony of other witnesses in the trial—can be distressing to witnesses. The intent is to prevent witnesses from refreshing their memory or shaping their testimony to fit other testimony. The rule is particularly frustrating to health care practitioners acting as expert witnesses. They will be asked to testify about the validity of other testimony that they are prevented from hearing. Since the attorneys are free to paraphrase the words of other witnesses, perhaps putting a different cast on them, the expert may be in the position of condemning another physician for something the physician did not say or do.

Cross-Examination

Cross-examination is the process of elucidating the truth through the examination of the contested information by adversary attorneys. The best example of cross-examination is the examination of witnesses. Each attorney questions the witness in turn, and each is allowed to requestion the witness on matters brought out by subsequent questioners. This may take a few minutes or several weeks, depending on the complexity of the testimony. In theory, this relentless questioning eventually flushes out the truth. This theory, however, is predicated on the assumption that the adversaries are sufficiently well versed in the technicalities of the witness's testimony to recognize the truth when it makes an appearance. In practice, cross-examination of witnesses frequently illuminates little more than the relative acting skills of the examining attorneys and the witness.

The Hearsay Rule

Few other concepts in law arise so often and yet are so inadequately understood as the concept of hearsay. The hearsay rule is important in the medical setting because the admissibility of the medical record into the court as evidence is governed by the hearsay rule. A basic understanding of this rule is necessary to an understanding of the legal significance of medical recordkeeping protocols. The *hearsay rule* holds that one person cannot testify about the truth of what another person said. Witnesses can testify only as to what they heard the person in question say. For example, a nurse may testify that she heard Dr. Jones say, "I must have been drunk to have nicked that patient's intestine!" The jury could accept this as evidence of what Dr. Jones said but not as evidence that she was drunk or had nicked the intestine. These facts would need to be proved through the testimony of

Dr. Jones herself or the testimony of appropriate expert witnesses.

The hearsay rule arises from the need for counsel to cross-examine every witness and document to determine its truthfulness. If a statement made out of court is accepted as evidence, the person making that statement cannot be cross-examined about the truthfulness of it. The court demands that the person who actually made the statement be brought into the courtroom, placed under oath, and asked to repeat the statement.

If this rule were applied to the medical record, everyone who made an entry in the record would have to be called into the courtroom and asked which entries they made, why they made them, and what information they based these entries upon—an extremely time-consuming process and maybe even impossible. Because of these practical difficulties, the courts have created the business records exception to the hearsay rule: documents may be admitted into evidence without the requirement that the persons who made the entries be available for cross-examination.

Business Records Exception to Hearsay

Documents are subject to cross-examination under the hearsay rule. Most documents are hearsay because they record what others did and said, and are generally maintained by someone who was not involved in matters in the records. There is an exception to the hearsay rules for business records. For health care practitioners, the medical record is the key business record. Medical recordkeeping procedures must fulfill the legal requirements of the business records exception if a medical record is to be admissible in court. This exception to the hearsay rule requires that the record meet four basic tests:

1. The record was made in the regular course of the business.
2. The entry in the record was made by an employee or representative of that business who had personal knowledge of the act, event, or condition that is being recorded in the record.

3. The record was made at or near the time that the recorded act, event, or condition occurred, or reasonably soon thereafter.
4. The records were kept in a consistent manner, according to a set procedure.

Entry in the Regular Course of Business

The first requirement is that the entry be made in the regular course of business. For a physician, the regular course of business is providing medical care, keeping medical records, and complying with state and federal health laws. The medical record will be admissible to prove the truth of activities related to the practice of medicine. Entries in the medical record that do not deal with the practice of medicine will not be considered to have been made in the regular course of business.

For example, if a patient seeks medical care after being involved in an automobile accident, the patient's physical condition, as described in the medical records, will be admissible as evidence in a legal proceeding. However, if the physician also entered the patient's description of the accident into the medical record, this would not be admissible because investigating accidents is not part of the regular course of business for a physician. Thus, the information about the accident would be excluded from the courtroom as hearsay.

In general, physicians should refrain from making entries into the medical record that are not directly concerned with the provision of medical care or with legal matters that are necessary to the rendering of medical care (for example, guardianship status or court orders bearing on the rendering of medical care).

Personal Knowledge

The requirement that the entry be made by someone who has personal knowledge of the event being recorded or that the information be transmitted directly to the person making the entry from someone who has personal knowledge allows a physician to dictate notes to be transcribed and put in the chart. The transcriptionist need not have any personal knowledge of the medical care rendered because he or she is getting the information from someone who is familiar with the care given.

The requirement of personal knowledge is a problem in teaching institutions. In some cases, a physician may write chart notes and summaries for a patient he or she has not personally cared for or discussed with the physician who did care for the patient. If the recording physician does nothing more than summarize data already in the medical record, there will be no problem with the personal knowledge requirement, because the physician, by reviewing the record, will have personal knowledge of the data in the record.

Problems arise when the physician draws conclusions about the patient's condition based on data in the record. Although these conclusions are incorporated in the medical record, they are not based on personal knowledge of the patient's condition. This failure of personal knowledge could be legal grounds for attacking the admissibility of the conclusions in court.

Timely Entry in the Usual Course of Business

The requirement of the law that is most frequently not complied with is that the entry be made at or near the time of the act, event, or condition described. The courts allow reasonable delay, given the circumstances of the business. Most hospitals use the Joint Commission on Accreditation of Healthcare Organizations 30-day standard for completing the chart, with certain time-critical entries to be completed in 72 hours. (This does not mean that entries can be backdated. Progress notes and other daily memoranda must be made on the day to which they pertain.)

Although the courts would generally ignore this delay, it is certainly questionable whether 30 days is a reasonable delay. Since both plaintiffs and defendants usually want the record admitted to court, there has been little litigation on whether medical records actually meet the requirements of the business records exception.

Standard Recordkeeping Procedure

In theory, the most important requirement is that the records be kept in the usual course of business. This is a twofold requirement: the records must be kept in a standard, well-defined form, and they must be kept as part of the day-to-day activities of the business. This requirement goes to the accuracy of the records. It is assumed that the business does not have an incentive to lie in its routine business records. Once the business's activities are under question, however, it is assumed that there may be some incentive to slant the entries. Self-serving entries that do not relate to the factual basis of a patient's care could be challenged under this requirement.

Expert Testimony and Professional Standards

Civil and criminal trials depend on live witnesses to present testimony. Even when the information being presented is in the form of documents, there must usually be a human witness to authenticate the documents. Witness's testimony can be divided into factual testimony about matters the witness has personal knowledge of and expert testimony, in which an expert testifies as to conclusions he or she draws from the records in the case. Most of the controversy about witness testimony concerns expert witness testimony. The most common medical care–related cases involve alleged negligent treatment of patients—medical malpractice—or injuries caused by medical devices or drugs—products liability. Both of these types of cases require expert testimony to establish the appropriate standards, to determine if the standards have been breached, and, most difficult in many cases, whether the alleged misconduct or defective product caused the plaintiff's injuries.

Fact Witnesses

Most witnesses are fact witnesses; they have personal knowledge of either the incident that underlies the lawsuit or the persons involved. Anyone may testify as to facts; only an expert may present opinions. Fact witnesses are usually laypersons who have little experience in the courtroom. Cross-examination is more effective with these witnesses than with experienced expert witnesses.

An expert, such as a physician, may be called as a fact witness in areas that are outside his or her expertise. For example, a physician may have witnessed an automobile accident. A physician may be a fact witness when a case involves a person whom the physician has treated. The physician may be asked to testify as to the fact of the patient's injury, the treatment rendered, the cost of the treatment, and the current condition of the patient. These are matters of fact contained in the patient's medical record. Questions about the patient's prognosis, however, require an expert opinion. It is this requirement of special qualifications to render opinions that separates fact from expert testimony.

The most important fact witnesses in civil cases are the parties themselves. The jurors' sympathy for the plaintiff versus the defendant is an important determinant of their ultimate verdict. Plaintiffs in medical malpractice cases must convince the jury that they have been injured and that they are deserving of compensation. Defendants must convince the jury that they deserve to be vindicated, both because they did nothing wrong and because they are good people. In criminal trials the dynamic is different. The defendant's right against self-incrimination means that the defendant may refuse to testify, and frequently does. The victim, if living, may testify, but in many cases the victim is dead or unavailable. In fraud cases, especially reimbursement fraud, the only victim may be a corporation or the government.

Expert Witnesses

Whereas anyone can be a witness to the facts they personally know, any testimony that requires either an opinion about the meaning of the facts that is based on a scientific analysis, or otherwise requires special knowledge not possessed by the average juror, must be presented by an expert. For example, in a dispute over the sale of land there may be testimony by an appraiser as to the value of the land. Personal injury cases will need an expert to testify about the seriousness of the patient's injuries and prognosis. In medical malpractice litigation, the plaintiff must present the testimony of an expert who believes that the defendant did not care for the plaintiff properly and that this breach of professional conduct caused the plaintiff an injury. A fraud case may require an expert on accounting standards. A products liability claim against a drug company may require an expert to testify as to whether the drug actually causes the type of injury that is alleged.

Evaluating Expert Witnesses

The key problem with the use of expert witnesses is that the jury is asked to determine the credibility of the expert testimony presented. In the typical case, plaintiff and defendant both have experts whose testimony conflicts. The conflict may be subtle, or simple and direct: the plaintiff's experts in the breast implant litigation say that silicone causes autoimmune disease and that women with implants have a high incidence of autoimmune problems. The defense says it does not and that women with implants have no more problems with autoimmune diseases than does a control group. The jury, of course, has been selected to ensure that no jury members have any special knowledge of medical epidemiology or autoimmune disease. They must evaluate highly technical, conflicting testimony to determine billions of dollars in liability.

Jurors cannot evaluate the scientific merits of such testimony. They have no alternative but to judge the testimony of expert witnesses based on the personal credibility of the witness. Positive factors such as academic degrees, specialty board certification, and publications influence credibility. So do factors such as physical appearance, race, gender, command of English, and personality. For an expert witness, the foremost qualifications are effective presentation and teaching ability. The expert must educate the jury in the technical matter at hand, just as he or she might educate an undergraduate physiology class. The objective is to convince the jurors that they understand the technical issues. Once there is a perception of understanding, the expert can convince them that they are making an independent decision that his or her testimony is correct, rather than just agreeing with him or her.

The risks of this system are that scientifically or medically unsound evidence, presented by credible-appearing witnesses, can supplant proper evidence.[6] There are legal rules that establish the standards that judges are to use in determining whether an expert should be allowed to testify and the extent of that testimony. Judges are charged with ensuring that this does not happen by excluding the testimony of experts who are not properly qualified, or whose testimony goes against known scientific principles.[7] Judges, however, are not any more scientifically knowledgeable than most jurors, and are subject to the same misunderstandings as jurors.

The Frye Rule

The traditional standard for the admission of medical testimony was established in the *Frye* case, which involved the appeal of a criminal defendant who was convicted based on a precursor to the lie detector. This machine measured changes in the systolic blood pressure and the operator of the machine would then correlate these changes with the defendant's truthfulness. The defendant argued that this was an unfounded technique that was not recognized by scientists in the field. The Court agreed, and established this standard:

> Just when a scientific principle or discovery crosses the line between the experimental and demonstrable stages is difficult to define. Somewhere in this twilight zone the evidential force of the principle must be recognized, and while courts will go a long way in admitting expert testimony deduced from a well-recognized scientific principle or discovery, the thing from which the deduction is made must be sufficiently established to have gained general acceptance in the particular field in which it belongs.[8]

The *Frye* rule became the standard for federal and state courts evaluating expert testimony. Before an expert witness could testify, the judge would have to determine if the testimony met the *Frye* test and, if it did, if the witness was properly qualified to be an expert. For example, in a medical malpractice case against a surgeon for negligence in the performance of a surgical procedure, the plaintiff would have to have an expert who was well versed in surgery and knowledgeable in the procedures at issue. If the plaintiff tried to use a pharmacist to testify, the judge would exclude the testimony because a pharmacist does not have the training and expertise of a surgeon. If the plaintiff had a surgeon as an expert, but the surgeon wants to testify that the defendant should have used a surgical procedure that no one but the plaintiff's expert uses, the judge would exclude the testimony because it was not generally accepted.

The *Frye* rule has several shortcomings. General acceptability excludes many new discoveries that have not had time to become generally accepted. General acceptability is hard to establish for narrow areas of inquiry where there may only be a few experts. It is also problematic if the plaintiff is arguing that what is generally accepted is not true. In contest to *Frye*, the tort law recognizes that there are situations where what is generally accepted is not proper behavior.[9] Finally, the *Frye* rule proved difficult to administer, encouraging judges to allow broad latitude for the admission of questionable evidence.

The **Daubert** *Case*

The *Frye* rule was reviewed by the U.S. Supreme Court in the *Daubert* case.[10] This was a case brought by two children born with birth defects that they claimed were caused by an anti-nausea drug, Bendectin. The only such drug approved by the FDA (Food and Drug Administration) for pregnant women, it had been given to more than 17,500,000 women before being taken off the market. Plaintiffs' attorneys argued that thousands of children were born with birth defects to mothers who had taken Bendectin and this proved that Bendectin caused birth defects. Although extensive studies had not shown Bendectin to have any teratogenic effects, plaintiffs had "experts" who disagreed with these studies, based on their own unpublished and unreviewed work. Using these experts, plaintiffs had filed many cases against the manufacturer, Merrell Dow Pharmaceuticals.

Plaintiffs had not been successful in any of the Bendectin lawsuits at the time of the *Daubert* case, but the costs of defense were so high that Merrell Dow had taken the drug off the market. It was assumed by plaintiffs that they would eventually get a substantial settlement from Merrell Dow, either because they would finally win one of the cases, or just to end the defense costs. In the *Daubert* case, the trial judge determined that plaintiff's experts were not credible because their evidence did not meet the *Frye* test requirements of general acceptability. Such a finding is critical to the defense because it stops the lawsuit before the costs are too high, plus it eliminates any chance of a sympathy verdict from the jury.

The plaintiffs appealed, claiming that the revised federal rules of evidence abolished the *Frye* rule and allowed the presentation of evidence that was not generally accepted by the medical or scientific community. The appeals court upheld the trial judge's decision and the plaintiffs appealed to the U.S. Supreme Court.

The **Daubert** *Test*

The U.S. Supreme Court agreed with the plaintiffs that the *Frye* test had been replaced by the Rule 702 of the Federal Rules of Evidence: "If scientific, technical, or other specialized knowledge will assist the trier of fact to understand the evidence or to determine a fact in issue, a witness qualified as an expert by knowledge, skill, experience, training, or education, may testify thereto in the form of an opinion or otherwise."[11]

As compared with the *Frye* rule, Rule 702 transfers the responsibility for evaluating the credibility of the evidence from the general scientific community to the judge. Rather than determining general acceptability, the judge must decide if the evidence is credible enough to assist the jury in making its decisions, or whether it would only mislead the jury. The Court cautioned that this should be a flexible process and that the trial judge has great discretion in making this determination. The Court recommended a set of criteria that the judge should look to in determining whether evidence should be allowed to go to the jury:

1. whether the expert's theory can be or has been tested

2. whether the theory has been subject to peer review and publication
3. the known or potential rate of error of a technique or theory when applied
4. the existence and maintenance of standards and controls
5. the degree to which the technique or theory has been generally accepted in the scientific community[12]

The court clearly states that the intent of the *Daubert* test is to broaden the judge's authority to admit evidence that was not acceptable under the *Frye* test, because, although credible, it was not generally accepted. Paradoxically, the result has been very different in many courts. Spurred on by the U.S. Supreme Court's insistence that the trial judges should be more active in reviewing evidence, trial judges have been much more willing to disqualify experts and testimony than they were in the *Frye* days. The lower court in the *Daubert* case, reexamining the evidence in view of the Supreme Court's ruling, again dismissed the plaintiff's case. This is not universal. Some judges use the *Daubert* test to admit very questionable evidence that clearly would not have been allowed under a strict reading of *Frye*. This has less impact than would be expected because these judges tended to apply the *Frye* test so generously that it also gave little protection against the admission of improper evidence.

Qualifying a Medical Standards Expert Witness

The *Daubert* rule is directed at evaluating scientific evidence, especially epidemiologic and statistical evidence. Whereas such evidence is frequently at issue in medical care–related cases, the most common evidentiary question is the determination of the proper standard for medical treatment. In a medical malpractice case, the plaintiff must present expert testimony as to the proper standard of care, how the health care practitioner defendant deviated from that standard, and how the deviation caused the patient's injury. These are matters that are generally not the subject of rigorous scientific investigation and are thus less

susceptible to the *Daubert* rule. Their proof depends on the testimony of experts who give an opinion, based on their experience, as to what the reasonable physician would have done in the same or similar situation as the defendant (see Chapter 2).

The attorney offering the testimony of an expert witness must follow certain legal formalisms to have the expert's testimony accepted in court. The attorney must first establish that the witness has the proper medical qualifications. When the witness is presented, the opposing counsel may ask to stipulate that the witness is qualified. This is done when the witness is clearly qualified and opposing counsel would prefer that the jury not dwell on the witness's background. If the defense does not stipulate to the witness's qualifications, the expert witness must describe his or her background, practice, or academic experience and any other training or experience that is relevant to the case. Most important, the expert must assert familiarity with the treatment of patients with the plaintiff's complaint by physicians similarly situated to the defendant.

The attorney offering the expert witness will tailor the testimony to the expert's qualifications. If the expert is a general practitioner testifying against a specialist, the testimony will be heavily weighted toward establishing that any competent physician would have avoided the defendant's error. If the expert is a specialist testifying against a general practitioner, the expert will be questioned whether the general practitioner had a duty to refer the patient to a more skilled physician.

If both the expert and the defendant are specialists, the jury must be convinced that the defendant delivered substandard care, as opposed to making a well-reasoned but incorrect judgment. The plaintiff's expert will try to explain the plaintiff's medical condition and the standard of care question in simple terms. This allows the jurors to convince themselves that there was no acceptable excuse for the defendant's failure to render the care described by the plaintiff's expert.

An alternative tactic is to attack the defendant's qualifications to treat the plaintiff's condition. This may be done with either a same-specialty expert or, preferably, an expert from a different and more appropriate specialty. The best situation for this approach is when the patient's condition is usually managed by a different specialty: for example, a surgeon defending his supervision of a certified registered nurse anesthetist against damning testimony by an anesthesiologist. The hope is to force the defendant to abandon his posture of special knowledge. If the plaintiff is successful in establishing the defendant's lack of special knowledge, then the defendant must contend that the treatment of plaintiff's condition was a matter of general medical knowledge. Even if the plaintiff is not wholly successful, he or she will still force the defendant to expend credibility on refuting the allegation that he was unqualified to manage the patient's condition. For guidelines for expert witness testimony in medical liability cases, see Appendix 5–A.

POSTTRIAL

At the conclusion of the trial, the judge or jury will render a *judgment:* a decision on whether the defendant owes the plaintiff money. In a *take nothing judgment,* the defendant owes the plaintiff no money. For a certain period, the judgment may be appealed. If it is not appealed or if the court rejects the appeal, the judgment becomes payable. In some situations, the judgment is apportioned into periodic payments, but in most cases the full value of the judgment is due in cash.

The judgment entered in a case is final unless an affected party can convince the appeals court that it should be reversed or modified because of legal errors. A common request is that a large judgment be reduced (*remitted*) as being unsupported by the facts. In most states, the judge who tried the case has the right to order that the plaintiff take less money than the jury has awarded. If the plaintiff refuses, the judge can order that the case be retried. When a case is accepted for review by a higher court, the attorneys prepare detailed legal analyses of the alleged errors in the case. They must also provide the appeals court with a transcript of some or all of the trial testimony. This transcript can cost $10,000 or more,

making an appeal an expensive proposition. The losing party must usually post a bond in the amount of the verdict. In some cases, the defendant cannot get such a bond and thus cannot appeal the case. Appeals also take time—usually two or more years. For these reasons, plaintiffs often agree to settle a case for less than the jury award if the case is accepted for appeal.

If the defendant does not pay the judgment, the plaintiff may levy on (have the sheriff seize) such of the defendant's property as is necessary to pay the judgment. What may be seized is a matter of state law. In addition, in some states, the plaintiff may be able to attach a part of the defendant's earnings to pay the judgment. If the defendant is unable to pay the judgment he or she may declare bankruptcy. In this event, the bankruptcy court apportions the defendant's nonexempt assets (those subject to sale to pay creditors) as determined by state and federal law. When the bankruptcy is complete, tort judgments are usually discharged. Bankruptcy is a harsh remedy, but it provides the ultimate control over tort judgments.

THE COST OF LITIGATION

Justice is expensive in the United States. Every citizen has the right to seek redress for his or her grievances in the courts. The problem is paying the bills. Lawyers' fees are typically $75 to $1,000 an hour, and associated costs can amount to tens or hundreds of thousands of dollars, depending on the nature of the case. In the criminal justice system, where successful plaintiffs only get their freedom and the government only pays a small amount toward the defense of indigent persons, access to the best criminal defense in a serious case is restricted to the very rich and a very few high profile cases, such as the Oklahoma bombing defendants.

A medical malpractice trial can take one to six weeks. A trial of a complex business case frequently takes months; some have gone on for more than a year. Trials cost each party $2,000 a day and up, depending on the number of attorneys representing the party. Expert witnesses' fees and expenses can add another $2,000 to $3,000 a day for every day or part of a day that the witness must be in court. For parties paying their own lawyers, a trial can be so expensive that any victory will be Pyrrhic. For plaintiffs represented on contingency contracts, a trial increases the expenses that they must pay out of any money they receive, but it is their attorneys who bear the major expense of the trial. The time, expense, and uncertainty of a trial is the major justification for the 30% to 50% of the award that a contingent fee client must give up to the attorney. Even defendants represented by counsel paid by an insurance company can lose large amounts of money because of the business they lose while tied up in the trial.

Although the insurance company pays all of the direct costs of the trial and these costs do not directly raise the defendant's insurance premium, they must be recouped from all of those insured in the defendant's insurance pool, including the defendant. Defense costs are a major factor in the decision to settle any lawsuit. An insured defendant may want to fight a case on principle, but it is usually a bad business decision to spend $150,000 to fight a case that could be settled for $25,000, if the defendant was negligent.

The most disturbing consequence of trial costs is that they allow a very well-funded party to punish an opponent, irrespective of the merits of the case. A wealthy surgeon can use litigation to force colleagues on a peer review panel to back down from limiting his or her privileges. A tobacco company can devote unlimited resources to fighting persons who sue for injuries caused by smoking.

Contingent Fees

Except for large businesses and wealthy individuals, most potential plaintiffs do not have the money to pay the costs associated with litigation. There are third-party payers in law, but they are insurance companies, which usually limit their payments to defense lawyers. Since few people have the resources to hire an attorney on an hourly basis, persons with valid personal injury claims would be denied their day in court if this were the only payment system. This would be an injustice.

The solution adopted in the United States is the contingent fee contract. In this arrangement, attorneys take a percentage of the winnings as their fee. The clients make their claims, the attorneys have a chance to earn a fee, and the contingency aspect gives attorneys added incentive to work hard for their clients.

If the lawyer works for a contingent fee, the fee must cover three costs of litigation. The first is the out-of-pocket costs and the salaries for the support personnel in the lawyer's office. Out-of-pocket costs include filing fees, court reporters, expert witness fees, copying charges, and payments for other goods and services necessary to prosecute a case. The second is the value of the attorney's time. In a contested malpractice case, the attorney may invest hundreds of hours of work that will never be paid for if the suit is unsuccessful. The third component is economic value of accepting the uncertainty and delay in litigation.

The contingent fee contract provides that the fees will be paid out of the money received from the defendant when a case is won or settled. Most contracts also provide that the attorney will loan the client the money to pay the out-of-pocket expenses of the case. Although the money for these expenses is styled as a loan, few attorneys attempt to collect it from the client if the recovery is less than the expenses in the case. The attorney's fee is based on a percentage of the gross recovery, without regard to the number of hours actually worked on the case. The fees are typically staged—perhaps 33% if the case is settled without filing a lawsuit, 40% after a lawsuit is filed, and 45% if the case must be defended on appeal. Most cases are settled after the filing of a lawsuit but before the rendering of a judgment by a court. Under this schedule, the attorney would receive 40% of the settlement and would be reimbursed for expenses out of the client's share.

Problems with Contingent Fees

Contingent fees are unfair because plaintiffs are not allowed to recover the cost of the fee from the defendant—that is, add the fee to the judgment awarded. Plaintiffs must prove the economic worth of their injuries. In a simple case, this might be the extra medical bills and lost wages incurred as a result of the negligence. If these total $20,000 and there are no other alleged injuries, then the jury will be limited to awarding $20,000. Approximately half of that will go to paying the attorney and the costs of the litigation. Therefore, the purpose of tort law—to make the plaintiff "whole" by compensating him or her for the losses due to the defendant's negligence—is not fulfilled. The plaintiff is able to recover 50% of the actual losses because the defendant does not have to pay the plaintiff's attorney's fees and costs of court. The problem of recovering litigation costs drives many of the claims for imaginative damages.

Contingent fees create an incentive to exaggerate the plaintiff's damages, and they encourage the filing and prosecution of cases with large damages but little negligence. Take the case of parents who come to the attorney's office with a brain-damaged child requiring custodial care. The potential recovery is so large that it is worth searching for any possible negligence to justify a lawsuit. Conversely, contingent fees deny access to the courts to plaintiffs with meritorious claims but low damages. Every plaintiff's medical malpractice lawyer has turned away cases in which the patient was injured by clear, even gross, negligence, but the potential recovery was too small to cover the cost of litigation. In general, if the provable damages are not in excess of $100,000, it does not make economic sense for an attorney to take the case.

In both law and medicine, it is ethically questionable to stop providing services to a client because the client cannot afford the fee. In criminal cases, the courts make it nearly impossible for an attorney to withdraw once representation has begun. As a result, criminal attorneys demand fees, which are nonrefundable, in advance. (There is also the problem of collecting from the incarcerated client.) In civil lawsuits, it is difficult to withdraw after the lawsuit has been filed. Ideally, every case will be investigated before a lawsuit has been filed. The problem is that the defense often refuses to cooperate in the investigation of a case. The plaintiff's attorney must decide whether to sue based on limited information. This encourages the filing of a case with large damages in the hopes that liability can be found as the case proceeds. For an attorney, this is the most ethically responsible step. Refusing to represent the client because the defense makes it difficult to investigate the case would compromise the client's rights.

Many state legislatures are capping the fees of plaintiffs' attorneys,[13] typically in two ways: sliding scale caps and limits on the percentage that the attorney may charge. In the sliding scale system, the fees that the attorney may charge for small cases—those under $100,000—are unaffected. Using the previous example, in a case settled before trial, the attorney would get 40% ($40,000) and be reimbursed for expenses (perhaps $5,000). As the award increases, the allowable fee, as a percentage of the award, is diminished, falling to perhaps 10% of the proceeds over $1 million. This type of cap does not affect the initial decision to accept the case; rather, it encourages the attorney to settle the case at a discount. After a certain point in the history of a case, it acquires a settlement value. In the traditional contingent fee contract, the attorney is provided an incentive to continue to invest work and money to raise that settlement value. With a sliding scale cap, the reduced reward for increasing the value from, say, $900,000 to $1 million may not offset the work involved.

Limiting the percentage of an award that the attorney may claim as a fee affects the litigation process in a different way. Capping the percentage charged (perhaps at 25%) raises the threshold value for accepting a case. A case that was profitable at 40% (of $100,000) would have to be worth $160,000 to yield the same fee at 25%. It has been argued that sliding scale caps prevent attorneys from gaining windfalls. Percentage caps, however, serve only to deny access to the courts.

Costs in Other Countries

The European countries, Canada, and the United Kingdom allow only limited contingent fees. They have little medical malpractice litigation as compared with the United States, and little personal injury litigation of any type. It is assumed that the limitation on contingent fees is responsible for the dearth of litigation. This underlies the call by many physicians and others to limit or abolish contingent fees in the United States. Although it is true that contingent fees are necessary to ensure that most individual plaintiffs have access to the courts, the important question is why other counties have not adopted contingent fees. The answer is that there is a quid pro quo for this lawsuit-free climate.

In the medical context, other developed countries are less dependent on litigation because their citizens have some level of guaranteed access to medical care and rehabilitation services. In the United Kingdom, for example, the National Health Service provides medical services without regard to the cause of the injuries or the patient's personal financial status. Other social welfare agencies help with disability relief. Therefore, there is no need for patients to sue to force negligent third parties to pay for the cost of their injuries. The disciplining of physicians is separate from compensating the plaintiff. A physician found to be incompetent is struck off the register rather than incurring a large litigation loss that will ultimately be paid by the other physicians in the same insurance pool.

In the United States, patients are responsible for their own medical bills and rehabilitation services. Many persons have medical insurance through their employers, but a substantial number do not. Moreover, this employment-based insurance is lost if the patient's injuries interfere with his or her ability to do the job. Politically, it is easier to leave compensation to an entrepreneurial law system rather than to address the problems of an incomplete medical care delivery system.

EMOTIONAL RISKS OF A TRIAL

Health care practitioners who are criminal defendants are usually facing imprisonment and professional ruin. This is understandably stressful. Yet physicians being sued for medical malpractice (most cases are still against physicians),

where the odds of wining are 60% to 80% if the case goes to trial, are also affected. Even when they lose, their insurance company nearly always pays the settlement. Considering these odds in their favor, physicians should view a trial with some equanimity. Most do not. Some have even committed suicide before their cases came to trial.

One of the roots of this fear is the belief that the physician's personal worth, rather than the quality of the medical care, is on trial. Most physicians believe that being found guilty of malpractice is a moral judgment equivalent to being found guilty of a crime. This belief partly reflects a misunderstanding of civil law. One is not found guilty of malpractice; one is only found liable to pay money for the injuries attributable to the malpractice.

More fundamentally, though, it reflects the correct perception that trials are about people, not actions. Although every case must meet technical legal requirements—otherwise the judge will not allow the case to go to the jury—the plaintiff must do more than present evidence on the technical elements of the case. The critical issue is that the jury must be persuaded to rule for the plaintiff.

Persuading the jury to agree with the client is the heart of the trial lawyer's art. Facts are sometimes persuasive on their own, but usually it is their presentation that is critical. Creating empathy for one's client is critical to successful litigation. (This is true even in business litigation, where the legal questions may be complex and the actual injured party a faceless corporation.) Lawyers want to focus on people rather than legal technicalities.

The best example of this technique is the case of *Texaco, Inc. v. Pennzoil Co.*,[14] whose $10 billion verdict is the largest in U.S. history. The legal issue in this case was whether, and when, a contract to sell a company was formed. The damages were the loss of the value of the contract by Pennzoil, a large corporation. The beneficiary of the contract was Texaco, another large corporation. The plaintiff's attorney (representing Pennzoil) presented the necessary technical evidence on the contract questions, but he persuaded the jury to give his client money by personalizing the case.

He was able to vest the corporate identity of Pennzoil in its chairman, ostensibly a lovable Texas businessman. Texaco was identified with its New York investment bankers. The defense exacerbated its problems by rebutting the plaintiff's presentation of a human drama with dry financial and legal niceties. The verdict was achieved through trying the personalities in the case as much as trying their actions.

Attacking the Defendant

To prevail in a medical malpractice trial, the plaintiff's attorney must convince the jury that the plaintiff is more deserving than the defendant. Ideally, this would be done by building up the plaintiff; practically, it always involves some level of attack on the defendant. The plaintiff must provide testimony that the defendant's actions were below the acceptable standard of care (see Chapter 6). This in itself is a morally loaded accusation. The defendant's justification for his or her behavior affects the level of personal attack necessary for the plaintiff's case.

The most important consideration in assessing the strategy in a medical malpractice case is that physicians are held in high esteem in the community. Physicians win most malpractice cases that are tried because of this community respect. If the plaintiff maligns a physician whom the jury respects, the jury will be more difficult to persuade on the factual issues of the case. Conversely, if the plaintiff can successfully undermine the jury's confidence in the defendant, the defendant will suffer from the jury members' implicit comparison with their idealized notion of physicians.

These considerations also apply to attacks on the plaintiff. Attacks on the plaintiff's technical case can defeat the plaintiff entirely. Attacks on the plaintiff's character can reduce the potential damages in the case by lowering the value that the jury puts on the plaintiff's future earnings and so forth. Attacks on the plaintiff's character, if believed, can also reduce the credibility of the plaintiff's expert witnesses. Although the testimony of witnesses should be seen as independent of the character of the plaintiff, if the plaintiff is not credible, it will be assumed that his or her witnesses are not credible either. There are plaintiffs (and defendants) whose personalities destroy their cases, irrespective of the underlying merits.

Surviving a Trial

The more a party knows about what is happening at the trial, the easier it is to stay intellectually involved. An informed client, particularly a defendant in a medical malpractice case, is also an asset to the attorney. The client can assist with the review and organization of records, the evaluation of witnesses, the analysis of testimony, and other tasks that require special knowledge of medicine or the facts of the case. In addition to the advantage that this gives the physician's attorney, it reduces the anxiety associated with litigation by reducing the uncertainty.

Despite the salutary value of becoming a partner in their litigation, few physicians involve themselves in the preparation of their cases. There are several reasons for this lack of involvement. If the attorney is being paid by the insurance company, the physician has no short-term financial incentive to assist in the case. The attorney will hire the necessary personnel to prepare the case and bill the insurance carrier. Even when physicians are paying their own legal bills, it is unusual for an attorney to explain the potential benefits that might accrue if the client assists in the case.

Attorneys cannot completely control the progress of a case through the courts. For example, an attorney may work diligently at setting the depositions in a case. If all the witnesses are available, the case can proceed; if a witness is not available, it may delay the case for months. Whenever an attorney files a motion with the court requesting action from opposing counsel, the opposing counsel has 10 to 60 days to reply. Ideally for the client, the attorney will push the case forward at every opportunity. The reality of law practice is that attorneys work on so many cases simultaneously that they cannot push every one forward. This differential attention helps level out the work flow in the attorney's office, but it slows the resolution of each case. In the worst situation, the attorney becomes reactive, only responding to actions by the court or opposing counsel. If opposing counsel on the case is also in a reactive mode, the case can languish for years.

All attorneys share the problem of getting good expert witnesses and help with the preparation of cases. Even when experts are available, they are expensive and time consuming to deal with. Few clients, insurance companies included, are willing to hire an expert witness to do more than testify in a case. Attorneys in medical malpractice cases often get by with the help of nurses and their own expertise. But even attorneys with medical degrees find that there is not enough time to be both a good lawyer and a good doctor.

REFERENCES

1. *Gaither v. City Hosp., Inc.*, 487 S.E.2d 901 (W. Va. 1997).
2. *United States v. Salerno*, 481 U.S. 739 (1987).
3. *Brady v. Maryland*, 373 U.S. 83 (1963).
4. *United States v. Clark*, 928 F.2d 733, 738 (6th Cir. 1991).
5. *United States v. Bagley*, 473 U.S. 667, 682 (1985).
6. Huber PW. *Galileo's Revenge: Junk Science in the Courtroom*. New York: Basic Books;1991.
7. Federal Rules of Evidence Rule 104, 28 U.S.C.A.
8. *Frye v. United States*, 293 F. 1013, 1014 (App. D.C. Dec. 03, 1923).
9. *The T.J. Hooper*, 60 F.2d 737 (C.C.A.2 1932).
10. *Daubert v. Merrell Dow Pharm., Inc.*, 509 U.S. 579 (1993).
11. Federal Rules of Evidence Rule 702, 28 U.S.C.A.
12. *Moore v. Ashland Chemical Inc.*, 151 F.3d 269 (5th Cir. [Tex.] 1998).
13. Birnholz RM. The validity and propriety of contingent fee controls. UCLA Law Rev. 1990;37:949.
14. *Texaco, Inc. v. Pennzoil Co.*, 729 S.W.2d 768, 822 (Tex.App.—Houston [1st Dist.] 1987, *writ ref'd* n.r.e.).

SUGGESTED READINGS

Aksu MN. Expert witness or "hired gun?". *J Am Coll Dent.* 1997;64:25–28.
Allen AM. The nurse and the deposition. *Orthop Nurs.* 1987;6:50–51.
American Psychiatric Association resource document on peer review of expert testimony. *J Am Acad Psychiatry Law.* 1997;25:359–373.
Annas GJ. Medicine, death, and the criminal law. *N Engl J Med.* 1995;333:527–530.
Beckman HB, Markakis KM, Suchman AL, Frankel RM. The doctor–patient relationship and malpractice: lessons from plaintiff depositions. *Arch Intern Med.* 1994;154:1365–1370.
Berlin L. On being an expert witness. *AJR.* 1997;168:607–610.
Bertin JE, Henifin MS. Science, law, and the search for truth in the courtroom: lessons from Daubert v. Merrell Dow. *J Law Med Ethics.* 1994;22:6–20.
Black B. Subpoenas and science—when lawyers force their way into the laboratory. *N Engl J Med.* 1997;336:725–727.
Black E. What to expect at your deposition: a guide for physicians and health care professionals. *Pa Med.* 1998;101:24.
Blake BL. Sgt. Friday, Dr. Welby, and the demand for patient information: what to do when the police knock. *Mo Med.* 1998;95:567–573.
Boyarsky S. Practical measures to reduce medical expert witness bias. *J Forensic Sci.* 1989;34:1259–1265.
Brennan TA, Leape LL, Laird NM, et al. Incidence of adverse events and negligence in hospitalized patients: results of the Harvard Medical Practice Study I. *N Engl J Med.* 1991;324:370–376.
Brent RL. Bringing scholarship to the courtroom: the Daubert decision and its impact on the Teratology Society. *Teratology.* 1995;52:247–251.
Breyer S. The interdependence of science and law. *Science.* 1998;280:537–538.
Carter R. The subpoena: coping with the anxiety and stress. *NY State Dent J.* 1997;63:16–17.
Clifford R. Deposition abstracts provide insights into personal injury cases. *Natl Med Leg J.* 1997;8:4.
Craft K, McBride A. Pharmacist–patient privilege, confidentiality, and legally-mandated counseling: a legal review. *J Am Pharm Assoc (Wash).* 1998;38:374–378.
Francisco CJ. Confidentiality, privilege, and release of medical records under a subpoena duces tecum. *Tex Med.* 1991;87:34–35.
Gilbert JL, Whitworth RL, Ollanik SA, Hare FH Jr. Evidence destruction—legal consequences of spoliation of records. *Leg Med.* 1994:181–200.
Hood RD. Some considerations for the expert witness in cases involving birth defects. *Reprod Toxicol.* 1994;8:269–273.
Hupert N, Lawthers AG, Brennan TA, Peterson LM. Processing the tort deterrent signal: a qualitative study. *Soc Sci Med.* 1996;43:1–11.

Karp D. Deposition preparedness is essential to malpractice defense: experienced defense attorneys offer advice for physicians. *Mich Med*. 1994;93:27–29.

Kern SI. Responding to subpoenas and other demands for records and testimony. *NJ Med*. 1996;93:85–88.

Licata LJ, Allison TH. Subpoenas for medical records served upon physicians. *Ohio Med*. 1989;85:48–51.

Lindauer C. The video deposition—"you are the witness". *Natl Med Leg J*. 1990;1:7–8.

Localio AR, Lawthers AG, Brennan TA, et al. Relation between malpractice claims and adverse events due to negligence: results of the Harvard Medical Practice Study III. *N Engl J Med*. 1991;325:245–251.

Mandell MS. 10 legal safeguards for giving a deposition. *Nurs Life*. 1988;8:50–51.

McAbee GN. Improper expert medical testimony: existing and proposed mechanisms of oversight. *J Leg Med*. 1998;19:257–272.

Meadow W, Lantos JD. Expert testimony, legal reasoning, and justice: the case for adopting a data-based standard of care in allegations of medical negligence in the NICU. *Clin Perinatol*. 1996;23:583–595.

Millock PJ. The Harvard Medical Malpractice Study and the malpractice debate in New York State. *Leg Med*. 1991:111–125.

Neoral L. Forensic medicine, its tasks and duties in medical malpractice and medico–legal litigation. *Med Law*. 1998;17:283–286.

Perry C. Admissibility and per se exclusion of hypnotically elicited recall in American courts of law. *Int J Clin Exp Hypn*. 1997;45:266–279.

Peters BM, Rosenbloom AG. The physician's deposition: preparation and testimony of the medical malpractice defendant. *Pediatr Emerg Care*. 1987;3:194–201.

Plunkett LR. Anatomy of a dental malpractice case: subpoenas and confidentiality. *NY State Dent J*. 1997;63:8–11.

Purnell L. What to do if called upon to testify. *Accid Emerg Nurs*. 1995;3:19–21.

Rappeport JR. Effective courtroom testimony. *Psychiatr Q*. 1992;63:303–317.

Reed ME. Daubert and the breast implant litigation: how is the judiciary addressing the science? *Plast Reconstr Surg*. 1997;100:1322–1326.

Richards EP, Walter C. Science in the Supreme Court: round two. *IEEE Eng Med Biol Mag*. 1998;17:124–125.

Rosenbaum JT. Lessons from litigation over silicone breast implants: a call for activism by scientists. *Science*. 1997;276:1524–1525.

Smith RH, Griffin M Jr. A keep-your-cool guide to giving a deposition. *RN*. 1988;51:77–79.

Stinson V, Devenport JL, Cutler BL, Kravitz DA. How effective is the motion-to-suppress safeguard? Judges' perceptions of the suggestiveness and fairness of biased lineup procedures. *J Appl Psych*. 1997;82:211–220.

Strasburger LH, Gutheil TG, Brodsky A. On wearing two hats: role conflict in serving as both psychotherapist and expert witness. *Am J Psychiatry*. 1997;154:448–456.

Tammelleo AD. Nurse asks "Should I get a lawyer"? *Regan Rep Nurs Law*. 1994;35:1.

Ventura MJ. Are these nurses criminals? *RN*. 1997;60:26–29.

Walter C, Richards EP. Keeping junk science out of the courtroom. *IEEE Eng Med Biol Mag*. 1998;17:78–81.

Walter C, Richards EP. The social responsibility of scientists: the scientific impact statement. *IEEE Eng Med Biol Mag*. 1998;17:94–95.

Weirich AM. The deposition. *Home Health Nurse*. 1996;14:876–877.

Zonana H. Daubert v. Merrell Dow Pharmaceuticals: a new standard for scientific evidence in the courts? *Bull Am Acad Psychiatry Law*. 1994;22:309–325.

APPENDIX 5–A

Guidelines for Expert Witness Testimony in Medical Liability Cases

American Academy of Pediatrics Committee on Medical Liability

The American Academy of Pediatrics joins with other medical organizations in emphasizing the obligation of objectivity when its members respond to requests to serve as expert witnesses in the judicial system. Regardless of the source of the request, such testimony ought to embody the relevant facts and the expert's knowledge, experience, and best judgment regarding the case. At the same time, the Academy reiterates that it cannot condone participation of its members in legal actions in which their testimony will impugn some performances that clearly fall within the accepted standards of practice or, conversely, will endorse some obviously deficient practices.

The role of an expert witness in a medical liability case is to testify to the standards of care in a given case, and to explain how the defendant did or did not conform to those standards. An expert witness may be asked to testify as to whether a deviation from the standard of care caused the injury. Expert witnesses are also called upon to help

an attorney determine if a case has merit, and in several states attorneys are required by law to consult an expert before a suit is filed. Because experts are relied upon to help courts and juries understand the "standards of practice" as applicable to a given case, care must be exercised that such "expert testimony" does not narrowly reflect the experts' views about applicable standards to the exclusion of other acceptable and perhaps more realistic choices. The standards of care for generalists may not necessarily be the standards of care for subspecialists. The Academy considers it unethical for any expert to provide testimony that does not adhere scrupulously to the goal of objectivity.

The Academy also recognizes its responsibility and that of its Fellows for continued efforts to improve health care for children. However, some claims of medical malpractice may represent the response of our society to a technologically advanced form of health care that has, unfortunately,

Acknowledgment: The Committee on Medical Liability gratefully acknowledges the contributions of the American College of Obstetricians and Gynecologists (Ethical Issues Related to Expert Testimony by Obstetricians and Gynecologists) and the Council of Medical Specialty Societies (Statement on Qualifications and Guidelines for the Physician Expert Witness) in the development of this policy statement.

Note: The recommendations in this statement do not indicate an exclusive course of treatment or serve as a standard of medical care. Variations, taking into account individual circumstances, may be appropriate. PEDIATRICS (ISSN 0031 4005). Copyright © 1994 by the American Academy of Pediatrics.

Source: Reprinted with permission from Guidelines for Expert Witness Testimony in Medical Liability Cases, *Pediatrics*, Vol. 94, No. 5, pp. 755–756, © 1994, American Academy of Pediatrics.

fostered some unrealistic expectations. As technology continues to become more complex, risks as well as benefits continue and sometimes increase, making the practice of medicine more and more complicated.

Under such circumstances, it becomes most important to distinguish between "medical maloccurrence" and "medical malpractice."[1] "Medical malpractice," according to *Black's Law Dictionary*,[1(p864)] is defined as follows:

> In medical malpractice litigation, negligence is the predominant theory of liability. In order to recover from negligent malpractice, the plaintiff must establish the following elements: (1) the existence of the physician's duty to the plaintiff, usually based upon the existence of the physician-patient relationship; (2) the applicable standard of care and its violation; (3) a compensable injury; and (4) a causal connection between the violation of the standard of care and the harm complained of.

In contrast, medical maloccurrence is a less-than-ideal outcome of medical care, which may or may not be related to the reasonableness of the quality of care provided. Whereas a medical maloccurrence is always present in cases of malpractice, the converse is not true. Certain medical or surgical complications can be anticipated and represent unavoidable effects or complications of disease. Still other unavoidable complications arise unpredictably for the individual patient. Of course, others occur as a result of judgments and decisions carefully made by physicians and patients with informed consent but that turn out, in retrospect, to have been the least desirable of several options considered. Each of these situations represents maloccurrence rather than malpractice and is a reflection of the innate uncertainty inherent in medicine.

The potential for personal satisfaction, professional recognition, or financial reward appears to encourage "expert testimony" that overlooks the distinction between a simple maloccurrence and actual malpractice. The Academy considers it unethical for an expert to distort or misrepresent a maloccurrence in which the applicable standard of care was not violated as an example of medical malpractice—or the converse.

The Academy supports the concept of appropriate, prompt compensation to patients for injuries due to medical negligence. Under the present legal, insurance, and social tenets, such remuneration is sometimes made for medical maloccurrence in which no malpractice is present, on the assumption that the larger society should bear financial responsibility for such injuries.

The moral and legal duty of physicians to testify as called upon in a court of law in accordance with their expertise is recognized and supported. This duty implies adherence to the strictest ethics. Truthfulness is essential and misrepresentation or exaggeration of clinical facts or opinion to attempt to establish an absolute right or wrong may be harmful, both to the individual parties involved and to the profession as a whole. Furthermore, the acceptance of fees that are disproportionate to those customary for such professional endeavors is improper as the payment of such fees may be construed as attempting to influence testimony given by a witness.

The 1992 opinion of the American Medical Association on Medical Testimony states as follows:

> As a citizen and as a professional with special training and experience, the physician has an ethical obligation to assist in the administration of justice. If a patient who has a legal claim requests a physician's assistance, the physician should furnish medical evidence, with the patient's consent, in order to secure the patient's legal rights.
>
> The medical witness must not become an advocate or a partisan in the legal proceeding. The medical witness should be adequately prepared and should testify honestly and truthfully. The attorney for the party who calls the physician as a witness should be informed of all favorable and unfavorable information developed by the physician's evaluation of the case. It is unethical for a physician to accept compensation that is contingent upon the outcome of litigation.[2(p46)]

The Academy encourages the development of policies and standards for expert testimony. Such policies should embody safeguards to promote the accuracy and thoroughness of the testimony and efforts to encourage peer review of the testimony.

The following principles have been adopted as guidelines for the American Academy of Pediatrics and its members who assume the role of expert witness:

1. The physician should have current experience and ongoing knowledge about the areas of clinical medicine in which he or she is testifying and familiarity with practices during the time and place of the episode being considered as well as the circumstances surrounding the occurrence.
2. The physician's review of medical facts should be thorough, fair, objective, and impartial and should not exclude any relevant information in order to create a perspective favoring either the plaintiff or the defendant. The ideal measure for objectivity and fairness is a willingness to prepare testimony that could be presented unchanged for use by either the plaintiff or defendant.
3. The physician's testimony should reflect an evaluation of performance in light of generally accepted standards, neither condemning performance that clearly falls within generally accepted practice standards nor endorsing or condoning performance that clearly falls outside accepted practice standards.
4. The physician should make a clear distinction between medical malpractice and medical maloccurrence, which is not the result of a violation of the applicant standard of care when analyzing any case. The practice

of medicine remains a mixture of art and science; the scientific component is a dynamic and changing one based to a large extent on concepts of probability rather than absolute certainty.

5. The physician should make every effort to assess the relationship between the alleged substandard practice and the patient's outcome, because deviation from a practice standard is not always the cause of the less-than-ideal outcome at issue in the case.
6. The physician should be willing to submit transcripts of depositions and/or courtroom testimony for peer review.
7. The physician expert should cooperate with any reasonable efforts undertaken by the courts or by plaintiffs' or defendants' carriers and attorneys to provide a better understanding of the expert witness issue.
8. It is unethical for a physician to accept compensation that is contingent upon the outcome of the litigation.

Committee on Medical Liability, 1993 to 1994

Bradford P. Cohn, MD, Chairperson
Jan Ellen Berger, MD
Ian R. Holzman, MD
Jean Lockhart, MD
Mark Reuben, MD
William O. Robertson, MD
Steven Selbst, MD

Consultant

Holly Myers, Esq

REFERENCES

1. *Black's Law Dictionary.* 6th ed. St. Paul, MN: West Publishing Co; 1990.

2. Current Opinions of the Council on Ethical and Judicial Affairs of the American Medical Association. Chicago: American Medical Association; 1992.

SUGGESTED READINGS

Ackerman AB. The physician expert witness: Is peer review needed? *Generics.* 1985;37–52.

Brennan TR. Untangling causation issues in law and medicine: Hazardous substance litigation. *Ann Intern Med.* 1987;107: 741–747.

Brent RL. The irresponsible expert witness: A failure of bio-medical graduate education and professional accountability. *Pediatrics*. 1982;70:754–762.

Dyer C. Judge "not satisfied" that whooping cough vaccine causes permanent brain damage. *Br Med J*. 1988;296:1189–1190.

Ethical Issues Related to Expert Testimony by Obstetricians and Gynecologists. American College of Obstetricians and Gynecologists; 1987.

Fish R, Rosen P. Physicians should be expert witnesses. *J Emerg Med*. 1990;8:659–663.

Higgins LC. MD (medical director) witnesses: who are these experts? *Med World News*. 1988;29:28–36.

Lundberg GD. Expert witness for whom? *JAMA*. 1984;252:251.

Miller D. Courtroom science and standards of proof. *Lancet*. 1987;2:1283–1284.

Robertson WO. *Expert Witness Controversies in Medical Malpractice: A Preventive Approach*. Seattle, WA: University of Washington Press; 1985:124–136.

Robertson WO. Some 'experts' may not be all that expert. *WSMA Rep*. June 1988:4.

Statement on Qualifications and Guidelines for the Physician Expert Witness. Council of Medical Specialty Societies; 1989.

CHAPTER 6

The Law and Lawyers

HIGHLIGHTS

- Health care practitioners have many legal relationships.
- The attorney–client relationship is fundamentally different from the physician–patient relationship.
- Few attorneys are experts in all aspects of medical care law.
- Health care practitioners must learn to be active participants in managing their own legal problems.
- Legal clients must request preventive law if they want more than symptomatic treatment for their legal problems.

INTRODUCTION

Health care practitioners must understand the basics of the law if they are to avoid legal problems. They do not need to become lawyers, or to understand the law in the same way that lawyers understand the law. In some narrow areas, such as Medicare reimbursement, they must know more law than all but the most specialized health care lawyers do. In most areas, health care practitioners just need a well-informed layperson's knowledge of the law as it regards medical practice in general and their practice area in specific. The goal is not to have health care practitioners act as lawyers. They should be able to recognize when there is a potential legal problem and whether they need expert legal advice to manage the problem.

This chapter introduces the basic legal relationships involved with providing health care services. These are important to understanding the subsequent materials because legal rights and duties depend on the context of the legal relationship between the parties. For example, the legal rela-

tionship between a physician and a nurse depends on whether the physician employs the nurse, whether the physician and the nurse are employed by the same corporation, whether they have separate employers, and, if so, on the legal relationships between their employers.

Health care practitioners must also understand how to work with lawyers. As professions, law and medicine share many characteristics: the expectation of confidentiality; a fiduciary duty to put the client/patient's interests first; and a concern with matters of great personal and societal importance. The professional norms of law and medicine are very different, however, and health care practitioners must understand this difference if they are to work successfully with lawyers. These are introduced in this chapter, and discussed more specifically in later chapters.

LEGAL RELATIONSHIPS

In health care, the basic legal relationships are between health care practitioners and patients, between individual health care practitioners, between individual professionals and their employers or contractors, and between health care practitioners and the state. Some legal rules apply equally to all relationships; others depend on the particulars of the relationship. The rules that apply equally to all persons—business law, constitutional rights, criminal law, and family law—define the civic role of citizens of society, as well as the specific roles of health care practitioners.

Health care delivery involves several types of legal relationships. While most of these relationships can involve any licensed health care practitioners, the legal rules that govern them are often dependent on the practitioner's license and specific training, with different rules for physicians and midlevel practitioners, or between medical specialties. For example, in many circumstances the law gives patients broader rights of privacy in their records of psychiatric care than in general medical care records. Health care practitioners must be aware of the general rules on legal relationships and which rules differ, based on the status of the specific practitioner. The first step is understanding the general classes of legal relationships that all health care practitioners share.

The State

The fundamental legal relationship is between health care practitioners and the state and federal governments. In the United States, most of the law governing medical practice and general health care delivery, exclusive of payment issues, is state law. All health care practitioner licenses are issued by the states, rather than by the federal government. State laws define the practice of medicine and nursing, who can write prescriptions, the supervision requirements for nonphysician practitioners, and the other parameters that establish the bounds of health care delivery. These laws are subject to any applicable federal mandates, such as the special restrictions on controlled substance prescriptions, or requirements tied to reimbursement for care paid for with federal funds. While the state regulation and licensing of health care practitioners is taken for granted, there is no legal

principle that would prevent a state from allowing a layperson to practice medicine.

Health care practitioners owe the state certain duties in return for the right to their professional licenses: the duty to protect the public health through various reporting and recordkeeping functions, the duty to practice competently and within the constraints established by the state laws, and the duty to help ensure that other health care practitioners maintain proper standards of practice.

Patients

The physician–patient relationship arises from state statutes and common law rules and is the model for the legal rules governing the relationship between other health care practitioners and patients. The courts recognize some form of special relationship between midlevel practitioners and patients, and even between hospitals and patients, but the legal dimensions of these relationships are usually less extensive than those of the physician–patient relationship. The doctrine of informed consent and the patient's rights movement have increased the rights of patients in the practitioner–patient relationship. At the same time, the special nature of the relationship is under pressure from medical businesses and third-party payers who seek to influence the decisions of health care practitioners.

Other Practitioners

Health care practitioners, especially physicians, work with other practitioners in three roles: as colleagues, supervisors, and competitors. These roles have become more important as health care delivery moves from the small private physician's offices to managed and team care settings. As supervisors, practitioners must comply with same workplace laws and regulations as supervisors in non–health care businesses, while also dealing with the issues that are unique to health care delivery. These include the duty to consult with other practitioners when it is necessary for a patient's welfare, the duty to ensure that subordinates and other team members deliver good medical care, and that state and federal law and regulations are followed.

Physician-Owned Businesses

Historically, most states have limited the ability of physicians to work as employees of hospitals or other businesses that are not controlled by physician owners. Until recently, this meant that physicians tended to work as solo practitioners, in small groups, or for physician-owned clinics. These businesses employ both physicians and other personnel to aid in the practice of medicine. These persons are protected by the usual business laws governing the employer–employee relationship. In addition, they pose some special legal problems related to medical licensure, the supervision of personnel, and antitrust considerations.

Physicians often employ nonphysician medical personnel, such as nurses, laboratory technicians, physician's assistants, and respiratory therapists. As employers, the physicians assume both the general employers' vicarious liability for the acts of its employees, and the special duties of supervision of medical personnel that are imposed by state and federal law. They must be concerned with the appropriate level of delegation for medical care services provided in their offices. Physician–employers must also recognize that while physicians are licensed to perform all medical services, they are often not as skilled as the midlevel practitioners in many routine procedures.

Finally, physicians must compete fairly with other physicians, resisting the temptation to use quality-of-care issues as a cover for anticompetitive activities. This has become a major area of legal conflict as medical practice has become more competitive. The United States has traditionally valued free enterprise and has strict laws governing attempts to restrict competition. Physicians must balance the need to preserve good quality medical care against the policy of allowing the market to regulate business activities.

Corporate Employers and Institutions

The great majority of midlevel providers are employees. Most physicians now become employees as they enter practice, and many of the older private practices have been sold and their owners have also become employees. Health care practitioners may work for hospitals and clinics providing medical services to the general public, in the medical departments of nonmedical businesses providing occupational and general medical care to the other employees, or in governmental institutions such as prisons and schools. They are subject to the same rules as other professional employees. This means that while the employer can set the general workplace rules, the employer may not require health care practitioner employees to violate the terms of their license or to violate professional norms of practice.

While some physicians now work as employees of hospitals, most physicians who practice at hospitals are independent contractors whose relationship with the hospital is governed by the medical staff bylaws. The effect of this contract is to ensure that the nonemployee physician is subject to the rules of the institution. Many managed care companies use this same model for their relationships with physicians. These contracts pose difficult legal issues. They may impinge on the physician's professional decision making and may limit the patient's right to information or alternative treatments. Since the physician is not an employee, there are few protections available if the contract is terminated because the physician is unwilling to comply with improper practices.

WORKING WITH LAWYERS

Medicine and law are uncomfortable bedfellows. Traditionally, it was the acrimonious nature of medical malpractice litigation that shaped the views of health care practitioners toward law and lawyers. Now this is mixed with the hostility they feel toward government agency regulators who are often seen as making reimbursement and facility management overly complex. More fundamentally, the professions are similar in that both deal with intensely personal and life-affecting matters, but very different in their professional paradigms. This leads to tension whenever they come into conflict, and requires considerable effort for health care practitioners and attorneys to work together. The result of this uneasy relationship is that health care practitioners do not make effective use of legal services and take unnecessary legal risks. On the legal side, attorneys often give advice that does not properly address the special nature of medical practice.

These issues must be managed if health care practitioners are to take full advantage of legal advice and to enjoy the full confidentiality protections of the attorney–client relationship. This chapter discusses several issues that make it more difficult for health care practitioners and attorneys to work together, and provides guidance on resolving these issues.

CLASH OF CULTURES

Law and medicine are both learned, licensed professions, practiced by demographically similar individuals. Each profession has a well-developed paradigm that governs the relationship between independent professionals and their clients. The attorney–client relationship shares many characteristics with the physician–patient relationship: attorneys have special education and experience not possessed by clients; attorneys have a license that allow them to perform tasks that a layperson may not perform; attorneys must keep clients' matters confidential; and attorneys owe clients a special duty to put clients' interests before their own interests (a fiduciary duty). It is these shared values that lead health care practitioners to assume that attorneys deal with clients' needs in the same way as they do. This is not a correct assumption. The attorney–client relationship is profoundly different from the physician–patient relationship. This difference can lead to hostility and dangerous misunderstandings between health care practitioners and attorneys.

The key difference between legal and medical relationships is that law is not based on a scientific paradigm. There have been efforts to bring social science and economic analysis techniques to bear on legal problems, but these have been of limited utility. The evolution of legal theory is a nonrational social process that most resembles religious disputation. One accepts a premise and then develops an intricate set of rules and theories based on that premise. We see Marxist-based legal systems, democratic-based legal systems, and legal systems such as Islamic law that are openly derived from religious beliefs. Understanding law and lawyers requires an appreciation of legal belief systems, as well as the statutes and cases.

Paternalism in Medicine

Paternalism has become a politically unpopular word because of its association with physicians telling patients what is good for them, without regard to the patient's own needs and interests. This limited sense of paternalism is improper and has been obviated by informed consent requirements. In the larger sense, however, the relationship between health care practitioners and patients is a paternalistic, beneficent relationship: the health care practitioners are expected to do what is medically best for the patient. While that might even include assisted suicide in an extreme case, it never includes improper medical care given only because the patient requests it. Despite the importance of patient involvement and informed consent, health care practitioners are expected to do what is best for their patients. In certain public health situations, they are also expected to consider what is best for society, even if that may not be in the best interests of the patient.

The courts' skepticism in cases in which patients allegedly make an informed choice of medically improper treatment highlights the expectation that physicians will offer patients only the choice of medically proper and indicated treatments. This reflects a general societal consensus on what constitutes acceptable medical care. In most cases, physicians, patients, and society agree on the desired outcome and the appropriate spectrum of treatments to accomplish that outcome. While this is not meant to minimize the very real conflicts between physicians and patients, debates over contentious issues such as abortion, right to die, and entrepreneurial medical practice tend to obscure the congruence of interests that define the vast majority of patient care.

Attorneys and Autonomy

The attorney–client relationship, in contrast, is based on autonomy rather than paternalism. Law is an adversarial process with many areas in which there is no clear societal consensus on the correct role of the attorney. Respecting a person's autonomy can mean protecting a mentally ill homeless person's right to freeze under a bridge or the right of a person to refuse simple, life-saving medical care. Short of helping clients commit crimes, attorneys are expected to advocate their clients' wishes zealously, not limit their services to those that are good for the client. Unlike health care practitioners, attorneys have only a very limited role in controlling the impact of their client's actions on society.

Beyond this philosophical prejudice toward client autonomy, traditional codes of legal ethics limited the attorney's obligation to do the legal equivalent of a complete history and physical. These ethical codes created the *limited engagement doctrine*. The limited engagement defined the attorney's role as providing the specific legal services sought by the client. In its strictest form, the limited engagement doctrine prohibited the attorney from asking the client about other potential legal problems. This prohibition was intended to prevent barratry, the stirring up of litigation. Such a prohibition was beneficial to attorneys because it greatly limited their liability for legal misdiagnosis. Given that it is difficult to police barratry prohibitions, the limited engagement served to limit attorneys' liability without greatly limiting their ability to stir up litigation.

If the physician–patient relationship was a limited engagement, a physician might prescribe cough medicine to a coughing patient without inquiring into the underlying cause of the cough—ethically and legally proper care under the traditional standard of the limited engagement. The physician–patient relationship is not a limited engagement because the physician is ethically bound to consider the patient's overall medical needs. An attorney held to the standards that govern the physician–patient relationship would be required to do a legal checkup on clients to ensure

that the services requested by the client were appropriate for the client's total legal health.

The limited engagement is beginning to erode for both business and professional reasons. For example, severe tax consequences of divorce are so pervasive that it is considered unprofessional not to counsel divorce clients about tax problems. This benefits the client and generates an opportunity to deliver additional legal services. In most areas of law, however, the client cannot assume that the attorney will inquire into hidden but related legal problems. Since the law has not developed a comprehensive doctrine of informed consent, the attorney is not required to inform the client of the implications of the limited engagement. A physician seeking legal services must be sure that the attorney addresses the underlying legal disease rather than just providing symptomatic treatment.

LEGAL EDUCATION

The Limitations of Legal Education

Unlike the combination of medical school and residency, most law schools do not prepare graduates for the practice of law. Becoming skillful at a learned profession requires both technical knowledge and judgment, which take time and practice to develop. The problem is the short duration of law school and the absence of a legal equivalent to medical residency training. There are no prerequisites for law school admission, beyond a college degree in any subject. Law school training is usually three years, excluding summers. If the school offers a summer program, it is possible to finish in just over two years. In contrast, medical students are expected to take some medical science–related courses before medical school. Most medical schools are four years, including all but one summer, making basic medical education almost twice as long as legal education. Graduates must then complete at least one more year of residence training before licensure in most states, and the vast majority goes on for several more years of specialty training. Law students get the "basic sciences" and a smattering of classroom-based "clinical education." They get almost no intensive, problem-oriented clinical experience. The parallel would be licensing physicians and putting them into unsupervised practice after the basic science phase of medical school. Even law schools with extensive clinical education programs expose law students to clients with only simple legal problems.

This model of education is based on the assumption that law school graduates will go to work for large law firms who will train the new lawyers and supervise their work. It is not clear that this was ever valid for the majority of law school graduates, but it is certainly not true now. Even the big firms no longer have significant, supervised in-house training. While law schools are aware of the problem and are seeking ways to correct it, any changes will take years to implement. This is partially due to the inertia that affects all higher education, and partly due to the lack of incentives from the community to profoundly change legal education.

Pitfalls in On-the-Job Legal Education

Health care practitioners, especially physicians, must learn their skills on their patients. The first several years of this training are done in formal education programs where the hospital or other institution pays the student as an employee to take care of patients as part of their training. The patients are supposed to be notified that they are being examined and treated by students, and most programs do inform them. The care is supervised and signed off by staff physicians who are expert in the area. The federal government pays most of the costs of this training. The patients, or the government on their behalf, pay the costs for the care, but this is generally limited to the work performed by the attending physicians, not the student. If the resident does not know how to do a procedure, the patient is not charged extra for time needed to train the resident. After formal clinical training, physicians and other health care practitioners, like all professionals, must continue learning on the job. The cost of this training is amortized over all the patients treated. No individual patient is

charged extra because the physician spends an hour reading a journal article about his or her disease, or bought a new reference text. There may even be a duty to inform the patient if the practitioner is trying a new technique in which he or she is not skilled.

Attorneys, however, charge each client for the time the attorney spends learning about the law governing the client's problem. Attorneys working in an area of law new to them not only have no duty to warn the client; they may be paid extra for the additional time needed to research this unfamiliar area. Attorneys working in an unfamiliar area spend time researching irrelevant issues, miss important issues, and have difficulty in translating legal research into useful legal advice. Once it is accepted that clients should pay for educating senior attorneys, then it is a logical extension to expect clients to pay for educating junior attorneys. Thus, the client's financial advantage of hiring an attorney expert in a particular problem often evaporates. The client may get the advantage of the senior attorney's judgment but have to pay junior attorneys to duplicate this knowledge. In the worst case, the client pays the junior attorneys to learn judgment and there is no expert senior attorney supervising the work.

A more fundamental problem is that law has only limited formal specialty certification boards and no formal specialty training analogous to medical residency training. Attorneys are deemed specialists because they have worked in the area for some time, or because they happen to work for a law firm that has the reputation of having expertise in a given area of law. There is no credentialing process by legal institutions in the way physicians have to be credentialed to ensure their competence. This makes it difficult for a client to ensure that an attorney is really expert in an area such as health law.

Choosing an Attorney

There are law firms that do a lot of health care work, who have expert attorneys on staff, and who only have those attorneys work on health care matters. There are also law firms who do a lot of health law work that have limited expert staff and who allow unskilled attorneys to work on complex health law matters, sometimes with little effective supervision. There are even law firms that claim to do health law work, who have no expertise and plan to learn as they go along, on the client's tab. Size is no guide. If anything, the conflicts of interest in a large firm representing many health care competitors can be more problematic than the lack of expertise in a smaller firm.

Personal friendships, club memberships, and financial success are no better (or worse) a measure of attorney competence than they are of physician competence. Physician clients must try to determine their attorneys' general competence, as well as their expertise in the specific legal problem at issue. Clients should inquire into the attorney's experience in the problem area. They should pay attention to how effectively the attorney questions them about their legal affairs. If the attorney does not appear knowledgeable, the client must question the attorney's experience in the area. For example, if the problem involves a medical joint venture, it is important that the attorney ask about the impact of this venture on professional decision making and referrals. If the arrangement might create a conflict of interest with certain patients, the specific constraints that the state imposes on the physician–patient relationship should be discussed in the interview.

HOW TO APPROACH THE LAW AND LAWYERS

Where law once had little day-to-day impact on medical practice, law now permeates every corner of medical care and affects all health care practitioners. The penalties have also changed. Not long ago most medical legal issues just involved a medical malpractice claim. Now providers can face huge, uninsured civil fines and even jail time. Health care practitioners now accept that patients should learn about their diseases and treatments. This facilitates more effective informed consent and makes patients more effective partners in their own care. It is common to find patients with chronic conditions who know more about their

diseases than most physicians. Health care practitioners must adopt this same attitude themselves about the law.

Just as patients need not become doctors or nurses to take some responsibility for the management of their medical conditions, a health care practitioner need not know as much as an attorney about law in general. However, it is critical to know how to recognize and avoid the legal problems that are specific to the professional's own practice. This is a different type of knowledge than that of the attorney. Just as one does not need to know how to work on a car to avoid hitting a jay-walking pedestrian, one does not need to understand the nuances of antitrust law to avoid illegal conversations at the local medical society meetings.

Preventive Law

There are two fundamentally different ways to approach law. One is to deal with legal problems as they arise. A classic example is the defense of medical malpractice litigation. The first the physician thinks about the lawsuit is when he or she is served with the plaintiff's complaint or notice of a claim. At that point the physician engages a defense lawyer, usually through the physician's medical malpractice insurance carrier. This approach deals with "cold facts," facts that have already happened and cannot be changed. The law must be fit around these facts. If it does not fit, the physician loses.

The alternative is called preventive law. Preventive law, like preventive medicine, is based on preventing problems before they arise. This is called dealing with "hot facts," facts that have not yet arisen and thus can be changed. A simple preventive law example is a consent form for medical treatment. The consent form serves both to reduce the chance of patient injury (being denied adequate information) and to help prevent legal disputes by clearly establishing what information the patient was given. Properly kept medical records serve many preventive law functions. They help prevent medical malpractice litigation by documenting the patient's condition and treatment. They provide protection against false claims prosecutions by providing the documentation necessary to substantiate claims for payment from Medicare.

The key to preventive law in health care is integrating the law into the health care practitioner's routine practice. This requires that the health care practitioner learn some legal basics about day-to-day care. These basics will solve many of the first line legal problems that arise and will help the practitioner know when to get expert legal advice. A preventive law approach has always made good business sense. It is now a federal requirement for hospitals that receive Medicare/Medicaid funds. As discussed in Chapter 5, the Conditions for Participation for the Medicare program now require hospitals and certain other providers to have a "compliance" program to ensure that the hospital and all affiliated providers comply with the laws governing receipt of federal health care funds. These compliance plans are classic preventive law plans.

The Hazards of Ignoring Legal Risks

All health care practitioners know the value of the early detection of chronic medical problems. Whether it is cancer or hypertension, the prognosis is usually better when the disease is dealt with earlier, rather than later. Many legal problems also become more severe and difficult to treat with time. A current example is federal prosecutions for Medicare/Medicaid fraud and abuse. Many hospitals, medical schools, and health care practitioners have found themselves facing huge fines and potential criminal prosecution for not complying with federal reimbursement rules. In most cases, these problems arise from business arrangements or practices that were clearly in violation of the law, and had been for many years. Yet the legality of the practices was not questioned because federal enforcement was very lax. Providers and their lawyers assumed that since "everyone" was doing it and very few people were being prosecuted, that they did not need to worry about the legal liability.

This all changed in the mid-1990s, when the Office of Inspector General (OIG) at the Depart-

ment of Health and Human Services (DHHS) and the Department of Justice (DOJ) began to enforce these laws. Suddenly targeted institutions were faced with multimillion-dollar fines and individuals were facing prison. The worst shock came when institutions and individuals realized that they were liable for things they had done up to six years before. This is an example of the legal problem of pipelining: the accumulation of legal liability for past improper actions. Pipelining usually becomes an issue when there is some change in the legal system. For fraud and abuse, the pipeline was created when the federal government shifted from very lax enforcement policy to a very aggressive one. Sometimes pipelining results when otherwise hidden legal risks come to light because of lawsuits or adverse media coverage. A large, well-publicized jury verdict or settlement will cause attorneys to look for more cases against the defendant, perhaps uncovering substantial additional liability. Again, in the false claims area, once the first plaintiffs had been awarded multimillion-dollar fees for bringing false claims lawsuits, attorneys started looking for these claims and employees who had not been able to get their institutions to adopt proper claims practices now had attorneys eager to file a lawsuit on their behalf.

CONFLICTS OF INTEREST

Exercising independent legal judgment requires an objective detachment from the client's interests. This objectivity may be compromised by financial or personal conflicts. Conflicts of interest are usually thought of as limited to situations in which an attorney attempts to represent parties with conflicting interests in the same piece of litigation, such as both parties in a divorce. Attorneys usually avoid such obvious conflicts. The more common problems are conflicts with other clients in other matters, conflicts between clients who seemingly have the same interests, and conflicts between the attorney's own interests and those of the client.

Another problem is that attorneys often identify with health care professional clients. They have common educational backgrounds, interests, and sometimes even friends, especially in smaller communities. Because of this identification, the attorney may not evaluate the physician's legal problems objectively. This loss of objectivity can hurt the client in many ways. The attorney may not investigate the physician's recitation of the facts diligently or appreciate how a jury will view the physician's actions. These misperceptions increase the risk of poor legal advice. Just as physicians are cautioned about treating their close friends and family members, so should physicians take care to ensure that their attorneys are objective.

Doing Business with Your Clients

Whenever a client is in a business venture with an attorney, there is potential for confusion of roles. If the attorney acts only as a businessperson, there is no conflict of interest. However, if the attorney also provides legal services or makes legal decisions, there is a conflict with the other participants in the venture. It is not unusual for attorneys to be partners or shareholders in business ventures in which the attorney also provides legal advice. The attorney may be an investor as well as counsel, or he or she may provide legal services as his or her contribution to the venture.

As long as the interests of all of the participants are the same, this conflict will not be a problem. But in most ventures, the interests of the participants are not the same. It is best if the legal work for the business is done by an attorney who has no financial or other interest in the business. If this is impractical, the nonattorney participants should have an uninvolved separate attorney review the basic business documents. They should also consult with their personal attorney whenever there are changes in the business organization.

Conflicts with Other Clients

Attorneys who represent clients with adverse interests eventually will be forced to compromise the interests of at least one of the clients. This is a particular problem in legal specialty areas such as

medical law. There are advantages to the client in hiring a law firm that has experience in the problems at hand. In medical law, this often means a law firm with experience in representing health care providers. Twenty years ago, there were few conflicts between medical clients. Now, with the competition between hospitals and between individual physicians, it is important to ask the identity of the law firm's other health care clients. (This is not privileged information.) If the law firm represents real or potential competitors, it is best to hire a different law firm. Sometimes it is impossible to find another law firm with the appropriate expertise. It is then up to the law firm and the client to discuss the potential conflicts and establish a plan for avoiding them. This is especially important in medical malpractice defense.

Medical Malpractice Defense

In most medical malpractice cases, the physician is insured. A condition of this insurance is that the insurance company pays for the defense of a case. This benefits the insurance company because it is mostly its money that is at risk. It benefits the physician because attorneys are expensive, and a principal reason for buying insurance is that it pays defense costs. The problem is that the defense attorney represents the insurance company, not the physician. This becomes obvious when the potential recovery is substantially larger than the coverage provided by the insurance policy. If the insurance company misjudges the case, the physician also pays. The physician can also suffer if the insurer wants to settle a case to reduce their risk, but the physician did not commit malpractice. This may be a valid business decision for the insurer, but it can hurt the physician because it must be reported to the National Practitioner Databank. In these situations, physicians should retain their own attorneys to ensure that the insurance company protects their interests as well as its own.

The most serious potential for conflict arises in self-insurance trusts administered by hospital or other health care employers. Even when these trusts are properly constituted and supervised, they have limited assets. This is most serious in smaller facilities and single hospital trusts. Since the medical malpractice litigation risk for hospitals and their employees and physicians is not independent—factors such as adverse publicity increases everyone's risk of being sued—there is a chance that the plan will go broke, leaving the insured without coverage. If the plan is not properly organized, the risk of insolvency is much greater because of the temptation to use the funds for other purposes when the institution is in financial trouble. In some cases the health care practitioner's interests and that of the employer conflict, such as when the health care practitioner is a whistleblower who was attempting to prevent the patient's injury. In these situations, the employer may use threats of termination of coverage to coerce or punish the insured. Even when the pressure is not direct, the employer is often a big client of the defense firm and the firm cannot avoid pressure to favor the employer over the insured when there are conflicts. Ideally, health care practitioners should have their own insurance rather than being tied to an employer-controlled plan. If this is not possible, and the health care practitioner suspects a conflict, it is a good idea to hire a private attorney to monitor the defense counsel.

In-House Counsel

In-house counsel try to serve the interests of the institution and of the individuals in that institution. They will do their best to protect everyone associated with the institution who is not involved in wrongdoing. However, when there is a conflict, in-house counsel only have one client: the institution that employs them. While there is some learned debate on what this means in the context of the CEO, the board of directors, and the stockholders, for everyone else it is clear that the hospital or health care institution's attorney does not represent their interests. Thus a nurse interviewed about an incident by the hospital counsel could not claim attorney client privilege for the information given the attorney, even if the attorney was going to use it in a way that harms the nurse. The nurse must also be aware that the attorney's advice is intended to protect the institution, not his or her interests, if they conflict with the institution's interests.

With the growth of criminal law investigations and prosecutions in health care, the conflict between health care practitioners and in-house counsel becomes much more serious. As discussed in Chapter 5, attorney–client privilege is much more important in criminal matters than in civil cases. If a health care practitioner is concerned about being the target of a criminal investigation, he or she should get a personal attorney, rather than relying on in-house counsel.

PAYING FOR LEGAL SERVICES

As professionals, physicians and attorneys charge for the exercise of professional judgment. Most physicians charge based on procedures and patient encounters. These tend to be fixed charges that are independent of either the results or the time actually spent on the procedure. Some physicians, such as anesthesiologists, have charges that are related to the time spent with the patient. Physicians also charge for services performed by their staff. Physicians record their diagnoses and procedures in complex, standardized notations. Physicians throughout the world use the standard taxonomy for medical diagnoses, the ICD-9 (international classification of disease, revision 9). In the United States, physicians use the American Medical Association's current procedural terminology (CPT) system to classify medical procedures.

In contrast to physicians, attorneys do not have any standardized system for billing, for keeping records, or for describing legal work and legal diagnoses. Without such a formal structure, it is difficult for clients to track and manage legal services. It is also very difficult to audit legal records for either quality assurance (QA) or to ensure that the charges were necessary and proper. From the client's perspective, the absence of a standard procedure code for legal procedures is more noticeable than the lack of a standard diagnostic code. While attorneys' hourly bills may be intricately detailed, they are seldom comparable among law firms or even from attorney to attorney in the same law firm. This lack of standardization prevents clients from comparing their legal services with those rendered to other clients and makes it impossible to relate the billing entries to the progress of the client's case.

Plaintiff's attorneys usually work on a contingent fee. Fixed fees are used in certain routine matters such as divorces and in most criminal defense cases. Criminal attorneys also demand the fee in advance, since unsuccessful clients have little incentive to pay the attorney's fees. Attorney's fees range from $75 to $400 per hour, with certain specialists charging up to $1,000 an hour. Within a large law firm, the younger, less experienced attorneys are billed at a lower rate than the senior members of the firm. Nonattorney support personnel are also billed on an hourly basis. These may include nurses, physicians, engineers, certified public accountants, and other nonattorney professionals whose expertise is necessary for the proper preparation of a case. They also include law students and paralegals who work on client matters. The client is billed for every minute that law firm personnel spend on activities related to the client's case. If an attorney does the work, the client pays the attorney's hourly rate. It does not matter that the attorney is doing work that does not require the exercise of legal judgment. The rates are the same for solving a difficult analytical issue, making telephone calls to schedule a deposition, or organizing the papers in a file.

Lawyers working on a contingency do not charge the client an hourly rate, but they do pass on the expenses of the case. Attorneys working for an hourly rate pass all expenses through to the client, in addition to the charges for their time. These expenses range from a few dollars for photocopying and messenger charges to expert witness fees in the thousands of dollars. The client sometimes pays the bills directly, although in most cases, the law firm includes the expenses with the professional services bill. The client pays the aggregate charges, and the law firm pays the outside vendors. Expenses in a simple collection matter may be $100. Expenses in the defense of a medical malpractice case may be $30,000 or more. Ex-

penses in a complex antitrust case can run to millions of dollars, plus tens of millions in attorney's fees.

Legal Bills

The attorney bills the client for each increment of time the attorney spends on the case. Since law does not have standardized diagnoses or procedures, the delineation of these increments may seem arbitrary, and they may not appear to match the tasks that must be completed to solve the client's problem. Attorneys bill the client based on the physical task the attorney performs: charges for talking on the telephone, reading documents, traveling, reading cases, and the other physical things attorneys do. It is as if a carpenter charged by how long he or she pounded nails, sawed boards, climbed ladders, and so forth. If you have hired this carpenter to remodel your house, knowing how long he or she spends on each carpenter task does not tell you whether the stair is finished and how much work remains on the kitchen.

When a client reads an attorney's bill, he or she may not care how much time the attorney spent doing research, talking on the telephone, and so forth. The client wants to know how the course of the legal work has been furthered by the work he or she is being asked to pay for. Ideally, he or she would pay the attorney progress payments, in the same way that he or she would pay the carpenter. This analogy breaks down, however, because attorneys expect clients to pay them for learning their trade, as well as completing the client's work.

Chronological Billing

Most attorneys bill chronologically rather than aggregating the charges for a given task. As attorneys work, they fill out time slips that document the client, the task, the attorney, and the time spent on the task since the last time slip was completed. Assume that the attorney is reviewing your file:

- Looking at the correspondence (*review correspondence—.25 hr.*).
- Making three telephone calls in response to the correspondence (*phone call, Sara*

Smith—.25 hr.; phone call, Jack Jones—.25 hr.; phone call—Dr. Alexander—.25 hr.).
- Looking over the pleadings (*review pleading—.25 hr.*).
- Dictating a motion (*prepare motion—.25 hr.*).
- Reading an article on the use of thermography to see if it would help in your case (*research—.5 hr.*).
- Spending a few minutes rearranging the papers (*reorganize file—.25 hr.*).

This single work session generates eight billing entries, most of which are for the law firm's minimum billing increment, a quarter-hour. None of these entries is of value in determining the status of the case.

Legal bills also fail to give the client proper information on the cost of the discrete elements of the case. The information is in the bills, but it is just not aggregated in time. Assume that you want to know the cost of a deposition. The monthly charges for a deposition might resemble the following:

May

- Telephone conference with an expert: 1 May—.5 hr.
- Research on the factual issues: 15 May—.75 hr.
- Research on the factual issues: 21 May—1.5 hr.
- Phone calls to schedule the deposition: 30 May—.25 hr.

June

- Research on the factual issues: 30 June—1.0 hr.
- Phone calls to schedule the deposition: 10 June—.25 hr.

July

- Research on the factual issues: 12 July—.5 hr.
- Research on the factual issues: 14 July—.75 hr.

- Phone calls to schedule the deposition: 13 July—.5 hr.

August

- Research on the factual issues: 1 August—.5 hr.
- Review the file before the deposition: 21 August—2.5 hr.

September

- Predeposition client conference: 10 September—2.0 hr.
- Travel to deposition: 11 September—3.5 hr.
- Take deposition: 11 September—5.5 hr.
- Return from deposition: 12 September—3.5 hr.

October

- Summarize deposition: 10 October—1.5 hr. (paralegal).

November

- Court reporter's bill: 10 November—$637.00.
- Charge for airline tickets: 12 November—$560.00.
- Charge for hotel room and meals: 12 November—$150.00.
- Review deposition summary: 30 November—1.0 hr.

This deposition accounts for 20 billing entries spread over seven monthly bills. If this is a typical litigation case, these seven bills may each have 150 other entries. It would easily take an hour to locate and tabulate the entries for this single deposition. It would be impossible to tabulate them in most bills because the individual entries do not reference the deposition that they are associated with. Importantly, each monthly bill has had more charges for the deposition. The client has no way to know how long these charges will go on.

Legal Practice Styles

Legal fees are determined by the amount of time spent on the client's problem. Ideally, the amount of time is a function of the complexity of the client's problem. However, an important secondary determinant, which can account for 50% or more of the fee in a case, is the practice style of the law firm. Law firms have a powerful incentive to generate hourly billings.

Clients should be especially wary of "wolf packing," which occurs when the law firm assigns more than one attorney to the same piece of work. This is most obvious when several attorneys attend the same meeting or court hearing. It is less obvious when the client is billed for conferencing by several different attorneys, when the conference is actually a firm meeting. The client should ask the attorney to explain which additional firm members may be involved in the case and their specific expertise. If possible, the client should be introduced to everyone who will work on the case, including the paralegals.

A more controversial practice is the padding of hours. For example, an attorney who is supposedly being paid by the hour will charge for drafting a document that is actually printed up by a secretary from a form file. He or she may charge, say, 5 hours for a piece of work that takes only 30 minutes. This practice is justified as amortizing the cost of the work over all the clients who benefit from it. Unlike traditional amortizing, the first client to request the work probably paid the full cost of drafting the document. Moreover, there is no time when the document is deemed fully amortized and becomes a free service to future clients.

"Dilatory practice" is the legal euphemism for wasting time. It occurs for a number of reasons: time may be wasted because a witness, or even the client, cannot be found or it may occur because of disorganization and a failure to do long-range planning. Plaintiffs' cases usually deteriorate with time. In the worst case, the plaintiff or a critical witness will die, making it difficult to try the case effectively. Unless there is a strategic reason for the delay, wasted time costs plaintiffs and their attorneys money.

In contrast, delay can be rewarding for defense attorneys. Defenses get stronger as time erodes the plaintiff's case. Death can transform a multi-million-dollar injured-baby case into a "dead baby" case worth very little. Witnesses disappear, lovable children turn into surly adolescents, and grieving widows remarry. The insurance company benefits from the delay if the cost of reinsuring the risk of the unpaid claim is less than the income they can earn on the money that will be needed to pay the claim. Defense lawyers personally benefit because delayed cases require constant maintenance, with the attendant opportunities to bill the client.

BEING AN EFFECTIVE CLIENT

Attorneys advise clients that contracts for services should be clear and specific about work to be done, how much it will cost, and how to resolve disputes if the client is dissatisfied with the services. Unfortunately, legal representation contracts are usually vague about charges and the work to be done. The legal client should require that the representation agreement provide the same information as any other contract for services: the work to be done and what it should cost.

An effective client must understand the dimensions of his or her legal problems and the specific tasks that must be performed. The attorney must teach the client about the legal problem just as the physician must teach patients enough about their medical problems to allow them to make informed decisions. Simple legal services do not require a lengthy explanation, but many legal services are complex, requiring months to years of work. These services may cost the client tens to hundreds of thousands of dollars. A client engaging an attorney for such a prolonged relationship is entitled to considerable detail about the strategy and progress of his or her case.

The client should ask the attorney to document the information the client is given about the case: the work to be done, who will do the work and their expertise, the billing rates for various personnel, and estimated costs of the different services to be performed. The client may want to ask the attorney to draw a diagram of all the steps in resolving the legal problem. This graphic display of the chronology is effective in eliminating uncertainty about what needs to be done. This diagram should be included in the client's documentation.

In addition to the traditional bill, the client should ask for a running total for each task outlined on the legal road map. For a deposition, each month's bill should include the total of all charges relating to the deposition that have been incurred to date. The bill should also group hourly charges for the deposition together rather than presenting all the hourly charges in chronological order. If the client's road map of the case includes the various steps in a deposition, the client can reconcile the road map with the bill each month.

PREVENTIVE LAW AND COMPLIANCE

Clients must specifically discuss whether they want the attorney to review their general legal situation. This process, called a *preventive law audit*, is meant to assess the client's legal condition in the same way that a history and physical examination is meant to assess a patient's medical condition. Preventive law audits have been a mainstay of environmental law for many years. If there is an allegation of criminal wrongdoing, such as an intentional violation of a dumping regulation, the presence of an effective preventive law plan can serve to mitigate the charges. While calling them compliance plans, rather than preventive law plans, the OIG has now mandated that health care providers institute preventive law audits for potential violations of federal health care regulations.

A preventive law audit has three goals: identifying mature, previously undetected legal problems; identifying legally risky situations; and identifying potential legal risks. The audit is usually performed by an attorney, and it requires the client's cooperation and participation. The client will have to provide partnership agreements, insurance policies, leases, and all other legal agreements, answer questions, and fill out legal audit forms. The result is the legal equivalent of a complete history and physical examination.

Undetected Legal Problems

These are situations in which the legal risk has already occurred but the client is not aware of the problem. This is what has been happening with Medicare/Medicaid fraud and antikickback prosecutions. While the law has been on the books for many years, it is only in the last 5 years that the government began enforcing the law (see Chapter 5). Many health care institutions and practitioners are involved with questionable practices that have been going on for years, which now pose significant legal risks. Detecting such problems is an unalloyed benefit because of the near certainty that the client's failure to comply will eventually be detected and penalized.

Legally Risky Situations

Some situations may result in legal problems in the future—for example, a partnership agreement that did not provide for an orderly dissolution if a partner dies. This is not a problem until the partner dies. Once the death occurs, it is difficult and expensive to remedy the problem.

When a legally risky situation is identified, the client must decide if the remedy is cost-effective. The incomplete partnership agreement would cost little to correct, and the benefit would be great. In cases in which the potential costs are both well known and small, it may be cheaper to accept the risk than to invest in a remedy. An example is the purchase of an inexpensive, easily replaced office machine. The warranty provisions of a sales contract for an adding machine may be ambiguous, but it is not worth the trouble to have an attorney redraft the contract.

Potential Future Risks

These are risks that may arise from changed circumstances. The client may get divorced, necessitating a new will. The law governing medical practice may change, necessitating changes in the office routine. It is impossible to anticipate all future problems. The objective of the legal audit is not to predict the future but to compile an inventory of the client's legal relationships. This inventory will help both the client and the attorney to recognize when they need to take action to protect the client's legal health.

Remedying Problems

The client may make an informed choice and decide not to remedy all of the legal problems that are detected, just as a patient may make an informed choice to forgo treatment for conditions detected in a general history and physical. However, once a legal problem has been identified, it becomes more dangerous to ignore. Conduct that was negligent when done unknowingly becomes intentional or reckless once the physician is notified that the behavior is questionable. This does not mean that ignorance is defensible. Health care practitioners who violate the law can be prosecuted irrespective of whether they know the specifics of the law that they break. The constitutional requirement is that the law be specific enough to define illegal behavior clearly, not that defendants personally know they are breaking the law.

CONFIDENTIALITY AND LEGAL PRIVILEGE

There is a strong public policy to encourage people and institutions to seek legal advice. In civil and regulatory matters it is assumed that legal advice will encourage them to be more law abiding. In criminal matters there is a constitutional right to counsel and any undue restrictions on the attorney–client relationship would violate that right. It is assumed that clients cannot work effectively with counsel unless their confidences are protected. Ten years ago, discussions of legal privilege in health care were centered around discovery of hospital incident reports and peer review records in civil litigation. While these are still significant issues, federal and state criminal prosecutions for health care fraud have made health care practitioners much more concerned with legal privilege as related to business records and compliance audits.

There are two types of legal privilege: the attorney–client communication privilege, and the attorney work product privilege. These provide varying amounts of protection, but they do not automatically attach just because an attorney is involved with a transaction. They depend on both the client's behavior and whether the attorney is acting as independent legal counsel.

Attorney Independence

Attorney independence is usually not an issue for attorneys in private practice representing clients in traditional litigation or transaction practice, unless the attorney is in business with the client, or becomes a participant in the client's wrongdoing. There is no protection if the court determines that the attorney–client relationship was a sham to conceal illegal activities involving the attorney. There has already been one case in which health care attorneys were indicted, along with their clients, for materially participating in the clients' alleged scheme to defraud the federal government. The physicians were accused of taking kickbacks to steer nursing home patients needing hospital care to hospitals that paid the physicians' bribes. These bribes were in the form of consulting fees pursuant to contractual agreements drawn up by counsel. The allegation was that the attorneys knew that these deals were illegal. This would mean that there would be no privilege between the accused attorneys and their clients.

Most questions about attorney independence involve in-house counsel. If the attorney is found to be acting as an administrator, rather than an attorney, there will be no privilege. The first step to preserving privilege for in-house attorneys is to ensure that they are licensed in the jurisdiction where they are giving advice. While there are circumstances were privilege might attach when the attorney is not properly licensed and not under the close supervision of a licensed attorney, these are unusual and would not apply to an in-house counsel who was not closely supervised as part of a legal department.

The possession of a license is not enough, however; the attorney also must be free to exercise independent legal judgment. The free exercise of independent judgment is a distinguishing characteristic of a professional. Whether it is certifying a bridge as sound, diagnosing an illness, or giving a legal opinion, only the person holding the appropriate license can legally make the professional decision. A corporation cannot hold a professional license; neither can an unlicensed individual practice a profession by employing a license holder to ratify the layman's decisions. These strictures apply equally to physicians and attorneys, although the nature of professional judgment is easier to define for physicians. Since hospitals constantly deal with the issue of independent judgment with regard to physicians' services, this situation will be used to illustrate the principle of free judgment.

The medical situation that is closest to the role of in-house counsel is that of a company physician. Despite the often-held belief that physicians cannot be employed by nonphysicians, most large corporations employ physicians to treat employment-related illnesses and manage employee health programs. The physician is employed to provide services as defined by the employer. The employer may tell the physician how many hours to spend seeing patients, or not to see patients at all. These are administrative decisions. The employer cannot tell the physician how to treat the patients that the physician does see. When seeing patients, the physician is exercising medical judgment, an area that the employer cannot infringe upon. In the same way, an attorney cannot let a nonattorney client dictate his or her decision making. To do so would be legal malpractice, and would forfeit privilege.

To preserve this independence, the head of a legal department, or, if there is just one in-house attorney, that attorney, must report to the CEO or to the board, rather than to a lower-level administrator. The attorney must be acting as an attorney, not just as an administrator with a law license.

Attorney–Client Privilege

The attorney–client privilege is the strongest legal privilege. It is limited to communications between attorney and client made as part of the attorney–client relationship. To be legally privileged, a communication must pass directly from one party to the other, and it must pass intentionally. It may be written, spoken, signed, or otherwise communicated. It extends only to the communication itself, it cannot be used to hide information that was not previously privileged. The privilege only prevents the court from forcing the attorney to testify. For example, if the client tells the same information to a friend as to the attorney, the friend may be forced to testify about the information. The privilege cannot be used to hide documents that were not prepared by the attorney, and it does not extend to physical evidence.

This example from criminal law will help illustrate the nature of a communication. One of the traditional privileges in criminal law is the protection of communications between husband and wife. This privilege is intended to preserve domestic relations. It prevents people from testifying about information they were told by their spouse. If a husband is told by his wife that she has been filing fraudulent Medicare claims, he may not testify if she is prosecuted for criminal Medicare fraud. However, if he actually watches her filling out fraudulent forms on their home computer, he may be compelled to testify as to his observations.

The only exception to the attorney–client privilege is the threat of future harm. The attorney may alert the police if the attorney believes the client is going to commit a crime that would endanger others. The state may also require attorneys to report child abuse and other public health problems, but few states do.

Attorney Work Product Doctrine

Attorney work product is the work that an attorney performs, other than communication with the client. Notes that the attorney prepares from a client interview would be related to the client communication and would be protected by the attorney–client privilege. An independent investigation that the attorney carries out for the client would not be a communication, but would be work product. The U.S. Supreme Court found that there would be privilege if the communications were sought or given in "anticipation of litigation," a term of art from a key case establishing the bounds of privilege for attorneys conducting an investigation of corporate behavior.[1] Anticipation of litigation is a broad umbrella. The threat of litigation need only be potential, not imminent. For example, a severe medication reaction would carry the potential of litigation. An investigation of a medication error could satisfy the criterion of anticipation of litigation. If the attorney directs the investigation, the information that is communicated to the attorney would be privileged, if it is not otherwise available to others.

The key distinction between attorney–client privilege and attorney work product involves whether the document in question contains information obtained from the client. The reason for making this distinction is that information protected by the attorney–client privilege is (almost) never available to discovery. Attorney work product is available, however, if the opposing party can show that justice would be denied if the work product was unavailable. For example, if an attorney made detailed summaries of important documents that then disappeared, the opposing counsel would be denied information about the contents of the documents if the work product was not available. In practice, the distinction between attorney work product and attorney–client communications is rarely of issue, judges tending to protect both equally.

Attorney as Witness

When the attorney acts as an administrator, the activities are neither attorney work product nor attorney–client communications. For example, assume that one of the duties of the attorney is to act as an intermediary between the patient and the physician, attempting to defuse the situation and prevent litigation. As part of this process, the attorney prepares a report for the hospital's medical staff committee. This report would not be an attorney–client communication because neither the patient nor the physician is a client. It would also not be attorney work product because the attorney would be acting as an administrator.

The most serious problem for the administrator/attorney arises in the inadvertent witnessing of an adverse incident. Just as the spouse who witnesses the fraud must testify, an attorney who becomes a fact witness cannot avoid testifying in a lawsuit. This can occur by observing a negligent act or by participating in a negligently conducted review process. The attorney may advise a review committee on the due process aspects of its work; but if the attorney takes part in the review process, the attorney may not protect communications from patients, physicians, and other nonclients, if they are not otherwise protected. In the same way, an attorney who routinely inspects equipment such as anesthesia machines could be called as a witness to the condition of the equipment.

The problem of too many administrative levels between the attorney and the person generating the sensitive information usually involves a nonattorney administrator who decides what information is passed on to the attorney. This is often a nonattorney "risk manager" who sends only "important" incident reports to the attorney. The problem is that the incident reports not sent to the attorney will be discoverable. The attorney cannot delegate legal decision making to the risk manager, nor can work involving the judgment of the risk manager be considered attorney work product.

Protecting Investigations

This example of an investigation of an incorrect medication incident illustrates the role the attorney must play to preserve legal protection for the process. (In many states there are specific statutes that will also make this information privileged.) Assume the risk manager is given an incident report that contains the patient's name, the nurse who gave the medication, the intended medication and its dosage, the medication actually given and its dosage, and the patient's reaction. The intended medication was a mild sleeping pill; the medication actually given was a powerful diuretic. The error was not noted at once but was detected only after the patient began to diurese at a very high rate and became unresponsive. The attending physician was notified, and the risk manager was immediately sent the incident report. The administrator realizes the possible severity of the mistake and decides that the incident must be investigated at once. It is important to get the facts while everyone's memory is fresh. Also, in an incident whose outcome is still unsettled, it is necessary to decide the hospital's position in dealing with the patient. The hospital may be able to mitigate the damages and avoid alienating the patient. If possible, the administrator would also like to protect the information developed by the investigation from being discovered by the plaintiff in a lawsuit.

For the results of the investigation to be protected from discovery, it must be clear that the investigation was conducted in anticipation of litigation and not as a part of normal recordkeeping. A good way to establish this distinction is to open a potential claims file on each incident that is investigated. This file should be sent to the hospital counsel when the investigation has been completed, or sooner if difficulties arise in completing the investigation. The administrator should also consult the attorney about whether a claim should be investigated. Standard investigation forms should be prepared to ensure that all pertinent information is collected. The use of such forms will provide evidence that the intent of the investigation was to prepare for a potential claim. If the incident results in serious injury, the potential claim file will be a valuable asset when the counsel becomes involved.

The actual investigation involves collecting all of the standard information required on the potential claims forms and getting statements from the parties to the incident. In our example, the investigation may show that the patient noticed that the medication "did not look right" and questioned the nurse about it, but the nurse ignored the complaint and gave the patient the medicine. This information should be put in the report of the investigation. This report is not discoverable, and the investigator cannot be personally asked about the contents of the report. The plaintiff can ask the nurse who gave the medication what was said. The nurse must answer the question truthfully, relating that the patient said that the medicine "did not look right."

It may not seem to matter whether the plaintiff gets the investigation report if the plaintiff is free to investigate the incident by directly questioning the nurses. While it is true that a well-prepared attorney who investigates the case carefully may find out the same information that the investigator finds, few attorneys are willing to devote the necessary time to carry out this type of investigation. It is also to the benefit of the investigator to collect information in a nondiscoverable form, because it encourages the cooperation of other staff members, especially physicians. The physician will be reluctant to help with an investigation if it could be discovered by the plaintiff's attorney, who may also be suing the physician.

Preserving Physical Evidence

A very important part of the investigation is preserving physical evidence. If the patient was injured by a defect in a piece of equipment, the proper party to sue may be the equipment manufacturer. The risk manager must be very careful to determine if the injury resulted from the design or construction of equipment rather than from an error by the hospital staff. Defective equipment can range from a multimillion-dollar X-ray therapy machine to a surgical needle. The entire hospital staff, both nursing and medical, should be carefully informed about the product liability issues in medical lawsuits. An extremely important part of any incident investigation is the recognition of risks that parties other than the health care providers are legally responsible for.

The modern hospital acts as both a nursing service and a medical supply house. The hospital supplies drugs, surgical equipment, diagnostic equipment, toilet tissue, and an enormous list of other items. In most cases, the hospital passes these items along to the patient without altering them from their manufactured state. There is not even much presterilization since the advent of disposable medical supplies. If an item that the hospital dispenses injures a patient, the hospital wants the patient to sue the manufacturer of that item rather than the hospital. If the patient does sue the hospital, the hospital should then sue the manufacturer for whatever damages the lawsuit causes the hospital to suffer. The investigator must ensure that the identity of the item that injured the patient is determined, and that the item is preserved for future testing and investigation. This should be part of the incident reporting process. The staff must be encouraged to save the defective item and any packaging material that has not been destroyed. These items should be sealed in clear plastic bags and carefully labeled as to the patient and the incident. The risk manager should immediately determine who the manufacturer is and check the remaining stock of the item for defects. The remaining units should be impounded and the manufacturer asked to replace them. It is very important not to allow a second patient to be injured by the same item. The first injury may be the manufacturer's fault, but the second injury will be the hospital's fault.

An incident involving a defective product should be brought to the attention of the hospital's counsel. While it may be possible to prevent the discovery of information about the defective product, such prevention is not desirable. The attorney may need to institute legal action against the product's manufacturer to protect the hospital's interests. The attorney may also want to cooperate with the patient's attorney. If the patient's attorney can sue the manufacturer of a defective product, that attorney will be more likely to settle with the hospital. This occurs because it is much simpler (and more lucrative) to litigate a defective product claim than a medical malpractice claim. To take advantage of this, the hospital must be prepared to share information with the patient's attorney. To make these types of action more effective, the quality control program must be coordinated with the hospital's purchasing program. The purchasing agent should know the manufacturer and distributor for each item that is purchased. The hospital must avoid purchasing items that have an unclear origin or are manufactured by a company against which it would be difficult to obtain a judgment. This may not be important for items such as tissue paper, but for items with great potential for harm, such as IV (intravenous) solutions or disposable needles it can be cheap insurance to pay a few cents more for an item from an established manufacturer. Even if the two products are equally good, it is to the hospital's benefit to have a responsible party to sue if there is a defect.

CONCLUSIONS

Health care practitioners must understand basic health care law to practice in the modern health care environment. Health care practitioners do not need to become lawyers, but they need to be able to recognize legal problems and triage them into those that they can manage themselves, those that need more detailed legal advice, and those that constitute legal emergencies. Law must be part of the routine practice of health care delivery, not just something that the lawyers do. Health care practitioners need to practice in ways that are consistent with their legal and ethical duties, and they need to create a culture that encourages others to do the same.

REFERENCE

1. *Upjohn Co. v. United States*, 449 U.S. 383 (1981).

SUGGESTED READINGS

Bahner TM, Gallion ML. Waiver of attorney–client privilege via issue injection: a call for uniformity. *Defense Counsel J.* 1998;65:199–207.

Ball FR. Corporate clients and the attorney–client privilege in Illinois state and federal courts. *Ill Bar J.* 1998;86:426–430.

Burman JM. The attorney work product privilege. *Wyo Lawyer.* 1996;19:15–17.

Cerven JM. Court extends attorney–client privilege to psychiatrist-client communications. *Ill State Bar Assoc.* 1995;83:598–600.

Dunson KC. I. The attorney–client privilege. *J Legal Prof.* 1996;20:231–238.

Flaming TH. Internet e-mail and the attorney–client privilege. *Ill State Bar Assoc.* 1997;85:183–184.

Floyd DH. A "delicate and difficult task": balancing the competing interests of federal rule of evidence 612, the work product doctrine, and the attorney–client privilege. *Buffalo Law Rev.* 1996;44:101–138.

Gruber HM. E-Mail: the attorney–client privilege applied. *George Washington Law Rev.* 1998;66:625–656.

Hardgrove JA. Scope of waiver of attorney–client privilege: articulating a standard that will afford guidance to courts. Board of Trustees of the University of Illinois. 1998;1998:643–681.

Hellerstein AK. A comprehensive survey of the attorney–client privilege and work product doctrine. *Practising Law Inst.* 1996;540:589.

Higgason RW. The attorney–client privilege in joint defense and common interest cases. *Houston Bar Assoc.* 1996;34:20.

Higgins AS. Professional responsibility—attorney–client privilege: are expectations of privacy reasonable for communications broadcast via cordless or cellular telephones? *Univ of Baltimore Law Rev.* 1995;24:273.

Hyland TW, Craig MH. Attorney–client privilege and work product doctrine in the corporate setting. *Int Assoc Defense Counsel.* 1995;62:553–563.

Jones E. Keeping client confidences: attorney–client privilege and work product doctrine in light of United States v. Adlman. *Pace Law Rev.* 1998;18:419–491.

Keeley M. The attorney–client privilege and work product doctrines: the boundaries of protected communications between insureds and insurers. *Tort Ins Law J.* 1998;33:1169–1199.

Libby, FA. Inadvertent waiver of the attorney–client privilege and work product doctrine in the first circuit. *Boston Bar Assoc.* 1997;41:16–17, 28.

Needham CA. When is an attorney acting as an attorney: the scope of attorney–client privilege as applied in corporate negotiations. *S Tex Law Rev.* 1997;38:681.

Rice PR. Attorney–client privilege: the eroding concept of confidentiality should be abolished. *Duke Law J.* 1998;47:853–898.

Sadler CM. The application of the attorney–client privilege to communications between lawyers within the same firm: evaluating United States v. Rowe. *Ariz State Law J.* 1998;30:859–873.

Scannell TJ. Attorney–client privilege-crime-fraud exception. *Mass Bar Assoc.* 1997;82:310–312.

Stephens WL Jr. Convenience vs. confidentiality: an evaluation of the effects of computer technology on the attorney–client privilege. *Duquesne Univ.* 1997;35:1011–1022.

Stevenson AMF. Making a wrong turn on the information superhighway: electronic mail, the attorney–client privilege and inadvertent disclosure. *Capital Univ Law Rev.* 1997;26:347–377.

Van Deusen MC. The attorney–client privilege for in-house counsel when negotiating contracts: a response to Georgia-Pacific Corp. v. GAF Roofing Manufacturing Corp. *William & Mary Law Rev.* 1998;39:1397–1439.

CHAPTER 7

Medical Records

HIGHLIGHTS

- Improper medical records can subject health care practitioners to civil and criminal liability.
- Medical records must meet federal standards for documentation.
- Even informal medical encounters should be documented.
- Patient confidentiality must be respected when releasing medical records.
- Medical records must never be altered or fabricated.

INTRODUCTION

Ten years ago there were two major legal issues in medical records management: how would the medical record be used in possible medical malpractice litigation; and who should have access to the record. These are still important issues, with access having become even more difficult a problem in the face of managed care and electronic records. A third problem has now arisen from the growing concern with insurance fraud: does the record contain the necessary information to justify the bill for services rendered, and to prove that they were provided by the appropriate health care practitioner. Failing to meet these standards can result in criminal prosecution, as well as substantial fines.

This chapter deals primarily with medical office records, rather than hospital records. Hospital records are governed and audited by many organizations, with the most common being the Joint Commission on Accreditation of Healthcare Organizations (Joint Commission). Most state laws and regulations also apply to hospital records. In contrast, relatively little attention has been paid to

medical office records, at least until the Office of the Inspector General (OIG) began to audit them as part of Medicare/Medicaid fraud prosecutions. With the increasing pressure to keep patients out of the hospital, and to do as much care as possible in the medical office, practitioner records contain the greatest share of modern medical information.

A HISTORICAL PERSPECTIVE

Medical recordkeeping evolved during the early part of the twentieth century, before there were health care delivery teams and free-floating hospital-based specialists. Physicians took care of their own patients, and patients generally had only one physician. When consultants were used, they consulted; they did not take over the care of the patient. Neither patients nor physicians moved very often, so the composition of the practice was stable. Physicians would know most of their patients by sight and would have some memory of their conditions. Office records served more as a reminder than as the only source of information about the patient and the patient's care. With a very limited pharmacopeia, and few outside services such as physical therapy or laboratory tests, there was much less to record.

Hospitals provided nursing, custodial, food, and hotel services. Nursing was low-technology patient care. Little laboratory work was performed, and the physician often participated in this work himself. The nurses, often nuns, were available night and day. They knew the patient's condition and needs, and they talked to the physicians. Medical records served as documentation but were not a primary vehicle for communication between health care providers. Simple narrative reporting was used because there were few events to record and little need for retrieving information from the record.

Health care has changed in two ways that dramatically altered the significance of medical office and clinic records. The most fundamental change has been the destruction of the traditional long-term physician–patient relationship. It is not unusual for patients to change primary care physicians every year, as their health insurer changes its panel of physicians. The patient may go for years without ever seeing the same physician for two different medical problems. The patient will be known by no physician, and the only information about the patient's medical care will be in the office records of several different physicians. In many cases, no one will have a complete record of the patient's care.

The second change is the growth of team care. A patient will have many health care providers caring for different medical problems, often on a one-time basis. In the past, either patients selected their own consultants, or these consultants were known to the patient's primary care physician, who made the referrals and coordinated the care. Now the panel of consultant physicians will be set by the patient's insurance plan, and the plan itself may make the referral. The primary care physician may get back a note from the consultant explaining the patient's treatment, or there may be no follow-up at all. In the hospital setting, nurses are now employees with regular shifts and multiple responsibilities, and many of them are agency nurses who move between different hospitals. There are many other technicians involved in pa-

tient care who provide services without the direct supervision of either the nursing department or the patient's physician. The medical record is now the basic vehicle for communication among members of the health care team.

These nonpatient care demands have distracted providers from the three primary uses for a medical record: (1) providing rapid access to recent information (about the patient's condition, laboratory tests, and drugs, for example); (2) ensuring continuity of care as responsibility for patient care shifts between different providers; and (3) as an audit tool to gauge the quality of medical care. These primary uses for medical records must not be sacrificed to facilitate secondary goals such as medical malpractice defense and billing.

LEGAL USES OF MEDICAL RECORDS

Medical records have an unusual legal status. They are health care practitioners' primary business records, but they are also confidential records of information whose dissemination is at least partially controlled by the patient. This is further complicated by the ambiguous nature of rules governing physician–patient communications. Unlike the lawyer–client privilege, which is a traditional common law privilege, there is no common law physician–patient privilege. Although medical ethics has always demanded that the physician respect the patient's confidences, violations were punished, if at all, as general invasion of privacy cases. In the last 30 years, most state legislatures have enacted medical privacy laws. These laws are similar in that they limit the dissemination of medical information without the patient's consent, and they provide certain exceptions for this protection, such as allowing the discovery of medical information when the patient has made a legal claimed based on that information or when the patient poses a threat to the public health. The federal government does not provide a general protection for medical privacy outside of federal institutions, but there is a federal law that protects records dealing with treatment for alcoholism and substance abuse.[1] As part of the Conditions of Participation for Medicare/Medicaid and Joint Commission requirements, providers must protect patient confidentiality.

These state and federal privacy laws modify the usual presumption that medical records, as a business record, are subject to discovery in civil and criminal matters against the health care practitioner. When a medical record is at issue in state litigation against a health care practitioner, other than cases brought by the patient, medical records will be protected from discovery unless the plaintiff can show a compelling reason why the records are necessary to prove its case. Even then, the court will supervise the discovery and generally require that all patient-identifying information be removed. If the case is brought in federal court, under federal law, such as an antitrust or false claims case, then the state law protections do not apply. Although federal judges do try to protect patients' confidential information when possible, there are many situations, such as a Medicare fraud prosecution, where the records, patient identifiers and all, will be discoverable.

Medical Malpractice Litigation

The medical record is the basic legal document in medical malpractice litigation. A poorly written, disorganized record is strong evidence of an incompetent health care provider. The poorly kept record is not, in itself, proof of negligence on the part of the health care provider, but it is proof of substandard care. Conversely, medical personnel, constantly told that "the good medical record is the best defense," miss the point that the good medical record is valuable only to the extent that it documents the actual rendering of good medical care. A medical record can be legally disastrous if it demonstrates the incompetence of the underlying medical care. Poor documentation is actually an advantage to an incompetent defendant whose best defense is obfuscation. A poor record may prevent the medical care providers from establishing the good care they gave the patient, but a good record is not a substitute for good care.

Medical Records as a Plaintiff's Weapon

When an injured patient seeks legal advice about filing a medical malpractice lawsuit, the attorney's first task is to review the medical records. Medical malpractice litigation is built around the medical record, which provides the only objective record of the patient's condition and the care provided. The attorney is looking for specific acts of negligence and at the overall quality of the record. The strongest medical malpractice lawsuits are based on well-documented, specific acts of negligence. In most cases, however, the negligence is inferred from documented and undocumented events. If the patient's case depends at least partially on assuming that certain events were not recorded, the attorney must be able to cast doubt on the credibility of the record.

Records are particularly important for a physician's defense. The patient has injuries to show the court; the physician or other health care practitioner has only the medical records to prove that the injuries were not due to negligence. If the record is incomplete, illegible, or incompetently kept, this is the health care practitioner's failure. Although courts and juries usually give a defendant the benefit of the doubt on ambiguous matters, this does not extend to ambiguities created by incompetent recordkeeping. The least credible records are those that are internally inconsistent—for example, the physician's progress notes report that the patient was doing well and improving steadily, but the nurses' records indicate that the patient had developed a high fever and appeared to have a major infection. More commonly, the credibility of the records is attacked through demonstrating that it is incomplete. If it is clear that medically important information is missing from the record, then it is easier to convince a jury that the missing information supports the patient's claims.

Defensible Records

Viewing the medical record from outside, without reference to its role in medical care, leads to the *defensible record,* one that does not facilitate good care but does contain enough information to allow a plausible defense for the physician's actions. For example, recording a child's height and weight without plotting a growth chart would allow the defense that the physician was aware of the child's development. Plotting the information, however, might have caused the physician to investigate growth retardation and treat underlying medical problems. This would mitigate the child's injury and reduce the probability of litigation.

From the point of view of prevention, the best medical record is one that facilitates good care. If the patient's care is good, the probability of a successful medical malpractice lawsuit is low. If, in addition to facilitating good care, the record fully documents the patient's course and the care provided, then it is unlikely that a knowledgeable plaintiff's attorney will even proceed with a case. This appears to be happening with structured prenatal care records. These are printed medical records with checkoffs for all routine prenatal care, combined with extensive patient education handouts. There have been many fewer than expected claims against physicians using these records (see Chapter 14). Given the financial and emotional cost of medical malpractice litigation, the best record is the one that convinces a plaintiff's attorney that it is not worth filing a lawsuit.

Administrative Review of Records

Health care providers who are subject to state or federal regulation, including Medicare/Medicaid Conditions of Participation, must allow inspectors from these programs access to their medical records. These inspectors may view the entire record, including the patient identifiers, without the permission of the patients. This is justified under the police powers as a reasonable intrusion based on a greater societal need, the same legal basis as that used for requiring patient information to be reported for various statistical and disease control purposes (see Chapter 12). State health care practitioner licensing agencies have the right to inspect medical records under certain circumstances.

Criminal Discovery

Prosecutors may seek medical records with a search warrant if the content of the medical record is relevant to the underlying criminal case. This is common in Medicare/Medicaid fraud prosecutions, where the record is relevant to determining if the care that was billed was necessary and proper. Search warrants must be approved by a court to ensure that there is probable cause to believe that the search will turn up evidence of a crime. When medical records are being sought, the court will also consider "... the type of record requested, the information it does or might contain, the potential for harm in any subsequent nonconsensual disclosure, the injury from disclosure to the relationship in which the record was generated, the adequacy of safeguards to prevent unauthorized disclosure, the degree of need for access, and whether there is an express statutory mandate, articulated public policy, or other recognizable public interest militating toward access."[2]

In most cases that involve billing fraud, the court will allow the discovery of the Medicare/Medicaid patients' medical records. The Health Insurance Portability and Accountability Act (also known as the Kassebaum-Kennedy bill) makes fraud against private health care insurers a federal crime. This means that in the future, health care practitioners can expect to see search warrants for private patient records, as well as for Medicare/Medicaid patients. The courts do recognize that the physician has the right to contest these orders on behalf of the patients because the patients have no way of knowing about the order and thus cannot assert their rights.[3]

Quality Assurance and Accreditation Review of Records

State confidentiality laws anticipate that medical information must be shared when taking care of the patient. (Some states enacted restrictions on entering information about AIDS/HIV into the medical chart that made it very difficult to care for these patients.) This is assumed to include quality assurance activities and accreditation, and the review of medical records and confidential patient information by private accrediting associations such as the Joint Commission. Interestingly, there is no clear legal mandate for this release of confidential medical information to a private group. In many states it could be argued that this release comes under the exception for quality assurance review.

This exception is not an unlimited right to use medical information for all administrative purposes. In one case, plaintiffs sued a hospital for releasing records to its law firm so that the attorneys could determine if any patients were eligible for additional federal benefits. The hospital moved for summary judgment, claiming that the general consent patients sign on admission covered this release of information. The court disagreed, noting that the general consent mentioned only releases to insurers. The court also rejected the defendant's claim that this release was allowable under their attorney–client relationship. The court held that the hospital could be sued for releasing the records.[4]

Perhaps most interestingly, the court also found that the law firm may have improperly induced the hospital to violate its fiduciary duty toward the patient by releasing confidential medical information. The court applied a standard drawn from a case involving an improper disclosure of psychiatric information to an employer, who was alleged to have induced the psychiatrist to disclose the information: "(1) [T]he defendant knew or reasonably should have known of the existence of the physician–patient relationship; (2) the defendant intended to induce the physician to disclose information about the patient or the defendant reasonably should have anticipated that his actions would induce the physician to disclose such information; and (3) the defendant did not reasonably believe that the physician could disclose that information to the defendant without violating the duty of confidentiality that the physician owed the patient."[5] Such a standard raises questions about many consulting schemes designed to increase billing by reviewing records and tuning up the billing.

MEDICAL OFFICE AND CLINIC RECORDS

Most medical practices have changed dramatically in the last 10 years. Their patient panels turn over rapidly, they no longer control referrals to specialists, and they are treating sicker patients in the office because of the pressure to keep patients out of the hospital. Malpractice risks have not changed in the last decade, but the risk of being prosecuted for billing fraud has gone from negligible to significant. Yet, with all the changes, many health care practitioners keep patient medical records in a manner that assumes that they know each patient personally and that the patient will be there forever—records that would not look out of place in an office of 50 years ago.

The Joint Commission provides detailed requirements for the maintenance of medical records in the hospital and in ambulatory care centers. There are no corresponding, uniformly recognized standards for physician's office records. Consequently, there is a tremendous variation in the quality of physicians' office records. Physicians should use a standard medical record format such as the problem-oriented medical record for all their medical records. Whereas the Joint Commission does not certify physician's offices, the standards for ambulatory care centers provide useful guidance for records management in the physician's office.[6]

Basic Patient Information

Although proper charting of medical and treatment information has always been important for medical malpractice prevention, it is now also important as a compliance measure for billing fraud issues. The old rule in medical malpractice was that if it was not in the chart, it was not done. Auditors looking for insurance or Medicare fraud use the same standard: if the medical necessity of the care is not documented along with the care, then the bill for the care is fraudulent. In the best case, the health care practitioner will have to refund the amount paid. In the worst case, there is a $5,000 fine per fraudulent bill, plus jail time.

The most important information is the basic patient data. The chart must contain enough information for a health care practitioner unfamiliar with the patient to provide appropriate care. This should include physiological information, therapeutic information, and any special patient characteristics such as allergies or handicaps. This information should be summarized on a cover sheet. There are several acceptable styles for providing this summary, but they share an emphasis on rapid identification of abnormal findings, the recording of problems that will require attention on future visits, and a way to ensure that the physician is notified if the patient misses a follow-up visit.

The record should also contain family and legal information. For minors, the names of the parents or guardians should be in the chart, and a prominent notation as to who is legally able to consent to the child's care. Most important, the chart should note any special legal constraints, such as a parent who is not allowed to consent to care, who is not allowed to pick up the child from the clinic, or who is not allowed to have access to the child's medical information. If patients have a living will or durable power of attorney, this should be noted in the chart and a copy attached, if available. Adult family information—spouses, children, significant others—should be recorded and a note made if other members of the family are patients of the practice. The health care practitioner may review the other patients' charts to look for medically significant information, such as the risk of spreading infectious diseases between family members. However, the health care practitioner must not share one adult's medical information with another without the patient's consent. If there is consent to share information, it should be in writing and filed in the chart. As discussed in Chapter 12, if the health care practitioner believes that a patient may endanger others by spreading disease, then the proper response is to report this to the public health authorities and ask for their help and advice.

Team and Managed Care

In clinics with several physicians and other health care practitioners, the demands on the medical record begin to resemble those of a hospital medical record. All of the health care practitioners in the group must keep records in the same format, record enough information to allow any other health care practitioners in the group to treat the patient, and identify patient problems with great specificity to ensure continuity of care. It is very important that the each person who cares for the patient be clearly identified in the chart. If nonphysician health care practitioners are treating patients under a physician's supervision, the supervising physician should be clearly identified in the chart. This can be a very important issue in Medicare billing because of the rules on what care may be billed by what class of provider. It is important for medical malpractice risk management to establish that state laws governing supervision of nonphysician personnel are followed.

Clinics where the patient sees whichever health care practitioner is available at the time the appointment is made create the opportunity for patient problems to be ignored through shared authority for patient care. As with hospital-based care, the ideal is that there is one physician in charge of the patient's overall care, and that the chart identifies this physician. The chart will be returned to this physician for review whenever the patient is treated by another member of the clinic group. This review allows the primary physician to reconcile the care of the other providers. If there are problems, the patient can be contacted. If there are no problems, the reviewing physician can add whatever notes are necessary to ensure that the next physician to see that patient has the proper information. In systems where this is impossible, the charts must kept in such as way as to preserve all the relevant data so that the health care practitioner who treats the patient can try to make sense out of the previous care.

Maintaining the Records

Chapter 5 discusses the hearsay rule and medical records as business records. As such, medical records are subject to the specific legal requirements for keeping records that may be used in court: (1) the record must be made in the regular course of the business; (2) the record must be kept by a person who has personal knowledge of the act, event, or condition being recorded; (3) the record must be made at or near the time that the recorded act, event, or condition occurred or reasonably soon thereafter; and (4) the record must be kept in a consistent manner, according to a set procedure.

Readability

An illegible medical record is doubly damaging to a physician: it obscures necessary information, and it makes the physician who wrote the entry look less than professional. A favorite strategy of plaintiffs' attorneys is to make enlargements of illegible medical records and use them to belittle the defendant physician in front of the jury. Despite the jokes about physicians' handwriting, juries are not tolerant of illegible records.

The best way to ensure that records are legible is to dictate them. This may be done on a pocket tape recorder while the physician is still with the patient or immediately after. In all cases, the dictation should be done before the physician sees another patient. If recordkeeping is delayed, it is inevitable that entries will be lost or distorted. The tape should be transcribed daily and the transcription entered into the chart. This entry may be made by affixing the actual typescript to the medical record. If a computer or memory typewriter is used for the transcription, then the entry, after proofing, may be printed on the chart page itself.

Handwritten notes should always be made in the chart in case the transcription is delayed or lost. The transcribed notes should not be pasted over the handwritten notes; both sets of notes are part of the legal record and must be preserved. If the chart entries are not dictated, all entries should be made in black ink—*never* in pencil. It is best if they are printed, but legible cursive handwriting is acceptable. The records should be spot-checked for legibility from time to time. Taking the time to write one legible sentence makes for a better record than a hastily scrawled page of illegible notes.

Altered Records

It is important to be consistent in the keeping of records. The essence of a credible record is that it appears to have been maintained in the regular course of business. Anything that indicates special treatment for a record reduces its credibility. Attorneys and juries are suspicious of inconsistencies. If records are usually handwritten, a dictated note will be questioned. Conversely, a handwritten note in a series of dictated notes will be suspect.

Health care practitioners should not alter their medical records under any circumstances. Hospitals protect medical records from alterations, but there is no such watchdog in a physician's office. Even an inconsequential alteration throws the validity of the entire record into question. Innocent mistakes, such as the loss of a few pages of a record, will be construed as an intentional cover-up. Under no circumstances should liquid correction fluid be applied to the record in order to correct an entry. If an entry must be changed, a single line should be drawn through the entry, taking particular care to make sure that the original entry is clearly legible.

The new entry should be written above or next to the old entry, with the date of the new entry and the initials of the person making the entry recorded. It is important that the new entry include the reason for its inclusion—perhaps newly available laboratory information, addenda to explain a previous note, or just that it is a supplemental note. As long as it is clear that no deception is intended, physicians should not hesitate to supplement chart notes. A note supplemented two weeks after the original entry is more credible than attempts to supplement it on the witness stand five years later.

Protecting Records

Medical records are the basic tangible assets of a private practice. If these records are lost through fire or theft, the medical care of many patients may suffer. If medical office records were to be lost, it could be difficult to defend a claim brought by a patient who had been treated by the physician. As with any other business, the health care practitioner will also face potential financial ruin from the loss of the customer information contained in the medical records. Unlike many other businesses, however, health care practitioners often fail to use standard business techniques for protecting their records.

Paper records should be stored in fire-resistant filing cabinets that are locked whenever the office is closed. This provides some protection from fire and theft. Computer records should be copied (backed up) to removable media, either disks or tape, daily, with at least two sets of backup media. This practice ensures that one set will be preserved if a mistake is made in the backup process. These sets are alternated, with one being used on Monday, Wednesday, and Friday and the other on Tuesday, Thursday, and Saturday. It is better to have a set of backup media for each working day. Most businesses keep at least one set of backup media in a different building from the computer. A duplicated backup is made on this remote set at least once a week to prevent a complete loss of information if the building is destroyed.

If the medical office is destroyed, the first step is to contact all of the patients: (1) to remind patients in need of continuing care that they must contact the new office for an appointment; and (2) to reassure patients that the physician will reopen the office and that they need not seek medical care elsewhere. Contacting the patients will be much easier if the medical office maintains a patient list in a secure place away from the office in which the records are kept. This list should contain enough information to locate patients and, ideally, to reconstruct a skeleton of the patient's medical history. Keeping such a list is time consuming, but it can be an effective marketing tool. A physician can use routine mailings to established patients to build loyalty. Mailings directed at patients with chronic conditions can be used to remind them to come in for follow-up care. This is good business and good medical management.

Retention of Records

There are few statutory requirements on how long a medical office must retain private office records. From a risk management point of view, it is desirable for all records to be retained indefinitely in the office. Unfortunately, this may be economically unfeasible and interfere with access to active records. All medical offices should have a formal records retention policy that balances convenient and economic storage with easy access to active records.

Records for any patient seen in the last two years must be considered active unless the patient has died. If the patient has not been seen for two years and does not have a continuing medical condition, the health care practitioner may consider putting the patient's records into less accessible storage while retaining the cover sheet of the chart in case the patient is seen again. The cover sheet will facilitate urgent care in either the office or the emergency room before the full record can be retrieved.

The health care practitioner must maintain a separate tracking system for all patients with implants of any kind. Although this has always been done for heart valves and pacemakers, it is important for other implants that either need replacing or are subject to FDA (Food and Drug Administration) recalls or reviews. This includes intrauterine devices and implantable contraceptives, including Depo-Provera. The tracking system should identify each patient with an implant, the type of implant, the last patient visit, and any necessary review dates. For implantable contraceptives, such as Norplant, the patient should be seen each year and should be notified in the fourth year that the contraceptive effect is wearing off. For Depo-Provera, the patient must be followed up every three months, or whatever is the effective length of the preparation that is used.

The physician should contact patients with chronic medical problems who have not been seen recently. If the patient is being treated by a new physician, that physician's name should be noted in the chart. If the patient cannot be found and is not in need of specific follow-up care, the physician should send a postcard to the patient's last known address. If the card is returned as undeliverable, it should be put in the chart to document that the physician tried to keep track of the patient. Once the patient has been accounted for, the chart may be moved to storage. If there are patients in need of follow-up care, they should be managed as discussed in Chapter 8.

From a strictly legal point of view, the statute of limitations for medical malpractice in the state where the physician practices is the absolute minimum period that records should be maintained. Depending on the local state laws, adults have from one to four years after the occurrence of an injury to file a claim for medical malpractice. For children, this period is usually extended until the patient reaches age 20 to 24.

The problem with the statute of limitation is that states tend to measure the period differently. The statute of limitations may begin to run: (1) on the date when the malpractice occurred, whether the patient knew about the malpractice or not; (2) on the date when the physician last treated the patient for the condition at issue; or (3) on the date the patient knew, or should have known, that he or she was a victim of malpractice. In states in which the running of the statute of limitations starts from the discovery of the malpractice, it is conceivable that a malpractice suit could be filed 10, 15, 20, or more years after the patient was treated.

Statutory Requirements on Recordkeeping

Federal and state laws govern the retention and release of medical records. Some Medicaid/Medicare records must be available for verification of charges for a five-year period. OSHA (Occupational Safety and Health Administration) regulations govern the retention and release of certain occupational health records (see Chapter 15). Any health care practitioners involved in substance abuse treatment or occupational medicine should request more information about these laws from their attorneys. A federal law strictly regulates the release of medical information and the management of records for persons undergoing treatment for substance abuse. Health care practitioners who treat patients for substance abuse should seek assistance in complying with these regulations from the participating governmental agency or a private attorney.

Destroying Records

Records may be destroyed only in limited circumstances. The clearest is when the patient dies. A reasonable period of time after the patient's death—perhaps the statute of limitations for medical malpractice in the state—the chart may be destroyed if it is not subject to any laws requiring preservation. It is always recommended that the family of a deceased patient be given a chance to request a copy of the chart before it is destroyed because it may provide invaluable medical information for other family members. If a physician dies and his or her records are not transferred to another physician, these records must be preserved as long as required by applicable laws, then they may be destroyed. The executor of the physician's estate should attempt to contact all patients before destroying the records. All patients should be sent a certified letter at the time of the physician's death notifying them that the physician has died and that they may claim their medical records within a set time, say, three months. Once the time for claiming records has elapsed, the executor may move records that must be preserved to long-term storage.

Telephone Encounters

The same basic information must be recorded for every telephone call: date; time; name and age of the patient; telephone number; symptoms; disposition of the call; whether it is a repeat call; and the person handling the call. In most offices, the only practical way to record this information is in a telephone log. It is too difficult to pull patient charts for every call. Using a central telephone log also allows the supervising physician to monitor the management of calls in the office. The problem with telephone logs is that they can prevent important medical information from being incorporated into the patient's chart.

There must be a protocol to determine what information should be transcribed from the telephone log into the patient's chart. This problem will be eased considerably if the physician uses a telephone log with a preprinted information form on 2-part carbonless paper. Ideally, the copy of every call slip will be filed into the patient's chart. If this is impossible, it is critical to transfer all treatment recommendations, prescriptions, refill call-ins, referrals to the emergency room, and repeat calls for the same problem.

Off-Chart Records

Poor organization, combined with illegible handwriting, leads many medical care providers to use temporary notes, such as index cards, to coordinate care. These notes are used as a source of immediate information. Entries in the official medical record may be written long after the care is delivered. Given the added dimension of hindsight, it is impossible to avoid slanting entries to reflect what should have happened, as opposed to what did happen. This is legally dangerous because it is difficult to maintain consistency in entries that are biased by hindsight. It is very damaging if a patient's attorney can discredit the record through internal inconsistencies and thereby raise questions about the good faith of the providers, as well as the quality of care.

Physicians in training and nurses maintain most extra-chart records. Residents often use 3×5-inch index cards with a brief history, the attending physician, recent test results, pending test results, and what needs to be done next. Residents keep their own cards, and these may be passed on at shift change or may serve as a memory jogger to fill in the new residents in charge, who transfer the information to their own set of cards.

Nursing personnel keep elaborate extra-chart bedside records. Individual nurses keep personal notes, and often the nursing service maintains a centralized extra-chart recordkeeping system. These records exist outside both legal and administrative control. The records are kept in pencil, and old data are erased to make room for new data, ensuring that decisions are based on current information. This process of creating and erasing temporary records also carries over to the processing of physician orders, which are transcribed from the medical record into the extra-chart record. Once in the extra-chart system, it is easy to erase or mark out orders as they are performed.

From a patient care perspective, extra-chart records provide a way to coordinate patient care and provide ready access to laboratory test results. But these records are deficient in that they provide no historical information. Extra-chart records inevitably corrupt the accuracy of the chart itself because the extra-chart record becomes the record that is filled out first, with the chart becoming a secondary record, filled out when time allows. Secondary records often reflect what should have been done rather than what was done. This causes medical problems if the extra-chart system breaks down (someone loses the index cards, for example) and legal problems if the care is challenged in court.

Physicians should never use off-chart records. All patient information must originate in the chart and be transferred to notecards or other temporary records from the chart. If notes are made separate from the chart, these notes should be glued into the chart. They should not be copied over into the chart. Notepaper with strippable adhesive should never be used for keeping medical notes. If they are inadvertently used, they should be glued into the chart with a permanent adhesive.

Releasing Medical Records

Medical records are a peculiar type of business record. The physical record (paper, microfilm, or something else) belongs to the physician making the record or the employing clinic. The information belongs to the patient in the sense that the patient has a right to control the release of the information to self and others. Some states limit the patient's access to potentially damaging psychiatric information, but in general the patient has a right to the information in the medical record. The parent or legal guardian of minors and the guardian of an incompetent adult may exercise this right on behalf of the minor or ward.

Authorizing Release of Medical Information

The physician does not need the patient's permission to report communicable diseases, unusual outbreaks of illness, child abuse, violent injuries, or other legally reportable conditions. In most other situations, the physician should not release information from the patient's chart without the patient's written permission. At the first patient encounter, the physician should have the patient sign an authorization to release information as necessary for the patient's treatment. This includes release to consulting physicians, laboratories, and other health care providers.

The physician must always have the patient's permission to release information for nontherapeutic purposes—for example, collecting insurance, determining job fitness, documenting sick leave, and other situations in which the release of information is not related to the patient's medical treatment. The physician should ask the patient to sign a written authorization to release this nontherapeutic information. The written permission should be dated, state to whom the information is to be released, which information may be passed on to that party, and when the permission to release information expires.

With the growing concern over AIDS-related discrimination, some patients will not authorize the release of their medical information to third parties. If the patient refuses to release information to consultants or other necessary medical care providers, the physician may not be able to manage the patient's condition properly. (This is the same ethical dilemma as a patient who refuses necessary medical treatment.) The physician has no right to release the information without the patient's permission. Conversely, the patient may not coerce the physician into rendering improper care. The physician should inform the patient of the problem and document this in the chart. If the physician refuses to treat the patient on this basis, the patient must be informed of the medical rationale for this refusal.

Preventing Unauthorized Release

A physician has a duty to ensure that information is released only to properly authorized individuals. Assume, for example, that a patient has signed an authorization to release information to an employer. The health care practitioner can legally release information to the employer, but he or she must ensure that the person requesting the information is the one authorized to have it. This might require that the information be sent to the personnel department rather than be given to a caller on the telephone.

If someone presents an authorization that the patient has signed, the health care practitioner should endeavor to determine if the release is valid. If the release is over a few months old or appears irregular, the health care practitioner should attempt to contact the patient before releasing the information. If the patient cannot be located, the health care practitioner should contact the person seeking the information and try to verify the authenticity of the release. If the health care practitioner is still suspicious, he or she should request that the person seeking the information have the patient contact the office. Health care practitioners should also be wary of subpoenas. In many states, these can be issued without supervision by a judge, and they are very easy to forge. The health care practitioner should insist on a signed release from the patient, and should call the law office listed on the subpoena to assure that the subpoena is valid. The best policy is to have the office staff contact the patient and tell them about the subpoena before turning over the records.

A physician has a right to charge a nominal fee for a copy of the patient's medical record. This fee should reflect the actual charge for copying the chart. If the patient is indigent, the physician should provide the chart or an appropriate summary at no cost. Under no circumstances should the physician attempt to hold the chart hostage for an unpaid medical fee or to prevent the patient from seeking care elsewhere. This is bad public relations and may cause the patient to sue to obtain the record.

Selling Medical Records

In many situations, the selling of a private medical practice is little more than selling patients' medical records. Interestingly, there have been few legal actions against physicians who sell medical records. In many states, it is illegal to transfer medical information for nontherapeutic purposes without the patient's explicit permission. In these states, the law would seem to require that each patient be contacted for permission to transfer the records. If the permission is denied, the selling physician will have to retain the records. If the patient cannot be located, then the record might be transferred under seal to the buying physician, to be opened only if the patient contacts the physician in the future.

It is expected that HIV/AIDS will precipitate a reexamination of the selling of medical records. This will be especially threatening in states that make violations of patient confidentiality a criminal act. Even in states that allow the transfer of medical records as part of the sale of a practice, this transfer is limited to another physician, not a lay practice broker.

PEDIATRIC RECORDS

With the exception of intensivists treating neonates, the care of children is a legally low-risk endeavor. General pediatricians tend to get in trouble more for what they do not do than for what they do. This is to be expected in any area of medicine in which the vast majority of patient encounters are either preventive in nature or are for minor illnesses. Many of the cases in which pediatricians are charged with failure to diagnose a condition actually involve a systems failure in the physician's office routine rather than an error in medical judgment. As with all other physicians who have highly routinized practices, pediatricians must take special care to document all findings and ensure that atypical events are identified.

Pediatric recordkeeping has two complicating aspects. First, most visits are for minor illnesses. Second, the records must track growth and development, which is not an issue in adult medical practice. The difficulty with a practice that is overwhelmingly devoted to minor illnesses and well-child care is that it is easy to miss subtle developmental problems and rare, fast-evolving illnesses such as meningitis. This is particularly a problem in children with atypical presentations. It can be impossible to tell the early onset of meningitis from an upper respiratory infection. If the disease progresses very quickly, the child may be permanently injured before the physician could reasonably have expected to make the proper diagnosis.

Pediatric practice is telephone intensive. This is consistent with the minor nature of most pediatric illnesses. Most calls to the pediatrician are for reassurance that the child is not seriously ill. More problematically, most calls are handled by office personnel other than the physician in charge. These calls are seldom recorded in the patient's chart, and calls are often answered without reference to the chart. This leads to the most common telephone-related legal problem: misunderstanding about the severity or progression of the child's illness.

One of the most important diagnostic indicators for children is the parent's level of concern. If a parent calls the physician's office repeatedly over a period of hours or days, this should alert the physician that the child should be seen immediately. Legally, it is very difficult to defend cases in which the parents have repeatedly called the physician's office. If the child is injured due to a missed diagnosis or treatment failure, the jury will assume that the problem could have been managed if the child had been seen.

Physicians must know what their office personnel tell patients who call with medical questions. There must also be a protocol to identify the cases that must be handled by the physician and potential emergencies. In addition to the general telephone problems discussed in Chapter 9, pediatric telephone advice poses special problems that are beyond the scope of this book.[7]

When the physician on call has not had an uninterrupted meal or night's sleep in a week, it is easy to forget that one cannot look at a rash, listen to a chest, or palpate an abdomen over the telephone. The mother's description is not a substitute for a physical examination. If the child potentially has any condition where proper care decisions would require a physical examination, the child should be sent to the office or the emergency room immediately. If the mother is unreliable, then her descriptions over the telephone are also suspect. If the mother is reliable, then she would not call late at night unless she has a serious concern.

Juries will be unsympathetic to a physician's claims unless the medical record carefully documents the child's condition and the physician's plans. The problem is that many physicians keep sketchy records on children with minor illnesses. These records are adequate for the vast majority of patients who are not seriously ill, but they may mask the progress of a severe illness. This increases both the chance of prolonging the misdiagnosis and the probability that a jury will rule against the physician. Physicians caring for children must make a special effort to record the presence and absence of diagnostic signs that indicate serious illness.

Acute Illness Observation Scale

P.L. McCarthy's technique of evaluating pediatric patients focuses on six easily observed factors that, taken together, are a sensitive indicator of serious illness in an infant (see Exhibit 7–1). Ideally, each of these factors would be noted on every pediatric patient seen for an illness. This could be accomplished by using a rubber stamp to enter the list into the medical record. Even if the individual factors are not recorded for each visit, they should always be recorded for patients in whom they are abnormal:

Recording Physical Growth and Development

Carefully recorded charts of a child's growth and development are critical to detecting long-term developmental problems and chronic illnesses with gradual onset. The child's physical development should be recorded on height and weight charts. Height and weight should be recorded at regular intervals, and weights should be taken at every visit. Weights should be measured at every pediatric visit for acute illness. A physician cannot access hydration or weight loss in a small child if there is no record of the child's weight before the onset of the illness.

The data should be plotted at the time they are taken. The most legally damaging situation is to have height and weight information recorded in the child's chart but not plotted. It is impossible to evaluate changes in these data without comparing

Exhibit 7–1 P.L. McCarthy's Technique for Evaluating Pediatric Patients

QUALITY OF CRY

1—strong cry with normal tone or contented and not crying

2—whimpering or sobbing

3—weak cry, moaning, or high-pitched cry

REACTION TO PARENTAL STIMULATION

1—cries briefly and then stops, or is contented and not crying

2—cries off and on

3—cries continually or hardly responds

STATE VARIATION

1—if awake, stays awake, or if asleep and then stimulated, awakens quickly

2—closes eyes briefly when awake, or awakens with prolonged stimulation

3—falls asleep or will not arouse

COLOR

1—pink

2—pale extremities or acrocyanosis

3—pale, cyanotic, mottled or ashen

HYDRATION

1—normal skin and eyes, moist mucous membranes

2—normal skin and eyes, slightly dry mouth

3—doughy or tented skin, dry mucous membranes and/or sunken eyes

RESPONSE (TALK, SMILE) TO SOCIAL OVERTURES, OVER 2 MONTHS

1—smiles or alerts

2—smiles briefly or alerts briefly

3—no smile, anxious face, dull expression, or does not alert them with previous measurements and the norms on the charts. When the physician's care is questioned, the plaintiff's attorney will plot the data to demonstrate to the jury that the physician should have seen problems.

Recording Neuromuscular Development

The child's neuromuscular development should be tracked with a standard assessment tool such as the Denver Developmental Screening Test. If these tools are used conscientiously, they can illustrate subtle developmental problems that might otherwise go unnoticed. They also allow the early detection of medical problems, such as hearing impairment, that must be treated promptly to prevent disruption of the child's development.

The standards of care for pediatric preventive medicine are stringent. The federal maternal and child health programs set explicit standards for developmental screening. A physician in private practice cannot justify a lower standard of care for health assessment than the child would receive in a community health center or from the local health department.

HOSPITAL MEDICAL RECORDS

Each hospital has its own rules for maintaining medical records. Most of these derive from the standards set by the Joint Commission, which provide a detailed guide to keeping records. Health care practitioners who practice in hospitals should become familiar with these rules. Under recent regulations from the OIG, hospitals are now required to audit chart entries to assure that they meet the standards for Medicare/Medicaid billing. These regulations also extend to outpatient clinics run by the hospital, or in which the hospital has an interest. Unlike failure to comply with Joint Commission medical records rules, which usually only merits a slap on the wrist, failure to comply with Medicare/Medicaid rules will require the facility to dismiss the health care practitioner or face federal fraud charges on the bills submitted for improperly documented care.

ELECTRONIC MEDICAL RECORDS

For more than 30 years electronic medical records have been the holy grail of medical informatics. In the last few years they have become a practice reality and their use will increase dramatically over the next decade. Electronic records offer quick retrieval, compact storage, and the ability to aggregate huge amounts of medical data to look for trends and statistical correlations.

There are four major hurdles to the effective use of electronic medical records. The first is that they demand highly structured input if the output is to be useful. This is not unique to electronic records, it is just that the expectations are higher. Everyone who does research in traditional paper records quickly learns that the data are very difficult to retrieve and require a sophisticated review to decipher and code into standard format so they can be analyzed. There is an expectation that data in electronic records will automatically be in a standard form for searching and use, even if the health care practitioners who use the electronic records type in the same stuff they hand-wrote or dictated into the paper records.

The second problem is getting the health care practitioners to complete the electronic records properly. This is deadly work for those who do not type because there is only so much you can do with checkboxes. Paper records, especially dictated ones, are easier, especially because there is no electronic nanny making you really enter all the data. This will only be solved by time and the demand that all health care practitioners learn how to type.

The third problem is that electronic records are especially easy to alter or otherwise manipulate, unless they are designed to make this impossible. They are also difficult to authenticate, unless the computer entry ports have biosensors, such as fingerprint or retina scanners. This makes it hard to tell if the correct provider really entered the data. Electronic records also allow the use of form data such as a canned review of systems designed to support billing for a given diagnosis. Again, properly designed records will prevent this, but it will be years before there are adequate standards and certifications for medical records software.

The fourth problem is privacy. All health care practitioners know that medical privacy is more of a myth than a reality. Too many people see records and it is too hard to secure them to ensure real privacy for any specific record. On balance, however, the system is fairly secure because the difficulty of retrieving and copying more than a few records makes large-scale information theft impossible. In an electronic system, however, a breach in security can mean the theft of all of the data, without even a warning that it is gone. Given a big enough selection of records and the means to fish through them electronically, an infovandal could do real harm. This might be in the form of public embarrassment or humiliation, or in blackmail demands to keep the information secret.

Health care practitioners who use electronic records systems must ensure that the records are secure. This means both electronic security and physical security—many serious breaches of computer security can be traced to passwords and operating information that was retrieved from dumpsters or stolen by cleaning staff. In many offices the easiest way to steal the data is to just walk out with a backup tape. The requirements for proper computer security are beyond the scope of this book. Any office that uses electronic records must work with a computer security expert to ensure that the system is secure. It is important to not just take the word of the vendor, but to get an independent evaluation of both the system and the general security in the offices.

REFERENCES

1. 42 U.S.C.A. § 290dd-2.
2. *United States v. Westinghouse Elec. Corp.*, 638 F.2d 570, 578 (3d Cir. 1980).
3. *In re Search Warrant (Sealed)*, 810 F.2d 67 (3d Cir. 1987).
4. *Biddle v. Warren Gen. Hosp.*, 1998 W.L. 156997 (Ohio App. 11 Dist. Mar. 27, 1998).
5. *Alberts v. Devine*, 479 N.E.2d 113, 121 (Mass. 1985).
6. *Standards for Ambulatory Care*. Oak Brook, IL: Joint Commission on Accreditation of Healthcare Organizations; 1998.
7. Schmitt BD: *Pediatric Telephone Advice*. 2nd ed. Boston: Little Brown; 1998.

SUGGESTED READINGS

Barrows RC Jr, Clayton PD. Privacy, confidentiality, and electronic medical records. *J Am Med Inform Assoc*. 1996;3:139–148.

Barton HM. Medical records can win or lose a malpractice case. *Tex Med*. 1990;86:33–36.

Berlin L. Alteration of medical records. *AJR*. 1997;168:1405–1408.

Burton K. Your memory/your patient's memory and your medical records. *WV Med J*. 1996;92:308–309.

Butler RN. Who's reading your medical records? *Geriatrics*. 1997;52:7–8.

Campbell SG, Gibby GL, Collingwood S. The Internet and electronic transmission of medical records. *J Clin Monit*. 1997;13:325–334.

Carman D, Britten N. Confidentiality of medical records: the patient's perspective. *Br J Gen Pract*. 1995;45:485–488.

Corker D. Involuntary disclosure of private medical records to the defense in criminal proceedings. *Med Sci Law*. 1998;38:138–141.

Francisco CJ. Confidentiality, privilege, and release of medical records under a subpoena duces tecum. *Tex Med*. 1991;87:34–35.

Gilhooly ML, McGhee SM. Medical records: practicalities and principles of patient possession. *J Med Ethics*. 1991;17:138–143.

Henry PF. Legal issues relating to access to medical records. *Nurse Pract Forum*. 1993;4:120–121.

Jones TL, George T. Private matters: will electronic medical records doom confidentiality? *Tex Med*. 1996;92:46–50.

Karp D. Dictated medical records reduce liability. *Alaska Med*. 1991;33:42.

Kluge EH. Advanced patient records: some ethical and legal considerations touching medical information space. *Methods Inf Med*. 1993;32:95–103.

Knox EG. Confidential medical records and epidemiological research. *BMJ*. 1992;304:727–8.

Markus A, Lockwood M. Is it permissible to edit medical records? *BMJ*. 1991;303:349–51.

Markus AC. Medical confidentiality and records in general practice. *Br J Gen Pract*. 1991;41:136, 138.

Melton LJ 3rd. The threat to medical-records research. *N Engl J Med*. 1997;337:466–470.

Mitchell MW. Physician medical records patient access revisited. *J Ark Med Soc*. 1991;88:89–90.

Miya PA, Megal ME. Confidentiality and electronic medical records. *Medsurg Nurs.* 1997;6:222–224, 212.

Philipsen N, McMullen P. Medical records: promoting patient confidentiality. *Nursingconnections.* 1993;6:48–50.

Prosser RL Jr. Alteration of medical records submitted for medicolegal review. *JAMA.* 1992;267:2630–2631.

Richards BC, Thomasson GO. Medical records figure prominently in malpractice cases: a closed liability claims analysis. *Colo Med.* 1992;89:398–401.

Rind DM, Kohane IS, Szolovits P, Safran C, Chueh HC, Barnett GO. Maintaining the confidentiality of medical records shared over the Internet and the World Wide Web. *Ann Intern Med.* 1997;127:138–141.

Rosenblum JB. Legal aspects of computerized medical records. *Leg Med.* 1995:205–225.

Smith J. Good medical records key to prevention, defense against malpractice claims. *Mich Med.* 1993;92:14–15.

Sokolov KI. Medical records of minors—procedures regarding disclosure. *J Med Assoc Ga.* 1989;78:718–721.

Start CA. Patient records and medical history: tips to avoid liability. *J Mich Dent Assoc.* 1996;78:22, 24.

Tadd V. Medical records: off the record. *Nurs Stand.* 1996;10:44.

Tilton SH. Right to privacy and confidentiality of medical records. *Occup Med.* 1996;11:17–29.

Wald N, Law M, Meade T, Miller G, Alberman E, Dickinson J. Use of personal medical records for research purposes. *BMJ.* 1994;309:1422–1444.

Weil Z. Evidential damage as a result of improper medical records. *Med Law.* 1998;17:13–24.

Wernert JJ. Maintaining confidentiality of computerized medical records. *Indiana Med.* 1995;88:440–444.

Williams RC. Privacy and computerized medical records. *Ala Med.* 1995;65:29–37.

Wooddell J. Medical records and their use in litigation. *Mo Med.* 1997;94:168–170.

CHAPTER 8

The Physician–Patient Relationship

HIGHLIGHTS

- The law of all health care practitioner–patient relationships is based on the physician–patient relationship.
- The core of the physician–patient relationship is the exercise of medical judgment.
- Consultants also have a legal relationship with patients.
- Good Samaritan laws protect physicians who stop at accidents.
- Contracts with health plans restrict the health care practitioner's right to choose the patients they will treat.

INTRODUCTION

The basic legal relationship in medicine is between the physician and the patient. Although recognizing that there are many nonphysicians delivering health care services, the courts and the legislatures still use the physician–patient relationship as the paradigm for the legal rights and responsibilities that flow between health care practitioners and patients. At this point in time, it is unclear how much of the law developed for the physician–patient relationship will be applied to other health care practitioners. Some duties, such as the duty to protect the patient's confidence, clearly apply to everyone who provides medical services. Some do not—the courts have not applied the "learned intermediary" doctrine to nurses.[1] Until the courts rule on more cases involving the legal relationship between nonphysician health care practitioners and patients, it is difficult to predict which direction the law will go.

MANAGED CARE AND THE PROFESSIONAL RELATIONSHIP

This chapter deals with traditional physician–patient relationship law. The core legal assumption about the physician–patient relationship is that it is a fiduciary relationship. The law expects physicians to put their patients' financial and other interests first. Managed care is dramatically changing the nature of the physician–patient relationship in ways that are not contemplated by existing law. This is resulting in litigation and increased scrutiny by state regulatory agencies. Physicians and other health care practitioners are caught between the economic power of the managed care organizations with their control of the stream of patients, and the demands of patients and consumer advocates that they live up to the traditional values of the physician–patient relationship. There are several specific problem areas that will be discussed in this chapter. In general, health care practitioners must assume that the traditional physician–patient relationship applies in the managed care setting until the courts or legislatures change the law.

ESTABLISHING THE RELATIONSHIP

Historically, the primary legal characteristic of the physician–patient relationship was that it was voluntary. The physician was free to choose which patients to treat. The patient, in theory, was free to choose a physician. Unfortunately, this voluntariness permitted racial, religious, and economic discrimination against patients. Federal and state civil rights laws and health care regulations such as the Emergency Medical Treatment and Active Labor Act prohibit discriminatory treatment and in that sense limit the ability of health care practitioners to refuse to treat patients. There are other exceptions involving physicians who have contractually agreed to treat certain classes of patients, such as those in managed care organizations (MCOs) or emergency room staffing groups. These exceptions have greatly reduced the latitude of most physicians to refuse to treat a given patient. Within these constraints, the law still assumes that a physician must accept a patient voluntarily before the physician–patient relationship is legally binding.[2]

Explicitly Accepting the Patient

The clearest way to form a physician–patient relationship is for the physician to accept the patient explicitly. The physician and the patient may enter into a written contract, or the physician may just say that he or she accepts the patient. This explicit acceptance happens most frequently when the patient is seeking elective medical care that is not reimbursable by a third-party payer. Physicians delivering such care use written contracts to ensure that the patient will pay for the treatment. Outside of uninsured elective care, these explicit agreements are uncommon. Usually the physician's acceptance of the patient must be inferred from the physician's conduct.

One way to trigger a physician–patient relationship is to evaluate the patient's medical condition—perhaps in an examining room, talking to him or her in an emergency room, or taking his or her pulse at an accident site. In general, the physician's right to refuse to accept the patient must be exercised before the physician evaluates the patient. If the physician evaluates the patient and determines that he or she is in need of immediate care, then the physician is responsible for ensuring that the necessary care is provided. If the patient is not in need of immediate care, the physician may terminate the relationship.

When patients make appointments with physicians, patients assume that they have been accepted for treatment. This expectation does not create a problem if the physician sees every patient who makes an appointment. The patient's expectations become an issue when the physician evaluates the patient's insurance status after making an appointment. The physician may refuse to accept a patient for financial reasons, but this right is limited once a physician–patient relationship is initiated. Making an appointment may create a limited physician–patient relationship. The test would be the extent to which the patient will suffer because he or she has relied on the appointment. This requires balancing the severity of the patient's condition with the delay between making the appointment and seeing the physician. If the patient must wait two months to see the physician and will have to wait two months to see another physician, a jury is likely to find that the patient should have been seen, irrespective of financial considerations. Conversely, if the patient has waited only a few hours and other care is readily available, the physician has greater freedom to refuse to see the patient. If the patient has an emergent condition, such as chest pain or a threatened miscarriage, the physician must attend to the patient irrespective of the availability of alternative care.

Exercising Independent Medical Judgment

Legally, a physician–patient relationship is formed when the physician exercises independent medical judgment on the patient's behalf. *Independent medical judgment* is a vague term that is defined by the facts of the given situation. It may involve making a diagnosis, recommending treatment, or implying that no treatment is necessary. As a legal concept, the key is reliance: Did the patient reasonably rely on the physician's judgment?

A physician may exercise independent medical judgment explicitly or implicitly. A physician who evaluates a patient and establishes a differential diagnosis recognizes that he or she has exercised independent medical judgment. Legal problems usually arise from the implicit exercise of medical judgment. If a physician is not aware of initiating a physician–patient relationship, he or she may injure the patient through inattention. The implicit exercise of medical judgment is best understood through a discussion of common practice situations in which medical judgment is at issue. Since telephone calls pose the most difficult problems in determining whether a physician–patient relationship has been formed, they serve as a useful model to discuss these issues.

Telephone Calls

Telephone calls are problematic because the caller and the physician often have different expectations. Some patients call physicians day or night about every minor medical question that comes to mind. Many patients call physicians after office hours only when they believe that they have a serious problem. From the physician's perspective, most calls involve minor problems. This creates a sense of complacency that may lead physicians to mishandle telephone calls by underestimating the severity of the patient's condition.

From a medical perspective, new patients and new problems should not be evaluated over the telephone. If the patient has a medical complaint, the only question would be whether an ambulance should be sent to pick up the patient or whether the patient can find transportation to a medical care facility. Patient and physician resources make this an unreasonable ideal. In many situations patients must be evaluated without a hands-on examination. This should not blind physicians

to the medical and legal hazards implicit in such indirect evaluations.

A physician who listens to the patient's complaints assumes the duty to make a triage decision about the patient's condition: recommending treatment, no treatment, or that the patient see a physician in person. Physicians have an ethical duty to see that patients with emergent conditions get proper treatment. For persons who do not have a preexisting relationship with the physician, this duty can be fulfilled by sending the patient to a properly equipped emergency room. If the physician becomes more involved, such as by calling the ambulance, he or she must carry out these actions correctly—perhaps by calling the emergency room later and inquiring after the patient.

A physician who listens to a patient's complaints and then recommends no treatment is implicitly telling the patient that he or she does not need immediate medical services. Usually the physician does intend for the patient to assume that he or she does not need further medical care. Occasionally, however, the physician does not want to treat the patient personally; he or she does not intend to imply that the patient does not need medical care. Once a physician has listened to the patient's complaints, he or she has assumed a limited duty to that patient. It is this limited duty that creates the inference that not prescribing treatment is the same as telling the patient that he or she does not need treatment. A physician who does not want to accept responsibility for the patient must pass the patient on to another physician. This must be done expeditiously to avoid responsibility for determining that the patient is not in need of immediate care.

Prescribing medication is an exercise of independent medical judgment and creates a physician–patient relationship. It does not matter whether the physician recommends a prescription drug or an over-the-counter medication. Recommending aspirin is just as much as an exercise of judgment as prescribing digitalis. Telling the patient to "take two aspirin and call the office in the morning" assumes that the physician has ruled out the presence of any serious conditions that would require prompt attention. Recommending treatment over the telephone is best reserved for patients with whom the physician already has a relationship. If the physician has not seen the patient before, he or she does not have the necessary context to judge the patient's condition. Is a headache due to a cold or out-of-control blood pressure? When dealing with existing patients, the physician must ensure that he or she has enough information to evaluate the patient's condition properly. If the physician has not seen the patient recently enough to remember him or her accurately and does not have the patient's chart available, the patient should be seen or referred to an emergency room.

All telephone conversations that involve medical decision making should be documented. If the call concerns an existing patient, the record of the call should be added to the patient's chart. If the call involves a person that the physician accepts as a new patient, a preliminary record should be opened for that patient. If the call involves a person whom the physician refers to another medical care provider, including an emergency room, a referral record should be created. These records have two purposes. For existing patients, recording telephone calls is necessary to ensure that the patient's medical chart is complete. For persons who are not patients, the record of the call prevents later misunderstandings about what the physician told the patient. The record should contain the time and date of the call, the identity of the caller, how he or she came to call the physician (name out of the telephone book, for example), the nature of the complaint, exactly what the physician told the person, and where the patient was referred.

Private Office Walk-In Patients

The most basic consideration in patient screening in the office is whether the patient is calling for an appointment in the future or is standing in the office requesting care. There are many options for dealing with a patient on the telephone, but the patient in the office requires an immediate decision. The law does not impose a duty to treat every patient who walks into a private medical office; however, there are several exceptions that do recognize a duty to treat certain patients. More important, it would be ethically impermissible to turn away a patient for whom this would mean certain injury.

The basic duty to a walk-in patient is to determine whether the patient needs immediate treatment to forestall further injury. In the private office, this duty is limited to situations in which a patient presents with a major problem such as a heart attack in progress or anaphylactic shock. The situation is most likely to occur if the physician's office is in an office complex with nonphysician tenants—a risk particularly for physicians in shopping center offices. This type of event is unusual, but it is potentially catastrophic and demands some type of screening for all walk-in patients. For most patients, this simply requires asking the patients why they want to see the physician. Patients should not be relied upon for a definitive diagnosis, but they can recount the natural history of the complaint. If the symptoms were of sudden and recent onset or if the patient appears seriously ill, it is critical that a more complete medical examination be done at once.

If the patient is found to need urgent care, that care must be rendered to the extent that the practitioner is capable. The central problem for a physician facing a medical emergency outside his or her expertise is determining the extent of care that must be rendered before the patient can be transferred. For example, any physician should be able to manage anaphylactic shock; a dissecting aneurysm will require emergency transport to a fully equipped surgical center. The issue is the physician's general knowledge and the available facilities, not his or her self-selected specialty. A gynecologist and an allergist would have the same duty to treat a patient in anaphylactic shock, although the gynecologist would have no obligation to treat a routine allergy patient. If the patient can be managed without transport to an emergency room, the physician may determine later if he or she wants to continue the physician–patient relationship beyond the acute episode.

If the physician determines that the patient is not in need of urgent treatment, certain obligations remain. If the physician chooses to accept the person as a regular patient, these obligations will be discharged. If the physician chooses not to continue treating the patient, then he or she must ensure that the patient is told all the pertinent information about the condition, including the need for further treatment. If the condition requires continuing treatment, the physician must be sure that the patient understands the need for this treatment. The physician must be careful to distinguish between telling the patient that no treatment is required and telling this person to seek treatment elsewhere. The best course is to refer the person formally to the appropriate physician or hospital for treatment.

Informal Consultations

One of the banes of physicians is the curbside consult. These are best handled in the same way as a telephone call. A nonpatient who needs care should be referred in a manner appropriate to the urgency of the presenting condition. If the physician consults with a patient, appropriate records should be kept. With one caveat, informal consultations should be documented in the same manner as telephone calls. When a person telephones a physician, that person has demonstrated a much greater level of concern than someone who just makes conversation with a physician at a party. All telephone calls should be documented, but it is not necessary to record every social conversation that turns to a person's medical condition. The physician should record substantive discussions with existing patients in the patient's medical record and any consultations in which he or she recommended treatment or referred the patient for evaluation of an emergent condition.

Financial Considerations

The most common reason for refusing to accept a patient is the patient's potential inability to pay for the necessary medical services. Patients should be given some indication of the financial requirements when they make an appointment for treatment to prevent them from delaying making other arrangements for care while waiting for an appointment at which they will receive no treat-

ment. A defensible decision not to accept a patient for financial reasons can appear questionable in retrospect if the person was injured by the subsequent delay in receiving medical care.

Some physicians will not treat certain individuals or classes of patients. Perhaps the most common restriction is refusing to treat patients involved in accidents that will lead to litigation. Some physicians refuse to treat attorneys. Many obstetricians refuse to treat a pregnant woman who first seeks care after the sixth month of pregnancy. These decisions are shortsighted in a competitive market and ethically questionable in a market where they may make it difficult for the affected persons to obtain care; but they are not illegal.

Assisting at Accidents

A physician has no duty to help an injured or sick individual unless there is a preexisting physician–patient relationship or other statutory or contractual relationship. Although morally reprehensible, it is not illegal for a physician to drive past the scene of an accident where his or her services could be lifesaving or to refuse to provide cardiopulmonary resuscitation to a fellow diner at a restaurant. If the physician does choose to help, there is one central rule for volunteers: do not make the victim worse off.

The classic legal example is the person drowning in a lake. There are several boats within sight of the victim, and one of them heads toward the victim. The others stay away so as not to complicate the rescue. The original rescuing boat now has a duty to continue the rescue because it has interfered with the victim's chance to get other help. In the same way, once a physician stops to help at an accident, the help must be continued until the patient may be safely transferred to another medical care provider or until the patient is no longer in need of medical attention.

Physicians should be careful not to interfere with other persons who have superior skills for the task at hand. If there is ambulance service available, it should be summoned. The paramedic on the ambulance may be much better at resuscitation than the physician is. And a veterinarian with an active farm practice may be a much better candidate for delivering a baby than an internist who has not seen a delivery in 20 years. The internist should stand by, however, in case the veterinarian needs advice or assistance in the care of a human.

Physicians should not be offended if they are asked to provide identification at the scene of an accident. All emergency professionals are plagued by people who join in the excitement. Following the fire brigade is as old as organized fire fighting; impersonating a police officer has been criminalized because it is common and dangerous to society. There are also people who impersonate physicians in hospitals and at the scenes of accidents. Many states provide wallet-sized copies of the medical license to use as identification. Physicians should understand the need for such identification and be willing to provide it.

Although physicians do not have a duty to carry medical equipment with them, it is recommended that they carry basic equipment when traveling. If the physician does volunteer help in an emergency, it is extremely disconcerting not to have the necessary tools available. Many emergency medical technicians, nurses, and doctors keep first-aid equipment in their cars or at home because they do not want to be in an emergency situation without the equipment necessary to save a life. This is especially important for physicians who practice in small towns where there are no paramedics with a readily available and fully equipped ambulance.

Once a physician has assumed the care of a patient in an emergency, the duty to the patient does not end until the patient is assured of proper follow-up care. If the patient is taken away by ambulance, it is wise to notify the hospital that the patient is coming and to pass on medical information. A follow-up call to make sure the patient arrived is also a good idea. Unless there is no question of undetected injury, the patient should not be allowed to assume that the roadside care is all that is required. An emergency room record with notations from the physician at the scene will improve the quality of care a patient receives if late complications develop.

Physicians may be faced with rendering emergency care in a state where they are not licensed. The drowning on the beach, the car accident, or the call for a physician in the air terminal may expose the vacationing physician to the need to practice medicine without a license. Considerations of licensure should not stop a physician from saving a life. The physician should make a good-faith effort to help and should turn the case over to qualified medical personnel as soon as possible. The same rules on relinquishing care and follow-up should be followed as if the physician were licensed. Most state licensing laws explicitly allow for emergency care by nonlicensed personnel, and no state would prosecute a physician for volunteering emergency medical care.

Good Samaritan Laws

There is a widespread myth that physicians will be sued for a poor outcome if they stop to help a stranger in need. Despite the reality that no physician has ever lost a suit over a Good Samaritan act, it is hard for most physicians and nurses to believe that physicians do not get sued for volunteering medical care. Millions of people watched Dr. Kildare lose a suit for helping at the scene of an accident. Every physician has heard a story over coffee about some other physician who got sued. It may have happened to Dr. Kildare, but it has not happened to any real doctors. There have been many cases filed in which poor care was rendered in an emergency, but they were cases where the physician had a duty to treat that patient, not cases of volunteer care. Even before the enactment of Good Samaritan laws, there was a common law protection and a social policy against such suits. Unfortunately, the myth persists because it is an excuse for some physicians who refuse to inconvenience themselves by helping others in emergencies.

Because of the pervasive myth of liability in the medical professions, most states have enacted some form of Good Samaritan law prohibiting a patient from suing a physician or other health care professional for injuries from a Good Samaritan act. To trigger the protection of such an act, two conditions must be satisfied: it must be a volunteer act, and the actions must be a good-faith effort to help. Displacing a neck fracture in an effort to do rescue breathing might be malpractice in the emergency room, but it is not bad faith on the roadside. Trying an unnecessary tracheostomy just for the practice would be bad faith.

The legal problem with Good Samaritan laws is that they were unnecessary. If the common law was a perfect protection against a Good Samaritan lawsuit, then specific Good Samaritan legislation cannot improve the situation. Conversely, by passing statutes, legislatures encourage attorneys to look for loopholes. An attorney who can find a way to convince a jury that a physician was not covered by the Good Samaritan law may be tempted to sue.

In the medical sense, a Good Samaritan is a medical care professional who volunteers to help someone in need of emergency medical care. The act must be done without there being any duty to care for the patient and without any expectation of compensation. The classic case is the physician who comes upon the scene of a car accident. A physician who stops and renders aid to the victims of the accident has acted as a Good Samaritan. If the physician later sends a bill for the emergency services, this is no longer a Good Samaritan action. If the victims spontaneously send the physician a dozen roses as a thank-you gift, this does not affect the voluntary nature of the act.

Conversely, if the physician is being compensated for the work, either with payment or in kind, most Good Samaritan laws will not cover the physician's actions. It is a closer call whether physicians agreeing to provide volunteer care, such as at a Girl Scout camp or a rock concert, are covered by Good Samaritan laws. This will depend on the wording of the specific state law. Some laws stick to the limited definition of a Good Samaritan as someone who volunteers at the scene of an accident or other unexpected site where medical care is necessary. This would not include situations where the physician explicitly assumed the duty to care for a group of people, even for no pay. Physicians who plan on providing this type of care should check with their medical malpractice insurers to be sure it is covered by their policy. Their insurer should also be able to explain the provisions of the applicable Good Samaritan law.

Emergency Care in the Office

Emergencies occur in every type of medical practice. The dermatologist may not treat anaphylaxis as often as the emergency physician, but there is always the chance that a patient will react to a drug. All physicians must consider the types of emergencies that may arise in their practices and be prepared to deal with them. Some minimum standards for all physicians are set by professional organizations and hospital staff rules. Proficiency in basic life support at the level necessary to maintain certification with the American Heart Association or the American Red Cross has become such a common requirement for employment or staff privileges that it is arguably a standard of care for all practicing physicians.

The same general standards of care apply for emergencies as for routine care in the office or the hospital. Specialists are expected to work to the standards of their specialty and to have general competence in other areas of medicine. This can be a problem for subspecialists who were not trained as general practitioners before they did their specialty training. The law assumes that there is a core body of medical knowledge shared by all physicians. This includes the management of basic emergency conditions such as heart attacks and the management of iatrogenic complications of specialty practice, such as anaphylactic shock from a drug administered in the physician's office.

Physicians should have appropriate emergency equipment available where they practice, with the specific equipment needed tailored to the practice and the patient panel. For example, physicians who give injectable drugs should have all the equipment necessary to treat anaphylaxis. If the physician does not treat anyone under the age of 16, pediatric-sized airways are not necessary. If the physician does not treat anyone over the age of 10, a kit full of 18-gauge needles and liter bottles of fluid would not be appropriate. Physicians whose practices include older individuals should have the equipment and training to deal with a myocardial infarction. Although the physician may not cause the patient's heart attack, heart attacks are an expected occurrence in the patient group.

The manufacturers of emergency kits are working to raise the standard of care for office emergency equipment. A bite block made from a tongue depressor and a syringe full of epinephrine taped to the wall is no longer acceptable emergency preparation. Oxygen, intravenous fluids, and steroids may be lifesaving. They are readily available in a suitcase kit that contains protocols for the use of all the equipment. Appropriate drugs and equipment should be readily available in usable form to treat a patient in a foreseeable emergency. Losing a patient to anaphylaxis because there is no oxygen available or the epinephrine is out of date is inexcusable.

Physicians should accompany their patients to the hospital in the emergency transport vehicle if there is no proper paramedic service. Many helicopter transport systems will not allow the attending physician to ride in the helicopter, but these systems usually have appropriate personnel on board. The attending physician should call ahead while the helicopter is en route and talk to the staff physician at the receiving hospital.

Physicians rendering emergency medical care in the office should recognize the limitations of the situation and of their skills. Physicians should not hesitate to call an ambulance to transport a patient to an emergency room. If the physician cannot manage the emergency, it is negligent not to transport the patient to a proper emergency facility. The physician should never send a patient with a serious condition to an emergency room in private transportation. If the condition requires emergency care, the patient should be transported in an ambulance. (This may not hold true in rural areas without available ambulance service. In this case, the physician may need to accompany the patient.) The ambulance personnel may not be able to keep the asthmatic patient from dying, but a jury would never believe that the ambulance would not have helped.

REFERRAL AND CONSULTATION

The legal rules governing referral and consultation evolved in earlier times when patients tended to have long-term relationships with individual physicians. With the advent of team care and the corporatization of medical practice, sorting out the individual responsibilities for a patient's care has become a difficult problem, complicated by the economics of current medical practice (see Chapter 10). Referrals are sometimes a battleground in the fight to retain well-insured patients while minimizing responsibility for uncompensated care. These financial issues complicate malpractice litigation arising from referral-related injuries.

The distinction between a consultation and a referral has become blurred. Nevertheless, it is legally important because it determines whether the responsibility for the patient's care shifts from one physician to another or whether it simply encompasses more physicians. In a *consultation,* the original physician retains the duty to oversee the patient's care. Consultants have an independent duty to the patient, but this does not supplant the duty of the attending physician. In a *referral,* the responsibility for the patient's care shifts from the original physician to the recipient of the referral, who then becomes the attending physician. The consultant relationship is problematic because consultants such as pathologists and radiologists mistakenly assume that they work for the attending physician rather than the patient.

Obtaining a Consultation

Virtually every physician sometimes relies on specialty consultants because of the nature of modern medical practice. No physician can be all things to all patients. Consultations can offer patients the comfort and continuity of receiving care from a single physician, while benefiting from the expertise of specialists. The attending physician benefits from the help and advice of other physicians but retains the primary relationship with the patient.

Consultations have two functions. More commonly, they allow physicians to manage problems that require additional expertise but are within the physician's general area of skill. They are also useful in helping physicians determine if a patient's problem is beyond their skills or available facilities, thus necessitating a referral. The consultation itself does not transfer the responsibility for the patient's care, but the consultant does assume certain duties to the patient. Since the primary physician retains the responsibility for the patient's care, it is this physician, not the consultant, who makes the final treatment decisions. Responsibility becomes an issue only when the consultant and the attending physician disagree about the proper course of action.

The attending physician's better knowledge of the patient and the history of the condition may lead him or her to decide against the recommendations of a consultant, or the attending physician may find that the consultant is not as knowledgeable or skilled as was thought at the time the consultation was requested. When the attending physician disagrees with the consultant, both parties should discuss the disagreement with the patient and their reasons for recommending differing courses of action. It is best for the attending physician and the consultant to talk with the patient at the same time. In discussing the differing recommendations, it is important to differentiate between facts, such as laboratory tests, and opinions, such as interpretation of a panel of tests. This avoids misunderstandings and can sometimes result in a negotiated care plan that meets the needs of all parties. The attending physician should consider a second consultation, but this should not be seen as a poll of the best two out of three. No matter how many consultations are obtained, the medical responsibility remains with the attending physician. It is critical, however, to obtain the patient's informed consent when choosing to ignore the recommendations of a consultant. If the patient decides to follow the advice of the consultant rather than that of the attending physician, the latter should discuss whether the patient needs a different attending physician.

Requesting a Consultation

In most cases the decision to ask for a consultation is a medical judgment. A physician who be-lieves that the patient's care would benefit from another opinion should ask for a consultation. Sometimes hospital or insurance company rules require a consultation before certain therapy begins. For instance, if a patient may not be admitted to the coronary care unit without a cardiology consultation, the general internist has a duty to obtain the consultation to provide the patient with the needed care.

Often a physician must consult another physician to obtain a certain test for a patient. The attending physician may believe that a specific cardiologist is skilled at doing stress tests and cardiac catheterizations but is too quick to recommend bypass surgery. In this case, the attending physician should let the patient know in advance why his or her recommendations may differ from those of the consultant. The attending physician should ensure that the cardiologist understands that this is a consultation, not a referral. Conversely, the cardiologist may believe that the attending physician is endangering the patient by downplaying the seriousness of the condition. The cardiologist has a duty to inform the patient of this opinion, but it is better if this is done in cooperation with the attending physician.

Physicians often obtain informal consultations from colleagues without appreciating the legal significance of this process. Informal consultations are valuable and should be used, but they have limitations. First is the patient's right to privacy and to choose physicians. An informal consultation should be anonymous. Any information that would disclose the identity of the patient should be withheld. In small communities, the physician should ask the patient to consent to an informal consultation. The physician should ensure that informal consultations do not violate any state or federal laws, as might be the case for substance abuse patients.

Patient Choice

Most practitioners are aware of the patient's right to choose a physician for consultation. In the outpatient setting, the patient is unlikely to go to another physician if he or she does not want the consultation. A hospital patient has this same right to choose whether another physician will be consulted. When a consultation is considered, the patient should be informed and given the opportunity to refuse the consultation or the consultant proposed.

When a patient refuses a necessary consultation, the physician should first determine whether the refusal is based on financial concerns. If the patient's insurer will not pay for consultation, the physician has a duty to try to persuade the insurer that the care is necessary. If this fails, the physician should try to persuade the consultant to waive or reduce the fee. If the patient's refusal is not based on financial concerns, the physician should carefully explain (and document) the necessity of the consultation. The problem then becomes the general problem of a patient who refuses necessary care. Although the physician should try to continue treating the patient, this may be impossible; the physician may be forced to terminate the physician–patient relationship (see Chapter 9).

Using Consultants Properly

An attending physician has the legal responsibility to obtain consultations when necessary for the patient's well-being. Physicians must choose consultants carefully, both as to specialty and personal competence. The attending physician must then oversee the actions of the consultant while continuing to provide the patient's general care. When orders are written or accepted by the attending physician, he or she has implicitly ratified the correctness of those orders. It is not a defense to say that the order was written at the suggestion of a consultant.

Physicians may be held liable for substandard care if they fail to obtain a consultation in a case that falls outside their areas of expertise or in a case in which only a consultant can provide necessary tests or procedures. If an internist who cannot do endoscopy is caring for a patient with occult intestinal bleeding, the internist has a duty to consult an endoscopist to obtain the procedure for the patient. The attending physician cannot force a patient to undergo the procedure but must ensure that the test and the consultation are available. If the attending physician leaves the arrangement of the consulta-

tion to the patient, the patient may later contend that he or she had no real opportunity for this care.

A physician has a duty to choose consultants wisely. The physician should know the consultant's qualifications and be assured of the person's competence before asking for a consultation. Usually the attending physician can rely on the process of admission to hospital staff as adequate verification of another physician's qualifications. This reliance assumes that the attending physician has no reason to suspect the consultant. If a consultant does not appear to have appropriate skills or is impaired, the attending physician has a duty to investigate before consulting that particular physician. For example, a surgeon typically may accept as an anesthesiologist any member of the anesthesia group that serves the hospital; the qualifications of the individual anesthesiologists have been checked by the hospital staff committee and the anesthesia group. If, however, the surgeon has reason to suspect the competency of the anesthesiologist, the surgeon has a duty to protect the patient by refusing the anesthesiologist's services.

An attending physician is liable for negligent care that a patient receives from a consultant because the attending physician retains responsibility for the patient's care. An attending physician should never simply turn over the care of the patient to a consultant. The attending should be informed of all actions taken by the consultant and should order all tests, medications, and other changes in the patient's care. If the attending physician does not wish to accept responsibility for the patient's care, the patient should be referred to the consultant or another physician.

Documenting a Consultation

The entire process of consultation should be documented in the patient's chart: the request for consultation or, in the hospital, an order for the consultation; all physical findings and test results; a clear evaluation and recommendation; the attending physician's evaluation of the consultation and his or her own recommendations; and any differences of opinion between the physicians and the basis for the difference. The last should be done clearly and factually, without subjective comments. The chart should reflect that the attending physician appreciated and differed with the consultant's findings. Neither party should denigrate or belittle the other's analysis. Offhand remarks can take on unintended significance when presented in a legal proceeding.

Referral

A referral is the correct choice for a physician when a patient's condition requires care that the attending physician cannot provide—perhaps because of a lack of proper facilities, because it is an area in which the physician lacks sufficient training, or because the physician does not choose to practice medicine in that area. By a proper referral, the original physician may shift the responsibility for the patient's general care or refer the patient only for specialty treatment. In either case, the physician who accepts the referral accepts responsibility for care of the patient.

A physician may refer a patient for specialty care without transferring all responsibility for care. For example, a pediatrician may refer a patient to an otorhinolaryngologist for evaluation and insertion of tympanotomy tubes. This referral is necessary if the pediatrician lacks the training and surgical privileges necessary to provide the needed service. The referring pediatrician could remain the primary physician for the child's preventive care and for other acute problems.

After the surgery and necessary postoperative care, the otorhinolaryngologist sends the child back to the referring pediatrician. However the responsibility for the patient's future care is allocated, it is critical that the physicians involved understand their continuing areas of responsibility. The pediatrician should not assume that the otorhinolaryngologist will provide general medical care to the child; the otorhinolaryngologist should not assume that the pediatrician can manage postoperative complications. Both physicians must take responsibility for the care of the whole patient, with each concentrating on his or her appropriate area of expertise.

The referring physician has a limited duty to ensure the competence of the receiving physician. This is primarily a duty to determine if the physician provides the type of care the patient requires. If the referring physician has reason to believe that the receiving physician is incompetent, there may be liability for negligently selecting the receiving physician. This is a problem in MCOs that dictate the panel of referral physicians. While the primary physician may have no control over the referral, the court may find that there is still a duty to not refer to a physician who is known to be incompetent. If there are questions about the appropriateness of the referral, the referring physician should follow the patient's progress until he or she is confident that the patient is receiving appropriate care.

Duty To Refer

A physician may have the personal skills necessary to provide certain types of specialty care but lack the necessary resources. For example, an internist may be trained in cardiology but be practicing in a hospital that does not have an intensive care unit, or a patient may have a rare disease that can be treated by experimental drugs, but the drugs are licensed only to research centers. In such cases, the patients should be referred to a physician and medical center that have the necessary resources. Physicians must resist institutional pressures not to transfer insured patients if the original institution cannot provide appropriate facilities.

Providing very specialized care may require transferring the patient to a specialty hospital or regional center where none of the staff is known to the referring physician. In this case, the referring physician may have difficulty ensuring the quality of care that the patient will receive. To a large extent, the referring physician may have to rely on the reputation of the center; nevertheless, it is always a good idea to keep in touch with the patient and to request reports from the caregivers to ensure that the referral was appropriate and that the patient is receiving appropriate care.

Duty To Refer to a Nonphysician

In many situations a physician has a duty to refer a patient to a nonphysician for special care. In some cases, such as patients with psychological problems, there may be physicians who could provide the care, but better or more cost-effective service may be available from a psychologist or professional counselor. Many problems are treated only by nonphysicians. A pediatrician who detects a speech defect in a school-aged child has a duty to see that the child is evaluated and treated by a qualified speech therapist, although the speech therapy itself is beyond the realm of pediatric practice. As with other referrals, a referral to a nonphysician should be discussed with the patient.

A physician has the same duties to ensure quality care for patients with referrals to nonphysicians as when referring to another physician. The attending physician must know that the party accepting the referral is qualified to provide the needed care and willing to accept the care of this patient. The physician does not have an ongoing responsibility to monitor the care provided by the nonphysician but should intervene if there are problems with the care rendered.

Referring to Institutions

Physicians often refer patients to institutions rather than to other physicians, a situation that can pose some difficult problems for both the patient and the physician. Most major specialty institutions have specific eligibility criteria and various funding requirements. A children's hospital may not accept patients who are more than 18 years old but make exceptions for patients who have had surgical repairs of congenital defects in that hospital. A cancer center may not accept patients who do not have private health insurance unless the patient is willing to participate in a research protocol that has outside funding. A physician who wishes to refer a patient to such an institution must make sure that the patient is eligible for care and that the institution is willing to accept him or her. The best way to do this is to call someone in charge of admissions at the institution and follow up the conversation with a letter. If the patient is not eligible for that institution, care can be sought elsewhere quickly and without the inconvenience of being turned away.

Eligibility may be based on the patient's financial status or residence. Public charity hospitals normally serve residents of a specific area who have incomes below a certain level. These hospitals do not provide free care to everyone. A patient who has no medical insurance may be considered indigent by a private hospital but not be eligible for free services at the county hospital. Before referring a patient to a charity hospital, the physician should check to make sure that the patient will be accepted, as he or she would with any other institutional referral. The referring physician also must be aware of federal antidumping regulations that carry a fine of up to $50,000 against the physician personally for improper transfers to charity hospitals. The fine is beyond any malpractice claim that might be paid by insurance (see Chapter 4).

The Duty To Find Care

The regionalization of care poses problems for even the best-insured patients. A regional facility, with its complement of subspecialist practitioners, has a substantial stake in keeping specialty beds full. This situation can lead to overinclusive policies on the necessity for specialty care. Neonatologists in some centers, for example, establish standards of care that require pediatricians to refer as many infants as possible to the neonatologists for care. A failure to make these referrals could be malpractice by a pediatrician. The pediatrician, however, does not have the power to force acceptance of a particular patient. If the regional care system is full, the problem of finding a place for a severely premature infant falls to the pediatrician because there is no duty for the neonatologists to transfer less-ill infants to make room for more-ill patients.

A physician with a patient who needs special care must pursue all options until a place is found for that patient. In some celebrated cases involving indigent, premature infants, this has required searching in several states and calling on the military for emergency transport. The physician's best allies in such situations are a newspaper reporter and a public interest attorney. The threat of adverse publicity and litigation can work wonders in finding care for an individual patient.

If rejections happen too frequently, community physicians should work with the regional centers to correct the problem. Specific guidelines should be established that specify which patients have priority for the space available and which patients will be moved or discharged first when a higher-priority patient comes in. It is hard to defend keeping a terminal cancer patient in the only intensive care bed available if it means that a patient with a heart attack may die for lack of care. Physicians who practice in communities that do not provide adequate indigent or specialty medical care services must warn their patients that they may be denied necessary care. Physicians in these areas also should assist patients in using the federal and state laws to gain access to medical care.

Continuing Care

Before referring a patient to a specialty institution, the physician and the patient should decide to what extent the physician will provide continuing care to that patient. Even physicians who no longer provide care after the referral should follow up to make sure that the referral was received and that the patient is being cared for. If the original physician will continue to provide some care for the patient or take the patient back after the special care, he or she should keep abreast of the patient's care at the referral center. Too often, the patient is the only source of information the community physician has. Checking with the patient or family during the course of treatment helps maintain a good relationship and may allow the physician to intervene if necessary.

The referring physician should make sure that complete records on the treatment provided at the referral center accompany the returning patient. The referring physician should insist on receiving copies of any operative reports, significant test results, and discharge summaries. If it is difficult to get such information from the referral center, the physician should consider getting a release from the patient and formally requesting a copy of these sections of the record. The medical records administrator of a large hospital is likely to be prompter and more thorough in honoring such requests than a resident who has moved to another service.

Liability for Improperly Managed Referrals

Referring a patient to another physician generally relieves the original physician of responsibility for the patient's care and reduces his or her liability. However, if the referral is not made correctly, the liability of the referring physician may increase. The referral must be acceptable to all three parties involved: the referring physician, the receiving physician, and the patient. (If the patient requires emergency care or is in labor, the referring physician must comply with the federal laws discussed in Chapter 4.)

Patients have the right to refuse referral without relieving their attending physician of responsibility for their care. To refer patients against their wishes and then withdraw from the patient's care constitutes abandonment. Historically, abandonment did not result in substantial tort losses because patients could usually find substitute care. This is no longer true in many parts of the United States. Abandoned patients, particularly pregnant women, may not be able to find care until they can qualify for emergency care under the federal laws. Referrals must be made so that the patient is ensured of the availability of ongoing care.

When a patient refuses to be referred to another physician, the attending physician should find out why and attempt to correct any problem. If the patient is opposed to the specific physician recommended, another physician should be sought. If the patient's insurance will not pay for the care, the attending physician should help the patient deal with the insurance carrier. If the patient does not want to change physicians, the attending physician should carefully explain to the patient why this change is necessary. (Perhaps the physician does not have the skills or resources needed to continue the case.) The patient should understand that after making appropriate care available, the attending physician will withdraw from the case.

A physician may refuse a referral for a variety of reasons but not if he or she has a preexisting duty to care for the patient (see Chapter 9). The neurosurgeon whose hospital staff privileges are dependent on his accepting referrals from the emergency room, for example, has a duty to treat an accident victim referred from the emergency room. In practice, this duty does not help the emergency room physician or the patient if the neurosurgeon refuses to come in. The emergency room physician must care for the patient until appropriate specialty care becomes available.

The attending physician should ensure that the receiving physician will accept the patient before making the referral. This may be on a patient-by-patient basis or through an ongoing agreement. If the receiving physician refuses to accept the patient, the referring physician must make other arrangements. If the physician refusing the referral has an obligation to accept the referral and still refuses, the referring physician should report the refusal to the proper agency: a hospital medical staff committee, a contractual provider of medical services such as an MCO, or the state board of medical examiners. Physicians should keep in mind that they may become liable for the lack of adequate staff coverage or the misbehavior of other physicians if they acquiesce in the misbehavior.

Being a Consultant

As attorneys become more sophisticated about team medical care delivery, plaintiffs are increasingly suing consultants (see Chapter 10). Hospital and laboratory-based consultants commonly assume that they work for the physician who orders the tests. Legally, this is not so: physician consultants who do individual patient evaluations for the welfare of the patient enter a physician–patient relationship, with all its attendant duties. If a consultant relies on the treating physician to communicate with the patient, there are situations when the consultant can be liable if the patient does not receive the necessary information. The consultant must balance the conflicting roles of adviser to both patient and treating physician. This can lead to some difficult decisions for the consultant when an attending physician does not follow recommendations. Consequently, a consultant must be as careful in choosing which physicians to consult for as an attending physician must be in choosing consultants.

The Consultant–Patient Relationship

Traditionally, the consultant relationship is seen as a physician-to-physician relationship, a view that derives from the business side of consultant practice. Until the recent growth in managed care plans, consultants were dependent on the good will of attending physicians for referrals. Specialists who took patients from primary care physicians by turning consultations into referrals saw their consultations dry up, as did those who questioned the probity of the attending physician's care of the patient. The law, however, insists that the consultant's primary duty is to the patient, not the treating physician: the attending physician is seen as the patient's agent, with the delegated authority to hire other physicians on the patient's behalf.

A physician who is requested to consult on a particular case that involves contact with the patient must first establish a physician–patient relationship with the patient—usually accomplished by an introduction to the patient and an explanation of the consultation requested. A consultant should not assume that the patient has consented to the consultation simply because the attending physician has requested it. Consultants should not rely on blanket consents such as those that authorize treatment from "Dr. Smith and other physicians he or she may designate." Although these are adequate for radiology and pathology consultations and others that do not require direct patient contact, they should be avoided by other consultants. Observing the courtesy of consultation is important. Treating the patient rudely increases the probability of a lawsuit if anything goes wrong and will encourage the patient to refuse to pay for the consultant's services if they are not fully covered by insurance.

The consultant should explain the nature of the consultation and any tests or procedures that will be done. It is wise to make sure that the expectations of the patient and the attending physician are not unreasonable. The consultant should dissuade the patient from the idea that specialists can work miracles. A patient who has a close and long-standing relationship with his or her attending physician is likely to blame the impersonal consultant for problems that arise. This is sometimes implicitly encouraged by attending physicians, who may oversell the consultant's services.

Consultants should do a complete evaluation of the case as soon as the patient accepts the consultation: reviewing the patient's chart, examining the patient fully, and talking with both the patient and the attending physician. Relying on information gathered secondhand is dangerous. The assumption in bringing a consultant into a case is that the attending physician is not as skilled or as knowledgeable about the problem as the consultant. This makes it unacceptable to rely entirely on the history and physical in the chart. Items critical to the specialty consultation should be verified by the consultant.

Tests and Procedures

Consultants who conduct tests or procedures on a patient must first obtain proper informed consent. They must inform the patient of any risks involved and any available alternatives. In the case of diagnostic tests, the patient should be told about the reliability of a test and whether it will make any difference in the choice of therapy. A patient is likely to be angry if he or she is injured by a test that is of diagnostic interest to the physician but has no bearing on how the patient will be treated. Informed consent to dangerous tests is sometimes complicated by the unwillingness of the attending physician to acknowledge the risks of the procedure, thus undermining the consent obtained by the consultant.

Consultants should always determine for themselves if any contraindications exist to a particular procedure or therapy. For example, it is not a defense to say that the chart did not record that a patient was allergic to iodine. The radiologist is responsible for taking an adequate history to determine that it is safe to do an iodine dye study. And the nephrologist who orders an intravenous pyelogram (IVP) should personally ascertain that the patient is not dehydrated, is not pregnant, and is not allergic to the dye. The legal expectation is that all the physicians involved in the procedure will exercise caution to prevent avoidable injuries to the patient.

The results of tests and the recommendations of the consultant must be transmitted to the attending physician in a manner consistent with the urgency of the patient's condition. For example, a cardiologist who reads all electrocardiograms in a hospital may have the reading posted on the chart by the next morning. If a routine ECG turns out to have a life-threatening arrhythmia on it, the cardiologist must ensure that the patient is treated immediately. This duty is not discharged by noting the arrhythmia on the report and sending the report to the patient's chart, to be seen many hours later.

Informing the Patient

Consultants who personally examine and talk to the patient have a duty to make sure that a patient is informed about the results of the consultation. Since a consultation is intended to assist the attending physician in making medical decisions, it may seem that informing the attending physician should be sufficient. It may not be when the consultant has established a direct physician–patient relationship with the patient. Discussing findings with the patient gives the consultant the opportunity to ensure that his or her recommendations and findings are known and understood by the patient. It also gives the consultant the opportunity to withdraw explicitly from the case and relinquish responsibility to the attending physician. This gives the patient and the nursing staff a clear understanding of who is in charge of the care of the patient.

Sometimes a consultant has a duty to intervene in a patient's care. In the case of the cardiologist who discovers a life-threatening arrhythmia, it is unlikely that the patient or the attending physician will object to emergency orders if the attending physician is not available. When the attending and consulting physicians do not agree, the consultant usually should not countermand the orders of the attending physician. It is best to discuss the problem with the attending physician before talking to the patient. The attending physician may be able to provide additional information or insight that will obviate the disagreement. If the consultant and the attending physicians still disagree, the consultant must fully inform the patient, or the person legally authorized to consent to the patient's medical care, about the disagreement and the options for care.

Patients retain the right to choose their physicians and their care. In some cases, the patient will choose to follow the advice of the attending physician. If so, the consultant should document any disagreements and the patient's choice and then formally withdraw from the case if the disagreements are important enough to warrant this decision. With a hospitalized patient, the consultant should file an incident report if he or she believes the patient is at risk. If the patient chooses to follow the advice of the consultant, the consultant should be prepared to act as attending physician for the patient. If the consultant cannot act as attending physician, both physicians should be ready to assist the patient in finding another physician who meets the patient's needs. Neither physician should abandon the patient.

Recordkeeping

Consultants are held to the same standards for recordkeeping as attending physicians. All pertinent information—history, physical findings, consent, test results, and contacts with the patient—should be reflected in the chart. In addition, the consultant should provide a written consultation report to the attending physician. The consultant's report should be complete and understandable and avoid the use of abbreviations and specialty jargon. A PPD, for example, is an intradermal test for tuberculosis infection to an infectious disease physician, but postpartum depression to a psychiatrist. Distinguishing the two is very important in a postpartum patient suffering from fatigue. Consultants create unnecessary legal liability when their recommendations are not clear and understandable.

Public Duties

The practice of medicine encompasses specific duties to the public and society. These duties apply to all physicians, attending and consulting. Every jurisdiction in the United States requires the reporting of certain infectious diseases and certain types of injury that may result from a criminal act (see Chapter 12). A radiologist who sees suspicious injuries on a child's X ray has the duty to report these findings to the child protection agency. The consultant's duty to report is independent of previous reports by the attending physician. The consultant should not be a party to any agreements by the attending physician not to comply with the reporting laws.

Institutional Consultants

Physicians whose specialty requires a hospital-based practice are often practicing as consultants without realizing it. The contracts under which they practice in the hospital make them formal consultants for most of the patients admitted. The consultations are done as a matter of routine, often without the patient and physician ever seeing one another. Nevertheless, the consultations and the accompanying charges for service establish a physician–patient relationship, with all its attendant duties. When they exercise independent medical judgment, they enter into a physician–patient relationship with their invisible clientele.[3] Because these specialists usually perform their work at the request of a primary treating physician, they often see their duty as flowing to the physician rather than to the patient—a concept that creates risks for the patient and both physicians.

Most of the work of radiologists and pathologists does not involve directly dealing with the patient. Nonetheless, they have a relationship with the patient to the extent that they interpret tests or otherwise exercise medical judgment on the patient's behalf. In these cases, the courts consider the physician who ordered the test as the patient's agent who creates a physician–patient relationship with the consultant on the patient's behalf.[3] If the test is negligently interpreted, the consultant will be liable for whatever damages the patient suffers.

Generally the courts find that passing the information about abnormal test results on to the ordering physician satisfies the consultant's duty to the patient.[4] The problems arise in how this is done in situations where the consultant finds a condition that requires urgent treatment, but has reason to know that the ordering physician is unaware of the urgency. This will usually involve either ancillary findings, or unanticipated findings. Although there has been little litigation on the point, at least one court has found that there can be a duty to directly contact the ordering physician or the patient.[5] In another case, the report the radiologist sent never reached the ordering physician. The court found the radiologist could be liable for any injuries occasioned by delay or improper treatment due to the miscommunication.[6]

This is an area where managed care and its weakening of the relationship between the patient and the treating physician can be expected to increase liability. The legal opinions on duty to inform patients of test results make it clear that the remedy lies against the treating physician if that physician has been properly informed by the consultant, but against the consultant if there has not been a proper warning. To the extent that the consultant cannot reasonably expect that reports will be promptly acted on by the receiving physician, or that the reports may not reach the treating physician at all, the courts will probably be willing to find that there is a duty to inform the patient directly. A report addressed to a clinic, or to the physician of the day, may not be seen by a jury as properly discharging the duty to inform the patient.

Radiology

The usual system for providing radiology services in a hospital is a contract between the hospital and an individual physician or a practice group. The group agrees to supervise technical personnel and to read and interpret all tests. The hospital gives the group an exclusive contract to provide these services and requires that all tests done in the hospital be done through the group. Patients eventually receive a bill from the radiology group.

One source of liability for radiologists is improper supervision of nonphysician technical personnel and equipment. Physicians are responsible for ensuring that the personnel are adequately trained and doing their jobs properly. Patients must be protected from falls and other simple injuries.

The radiologists must ensure that all equipment is functioning, that the tests are technically adequate, and that patients are not exposed to excessive doses of radiation.

Radiologists must carry out special tests and invasive procedures safely and accurately. Whenever there are invasive procedures, the radiologist should review the patient's history, do a physical examination as necessary to verify critical information, and obtain informed consent for the procedure. For example, if the attending physician has ordered an IVP and the patient is dehydrated, the radiologist has a duty to cancel or postpone the test until the patient is able to tolerate it. If the IVP was done by a technician without the radiologist's evaluating the patient, the radiologist is responsible, not the attending physician. The attending physician would argue that determining the patient's fitness for the test at the scheduled time is the radiologist's responsibility.

Radiologists should interpret tests as completely as possible. There is an unfortunate tendency to equivocate on reports as a way of avoiding responsibility. Giving a report of "possible pneumonitis" instead of "right lower lobe infiltrates consistent with bacterial pneumonia" does not provide the attending physician with the benefit of the expert opinion that a radiologist is expected to provide. Vague readings increase the consultant's liability when they mask serious conditions or substitute for an in-depth review of the film.

Radiologists have a duty to make sure attending physicians are informed quickly of any serious or life-threatening conditions found on a test. Technicians should routinely inform their supervising radiologists about any serious results or results that are strange or unusual. Radiologists also must ensure that the patient is informed of test results and their significance. Usually this is done by alerting the attending physician, who in turn informs the patient and recommends any necessary care. This generally discharges the radiologist's duty to inform the patient personally.

Pathologists

Pathologists' liability stems primarily from quality control and communication problems. Pathologists depend on the attending physician for the collection of samples to be analyzed. When mistakes in labeling result in a patient with a benign condition being subjected to a mutilating surgical procedure, or a serious condition being misdiagnosed, lawsuits are inevitable. Pathologists should ensure that samples are unambiguously labeled upon receipt, when it may still be possible to correct mistakes. If there is any question about the origin of a sample, the attending physician must be notified at once.

Pathologists should follow the same procedures as radiologists to determine that significant laboratory findings are received and appreciated by the attending physician. This is particularly important for rapidly evolving conditions or life-threatening conditions. This type of information should be handled differently from information that is not time critical. Pathologists who practice alone in small laboratories should see to it that the laboratory has formal mechanisms for communicating time-critical information. If the communication of these results depends on ad hoc calls to the attending physician by the pathologist, there is a high probability that the system will break down if a substitute pathologist fills in during a vacation or illness.

Cardiology

Many hospitals have instituted quality assurance systems that require that all ECGs be read by a hospital cardiologist, just as X rays are read by a hospital radiologist. Cardiologists who review routine ECGs must realize that this creates a duty to ensure that the results of the reading are acted on properly. These duties may be more extensive than the duties of a pathologist or a radiologist because cardiologists also act as treating consultants. A cardiologist is expected to know whether the drugs the patient is taking are appropriate to someone with particular ECG findings and to intervene if they are not. A dangerous finding on an ECG may create a duty for the cardiologist to do a full evaluation and consultation in order to ensure that the patient is being cared for properly.

LIMITED DUTY RELATIONSHIPS

The previous discussion presumed that the physician would be treating or at least directly dealing with the patient in a situation where the patient has an expectation that there is a traditional physician relationship. There are many physicians, such as radiologists and pathologists, who make professional judgments about patients, but who do not have a direct relationship with patients. Occupational medicine physicians have a direct relationship with the patient, but not in a situation where the patient has the reasonable expectation of a traditional physician–patient relationship (see Chapter 15). Specialty practitioners of all types have relationships circumscribed by the specialty.

Specialty Care

Most physicians engage in a specialty practice, with almost all new licensees being specialists. Specialties range from narrow interests in an obscure disease to family practice. The more narrow the specialty is, the smaller is the potential patient population. If patients selected physicians at random, then narrow interest specialists would spend all their time turning away patients. The reality is that specialists with narrow interests traditionally depend upon referrals from other physicians rather than marketing their services to patients directly.

The most important limitation on a physician's willingness to accept a patient is that of a self-imposed specialty. Although there is nothing in the law to prevent a dermatologist from practicing general medicine, most dermatologists will decline to regulate a patient's diabetes. In the same sense, a family physician may be willing to treat acne and diabetes but unwilling to perform surgery. These limitations cause a problem only if they are not known to the patient when making an appointment. For example, a patient with severe hypertension makes an appointment with an internist. After taking the patient's medical history, the physician tells the patient that he limits his practice to gastroenterology. The patient would be justified in refusing to pay for the visit. More important, this unnecessary appointment may delay proper treatment for the patient's condition. In this situation, the physician should arrange for a referral and send the patient to an emergency room if he is concerned with the delay in seeing the second physician.

The Treating Specialist

Treating specialists have limited their practice to a certain specialty area but treat patients independent of a primary care physician. This includes most of the non–hospital-based specialties, such as endocrinology, gastroenterology, and gynecology. The duty to treat is more stringent for treating specialists because of the prescreening that their patients undergo. Unlike family practitioners, whose patients are mostly self-selected, specialists evaluate a patient before determining if they will accept the patient. Thus, the specialists have much more freedom to refuse to treat a patient, creating a greater duty to continue treating the patient once the patient has been accepted.

Within certain limitations, a specialist may examine and diagnose a patient without creating a physician–patient relationship. Assuming non-emergency care and no contractual obligations to the patient (such as MCO relationships), the specialist may determine if the patient falls into his or her chosen area of expertise. This opportunity to evaluate a patient before accepting him or her carries a corresponding duty to continue treating the patient. This duty is predicated on the patient's greater reliance on the specialist, as evidenced by the greater amount of time and money expended to be accepted for care by the specialist. This greater duty is tempered by the specialist's greater freedom to transfer the patient for complaints unrelated to the original disease that brought the patient under the specialist's care.

Referral is one of the most difficult judgments in specialty practice. Specialists have a duty to continue treating a patient until the person may be safely released from treatment or until a proper transfer of care may be arranged. The problem is the patient who develops conditions outside the specialist's area of expertise but for whom no substitute physician can be found. The choice is between treating a condition outside the specialist's chosen area or not treating the secondary problem. For example, assume that an obstetrician has a patient who is several months pregnant. This patient develops serious thyroid disease, but the obstetrician is unable to find a specialist willing to see the patient. In this situation, the obstetrician would be obligated to treat the thyroid disease, despite its being outside his or her chosen area of expertise.

The more difficult problem is the patient who develops a condition that the specialist cannot treat alone, but the management of which is part of his or her specialty—for example, a gastroenterologist who finds that the patient has acute appendicitis. The physician cannot perform the surgery, but it would be unacceptable to try to treat the patient without surgery. The gastroenterologist must be able to arrange proper surgical referrals as part of his or her duty to the patient. The patient is entitled to assume that the specialist is prepared to coordinate all of the personnel necessary to treat the patient's gastrointestinal problems.

Occupational Physician–Patient Relationship

Most of the law on occupational medical services involves full-time employee physicians working for the employer, or contract physicians who only perform screening examinations. In these cases, the courts have found that patients receiving occupational medical services and examinations do not have the expectation of a full physician–patient relationship in all situations. If the physician is performing a screening examination for someone other than the patient, such as an employer or insurer, there is no physician–patient relationship. The patient must be told of abnormal results that the health care practitioner knows of, but may not sue for failure to detect problems.[7] The physician can be liable if he or she injures the patient during the examination.[8] If the occupational medicine physician treats the patient, there is a physician–patient relationship for that treatment and the physician will be liable for any medical malpractice. The physician's duty will be limited to the injury and conditions related to it. There is no broader duty to evaluate the patient's condition, even if such evaluation would be standard of care in a non–occupational medicine setting.

CONTRACTUAL AND STATUTORY DUTIES TO TREAT

Under the traditional common law, physicians and patients entered into voluntary contracts for services. Patients could choose their own physicians, and physicians were free to refuse to treat patients for any reason they chose. This right to refuse to treat was substantially limited by the Civil Rights laws in the 1960s. Health care practitioners and institutions could no longer refuse to treat based on race, religion, or ethnicity. Subsequent to the Civil Rights Act, the government further limited physicians' right to refuse to treat in the Americans with Disabilities Act (ADA) and the Emergency Medical Treatment and Active Labor Act (EMTALA) (see Chapter 4). However, the greatest change in the freedom of physicians and patients to contract for health care has been brought about by private health plans, not statutes. As private insurance plans have moved to the MCO model, they have limited both the physician's right to refuse to treat and the patient's right to choose his or her physician.

Emergency Medical Treatment and Active Labor Act (EMTALA)

Hospitals with emergency facilities must provide medical screening and needed treatment to all persons who request emergency medical care, including delivering the infant of a woman in labor (see Chapter 4). The important consideration for physicians is that the law is structured to trigger the physician–patient relationship: whenever a patient presents with a request for emergency care, the patient must receive a medical screening examination from either a physician or someone under the supervision of a physician. Once the patient receives this examination, the physician will have exercised independent medical judgment on

behalf of the patient, the patient will have relied on that judgment, and the physician will be required to provide all necessary care until the patient can either be discharged from the hospital or transferred to another physician.

This duty is not limited to the physicians on duty in the emergency room. Most hospital by-laws require medical staff members to assist in the delivery of emergency care if needed or to participate in a specialty call system. This contractually obligates the physician to treat persons in the emergency room when called on by the hospital. If a physician refuses to treat a patient when requested under this agreement, the hospital has the contractual right to cancel the physician's medical staff privileges. Such a refusal also violates the physician's duty under EMTALA and will subject the physician to sanctions under the Act. Even if the hospital wants to avoid this by not calling the physicians for indigent patients, EMTALA requires that the hospital provide on-call physicians for specialty care.

Physicians can violate EMTALA in three ways: they can refuse to do screening examination; they can refuse to provide needed care; and they can improperly transfer the patient to another facility. A proper transfer can only be done when the patient is stable, when there is a medical justification for the transfer, when the receiving hospital agrees to accept the transfer, and when all of this has been properly documented according to the standards of EMTALA. If the physician violates EMTALA, the government can impose a fine of up to $50,000 and ban the physician from participating in federal reimbursement programs. Other federal rules prevent the physician from working with any health care institution that participates in federal reimbursement programs, making it impossible to work in most health care jobs.

EMTALA does not create a cause of action against the physician, although it does create one against the hospital. The only basis for a patient lawsuit against the physician is medical malpractice. Unfortunately, since the physician has a physician–patient relationship with the patient, actions that violate EMTALA will probably also be medical malpractice. In addition, the hospital can sue the physician for indemnification for any losses it sustains because of the physician's failure to comply with EMTALA. This means that the physician could end up paying for a patient's lawsuit against the hospital for the EMTALA violation. Most troubling for physicians, a recent U.S. Supreme Court case found that EMTALA applied to the transfer of a patient to a nursing facility several months after the patient's initial admission to the hospital.[9] This was based on the fact that she had never been stabilized after a very severe automobile accident and did suffer injuries secondary to her transfer. It raises the issue of whether EMTALA applies to every discharge or transfer of a patient, not just those that occur in the emergency department.

Americans with Disabilities Act

As discussed in Chapter 15, the ADA's employment provisions applies to all businesses with 15 or more employees, which would include many medical practices. (It would include all practices that are owned by a hospital because the count is of all the employees in the entire corporation.) The ADA also has access provisions that apply to all businesses that are deemed a public accommodation, irrespective of how many employees they have. Physicians' offices are deemed a public accommodation under the Act and must meet the standards for handicapped access, such as wheelchair-accessible offices. The Act also bars discrimination in treatment based on disability. There was only one Supreme Court case on point at the time this was written, and it concerned a dentist who wanted to fill the cavity of an HIV (human immunodeficiency virus)-infected patient at the hospital, rather than in his office. (See Chapter 15 for a detailed discussion of the case.) The Court found that a health care practitioner could not refuse to treat a patient, or treat a patient differently, based on a disability, unless there was a valid medical reason for the disparate treatment.

In this case, the dentist invoked the exception in the ADA for situations that pose a risk to others. The dentist argued, with little support, that filling a cavity would pose an infection risk because of the aerosolized blood and tissue containing HIV. The dentist said he would rather do this in the hospital operating room because it had better protections against contamination. The U.S. Supreme Court said that he must treat the patient unless he could prove that there was a risk of transmission and sent the case back to the lower court to investigate the evidence of risk. The lower court found that the dentist did not prove his case for risk and sanctioned him for failing to treat the patient.[10] (The dentist did not put on a very strong case, and it is not clear whether he might have prevailed with better evidence.)

What the Court left unsaid was the extent to which the ADA prevents physicians from refusing to treat patients with disabilities when the objection is because the physician does not want to treat the underlying condition. Can an internist choose to not treat diabetics because he or she does not want keep up with diabetes treatment? What if a family practitioner does not know how to handle the new drugs for HIV? Does he or she have to treat HIV patients anyway, with the risk that they will not receive optimal treatment?

MCOs

With the recent growth of MCOs, many physicians have contracted with insurance carriers to treat any patient insured by that carrier. This obviates the physician's right to refuse to treat. A person who is injured because a physician wrongfully refuses to accept him or her as a patient may sue the physician based on this contractual agreement with the insurance company. Unlike traditional physician–patient relationship law, which is based on the physician–patient dyad, MCO contracts can create a physician–patient relationship with a class of persons rather than with a single individual. When a member of this class requests treatment, the physician has the responsibility to treat that person as an accepted patient.

Closed-panel MCOs are the most restrictive type of health insurance scheme. The degree of restriction on the patient's choice of physicians varies among organizations, but in general, closed

HMO patients have a physician assigned to care for them. The physicians have even less choice of which patients they may treat. In this situation, the traditional assumption of a freely determined physician–patient relationship is inapplicable, and the physician's duty to the patient probably begins when the patient is assigned as part of the physician's panel. In preferred provider organizations (PPOs) and other MCO arrangements in which the patients have a smaller copayment if they are treated by certain physicians, the choice of physicians is limited, but unless the list is very short, the patients still perceive that they are choosing the physician. The physicians' position is more ambiguous. They may retain the right to refuse to treat patients of their choosing, but it is more usual that the PPO contract requires them to treat any PPO patient who presents in the office, subject to limitations of scheduling and specialty practice.

EXPECTATION OF CONTINUED TREATMENT

There is a presumption that treating a patient creates an ongoing physician–patient relationship. This presumption derives from the traditional relationship between physicians and their patients. It is questionable how effectively it describes modern innovations such as ambulatory care centers in shopping malls and contract emergency room physicians. The extent of the physician's continuing responsibility to the patient is predicated on whether the patient has a reasonable expectation of continued treatment, the nature of the patient's illness, and whether the physician explicitly terminates the relationship.

The family doctor is the idealized physician–patient relationship beloved by nostalgia buffs and television script writers. In this romantic notion of medical practice, these physicians are intimately acquainted with all the details of their patients' lives, payment is never an issue, and the patients have unlimited resources to comply with the physician's recommended treatment. Life was never this way. The central problem for family physicians or general practitioners is to reach an accommodation between their style of practice and patients' expectations. This accommodation helps prevent legal misunderstandings, but its most important goal is preserving trust and mutual respect between physicians and their patients. How this accommodation is reached depends on the type of practice each physician is engaged in.

The law requires a physician to provide treatment to a patient until that patient can be transferred to another physician safely or can be released from care. The physician is not required to provide that treatment personally, but responsibility for after-hours care and emergency care is always a vexing issue. This is easier to manage in urban settings because of the availability of alternative medical care. Urban physicians usually have arrangements with other physicians to share calls, reducing the burden of 24-hour responsibility for patient care. The availability of emergency room facilities can relieve the burden of after-hours care as well as provide care for patients who may need more extensive services than are available in the office. The problem of urban practitioners is educating patients about the use of these alternative sources of care.

The main problem with small town practice is the lack of backup coverage, either through fellow practitioners or through easily accessible emergency room facilities. Physicians in this situation will face the "super doc" dilemma: the "If I don't treat them, nobody will!" mind-set. Although there is great ego gratification in being indispensable, this leads to burnout and the compromising of professional standards. Physicians must take personal time for relaxation and education and arrange for backup medical care for those times.

TERMINATING THE RELATIONSHIP

The initiation and termination of physician–patient relationships are legally risky events. At both times, it is critical that the physician and the patient have the same expectations and that the patient's health not be compromised by the physician's actions. Terminations are becoming increasingly risky because market pressures are making it more difficult for physicians to maintain long-term relationships with their patients.

Abandoning Patients

Abandonment is the legal term for terminating the physician–patient relationship in such a manner that the patient is denied necessary medical care. This should always be avoided. The legal liability becomes significant when the patient is injured by the failure to receive medical care. Abandonment can be intentional or inadvertent. *Intentional abandonment* is legally riskier because a jury may choose to award punitive damages as punishment for intentionally putting a patient's health at risk.

The most common reason for intentional abandonment of a patient is failure to pay the physician's fees, either by the patient or by the patient's insurance company. This is also legally the least justifiable. Juries have little sympathy for physicians who deny a patient necessary care because the patient is unable to pay the bill. Perhaps the worst case occurs when the physician denies the patient care because the patient's insurance company has refused to pay. If the insurance company has mistakenly denied coverage, the jury may take its anger out on the physician for allegedly conspiring with the insurance company to deny the patient medical care. A physician who is considering refusing to treat a patient for any reason, including failure to pay, should make sure that he or she can ensure that the patient will not be injured by this action.

Inadvertent abandonment usually occurs through misunderstandings about backup coverage when the physician is unavailable. Although a jury will be much more sympathetic if the physician was unavailable because of a medical emergency, as opposed to a social event, the reason makes little difference to the patient in need of care. Many physicians would never go to a party without arranging to receive their calls or providing someone else to cover emergencies, but they may become involved in lengthy hospital procedures that render them unavailable without arranging any coverage.

Failure of the system for backup coverage can result in constructive abandonment. A physician who is part of a group that shares calls on a set schedule can get in trouble if the person on call does not show up. The physician's duty is to his or her patient. If the patient is injured because of a problem with the call schedule, it is the patient's original physician, not the on-call physician, who is ultimately liable. It is important to verify call arrangements each time, rather than relying on habit or custom.

Patients may be abandoned through failures in the scheduling system. The appointment clerk may functionally abandon a patient by refusing to let a patient talk to the medical personnel, by scheduling an appointment too far in the future, or by filing away the chart of a patient who failed to keep an important follow-up appointment.

Patient-Initiated Terminations

In the simplest scenario, the patient voluntarily terminates the physician–patient relationship and seeks care from another physician. Unfortunately, patients sometimes stop coming before they are fully recovered from the acute condition that brought them to the physician. When this happens, the physician must make some effort to determine whether the patient is knowingly forgoing further care, has found another physician, or is staying away out of ignorance or a misunderstanding of the physician's instructions. As discussed later under "documentation," the process of investigating the patient's disappearance also generates the necessary record that the physician has discharged the duty to the patient.

An adult patient has the right to refuse to follow the physician's advice. If this person understands the need for further treatment and the consequences of not having that treatment, the physician has no legal liability for the patient's subsequent course. (The physician's duty is different for minor and incompetent patients.) The problem arises in establishing what the patient was told. A jury will presume that a severely injured patient would not have refused to follow the physician's instructions if he or she had understood the consequences of the refusal. An example of this problem arose when a woman died of cervical cancer and her family sued the physician for failure to diagnose.[11] The physician argued that she had refused a Pap smear, and this prevented him from making a proper diagnosis. The physician lost. The jury did not believe that he had properly informed her of the value of the test. His credibility was undermined because she had dutifully returned for gynecological checkups, including pelvic examinations, and he had never documented the refusal of the test in the medical record. It was hard to believe that she would go to this much trouble and refuse a minor diagnostic test.

Problems also arise if the patient has misunderstood either the physician's directions as to the need for further care or the seriousness of forgoing further care. In this situation the patient is not intentionally accepting the risk of injury. The physician may be liable if it can be established that the patient was not properly informed about the need for further treatment. There are steps the physician may take to ensure that the patient receives the proper information, but nothing can ensure that the patient understands this information. Since the goal of the physician is to prevent patient injuries whenever possible, he or she should make some effort to follow up with patients who do not return for needed visits.

Patients sometimes discharge their physicians explicitly. They may fire the physician over a disagreement or courteously inform the physician that they are seeking care elsewhere. In either case, the physician should endeavor to identify the subsequent treating physician and document the patient's decision to seek care elsewhere. If the patient has a new physician, the patient should be asked to write down the name of the new physician so that records may be forwarded. If the patient has not made arrangements for care, the physician should reiterate the need for care and offer to help the patient find a new physician. These efforts will help ensure that the patient receives proper care. If, despite the physician's efforts, the patient does not follow through in seeking proper care, there will be evidence that the original physician made a good-faith effort to help the patient.

Many medical insurance schemes use financial incentives to coerce patients into abandoning their usual physicians. The purpose is to shift patients to the care of physicians who have agreed contractually with the insurance company to accept reduced fees, modify their way of practice, or both. The effect is that the patient is forced to discontinue an established medical relationship and seek care from a new physician who is unfamiliar with the patient's condition. This poses a legal risk to physicians who subsequently treat these patients. Patients who are forced to abandon a long-standing relationship with a physician may be very demanding of a physician they see under duress. This increases the probability that misunderstandings and bad results will escalate to litigation. It also puts the physician at a medical disadvantage. He or she is expected to pick up the patient's care exactly where the previous physician left off, without the benefit of the previous physician's knowledge of the patient.

The physician who accepts a new patient who has sought care voluntarily is not expected to have all the knowledge of the patient's condition that the previous physician possessed.

Physician-Initiated Termination of Care

When a physician–patient relationship must be terminated, the physician must carefully document the circumstances in the patient's medical record. This termination note should review the patient's previous medical treatment and the current state of the patient's health. If the termination will not affect the patient's health, this should be stated and explained. If the patient is in need of continuing care, the note must explain how the physician has ensured that the termination will not compromise the patient's health. For patients in need of continuing care, there must be documentation of the arrangements made for the patient's subsequent care. If no arrangements have been made, there needs to be a detailed discussion of why the relationship is being terminated and why it was not possible to make follow-up arrangements.

There are several acceptable reasons for terminating the relationship with a patient who is still in need of medical care for an acute problem. One is that the patient has refused to follow the physician's advice to the extent that it becomes impossible to care for the patient in a professional manner.[12] For example, a severely hypertensive patient may refuse to take medication. Assuming this refusal is not based on a reasonable concern with the side effects of the medicine, the physician is not bound to try to continue treating a patient who refuses what the physician believes to be essential therapy. The case of *Bouvia v. Superior Ct.*,[13] in which a person with cerebral palsy sought the legal right to force a hospital to starve her to death, is an extreme example of this problem.

Physicians may also terminate the physician–patient relationship when changing circumstances in a physician's practice may make it difficult to care for a patient in a professional manner. The physician may be changing the nature of the practice (such as working part time), moving to a different geographic area, or joining a corporate practice that will make it difficult to continue treating former patients.

DOCUMENTING THE TERMINATION

When the relationship between a physician and patient is terminated, the exact circumstances of the termination must be documented. The patient's condition should be summarized in the same manner as a discharge note in a hospital record. For each ongoing medical problem that is identified, there should be evidence that the patient was notified of the problem and the need for further care. If the physician knows who the patient is transferring to, this should be recorded in the termination note.

A physician who terminates the physician–patient relationship must document that the patient was properly notified. The physician should write a termination note in the patient's chart documenting that the patient was contacted and told of the physician's decision, its medical implications, and where to obtain further care, if needed. This information should also be put in a letter to the patient. If possible, the patient should sign a copy of this letter during a visit with the physician. The physician should give the patient the original letter, keeping the signed copy for the files. If this is

not possible, the letter should be sent by certified mail, with a return receipt requested. The certified mail number should be noted in the letter, and a copy of the letter and the return receipt should be put in the patient's medical record. If the letter is returned and efforts to find a correct address fail, the unopened letter in the patient's record will document that a diligent effort was made to contact the patient.

Patient-initiated terminations must be carefully documented. Although the patient always has the right to terminate the physician–patient relationship, this is usually done not by confronting the physician but passively by not returning for care. It is the physician's responsibility to follow up on patients who disappear if they have conditions that require continuing medical care. (It is also good business to keep track of patients and their reasons for seeking care elsewhere.) These conditions may be acute, such as an orthopaedic patient who does not return to have a cast removed, or chronic, such as a diabetic.

Following up on missing patients requires that medical records be kept in such a manner that the physician is aware that a patient has been lost to follow-up. Tickler files serve as reminders that a patient is due to return for care. These may be computerized, or kept in a manual tickler file. When a patient misses an appointment, the physician should call to find out what has happened to the patient. If the patient cannot be located, refuses to come back, or has found care elsewhere, the physician should document this information in the chart. The physician should send the patient a certified letter explaining why the patient should return or find alternate care.

TELEMEDICINE AND INTERNET MEDICINE

Since the 1950s, health planners and medical informatics sages have wanted to link local practitioners in remote areas with specialists in academic medical centers. Despite several pilot projects and substantial federal monetary support, practical remote medical consultations remained beyond reach until recently. The revolution in personal computers and Internet communications makes it possible to piggyback telemedicine on multiuse computers and communications channels. This solves the key technological problem that stalled the routinization of telemedicine—access to sufficient audio and video processing power and communications bandwidth at an affordable cost. With the technological barriers lowered, the implementation of effective telemedicine now depends on solving legal and reimbursement policy questions. Until these questions are resolved, telemedicine poses substantial legal risks, making it essential that health care practitioners who are involved with telemedicine understand the basic legal constraints on such practice.

Traditional Electronic Physician–Patient Relationships

Physicians and patients have used electronic consultations since Alexander Graham Bell invented the telephone. Patients call their physician for medical advice and physicians call other physicians for consultations. Records have also moved electronically between physicians, first as photocopies, then as faxes. For decades, laboratory tests, X rays, and ECGs have been evaluated by physicians who never see or talk to the patient. As discussed elsewhere in this chapter, the law has developed criteria for the legal duties that attach to these relationships, including when a physician–patient relationship is formed and when the remote physician has a duty to report directly to the patient.

Some of the current concerns with video and computer-based telemedicine are no different than they were with traditional telemedicine; the change is that we ignored them when it was the telephone and we now worry about them when it is the computer. Foremost among these is the issue of state licensing. Health care practitioners are licensed to practice medicine by the state, and one state's license does not allow practice in a different state. There has been a great deal of concern about the legal problem of telemedicine over state lines. The concern is legitimate, it is just not new: physicians and patients have been talking on the tele-

phone across state lines for as long as they have been using the telephone. This is especially evident in cities such as Kansas City, where the state line dividing Kansas from Missouri runs through the middle of the city. Although most physicians in one state know they cannot set up an office in the other state without getting a second license, none hesitates in giving patients across the state line advice over the telephone. This is true in all communities near state lines, although it is technically practicing medicine without a license because most states regard the location of the patient as the location where the care is delivered.

Traditional phone consultations and the review of tests and records by consultant physicians are predicated on there being either an existing relationship with a physician who was physically present, or that such a face-to-face relationship would follow the phone conversation if it was a patient asking a new physician for advice. Patients calling across state lines does not concern state licensing agencies as long as this is just an adjunct to the primary physical physician–patient relationship that is within the state where the physician is licensed. In contrast, telemedicine has been promoted as a way to bring physician services to remote areas without physicians, and to allow patients to have consultations with specialists that are not available in their area.

Licensure Issues

Health care practitioners, lawyers, and many other professionals are licensed by the states, rather than the federal government. Historically, the federal government had little or no role in the licensing of professionals, with the exception of patent agents and persons involved in shipping and, later, aviation. This made sense because, at one time, there were substantial differences in medical practice among the states. With the advent of modern medical training, national certification of medical schools and residencies, and national licensing exams, state standards for medical practice and for licensing have become very uniform, weakening the rationale for state licensing. (States do differ on whether physicians who have been out of school for more than 10 years have to retake a certifying examination and in certain other requirements that can make getting a license much more time consuming in some states than in others.)

The best rationale for continuing to license physicians at the state, rather than national, level is that the practice of medicine has been a very local activity and that local regulators are in a better position to supervise it. This is certainly true as regards consumer complaints. It is less true for professional review actions, since the information available to the state licensing agency is usually provided by reports to the National Practitioner Databank. There is also a strong component of trade regulation in the licensing of health care practitioners, which is expressed through the legislature's and the licensing agency's definition of the scope of each license. Each licensed group seeks to expand their license, usually at the expense of other licensed and unlicensed groups. A recent example is the fight over the licensing of acupuncture practitioners. If acupuncture is restricted to physicians, then the traditional healers will be unable to practice unless associated with a physician. Although this has the benefit of ensuring that the patient receives the full spectrum of medical care, it increases the cost of such care. (It also raises the issue of how physicians can supervise an activity that they know nothing about.)

Interstate Enforcement Issues

The concern with licensing remote practitioners who do not have a presence in the state involves both considerations of quality control and trade restrictions. Assuming that the practitioner is properly licensed in a remote state, the history of interstate enforcement of state regulations is not promising: it is very difficult to get a state agency to act on out-of-state complaints or help with interstate enforcement actions. As an example, even with massive federal intervention, it is still difficult to get child support orders enforced on out-of-state parents. This is understandable because most state agencies are underfunded and understaffed. They have to direct their primary efforts to the citizens of their own state. Given that most state medical licensing agencies are unable

to manage the complaints in their own states, it is unrealistic to assume they can cooperate effectively in the interstate regulation of telemedicine.

The darker side of telemedicine is already obvious on the Internet—physicians running Internet sites to sell prescriptions for popular drugs such as Viagra. This is possible because the drug enforcement laws are really only intended to manage the distribution of controlled substances, i.e., psychoactive drugs such as tranquilizers and narcotics. There is little concern with or regulation of the distribution of other drugs, which has been tacitly endorsed by the federal regulations allowing the importation and personal use of unapproved substances and drugs diverted from commercial pharmacy channels. The proper method of enforcement against these providers is by the licensing agency in their own state. The pharmacy-licensing agencies in the states where the prescriptions are filled should also enforce state law prohibitions on filling prescriptions by out-of-state physicians. The difficulty in these enforcement actions is that unethical telemedicine providers do not have physical offices and do not generate the medical records that are at the heart of most medical enforcement actions.

The most troubling aspect of telemedicine, especially Internet medicine, is that it is very difficult to determine if the provider is licensed anywhere, or is even medically trained. When a kid in high school can produce a professional appearing WWW (World Wide Web) site, all the traditional cues that indicate a legitimate practitioner disappear. Even insurance coverage is not a good indicator as more people turn to cash-based medical care, either because of the referral restrictions in their health plans or to get alternative medicine. In theory, consumers could call the licensing agency to see if someone with that name was licensed, but they would have to know the state of licensure and have some way to verify that the Internet physician was not an impostor. Even these protections fail for offshore operations.

Trade Regulation Issues

All professional licensing laws have some component of trade regulation that is driven by the affected profession's interest in limiting competition. State licensing agencies for lawyers have fought to prevent nonlawyers from helping people with divorce filings, to prevent the publication of self-help legal books on estate planning, and to limit the extent that real estate brokers can assist with the documents for selling real estate. In medicine, trade restrictions were the traditional focus of regulations. It is only in the last few decades that medical licensing agencies in many states have even had the legal authority to discipline a physician for incompetence.

Telemedicine has been promoted as a way to deliver medical services to remote areas that would otherwise not have access to expert physicians. Politically, this is the best way to diffuse criticism because it does not threaten the livelihood of other physicians. Realistically, however, it will be impossible to restrict telemedicine to such areas. If I am an insurer, I can lower costs and perhaps improve the quality of care for my insureds by contracting with a leading medical center for specialty consultations with local general practitioners. Thus a patient in Atlanta might be able to get a consultation from a Mayo Clinic physician, but at a lower cost than a local specialist because the patient's primary care physician will manage the consultation. The specialists will be under pressure to price these consultations attractively. They are already losing business because MCOs are unwilling to send patients to regional centers for specialty care. The specialists can essentially extend their franchise at the cost of a fast Internet connection, with no added office expense or capital expenditures.

Given that many specialties have more practitioners than the patient flow warrants, especially if the patients could shop over a broader region, telemedicine is very threatening. This extends down to the primary care physician level: one of the claims for telemedicine is that it will enable communities that can only support a nurse to have physician care available under the direction of the nurse. Once this is accepted, there is no reason why MCOs would not want to use it for all their primary care patients.

Medical licensing agencies and health care practitioner professional organizations must work out a balance between the importance of hands-on physician care and the obvious advantages of leveraging medical expertise. Such leveraging can both reduce costs and increase the quality of patient care, although at the expense of local practitioners.

Practicing Telemedicine

There are three possible roles for a telemedicine practitioner: local patient contact; remote consultant; and remote operator. All of these imply contact and decision making for a specific patient and trigger the formation of a physician–patient relationship with its attendant legal duties. Running an Internet site that provides medical information to the general public, rather than specific advice to individual patients, does not trigger the physician–patient relationship and is legally more like publishing a book. Such activities are generally protected by the First Amendment and cannot be the basis of tort liability, other than for publication related torts such as defamation. Giving advice to specific patients can trigger a physician–patient relationship, as would any medical decisions such as writing a prescription or providing medications by mail order.

Some telemedicine consultations mimic classic phone consultations—the patient's local physician knows the consultant and his or her expertise and all the medical recommendations are given to the local physician, who implements them as he or she sees fit. As long as the consultant in these consultations does not do any independent testing or evaluation of data (as would a cardiologist or radiologist), most states would see this as advice to the local physician and would not assume that a physician–patient relationship was formed. This starts to change when the patient is introduced into the consultation. When the remote consultant makes direct contact with the patient, either by video or audio, or perhaps even email, there is a strong presumption that a physician–patient relationship has been formed.

The Telemedicine Physician–Patient Relationship

Once there is contact between the patient and the telemedicine practitioner, the question shifts from whether there is a physician–patient relationship to the nature of the physician–patient relationship. As is demonstrated by occupational medicine, the law recognizes that there are physician–patient relationships with limited duties to the patient. Just as an occupational medicine physician may examine a patient or treat a workplace injury without triggering a duty to evaluate the patient's general medical status, the courts are likely to hold that the telemedicine practitioner's duty is limited to the extent of the matter that is the subject of the consultation. This will probably depend on the status of the local practitioner.

If the patient is cared for locally by a physician, then that physician will have primary responsibility for the patient's care and the court is more likely to find that the telemedicine practitioner's duty is limited. Conversely, if the patient's local contact is not a physician, then the court is more likely to find that the local practitioner has become the borrowed servant of the telemedicine practitioner and that the telemedicine practitioner is responsible for all aspects of the patient's care. This would be moderated if the local contact was under the supervision of another physician, who would then have primary legal responsibility for implementing the telemedicine practitioner's recommendations.

Physicians who conduct remotely controlled surgical and medical procedures will have the same legal duties as they would if they were in the operating room with the local physician. At least for the next several years, until these procedures become commonplace, remote physicians can also assume that they will be held liable for problems with the equipment and the other aspects of the procedure that deviate from ordinary practice. This expanded liability mirrors the situation in experimental medicine, where the supervising physician must ensure the integrity of the entire process. They may be able to counterclaim against the manufacturers of the equipment, but these counterclaims may be limited if it was not specifically manufactured for telemedicine. For example, if a standard desktop computer were used as a monitoring terminal for a remote surgical procedure, the manufacturer could reasonably claim that this was not an intended use and that it should not be responsible for personal injuries flowing from the monitor's failure.

Being the Local Contact

Traditional consultations are premised on a relationship of trust between the primary physician and the consultant. If either does not know the other, or does not trust the other, these consultation become problematic. Putting aside telemedicine, many MCOs are already raising this issue by forcing primary care physicians to consult with specialists they know nothing about, and putting consultants in the position of not knowing the capabilities of the primary physician. This will be exacerbated by telemedicine. Local practitioners could be in the same position as the consumer as regards determining the competence and license status of the remote practitioner, with the caveat that the courts are likely to find that there is a duty to ensure the competence of the remote consultant.

Practitioners who work with remote consultants, especially those across state lines, should document the training and licensure of the consultant as part of their office records. This does not need to be duplicated in each patient's record, but it must be available to show proper diligence in screening the consultant. There should also be a record of the consultation and any recommendations of the consultant. This could be in the form of ordinary chart notes and a letter from the consultant. If the consultation is conducted through a computer, then the session could be recorded by the computer and stored as an electronic file. These files can be compressed and transferred to a CD-ROM that is kept with the patient's other medical records.

Being the Remote Consultant

If there is a physician–patient relationship between the remote consultant and the patient, then the consultant has certain duties to the patient. Consultants will be liable for negligent diagnosis or advice to the patient. Since they must depend to some extent on information from and observations by the local practitioner, they should be concerned with whether the local practitioner is competent and reliable. The more difficult questions involve the extent of the relationship. If the local contact is the patient's primary physician, and the consultation is for a specific purpose, then the consultant's legal duties will be limited to the correctness of his or her own advice. To establish this in court, the consultant will need to keep a good record of the consultation and should draft a specific consultation letter that is provided to both the patient and the local practitioner. The consultant should preserve any medical records that he or she is provided as part of the consultation. These can be imaged and stored electronically with the record of the consultation.

The consultant should have the patient execute an informed consent to the consultation. Ideally this would be done prior to the consultation and could be done electronically. This should include a specific release for the medical information that the consultant needs to review, and a clear statement of the purpose of the consultation and limitations on the relationship between the patient and the consultant. Patients should be informed of whether they may contact the consultant directly or whether all contact must be through the local practitioner. Patients must also be informed that they do not have an ongoing relationship with the consultant, if this is the case. If the local practitioner is not a physician, then the consent should specifically identify the physician who is responsible

for supervising the local practitioner, how the patient can get in touch with the physician, and that this physician, not the consultant, is responsible for the patient's ongoing care. It is critical that patients always know who is responsible for their care, otherwise the consultant could be held to have abandoned the patient.

Legally, the greatest risks occur when the remote consultant is the only physician involved in the patient's care. The worst case is when the patient contacts a remote physician without any local medical practitioner to mediate the consultation and without having seen the practitioner in person. In these situations the courts are most likely to assume that the telemedicine physician has an unlimited physician–patient relationship with all the attendant legal duties of follow-up and general evaluation of the patient's condition. Physicians who advise patients in these situations should be very careful to collect as much medical information as possible about the patient, and to record the consultations. The informed consent for the consultation should address the special problems of remote consultation and the reasons that it is being used in the specific patient's case. These will be very important if a court is called on to evaluates the consultation. Providing medical advice to a sick person in a remote location who has no access to any other health care providers is a powerful argument for a court to find that consultation serves an important societal function and deserves legal protection. Conversely, running up big charges as Dr. Internet to the confused and gullible will be less sympathetic to the jury if something goes wrong.

REFERENCES

1. *Mazur v. Merck & Co.*, 964 F.2d 1348 (3d Cir. [Pa.] 1992).
2. *Reynolds v. Decatur Mem'l Hosp.*, 660 N.E.2d 235 (Ill. App. 4 Dist. 1996).
3. *Bovara v. St. Francis Hosp.*, 700 N.E.2d 143 (Ill. App. 1 Dist. 1998).
4. *Townsend v. Turk,* 218 Cal. App. 3d 278, 266 Cal. Rptr. 821 (Cal. App. 4 Dist. 1990).
5. *Phillips v. Good Samaritan Hosp.*, 416 N.E.2d 646 (Ohio App. 2 Dist. 1979).
6. *Merriman v. Toothaker,* 515 P.2d 509 (Wash. App. Div. 2 1973).
7. *Tumblin v. Ball-Incon Glass Packaging Corp.*, 478 S.E.2d 81 (S.C. App. 1996).
8. *Mero v. Sadoff,* 31 Cal. App. 4th 1466, 37 Cal. Rptr. 2d 769 (Cal. App. 2 Dist. 1995)
9. *Roberts v. Galen of Va., Inc.*, 119 S. Ct. 685 (1999).
10. *Abbott v. Bragdon,* 163 F.3d 87 (1st Cir. 1998).
11. *Truman v. Thomas,* 611 P.2d 902 (Cal. 1980).

12. *Payton v. Weaver,* 131 Cal. App. 3d 38, 182 Cal. Rptr. 225 (Cal. App. 1 Dist. 1982).

13. *Bouvia v. Superior Ct.,* 179 Cal. App. 3d 1127, 225 Cal. Rptr. 297 (Cal. App. 2 Dist. 1986).

SUGGESTED READINGS

General

Barratt K. Avoid patient abandonment—how to properly end a relationship with your patient. *Wis Med J.* 1996;95:875–877.

Barton HM. Creation of the physician–patient relationship. *Tex Med.* 1994;90:39–42.

Barton HM. Terminating the physician–patient relationship. *Tex Med.* 1994;90:46–49.

Berlin L. Communication of the significant but not urgent finding. *AJR.* 1997;168:329–331.

Borowitz SM, Wyatt JC. The origin, content, and workload of e-mail consultations. *JAMA.* 1998;280:1321–1324.

DuVal G. Liability of ethics consultants: a case analysis. *Camb Q Healthc Ethics.* 1997;6:269–281.

Epstein RM. Communication between primary care physicians and consultants. *Arch Fam Med.* 1995;4:403–409.

Eser A. The role of law in the patient–physician relationship. *Forensic Sci Int.* 1994;69:269–277.

Eyers K, Brodaty H, Parker G, et al. If the referral fits: bridging the gap between patient and referrer requirements in a tertiary referral unit. *Aust NZ J Psychiatry.* 1996;30:332–336.

Eysenbach G, Diepgen TL. Responses to unsolicited patient e-mail requests for medical advice on the World Wide Web. *JAMA.* 1998;280:1333–1335.

Finkelstein D, Wu AW, Holtzman NA, Smith MK. When a physician harms a patient by a medical error: ethical, legal, and risk-management considerations. *J Clin Ethics.* 1997;8:330–335.

Fox BC, Siegel ML, Weinstein RA. "Curbside" consultation and informal communication in medical practice: a medicolegal perspective. *Clin Infect Dis.* 1996;23:616–622.

Gallagher TH, Lo B, Chesney M, Christensen K. How do physicians respond to patient's requests for costly, unindicated services? *J Gen Intern Med.* 1997;12:663–668.

Garrick TR, Weinstock R. Liability of psychiatric consultants. *Psychosomatics.* 1994;35:474–484.

Golden GA, Brennan M. Managing erotic feelings in the physician–patient relationship. *CMAJ.* 1995;153:1241–1245.

Grana WA. An essay on managed care and the patient–physician relationship. *J Okla State Med Assoc.* 1997;90:450–452.

Haney C. Guidelines for the physician–patient relationship. *J Med Assoc Ga.* 1992;81:607–609.

Kelly CE. Bringing homophobia out of the closet: antigay bias within the patient–physician relationship. *Pharos.* 1992;55:2–8.

Larsen JH, Risor O. Telephone consultations at the emergency service, Copenhagen County: analysis of doctor–patient communication patterns. *Fam Pract.* 1997;14:387–393.

Levinson W, Roter DL, Mullooly JP, Dull VT, Frankel RM. Physician–patient communication: the relationship with malpractice claims among primary care physicians and surgeons. *JAMA.* 1997;277:553–559.

Lloyd BW. A randomized controlled trial of dictating the clinic letter in front of the patient. *BMJ.* 1997;314:347–348.

Martz EW. Sexual misconduct in the physician–patient relationship. *Del Med J.* 1993;65:451–452.

McMillan RC. Responsibility to or for in the physician–patient relationship? *J Med Ethics.* 1995;21:112–115.

Olive KE. Physician religious beliefs and the physician–patient relationship: a study of devout physicians. *South Med J.* 1995;88:1249–1255.

Schreiber K. Religion in the physician–patient relationship. *JAMA.* 1991;266:3062, 3066.

Schwenk TL, Romano SE. Managing the difficult physician–patient relationship. *Am Fam Physician.* 1992;46:1503–1509.

Spielberg AR. On call and online: sociohistorical, legal, and ethical implications of e-mail for the patient–physician relationship. *JAMA.* 1998;280:1353–1359.

Stratton WT. Medical abandonment. *Kans Med.* 1988;89:250, 253.

Swee DE. Health care system reform and the changing physician–patient relationship. *NJ Med.* 1995;92:313–317.

Tate P. Current thinking on the consultation. *Practitioner.* 1995;239:454–456.

Thieman S. Avoiding the claim of patient abandonment. *Mo Med.* 1996;93:634–635.

Torres A, Wagner R, Proper S. Terminating the physician–patient relationship. *J Dermatol Surg Oncol.* 1994;20:144–147.

Williams S, Dale J, Glucksman E. Emergency department senior house officers' consultation difficulties: implications for training. *Ann Emerg Med.* 1998;31:358–363.

Yeo M, Longhurst M. Intimacy in the patient–physician relationship; Committee on Ethics of the College of Family Physicians of Canada. *Can Fam Physician.* 1996;42:1505–1508.

Telemedicine

Allaert FA, Dusserre L. Legal requirements for tele-assistance and tele-medicine. *Medinfo.* 1995;8:1593–1595.

Balas EA, Jaffrey F, Kuperman GJ, et al. Electronic communication with patients: evaluation of distance medicine technology. *JAMA.* 1997;278:152–159.

Bradham DD, Morgan S, Dailey ME. The information superhighway and telemedicine: applications, status, and issues. *Wake Forest Law Rev.* 1995;30:145.

Brannigan VM, Beier BR. Patient privacy in the era of medical computer networks: a new paradigm for a new technology. *Medinfo.* 1995;8:640–643.

The Center for Telemedicine Law. Telemedicine and interstate licensure: findings and recommendations of the CTL licensure task force. *ND Law Rev.* 1997;73:109.

Darr JF, Koerner S. Telemedicine: legal and practical implications. *Whittier Law Rev.* 1997;19:3.

Forslund DW, Phillips RL, Kilman DG, Cook JL. Experiences with a distributed virtual patient record system. *Proceedings / AMIA Annual Fall Symposium.* 1996:483–487.

Frank AP, Wandell MG, Headings MD, Conant MA, Woody GE, Michel C. Anonymous HIV testing using home collection and telemedicine counseling: a multicenter evaluation. *Arch Intern Med.* 1997;157:309–314.

Franklin PL, Hanson PC. MMA releases comprehensive telemedicine report. *Minn Med.* 1996;79:52–53.

Granade PF. Medical malpractice issues related to the use of telemedicine—an analysis of the ways in which telecommunications affects the principles of medical malpractice. *ND Law Rev.* 1997;73:65.

Kearney KA. Medical licensure: an impediment to interstate telemedicine. *Health Lawyer.* 1997;9:14.

Laske C. Health care telematics: who is liable? *Comput Methods Programs Biomed.* 1997;54:1–6.

Laster F. Lurking under the bridge to 2001: telemalpractice. *Hosp Prac (Off Ed).* 1997;32:183–184.

Llaurado JG. Commentary on a futuristic model of patient record systems and telemedicine. *Int J Biomed Comput.* 1996;43:155–160.

Malpractice in the new millennium: better than today? Managed care, telemedicine, genetic tests create new liabilities. *Alaska Med.* 1996;38:106–108.

McMenamin JP. Does products liability litigation threaten picture archiving and communication systems and/or telemedicine? *Digital Imaging.* 1998;11:21–32.

Orbuch PM. A Western state's effort to address telemedicine policy barriers. *ND Law Rev.* 1997;73:35.

Reichertz PS, Halpern NJL. FDA regulation of telemedicine devices. *Food Drug Law J.* 1997;53:517.

Sanders J. The revolution in health care delivery. *ND Law Rev.* 1997;73:19.

Smith MF. Telemedicine and safety. *J Telemed Telecare.* 1996;2:33–36.

Telemedicine presents new malpractice concerns according to physician insurers association. *J Okla State Med Assoc.* 1997;90:101–102.

Ziel SE. Telecommunications in health care. *AORN J.* 1998; 67:458–459.

CHAPTER 9

Consent to Medical Treatment

HIGHLIGHTS

- Informed consent is the core principle of modern medical practice.
- In some very limited circumstances, care can be provided without consent.
- Health care practitioners must disclose conflicts of interest that might affect their clinical judgment.
- There are special laws governing consent for minors and incompetents.
- Patients have the right to refuse medical care, even when it means they will die.
- Patients do not have a right to improper care or assisted suicide.

INTRODUCTION

The doctrine of informed consent is the cornerstone of modern medical jurisprudence. Although the need for bare consent to treatment is old, informed consent arose after World War II, driven by the Nuremberg Doctrine and the rise of technological medicine. It has been one of the most misunderstood principles in medical law, sometimes driving a wedge between patients and physicians. Now it is returning to its roots in the physician's fiduciary duty to the patient, as consent issues shift from concerns about unnecessary or inappropriate treatments to denial of treatment driven by managed care organizations' cost cutting.

This chapter reviews the history of informed consent and discusses the different standards governing simple and informed consent. These standards reflect the conflict between legal ideals of medical care and its reality. Patient advocates and many physicians view informed consent as a way to empower patients, thereby making them equal partners in the therapeutic relationship. This is a naive view of informed consent. Informed con-

sent does not affect the disparity in power and knowledge between physicians and patients. Informed consent is very important at the margin, when there are clear, simple-to-understand choices. It cannot protect patients from overreaching by physicians or from antiscientific delusions about medical treatments. Good science and proper standards for medical practice are more empowering than elaborate informed consent rituals. Informed consent is a laudable goal, but it is possible to comply with the legal standards for informed consent without effectively involving the patient in the decision-making process. When this happens, physicians lose the true value of informed consent: reducing conflicts with patients through dissipating unreasonable expectations.

BATTERY—NO CONSENT

As a pure legal issue, forcing treatment on an unwilling person is no different from attacking that person with a knife. The legal term for a harmful or offensive touching without permission is *battery*. Battery is a criminal offense, and it can also be the basis of a civil lawsuit. The key element of battery is that the touching be unauthorized, not that it be intended to harm the person. Thus forcing beneficial care on an unwilling patient would be battery. The classic statement of a physician's duty to get the patient's consent is Justice Cardozo's opinion in *Schoendorff v. Society of New York Hospital*:[1]

> Every human being of adult years and sound mind has a right to determine what shall be done with his own body; and a surgeon who performs an operation without his patient's consent commits an assault for which he is liable in damages. This is true except in cases of emergency, where the patient is unconscious and where it is necessary to operate before consent can be obtained.[1]

Yet even this statement is hedged. The strong language mandating consent for every person is qualified with the right to treat a person without consent in an emergency. In fact, battery is only an issue in very limited circumstances where there is a complete failure of consent and no other legal justifications for treating the patient without consent. In most circumstances, where a patient voluntarily seeks treatment, the patient will be found to have implied his or her consent to the treatment by merely submitting to the treatment. Only consent is implied, however, not informed consent.

Battery is a legal threat in three situations. If the patient has been lied to about the treatment or there is other fraud in the informed consent, then the entire consent is invalid. The second situation is when the patient is incompetent to consent and receives improper care. The most likely scenario is the third: the patient has refused care and the care is forced on him or her, typically in an involuntary setting. As discussed later, a patient who refuses care may not be treated without the authorization of a court. This can support a civil lawsuit for battery. Yet even when a patient has refused care, the physician is unlikely to be charged with the crime of battery if the treatment was meant to be beneficial. This is not an endorsement for acting against a patient's will. It is a recognition that the criminal law is reticent to punish physicians unless it is clear that they intended to cause harm.

EXCEPTIONS TO THE REQUIREMENT OF CONSENT

There are two well-recognized exceptions to the need for consent to medical treatment. The more common is a medical emergency, in which an unconscious or delirious patient cannot consent. The second is less common and involves certain court-ordered treatments or treatments and tests mandated by law. It is important to note that these are exceptions to the need for any consent at all, not just exceptions to the need for informed consent.

The Emergency Exception

The emergency exception to the need for consent is based on the premise that a reasonable person would not want to be denied necessary medical care because he or she happened to be too incapacitated to consent to the treatment.

The major abuse of the emergency exception to the need for consent is its use as a justification for treating chronically ill patients who are incompetent to consent to medical care. The emergency exception is just that—an exception limited to emergencies. These may be in the emergency room, or they may involve patients in the hospital who have an unexpected event such as a cardiac arrest. The emergency exception does not apply to an incompetent patient in need of routine care. Chronically incompetent patients should have a legal guardian.

When Does the Emergency Exception Apply?

There are very few cases that directly address the emergency exception. It usually is only discussed indirectly in cases that really involve failure of informed consent. Because these cases do not involve emergency treatment facts, the judges usually present the emergency exception as only applying when the patient is incompetent and in need of treatment to save his or her life or to prevent permanent disability. Although this is a correct statement of the law, the actual application of the emergency exception includes procedures to determine whether the patient might need medical care. For example, one of the few cases to directly litigate the emergency exception involved a very drunk patient (blood alcohol of .233%) who was brought into the emergency room after an automobile accident.

Based on the patient's complaints, the nature of the accident, and the physical examination, the emergency room physician decided to do a diagnostic peritoneal lavage. The patient asked what was going to be done, and when told, became belligerent and tried to leave the emergency room. The patient was restrained and sedated, and the procedure performed. The patient later sued for battery and failure of informed consent. The trial court would not allow the defendant hospital to assert the emergency exception as a defense. After an excellent review of the emergency exception doctrine, the Rhode Island Supreme Court found that this was an appropriate use of the emergency exception.[2] This comports with the usual emergency room practice of evaluating all patients who are unable to consent to determine if they are in need of emergency care. It is not unusual for patients, especially drunks, to fight the evaluation. It is likely that if the emergency room let a very drunken and potentially seriously injured patient leave without evaluation, and that patient died from lack of care, the emergency room would be sued for failing to restrain the patient.

Children in the Emergency Room

A classic problem is children brought to the emergency room with conditions that are not life-threatening. The child, who may be medically able to consent to treatment, is legally unable to consent because of his or her age. An example is the problem of the 14-year-old who has broken an arm and is brought to the hospital by a neighbor. Neither the child nor the neighbor is legally able to consent to treatment. The cases hold that the physician may rely on the emergency exception to consent only if immediate care is necessary to preserve the use of the child's arm.

The case law on the definition of an emergency for the treatment of children is so restrictive because the only cases that are brought to court involve bizarre facts, such as children being brought in for elective surgery without, or against, their parents' consent. If parents were suing a physician because he or she relieved their child's suffering, the issue would quickly shift from the physician's liability for malpractice to the parents' liability for child abuse and neglect. In general, it is better for the physician to be explaining to a jury why he or she helped someone rather than stand by and watch the child lose life or limb. Most states have passed laws that allow family members other than parents to consent to care for children and otherwise make it easier to care for children in the emergency room.

Refusal of Care

A rare abuse of the emergency exception involves patients who have refused to consent to specific medical care. The refusal may be based on religious beliefs, such as refusing blood transfusions, or on a personal decision, such as refusing intensive care. If the physician disagrees with such a decision, the time to fight the decision is when it is made. There is no legal justification for waiting until the patient is unconscious or for physically or chemically restraining a patient and then rendering care against the patient's consent. This would not constitute an emergency exception to the need for consent. On the contrary, it would constitute battery. The solution in these cases, as discussed later in this chapter, is to apply to the courts for permission to treat against the patient's consent.

Legally Mandated Treatment

There are three situations when persons must submit to medical care or testing without their permission, outside of the emergency situation. The first are patients who are have been judged legally incompetent and have had a guardian appointed by the courts or who have been involuntarily confined in a mental institution. Whereas such patients do not give up all their rights, the guardian may consent to care for them and may even require them to submit to care that they have refused.[3]

The second situation involves public health orders, as discussed in Chapter 12. A court with proper jurisdiction may appoint a guardian to consent for a patient, or a court may issue an order for treatment under the authority of the public health laws.[4] The third situation is the testing of prisoners in the custody of law enforcement officials, and persons who are having blood drawn or other medical samples taken pursuant to a search warrant. In both of these situations, the courts or the legislature have the right to force the subject to be tested or submit to the treatment. Many health care practitioners are uncomfortable participating in involuntary treatment, however, because of the consent issues.

Medical treatment mandated under the criminal or public health laws poses a peculiar informed consent problem. The patient cannot refuse the treatment but is probably entitled to be informed about the nature of the treatment. This anomalous situation arises because a legal action for failure of informed consent requires the patient to prove that he or she would have refused the treatment if he or she had been properly informed. Since refusal is not an option, the legal action would fail. Conversely, it is repugnant to our sense of freedom to force treatment on a person without at least explaining what is being done and why.

Health care practitioners in emergency rooms should determine who is authorized in their jurisdiction to bring in people for involuntary treatment and testing to ensure that any requests are proper. The circumstances of the care should be carefully documented in the encounter record. This should include the names and badge numbers of the law enforcement officials, the stated reason for the medical care, and a copy of the search warrant, if one is being used.

The Therapeutic Exception

The therapeutic exception is an exception to the need for informed consent, rather than for any consent. It ostensibly allows the physician to withhold information from a patient if that information would psychologically harm the patient and thus imperil the patient's physical health. The therapeutic exception was first broached in one of the early informed consent cases, *Nishi v. Hartwell*, decided in 1970.[5]

Nishi involved consent to angiography for an elderly dentist. He was not told of the risks and was paralyzed as a result of the test. The defendants claimed that they did not tell him the risks because it was not the standard of care to disclose those risks, and because they were concerned he would be frightened and would refuse the test. At the time the case was decided, Hawaii used the community standard for informed consent, which requires plaintiffs to have expert testimony as to what the reasonable physician would have told the patient. The plaintiff had no expert, so the court dismissed the case. In doing so, however, it also discussed the duty of a physician to do whatever is best for the patient, citing older—pre–informed consent—cases as authority.

Thus the therapeutic exception to the need for informed consent arises from the now-discredited view that information about risks of treatment or the existence of diseases such as cancer should be withheld from patients to foster the proper mental attitude for recovery. Most of the court opinions and legal articles dealing with informed consent take care to acknowledge that there may be circumstances when it is in the patient's best interest not to be informed of the risks of the proposed treatment. Although the courts constantly reaffirm the existence of the therapeutic exception, they uniformly reject it as a defense in specific cases. Even Hawaii, which specifically overruled *Nishi* and adopted the reasonable patient standard for informed consent, still says that the physician can defend with testimony that a reasonable physician would have withheld the information.[6]

The public debate that surrounded the question of telling patients about their cancer has made the courts wary about establishing standards that would deny patients information. But the courts have not explicitly overruled the cases that discuss the therapeutic exception; they have just refused to find that a therapeutic exception existed in the cases where the defendant physicians have tried to use it as a defense. They have stated that the alleged harm cannot be the refusal of the treatment. Implicit in the narrowing of the basis for the therapeutic exception is the belief that if a patient is sufficiently psychologically fragile as to be harmed by the consent process, then perhaps that patient is not competent to consent to care. If a physician really believes that it would do significant harm to a patient to tell that person the risks of a proposed treatment, then it would be appropriate to consider petitioning the court to determine if that patient should have a guardian appointed to make medical decisions.

INFORMED CONSENT

Medical care, especially surgical care, is the most intrusive private action that may be done to a free person. Society may imprison or execute, but one private citizen may not cut or medicate another without permission from the intended patient and a license from society. A person's right to consent to medical treatment has always been an important part of medical care. It was not a topic of general interest until the war crimes trials at Nuremberg shocked the world medical community with revelations about the experiments carried out by physicians in the death camps. Blurring the line between experimentation and torture, these experiments moved the discussion of consent to medical care from the philosophical to the practical.

Social Trends behind Informed Consent

The broad acceptance of informed consent to medical treatment as a routine part of medical practice is less than 20 years old. Despite many physicians' belief that informed consent is a creature of legal fiat, it is the natural societal response to the demystification of medicine. As medicine has moved from the shaman's tent into the research laboratory, it has adopted the cloak of logical decision making. A natural response is the assumption by the lay public that, given enough information, they may rationally make their own medical decisions.

Technology-Oriented Medicine

The post-Nuremberg period coincides with the growth of technology-based medicine. Although the Nuremberg Doctrine provided the moral force for transforming consent to medical treatment, the growth of technology determined the direction of this transformation. The interval between the advent of scientific medicine in the late 1890s and the rise of technological medicine in the 1950s was a period with relatively few effective treatments. The patient's choices were usually limited to one treatment or no treatment at all. Perhaps most important, fewer conditions had been medicalized. Symptomatic disease, rather than laboratory values, drove patients to seek treatment.

In this context, patients expected physicians to make all necessary medical decisions. This was an extension of the traditional paternalistic physician–patient relationship. It was also a reasonable response. The decision on treatment was based mostly on technical medical considerations. Without the luxury of several effective treatments, the paternalistic model of medical decision making did not deprive patients of meaningful autonomy.

The Demise of Paternalism

Traditional medical paternalism was based on the importance of faith in the absence of effective treatments. Physicians occupied a quasi-religious role, providing solace rather than salvation. With the rise of more invasive medical procedures, more finely tuned but highly toxic drugs, and more diseases defined by a medical finding rather than by a patient's symptoms, the underpinnings of this paternalistic role deteriorated. Choosing treatments is no longer the simple exercise of diagnosing the patient's condition and having that diagnosis determine therapy. A diagnosis now triggers a universe of possible actions. The selection of a treatment from this universe becomes a value judgment based on the relative risks and benefits of the various actions. The risks to be considered include patient-specific psychological and social risks.

Physicians may be expert in determining the medical risks of a treatment, but it is only the patient who can determine the relative acceptability of these risks. For example, some patients will risk substantial disability on a chance of a complete cure of chronic pain. For others, chronic but bearable pain is preferable to the chance of disability secondary to treatment. This weighing of risks is idiosyncratic to the patient's individual risk-taking behavior and cannot be predicted by a physician. Following the paternalistic model, physicians assumed the task of making these risk–benefit decisions for the patients. Problems arose as patients began to question the consequences of these decisions. Once patients realized that there might be more than one way to treat their conditions, they began to question the physician's authority to make unilateral treatment decisions.

Changing Values

Patients expressed their dissatisfaction with paternalism through lawsuits. In a small number of cases in the 1960s and early 1970s, physicians were sued for obtaining consent without informing patients of the risks of the proposed treatments. In almost every one of these cases, the failure to inform the patient properly was only one facet of substandard care. A few courts held that a patient was entitled to be informed of the risks of treatment as part of the consent process. These opinions were seized upon by legal scholars, who then fashioned the theory of informed consent to medical care.

As more courts began to recognize a patient's legal right to be informed about the risks of treatment, this was transformed into an individual liberties issue. Physicians who did not inform patients adequately have been accused of oppressing their patients. This legal view of informed consent as a liberty issue created a bitter dispute over the role of the physician. Physicians felt that their integrity was being challenged over their good-faith attempts to shield patients from unpleasant medical information. The courts, despite much language about the special relationship between physicians and patients, have inexorably moved to the position that physicians who assume the right to make decisions for their patients also assume the consequences of those decisions.

Legal Standards for Informed Consent

The core of the controversy over informed consent is the choice of a standard by which informed consent is judged. Physicians argue, correctly, that they have always talked to patients about proposed treatments. It is not talking to patients that they object to; it is the court's intrusion into what is said. Many states have sought to minimize this intrusion by adopting disclosure standards based on physician expectations: the community standard. Other states have adopted standards based on patient expectations: the reasonable-person standard.

Who Must Get Consent?

The legal doctrine of informed consent is directed at physicians. The courts have not found a duty for hospitals or other providers to get informed consent, holding that this always flows to the physician.[7] This has interesting ramifications as MCOs increasingly provide care without direct physician involvement. From the court decisions, it is clear that any failures in informing the patients of the risks of such treatment will be charged against either the supervising physician, or, in the absence of a clearly identified supervising physician, against the medical director.

In a great irony, the courts have not extended the duty of informed consent to alternative healers or chiropractors. Many states impose only a limited duty on them to inform the patient of the risks of their treatments or the advisability of seeking medical care for conditions that cannot be treated by the modalities offered by the alternative healer.

The Community Standard

The community standard is the older standard and reflects the traditional deference of the law toward physicians. It is based on what physicians as a group do in a given circumstance. The community standard requires that the patient be told what other physicians in the same community would tell a patient in the same or similar circumstances. "Community" refers both to the geographic community and to the specialty (intellectual community) of the physician.

The community standard usually requires that the patient be told little about the risks of the treatment or possible alternatives. In the extreme case, the community standard can shelter, telling the patient nothing other than the name of the proposed treatment and a brief description of it. In this extreme situation, physicians choose not to inform patients about the risks of the treatment.

The community standard has the most extreme results in very limited subspecialty areas of practice. In these areas, the number of practitioners is small, and there are only a few training centers. This results in an intellectually homogeneous group of physicians who tend to approach patient care in a similar manner. It is common for subspecialty practitioners to become true believers in the efficacy of a given treatment and to promote that treatment to patients. In this situation, the community standard will be to offer the patient only enough information to convince him or her to have the treatment. Risks will be ignored because the physicians have convinced themselves that it would be unreasonable to refuse the treatment.

Another area in which the community standard becomes a problem occurs when a small group of a larger specialty adopts a therapy that is rejected by the majority of the specialty. Since informing their patients of the majority view would make it impossible to perform the procedure, the minority-view physicians must ignore the controversy. For example, there has been a great controversy in ophthalmology over performing radial keratotomies. A small group of ophthalmologists began performing this procedure on large numbers of patients without traditional controlled studies on the benefits and long-term risks of the procedure.[8] A disclosure based on the views of the majority of the profession would have required that the patient be told that this was an unproved, experimental treatment that carried potentially severe long-term risks. Fewer patients would consent to an essentially cosmetic procedure if given this information. As a result, the majority view was discounted, and patients were told little about the uncertainty concerning the existing and future risks of the treatment. When a national study panel disputed this practice and called for proper

studies of the procedure, the advocates of radial keratotomies sued the members of the study panel for antitrust violations.[9] The court found these allegations groundless and ruled for the study panel members.[10]

Fraud in Consent

Both the community standard and the reasonable-person standard are used for judging the information to be given to passive patients, who do not ask questions. If the patient does ask questions, the physician must answer these questions truthfully. More important, the answers must be sufficiently complete to convey the requested information accurately. The physician cannot hide behind the patient's inability to phrase a technical question properly. Under either standard, a patient who asks to be told all the risks of a procedure is entitled to more information than a patient who sits mute. Failure to disclose a risk in reply to a direct question may constitute fraud, even if the appropriate standard for judging informed consent would not require that the risk be disclosed.

The Uncertainty of the Community Standard

From a physician's perspective, the community standard provides little guidance in deciding what to tell patients. Physicians do not routinely discuss what they tell patients; medical journals do not publish articles on the proper disclosure for specific treatments; professional societies do not promulgate standards for disclosure because they fear antitrust litigation by physicians who are offering unorthodox treatments. A physician who wants to comply with the community standard has a difficult task in establishing what disclosure the standard would mandate for a given treatment.

This uncertainty arises because the community standard is not rooted in medical practice. It is a legal rule that determines how a jury is to decide if a specific patient was given enough information. The community standard is a defensive standard. The jury is not allowed to judge the physician's disclosure on a common sense basis. The patient must find a physician to testify that certain disclosures should have been made. It is usually possible to find a physician to testify that whatever complication the patient suffered is part of the community standard for disclosure. This leaves a physician who has not disclosed the risk, based on a good-faith belief that the disclosure was not required, without an objective standard to argue to the jury.

Reasonable-Person Standard

The courts and legislatures of several states have abandoned the community standard in favor of the more patient-oriented reasonable-person standard. The reasonable-person standard requires that a patient be told all of the material risks that would influence a reasonable person in determining whether to consent to the treatment. Although hardly less ambiguous than the community standard, the reasonable-person standard has the advantage of encouraging physicians to discuss the proposed treatment with the patient more fully.

This new standard is not accepted by all states, but it is spreading. As courts in community standard states grapple with the perceived abuses of corporate medical practice, it is expected that they will move to the reasonable-person standard. Even in states that retain the community standard, a plaintiff's expert will present a hybrid standard to the jury based on the increased information given patients in states that have adopted the reasonable-person standard. Since the standards for specialty practice are national, physicians in reasonable-person jurisdictions will set the minimum disclosure, which will then have to be followed in the community-standard states. By this incremental increasing of the standards for disclosure, the reasonable-person standard will become the de facto national standard.

When a standard is based on reasonableness, it means that jurors are allowed to use their common sense to determine what should have been done. In an informed consent case, the jurors decide what they would have wanted to be told about the proposed treatment. This weights the standard toward disclosure, since each juror is more likely to add to the list of necessary information than to argue that another's concerns are unreasonable.

Alternative Treatments

The reasonable-person standard both increases the amount of information that the patient must be given and changes the substance of that information. The community standard is concerned with the old question of treatment versus no treatment. The reasonable-person standard is concerned with the modern problem of choosing among alternative treatments. To make an informed choice, the patient must be told about the risks and benefits of all the acceptable treatments and the consequences of no treatment. This becomes a sensitive issue because specialty practice lines are often based on a particular approach to treatment. Surgeons do not like to discuss the medical management of patients, and family practitioners are reticent to recommend highly technical procedures for conditions that may be managed more conservatively.

The disclosure of alternative treatments is crucial when the physician is being pressured by a third-party payer to steer the patient to less expensive treatments. The patient must be informed of alternative treatments and their relative benefits. If the physician believes that an alternative treatment is preferable to the treatment that the third-party payer is advocating, the patient must be told of this conflict. The physician must never imply that a financially motivated treatment decision is medically preferable. Financial considerations must be explicitly discussed, or the physician commits a fraud on the physician–patient relationship.

Perhaps the most significant difference between the community standard and the reasonable-person standard is the presentation of the physician's personal recommendations. The community standard rests on the inherent coercion of forcing the patient to choose between treatment and no treatment: between continued care by the physician and loss of care. The reasonable-person standard, with its emphasis on alternatives, allows the patient to reject a given treatment without rejecting the physician. This change in emphasis reflects the reality of contemporary medical practice. In a competitive marketplace, physicians need patients as much as patients need physicians. This recognition of mutual dependence is beneficial unless it results in physicians' advocating trendy treatments to gain a marketing edge.

Statutory Disclosure Standards

Certain states and the federal government mandate specific disclosures in certain situations. Texas is a good example because it has the most detailed requirements. The Texas Medical Disclosure Panel, a statutory body consisting of physicians and lawyers, promulgates lists of procedures and the risks that a patient must be told about each procedure. In some cases, the panel mandates more disclosure than was usual in the community, and in others it has lowered the level of disclosure.

This law was passed to reduce the threat of informed consent litigation. It is difficult to determine if it has been effective because there was very little informed consent litigation in Texas before the law was passed. What it has done is make it easier to sue physicians who do not comply with the statutory requirements. It has also reduced the effectiveness of informed consent as a risk management tool. Rather than using the consent process to ensure that the patient understands what is to be done, physicians simply have patients sign the promulgated forms.

The best risk management advice for physicians in states with statutory disclosure standards is to tell the patient everything a reasonable person would want to know and then be sure that the patient signs the appropriate statutory consent forms. Physicians should ask their attorney if their state has any statutory disclosure requirements. If so, these should always be complied with. They are not, however, a substitute for obtaining a full informed consent.

Fraud

Fraud arises when a physician intentionally misleads a patient about the risks and benefits of a treatment. It becomes a serious legal (and criminal) issue when a patient is induced to accept substandard care by forgoing beneficial treatment or submitting to an unorthodox treatment. Concerns about fraud often arise when a physician begins to specialize in an unorthodox treatment. The most common examples are weight loss clinics that employ unusual and unapproved regimens, such as giving patients human chorionic gonadotrophin injections or pesticide pills. A patient who can establish fraud may be entitled to punitive damages. Fraudulent dealings may also subject the physician to criminal prosecution and the loss of his or her license. One physician who was involved with a fraudulent weight loss clinic was successfully prosecuted under the federal racketeering laws.[11]

The Commonsense Approach

The doctrine of informed consent is a special case of the broader notion of assumption of risk. Whenever a person knowingly engages in a risky activity, that person consents to the risks of the activity. For this consent to be effective, (1) the person must know the risks that are being assumed; (2) he or she must assume these risks voluntarily; and (3) it must not be against public policy to assume the risks. When a person makes a formal agreement (usually written) to accept the risks of an activity, that agreement is called a *waiver*. A properly executed informed consent is a waiver of the risks of medical treatment. To be effective, a waiver of the risks of medical treatment must meet the same three criteria as other waivers. Informed consent serves an additional, perhaps more important, purpose. In the process of discussing the risks, benefits, and potential alternatives to a given treatment, the physician and the patient have an opportunity to ensure that there are no misunderstandings about the patient's complaint and the proposed treatment.

Knowable Risks

People can assume only risks that they know about. For most commonplace activities, such as driving a car, the risks are well known and are implicitly assumed by engaging in the activity. It is possible to assume implicitly the risks of medical care. For example, a physician undergoing general anesthesia would be assumed to know that general anesthesia carries a risk of anoxic brain damage. He or she would implicitly assume this risk without the need for an explicit informed consent.

Most patients do not have the background medical knowledge to assume specific risks of treatment implicitly. Prior to the advent of informed consent, the patient was assumed to know that medical treatment was risky. Since the person had sought treatment knowing that it was risky, he or she was assumed to have accepted that the risk of treatment was less than the risk of the medical condition. The law was not concerned with the particular form that a risk might take.

Advances in medical technology have caused a proliferation of choices in medical therapy. Patients are no longer limited to the choice between treatment or no treatment. This undermines the theory that the patient has accepted that the undifferentiated risks of medical therapy outweigh the risks of the condition. With many possible therapies for a given condition, the courts have rejected this implicit assumption of risk. A patient must now be told of the risks that he or she is assuming. The more particularized the information is about the potential adverse consequences of a treatment, the more effective is the assumption of risk.

Unknowable Risks

Medicine is not a perfect science. All medical care is associated with unknown, and perhaps unknowable, risks. The physician must tell the patient of the known risks of treatment, but this is not a guarantee that other problems cannot occur. Patients may assume these unknown risks if three conditions are met:

1. The risk is unknown (or of such a low probability that it is not known to be causally related to the procedure).
2. The patient is informed that the disclosed risks are not the only possible risks.
3. The medical rationale for the treatment is sound.

Condition 3 means that a patient cannot assume the risks of a negligently recommended treatment, an important issue with marginal treatments and vanity surgery. A patient who suffers a complication from an improper treatment may always sue the physician who recommended the treatment. A detailed consent form, listing all the risks of a treatment, is no protection if the treatment is unnecessary. If a patient can prove that a treatment was unnecessary or contraindicated, then the consent to risks of the treatment becomes ineffective.

Voluntariness

Consent to medical care can be truly voluntary only when it is reasonable to reject the care. Certain religious groups aside, a patient can be assumed to accept the risks of lifesaving care. The law recognizes this in its requirement that a patient convince the jury that he or she would have forgone the treatment had the risk in question been made clear. The more clearly necessary a treatment is, the less meaningful is the idea of informed consent. Yet even in life-threatening situations, voluntariness can be an issue if there is more than one appropriate treatment. The patient might not reasonably reject all treatment but may justifiably argue that he or she might have chosen a different treatment.

Voluntariness becomes a legal issue if the physician coerces the patient into accepting a treatment for which there are acceptable alternatives. This coercion may be explicit—telling the patient that he or she will die without the proposed treatment at once—or implicit—ignoring the discussion of alternatives or financial intimidation. Physicians who cooperate with third-party payers to limit patients' treatment options undermine the voluntariness of patient consent. They should not be surprised if a court determines that this renders the patient's informed consent invalid.

Public Policy

A patient may assume only risks that arise from appropriate care. For example, any operation done under general anesthesia carries a small risk of anoxic brain damage. Assume that a patient consents to general anesthesia, including acknowledging the risk of brain damage. The anesthesiologist then negligently overdoses the patient with an anesthetic agent, fails to monitor the patient, and discovers the mistake only after the patient is brain injured. The patient's informed consent to the risks of anesthesia would not prevent the patient from suing for the negligent administration of anesthesia.

The law does not allow a provider to force a patient to assume the risks of negligent medical care because of the involuntary nature of medical care. A person providing a necessary service has a duty to provide that service in a proper manner. This policy is intended to preserve the quality of necessary services. Conversely, it does not apply to services that the consumer may freely reject. For example, in most states, a skydiving service can successfully require that a customer waive the right to sue for all risks, including those from negligent acts of the service. This is accepted because skydiving is a purely voluntary activity.

Medically Unnecessary Procedures

The most difficult informed consent problems are those that arise from competently performed but medically unnecessary procedures. The extreme cases are those that involve vanity procedures, such as facelifts, liposuction, and breast enhancements. These procedures pose an informed consent dilemma. As medically unnecessary procedures, they may be rejected in the same way that skydiving may be rejected. From this perspective, a physician should be allowed to require a patient to assume all the risks of a vanity procedure, including the risks of negligent treatment.

A more moralistic perspective is that it is improper for physicians to use their skills and position of respect to perform purely commercial treatments. This attitude would view the vanity surgery patient as a victim who should not bear the risks of the physician's greed. This would lead to the rejection of assumption of risk for all risks, leaving vanity surgeons as guarantors of a good result.

Jurors tend toward the moralistic view. Although they are constrained to accept a proper informed consent, they are very suspicious of the motives of vanity surgeons. If the consent has any ambiguities or if there is evidence of overreaching (such as aggressive advertising that implies that the risks are minimal and the benefits fantastic), then they tend to rule against the physician.

Duty to Inform of HIV

Traditionally there have not been informed consent cases predicated on the physician failing to warn the patient about personal risks the physician might expose the patient to. These could include infection with hepatitis b, Parkinson's disease in a surgeon, or other mental or physical impairments that interfere with the physician's abilities. The presumption was that a physician who had a condition that might injure a patient should refrain from putting patients at risk, and if the physician did injure the patient, it would be malpractice, rather than informed consent. (There are few reported cases, probably because if the disability and its adverse impact on the patient could be proven, the case would be settled.)

Professional Standard

This has changed with HIV infection. Medical professionals have decided that physicians with HIV only pose a risk to patients in very limited circumstances, such as invasive procedures. Even in those situations, many experts believe that the physician can take various precautions and not subject the patient to risk. Since these experts believe that there is little risk, they do not believe physicians have a duty to disclose their HIV status. Most physicians agree, but more because of the fairness issue: many state laws make it very difficult for a physician to determine if a patient is infected with HIV. It seems unjust to make the physician disclose, with the potential of professional ruin, when the patient, who, in most circumstances, poses a much greater risk to the physician than the physician does to the patient, can withhold the information.

Reasonable-Patient Standard

This analysis would be valid in states that judge informed consent by the community standard. Unfortunately, it is not sound in states with a reasonable-person standard. Patients are terrified of being exposed to HIV. They believe that any reasonable patient would want to know that their physician was infected, at least if the physician was performing any procedures that could put the patient at any risk of HIV transmission. This is mirrored by huge judgments in the few decisions involving persons who were infected with HIV in medical settings: a jury awarded $12.2 million to a doctor who was infected with HIV as an intern, allegedly because she had not been properly trained to handle sharps.

There have been two cases decided so far on the specific issue of whether a physician should inform the patient of the risk of HIV.[12] Neither patient become infected with HIV. In a traditional informed consent case, this would be a complete defense: the patient must prove that he or she suffered the complication that the physician failed to provide information about. The patients pled that they suffered emotional distress because they were exposed to the risk of HIV transmission and should be allowed to recover for that distress irrespective of whether they were infected. The judges accepted this theory because of the latency between HIV infection and the time when HIV tests can confidently rule out infection is estimated to be about six months. (Although polymerase chain reaction [PCR] testing might shorten this, it will be difficult to prove to the courts that it detects all infections in their earliest stages.) The damages were limited to the interval between the exposure and the final determination that there was no transmission. In one case there was also a claim against the hospital, which the judge allowed to stand.[12]

The Medical Value of Informed Consent

The informed consent document, carefully filed in the patient's medical records, has only legal value. It is the process of obtaining the informed consent that is medically valuable. Obtaining an informed consent should be seen as a quality control review of the patient's care. A proper informed consent must deal with the key elements in medical decision making: the patient's physical condition, the patient's subjective complaints and expectations, and the appropriateness of a proposed treatment.

Few patients are sophisticated health care consumers. They lack technical knowledge about medicine, and it is difficult for them to be objective about their health. Despite a physician's best efforts, questioning about medical history sometimes leads to an incorrect assessment of the patient's condition. This may arise because the patient misstates the severity of the condition, either denying or overstating its seriousness, or because the physician unconsciously directs the patient's answers toward the medical conditions that the physician is most interested in. Irrespective of how these misunderstandings arise, they dangerously distort the factual basis for medical decision making.

A careful discussion of the risks of the proposed treatment may cause the patient to reconsider the actual severity of his or her problem. The physician must be open to indications that the patient is growing uncomfortable about undergoing the proposed treatment. Synergistic misunderstandings can arise when the physician overestimates the severity of the patient's problem and recommends a major intervention. The patient then believes that the problem must be serious because the physician has recommended such a major treatment. Unless the physician carefully questions the patient after the treatment has been proposed but before it is carried out, the patient's belief that he or she must be sick because the physician wants to treat him or her as sick will not surface until the patient is injured.

The Patient's Expectations

Unreasonable expectations are at the heart of most medical malpractice lawsuits. It is important not to overstate the benefits of a proposed treatment, most critically if the treatment is for a minor condition or if there are effective alternative treatments. It is simple enough for a physician to avoid overstating the benefits of a treatment in talking with the patient. It is much more difficult to combat the unreasonable expectations that patients get from the constant news about medical breakthroughs. With patients treated to the spectacle of routine heart transplants and perfect test-tube babies on the evening news, it becomes very difficult to explain that heart disease is a chronic illness without a quick fix and that a certain percentage of all infants have some type of birth defect.

A physician must assume that every patient has an unreasonable expectation of the benefits of medical treatment. Whether these unreasonable expectations arise from overly optimistic news reports or medical advertising, they must be rooted out and dispelled. The physician must specifically ask the patient what the patient expects the treatment to do and believes the risks to be. This will allow the physician to deal explicitly with the patient's misinformation rather than blindly giving the patient more facts to confuse. In a variant of Gresham's law, it is clear that bad information drives out good information by increasing a patient's misperceptions. Patient misperceptions should be documented and a notation made about the correct information given.

Even when the physician and the patient agree on the severity of the complaint and the risks of the treatment, they will not necessarily make the same decision about undergoing the treatment. Physicians and patients have different risk-taking behavior, and patients differ in their risk-taking behaviors. Some are gamblers, and some keep their money under the mattress.

One patient will present with chronic pain and be satisfied to find out that it is only a bone spur, having assumed it must be cancer. Another patient with the same problem will want the physician to try to correct the spur surgically, despite the risks of anesthesia and potential disability. Patients who do not like to take risks are poor candidates for treatment if their untreated prognosis is good and the available treatments are risky. Patients who are aggressive risk takers may want "kill-or-cure" treatments, but they may also be more aggressive about suing when the treatments fail.

The patient's occupation and avocation can strongly affect his or her tolerance of certain risks. People who engage in activities that involve fine motor skills are susceptible to subtle injuries that might not be noticed by other patients. Complications of a routine arterial blood gas sample drawn from the radial artery could diminish the coordination of an accomplished violinist. The same injury in an attorney whose hobby was gardening would go unnoticed. Accommodating treatment to the patient's lifestyle should be part of medical decision making but is sometimes overlooked. Moreover, for esoteric skills, the patient who is an expert in the skill will be a better judge of its demands than the physician who may never have encountered the problem before. In this situation, the patient may teach the physician, if the physician is careful to listen to the patient.

CONFLICTS OF INTEREST AND INFORMED CONSENT

When obtaining informed consent, the physician is expected to present an unbiased view of the proposed treatment, presenting the risks as well as the benefits. Although this informed consent is important, the most important decision is which treatments to recommend. If the physician's impartiality in the selection of treatments is compromised, then providing the patient with information about the compromised choice is meaningless.

Financial Conflicts of Interest

This problem is most extreme in the managed care plans that request the physician not to inform the patient about alternative treatments or tests, or that provide financial incentives that encourage the physician to deny the patient necessary care (see the discussion of the *Shea* case in Chapter 10). This benefits the plan by preventing patient complaints about being denied alternative treatments. It completely defeats informed consent, however, and leaves the physician in an indefensible posture if the patient is injured.

Physicians can also have financial and personal conflicts of interest in medical research. A patient with a rare condition can make a physician's reputation as a scientist. In the biotechnology area, a patient's tissues can be the basis of extremely valuable commercial products. This was the subject of litigation in the *Moore* case,[13] which involved a physician treating a patient who was afflicted with hairy-cell leukemia. During the treatment, the physician determined that the patient's cells would be suitable for making into a cell line with commercial potential. The physician mislead the patient into consenting to numerous medical procedures to facilitate this research work by telling the patient that they were necessary for treating his medical condition. The patient eventually found out what was going on and sued the physician, claiming he was entitled to the value of the cell line derived from this tissue. The court found that whenever a physician has a financial conflict of interest with a patient, the physician's fiduciary obligations require the physician to make a full disclosure of all relevant information to the patient.

Treating Family Members

This is probably the most commonly recognized conflict of interest. It has been traditional for physicians to treat their colleagues' families without charge to discourage physicians from treating their own families.[14] This professional courtesy is a recognition that objective decision making is critical to medical care and that this objectivity is impossible for someone who is emotionally involved with the patient. Treating one's own family can lead to disharmony and guilt if the treatment is not successful. Although it is generally not illegal to treat a family member, many states limit the drugs that may be prescribed. Ideally, physicians and their family members will seek care from physicians who are not close friends or colleagues. This helps ensure objectivity and avoids the conflicts inherent in confiding personal information to colleagues or friends.[15]

Hospitals

Physicians were traditionally prohibited from owning an interest in a hospital. (There was always an exception for small towns in which the physician might be the only person able to finance and oversee the hospital.) It was accepted by a consensus of the profession that it would be difficult for physicians to evaluate the need for hospital care objectively if they would financially benefit from putting the patient in the hospital. The disappearance of this prohibition does not result from today's physicians' being more objective than their predecessors. It results from the increased profitability of hospital ownership, which may intensify the potential conflict of interest. Such interested should be disclosed and may also violate federal law.

Laboratories

Just as ownership in a hospital potentially interferes with the physician's objectivity when evaluating the need for hospital care, ownership in a laboratory can encourage the ordering of unnecessary laboratory tests. Since there is no legal evidence that defensive medicine (the ordering of diagnostically unnecessary tests) reduces the probability of a medical malpractice lawsuit, many critics of this practice attribute it to direct and indirect financial incentives to order tests. The extent to which test ordering is influenced by nonmedical considerations has become obvious as shifts to prospective reimbursement systems reverse these incentives and begin to penalize physicians for ordering tests. There are risks associated with ordering unnecessary tests but much greater risks in failing to order a necessary test.

Sexual Relationships with Patients

The sexual exploitation of patients has been a high-visibility malpractice issue for psychiatrists. In psychiatry the conflict of interest is clear because the patient is by definition at a psychological disadvantage. The conflict is also clear in any situation in which the sexual relations could be termed sexual assault (see Chapter 6). This includes any sexual relations in a medical care delivery setting with a patient who is not the medical care provider's spouse. The more common problem is the physician who becomes romantically involved with a nonpsychiatric patient. It is important that the physician not continue providing major medical care for such a patient, and it is preferable that the patient be referred to another physician for all medical treatment.

CONSENT FOR MINORS

Pediatrics, or more specifically, the medical care of children, is the most legally distinct of the medical specialties. This legal uniqueness has three threads. The first is consent to care. Children may not legally determine their own care, but neither are parents fully empowered to control their child's medical care. The second is communication with the physician. Very young patients are unable to communicate their medical needs to a physician effectively. Finally, childhood immunizations are the front line in protecting society from epidemic communicable diseases. Immunization, with the potential risk of serious sequelae, creates a conflict between the child's individual medical care needs and the protection of society.

Until the late 1800s, parents had almost unlimited power over their children. Physical abuse of children was tolerated, and neglect, even to the point of death, was common. Children were treated as the property of the father. This presumption of complete power over the child was challenged under the laws designed to prevent cruelty to animals. Specific child protective laws followed, and now all states attempt to protect children from abuse and neglect. These laws, combined with public health laws and the U.S. Supreme Court decisions on reproductive rights, have greatly limited parental rights to deny children needed medical care.

In general, persons under 18 years old do not have the right to consent to their own medical care. Unless the parents' legal rights have been terminated, the parents of a minor have the sole authority to consent to medical care for the minor. In most states, if the parents are married to each other, they have an equal right to consent to medical care for the children of that marriage. If the parents are divorced or were never married, the parent with legal custody of the child may have the sole right to consent to care for the child. This does not give the physician the legal right to force care on a mature minor, nor may the physician render medically questionable care, such as a sterilization, at the parents' request.

Documenting Who Can Consent for Your Patients

Documenting consent to medical care for minors is a special case of the general problem of documenting proxy consent: the person who may consent to the care is not the person receiving the care. The physician must first document the relationship between the person giving consent and the patient and then document the risks and alternative treatments that the consenting person was informed of. If the patient is a mature minor, the physician should also discuss the treatment with the minor and document this discussion.

One common problem is that pediatric patients are often brought to the office by someone other than the parent or legal guardian. In a busy pediatrics practice, it is easy to lose track of who has the legal right to consent to medical care for a child. As the divorce rate increases, more children have multiple parents with varying rights to consent to medical care. Ideally, the first time children are brought to the office, they should be accompanied by the parent or guardian who has full authority to consent to care. At that time, the physician should obtain written consent to care, including written authorization for any other persons who will be bringing the child in for care. This authorization should list who may consent to the child's care and whether there are any restrictions on what kind of care they may authorize. Although it sometimes cannot be avoided, the physician should check with the parents or guardian before accepting this proxy consent for surgical procedures or extensive nonemergency care. If there is disagreement between divorced parents over a child's medical care, it is important to find out which parent has the legal right to consent to the child's care. This can usually be determined by a call to the clerk of the court that has jurisdiction over the divorce. Child welfare services can also help in determining this information.

If there are disputes between the parents about the treatment or about who has the authority to consent, these disputes should be documented. It is important to document the rationale for deciding to accept the consent for treatment. The medical necessity of the treatment should be stressed. All contacts with child protective services should be documented. If the child is hospitalized, this information should be copied into the hospital medical record. Physicians who render necessary care to children are seldom sued for failure of consent. Proper documentation is important to reduce the chance that the physician will be sued as an ancillary party in child custody battles.

Special Circumstances

When a child's parents are divorced or legally separated, the physician can no longer assume that both parents have the right to consent to care for the child. The right to consent depends on the state law and the court's orders in the specific case. The parent with legal custody usually has the authority to consent to care for the child; however, the physician seldom knows which parent has legal custody. This is especially problematic in states that allow joint custody.

The child's legal status should be recorded in the medical record. The physician should tell the parents of minor patients to notify him or her of divorces and marriages, as well as address changes. If the physician knows that a couple is separating, he or she should ask who has the right to consent to the child's care. In states that do not allow the noncustodial parent to consent to care, the physician should discuss proxy consent with the custodial parent. A physician should not deny a child needed medical care because of uncertainty about the child's legal status. Conversely, the physician should not knowingly continue to treat a child with a questionable status without attempting to determine who has the legal right to consent to the care.

Many states give certain adult relatives of a child the right to consent to medical care for the child. The parents should be encouraged to use a proxy consent form to clarify their wishes and to broaden the emergency care authority granted in state statutes. If the child stays or travels with friends and neighbors, the parent or guardian should execute a proxy consent allowing these persons to consent to care for the child. If the parents are not comfortable with giving this proxy, they should reconsider whether they should leave the child with this person.

The extent of proxy consent for institutions depends on the proximity and availability of the parents and the medical resources of the school. If the institution has a physician available or if the parent will not be readily available, the proxy consent should be more encompassing. The maximum delegation involves institutions that stand *in loco parentis* ("in the place of the parent"). These institutions should ask the parent to delegate full rights to consent to the institution. The neighborhood public school needs little right to consent to care for a child. The boarding school that caters to diplomats' families needs full rights to consent.

Guardians

Many children are not in the custody of either biological parent. They may be in foster care, under the care of a relative, with a potential adoptive parent, or in other situations in which their caregiver is not a biological parent. If the child has a legally appointed guardian, the guardian must consent to the child's care in the same fashion as for an adult ward.

In some of these cases, no one has asked the court to appoint a guardian for the child. These children are in legal limbo; no one may consent to their care, but it is unthinkable to deny them necessary care because of their legal status. A child in need of immediate care should be treated as necessary while the hospital seeks to have the caregiver appointed as temporary guardian for the child. If the child is in need of simple elective care, that care should be postponed until a guardian is appointed. The physician should always notify child protective services when a child needs a legal guardian.

Conflict between Parents

Children can be pawns in marital battles. This becomes an issue in medical care if the child is being abused or if the parents disagree on medical treatment for a child. As discussed in Chapter 12, suspected child abuse must always be reported to child protective services. If the disagreement over medical care threatens to escalate into neglect or physical harm, this must also be reported to child protective services.

The most difficult cases are those involving disputes over elective care. Legally, consent from one parent is sufficient. When the child is too young to have an independent opinion, the physician may choose to treat the child based on the consent of one parent. If the physician has been refused consent by one parent, it is less clear that the physician may then seek consent from the other parent. Children who are mature enough to have an independent opinion should also be consulted. If the child and one parent agree on a medically reasonable course, the physician should follow that course. Conversely, since physicians should not force unwanted care on a mature minor in general, they should be especially reticent to do so if a parent agrees with the minor.

Conflicts between Parents and Children

The parents of a 17 year old may legally retain the right to determine the minor's medical care; however, the courts have been reluctant to allow parents to deny mature minors elective care. Although a physician should find out the legal requirements in his or her state, in general, physicians may provide birth control information and counseling, treatment for substance abuse, and treatment for communicable diseases to mature minors. In some states, minors may be entitled to consent to such care without their parents' being informed.

The more difficult cases involve attempts by parents to force care on mature minors. The most common scenario involves involuntary psychiatric care for an allegedly drug-abusing or crazy teenager. There is sometimes a fine line between self-destructive behavior and normal adolescent rebellion. Physicians have an ethical obligation not to allow psychiatric care to be used to manipulate or punish a recalcitrant child. Legally, the child could sue for malpractice against the physician who recommends unnecessary psychiatric care.

Statutory Right To Treat Minors

All states have laws that allow children to be treated without the parents' or guardian's consent in certain circumstances. These laws are designed to protect either the child or the public health of the community. All states allow persons in need of emergency care to be treated without consent; nevertheless, many hospitals and physicians have been reticent to treat children without parental consent. To encourage the prompt treatment of sick and injured children, many states have passed laws that allow certain relatives of a child to consent to emergency medical care when the parents are unavailable. Since consent to treatment is not required in true emergencies, the primary purpose of these laws is to assuage physicians' fears of litigation.

Most states allow a physician to treat a child who is suspected of being the victim of abuse or neglect, without the consent of the parents. These laws also require that the physician notify the proper authorities so that the case may be investigated and the child protected if necessary.

Most states allow a child to be treated for communicable and venereal diseases without parental permission. This treatment benefits the child and also helps prevent the spread of disease in the community. This exception to the need for parental consent is usually limited to diseases that are reportable under the state's communicable and venereal disease reporting laws. These diseases must be reported and the child welfare agency notified in certain cases where the disease (such as venereal disease in a young child) raises the suspicion of abuse.

Many states allow minors to seek treatment for alcohol and drug abuse without parental permission. These laws may or may not require child welfare agencies to be notified. Because of the prolonged nature of these treatments and the possibility of hospitalization, it is usually impossible to carry out the treatment without involving the parents. (Very few hospitals accept a minor without parental permission and a guarantee of payment.) These laws are most valuable when dealing with runaways and abandoned minors.

Pregnancy and childbirth pose the most legally difficult conflicts between the rights of parents and those of their children. State laws differ greatly and are frequently modified by U.S. Supreme Court decisions. The courts are attempting to balance the rights of the minor to determine her own medical care, the rights of a parent to control the medical care that a child receives, and the rights of the fetus. In general, the laws allow and encourage pregnant minors to seek prenatal care. There is also a more limited right to birth control information and devices. The most limited right is abortion, which is discussed in Chapter 13.

Emancipated Minors

Most states have a legal proceeding that allows a person under the age of majority to petition the court for full rights as an adult. This grant of adult rights is based on the maturity of the minor and the minor's need for adult status. This need is based on the minor's living alone or other factors that make it inappropriate for the minor's parents to retain control over the minor. Marriage usually qualifies the minor to consent to medical care, as does service in the armed forces.

Interests of the Child versus the Parents

Parents are presumed to have the best interests of their children at heart. In many cases, however, the values and interests of the child are not the same as those of the parents. This becomes a critical issue when evaluating consent to treatment. This problem becomes more common as children enter adolescence. Physicians who care for adolescent boys often see families in which the boy feels compelled to compete in sports to retain his father's affection. As long as this does not interfere with the child's growth and development, it is not a problem for the physician. However, parental enthusiasm becomes detrimental to the child if decisions about the care of injuries are made on the basis of ability to play rather than what is best for the long-term health of the child.

Physicians are increasingly pressured by parents to use medical treatments to alter characteristics of normal healthy children. One of the most controversial therapies is the use of human growth hormone to stimulate growth in children without intrinsic growth hormone deficiency. In most cases, the child is short for his or her age. Questions are being raised, however, about using growth hormone to help already tall children gain the extra height and size that is a critical edge in professional sports. Unlike the analogous problem of vanity surgery, the patient is not able to give an informed, legally binding consent to the treatment. This raises profound ethical questions about the role of the physician and the definition of health.[16]

Religious Objections to Medical Care

This is one of the most important areas of change in the law governing consent to medical care for minors. Where the religious beliefs of the parents once were paramount, the child's right to life and health now takes precedence over the parents' right to freedom of religion. An adult Jehovah's Witness, for instance, may have the right to refuse transfusion, even if it means certain death. That same person does not have the right to refuse transfusion for a child who will likely die. If parents refuse necessary care for a child, the physician or hospital administrator should immediately seek a court order for the care. If the care is needed urgently and cannot await the court order, then the physician should proceed with the care regardless of the parents' objections. The court order should be sought at the same time. The justification for this is the same as the emergency exception to consent. It is reasonable to assume that the court will uphold the child's right to life and health and grant the order for care. If the court cannot be contacted in time, the physician should go ahead with the care just as if it were the parents who are unavailable.[17]

Specific Types of Care

Parents may have many reasons for refusing specific types of care. Refusing the care offered by a particular physician or institution is not the same as neglecting the medical needs of the child. Parents may refuse a particular type of care because they do not believe it is in the child's best interests. Courts generally defer to the parents as the most appropriate judge of the child's interests; however, if the physician believes that the parents are not acting in the child's best interest, this should be reported to the child protection agency.

Physicians should be careful about the claims they make for the offered care. It is not unreasonable for parents to refuse medical care that is difficult or painful if it does not offer a substantial benefit to the child. Parents who refuse supportive care when there is little or no hope of cure are properly asserting the child's right to refuse unnecessary care. This is also true for discontinuing care. If parents refuse treatment for the first presentation of acute lymphocytic leukemia because they do not believe in treating cancer, the physician should seek court intervention. If the parents refuse a repeat course of chemotherapy when there is little hope of remission because they want the child to die at home in comfortable surroundings, the physician should probably do what he or she can to assist them. Physicians should not try to enforce their personal beliefs about hope or dying on the parents or the afflicted child.

CONSENT FOR MEDICAL RESEARCH

There has been more medical legal scholarship on the conduct of medical research involving human subjects than almost any other consent topic—in interesting contrast to the nearly complete lack of litigation alleging injuries from improperly conducted research. Medical research is controversial because of the abuses that occurred in the not-too-distant past, rather than a current litigation threat. Ranging from the medical experiments conducted by the Nazis to the Tuskegee syphilis experiment[18] conducted by the U.S. Public Health Service, these abuses resulted in the promulgation of two major international codes and extensive congressional regulation.[19] Any patient injured by an experiment that violates these

codes or regulations can sue the physician for medical malpractice. More commonly, however, investigators or their institutions are sanctioned by the Department of Health and Human Services (HHS) or the U.S. Public Health Service for not complying with governmental regulations.

In one area, litigation (and criminal investigation) is probable. The growth of joint research agreements between universities and medical businesses, combined with the involvement of medical scientists in for-profit ventures, has put many scientists in violation of laws dealing with conflicts of interest and stock fraud. The Public Health Service has also promulgated rules governing misconduct in science, which could be the basis for fraud-related litigation. Lawsuits asserting financial fraud are not covered by medical malpractice insurance and are especially dangerous to physicians. The physician-scientist must pay the defense costs for such actions and any fines or damages if the defense is unsuccessful.

International Codes

Two primary international codes govern the conduct of medical research involving human subjects. The Declaration of Helsinki is a document promulgated by the World Medical Association "as a guide to each doctor in clinical research." The Nuremberg Code arose from the Nuremberg trials of Nazi war criminals accused of conducting medical experiments on prisoners that caused great suffering and many deaths. The code sets forth principles designed to protect human subjects from abuses related to medical research. The code's statement of the ethical framework for medical research is considered to be the policy behind federal and state regulation of human-subject–based research.

Neither of these codes has the force of law, but they set the moral tone for all medical research, including research unregulated by state or federal law. These codes are admissible in court as evidence of the proper standard of care for medical experimentation. Every physician who is involved in medical research should read and be familiar with these codes.

The Nuremberg Code

The Nuremberg Code arose as part of the trial of the *United States v. Karl Brandt.* Karl Brandt and others were tried at Nuremberg for crimes against humanity committed in their roles as the Nazi high command. The code has 10 requirements:

1. The voluntary consent of the human subject is absolutely essential. This means that the person involved should have legal capacity to give consent, should be so situated as to be able to exercise free power of choice without the intervention of any element of force, fraud, deceit, duress, overreaching, or other ulterior form of constraint or coercion and should have sufficient knowledge and comprehension of the elements of the subject matter involved as to enable him to make an understanding and enlightened decision. This latter element requires that before the acceptance of an affirmative decision by the experimental subject there should be made known to him the nature, duration, and purpose of the experiment; the method and means by which it is to be conducted; all inconveniences and hazards reasonably to be expected; and their effects upon his health or person which may possibly come from his participation in the experiment. The duty and responsibility for ascertaining the quality of the consent rests upon each individual who initiates, directs, or engages in the experiment. It is a personal duty and responsibility, which may not be delegated to another with impunity.

2. The experiment should be such as to yield fruitful results for the good of society, unprocurable by other methods or means of study, and not random and unnecessary in nature.

3. The experiment should be so designed and based on the results of animal experimentation and a knowledge of the natural history of the disease or other problem under study that the anticipated results will justify the performance of the experiment.

4. The experiment should be so conducted as to avoid all unnecessary physical and mental suffering and injury.

5. No experiment should be conducted where there is a prior reason to believe that death or disabling injury will occur, except perhaps, in those experiments where the experimental physicians also serve as subject.

6. The degree of risk to be taken should never exceed that determined by the humanitarian importance of the problem to be solved by the experiment.

7. Proper preparations should be made and adequate facilities provided to protect the experimental subject against even remote possibilities of injury, disability, or death.

8. The experiment should be conducted only by scientifically qualified persons. The highest degree of skill and care should be required through all stages of the experiment of those who conduct or engage in the experiment.

9. During the course of the experiment the human subject should be at liberty to bring the experiment to an end if he has reached the physical or mental state where continuation of the experiment seems to him to be impossible.

10. During the course of the experiment the scientist in charge must be prepared to terminate the experiment at any stage, if he has probable cause to believe, in the exercise of the good faith, superior skill, and careful judgment required of him, that a continuation of the experiment is likely to result in injury, disability, or death to the experimental subject.[20]

World Medical Association

It is the mission of the doctor to safeguard the health of the people. His or her knowledge and conscience are dedicated to the fulfillment of this mission.

The Declaration of Geneva of the World Medical Association binds the doctor with the words: "The health of my patient will be my first consideration"; and the International Code of Medical

Ethics, which declares that "Any act of advice which could weaken physical or mental resistance of a human being may be used only in his interest."

Because it is essential that the results of laboratory experiments be applied to human beings to further scientific knowledge and to help suffering humanity, the World Medical Association has prepared the recommendations in Exhibit 9–1 as a guide to each doctor in clinical research. It must be stressed that the standards as drafted are only a guide to physicians all over the world. Doctors are not relieved from criminal, civil, and ethical responsibilities under the laws of their own countries.

In the field of clinical research a fundamental distinction must be recognized between clinical

Exhibit 9–1 World Medical Association Recommendations for Clinical Research

I. BASIC PRINCIPLES

1. Clinical research must conform to the moral and scientific principles that justify medical research, and should be based on laboratory and animal experiments or other scientifically established facts.

2. Clinical research should be conducted only by scientifically qualified persons and under the supervision of a qualified medical man.

3. Clinical research cannot legitimately be carried out unless the importance of the objective is in proportion to the inherent risk to the subject.

4. Every clinical research project should be preceded by careful assessment of inherent risks in comparison to foreseeable benefits to the subject or to others.

5. Special caution should be exercised by the doctor in performing clinical research in which the personality of the subject is liable to be altered by drugs or experimental procedure.

II. CLINICAL RESEARCH COMBINED WITH PROFESSIONAL CARE

1. In the treatment of the sick person the doctor must be free to use a new therapeutic measure if in his judgment it offers hope of saving life, re-establishing health, or alleviating suffering. If at all possible, consistent with patient psychology, the doctor should obtain the patient's freely given consent after the patient has been given a full explanation. In case of legal incapacity consent should also be procured from the legal guardian; in case of physical incapacity the permission of the legal guardian replaces that of the patient.

2. The doctor can combine clinical research with professional care, the objective being the acquisition of new medical knowledge, only to the extent that clinical research is justified by its therapeutic value for the patient.

III. NONTHERAPEUTIC CLINICAL RESEARCH

1. In the purely scientific application of clinical research carried out on a human being it is the duty of the doctor to remain the protector of the life and health of that person on whom clinical research is being carried out.

2. The nature, the purpose, and the risk of clinical research must be explained to the subject by the doctor.

3a. Clinical research on a human being cannot be undertaken without his free consent, after he has been fully informed; if he is legally incompetent the consent of the legal guardian should be procured.

3b. The subject of clinical research should be in such a mental, physical, and legal state as to be able to exercise fully his power of choice.

3c. Consent should as a rule be obtained in writing. However, the responsibility for clinical research always remains with the research worker; it never falls on the subject, even after consent is obtained.

4a. The investigator must respect the right of each individual to safeguard his personal integrity, especially if the subject is in a dependent relationship to the investigator.

4b. At any time during the course of clinical research the subject or his guardian should be free to withdraw permission for research to be continued. The investigator of the investigating team should discontinue the research if in his or their judgment it may, if continued, be harmful to the individual.

research in which the aim is essentially therapeutic for a patient, and clinical research the essential object of which is purely scientific without therapeutic value to the person subjected to the research.

Consent under the International Codes

The core value of both international codes is that medical research cannot be performed without the freely given (uncoerced) consent of the potential subjects. In a refinement of the Nuremberg Code, the Declaration of Helsinki distinguishes between therapeutic and nontherapeutic research, requiring the physician to exercise special care in performing research that cannot personally benefit the patient. Legally, informed consent shifts the risk of nonnegligent injury to the patient in therapeutic research. In nontherapeutic research, however, it is arguable that the physician–experimenter is strictly liable (regardless of negligence) for injuries to the patient. This distinction is reflected in the federal regulations with the requirement that the risk of the experiment be compared with both the benefits to the patient and to society.

HHS Regulations on Protecting Human Subjects

The Department of Health and Human Services has promulgated regulations for the protection of human research subjects, enforced through the creation of institutional review boards (IRBs) at each participating institution. They apply to all research done by covered institutions or individuals, including research done outside the United States. The regulations stipulate the composition and duties of an IRB, establish standards for informed consent, provide for sanctions against institutions and individuals who violate the regulations, and require more intensive scrutiny of research involving fetuses, in vitro fertilization, pregnant women, prisoners, and children. These regulations do not supersede other state and federal laws; they create additional duties for persons involved in research involving human subjects.

Researchers who run afoul of these regulations can lose their current research funding, can be-

come ineligible for future funding, and can be forced to repay funds improperly expended. In practical terms, a researcher who is disciplined under the regulations will be at a disadvantage for future funds from HHS and other government agencies. Researchers in competitive areas may find it impossible to continue their careers as principal investigators. For this reason, it is imperative that every person contemplating research involving human subjects have a basic understanding of the HHS regulations.

With certain delineated exceptions, the HHS regulations apply to all research conducted with HHS funds, both inside and outside the United States. All institutions receiving HHS funding in any area must have an ethical policy governing all human research conducted at that institution, regardless of the source of funding. Many institutions have also assured HHS that all research in the institution, irrespective of HHS funding, will be reviewed and conducted pursuant to the HHS regulations. These regulations require investigators supervising cooperative research projects to ensure that all other participants abide by the HHS regulations:

> Cooperative research projects are those projects covered by this policy that involve more than one institution. In the conduct of cooperative research projects, each institution is responsible for safeguarding the rights and welfare of human subjects and for complying with this policy. With the approval of the department or agency head, an institution participating in a cooperative project may enter into a joint review arrangement, rely upon the review of another qualified IRB, or make similar arrangements for avoiding duplication of effort.[21]

General Requirements for Informed Consent[22]

Except as provided elsewhere in this policy, no investigator may involve a human being as a subject in research covered by this policy unless the investigator has obtained the legally effective informed consent of the subject or the subject's legally authorized representative. An investigator shall seek such consent only under circumstances that provide the prospective subject or the representative sufficient opportunity to consider whether or not to participate and that minimize the possibility of coercion or undue influence. The information that is given to the subject or the representative shall be in language understandable to the subject or the representative. No informed consent, whether oral or written, may include any exculpatory language through which the subject or the representative is made to waive or appear to waive any of the subject's legal rights, or releases or appears to release the investigator, the sponsor, the institution, or its agents from liability for negligence.

(a) Basic elements of informed consent. Except as provided in paragraph (c) or (d) of this section, in seeking informed consent the following information shall be provided to each subject:

(1) A statement that the study involves research, an explanation of the purposes of the research and the expected duration of the subject's participation, a description of the procedures to be followed, and identification of any procedures which are experimental;

(2) A description of any reasonably foreseeable risks or discomforts to the subject;

(3) A description of any benefits to the subject or to others which may reasonably be expected from the research;

(4) A disclosure of appropriate alternative procedures or courses of treatment, if any, that might be advantageous to the subject;

(5) A statement describing the extent, if any, to which confidentiality of records identifying the subject will be maintained;

(6) For research involving more than minimal risk, an explanation as to whether any compensation and an explanation as to whether any medical treatments are available if injury occurs and, if so, what they consist of, or where further information may be obtained;

(7) An explanation of whom to contact for answers to pertinent questions about the research and research subjects' rights, and whom to contact in the event of a research-related injury to the subject; and

(8) A statement that participation is voluntary, refusal to participate will involve no penalty or loss of benefits to which the subject is otherwise entitled, and the subject may discontinue participation at any time without penalty or loss of benefits to which the subject is otherwise entitled.

(b) Additional elements of informed consent. When appropriate, one or more of the following elements of information shall also be provided to each subject:

(1) A statement that the particular treatment or procedure may involve risks to the subject (or to the embryo or fetus, if the subject is or may become pregnant) which are currently unforeseeable;

(2) Anticipated circumstances under which the subject's participation may be terminated by the investigator without regard to the subject's consent;

(3) Any additional costs to the subject that may result from participation in the research;

(4) The consequences of a subject's decision to withdraw from the research and procedures for orderly termination of participation by the subject;

(5) A statement that significant new findings developed during the course of the research which may relate to the subject's willingness to continue participation will be provided to the subject; and

(6) The approximate number of subjects involved in the study.

(c) An IRB may approve a consent procedure which does not include, or which alters, some or all of the elements of informed consent set forth above, or waive the requirement to obtain informed consent provided the IRB finds and documents that:

(1) The research or demonstration project is to be conducted by or subject to the approval of state or local government officials and is designed to study, evaluate, or otherwise examine: (i) Public benefit of service programs; (ii) procedures for obtaining benefits or services under those programs; (iii) possible changes in or alternatives to those programs or procedures; or (iv) possible changes in methods or levels of payment for benefits or services under those programs; and

(2) The research could not practicably be carried out without the waiver or alteration.

(d) An IRB may approve a consent procedure which does not include, or which alters, some or all of the elements of informed consent set forth in this section, or waive the requirements to obtain informed consent provided the IRB finds and documents that:

(1) The research involves no more than minimal risk to the subjects;

(2) The waiver or alteration will not adversely affect the rights and welfare of the subjects;

(3) The research could not practicably be carried out without the waiver or alteration; and

(4) Whenever appropriate, the subjects will be provided with additional pertinent information after participation.

(e) The informed consent requirements in this policy are not intended to preempt any applicable federal, state, or local laws which require additional information to be disclosed in order for informed consent to be legally effective.

(f) Nothing in this policy is intended to limit the authority of a physician to provide emergency medical care, to the extent the physician is permitted to do so under applicable federal, state, or local law.

DOCUMENTING CONSENT

There are two goals to achieve when documenting informed consent. The more important is using the process of documentation to ensure that the physician and the patient have the same understanding of the care being rendered—its risks, benefits, and alternatives. The secondary goal is to document this understanding in such a way that a third person, such as a juror, can determine both what the patient was told and whether the patient had some reasonable understanding of the implications of what was told.

Most of the literature on informed consent focuses on the consent form. Although it is true that an undocumented consent is legally difficult to defend, informed consent is more than just getting a form signed. A proper informed consent starts with a discussion between the treating physician and the patient. In this discussion, the physician discusses the risks of proposed treatment and its alternatives. Most important, these risks and alter-

natives must be discussed in the context of the patient's prognosis. For example, the same risks of general anesthesia have profoundly different implications for a patient having a tooth pulled compared with a patient with an ectopic pregnancy. The consent form serves to document the discussion between the physician and the patient. It cannot substitute for it.

The Form of the Documentation

There is no single best way to document informed consent. In some situations, such as an immunization clinic, having the patient sign a preprinted consent form is optimal. In other situations, such as elective experimental treatment, a videotape of the physician's talking to the patient may be desirable. The form of documentation must fit the circumstances of the actual transaction between the physician and the patient. The most important consideration is that the documentation reflect the physician's conversation with the patient. "The patient was given the appropriate information and consented to the treatment" is too brief and vague. Long preprinted forms tend to be so broad that it is not possible to establish that they describe the actual conversation with a specific patient.

Blanket Consent Forms

The worst solution to documenting informed consent is the form that blankets all possibilities. The typical blanket form recites that the physician and his or her designees may do what they think is necessary. These forms usually contain language about how the physician has discussed the treatment with the patient and that the patient has had an opportunity to ask questions. Such a form may protect the physician from accusations of battery. As the sole records of informed consent, these forms are worthless.

Treatment-Specific Consent Forms

These prepared forms act as an information sheet for the proposed treatment. They can be very useful as a patient education tool but must be part of a detailed conversation with the patient. If the form alone is used, the consent may be effective, but the risk management benefit of informed consent will be lost because the physician will not learn about the patient's special concerns.

Patient-Specific Consent Forms

These are the ideal consent forms. They contain information on the patient's condition, the proposed treatments and alternatives, and any special considerations. It is an administrative nightmare to collect this information and type up a form for each patient. The best solution is to write (legibly) a detailed note in the patient's medical record as the actual conversation takes place. The patient should be given the note to read and should sign it as part of the medical record. This makes a legally robust document and impresses the patient with the individualization of his or her care.

Non-English Speakers

It is possible to develop foreign language consent forms, but medical terms are often idiosyncratic to regional dialects. For example, there are many patient education materials available in Spanish. These materials may be in textbook Spanish, perfectly intelligible to nonnative Spanish speakers who learned Spanish in school. They may be in the dialect of the translator. They may be hybrid documents in a Pan-American patois. Whatever the case, they may be unintelligible to Spanish speakers who did not learn formal Spanish.

The major problem with dialects is not just that parts of a translated form will not be intelligible to the patient. The same idiomatic medical terms may be used in different dialects but with different meanings. Sometimes this is just embarrassing. Usually it results in the patient's believing that he or she understands the form, which he or she does in the context of the dialect, but misunderstands what is about to be done. This problem is similar to the functional illiterate who recognizes some words but cannot make out the subtle meaning of the document.

The best solution for non-English speakers who may not read standard-school Spanish or another well-defined national languange is to have someone who is medically knowledgeable explain the treatment to the patient in his or her own dialect, with the physician present to answer questions. Ideally the physician should be able to understand enough of the patient's language to know if the translation is appropriate. Real informed consent is very difficult if the patient and the physician have no common language.

Illiterate Patients

The ritual of the patient's reading and signing a form or chart note is meaningless if the patient is illiterate. Studies in the United States have found a substantial fraction of the population to be functionally illiterate—unable to read well enough to carry out day-to-day tasks. When the material that must be read is relatively technical in nature, such as a description of the risks and benefits of medical treatment, the number of persons capable of understanding the material drops substantially.

The first problem is determining if the patient is literate. This is not always easy, for there are some intelligent, successful people who have developed elaborate strategies to conceal their illiteracy. Moreover, many people in the United States are literate and well educated in a language other than English, so for them an English-language form is useless. Although this is obvious to the physician obtaining the consent, it seldom stops administrative personnel from having the patient sign the routine consent form. This undermines the documentation of the oral consent by calling into question the integrity of the process.

This problem requires a translator familiar with the patient's dialect and with the medical terms. The translator should be identified in the medical record. If possible, the translator's address and background should be on file with the hospital or physician. The translator may also serve as the witness if no one else fluent in the patient's language is available. The translator should be cautioned not to speak for the patient but to indicate if the patient's answer is inappropriate. The translator should write a brief note in the chart as to the patient's understanding and linguistic abilities.

Documenting the Oral Consent

The best form of documentation is a recording, either audio or video. These are cheap and easy to make but difficult to store. Medical records departments are equipped to store flat, relatively indestructible materials; lumpy items get lost or destroyed. This will change as medical images start being stored electromagnetically, but for the near future, the storage problems for recordings are a major impediment to their use. For this reason, recordings should be used only when the medical procedure or the patient poses particular problems. Unusual treatments include heart or liver transplants, experimental heroic measures such as artificial hearts, or refusal of lifesaving treatment by salvageable young people. Problem patients include minors undergoing nontherapeutic procedures (such as kidney donors), involuntary patients such as prisoners, patients with transient mental disabilities, and others for whom their state of mind at the time may become a significant issue.

When the person is illiterate but speaks and understands English, consent is usually documented with a witness. Ideally, this should be an impartial witness. The problem with an impartial witness is finding one. A family member may remember only what the patient remembers, whereas a nurse will be seen as an interested party. Clergy, a volunteer from a service agency, or another person not clearly identified with either the physician or the patient is the best choice. The witness must be present at the discussion with the patient and must make some independent record of his or her observations. This independent record may be simply initialing sections of the consent form or a note that certifies that the patient was asked a given question and made the appropriate reply.

PROXY CONSENT

Proxy consent is the process by which people with the legal right to consent to medical treatment for themselves or for a minor or a ward delegate that right to another person. There are three fundamental constraints on this delegation:

1. The person making the delegation must have the right to consent.
2. The person must be legally and medically competent to delegate the right to consent.
3. The right to consent must be delegated to a legally and medically competent adult.

There are two types of proxy consent for adults. The first, the power of attorney to consent to medical care, is usually used by patients who want medical care but are concerned about who will consent if they are rendered temporarily incompetent by the medical care. A power of attorney to consent to medical care delegates the right to consent to a specific person. The second type is the living will.

Power of Attorney To Consent to Medical Care

The basic vehicle for an adult to delegate his or her right to consent to medical care is the power of attorney to consent to medical care. In the simplest case, the person delegates all medical decision-making power to another competent adult, for a fixed period of time or an indefinite period. A competent patient may always revoke a power of attorney to consent to medical care.

Few states have laws forbidding the use of a power of attorney to delegate the right to consent to medical care. Conversely, some states do not specifically outline what a power of attorney may be used for. Although the U.S. Supreme Court has not ruled that the right to delegate medical decision making is protected by the Constitution, it has endorsed the use of powers of attorney to consent to medical care. In the absence of a specific state law or state court decision forbidding the use of a power of attorney to delegate the right to consent to medical care, this is a valid method of proxy consent for adults.

The person making the delegation must be legally and medically competent at the time the power of attorney is signed. These documents are usually notarized, but the notarization has little legal significance. The notary public may testify only as to the signer's identity, not the person's competency. If the person delegating the power to consent to medical care has a condition that might affect his or her competency, a physician, preferably not the patient's usual attending physician, should evaluate the patient and swear to the patient's competence. This should be incorporated into the power of attorney to forestall attacks on its validity. The person to whom the right to consent has been delegated must be medically and legally competent to exercise this right. If he or she is not competent, the patient must be informed and asked to appoint a new person to consent to care. If both the patient and the person to whom the right to consent has been delegated are incompetent, then a court order must be sought to determine who is legally able to consent to the patient's care. The patient may appoint an alternate decision maker in the power of attorney and may specify under what conditions this person will serve.

Conflicts of Interest

The person to whom the power to consent will be delegated should not have any conflicts of interest—emotional, financial, or professional—with the patient. The most obvious conflict is between the physician and the patient. Although the physicians caring for the patient certainly have the patient's best interests in mind, they cannot both propose treatments and consent to them. Physicians and other health care providers should not allow themselves to be given the right to consent to care by a patient for whom they may have to provide treatment. This does not prevent physicians' acting for friends or relatives when their role is to act as the patient's advocate.

There are two types of conflict of interest between family members: conflicts related to loss of objectivity about the medical problems of a loved one and conflicts related to interests in the property or authority of the relative. For example, assume that a woman authorizes her husband to consent to her medical care during a severe illness. When significant treatment decisions must be made, the husband will find it difficult to put aside his concern for his wife and make objective decisions. He may feel guilty that she is ill and he is not. He may feel that he has contributed to her ill-

ness. He may even resent her illness and seek to punish her for being ill. The result is irrational decision making. The husband may blindly accept the proposed treatments or, less frequently, unreasonably refuse to consent to necessary treatments.

This issue should be discussed with patients who seek to execute a power of attorney to consent to medical care. It is important that patients realize the heavy burden that accompanies the right to consent to medical care for a loved one. They should consider whether they have a close friend or more distant relative who would be better able to make objective decisions and weather the pressures associated with the decisions.

Financial conflicts of interest also are inherent in family relationships. Returning to the example of the husband who has power of attorney to consent to his wife's care, if their resources are limited or the proposed treatment is very expensive, the husband will have to choose between paying for his wife's care or the needs of other members of the family. A third party can make more reasoned decisions about allocating resources and is less likely to consent to questionable treatments that the couple cannot afford.

Limitations

A power of attorney to consent to medical care may be limited in whatever way the person delegating the right wishes, consistent with public policy. Put simply, a person may not use a power of attorney to force treatment decisions that would otherwise be improper. For example, the person with a power of attorney may not authorize active euthanasia or force the physician to provide care that the physician would not otherwise provide.

If the person delegating the authority to consent is suffering from a terminal illness, it is usual to state that the power of attorney to consent to medical care is to remain in effect until revoked. It is also usual for spouses to execute prospective powers of attorney that are of indefinite duration, called *durable powers of attorney*. A durable power of attorney remains in force if the patient becomes legally incompetent. In some states, a power of attorney expires when the patient is declared legally incompetent. In all states, the court may supersede a power of attorney by appointing a guardian for the person. The courts are interested in perpetuating the person's wishes and will usually honor a guardian who is proposed in the power of attorney. For the power of attorney to be durable, it must recite that the patient wants the power of attorney to remain effective if he or she becomes incompetent. If the person is concerned only with temporary incapacity secondary to medical treatment, the power of attorney to consent to medical care should have an expiration date.

A power of attorney to consent to medical treatment may be unlimited, or it may authorize only certain medical decisions. It is even possible to execute more than one power of attorney to consent to medical treatment, as long as each document is limited and does not conflict with the others. This might happen when the person executes a general power of attorney to consent to routine medical care and a specific power of attorney to refuse or terminate life support.

In some situations, it is difficult to determine what authority the patient intended to delegate. The patient may have delegated the right to consent to more than one person. The power of attorney may be inconsistent, delegating the right to consent to only part of the necessary care or delegating the authority to consent to improper care. A physician confronted with an ambiguous delegation of the authority to consent to treatment or with improper delegations should ask a court for clarification.

GUARDIANSHIPS

All states provide legal mechanisms to manage the affairs of persons who have become incompetent through illness or injury. Although the names of these proceedings vary, they have the common goal of determining whether the person is competent and appointing a surrogate if he or she is not. This surrogate is usually called the *guardian,* and the person who has been declared incompetent is usually called the *ward.* The guardian has a fiduciary duty to look out for the patient's best interests and may be required to have court approval

for decisions that have a potential adverse impact on the ward.

The guardian becomes the legal alter ego of the ward. When a court appoints a guardian for an individual, the physician must then obtain all consent to medical care from the guardian. The guardian must be given the same information that the patient would have been given. The guardian is also under a duty to ask questions and determine if the treatment is in the patient's best interests. The physician is no longer obliged to obtain consent from the patient. If the patient is conscious, the physician does have a duty to explain what will be done and to preserve the patient's dignity as much as possible.

Establishing the Authority of a Guardian

The most critical element in surrogate consent is establishing the legal standing of the surrogate. Physicians are frequently confronted with friends or relatives of an incompetent patient who claim to be the patient's guardian. It is imperative that these persons be asked to provide a copy of the legal order that establishes their status as guardian. A copy of this order should be made a part of the patient's chart and should be referred to in every consent form.

In most cases, guardianship proceedings are uncontested. The proceedings are instituted by a family member, social worker, health care provider, or other concerned person for the protection of the incompetent person. The incompetent's friends and relatives, if any, may testify that the appointment of the guardian is in the patient's best interests. In uncontested guardianships, consent for medical care should be documented in the same way as a consent from a competent patient. The same type of chart note and consent form should be used, with the additional language about the consent being obtained from the guardian.

Some guardianships are contested. The most common contest involves the appointment of a guardian to consent to medical care for a child whose parents do not want the child treated. The duty to inform the guardian is the same in these cases, but the necessary documentation is more extensive. In addition to incorporating the guardianship papers in the patient's medical record, an attorney should review these papers to ensure that they are in order. This review is to determine if there are any limitations on the guardian's authority. Since these cases usually involve hospitalization, the physician should also discuss the guardianship with the hospital's attorney.

Once a guardian has been appointed for a given purpose, the court does not second-guess the guardian's decisions. It does attempt to ensure that the guardian is acting properly, and persons may ask the court to remove the guardian if they believe that he or she is acting improperly. If a physician is treating a patient who has a guardian, the physician does not need to ask the court to approve each of the guardian's decisions. The physician should be prepared to explain how he or she and the guardian arrived at those decisions. Physicians treating patients with contentious guardianship arrangements should ensure that all decisions by the guardian are carefully documented in the medical record.

Emergency Guardianships

Two situations make it necessary to obtain an emergency guardianship: (1) when a parent refuses to authorize necessary care for a minor child and (2) when an adult refuses care in a situation in which the health care provider believes the refusal should not be honored. In both situations, the care at issue must be necessary to save life or limb or to prevent serious permanent injury. If the care is for a noncritical condition or has little hope of benefiting the patient, the patient's or parent's wishes should be heeded while applying for a guardianship on a nonemergency basis.

In an emergency guardianship, the judge appoints a temporary guardian for the patient. The appointment may be made over the telephone if the hospital has previously arranged a protocol with the appropriate judges. This protocol must address the care that is needed, the consequences of delaying the care while a hearing is scheduled, and an explanation of why the patient or parent

will not consent to the care. Ideally, the patient will be examined by an independent physician who can certify that the care is needed to preserve the patient's life or limb. The judge will often speak to the parents or the patient, if possible.

If the judge determines that an emergency guardianship is warranted, a temporary guardian will be appointed. The judge will usually limit the scope of the guardian's authority to consenting to care that is needed to prevent permanent harm or death. This guardian may be a hospital administrator, but it is preferable to appoint a person who is independent of the hospital and health care providers. The temporary guardian serves until the court can have a hearing with all the concerned parties. The hearing will be held as soon as the parties can be notified and a courtroom scheduled, sometimes within 24 hours.

Minors

When a parent refuses necessary medical care for a child, it is usually for religious reasons. Parents may refuse all care or just specific treatments, such as blood transfusions. They may belong to an organized religious group, such as the Christian Scientists, or have personal beliefs that may be shared with only a few other people. The strength and importance of their religious beliefs can sometimes be determined by how the child was brought to the health care provider. If the parents brought the child to the physician or emergency room, they should be assumed to want help. However, if the child is brought in by neighbors or the police, the physician should expect no cooperation from the parents.

The child should be evaluated at once to determine if immediate care is needed. If it is, a judge should be contacted to arrange a temporary guardianship. The child welfare department should also be notified because denying a child necessary medical care is neglect in most states (see the discussion of reporting child abuse in Chapter 12). Because many states allow children who are abused or neglected to be treated without parental consent, the child welfare agency may be able to authorize treatment for the child without a court order. Although the court may decide to accede to the parents' religious beliefs, the physician's duty is to advocate for the child until the court rules that the child need not be treated.

Adults

An adult who refuses emergency medical care poses a difficult problem. Society does not give parents the right to kill a child through neglect, but it does allow an adult to commit suicide by refusing lifesaving medical care. The only conditions are that the adult must demonstrate that he or she is mentally sound and that the care is being refused for a proper reason, such as a religious objection to care or the presence of a terminal illness (see Chapter 13). These two conditions often merge. If the court finds the reason for refusing care frivolous, this will be taken as evidence of an unsound mind.

As with a child, the patient should be evaluated to determine the needed care and the consequences of not providing that care. A judge should be contacted at once. If the patient remains conscious, the grounds for the refusal of care should be explored and carefully documented. A full mental status examination should be documented in the chart. A psychiatric consult can document the patient's fitness to make reasoned decisions. The attending physician should prepare a care plan that attempts to intrude as little as possible on the patient's beliefs, while still preventing permanent harm. Such a specific, limited-care plan will encourage the judge to allow the patient to be treated until the case can be reviewed in a formal hearing.

The Interim until the Judge Rules

Even an emergency guardianship takes time. The purpose of an emergency guardianship would be defeated if the patient were to die or be permanently injured before the guardianship could be obtained. This would be especially tragic for a child because the courts almost always appoint a guardian to consent to necessary care for children. If the child will suffer by a delay in care, then the child should be treated while the guardianship is being arranged. This is a technical violation of the parents' right to consent to the child's medical care, but it is unlikely that a jury would punish a physician for trying to help the child. Conversely, if the child is allowed to die or become permanently injured, the physician's behavior will be hard to explain to a jury.

Competent adults who refuse care because of religious beliefs pose a more difficult problem. If the physician chooses to treat the patient without consent, the treatment should not be limited in any way that will reduce its effectiveness. Legally, the most damaging outcome is ultimately to save the patient but only after he or she is permanently disabled.

REFUSAL OF CARE AND TERMINATION OF LIFE SUPPORT

Implicit in the right of patients to consent to their own medical care is their right to refuse medical care, even if this results in their death. Patients' right to die preoccupies bioethicists. The authors believe this is a misplaced concern: with the exception of a small number of well-publicized cases such as that of Nancy Cruzan, current reimbursement policies shift the concern from right to die to right to live. These cases mask the everyday ethical conflicts between MCOs, which make their profits by reducing care, and every patient needing expensive care that is not immediately curative.

Who Are the Stakeholders?

The ethical questions arising out of termination of life support for incompetent adults may be categorized by the interests of the various stakeholders: patients, physicians, hospitals, families, and society. These stakeholders have both conflicting and complementary interests. The shifting of these interests through time has shaped the history of thinking about termination of life-support decisions. Balancing these interests requires finding an ethical course of action within the constraints imposed by the legal system.[23]

Patients' Interests

The interests of patients have changed dramatically through time. In the medieval period, the church proscribed medical treatment by Christians. Religious orders were involved with caring for the sick, but this was palliative care intended only to smooth the transition into heaven. Life was seen as a veil of tears to be passed through, not an end in itself. Modern notions of prolonging life would have been considered blasphemous. (As is usually the case, these prohibitions fell mostly on the poor. Wealthy individuals and the nobility often had Jewish or Muslim court physicians.)

During the period between the development of modern medicine and the advent of life-support technologies, patients' interests shifted to curative, rather than merely palliative, care. After World War II, the U.S. government began to subsidize and otherwise encourage the construction of hospitals and the training of physicians. Technology became more important in medical practice, and private medical insurance companies proliferated as employers saw medical insurance as an attractive and inexpensive employee benefit. This trend continued through the 1950s, with technology-based medicine becoming the norm in the 1960s.

Two events in the 1960s had direct bearing on the problem of artificial prolongation of life. The first was the maturation of technology and its integration into routine practice. Ventilators, cardiac monitors, and other life-support devices were improved and became widely available. Physicians became comfortable with these devices and learned how to optimize their effectiveness through better infection control and nursing practices. The second event was the introduction of Medicare and Medicaid. Medicare was particularly important because it removed many of the cost constraints on the care of elderly patients, the class of patient most likely to need life support. This ushered in the era of patient demands for all possible medical technology.

The growth of technological medicine was accompanied by a developing concern for patient autonomy. The strongest force shaping demands for autonomy was the Nuremberg trials of the Nazi war criminals, which documented the medical experiments performed by physicians. Although directed at medical experimentation, the resulting Nuremberg doctrine set out the rights of patients to determine freely the course of their medical care. As discussed earlier in this chapter, the Nuremberg Code is the root of the informed consent doctrine. Patients' concerns with the right to make an informed choice of care began to include a concern for the right to refuse care as the risk of being reduced to a persistent vegetative state became better publicized.[24]

Physicians' Interests

From early Greece, physicians have been committed to curative treatment whenever possible. Physicians have always used whatever technology was available. The Hippocratic Oath's proscription of cutting for stone was based on the operation's uniform failure rate, not an aversion to technology. As anesthesia and antisepsis made surgery safer and much more effective in the late 1800s, modern hospitals and technology-based medicine were born. Physicians embraced life-support technologies as they became available in the 1950s and 1960s. Although originally intended to support metabolism while the patient recovered from a specific pathology, patient demands and insurance incentives soon made life support an end as well as a means.

Physicians made money by billing for patient visits and for doing procedures on patients in the hospital. Although physicians have financial interests in life-support decisions, their interests are not as great as those of hospitals. The physicians' stakes are as much emotional as financial. Physicians are torn between the urge to help specific identified patients avoid unnecessary suffering and a traditional reluctance to talk to patients about death and dying. Until diagnosis-related groups (DRGs) were introduced in the 1980s, physicians were rewarded by hospitals for keeping patients on life support as long as possible because the hospitals were paid based on the number of days the patient was hospitalized. Now irrespective of their personal feelings, physicians are under pressure from hospitals, managed care providers, and the federal government to save money by denying and terminating life support. This pressure is directed at all patients, not just those who are clearly terminally ill.

Hospitals

The growth of intensive care medicine has paralleled the growth of hospitals as businesses. Hospitals have evolved from "physicians' workshops" to independent agents in health care delivery. It is hospitals, rather than physicians, that bear the financial impact of termination of life-support decisions. Most legal challenges to termination of life-support decisions have been brought by hospitals rather than physicians.

The most controversial issue in critical care medicine is the extent to which financial concerns have driven hospital attitudes on termination of life-support decisions. Until the prospective payment system was put in place, termination of life support also meant the termination of a substantial income stream from the patient's insurer. Although it would be unfair to see reimbursement considerations as controlling, it is clear that they have had an impact on ethical decision making. It is likely that the technological imperative was greatly strengthened by its profitability.[25] The troubling question now is the extent to which prospective payment systems lead to the denial of necessary medical care.[26]

Families

Families often have deeply ambiguous feelings about termination of life support. In general, families want their loved ones given all the benefits of medical technology, including advanced life support. The family's interests become compelling when a patient with dependent children refuses life-saving treatment. At the same time, families are the main witnesses to the suffering and degradation that accompany the long-term life support of an incompetent patient. This creates a humanitarian urge to terminate life support, which is often complicated by unresolved feelings of guilt

over family issues unrelated to life support. For example, a family may want to use every possible avenue to prolong the grandmother's life because they feel guilty for putting her in a nursing home.

In the worst cases, family interests are shaped by potential inheritances. Since many wills contain clauses that shift the distribution of the estate depending on the time of death, there can be substantial financial interests in either artificially prolonging or shortening life. A major function of probate courts is to resolve family members' conflicts over estates. It would be unrealistic to assume that these conflicts had no influence on family decisions on termination of life support.

Society's Interests

Until recently, American society was uncritically committed to prolonging the life of all citizens. Insurance payments influenced physicians through direct financial incentives and through the indirect incentive of societal approbation. Insurance companies, as powerful representatives of society, clearly approved of the prolongation of life with advanced life-support technologies. The insurers ratified the life-at-any-cost mentality that physicians were adopting in the 1960s and 1970s. This is not surprising because the dominant insurers of this period—Blue Cross and Blue Shield—were controlled by physicians and hospitals.

This mentality lead to striking increases in the cost of health care. Employers, who buy most health insurance, and government, which pays for Medicare and Medicaid, became concerned with resource allocation. Resources expended on supporting the life of a patient are not available for other objectives, such as education or preventive medical care.[27] The enactment of the Medicare prospective payment system is one manifestation of this concern. Implicit in the prospective payment system is a repudiation of the life-at-all-cost signal sent by the previous cost-based reimbursement system.[28]

Societal interests have become more complicated as antiabortion forces have sought legislation that demands that the state favor life under all circumstances. Although intended to limit abortions, such statutory presumptions can also be read as limiting termination of life-support decisions. This is at issue in the *Cruzan* decision by the Missouri Supreme Court. The court held that its refusal of an order to terminate life support for an incompetent person was mandated by a pro-life statutory provision in the state's antiabortion law.

The *Cruzan* Case

On June 15, 1990, the U.S. Supreme Court rendered its long-awaited decision in the *Cruzan* "right-to-die" case. The actual law established by this case is very narrow and is only tangentially related to the termination of life support. This decision has discomfited many physicians because it does not establish an easy-to-administer, national standard for the termination of life support. *Cruzan* is an important decision because it clarifies several issues surrounding the termination of care for incompetent patients. Although it does not resolve the dilemmas posed by incompetent patients who have not properly formalized their wishes concerning continued care, *Cruzan* may prove to be a wise compromise for a difficult problem.

The specific facts of the *Cruzan* case are compelling: a young woman, brain injured in an automobile accident, was trapped in a persistent vegetative state for years. Brain atrophy made recovery or rehabilitation hopeless, and her family requested that her life support be terminated, but the state refused.

Cruzan is a hard case, and hard cases make bad law because they tempt judges and juries to help the injured party rather than follow the law. *Cruzan* was litigated by a Missouri attorney general seeking to gain support from antiabortion forces by enforcing a statutory provision saying the state favored life in all circumstances. Physicians are not strangers to hard cases. Every birth injury case tempts juries to help the infant by disregarding the legal standard for proof of malpractice. The facts in *Cruzan* call out to the court to ignore the traditional rule of patient autonomy and allow the family to terminate a patient's life support. This would be a good result in *Cruzan,* but would it best serve the needs of future patients and their health care providers?

The Missouri Supreme Court Ruling

The *Cruzan* case began in a Missouri public hospital. Nancy Cruzan was in a persistent vegetative state secondary to anoxia suffered during an automobile accident in 1983. She maintained sufficient brain function to breathe on her own and to respond to painful stimuli. She was fed through a gastrostomy tube but was not otherwise medicated or instrumented. Her parents, who had been appointed her legal guardians, sought to have her nutrition and hydration terminated. The state hospital, in consultation with the attorney general, opposed this request. A case was initiated in state trial court, and a guardian *ad litem* was appointed to protect the patient's interests.

The trial court sought to determine Nancy Cruzan's wishes. Since she had neither executed a living will nor used a durable power of attorney to appoint a surrogate to make decisions in her stead, there was no formal record of her intent. The trial court did find that she had once discussed termination of life support with a roommate, indicating in a general way that she did not want to live in a vegetative state. The trial court accepted this conversation as sufficient evidence of Nancy Cruzan's wish not to be maintained in a persistent vegetative state and authorized the termination of her feedings.

The Missouri Supreme Court accepted the guardian *ad litem*'s appeal of the trial court's decision. The Missouri Supreme Court reversed the trial court's authorization to terminate Nancy Cruzan's nutrition and hydration. This opinion addressed two central points: Were Nancy Cruzan's wishes knowable, and, if not, did her parents have the authority to terminate her life support as an independent decision?

The court found that Missouri law did not give Nancy Cruzan's parents, as guardians, the right to authorize the termination of her nutrition and hydration. The court did not find that such authority would be constitutionally impermissible, only that it was not explicitly provided in the state's guardianship statute. Having determined that Cruzan's parents did not have the authority to discontinue her life support, the Missouri Supreme Court sought to determine whether Nancy's own wishes were knowable.

The Missouri Supreme Court started with the premise that the traditional concept of informed consent applied to decisions to refuse care, as well as decisions to accept care. Under this standard, there would have to be evidence that Nancy Cruzan did not want to be maintained in a vegetative state and appreciated the significance of terminating her nutrition and hydration. The court also required that the patient's intentions be proved by "clear and convincing evidence." This is a standard that is stricter than the preponderance-of-the-evidence rule (51%) used in most civil cases but less strict than the beyond-a-reasonable-doubt rule required to prove guilt in criminal cases.

The clear-and-convincing-evidence standard is used in civil cases when an individual's liberty, rather than just money, is at issue. These situations include involuntary commitment for mental illness, deportation hearings, and proceedings to terminate parental rights.[29] Courts choose the clear-and-convincing-evidence rather the preponderance-of-the-evidence standard as "a societal judgment about how the risk of error should be distributed between the litigants."[30] The *Cruzan* court chose this standard because of the gravity of a decision to terminate life support.

Using this heightened standard of proof, the court then reviewed the evidence presented to the trial court. The court did not find that the testimony in the trial court's record provided clear and convincing proof of Nancy Cruzan's intentions. In particular, the court found that the reported conversations were only general reactions to other persons' medical care and not an informed statement of her intention to refuse life support if she were in a persistent vegetative state.

The disqualification of Nancy Cruzan's parents and the rejection of the evidence of her own desires forced the court to look for other sources of direction for determining whether it should authorize the termination of life support. The court's decision to reverse the trial court's order to terminate Nancy Cruzan's life support was compelled by a Missouri statute passed as part of the state's antiabortion laws: "At the beginning of life, Mis-

souri adopts a strong predisposition in favor of preserving life. Section 188.010, RSMo 1986, announces the 'intention of the General Assembly of Missouri to grant the right to life to all humans, born and unborn....'"[31] Although the legislators who passed this law had intended it to apply to abortions only, the court was compelled by its plain language to apply it to all human beings, including Nancy Cruzan. This decision was appealed to the U.S. Supreme Court.

The U.S. Supreme Court's Ruling

Chief Justice William Rehnquist wrote the majority opinion that establishes the legal rule of the *Cruzan* case. Four additional justices joined in this opinion, and four justices dissented. With the exception of Justice Antonin Scalia, all of the justices were willing to agree, for the purpose of this case, that a competent person has a right to refuse life-saving medical treatment. (When judges assume something for the purpose of a case, it means that what they are assuming is not critical to their decision and may be reevaluated in other cases.) Justice Scalia refused to accept this assumption because he believed that this would undermine the state's authority to forbid suicide.

Both the majority and dissenting opinions accepted that the patient's intentions should be controlling if they are known. The majority found it proper for Missouri to require these intentions be judged by a standard of clear and convincing evidence, preferably through a living will or durable power of attorney. The dissent found the requirement of such formality to be unconstitutionally burdensome, arguing that the court hearing a termination of life-support case should be bound by the testimony of the patient's family and friends. Although accepting such informal evidence would seem to ease the resolution of these cases, it conflicts with the general rule disallowing oral testimony:

> It is also worth noting that most, if not all, States simply forbid oral testimony entirely in determining the wishes of parties in transactions that, although important, simply do not have the consequences that a decision to terminate a person's life

does. At common law and by statute in most States, the parole evidence rule prevents the variations of the terms of a written contract by oral testimony. The statute of frauds makes unenforceable oral contracts to leave property by will, and statutes regulating the making of wills universally require that those instruments be in writing.[32]

The states prohibit oral testimony about wills because the person whose intentions are being sought is dead and thus unavailable to contest the testimony. This rule evolved as the courts found determining the wishes of dead people to be an invitation to fraud and family conflict. Given that a patient in a persistent vegetative state, is, for the purpose of contesting testimony, equivalent to a dead person, the majority did not find it unconstitutionally burdensome to require these same protections for termination of life-support decisions.

There is a contentious debate between the majority and dissenting opinions over the use of the clear-and-convincing standard for proving a patient's wishes. This debate is less important for its own merits than as a surrogate for the fundamental disagreement between the majority and dissenting opinions in *Cruzan:* Is Nancy Cruzan really dead? Justice Rehnquist's majority opinion and, more strongly, Justice Scalia's concurring opinion treat Nancy Cruzan as a living person with liberty interests that are entitled to constitutional protection. The dissenting justices, led by now-retired Justice Brennan, treat Nancy Cruzan as a dead person who has slipped through the cracks in the usual medical tests for death.

The majority opinion specifically rejected a constitutional right of family members to terminate care for patients whose wishes are not known. This ruling is consistent with the Court's previous cases protecting competent patients from requirements that husbands have a voice in determining their wives' medical care. The Court ruled that states, through their legislative processes, are empowered to establish guidelines for medical decision making for incompetent patients who have not otherwise properly documented their wishes. This ruling leaves existing state laws in place; *Cruzan* did not require any changes in established procedures to terminate life support.

The Persistent Vegetative State

The dissenting justices would give families a constitutional right to substitute their decisions for those of incompetent patients who had not made their treatment preferences known. The dissent rejected a state right to require that patients formalize their intentions in living wills or durable powers of attorney as too burdensome. In contrast to the majority, the dissenting judges would exclude the state from participation in termination of treatment decisions, finding families better judges of the patient's best interests. Ironically, in a case decided the same day as *Cruzan,* these same dissenting justices decried even notifying the family of a minor seeking an abortion.[33]

The apparent inconsistency of relying solely on the family for termination of life support but rejecting even limited family involvement in other medical decision making is resolved by a close reading of Justice Brennan's discussion of balancing the risks and benefits of medical treatment: "For many, the thought of an ignoble end, steeped in decay, is abhorrent. A quiet, proud death, bodily integrity intact, is a matter of extreme consequence.... A long, drawn-out death can have a debilitating effect on family members."[34] It is clear that Justice Brennan regards these patients as dying, or already dead, in the same way that brain-dead patients are legally dead although still physiologically functioning.

This assumption that Nancy Cruzan and other patients in her condition are effectively dead is a useful starting point for reconceptualizing the debate on substituted consent. It is the rare patient who survives in a persistent vegetative state while manifesting significant brain atrophy. Such patients should be dealt with by a modified definition of death. The courts and legislatures have been more willing to accept changing definitions of death than they have been to reduce the autonomy and protections of patients still considered alive.[35] A definition of death that includes Nancy Cruzan is more practical and ethically defensible than a definition of life that abets the denial of care to potentially salvageable patients.

Living with *Cruzan*

The *Cruzan* ruling is intrinsically limited because it is only permissive. It upholds Missouri's law that prohibits guardians from authorizing the termination of life support for their wards but does not prevent Missouri or other states from allowing guardians such authority. (Missouri subsequently passed a comprehensive "living will" law.) It upholds Missouri's right to require a patient's intentions to be proved by clear and convincing evidence but does not prevent states from using less rigorous criteria to determine a patient's wishes.

Justice Rehnquist, in a rare example of preventive law advice from the bench, stressed the importance of using living wills and durable powers of attorney. Since these were not at issue in the case, this advice is not law, but it is a useful prediction of the court's future direction.

Medical care providers in states such as Missouri should note that the majority opinion, and Justice Sandra Day O'Connor's concurring opinion, imply that the state may be bound to follow the requests of a patient-appointed surrogate. This would give a surrogate appointed by a patient's durable power of attorney more authority than a guardian appointed under restrictive state guardianship laws.[36]

It is critical to appreciate that the public debate over termination of life support is driven in part by a desire not to waste medical care on patients who will not benefit from it. The problem is determining just who these patients are. Nancy Cruzan clearly does not benefit (in the sense of improved prognosis) from her medical care. Yet there are thousands of close calls for everyone in a similar condition. Given the enormous pressure by medical insurers and the federal government on physicians' and patients' families to terminate medical care, relaxed rules for substituted consent may not be the best solution to the problems of those in Cruzan's condition.

Formalizing the Patient's Wishes

Every person, and especially every patient, should consider some formal provision for decision making should he or she become incompe-

tent. The implication of the *Cruzan* decision is that a durable power of attorney may be the strongest legal provision. There are other benefits to using a durable power of attorney rather than a living will.[37] Physicians do not like to discuss living wills with patients because it makes the patient face the issue of death. Living wills are also troublesome because they must anticipate future circumstances. Conversely, a durable power of attorney may be discussed in terms of the patient's potential temporary incompetence during treatment. Durable powers of attorney are also flexible because they substitute a fully empowered decision maker who can carry out the patient's intentions in the face of changing circumstances.

The Duty To Counsel

The Patient Self-Determination Act of 1990 requires health care providers to counsel patients about the use of living wills, advance directives, and powers of attorney to consent to medical care.

(1)...[T]he requirement of this subsection is that a provider of services or prepaid or eligible organization (as the case may be) maintain written policies and procedures with respect to all adult individuals receiving medical care by or through the provider or organization—

(A) to provide written information to each such individual concerning—

(i) an individual's rights under State law (whether statutory or as recognized by the courts of the State) to make decisions concerning such medical care, including the right to accept or refuse medical or surgical treatment and the right to formulate advance directives (as defined in paragraph (3), and

(ii) the written policies of the provider or organization respecting the implementation of such rights;

(B) to document in the individual's medical record whether or not the individual has executed an advance directive;

(C) not to condition the provision of care or otherwise discriminate against an individual based on whether or not the individual has executed an advance directive;

(D) to ensure compliance with requirements of State law (whether statutory or as recognized by the courts of the State) respecting advance directives at facilities of the provider or organization; and

(E) to provide (individually or with others) for education for staff and the community on issues concerning advance directives. Subparagraph (C) shall not be construed as requiring the provision of care which conflicts with an advance directive.

(2) The written information described [above] shall be provided to an adult individual—

(A) in the case of a hospital, at the time of the individual's admission as an inpatient,

(B) in the case of a skilled nursing facility, at the time of the individual's admission as a resident,

(C) in the case of a home health agency, in advance of the individual coming under the care of the agency,

(D) in the case of a hospice program, at the time of initial receipt of hospice care by the individual from the program, and

(E) in the case of an eligible organization ... [HMOs and certain other managed care providers] at the time of enrollment of the individual with the organization.

(3) In this subsection, the term "advance directive" means a written instruction, such as a living will or durable power of attorney for health care, recognized under State law (whether statutory or as recognized by the courts of the State) and relating to the provision of such care when the individual is incapacitated. (1395cc(f))[38]

Complying with a Patient's Refusal of Care

The American legal system is based on achieving politically acceptable rules within the limits posed by the Constitution. The courts are loath to interfere in the medical care decisions of competent adults, a product of the high value placed on patient autonomy. It also reflects judicial economy. Unlike attorneys, judges prefer to minimize the number and types of disputes that must be judicially resolved. The courts will upset the decision of a competent patient only when other stake-holders present a compelling argument for overriding the patient's interests.

Once patients have indicated their desires in a living will or by a surrogate decision maker appointed by a power of attorney, physicians should heed these instructions. Unnecessarily delaying the termination of life support, or forcing unwanted life support while contesting the patient's decisions in court is legally risky.

The Role of Courts

Until recently, decisions about the withdrawal or withholding of death-delaying treatment were debated by ethicists and civil libertarians but were not a fundamental problem for practicing physicians. Decisions were made, the courts were seldom involved, and there were few malpractice lawsuits or criminal prosecutions. With the advent of DRGs and other forms of prospective payment, the general public is beginning to be concerned that health care providers are doing less for patients for whom it is financially rewarding to do less. This erosion of public confidence, combined with the real pressure on physicians to do less for DRG patients, makes it imperative that decisions that will lead to premature death be carried out in a legally impeccable manner. Ultimately, adhering to legal principle is the best defense against administrative pressures to compromise patient care for the sake of optimal reimbursement.

Following the Patient's Wishes

If a competent patient refuses care, either directly or through a living will or surrogate, the physician is bound to respect those wishes. This does not apply to euthanasia or living wills that violate state law. Until recently, however, physicians have been able to treat critical care patients against their will because the courts were reluctant to punish a physician for delaying a patient's death. As the courts become more sophisticated about these cases, they are less willing to tolerate these intrusions on patient autonomy. One court has already assessed damages against a hospital that refused to terminate life support for a patient who was brain dead.[39] Courts are also likely to assess attorney's fees and damages against physicians who ignore clearly effective living wills in order to avoid terminating life support.

Physicians are already seeing patients and families who reject living wills and demand life support. Patients do not have the right to unnecessary medical care, including intensive care that cannot affect the outcome of their condition. If the patient demands all available care, the physician must be careful to document the therapeutic rationale behind decisions to deny or terminate life support for these patients. In all cases, it is easier not to start a therapy than to terminate it. This is a very slippery slope, however, as hospitals and third-party payers increase the pressure on physicians and families to refuse or terminate life support.

At least one hospital openly challenged the right of patients and their families to demand the application and continuation of life support. This hospital sought a court order to terminate life support for a patient whose clearly expressed wishes, and those of her husband, were to continue the life support. The court refused the order, finding no compelling reason to overrule the patient's decision. Most hospitals apply less open but nonetheless real pressure on families and physicians. Physicians should be careful that it is medical considerations and not financial pressures that underlie the decision to refuse life support to patients. Many physicians correctly worry about the denial of resources to other patients with a better prognosis. This does not make physicians who are determining the care for individual patients the proper agents to refuse care to benefit society. Although MCOs stress cost-effective care, this is under the constraint that the patient must receive the same quality care. Only the government can change the legal standard and allow classes of patients to be denied care to benefit society as a whole.

Judicial Intervention

There are two important caveats to nonjudicially supervised termination of life-support decisions. The first, and more critical, is that the patient must be a competent adult at the time the decision is made. The second is that the patient must clearly state his or her intentions, and these must be properly documented. Unless required by state law, this documentation need not be a witnessed living will. It can be a properly recorded conversation with the physician or the written request by a patient-appointed surrogate. The termination of life-support for minors, long-term medically incompetent patients, and patients who have not made their wishes known while competent are more complex and generally require the intervention of a judicially appointed guardian.

The most compelling cases for judicial intervention are those in which a patient who refuses curative therapy has dependent family members. These are almost exclusively persons with religious objections to some or all medical care. This may be because refusing curative treatment without a religious rationale results in the patient's being treated as an incompetent. Although courts have ordered treatment in some cases, recent case law, *Fosmire v. Nicoleau,*[40] affirmed the right of a pregnant woman to refuse blood transfusions despite the risk to her fetus:

> In sum, the patient as a competent adult, had a right to determine the course of her own treatment, which included the right to decline blood transfusions, and there is no showing that the State had a superior interest, in preventing her from exercising that right under the circumstances of this case.[41]

Cases such as *Fosmire* are ethically the most difficult to resolve. The case is brought on behalf of family members, usually minor children, who depend on the patient. If the necessary treatment is forced on the patient, the patient will recover and the issue will be resolved. The appellate judges in *Fosmire* had the luxury of upholding the patient's autonomy without having blood on their own hands: the trial court's order to give blood had been carried out immediately. The appeal sought only to second-guess its validity.

Physicians in a case like *Fosmire* would properly question whether it would be ethical, although legal, to stand by and not seek a court order to force treatment. Societal interest in the well-being of the dependents would also favor intervention. The trial court's ordering of the treatment might offend some people, but it would not shock the conscience of members of the general public. It is cases such as this that fuel ethical debates, yet these cases have little to do with termination of life-support issues.

Termination of life-support cases, in general, do not involve the refusal of curative therapy. If a competent adult refuses curative life support for religious reasons, these cases should be treated separately from the termination of noncurative life support. It is legally permissible to comply with such requests without legal process. It is ethically questionable, however, to accept a refusal of curative therapy without using judicial process at least to verify the sincerity of the request. In extreme situations, the patient's request is tantamount to a request for assistance in committing suicide.[42]

The Simple Cases

Few termination of life-support cases present irreconcilable ethical problems.[43] Most of the patients involved are going to die relatively quickly, irrespective of treatment. All but a few of the rest will be condemned to a persistent vegetative state, which they have previously rejected as unacceptable. Family members may have personal psychological reasons to resist the termination of life support. These are not compelling, however, because of the patient's inability to contribute either personally or financially to family life. Unlike refusal of curative therapy, there is no compelling ethical basis for a physician or hospital to resist the termination of essentially futile treatment. Once treatment becomes both ineffective and unacceptable to the patient, society's interest is to preserve its resources for other patients.[44]

This leaves a residuum of hard cases, cases such as that of Hector Rodas. Rodas suffered an accidental brain injury that left him mentally competent but otherwise totally dependent on life-support technology. He could neither speak nor swallow. He could respond to yes or no questions by nodding his head, which allowed him to spell out messages with the help of a therapist pointing to letters on a board. By this means, Rodas requested that he no longer be fed or hydrated. The hospital required Rodas, through his lawyer, to seek a court order discontinuing life support. The court ultimately ruled that Rodas could refuse nutrition and hydration while remaining in the hospital.[45]

The physicians and the hospital in this case were reluctant to terminate treatment without a court order, but it is difficult to imagine a court refusing Rodas's request to be allowed to die. According to Mishkin,[46] allowing Rodas to die without a court order is certainly legally proper. Considering the prolongation of Rodas's suffering caused by the court action and his extremely limited prognosis, it may be more than merely legal. In cases such as this one, where none of the stakeholders other than the patient has a compelling interest, the delays and suffering inherent in judicial process make such a course of action ethically questionable.

Living Wills in the Emergency Room

A patient who presents in an emergency room is presumed to be there for all necessary medical care. Patients who are conscious and able to make their wishes known may refuse unwanted medical care. But a living will should not be taken to forbid resuscitation efforts in the emergency room. Without knowledge about the patient, the physician should not assume that the document belongs to that patient or that it reflects the patient's wishes in that situation. However, at the same time that the resuscitation is being attempted, someone should try to clarify the status of the living will. The cardiopulmonary resuscitation (CPR) must be stopped at the point that it is reasonably certain that the living will is authentic. Once a terminally ill patient's wishes are known, there is no justification for rendering unwanted treatment.

Emergency room personnel should not circumvent living wills by demanding unreasonable proof that the living will is valid. It must be remembered that the burden is on medical personnel to disprove the will if it appears valid on its face. If the will is not over a few years old, is clearly written, is signed and witnessed (many states make notarization optional), and the identity of the patient is well known, the living will is facially valid. Yet even if the will is valid, it is not an absolute bar to the forbidden care. If there is a reasonable probability that CPR or other lifesaving care will be successful, then it should not be withheld if there is an indication that the patient would have wanted the care. For example, an elderly patient in currently good health may have signed a living will out of fear of a lingering cancer death. This patient might very well want to be given emergency treatment and CPR after an automobile accident.

The Impact of Cruzan

The *Cruzan* decision disappointed those who had hoped that the Supreme Court would find that families have a constitutional right to terminate a patient's life support.[47] The American Medical Association has supported substituted decision making for termination of life support, both because of concern with family suffering and because it is convenient for the physicians.[48] The dissent in *Cruzan* implied that without substituted decision making, physicians would be forced to keep most patients in critical care alive forever.

Would that we were so effective at keeping patients alive as the dissent in *Cruzan* implies. The dissent in *Cruzan* profoundly misinterprets the nature of most termination of life-support decisions. Cases like Nancy Cruzan's are rare rather than typical of termination of life-support situations. Most termination of life-support decisions for incompetent patients are questions of a few hours or days of extra care, not years or decades. Although not diminishing the familial suffering that can be caused by unnecessary delays of even a few days in terminating life support, this is not a problem that rises to constitutional significance.

The right-to-die debate blinds the public to the real crisis in intensive care: ensuring that every person who might benefit from medical care receives that care. Peter Medawar put it best:

> The tenacity of our hold on life and the sheer strength of our preference for being alive whenever it is an option is far better evidence of a life instinct than any element of human behavioral repertoire is evidence of a death instinct. It is odd, then, that nothing in modern medicine has

aroused more criticism and resentment than the lengths to which the medical profession will go to prolong the life of patients who need not die if any artifice can keep them going.... Charity, common sense, and humanity unite to describe intensive care as a method of preserving life and not, as its critics have declared, of prolonging death.[49]

The Drawbacks of Substituted Consent

The Judicial Council of the American Medical Association has endorsed the concept of allowing spouses and relatives to consent to the care of incompetent patients without first getting the patient's permission. Several state legislatures have considered or passed laws that empower physicians to seek informal consent from the relatives of incompetent patients. Physicians have supported these efforts because they make the physician's life simpler by limiting the need for guardianship proceedings. Unfortunately, these efforts may have profound and unintended consequences for the physician–patient relationship.

Substituted consent is a devil's bargain. First, the assumption that family members always have their relatives' best interests at heart is contradicted by the bulk of family law cases and many of the cases involving wills. Even a loving family is no insurance against conflicts:

> Close family members may have a strong feeling—a feeling not at all ignoble or unworthy, but not entirely disinterested, either—that they do not wish to witness the continuation of the life of a loved one that they regard as hopeless, meaningless, and even degrading. But there is no automatic assurance that the view of close family members will necessarily be the same as the patient's would have been had she been confronted with the prospect of her situation while competent.[50]

There is a particular irony in *Cruzan*. Justice Brennan's dissent in the case asserted that the family had a constitutional right to substitute its wishes for the unknown desires of the patient. This dissent was prefaced with a glowing description of the concern that all families feel for their loved ones and how it was cruel for the majority to imply that the family might not have the patient's best interests at heart. In a case decided the same day, Justice Brennan joined in a dissent portraying the families of girls seeking abortions as uncaring monsters who had no right to be informed or participate in the decision to have an abortion. Most bioethicists see a critical distinction between substituting consent for terminally ill incompetents and substituting consent for other patients. Unless this is based on the hidden belief that these incompetents are actually dead, it is legally unsupportable. There is no constitutional basis to believe that the Supreme Court will treat substituted consent for medical incompetents as a special case, separate from that of other situations where family interests conflict with those of the individual.

Although preserving patient autonomy is inconvenient for terminally ill incompetent patients, once autonomy is lost, the consent process will be a battleground for control of the physician–patient relationship. The legal basis of this relationship is the same personal autonomy that this substituted consent denies. If the Supreme Court creates a constitutional right for families to substitute their decisions for patients, this right will not be limited to termination of life-support cases. For example, such a constitutional right could be used as support for laws requiring husbands to be consulted about their wives' access to contraception or wives to be consulted about their husbands' cardiac surgery. It would be especially troubling for minors because minors are incompetents according to the law. The convenience of simplifying a limited number of termination of life-support decisions could be rapidly overshadowed by unprecedented intrusions into the physician–patient relationship.

The Problem of Relatives

If it is accepted that family members and spouses have a right to substitute their decisions for a patient, then physicians will find themselves talking to relatives in other situations, such as abortion counseling. Protecting patient autonomy has a great benefit to physicians: the physician always knows who has the right to consent to medical care. Although physicians dislike being involved in guardianship proceedings, the

alternative is uncertainty in obtaining consent. Relatives frequently disagree over the care a patient should receive. The physician must choose the relatives with whom to consult. This raises questions such as whether two children trump one spouse. Does any relative with an attorney trump the rest of the family?

If the physician chooses whom to consult for consent, he or she will also be legally liable if the choice is incorrect. If no family member has a right to consent, then no family member has the right to sue for failing to be consulted about the patient's care. Conversely, if family members may be consulted, then they have a right to sue if they are unhappy with the physician's decisions.

ASSISTED SUICIDE

The United States is conducting a national experiment with assisted suicide. At least one state has legalized it—Oregon[51]—albeit with substantial restrictions, and several others have specifically banned it. Some ethicists and law professors favor a right to assisted suicide as an extension of a patient's right to control their own medical care.[52] Many others oppose it on philosophical grounds in the individual case and as a dangerous slippery slope issue for society.[53] Given the pressures to cut costs in medical care, and the substantial savings that an early suicide of a patient with a serious illness can bring, it is inevitable that physicians will be pressured to recommend suicide, both by family members and by insurers.

History of Suicide Law

Assisted suicide was first before the U.S. Supreme Court in the *Cruzan* case, where one of the points urged on the court was that it should recognize a right to suicide because it was part of the Anglo-American legal tradition. In rejecting this claim, the Court outlined the history of suicide and assisted suicide:

> At common law in England, a suicide—defined as one who 'deliberately puts an end to his own existence, or commits any unlawful malicious act, the consequence of which is his own death,' 4 W.

Blackstone, Commentaries *189—was criminally liable. Ibid. Although the States abolished the penalties imposed by the common law (i.e., forfeiture and ignominious burial), they did so to spare the innocent family and not to legitimize the act. Case law at the time of the adoption of the Fourteenth Amendment generally held that assisting suicide was a criminal offense. See Marzen, O'Dowd, Crone, & Balch, Suicide: A Constitutional Right?, 24 Duquesne L. Rev. 1, 76 (1985) ('In short, twenty-one of the thirty-seven states, and eighteen of the thirty ratifying states prohibited assisting suicide. Only eight of the states, and seven of the ratifying states, definitely did not'); see also 1 F. Wharton, Criminal Law @ 122 (6th rev. ed. 1868). The System of Penal Law presented to the House of Representatives by Representative Livingston in 1828 would have criminalized assisted suicide. E. Livingston, A System of Penal Law, Penal Code 122 (1828). The Field Penal Code, adopted by the Dakota Territory in 1877, proscribed attempted suicide and assisted suicide. Marzen, O'Dowd, Crone, & Balch, supra, at 76–77. And most States that did not explicitly prohibit assisted suicide in 1868 recognized, when the issue arose in the 50 years following the Fourteenth Amendment's ratification, that assisted and (in some cases) attempted suicide were unlawful. Id., at 77–100; id., at 148–242 (surveying development of States' laws). Thus, 'there is no significant support for the claim that a right to suicide is so rooted in our tradition that it may be deemed 'fundamental' or 'implicit in the concept of ordered liberty.'' Id., at 100 (quoting Palko v. Connecticut, 302 U.S. 319, 325 (1937)).[54]

Physician-Assisted Suicide as a Constitutional Right

The question of whether there is a constitutional right to suicide was directly before the U.S. Supreme Court in two cases decided in 1997. These were brought by patients and physicians contesting state laws in Washington state[55] and in New York[56] that banned physician participation in assisted suicide. It is important legally that the cases were about the right of a physician to participate in assisted suicide, not about the general right of assisted suicide. Although it is clear from the Court's ruling that a state could ban assisted

suicide in general, the court did not need to reach this issue because the states have very broad authority under the police powers to regulate medical practice. There are many things that the state can prevent physicians from doing as a condition of licensure that it might not be able to do as a general rule for all citizens.

The Court found that there was no constitutional right to have a physician assist in a suicide, so that the states were free to prohibit physicians from participating in suicides. The Court found that converse was also true: there was nothing to prevent the states from allowing both assisted suicide and physician participation in assisted suicide, so long as Congress does not preempt their authority by passing a law banning physician-assisted suicide nationally.

Right to Pain Relief

The most persuasive evidence before the court was the scientific studies indicating that much of the demand for assisted suicide is driven by patients with inadequate pain relief and depression, with the depression complicated by the pain. These studies indicated that most patients with adequate pain relief and psychological treatment do not demand suicide. Advocates of assisted suicide countered that such levels of pain medication often shortened the patient's life and were, in themselves, a form of assisted suicide. Thus, if the Court banned assisted suicide, it must also ban dosages of pain medication that would shorten the patient's life. The Court rejected this argument, finding that the distinction between assisting suicide and providing care that might, as a side-effect, shorten life, was well established legally:

The distinction comports with fundamental legal principles of causation and intent. First, when a patient refuses life-sustaining medical treatment, he dies from an underlying fatal disease or pathology; but if a patient ingests lethal medication prescribed by a physician, he is killed by that medication. See, e.g., People v. Kevorkian, 447 Mich. 436, 470-472, 527 N.W.2d 714, 728 (1994), cert. denied, 514 U.S. 1083, 115 S.Ct. 1795, 131 L.Ed.2d 723 (1995); Matter of Conroy, 98 N.J. 321, 355, 486 A.2d 1209, 1226 (1985) (when feeding tube is removed, death "result[s]... from [the patient's] underlying medical condition"); In re Colyer, 99 Wash.2d 114, 123, 660 P.2d 738, 743 (1983) ("[D]eath which occurs after the removal of life sustaining systems is from natural causes"); American Medical Association, Council on Ethical and Judicial Affairs, Physician-Assisted Suicide, 10 Issues in Law & Medicine 91, 92 (1994) ("When a life-sustaining treatment is declined, the patient dies primarily because of an underlying disease").

Furthermore, a physician who withdraws, or honors a patient's refusal to begin life-sustaining medical treatment purposefully intends, or may so intend, only to respect his patient's wishes and "to cease doing useless and futile or degrading things to the patient when [the patient] no longer stands to benefit from them." Assisted Suicide in the United States, Hearing before the Subcommittee on the Constitution of the House Committee on the Judiciary, 104th Cong., 2d Sess., 368 (1996) (testimony of Dr. Leon R. Kass). The same is true when a doctor provides aggressive palliative care; in some cases, pain-killing drugs may hasten a patient's death, but the physician's purpose and intent is, or may be, *2299 only to ease his patient's pain. A doctor who assists a suicide, however, "must, necessarily and indubitably, intend primarily that the patient be made dead." Id., at 367. Similarly, a patient who commits suicide with a doctor's aid necessarily has the specific intent to end his or her own life, while a patient who refuses or discontinues treatment might not. See, e.g., Matter of Conroy, supra, at 351, 486 A.2d, at 1224 (patients who refuse life-sustaining treatment "may not harbor a specific intent to die" and may instead "fervently wish to live, but to do so free of unwanted medical technology, surgery, or drugs"); Superintendent of Belchertown State School v. Saikewicz, 373 Mass. 728, 743, n. 11, 370 N.E.2d 417, 426, n. 11 (1977) ("[I]n refusing treatment the patient may not have the specific intent to die").

The law has long used actors' intent or purpose to distinguish between two acts that may have the same result. See, e.g., United States v. Bailey, 444 U.S. 394, 403-406, 100 S.Ct. 624, 631-633, 62 L.Ed.2d 575 (1980) ("[T]he ... common law of homicide often distinguishes ... between a person who knows that another person will be killed as the result of his conduct and a person who acts with the specific purpose of taking another's life"); Morissette v. United States, 342 U.S. 246, 250, 72 S.Ct. 240, 243, 96 L.Ed. 288 (1952) (distinctions based on intent are "universal and persistent in mature systems of law"); M. Hale, 1 Pleas of the Crown 412 (1847) ("If A., with an intent to prevent gangrene beginning in his hand doth without any advice cut off his hand, by which he dies, he is not thereby felo de se for tho it was a voluntary act, yet it was not with an intent to kill himself"). Put differently, the law distinguishes actions taken "because of" a given end from actions taken "in spite of" their unintended but foreseen consequences. Feeney, 442 U.S., at 279, 99 S.Ct., at 2296; Compassion in Dying v. Washington, 79 F.3d 790, 858 (C.A.9 1996) (Kleinfeld, J., dissenting) ("When General Eisenhower ordered American soldiers onto the beaches of Normandy, he knew that he was sending many American soldiers to certain death.... His purpose, though, was to ... liberate Europe from the Nazis").[57]

The court discussed pain relief at some length, holding that there was clearly a right to adequate pain medication and that state laws to the contrary might be unconstitutional. This is the most important part of the ruling for the vast majority of health care practitioners and their patients: patients with serious, especially terminal, conditions must be given adequate pain relief, even at the risk of hastening death. (No one even raised the ludicrous issue of worrying about terminally ill patients becoming addicts.)

REFERENCES

1. *Schoendorff v. Society of New York Hosp.,* 105 N.E. 92, 93 (N.Y. 1914).
2. *Miller v. Rhode Island Hosp.,* 625 A.2d 778 (R.I. 1993).
3. *In re Conservatorship of Foster,* 547 N.W.2d 81 (Minn. 1996).
4. *Reynolds v. McNichols,* 488 F.2d 1378 (10th Cir. 1973).
5. *Nishi v. Hartwell,* 473 P.2d 116 (Haw. 1970).
6. *Carr v. Strode,* 904 P.2d 489 (Haw. 1995).
7. *Ward v. Lutheran Hosp. & Homes Soc'y of Am, Inc.,* 963 P.2d 1031 (Alaska 1998).
8. Freifeld K. Myopic haste? (100,000 plus have had new eye surgery). *Forbes.* May 6, 1985;95:135.

9. Norman C. Clinical trial stirs legal battles: legal disputes in Atlanta and Chicago over surgery for myopia raise issue of how controversial surgical techniques should be assessed. *Science*. 1985;1316:227.

10. *Schachar v. American Academy of Ophthalmology, Inc.,* 870 F.2d 397 (7th Cir. 1989).

11. *United States v. Bachynsky,* 934 F.2d 1349 (5th Cir. 1991).

12. *Faya v. Almaraz,* 438, 620 A.2d 327 (1993), and *Doe v. Noe,* 690 N.E.2d 1012 (Ill. App. 1 Dist. 1997).

13. *Moore v. Regents of Univ. of Cal.,* 793 P.2d 479 (Cal. 1990).

14. Wasserman RC, Hassuk BM, Young PC, Land ML. Health care of physicians' children. *Pediatrics*. 1989;83:319–322.

15. Lane LW, Lane G, Schiedermayer DL, Spiro JH, Siegler M. Caring for medical students as patients. *Arch Intern Med*. 1990;150:2249–2253.

16. Lantos J, Siegler M, Cuttler L. Ethical issues in growth hormone therapy. *JAMA*. 1989;261:1020–1024.

17. Holder AR. Minors' rights to consent to medical care. *JAMA*. 1987;257:3400–3402.

18. Jones JH. *Bad Blood: The Tuskegee Syphilis Experiment*. New York: Free Press; 1981.

19. Katz J, Capron AM, Glass ES. *Experimentation with Human Beings: The Authority of the Investigator, Subject, Professions, and State in the Human Experimentation Process*. New York: Russell Sage Foundation; 1972.

20. Nuremberg Code, Trials of War Criminals before the Nuremberg Tribunals under Control Council Law No. 10.

21. 45 C.F.R. § 46.114 (1998).

22. 45 C.F.R. § 46.116 (1998).

23. Carton R. The road to euthanasia. *JAMA*. 1990;263:2221.

24. Cranford RE. The persistent vegetative state: the medical reality (getting the facts straight). *Hastings Cent Rep*. 1988;18:27; Brody BA. Ethical questions raised by the persistent vegetative state patient. *Hastings Cent Rep*. 1988;18:330; and, Wikler D. Not dead, not dying? Ethical categories and persistent vegetative state. *Hast Cent Rep*. 1988;18:41.

25. Powerly KE, Smith E. The impact of DRGs on health care workers and their clients. *Hastings Cent Rep*. 1989;19:16.

26. Dougherty CJ. Ethical perspectives on cost containment. *Hastings Cent Rep*. 1989;19:5.

27. Murphy DJ, Matchar DB. Life-sustaining therapy: a model for appropriate use. *JAMA*. 1990;264:2103–2108.

28. Veatch RM. Justice and the economics of terminal illness. *Hastings Cent Rep*. 1988;18:34.

29. *Addington v. Texas,* 441 U.S. 418 (1979).

30. *Santosky v. Kramer,* 455 U.S. 745, 755 (1982).

31. *Cruzan v. Harmon,* 760 S.W.2d 408 (Mo. 1988).

32. *Cruzan by Cruzan v. Director, Mo. Dept. of Health,* 497 U.S. 261 (1990).

33. *Ohio v. Akron Ctr. for Reprod. Health,* 110 S. Ct. 2972 (1990).

34. *Cruzan,* 497 U.S. at 311.

35. AMA(1); Council on Scientific Affairs and Council on Ethical and Judicial Affairs. Persistent vegetative state and the decision to withdraw or withhold life support. *JAMA*. 1990;263:426–430.

36. Mishkin DB. You don't need a judge to terminate treatment. *J Intensive Care Med*. 1990;5:5201–5204.

37. Orentlicher D. Advance medical directives. *JAMA*. 1990;263:2365.

38. Cotton P. Providers to advise of "medical Miranda." *JAMA*. 1991;265:306.

39. *McVey v. Englewood Hosp. Ass'n,* 216 N.J. Super. 502, 524 A.2d 450 (N.J. Super. A.D. 1987).

40. *Fosmire v. Nicoleau,* 551 N.E.2d 77 (N.Y. 1990).

41. *Id.* at 84.

42. Kane EI. Keeping Elizabeth Bouvia alive for the public good. *Hastings Cent Rep*. 1985;15:5.

43. Weir RF, Gostin L. Decisions to abate life-sustaining treatment for nonautonomous patients: ethical standards and legal liability for physicians after Cruzan. *JAMA*. 1990;264:1846–1853.

44. Callahan D. Setting limits: Medical goals in an aging society. Washington, DC: Georgetown University Press; 1995.

45. Miller DH. Right to die damage actions. *Denver Law Rev*. 1988; 65:184.

46. Mishkin DB. You don't need a judge to terminate treatment. *J Intensive Care Med*. 1990;5:5201–5204.

47. AMA—Office of the General Counsel, Orentlicher D. The right to die after Cruzan. *JAMA*. 1990;264:2444–2446.

48. AMA, Council on Ethical and Judicial Affairs, American Medical Association. AMA ethical opinion 2.20: withholding or withdrawing life-prolonging medical treatment. *Curr Opin*. 1989;13.

49. Medawar, PB. The threat and the glory: Reflections on science and scientists. Quoted in Perutz, MF. *High on Science*. New York: Rev Books; August 16, 1990;37:12.

50. *Cruzan,* 497 U.S. at 286.

51. Egan, T. *In Oregon, Opening a New Front in the World of Medicine*. New York Times. November 6, 1997;A26.

52. Baron, CH. Pleading for physician-assisted suicide in the courts, *W N Eng Law Rev*. 1997;19:371.

53. Kamisar, Y. *The "right to die": on drawing (and erasing) lines*. Duquesne Law Rev. 1996;35:481; Arras, J. Physician-assisted suicide: a tragic view. *J Contemp Health Law Policy*. 1997;361. Brody, H. Compassion in Dying v. Washington: promoting dangerous myths in terminal care. *BioLaw*. July–Aug 1996; (special section): S-154; Burt, R. Constitutionalizing physician-assisted suicide: will lightning strike thrice? Duquesne Law Rev. 1996;35:159; Capron, AM. Liberty, equality, death! *Hastings Cent Rep*. May/June 1996;23.

54. *Cruzan,* 497 U.S. at 294.

55. *Washington v. Glucksberg,* 521 U.S. 702 (1997).

56. *Vacco v. Quill,* 521 U.S. 793, 117 S.Ct. 2293 (1997).

57. *Id.* at 2298.

SUGGESTED READINGS

General Consent Issues

Ackerman TF. Chemically dependent physicians and informed consent disclosure. *J Addict Dis*. 1996;15:25–42.

Agre P, McKee K, Gargon N, Kurtz RC. Patient satisfaction with an informed consent process. *Cancer Pract*. 1997;5:162–167.

Amet EM. Informed consent is a process, not a piece of paper. *J Oral Implantol*. 1996;22:2.

Aoki Y, Nakagawa K, Hasezawa K, et al. Significance of informed consent and truth-telling for quality of life in terminal cancer patients. *Radiation Med*. 1997;15:133–135.

Appelbaum PS, Grisso T. Capacities of hospitalized, medically ill patients to consent to treatment. *Psychosomatics*. 1997;38:119–125.

Artnak KE. Informed consent in the elderly: assessing decisional capacity. *Semin Perioper Nurs*. 1997;6:59–64.

Berlin L. Malpractice issues in radiology: informed consent. *AJR*. 1997;169:15–18.

Brennan M. A concept analysis of consent. *J Adv Nurs*. 1997;25:477–484.

Brick J. Informed consent and perioperative nursing. *AORN J*. 1996;63:258–261.

Brown V. Informed consent for PSA testing. *J Fam Pract*. 1996;43:234–235.

Bussey GD. Informed consent: its legal history and impact on medicine. *Hawaii Med J*. 1995;54:472–475.

Caulum SJ. Informed consent: advice from the trenches. *Wis Med J*. 1997;96:62.

Chambers T. Letting the patient backstage: informed consent for HMO enrollees. *J Am Geriatr Soc*. 1998;46:355–358.

Chiodo GT, Tolle SW. Informed consent across cultures. *Gen Dent*. 1997;45:421–424.

Clouser KD, Hufford DJ, O'Connor BB. Informed consent and alternative medicine. *Altern Ther Health Med*. 1996;2:76–78.

Cox JD. Paternalism, informed consent and Tuskegee. *Int J Radiat Oncol Biol Phys*. 1998;40:1–2.

Cunningham N. Fear and informed consent. *Am J Nurs*. 1996;96:66.

Etchells E, Sharpe G, Walsh P, Williams JR, Singer PA. Bioethics for clinicians: 1: consent. *CMAJ*. 1996;155:177–180.

Freda MC, DeVore N, Valentine-Adams N, Bombard A, Merkatz IR. Informed consent for maternal serum alpha-fetoprotein screening in an inner city population: how informed is it? *J Obstet Gynecol Neonatal Nurs*. 1998;27:99–106.

Gabel H. How presumed is presumed consent? *Transplant Proc*. 1996;28:27–30.

Gamulka BD. The need for true informed consent in pediatric teaching hospitals. *Acad Med*. 1998;73:628–629.

Geller G, Botkin JR, Green MJ, et al. Genetic testing for susceptibility to adult-onset cancer: the process and content of informed consent. *JAMA*. 1997;277:1467–1474.

Halva K. Minor consent to treatment. *Minn Med*. 1997;80:53–54.

Harrison A. Consent and common law. *Nurs Times*. 1997;93:52–54.

Hekkenberg RJ, Irish JC, Rotstein LE, Brown DH, Gullane PJ. Informed consent in head and neck surgery: how much do patients actually remember? *J Otolaryngol*. 1997;26:155–159.

Hill RB. Autopsy consent and family resistance: the role of the clinician. *South Med J*. 1996;89:1125–1126.

Hofmann PB. Physician experience as a measure of competency: implications for informed consent. *Camb Q Healthc Ethics*. 1996;5:458–459; discussion 459–466.

Holland PV. Consent for transfusion: is it informed? *Transfu Med Rev*. 1997;1:274–285.

Hood CA, Hope T, Dove P. Videos, photographs, and patient consent. *BMJ*. 1998;316:1009–1011.

Hopper KD, TenHave TR, Tully DA, Hall TE. The readability of currently used surgical/procedure consent forms in the United States. *Surgery*. 1998;123:496–503.

Jones MA. Ethical and legal responses to patients who refuse consent to treatment. *Br J Urol*. 1995;76(suppl 2):9–14.

Katz J. Reflections on informed consent: 40 years after its birth. *J Am Coll Surg*. 1998;186:466–474.

Kay NA, Barone BM. Optimizing the consent process for organ donation. *J SC Med Assoc*. 1998;94:69–75.

Kerns, AF. Better to lay it out on the table rather than do it behind the curtain: hospitals need to obtain consent before using newly deceased patients to teach resuscitation procedures. *J Contemp Health Law Policy*. 1997;13:581–612.

Khong TY. Improving perinatal autopsy rates: who is counseling bereaved parents for autopsy consent? *Birth*. 1997;24:55–57.

Kleinman I, Schachter D, Jeffries J, Goldhamer P. Informed consent and tardive dyskinesia: long-term follow-up. *J Nerv Ment Dis*. 1996;184:517–522.

Klepatsky A, Mahlmeister L. Consent and informed consent in perinatal and neonatal settings. *J Perinat Neonat Nurs*. 1997;11:34–51.

Lavoie FW. Consent, involuntary treatment, and the use of force in an urban emergency department. *Ann Emerg Med*. 1992;21:25–32.

Layson RT, McConnell T. Must consent always be obtained for a do-not-resuscitate order? *Arch of Int Med*. 1996;156:2617–2620.

Lescale KB, Inglis SR, Eddleman KA, Peeper EQ, Chervenak FA, McCullough LB. Conflicts between physicians and patients in nonelective cesarean delivery: incidence and the adequacy of informed consent. *Am J Perinatol*. 1996;13:171–176.

Liang BA. In initio invadere: issues in infant informed consent, i.v.s, and intubation. *J Clin Anesth*. 1998;10:73–76.

Lyttle J. Is informed consent possible in the rapidly evolving world of DNA sampling? *CMAJ*. 1997;156:257–258.

Mailhot CB. Culture and consent. *Nurs Manage* 1997;28:48P.

Marshall KG. Prevention: how much harm? How much benefit? IV: the ethics of informed consent for preventive screening programs. *CMAJ*. 1996;155:377–383.

McGleenan T. Affording brutality the cloak of law—consent to medical examination of suspects and children. *Med Sci Law*. 1996;36:9–14.

Meisel A, Kuczewski M. Legal and ethical myths about informed consent. *Arch Int Med*. 1996;156:2521–2526.

Mendelson D. Historical evolution and modern implications of concepts of consent to, and refusal of, medical treatment in the law of trespass. *J Leg Med*. 1996;17:1–71.

Molnar J. Consent in the 90's. *Med Law*. 1997;16:567–579.

Moustarah F. Organ procurement: let's presume consent. *CMAJ*. 1998;158:231–234.

Mulcahy D, Cunningham K, McCormack D, Cassidy N, Walsh M. Informed consent from whom? *J R Coll Surg Edinb*. 1997;42:161–164.

Murphy MF, Docherty S, Greenfield P. Survey of the information given to patients about blood transfusion and the need for consent before transfusion. *Transfus Med*. 1997;7:287–288.

Neptune SM, Hopper KD, Houts PS, Hartzel JS, Ten Have TR, Loges RJ. Take-home informed consent for intravenous contrast media: do patients learn more? *Invest Radiol*. 1996;31:109–113.

Nickerson CA, Jasper JD, Asch DA. Comfort level, financial incentives, and consent for organ donation. *Transplant Proc*. 1998;30:155–159.

Nora LM, Benvenuti RJ. Medicolegal aspects of informed consent. *Neurol Clin*. 1998;16:207–216.

O'Flynn N, Spencer J, Jones R. Consent and confidentiality in teaching in general practice: survey of patients' views on presence of students. *BMJ*. 1997;315:1142.

Orth OG. Virtues and informed consent. *Mo Med*. 1997;94:216–220.

Pang AH, Laf KY, Bailey V. Children's consent to psychiatric treatment: all or nothing? *Int J Clin Pract*. 1997;51:412–413.

Pape T. Legal and ethical considerations of informed consent. *AORN J*. 1997;65:1122–1127.

Pennels CJ. Consent and children. *Prof Nurse*. 1998;13:327–328.

Pennings G. Partner consent for sperm donation. *Hum Reprod*. 1996;11:1132–1137.

Pharris MD, Ledray LE. Consent and confidentiality in the care of the sexually assaulted adolescent. *J Emerg Nurs*. 1997;23:279–281.

Post LF, Blustein J, Gordon E, Dubler NN. Pain: ethics, culture, and informed consent to relief. *J Law Med Ethics*. 1996;24:348–359.

Power KJ. The legal and ethical implications of consent to nursing procedures. *Br J Nurs*. 1997;6:885–888.

Pryor F. Key concepts in informed consent for perioperative nurses. *AORN J*. 1997;65:1105–1110.

Qual S. Informed consent: still a physician's duty. *Minn Med*. 1997;80:51–52.

Stauch M. Consent in medical law. *Br J Nurs*. 1998;7:84.

Zinner SE. The elusive goal of informed consent by adolescents. *Theor Med*. 1995;16:323–331.

Impaired or Mentally Ill Patients

American Psychiatric Association. Resources document on principles of informed consent in psychiatry. *J Am Acad Psychiatry Law*. 1997;25:121–125.

Appelbaum PS. Missing the boat: competence and consent in psychiatric research. *Am J Psychiatry*. 1998;155:1486–1488.

Appelbaum PS, Grisso T. Capacities of hospitalized, medically ill patients to consent to treatment. *Psychosomatics*. 1997;38:119–125.

Artnak KE. Informed consent in the elderly: assessing decisional capacity. *Semin Perioper Nurs*. 1997;6:59–64.

Auerswald KB, Charpentier PA, Inouye SK. The informed consent process in older patients who developed delirium: a clinical epidemiologic study. *Am J Med*. 1997;103:410–418.

Batten DA. Informed consent by children and adolescents to psychiatric treatment. *Aust NZ J Psychiatry*. 1996;30:623–629; discussion 630–632.

Berg JW. Legal and ethical complexities of consent with cognitively impaired research subjects: proposed guidelines. *J Law Med Ethics*. 1996;24:18–35.

Billick SB, Della Bella P, Burgert W. Competency to consent to hospitalization in the medical patient. *J Am Acad Psychiatry Law*. 1997;25:191–196.

Brabbins C, Butler J, Bentall R. Consent to neuroleptic medication for schizophrenia: clinical, ethical and legal issues. *Br J Psychiatry*. 1996;168:540–544.

Chiodo GT, Tolle SW. Diminished autonomy: can a person with dementia consent to dental treatment? *Gen Dent*. 1992;40:372–373.

Christensen K, Haroun A, Schneiderman LJ, Jeste DV. Decision-making capacity for informed consent in the older population. *Bull Am Acad Psychiatry Law*. 1995;23:353–365.

Costa LM. Competency and consent. *Geriatr Nurs*. 1991;12:254.

Cournos F. Do psychiatric patients need greater protection than medical patients when they consent to treatment? *Psychiatr Q*. 1993;64:319–329.

Downes BR. Guardianship for people with severe mental retardation: consent for urgently needed treatment. *Health Soc Work*. 1992;17:13–15.

Fellows LK. Competency and consent in dementia. *J Am Geriatr Soc*. 1998;46:922–926.

Gendreau C. The rights of psychiatric patients in the light of the principles announced by the United Nations: a recognition of the right to consent to treatment? *Int J Law Psychiatry*. 1997;20:259–278.

Hoge SK. On being 'too crazy' to sign into a mental hospital:

the issue of consent to psychiatric hospitalization. *Bull Am Acad Psychiatry Law*. 1994;22:431–450.

Holzer JC, Gansler DA, Moczynski NP, Folstein MF. Cognitive functions in the informed consent evaluation process: a pilot study. *J Am Acad Psychiatry Law*. 1997;25:531–540.

Hundert EM. Autonomy, informed consent, and psychosurgery. *J Clin Ethics*. 1994;5:264–266.

Hunter J. Consent for the legally incompetent organ donor: application of a best-interests test. *J Leg Med*. 1991;12:535–557.

Janofsky JS, McCarthy RJ, Folstein MF. The Hopkins Competency Assessment Test: a brief method for evaluating patients' capacity to give informed consent. *Hosp Community Psychiatry*. 1992;43:132–136.

Kitamura F, Tomoda A, Tsukada K, et al. Method for assessment of competency to consent in the mentally ill: rationale, development, and comparison with the medically ill. *Int J Law Psychiatry*. 1998;21:223–244.

Krynski MD, Tymchuk AJ, Ouslander JG. How informed can consent be? New light on comprehension among elderly people making decisions about enteral tube feeding. *Gerontologist*. 1994;34:36–43.

Leung WC. Mental health and the law: parental consent to treatment is needed for those aged 16–18 who are incompetent. *BMJ*. 1998;316:70; discussion 71.

Manning SS, Gaul CE. The ethics of informed consent: a critical variable in the self-determination of health and mental health clients. *Soc Work Health Care*. 1997;25:103–117.

Marson DC, Chatterjee A, Ingram KK, Harrell LE. Toward a neurologic model of competency: cognitive predictors of capacity to consent in Alzheimer's disease using three different legal standards. *Neurology*. 1996;46:666–672.

Marson DC, McInturff B, Hawkins L, Bartolucci A, Harrell LE. Consistency of physician judgments of capacity to consent in mild Alzheimer's disease. *J Am Geriatr Soc*. 1997;45:453–457.

Marson DC, Schmitt FA, Ingram KK, Harrell LE. Determining the competency of Alzheimer patients to consent to treatment and research. *Alzheimer Dis Assoc Disord*. 1994;8:5–18.

Martin BA, Glancy GD. Consent to electroconvulsive therapy: investigation of the validity of a competency questionnaire. *Convuls Ther*. 1994;10:279–286.

McFadzean J, Monson JP, Watson JD, et al. The dilemma of the incapacitated patient who has previously refused consent for surgery. *BMJ*. 1997;315:1530–1532.

McKegney FP, Schwartz BJ, O'Dowd MA. Reducing unnecessary psychiatric consultations for informed consent by liaison with administration. *Gen Hosp Psychiatry*. 1992;14:15–19.

Melamed Y, Kimchi R, Shnit D, Moldavski M, Elizur A. Insight and competence to consent to psychiatric hospitalization. *Med Law*. 1997;16:721–727.

Morris CD, Niederbuhl JM, Mahr JM. Determining the capability of individuals with mental retardation to give informed consent. *Am J Ment Retard*. 1993;98:263–272.

Pang AH, Laf KY, Bailey V. Children's consent to psychiatric treatment: all or nothing? *Int J Clin Pract*. 1997;51:412–413.

Pepper–Smith R, Harvey WR, Silberfeld M, Stein E, Rutman D. Consent to a competency assessment. *Int J Law Psychiatry*. 1992;15:13–23.

Poythress NG, Cascardi M, Ritterband L. Capacity to consent to voluntary hospitalization: searching for a satisfactory Zinermon screen. *Bull Am Acad Psychiatry Law*. 1996;24:439–452.

Rikkert MG, van den Bercken JH, ten Have HA, Hoefnagels WH. Experienced consent in geriatrics research: a new method to optimize the capacity to consent in frail elderly subjects. *J Med Ethics*. 1997;23:271–276.

Silva MC. Competency, comprehension, and the ethics of informed consent. *Nursingconnections*. 1993;6:47–51.

Stagno SJ, Smith ML, Hassenbusch SJ. Reconsidering "psychosurgery": issues of informed consent and physician responsibility. *J Clin Ethics*. 1994;5:217–223.

Sugarman J, McCrory DC, Hubal RC. Getting meaningful informed consent from older adults: a structured literature review of empirical research. *J Am Geriatr Soc*. 1998;46:517–524.

Usher KJ, Arthur D. Process consent: a model for enhancing informed consent in mental health nursing. *J Adv Nurs*. 1998;27:692–697.

Wirshing DA, Wirshing WC, Marder SR, Liberman RP, Mintz J. Informed consent: assessment of comprehension. *Am J Psychiatry*. 1998;155:1508–1511.

Zaubler TS, Viederman M, Fins JJ. Ethical, legal, and psychiatric issues in capacity, competency, and informed consent: an annotated bibliography. *Gen Hosp Psychiatry*. 1996;18:155–172.

Research

Adshead G. Informed consent and psychiatric research. *Ann Ist Super Sanita*. 1997;33:497–503.

Altman DG, Whitehead J, Parmar MK, Stenning SP, Fayers PM, Machin D. Randomised consent designs in cancer clinical trials. *Eur J Cancer*. 1995;31A:1934–1944.

Auerswald KB, Charpentier PA, Inouye SK. The informed consent process in older patients who developed delirium: a clinical epidemiologic study. *Am J Med*. 1997;103:410–418.

Baskin SA, Morris J, Ahronheim JC, Meier DE, Morrison RS. Barriers to obtaining consent in dementia research: implications for surrogate decision-making. *J Am Geriatr Soc*. 1998;46:287–290.

Benatar D, Benatar SR. Informed consent and research. *BMJ*. 1998;316:1008.

Berg JW. Legal and ethical complexities of consent with cognitively impaired research subjects: proposed guidelines. *J Law Med Ethics*. 1996;24:18–35.

Berry DL, Dodd MJ, Hinds PS, Ferrell BR. Informed consent: process and clinical issues. *Oncol Nurs Forum*. 1996;23:507–512.

Biros MH, Runge JW, Lewis RJ, Doherty C. Emergency medicine and the development of the Food and Drug Administration's final rule on informed consent and waiver of informed consent in emergency research circumstances. *Acad Emerg Med*. 1998;5:359–368.

Brody BA, Katz J, Dula A. In case of emergency: no need for consent. *Hastings Cent Rep*. 1997;27:7; discussion 7–12.

Clever LH. Obtain informed consent before publishing information about patients. *JAMA*. 1997;278:628–629.

Daar AS. Ethics of xenotransplantation: animal issues, consent, and likely transformation of transplant ethics. *World J Surg*. 1997;21:975–982.

Davis TC, Holcombe RF, Berkel HJ, Pramanik S, Divers SG. Informed consent for clinical trials: a comparative study of standard versus simplified forms. *J Nat Cancer Inst*. 1998;90:668–674.

Doyal L. Informed consent in medical research: journals should not publish research to which patients have not given fully informed consent—with three exceptions. *BMJ*. 1997;314:1107–1111.

Doyal L, Tobias JS, Warnock M, Power L, Goodare H. Informed consent in medical research. *BMJ*. 1998;316:1000–1005.

Dukoff R, Sunderland T. Durable power of attorney and informed consent with Alzheimer's disease patients: a clinical study. *Am J Psychiatry*. 1997;154:1070–1075.

Elliott C. Caring about risks: are severely depressed patients competent to consent to research? *Arch Gen Psychiatry*. 1997;54:113–116.

Foster C. Commentary: ethics of clinical research without patients' consent. *BMJ*. 1996;312:817.

Geller G, Strauss M, Bernhardt BA, Holtzman NA. "Decoding" informed consent: insights from women regarding breast cancer susceptibility testing. *Hastings Cent Rep*. 1997;27:28–33.

Haimowitz S, Delano SJ, Oldham JM. Uninformed decisionmaking: the case of surrogate research consent. *Hastings Cent Rep*. 1997;27:9–16.

Hewlett SE. Is consent to participate in research voluntary? *Arthritis Care Res*. 1996;9:400–404.

High DM. Research with Alzheimer's disease subjects: informed consent and proxy decision making. *J Am Geriatr Soc*. 1992;40:950–957.

Hunter D, Caporaso N. Informed consent in epidemiologic studies involving genetic markers. *Epidemiology*. 1997;8:596–599.

Jezewski MA. Obtaining consent for do-not-resuscitate status: advice from experienced nurses. *Nurs Outlook*. 1996;44:114–119.

Koren G, Carmeli DB, Carmeli YS, Haslam R. Maturity of children to consent to medical research: the babysitter test. *J Med Ethics*. 1993;19:142–147.

MacKinnon B. How important is consent for controlled clinical trials? *Camb Q Healthc Ethics*. 1996;5:221–227.

Mader TJ, Playe SJ. Emergency medicine research consent form readability assessment. *Ann Emerg Med*. 1997;29:534–539.

Marson DC, Hawkins L, McInturff B, Harrell LE. Cognitive models that predict physician judgments of capacity to consent in mild Alzheimer's disease. *J Am Geriatr Soc*. 1997;45:458–464.

Mason S. Obtaining informed consent for neonatal randomised controlled trials—an "elaborate ritual"? *Arch Dis Child Fetal Neonatal Ed*. 1997;76:F143–F145.

McLean P. Biomedical research and the law of informed consent. *Can Nurse*. 1996;92:49–50.

Miller CK, O'Donnell DC, Searight HR, Barbarash RA. The Deaconess Informed Consent Comprehension Test: an assessment tool for clinical research subjects. *Pharmacotherapy*. 1996;16:872–878.

Montague J. Balancing caution & courage: physicians and regulators weigh informed consent issues in clinical research. *Hosp Health Netw*. 1994;68:50, 52–54.

Morgan A. Informed consent: finding a path toward prudent policy. *Pacing Clin Electrophysiol*. 1997;20:730–731.

Olson CM, Jobe KA. Reporting approval by research ethics committees and subjects' consent in human resuscitation research. *Resuscitation*. 1996;31:255–263.

Prows CA, McCain GC. Parental consent for bone marrow transplantation in the case of genetic disorders. *J Soc Pediatr Nurses*. 1997;2:9–18; quiz 19–20.

Reilly PR, Boshar MF, Holtzman SH. Ethical issues in genetic research: disclosure and informed consent. *Nat Genet*. 1997;15:16–20.

Resau LS. Obtaining informed consent in Alzheimer's research. *J Neurosci Nurs*. 1995;27:57–60.

Rikkert MG, van den Bercken JH, ten Have HA, Hoefnagels WH. Experienced consent in geriatrics research: a new method to optimize the capacity to consent in frail elderly subjects. *J Med Ethics*. 1997;23:271–276.

Sachs GA. Advance consent for dementia research. *Alzheimer Dis Assoc Disord*. 1994;8:19–27.

Silverman HJ. Ethical considerations of ensuring an informed and autonomous consent in research involving critically ill patients. *Am J Respir Crit Care Med*. 1996;154:582–586.

Susman EJ, Dorn LD, Fletcher JC. Participation in biomedical research: the consent process as viewed by children, adolescents, young adults, and physicians. *J Pediatr*. 1992;121:547–552.

Verheggen FW, van Wijmen FC. Myth and reality of informed consent in clinical trials. *Med Law*. 1997;16:53–69.

CHAPTER 10

Team Care and Managed Care

HIGHLIGHTS

- The physician–patient relationship is a fiduciary relationship.
- Managed care creates profound conflicts of interest between health care practitioners and patients.
- The law of the physician–patient relationship does not change in managed care.
- Most states require nonphysician practitioners to be supervised by physicians.
- Physician medical directors face special legal risks.
- Managed care poses new business risks to health care practitioners.

INTRODUCTION

The most legally significant change in medical practice over the last twenty years has been the corporatization of medical care services. This has accelerated in the last ten years with the growing dominance of managed care organizations (MCOs). In this book, an MCO is any organization with a financial interest in medical care delivered to a group of patients and that contracts with health care practitioners for the delivery of medical care and exercises some control over that medical care. These range from closed-panel health maintenance organizations (HMOs) with all employee physicians, to loosely structured preferred provider organizations (PPOs), and include hospital-owned physician's practices and other arrangements with noninsurers who nonetheless have a financial interest in the medical care that the health care practitioners deliver.

The legal consequences of the corporatization of medicine has been to broaden the legal threats facing health care practitioners from traditional medical malpractice litigation to include fraud, financial crimes, and other civil and criminal business litigation. The losses from such litigation are potentially much greater than from individual medical malpractice cases. Civil fines can run to the tens and hundreds of millions of dollars, and the individuals may be criminally prosecuted and face prison sentences.

This chapter deals with the special risks that arise from health care practitioners working with MCOs and in team care environments. Most of

---

these risks arise from the conflicts between the health care practitioner's fiduciary duty to the patient and the MCO's pressure to make the health care practitioner a gatekeeper who protects the interests of the MCO. Most of these risks run to physician health care providers because the vast majority of the statutes and case law dealing with fiduciary duty in health care are directed at physicians. Since informed consent law derives from the physician's fiduciary duty to the patient, Chapter 9 also deals with MCO-related issues.

THE CHANGING NATURE OF PHYSICIANS' PRACTICES

Traditionally, physicians practiced as sole proprietors or as small partnerships. A small number of physicians worked for employers such as railroads to provide care to the employees, and, in some cases, care to the employee's families. Patients paid directly for their care, usually in cash, but sometimes with barter. The physician's only institutional relationship was with the local hospital. Hospital privileges were simple independent contractor relationships, usually vetted by the local medical society. Medical law was simple, dealing mostly with medical negligence, hospital privileges, and perennially controversial areas such as abortion and narcotics prescriptions.

These patterns reflected the simplicity of the pre-World War II medical environment. There were relatively few effective drugs, technology was limited and not capital intensive, and hospitals were run mostly by religious orders and provided little more than nursing, laundry, and food services. Physicians worked alone and specialty practice, beyond surgery, was very limited. After World War II, medical specialization and advances in technology and pharmacology profoundly changed hospitals and physician practice patterns, but the old business organizations persisted beyond the point where they made business sense for anyone but the physicians. Business innovation was stifled by state laws, called corporate practice of medicine laws, that protected the private practice model.

Corporate Practice of Medicine

The evolution of business forms for physicians' practices has been limited by state anticorporate practice of medicine of laws.[1] These laws date back to the 1920s and 1930s. Interestingly, they evolved from laws intended to prevent the practice of law by corporations. Their purpose was to protect the independence of the professional's judgment from the pressures triggered by making money for the stockholders of a business. In a quote that presages many current criticisms of the more aggressive MCOs, a court in 1910 described the potential evils of allowing the corporate practice of law:

The relation of attorney and client is that of master and servant in a limited and dignified sense, and it involves the highest trust and confidence. It cannot be delegated without consent and it cannot exist between an attorney employed by a corporation to practice law for it, and a client of the corporation, for he would be subject to the directions of the corporation and not to the directions of the client. There would be neither contract nor privity between him and the client, and he would not owe even the duty of counsel to the actual litigant. The corporation would control the litigation, the money earned would belong to the corporation and the attorney would be responsible to the corporation only. His master would not be the client but the corporation, conducted it may be wholly by laymen, organized simply to make money and not to aid in the administration of justice which is the highest function of an attorney and counselor at law. The corporation might not have a lawyer among its stockholders, directors or officers. Its members might be without character, learning or standing. There would be no remedy by attachment or disbarment to protect the public from imposition or fraud, no stimulus to good conduct from the traditions of an ancient and honorable profession, and no guide except the sordid purpose to earn money for stockholders. The bar, which is an institution of the highest usefulness and standing, would be degraded if even its humblest member became subject to the orders of a money-making corporation engaged not in conducting litigation for itself, but in the business of conducting litigation for others. The degradation of the bar is an injury to the state.[2]

Corporate practice of medicine laws apply to physicians only. Any business may hire nurses or other nonphysician providers, subject to state law requirements of physician supervision. These laws are still in force in most states, although many states seem to have forgotten about their core purpose to protect physician decision making and ignore corporate practice arrangements as long as the physician technically works for a physician group that only contracts with the corporation. Attempts to avoid the prohibitions of corporate practice laws contribute to the complexity of the legal relationships between many MCOs and their physicians.

The effect on physicians was to lock them into simple partnership style practice arrangements, while the other players in the health care market, especially hospitals, became large, sophisticated corporations. This benefited physicians by prolonging their hold on power in the medical care system. The most important manifestation of this market power was that physicians controlled the physician reimbursement standards for major insurers such as Blue Cross and Blue Shield. When Medicare and Medicaid were originally formed, they used the same physician-driven reimbursement system as the private insurers. This reduced competitive pressures that might have constrained the rise in medical care costs years earlier. It kept the market entry costs low for physicians, which allowed new physician entrants to set up their own practices or work their way into existing practices. In the last few years, it has allowed some physicians to cash out by selling their practices to corporate providers while nominally remaining independent practitioners.

The downside of prolonging these simple business structures beyond the point where they made economic sense is that physicians were left unprepared for the onslaught of MCOs. The medical societies focused on medical malpractice reform—a small-practice issue—while MCOs were solidifying their legislative and political position. Physicians never developed the major business entities

that could better negotiate with MCOs. The physicians who cashed out are now finding that their corporate owners are starting to demand higher productivity and threatening to close practices that fail to turn a profit.

The Rise of MCOs

MCOs, in the broad sense of organizations that employ or contract with physicians to deliver care to defined groups of individuals as an alternative to private fee-for-service medicine, are as old as modern medical practice. The earliest cases establishing the ban on the corporate practice of the professions carved out exceptions for benevolent organizations that hired physicians or attorneys to look after their own members or those in need. These MCOs predated indemnity health insurance. Some were organized to ensure access to medical care for workers in isolated locations. Kaiser-Permanente Health Plan began as a method of providing medical care to the workers building Grand Coulee Dam. Others were integrated, member-owned mutual insurance plans that employed physicians to care for the members. Organized medicine opposed these early MCOs as unethical, and were sued by the government for antitrust for trying to restrict the competition in health care.[3] Although the courts supported MCOs, the concerted opposition of organized medicine kept them from making any substantial progress in the market until the 1970s.

In 1971, President Nixon addressed the rising cost of health care and predicted that it would cripple U.S. productivity. This prompted Congress to pass the Health Maintenance Organization Act of 1973 (HMO Act of 1973).[4] This act banned most state law impediments to the establishment of MCOs; it did not, however, preempt state laws on regulation of medical practice or state criminal laws dealing with bribing fiduciaries. With the legal framework in place, the rising cost of health care through the 1970s and 1980s fueled the growth of MCOs. By 1997, MCOs had become the predominant form of medical practice. Most physicians must participate in some form of MCO because it is estimated that less than

5% of individuals not under a government program have a traditional indemnification insurance plan.

The Structure of MCOs

It is difficult to generalize about MCOs because they take many different forms. Although most health care practitioners are familiar with the notions of whether MCOs are open panel or closed panel, an HMO or a PPO, these descriptions do not convey the variability of MCO organization. This variability makes it very difficult for physicians or the public to know with certainty what the MCO provides and how to best deal with it. The variability also causes legal problems for MCOs and their health care practitioners because administrative practices that might be legal under one organizational structure are illegal in others. For example, the rules governing physician incentives under Medicare prohibit practices that are legal for private pay patients.[5]

The Controlling Entity

The diversity of MCOs is more obvious if they are seen as multidimensional arrays, with each dimension corresponding to a different legal or economic parameter. The first dimension in describing MCOs is the interests of the controlling entity, characterized in the following listing.

- Insurers: An insurance company owns the MCO and uses it to provide care for its insured lives.
- Hospitals: The MCO is used to ensure that patients occupy beds and to increase leverage with insurers who pay for the care of the patients.
- Physicians: The MCO, often called a network, is formed by a group of physicians to increase their bargaining power with insurers and hospitals.
- Brokers: An MCO that is formed as a business venture by investors other than physicians, hospitals, or insurers.
- Governmental: Most governmental clinics are MCOs. The Veterans Administration

hospital system, for example, has been an MCO for years.

Relationships with Physicians

The second dimension is the legal relationship between the physicians and the MCO, as characterized in the following listing.

- Employees: Physicians are simple employees of the MCO, with no intervening physician group. Except for governmental MCOs, corporate practice of medicine bans make these MCOs less common than independent contractor MCOs.
- Physician Group: Developed in response to corporate practice of medicine bans, physicians are either employees, partners, or shareholders in a physician-controlled partnership or professional corporation, which in turn contracts with one or more MCOs. This is the most common organizational structure for the older HMOs, such as Kaiser-Permanente Health Plan in California.
- Independent Contractor: In this model, physicians may be either sole proprietors or members of a partnership or professional corporation, but they individually contract with one or more MCOs. The contracts are similar to those utilized in the physician group model. Interference with individual physician decision making is much more personal and intrusive when there is no physician group to function as a buffer between the physician and the MCO.

Additional Contractual Terms

Additional dimensions can be defined on the basis of intrusiveness of oversight of physician practice, and whether the physician is forced to assume some of the risks of insurance. Contractual arrangements vary from situations in which a physician group agrees to treat the MCO's patients for a set fee schedule, to situations in which there is a total capitation where physicians agree to assume the insurance risks for a panel of patients. MCO involvement in monitoring medical decision making may be minimal, but more often it involves a very intrusive review of all medical decisions that involve procedures, pharmaceuticals, or hospitalization—anything that costs extra. Enforcement mechanisms in these types of contracts may involve a pure financial incentive scheme, or the group may face contract termination for violating established norms.

How Do They Reduce Costs?

Finally, MCOs may be classified by how they reduce the cost of medical care below the premiums paid by the subscribers, that is, how they make money. Because MCOs have substantial administrative overhead, they must achieve substantial savings in physician, pharmacy, and hospital charges. This may occur in three ways: (1) reducing the price the MCO pays to providers, such as physicians and hospitals; (2) limiting access to care or shifting to cheaper care than would have been provided outside the MCO; or (3) in noninsurance company MCOs, providing more services that are profitable and fewer services that are not. All these strategies affect physician decision making. These changes are not always adverse to the patient's interests. One major effort of MCOs has been to reduce the profitability of Cesarean sections. This reduces the financial incentive to do them, which benefits patients who can deliver vaginally, but might otherwise be delivered surgically.[6]

MCO incentives are meant to counter traditional fee-for-service reimbursement incentives, which encourage physicians to provide more care for each patient, thus driving up the cost of care. Under managed care, physicians are encouraged to see patients more quickly, to use fewer tests and specialty referrals, to use less expensive drugs (and to let nonphysicians choose those drugs), and to keep patients out of the hospital. MCOs promise employers that cost-conscious physicians will provide better and cheaper care. Physicians who do not deliver cost-effective care generally are not allowed to continue to treat MCO patients.[7]

As discussed later, the denial of medically necessary care can put the physician in a legal quandary. However, it is the hidden incentives to deny care that pose the starkest conflict between the interests of physicians and those of their patients. These can breach the physician's fiduciary duty to the patient, which is actionable on its own, as well as support criminal law actions for fraud.

FIDUCIARY DUTY

Fiduciary law is an ancient legal device to protect the interests of relatively powerless persons:

"Courts of equity have carefully refrained from defining the particular instances of fiduciary relations in such a manner that other and perhaps new cases might be excluded. It is settled by an overwhelming weight of authority that the principle extends to every possible case in which a fiduciary relation exists as a fact, in which there is confidence reposed on one side and the resulting superiority and influence on the other. The relation and the duties involved in it need not be legal. It may be moral, social, domestic, or merely personal."[8]

Physicians as Fiduciaries

It is hard to imagine situations when one is more in the power of another than for treatment of serious illness and injury. In the words of one court,

[T]he physician-patient relationship has: ... its foundation on the theory that the former [physician] is learned, skilled and experienced in those subjects about which the latter [the patient] ordinarily knows little or nothing, but which are of the most vital importance and interest to him, since upon them may depend the health, or even life, of himself or family. [T]herefore, the patient must necessarily place great reliance, faith and confidence in the professional word, advice and acts of the physician.[9]

Nearly every state has case law holding that the physician–patient relationship is a fiduciary relationship. These cases are usually medical malpractice suits where on of the following questions may be posed: (1) Did the physician hide some negligent act to let the statute of limitations run?; (2) Did the physician provide the patient proper medical information about the patient's condition in other than informed consent situations?; (3) Was there sexual misconduct by the physician?; (4) Did the physician breach the confidential relationship?; (5) Did the physician fraudulently conceal information such as leaving a foreign body in a patient after surgery?; and (6) Did the physician fail to obtain a proper informed consent? (The role of the physician as fiduciary in informed consent is discussed in detail in Chapter 9.)

In addition to the case law holding that physicians are fiduciaries, the federal statutes and regulations implementing the Medicare and Medicaid programs have extensive provisions to protect independent medical decision making, and many states have adopted the commercial bribery section of the model penal code, which criminalizes financial incentives to affect physician decision making:

(1) A person commits a misdemeanor if he solicits, accepts or agrees to accept any benefit as consideration for knowingly violating or agreeing to violate a duty of fidelity to which he is subject as: ... (c)lawyer, physician, accountant, appraiser, or other professional adviser or informant; ...

(3) A person commits a misdemeanor if he confers, or offers or agrees to confer, any benefit the acceptance of which would be criminal under this Section.[10]

Training and Licensure

Physicians are fiduciaries because of their knowledge and their license. The physician has power over the patient by virtue of greater knowledge gained through training and experience. The physician must complete many years of professional training before being allowed to practice medicine. This training is available to only a small number of individuals in the population, and it consumes many societal resources. This contributes to the societal policy that physicians should not take advantage of patients by virtue of their superior knowledge. Even more important to this policy is the limitation of the right to practice medicine to persons with this professional training.

The medical license carries with it five rights: the right to diagnose illness, the right to treat that illness by medical means, the right to prescribe drugs, the right to supervise nonphysician practitioners in the provision of medical services, and the right to collect fees for medical services provided by oneself and others. Some of these rights are shared by other licensed health care practitioners, but taken together they give the physician a unique monopoly position in health care delivery. In return for these rights, particularly the unique right to prescribe drugs, society expects physicians to exercise concern for the interests of patients. If licensing and knowledge were the only sources of power in the physician–patient relationship, there would be no need to extend this fiduciary duty to physicians in need of medical care. In fact, the duty owed to physicians in need of medical care is only slightly less than that owed to laypeople because the law recognizes other factors that affect the bargaining power of the patient.

Market Factors

Another limitation on a patient's choice of health care services is the limited availability of market information. Although the Federal Trade Commission (FTC) has eliminated many of the traditional bans on physician advertising, the highly personal nature of medical care makes it difficult to compare prices and services. It is also difficult to obtain a personalized bid for medical services. This lack of information increases the physician's duty to provide the comparative information to the patient that is necessary to make an informed choice of treatment.

Even patients with information about the market for medical services are often financially limited in their ability to choose a physician. These financial limitations stem from attempts by employers and their insurance companies to limit the cost of medical care. The primary vehicles for reducing costs are managed care organizations. It is important to recognize that the more the patient's choice of physician is limited, the greater is the physician's duty to protect the patient's interests. If the plan is sufficiently restrictive (as is often true for specialty care in an MCO), this duty to guard the patient's interests may extend to the administrators of the plan and the employer that selects the plan.

Market models also assume that there is time to collect and evaluate market information, but many serious medical problems arise quickly and must be treated quickly, limiting the patient's choice of physicians to whomever is geographically available. Even in nonemergency cases, the discomfort and risk involved in shopping for physicians severely limit the patient's ability to choose a physician. An equally serious problem is financial limitations. The poor have always been limited in their choices of medical care providers—a limitation increasingly being felt by the middle class.

Finally, market models are based on the fungibility of goods: that one product is much the same as another, allowing them to be interchanged based on price. Patients do not like to treat physicians as fungible. One traditional definition of a profession was that it mattered who did the work, not just the price of the job. Although the medical profession does not like to stress the differing abilities of its practitioners, no health care practitioner would be comfortable picking a name from the phone directory if their family member needed treatment.

Duties of a Fiduciary

As a fiduciary, the physician has the legal duty to act on behalf of the patient. There have always been financial conflicts between physicians and patients, but they were of a different type than those that arise in the MCO setting. Physicians in private practice treating patients with traditional indemnification health insurance had an incentive to overtreat and perform unnecessary procedures. This is reflected in informed consent litigation. The pre-MCO cases are about whether a patient had enough information to consent to treatment. The post-MCO cases deal with whether the patient was informed that the physician had an incentive to deny treatment. Although unnecessary treatment can be bad for the patient, it is philo-

sophically different from a denial of treatment when denial of treatment is invisible.

When a physician recommends unnecessary treatment, the patient must be apprised of the indications for the treatment, the possible side effects, and the availability of alternative treatments. This acts as a check on the physician's financial interest in providing unnecessary care. When treatment is denied due to regulations or incentives provided by the MCO, the patient is not given a chance to balance the risks and the benefits of the forgone treatment. The check provided by informed consent is gone, and there is nothing to take its place. The physician is in a legally dangerous position because failure to provide the care may be found to be medical malpractice.

Legal Risks

Physicians who practice in MCOs with limited benefits face increased liability because the courts have not accepted the idea that a plan's failure to pay for care completely absolves the physician from liability for not providing the care. In *Wickline v. State of California*,[11] a leading case that arose from the California Medi-Cal program, the intermediary denied coverage for additional days in the hospital. The physician contested the denial, but then discharged the patient. The patient was harmed by the premature discharge and sued the physician and Medi-Cal. The plan defended by claiming that it did not discharge the patient, the treating physician did. Accordingly, this was a case of malpractice by the treating physician.

Although the court opined that a health plan could be liable for the adverse consequences of improper cost control decisions, it found that, in this case, it was the treating physician who made the decision to discharge the patient. Conceding that the physician was intimidated by Medi-Cal, it still held that the physician should have done more to keep the patient in the hospital if he thought it was necessary. Thus, the physician should have aggressively appealed the denial of authorization of care. The court was silent regarding what the physician should have done if the appeal ultimately was unsuccessful, but implied that he should have not have discharged the patient from the hospital.

In a subsequent case involving a utilization review contractor for a health plan, the court clarified its ruling in *Wickline* to make clear that a negligent decision to deny treatment by the treating physician would not automatically absolve the health plan and its contractors from liability. The court found that the insurer's decision to deny coverage for additional inpatient hospitalization was a substantial factor in the decedent's suicide:

> In the present case, there is substantial evidence that Western Medical's decision not to approve further hospitalization was a substantial factor in bringing about the decedent's demise. It was Western Medical which conducted the concurrent utilization review and directed that no further benefits be paid.... Once the insurance benefits were terminated, there were no other funds to pay for the decedent's hospitalization. The sole reason for the discharge, based on the evidence adduced in connection with the summary judgment motion, was that the decedent had no insurance or money to pay for any further in-patient benefits. Dr. Taff, the decedent's treating physician, believed that had the decedent completed his planned hospitalization there was a reasonable medical probability that he would not have committed suicide. The foregoing constitutes sufficient evidence to raise a triable issue of material fact as to whether Western Medical's conduct was a substantial factor in causing the decedent's death.[12]

California courts have gone on and allowed substantial awards against MCOs for breaching their duty to treat patients fairly. A jury awarded $89,000,000 in damages, including punitive damages, against a plan that delayed the patient's receiving what was then considered an experimental treatment.[13] Although the decision language would indicate that plans can be liable for the consequences of their reimbursement decisions, this is not the case for more than half of the total insured lives in the United States, the lives that are insured in health plans subject to the Employee Retirement Income Security Act (ERISA).[14] Had *Wilson* or *Wickline* been ERISA plans, the ruling of the courts on potential liability for denying coverage may have been very different.

ERISA HEALTH PLANS

The main function of ERISA is to protect and regulate pension plans. The ERISA provision dealing with health insurance was passed by Congress to allow large multistate companies such as automobile manufacturers to sign uniform labor agreements across all state lines. Prior to ERISA, an employer could not offer the same health insurance plan to all employees because state laws regulating insurance differed from state to state. Even if the terms of the plan could be worked out, there was a substantial cost in getting the plans approved in 50 different states. ERISA provides that health insurance plans that meet certain organization requirements are exempt from most state regulation. Since there is little federal regulation of insurance, this means that ERISA plans are essentially unregulated. The insulation from state regulation gives ERISA plans a competitive advantage so they are displacing non-ERISA plans for most employers.

ERISA plans are under more direct pressure to limit benefits than other types of health plans because they are not traditional insurance policies. To qualify under ERISA, the costs of the employee health care must be self-insured by the employer. The plan is often administered by an insurance company and the care is provided by either an owned or a contractor MCO. The role of the administrator is to process the claims and manage the care. The employer pays the administration fee and all the costs of the medical care. There is only a limited insurance component. If there are huge unexpected costs, then they are passed on to the employer. This puts pressure on the employer to limit coverage for expensive procedures and conditions.

Because employers attempt to limit losses, exempt treatment for given conditions, and limit options for conditions that they do cover, plans may fail to provide coverage that treating physicians believe is medically necessary. While ERISA plans are not insurers, if they do not keep the employer's health care costs low, then they risk losing the management contract to a competitor that promises greater savings. Thus, ERISA plans, like all MCOs, are under pressure to discourage unnecessary medical care if they are to make money.

ERISA Preemption

The text of ERISA does not mention medical malpractice lawsuits and there was no discussion of them in the congressional hearings preceding the adoption of ERISA. Nonetheless, the broad language of ERISA that exempts ERISA plans from state regulation has been construed by the courts to prevent state tort lawsuits against ERISA plans.[15] In most cases where a denial of benefits is challenged because the plan claimed they were excluded under the contract, courts find the claims to be preempted.[16] Some courts have gone farther and held that ERISA preempts medical malpractice claims against ERISA plans, although it is generally accepted now that ERISA does not preempt ordinary vicarious liability claims for physicians who are employees of the plan, rather than independent contractors. ERISA does not affect the employee or contract physician's liability for medical malpractice, so the physician is left as the target defendant when the plaintiff's case against the plan is dismissed.

Hidden Incentives

The clearest conflict between the demands of MCOs and the physician's fiduciary duty to the patient arise from the "gag" rules, which are MCO contract provisions intended to prevent physicians from telling patients medically significant information, or from indicating that the plan might not be treating the patient fairly. A typical clause reads as follows:

> Physician shall agree not to take any action or make any communication which undermines or could undermine the confidence of enrollees, potential enrollees, their employers, their unions, or the public in U.S. Healthcare or the quality of U.S. Healthcare coverage. Physician shall keep the Proprietary Information payment rates, utilization-review procedures, etc. and this Agreement strictly confidential.[17]

To the extent that gag rules prevent the patient from receiving full information about treatments and alternatives, they are in direct conflict with informed consent doctrine. Informed consent, however, is a doctrine that deals with medical risks, not financial information. This raises the difficult issue whether the physician or the health plan must disclose nonmedical information that might influence the physician's decisions about the patient's care. The traditional view is that the physician's conduct is judged only on the basis of whether it meets acceptable standards of medical practice. The courts generally have not allowed the plaintiff to inquire into whether the physician's decisions are motivated by financial considerations.

Preemption of Claims

In the *Lancaster* case,[18] the court reviewed the legality of hidden MCO provisions in a Kaiser health plan that provided financial incentives for physicians to deny patients care. In 1991, an 11-year-old child was taken to a physician complaining of nausea and severe, daily headaches on the right side of her head. She was examined, but no diagnostic tests were performed. The physician prescribed adult-strength narcotic painkillers. Her condition did not resolve and she continued to see the physician through 1995. During this time, the prescriptions were continued but the primary care physician never consulted with a neurologist. In 1996, the school psychologist, alarmed at the child's "intense, localized headaches, vomiting, and blood-shot eyes," persuaded the parents to demand that the child receive a proper neurologic workup and diagnostic testing. The child was found to have a tumor that had displaced 40% of her brain. After extensive surgeries, she still had substantial impairment and the prospect of more surgery in the future.

It appeared, under the facts of this case, that this systematic malpractice might have been financially motivated because there was evidence that throughout the nearly five-year period defendant physicians treated Lancaster, Kaiser and the Permanente Medical Group had in place a financial incentive program that paid physicians bonuses for avoiding treatments and tests.

The first counts of the plaintiff's complaint are simple malpractice allegations against the patient's treating physicians and a vicarious liability claim against the plan. As the court ruled, the malpractice claims against the treating physicians pose no ERISA questions because ERISA does not apply to medical care decisions made by the treating physicians, even if they are employees of the MCO. More interestingly, the court also found that ERISA did not preempt the vicarious liability claim against the plan. The plaintiff also asserted a claim against the plan "for negligently establishing the Incentive Program and for intentionally and knowingly concealing its existence from plaintiffs." This goes to the heart of the gag rule controversy: may a plan and its physicians agree to contractual terms that impact the patient's care, and then agree to hide these from the patient?

The court characterized this claim as attacking an administrative decision of the plan, not a medical decision by a plan physician. Because the court maintained that this was a case of first impression, it sought precedent in related cases involving utilization review decisions under ERISA. These cases involve claims that the utilization review organization denied the patient medical care or was involved in medical care decisions when it refused to certify that the plan would pay for the needed care. Because these decisions affect the benefits available to the patient, courts have found that they are administrative decisions and are thus preempted by ERISA. Having chosen this precedent, the court was driven to its decision on ERISA preemption:

> Finally, it is also plain that ERISA preempts the second section of Count IV, which alleges direct negligence against the Medical Group for promulgating the Incentive Program, as well as the fraud claims of Count V against Campbell, Pauls, and the Medical Group for concealing the cost containment policy's existence.... While the state laws on which these claims are based do not necessarily implicate ERISA, the substance of plaintiffs' direct negligence and fraud claims are directly "related to" the administration and

regulation of the Star Enterprises Employee Benefit Plan. Permitting these claims to proceed would undermine the congressional policies that underlie ERISA. Absent preemption, for instance, benefit plans would be subject to conflicting directives from one state to the next concerning the propriety of such financial incentive policies.[19]

The *Lancaster* court's ruling is clear: there is no remedy for an ERISA plan using an improper incentive plan or even hiding the incentive plan from its patients. The only recourse is a malpractice action against the treating physicians and a vicarious liability action against the plan, if the necessary agency relationship can be proven. In previous times, when a malpractice action was seen as perhaps the worst thing that could happen to a physician, this ruling might provide solace to the plaintiffs and ERISA health plan beneficiaries in general. In today's market, potential malpractice liability is much less threatening to physicians than the risk of deselection by the health plan, with the very real risk that there will be no other jobs available. Under *Lancaster*, improper physician incentives pose no risk to the plan as long as it properly distances itself from the physicians.

The Shea Case

The *Lancaster* court distinguished its holding from the decision in *Shea v. Esensten*.[20] Although the technical grounds, based on the plaintiff's pleadings, for distinguishing the cases may be sound, the courts reach profoundly different results, which cannot be reconciled on the facts. *Shea* also involved a secret incentive plan and a patient who was denied even marginally competent care. The court's summary of Mr. Shea's medical care is poignant:

> After being hospitalized for severe chest pains during an overseas business trip, Patrick Shea made several visits to his long-time family doctor. During these visits, Mr. Shea discussed his extensive family history of heart disease, and indicated he was suffering from chest pains, shortness of breath, muscle tingling, and dizziness. Despite all the warning signs, Mr. Shea's doctor said a referral to a cardiologist was unnecessary. When Mr. Shea's symptoms did not improve, he offered to

pay for the cardiologist himself. At that point, Mr. Shea's doctor persuaded Mr. Shea, who was then forty years old, that he was too young and did not have enough symptoms to justify a visit to a cardiologist. A few months later, Mr. Shea died of a heart attack.

Mrs. Shea brought a state law tort action under the Minnesota wrongful death statute. She filed against the treating physician, his medical group, and Medica, the health plan. The district court dismissed the plaintiff's complaint for failure to state a claim. The plaintiff appealed, resulting in the instant case. The appeals court found that ERISA preempted the plaintiff's state law claims against the plan because these clearly involved the administration of benefits. Unlike the *Lancaster* court, the *Shea* court found that the plaintiff was entitled to relief under ERISA itself.

ERISA allows a plan participant to bring an action for breach of the plan's fiduciary duty. This right extends only to plan participants. Medica argued that, because Mr. Shea was dead, he was no longer a plan participant and thus had no standing under ERISA. The court found that standing under ERISA continued if it was the plan's breach of duty that terminated the member's participation:

> We are persuaded that Mrs. Shea, as the representative of Mr. Shea's estate, has standing to assert her husband's ERISA claims. Any other result would reward Medica for giving its preferred doctors an incentive to make more money by delivering cheaper care to the detriment of patients like Mr. Shea, and "ERISA should not be construed to permit the fiduciary to circumvent [its] ERISA-imposed fiduciary duty in this manner."[21]

Having established that plaintiff had standing, the court considered whether Medica had a duty to disclose its incentive plan. ERISA itself has detailed disclosure requirements, but, with the exception of the rules for reporting on plans with Medicare and Medicaid subscribers, these are not specific to health plans and do not unambiguously answer the question. In the key case on the extent of an ERISA plan's fiduciary duties, the U.S. Supreme Court read ERISA as incorporating common law fiduciary duties: "In general, trustees' responsibilities and powers under ERISA reflect Congress' policy of 'assuring the equitable character' of the plans. Thus, rather than explicitly enumerating all of the powers and duties of trustees and other fiduciaries, Congress invoked the common law of trusts to define the general scope of their authority and responsibility."[22] As discussed in Chapter 9, a common law fiduciary clearly has the duty to disclose all material information to the patient, including an incentive plan that would affect the physicians' decision making:

> From the patient's point of view, a financial incentive scheme put in place to influence a treating doctor's referral practices when the patient needs specialized care is certainly a material piece of information. This kind of patient necessarily relies on the doctor's advice about treatment options, and the patient must know whether the advice is influenced by self-serving financial considerations created by the health insurance provider.[23]

This is the first major case to find that a health plan, as an ERISA fiduciary, has a duty to disclose incentive plans to the subscribers. The *Shea* case provides little benefit to the plaintiff in her claims against the plan because the statutory recovery under ERISA has not been litigated and may be limited to the value of the insurance premiums. For health care practitioners, however, *Shea* sends a clear message: health care practitioners, especially physicians, as fiduciaries, have a duty to disclose incentive plans that may negatively influence their decision making for individual patients' care.

TEAM CARE ISSUES

Medical care has become a team effort. Most of the laws dealing with responsibilities of physicians and nonphysician health care providers[24] (NPPs) are out of touch with modern practice patterns. This is most evident in MCOs where NPPs are widely used with very diffuse supervision. Unlike private practice settings where there are a few NPPs reporting to a smaller number of physicians, NPPs in MCOs are often used in situations where they have no single physician who is responsible for their practice. This is a legal problem because in many situations the law, as embodied in the cases and statutes of each state, is at odds with the routine practice of medicine. The law presumes that all patients will have a single, identified treating physician who will control all aspects of the patient's care, and who is the boss of all the nonphysician members of the medical care team. This is not the case in most MCO practice.

Vicarious Liability

In general, employers are responsible for the actions of their employees. This is *respondeat superior,* or the master-servant relationship, a term that dates the origins of the concept. More generally, liability for actions of others is called *vicarious liability.* MCOs are responsible for the actions of both physician and NPP employees. As discussed above, this responsibility is not affected by ERISA. Physicians who employ NPPs and others in their own offices will also be vicariously liable for their employees' actions, as long as these actions are in the *course and scope* of their employment. This rule poses two questions, Who is an employee? And what is the course and scope of employment?

Although it is commonly assumed that employment status is determined by how a person is paid, this is only one of several factors that are considered. Even unpaid volunteer workers may be classified as employees for the purpose of vicarious liability. The usual focus is on payment because most disputes about employment status involve the tax laws rather than the tort laws. The whole work situation is considered when determining whether there is vicarious liability for a person's actions.

Method of Payment

Persons who are paid as employees (the employer pays federal or state withholding tax, Federal Insurance Contributors Act [FICA], insurance, and so on) will generally be considered employees for determining vicarious liability. If the worker is a volunteer who receives no pay but does a defined job that is usually done by paid employees, the volunteer is also treated as an employee. If FICA should be paid but is not because the employee and the employer are trying to evade their tax liabilities, the court can still find the putative employer vicariously liable for the person's actions. In addition, the employer may have liability for tax evasion. The Internal Revenue Service has become intolerant of paying an individual as a contract worker to avoid employment taxes and FICA. If the worker is truly a contract worker, is a volunteer who is not displacing a paid worker, or is paid by someone else, then vicarious liability is determined by the extent to which the individuals control their own work.

Control

The fundamental issue that determines whether a person is legally treated as an employee is the extent to which the person hiring the work may control the details of the work. To illustrate this, consider the situation of hiring a licensed plumber to install a new sink in a physician's office. In this situation, the physician determines what type of sink to install and where to put it, but the plumber determines how to install the sink. If someone is injured because the sink is improperly installed, the physician is not vicariously liable for the plumber's work.

Conversely, assume that the physician hires an unskilled worker to install the sink. The physician tells the worker how to cut the hole for the sink, attach the pipes, and install the garbage disposal. In this situation, the physician would be vicariously liable for an injury caused by the unskilled worker's negligent installation of the sink. There will be vicarious liability when the employer directs the details of the work or has the responsibility for directing the details of the work.

Scope of Employment

An employee's scope of employment is the activities that the employee may properly carry out and that the employer is expected to supervise. Determining scope of employment is important because an employee can collect workers' compensation benefits only for injuries that arise within the scope of employment. It is also important if the employee injures another person. The injured person may recover from the employer only if the employee's actions were within the scope of employment. Disputes about scope of employment arise from actions, such as driving to a work site, that are not under employer supervision, or intentional actions, such as drunken driving or sexual assaults.

Intentional Acts

Intentional torts are usually not within the course and scope of employment. Employers may be vicariously liable for the intentional torts of their employees only if the employer tolerated the activities or did not properly screen the employees for dangerous tendencies. For example, assume a physician hires a physician's assistant who subsequently sexually assaults a patient. If the employee has no history of assaulting patients or other persons and the physician has not had any notice of problems, the physician will not be liable for the assault. If, however, the employee had assaulted persons in the past and the physician was negligent in not discovering this, the physician could be liable under the theory of negligent hiring. The physician could be liable for negligent retention if there were complaints about the behavior of the physician's assistant and the physician failed to act on them.

Physicians must have employment criteria designed to detect employees who are a potential hazard. They must take quick action if an employee is suspected of intentionally harming patients. Intentional injuries must never be covered up. Cover-ups can result in large financial losses through the assessment of punitive damages, and they undermine public confidence in the physician or medical institution. In one example, which occurred in a San Antonio teaching hospital,[25] a pediatric ICU nurse became so involved in the thrill of resuscitating patients that she began poisoning children with a muscle relaxant to create resuscitation opportunities, not all of which were successful. Rather than investigating the unex-

pected increase in deaths, the hospital and physician committees covered up the evidence pointing to murder and offered the nurse a good recommendation if she would resign. She continued to poison children in her subsequent job but was found out and convicted of murder. Through its participation in the cover-up, the hospital and physicians increased their liability for the nurse's actions while she was in their employ and may have assumed liability for the murders she committed later because the job was obtained with their false recommendation. They may have also committed crimes themselves by not reporting suspicious deaths and injuries under both the child abuse reporting laws and murder laws.

Hospital Employees

Physicians' liability for the actions of hospital employees is problematic because of the persistence of the *borrowed-servant* and *captain-of-the-ship doctrines*. These doctrines hold that all the actions of hospital employees are attributable to the patients' attending physicians. Under these doctrines, a physician may be found liable for the actions of a nurse whom the physician cannot hire, fire, or otherwise control. These doctrines evolved because until recently most hospitals were nonprofit corporations and the states gave them charitable immunity. This immunity was predicated on the assumption that a nonprofit hospital provided a community service that was financed through patient revenues. The courts ruled that it would be against the public interest to allow an injured patient to recover a judgment against a charitable hospital because the judgment would drain off resources that could be used to treat many other patients.

Since the patient could not recover against the hospital, the courts created doctrines that attributed the actions of hospital employees to the attending physicians. As private practitioners independent of the hospital and the charity, these physicians were susceptible to suit. Finding that nurses were always under the control of the patient's attending physician allowed the patient to sue the physician when the hospital employee was at fault. The borrowed-servant doctrine was useful because the courts are reluctant to deny injured persons their day in court. Because most states have abolished charitable immunity, the courts have modified the borrowed-servant doctrine to recognize that nurses have independent authority for many nursing tasks. The treating physician will not be liable for these independent actions. The borrowed-servant doctrine is still used when the physician is directing the actions of the nurse in an activity that the nurse cannot do independently, such as assist in an operation. Even in the operating room, however, there are still tasks such as the sponge count that are hospital rather than physician controlled.

The captain-of-the-ship doctrine is a special case of the borrowed-servant doctrine that applies in operating rooms. The theory was that the surgeon, as the captain of the ship, picked the crew and gave all the orders. As the captain of the ship, the surgeon was liable for the actions of all members of the operating room team. This made some sense in the early days of surgery when the surgeon was usually the only physician in the room, and the entire surgical team consisted of a nurse to assist and a nurse to give anesthesia. In a modern operating room, with a physician giving anesthesia and a team of highly trained nurses with independent responsibilities to the hospital, the idea that the surgeon controls all the activity in the room has become untenable. This has led most courts to abandon the captain-of-the-ship doctrine in favor of independently determining the liability of each person caring for the patient. Although this correctly reflects the shared responsibility in the operating room, it does reduce the incentive of the surgeon to ensure that all members of the team are competent.

Delegation of Authority

The practice of medicine and nursing is defined and regulated by state law. Most of the federal regulations on medical practice and payment for medical care defer to the state's rules on what is allowable practice. If one state allows nurses to do what another state restricts to physicians, a very common situation, the federal government will pay the nurse in the permissive state and not in the restrictive state. Since these rules vary greatly from state to state, physicians, nurses, and other NPPs should obtain their state's licensing laws and regulations and familiarize themselves with them.

All states reserve some aspects of medical care to licensed physicians, such as performing surgery. All states allow NPPs to do some activities without any physician supervision, such as changing wound dressings and taking blood pressures. Between these two extremes, the NPPs practice on the delegated authority of a licensed physician. For these activities, the physician is charged with supervising the NPP, either directly or through protocols and physician's orders. Depending on the activity and the state, the physician must be in the same room, in the same building, or may supervise at a distance, so long as he or she is available by telephone in emergencies. Physicians and NPPs who do not comply with their state's regulations on supervision and independent practice can lose their licenses,[26] be criminally prosecuted for unauthorized practice of medicine, or be prosecuted for Medicare/Medicaid fraud if they bill the government for improperly delegated tasks.[27]

There are three issues to consider when delegating authority: (1) the legality of the delegation, (2) the proper method of delegation, and (3) the physician's oversight responsibilities for the delegated duties. These issues must be considered within the context of the three classes of medical tasks. The first class is tasks that are freely assignable; they are not unique to medical care delivery and do not require the exercise of professional judgment. They include billing and patient accounts, maintaining simple medical equipment, and other nonpatient care activities that accompany the practice of medicine. The supervising physician must ensure that the activities meet the necessary legal standards for protecting patient confidentiality and any other statutory requirements, but they do not need to be done by licensed medical professionals.

The tasks in the second class are those that may be assigned to a limited class of persons. These tasks, such as nursing activities and laboratory analyses, require professional skills and judgment. They also may include activities that require physician supervision, such as recommending treatments to patients. Activities in the third class of medical tasks are reserved solely to physicians; delegation may violate criminal laws against aiding in the unauthorized practice of medicine. These activities include performing surgery, directly supervising nonphysician personnel in physician-only activities, and writing prescriptions for controlled substances. State law and tradition determine which specific activities cannot be delegated.

Explicit Delegation of Authority

Explicit delegation of medical authority occurs when a physician uses protocols to authorize NPPs to render medical care directly to patients. The physician is allowing the NPP to practice medicine by following written protocols that allow the extender to determine the physician's judgment in the specific limited situation. This works well if both physicians and extenders understand that all medical judgments must be made by physicians. Under the law in many states, NPPs may not substitute their personal judgment in any decision that requires medical judgment. Even if a state allows NPPs to practice independently, any physician nominally directing their actions will be legally liable for their malpractice if it involves an error in medical judgment that relates to the physician's supervision. For example, assume the physician is expected to perform periodic chart reviews. The physician could be liable for not discovering substandard care that injures a patient.

Implicit Delegation of Authority

Implicit delegation of authority occurs when the physician allows NPPs to act on their own initiative, by carrying out medical tasks without strict protocols. This is not a problem if these personnel are under the direct supervision of the physician, as a nonphysician surgical assistant is. Physicians are legally responsible for the actions of these personnel, but they also can recognize and correct any improper actions.

Problems arise in two situations: when NPPs initiate care outside the physician's direct supervision and when the physician allows these personnel to perform tasks that the physician is not competent to perform. The physician remains legally responsible but can no longer prevent improper actions. The classic example of this type of implicit delegation of authority was the medical equipment sales representative showing the surgeon how to place a hip prosthesis. The salesman scrubbed and participated in the operation, to the point of placing the prosthesis. There was much consternation about a sales representative in the operating room, but this was no more legally significant than the use of a nonlicensed surgical assistant. The physician could not supervise the sales representative's actions because the physician did not know how to do the procedure. Despite the proximity of the physician, knowledgeable supervision was impossible. (This action might also violate hospital rules on who is permitted in the operating room.)

Triage

Triage by the front desk clerk is a common and legally dangerous form of implied delegation of authority, particularly in large group practices and clinics. In this situation, the physician implicitly authorizes the appointments clerk to determine whether a patient needs immediate or follow-up care. Certainly this is not the physician's intent, but it happens when the office manager or clerk is permitted to deny appointments to patients who are behind in paying their bills or when there are no provisions for evaluating patients who may need to be seen more quickly than the physician's appointment calendar allows.

If the front office tells patients that they will not be seen until they pay their bills, this is implicitly determining that the patient does not need the return appointment. If, as frequently happens, the patient does not return for care, the physician could be liable for any consequences that flow from the denial of care. This is also the case when the patient is made to wait more than the medically acceptable time for a follow-up appointment. If the obstetrician tells a patient to come back in three days for a preoperative visit because it is time to put a stitch in her incompetent cervix, the appointment clerk must not schedule her for an appointment in three weeks. The obstetrician would be liable if the patient lost the fetus during this delay. Physicians must ensure that a patient's medical condition is considered when appointments are being scheduled. They should always be consulted before a patient is denied a timely appointment.

Triage is carried to an extreme in many MCOs. Patients cannot speak directly to a physician, or even to the office staff, but must go through a triage nurse system. These nurses, operating under some sort of protocols, call an ambulance for the patient, direct the patient to go to the emergency room, send the patient to an MCO-run urgent care center, or schedule the patient for an office visit. In some systems, these nurses are pressured to keep patients out of the emergency room. The result has been several deaths when patients with heart attacks or other emergency conditions were sent to poorly staffed and poorly equipped urgent care centers. As plaintiffs' attorneys litigate these cases, they will seek to tie the nurses back to both the MCO that employed them and to the physician who approved their protocols and carried out the oversight of their actions.

Evaluation of Medical Tests

Physicians sometimes implicitly delegate the evaluation of medical test results to their filing clerk. This happens when the office charting system is not set up to ensure that every test result is reported to the physician. From both a legal and a medical standpoint, a test should not have been ordered if the results do not warrant evaluation. Deciding that a report is normal for a patient is a medical judgment. A physician may reasonably delegate many of these evaluations to laboratory or nursing staff—the gynecologist does not need to see every normal Pap smear report that comes back—but there should be a formal system for checking in the reports, and it should be explicit about what can be filed and what must be evalu-

ated by the physician. If a laboratory report did not come back at all, it needs to be located or the test repeated. Physicians do not need to review every piece of paper that comes to the office, but there must be specific written orders or protocols for handling reports and for finding lost reports. The receptionist must have a tracking system that identifies and locates patients who miss appointments or fail to make return appointments the physician has recommended. For example, if a report comes back with a notation that the patient has a spot on a lung X ray, some action should be taken. Nurses in the office might have a protocol that allows them to arrange treatment and a follow-up visit, or the secretary might have instructions to pull the chart and leave it with the report on the physician's desk.

SUPERVISING NPPs

Physicians who employ NPPs should be very careful in their supervision. Because the physician is liable for negligent medical care rendered by NPPs, a physician should never accept responsibility for an NPP without having the authority to supervise or decline to practice with the person. The physician is also liable for nonmedical actions by the NPP, such as sexual assault, if the physician is negligent in screening or supervising the NPP.

The first step in selecting or accepting supervision of an NPP is to check the person's credentials personally and carefully. The NPP's license status must be checked in every state where the NPP has held a license, not just the state where he or she will work. The physician should find out the specifics of the NPP's training and previous experience to gauge skill levels. Finally, the physician should talk to other physicians who have worked with the NPP, asking specifically about his or her willingness to accept physician authority, clinical skills, and readiness to ask for consultation from the physician. An NPP who worked well with a physician who checks every patient and chart entry may not be compatible with a physician who prefers to delegate by written protocols.

The physician should observe a newly hired NPP in providing patient care and by repeating the physical assessment. It is not possible to know if the NPP recognizes a bulging eardrum until the physician has reevaluated both negative and positive findings by the NPP. This also gives the NPP the opportunity to learn the physician's preferences and practice habits, making both more comfortable with the arrangement. Many conflicts over supervision arise because the physician never clearly communicates his or her expectations to the NPP.

Scope of Practice

Every NPP should have a written scope of practice that specifically states what the NPP may do on his or her own initiative, what requires protocol authorization, and what must be referred to the physician. It should include specific instructions for handling emergencies and urgent situations when the physician is unavailable. It should specify types of patients that the NPP should or should not accept for care. If the NPP is a licensed nurse, the scope of practice should delineate which activities are nursing and which are delegated medical care. Like protocols, this scope of practice should be agreed upon and signed by both the physician and the NPP. The scope of practice should explicitly deal with both nursing diagnoses and what constitutes unauthorized practice of medicine.

Documentation

Careful documentation is particularly important when NPPs are practicing medicine under supervision, but it is not necessary or desirable to document every positive and negative physical finding. Such charts will be hard to read and are unlikely to be reviewed completely by the supervising physician. The important items to document are the subjective and objective findings that support the diagnosis under the protocol, the decision-specific assessment, and the treatment and instructions authorized under the protocol. (These recommendations must be modified by appropri-

ate Medicare evaluation and management [E&M] requirements.) Using the example of strep throat, an adequate visit entry might read as follows:

S: sore throat × 3 days
O: TMs clear, chest clear, throat red, no adenopathy, rapid strep +
A: strep pharyngitis
P: Penicillin V K 250 mg q.i.d. × 10—dispensed Tylenol, rest, liquids, RTC 2 weeks for recheck, sooner if problems

This chart entry, made in a timely fashion and legibly, provides all the necessary documentation for this encounter. It documents the trigger for the protocol and that the protocol was followed in testing, treatment, and follow-up. The protocol itself will provide the additional information to flesh out the chart note.

Quality Assurance

Quality assurance is as important in the private office as in large health care institutions. In hospitals or MCOs, there are many people who may observe the medical practitioner. In small offices, if the physician is not checking on the people he or she supervises, dangerous deficiencies may go unnoticed. The simplest form of quality assurance for NPPs is to have the physician read and sign every chart. This will allow correction of errors and ongoing education of the nurse or physician's assistant.

There should be a formal quality assurance program, usually a chart audit. Sample charts should be reviewed for every provider and for a range of patient problems. Each case should be evaluated to see if the protocols were followed and if the care was documented properly. General considerations, such as whether the entries were made at the time the care was rendered and whether they can be read by the other providers, should be included in the audit. At intervals, the actual care rendered should be checked. The chart entry may be perfect, yet bear no relationship to the patient's actual condition.

Every quality assurance program should have a system for correcting all identified deficiencies. It must have provisions for changing questionable practices and for immediately suspending anyone who may be dangerous to patients for any reason.

Drug Laws

Drug law violations account for most instances in which physicians lose their medical licenses or go to jail. Drug law enforcement against physicians is often done by the same agents who pursue drug dealers. These agents do not show the same deference to physicians as do boards of medical examiners' investigators.

Drugs are a particularly touchy area for NPPs. The states vary widely in the laws governing prescribing and dispensing drugs; some allow limited prescribing by nurse practitioners or physician's assistants, but many do not. Some laws are inconsistent. Pharmacy laws may allow prescribing or dispensing by individuals who are prohibited from this by the medical or nursing practice act. A physician should not allow an NPP to write prescriptions without a clear understanding of the applicable state laws and should not allow dispensing except under strict protocol.

Office dispensing has been very informal in the past, but heightened awareness of the role of prescription drugs in drug addiction is causing states and the federal government to tighten drug laws and their enforcement. For example, the federal regulations on distributing drug samples are much more restrictive than in the past. A physician must provide detailed information on a form mandated by the Food and Drug Administration (FDA) before the drug company representative may leave samples of prescription drugs. These samples must be kept secure and dispensed in the same manner as other prescription drugs. Some states require samples to be dispensed personally by physicians.

Physicians should contact their state board of pharmacy and local office of the Drug Enforcement Administration (DEA) to obtain a copy of the restrictions on prescribing drugs. If a clinic or physician group plans to buy drugs in bulk and package them for dispensing, it should inquire about a pharmacy or dispensing license and a federal repackaging permit. Most states allow physicians to dispense drugs if they bottle and label the pills personally and give them to the patient directly, but the state and federal government also impose substantial recordkeeping requirements on physicians who do this.

Protocols

The term *protocol* is widely used in health care to refer to a variety of documents. This book uses protocol to refer to written orders directing the practice of nurses and other NPPs. These protocols are not intended to be clinical algorithms; unlike clinical algorithms, which are intended to assist medical decision making, protocols are intended to circumscribe clinical decision making.[28]

Few medical offices use the detailed, deterministic protocols described in this chapter. Such protocols require substantial effort to compile and tailor to the needs of an individual physician's office. In the long term, however, they become time-effective by rationalizing quality assurance efforts and the analysis of work flow in the office. More important, systematically using structured protocols reduces the burden of routine documentation of patient encounters. If an office relies on standard protocols to determine the diagnosis and treatment of common conditions, these protocols become generic documentation for those conditions. As long as the physician can convince a court that the protocols are enforced, the protocol becomes evidence of a pattern of behavior. In this case, the burden of proof is shifted to the plaintiff, who seeks to dispute that the protocol was followed. If the office does not rigorously enforce the use of protocols, each patient encounter must be fully documented. In effect, the core of what would be the protocol must be written as a chart entry every time the condition is treated. Failing in this repetitive documentation shifts the burden of proving what care was rendered to the physician.

Physician Protocols

Many group practice organizations use physician protocols to standardize medical practice within the group. The goal may be to improve consistency of care when a patient is likely to be seen by different doctors, to limit the number of drugs in the formulary, or to ensure that the physicians are following recognized standards, such as Centers for Disease Control (CDC) protocols, in their practices. Physician protocols do not place legal limitations on the physicians; they are characterized by their allowance for independent medical judgment. They are a voluntary or contractual agreement by the physicians to follow certain patterns when practicing within the group.

A common example is a protocol for treating an MCO patient for essential hypertension. Typically this protocol would not include a definition of essential hypertension; every treating physician would be expected to be able to make the diagnosis. The protocol would contain a list of the diagnostic procedures to be done on a new patient. These might be arrived at by consensus after an analysis of the costs and benefits of each test. Every patient might have a blood count but only those over age 40 years would have an electrocardiogram. The protocol would then list the drugs to be prescribed for certain types of patients. A beta-blocker might be first choice, with an alpha-blocker substituted if the patient does not respond well or is over 60 years old. The drugs on the list also would be in the formulary.

The physician protocol guides rather than dictates patient care. If a physician wants to use a different drug from the established standard, the reasons for deviation should be documented, but the physician is legally free to make the change (subject, however, to discipline by the MCO). In contrast, an NPP would not be allowed to use such a protocol becasue it leaves the diagnosis open and allows choice in the use of medicines, both of which require exercising medical judgment.

Teaching Protocols

Teaching protocols, also called teaching algorithms, fall somewhere between strict protocols and physician protocols; they guide students through the exercise of professional judgment. Teaching protocols thus fill the dual purpose of providing consistency of care and helping students learn how to make good judgments.

The hallmark of a teaching protocol is a differential diagnosis list, which is generally unnecessary in a physician protocol and not proper in a protocol intended for NPPs. The classic example of a group of teaching protocols is the *Washington Manual of Medical Therapeutics,* often called the "intern's brain." The entries in this manual include a general definition of the condition and a list of other possible causes of the patient's problems. It then explains how to treat the patient, with reasons for some of the recommendations. Medical students use this source to learn about basic treatments. Residents use it as a treatment guide and for help in solving unfamiliar problems. Established physicians consult it when caring for patients with a problem they have not treated recently or for which treatment standards have changed. Each would learn from the protocols and use them according to their level of training and licensure.

Physician's Orders

The most common way of delegating authority is to write an order in a hospital chart or otherwise formally record orders for NPPs. The physician may write the order in person, or a nurse may enter it in the chart at the physician's direction. Formal orders are valuable for clarifying the delegation of authority in the hospital setting, though they are less commonly used in private offices.

Standing orders, which include protocols, are a special case of written physician's orders. A *standing order* is an order conditioned upon the occurrence of certain clinical events. The important characteristic of a standing order is that all the patients who meet the criteria for the order receive the same treatment. A common use of standing orders is in public health clinics that treat specific diseases. A venereal disease control program will use the CDC protocols for antibiotic dosages. Once the specific venereal disease is identified, the nurse administers the antibiotics as specified by the CDC protocol and authorized by the physician directing the clinic. In this situation, the CDC protocol is a standing order from the medical director, and the conditional event is the diagnosis of a specific venereal disease.

It is important to differentiate standing orders from *preprinted orders:* orders that the physician uses repeatedly and has photocopied to save the trouble and potential errors of rewriting each time they are used. Although the orders are the same for all patients, they are not standing orders because they are not conditional. The physician, not the nurse, determines whether the printed orders will be used in a given case. Unlike a standing order, until the physician incorporates the printed order into the chart, the nurse cannot initiate treatment. Preprinted orders are a useful tool, but they can lead to problems if a patient requires a variation in the usual printed order. These variations must be carefully marked on the orders and the nursing staff notified that the printed order has been modified.

Direct orders are voice orders that are given directly to NPPs. Sometimes these orders are documented in the medical records, but usually they are carried out at once and not recorded. For example, when a surgeon directs the operating room nurse assisting in a procedure, some of the surgeon's orders will be documented, but most will not. Documenting the individual orders is not a problem in this situation because the physician is directly supervising the nurse's work. The satisfactory completion of the nurse's work will be documented as part of the operative report.

In office practice, neither the voice orders nor their satisfactory completion will necessarily be documented in the patient's chart. This makes it difficult to determine whether the physician has given a direct order, or the NPPs are acting out of routine. Unless these routine actions are carried out according to a strict protocol, the physician will not be able to ensure that the proper nursing functions have been carried out. If the physician is sued over a question about the nurse's actions, there will be no record to establish what was done to the patient.

NPP Protocols: Strict Protocols

Protocols that are used to allow NPPs to do tasks that are generally reserved for licensed physicians must be much more rigid and specific than physician protocols or teaching protocols. The exercise of medical judgment remains with the physician who authorized the protocols. The NPP must follow the protocol to the letter, without deviation or the exercise of independent judgment. If state law allows NPPs to practice medicine without supervision, strict protocols are not necessary, but even in such a state, strict protocols are desirable for risk management, quality assurance, and compliance with federal laws.

Sample Protocol

This section works through a sample protocol (see Appendix 10–A) for strep throat to aid readers in understanding how to produce and use legal strict protocols for NPPs. In some states it may not be necessary for NPPs to act under strict protocol. Nevertheless, in any jurisdiction, physicians should use caution in authorizing practice by nonphysicians without strict protocols.

Diagnostic Criteria

This section defines the condition that triggers the use of the particular protocol. There may be more than one set of criteria that trigger the same protocol. The criteria will be very specific. A differential diagnosis has no place in a strict protocol.

Diagnostic Criteria for Strep Throat

1. Positive strep culture or rapid strep test on pharyngeal swab
2. Sore throat or cervical adenopathy in a household or day care contact to a laboratory-confirmed case of strep throat
3. Asymptomatic member of a household with two or more laboratory-confirmed cases of strep throat
4. Established patient with two or more laboratory-confirmed episodes of strep throat who now has symptoms that are typical for strep in this patient
5. Any sore throat in a patient with a history of rheumatic fever

This list gives five circumstances that trigger the protocol and allow the NPP to treat the patient for strep throat. The criteria take into account medical history, physical examination, patient complaints, laboratory tests, and living situation. The NPP may do the entire history, examination, and laboratory tests but is not called upon to judge what constitutes the need for treatment of strep throat. This diagnostic judgment is made by the physician in authorizing the protocol. A nurse who treated a patient for strep throat because he or she thought the throat was so red that it could not be anything else would be acting outside the protocol.

Examination/Laboratory

This section of the protocol specifies the extent of the examination and testing to be done to stay within the scope of the protocol. This should include everything necessary to establish that the diagnostic criteria have been met and everything that might require consultation or referral.

Examination/Laboratory
1. Examine throat, ears, neck, and chest in all patients.
2. Obtain a pharyngeal swab for strep testing on one family member at a time until two family members have positive tests.

The extent of examination required does not have to be this specific. The physician and the NPP may have decided on the type of examination that is appropriate in a particular type of case. Nevertheless, the NPP must take a history and do a physical examination extensive enough to gather the information required to meet the diagnostic criteria or the criteria for referral. In this example, the history must include household and day care information, and the physical must include examination of the throat and cervical lymph nodes and listening for a heart murmur.

Treatment

It is critical for legal protection and for quality of patient care that this section of the protocol be clear and specific. There may not be a selection of therapies. It should be clear from the specifics of the particular patient what course of therapy should be followed.

Treatment
1. Rest, humidity, acetaminophen for fever and body aches
2. Antibiotics
   a. Penicillin V potassium 250 mg q.i.d. in adults, 30 mg/kg per day in 4 divided doses for children.
   b. If the patient has red TMs or pustular tonsils, give amoxicillin 250 mg t.i.d. in adults and children over 45 lb, 125 mg t.i.d. in children over 15 lb.
   c. If the patient is allergic to penicillin, give erythromycin estolate 250 mg q.i.d. for adults, 30 mg/kg per day in 4 divided doses for children.
   d. If the patient is intolerant of both penicillin and erythromycin, consult the physician.

Following this treatment protocol requires reasonable skill by the NPP in determining the correct medicine and calculating doses. It does not, however, allow any exercise of judgment as to which drug to use. That is defined by the characteristics of the patient.

Follow-Up

When NPPs are working from protocols, it is particularly important that patients be given specific instructions about when to be rechecked. Because there is so much delegated medical judgment involved, it is important to ensure that the patient has received all the necessary and appropriate care.

Follow-Up
1. Return to the clinic if not improved in three days or if fever continues this long.
2. Return to the clinic in two weeks for recheck.
3. Return to the clinic immediately or go to the emergency room if you develop respiratory distress, rash, or fever greater than 102°F.

Referral

Inherent in the practice of protocol medicine is the need for physician backup when the problem falls outside the scope of the protocol or the particular practice. A family physician may make a practice of referring all patients with cardiac arrhythmias to a cardiologist. This is not a legal requirement; it is just good sense. A nurse practitioner who is working off protocols must refer patients who have problems beyond the scope of the protocols or the practice. The inclusion in the protocol of specific reasons for referring allows the physician to highlight conditions that are of particular concern. The protocol also may branch to other protocols if indicated.

Refer

1. Refer to the physician all patients with a rash, a heart murmur, or who appear toxic.
2. Consult the physician on all patients who cannot take penicillin or erythromycin.
3. Consult the physician on all patients under 6 months of age.
4. Refer to the emergency room by EMS all patients with respiratory distress or stridor. Do not examine.
5. Refer to the "Otitis Media" protocol all cases that involve concurrent ear infection.

Epidemiology

Any disease that is reportable or that involves the treatment of exposed individuals should have these requirements included in the protocol. This is as much a part of the treatment as doing laboratory tests or dispensing medicine.

Epidemiology

1. Strep infections are reportable weekly, by numerical totals only, to the health department at 555-1234.
2. Household members should be screened for all patients with more than one strep throat in two months.

Notes

This is the part of the strict protocol that should be used for all the educational information. It might include a differential diagnosis of the condition or the reasons for some of the choices made in establishing the protocol. This section also might contain prescribing information for the convenience of the physician. It should be clear to all parties involved that this section does not authorize any actions by the NPP.

Notes

1. There are no clinical signs or symptoms that differentiate strep throat from viral pharyngitis.
2. Sensitivities are not necessary since community-acquired strep is uniformly sensitive to all the penicillins.
3. Strep is not generally susceptible to sulfas.
4. The rapid strep now used by our lab is 85% sensitive.

SUPERVISING MEDICAL STUDENTS AND RESIDENTS

Although only a few physicians are full-time members of medical school faculties, most physicians have to deal with students and residents, at least occasionally, when they hospitalize or refer a patient. It is important for physicians to understand the extent to which they may rely on students and residents to care for patients. Improper delegation of authority to students and residents can subject attending physicians to medical malpractice liability, license review, and criminal investigation. The case of Libby Zion is a rare but poignant reminder of the risks of improper supervision in a medical teaching situation.[29]

Libby Zion, a young woman in generally good health, was admitted to a New York hospital for an acute illness. She died several hours later, after questionable care from residents who had been on duty for an extended period. A grand jury investigation found no criminal conduct but recommended shorter hours and more supervision for residents.[30]

Most private physicians do not appreciate the risks of working with an improperly supervised teaching program. Improperly billing for work done by students or residents may subject the physician to civil and criminal prosecution for Medicare/Medicaid fraud. In addition, teaching programs are increasingly the target of medical malpractice litigation and the courts have held that staff can be liable for the actions of the residents they supervise:

[m]edical professionals may be held accountable when they undertake to care for a patient and their actions do not meet the standard of care for such actions as established by expert testimony. Thus, in the increasingly complex modern delivery of health care, a physician who undertakes to provide on-call supervision of residents actually treating a patient may be held accountable to that patient, if the physician negligently supervises those residents and such negligent supervision proximately causes the patient's injuries.[31]

Patients' Rights

Physicians who work with teaching services should be careful to protect their patients' autonomy. Patients are entitled to control who is entrusted with their medical care and their medical information. Ethically, a patient's method of payment, or the absence of payment, does not affect the right to receive care from a licensed physician. This is also the legal rule unless modified by state law. Although a state might pass a law conditioning the provision of charity care on the acceptance of care by students and residents, this might pose equal protection problems under the Constitution. If a patient who is brought into a county charity hospital that uses students and interns extensively in first-line care demands a "real doctor," the hospital must produce a licensed physician to provide care. It is not acceptable to tell the patient that no physician is available.

Patients also are entitled to know, when they first seek care from a physician, whether they will be asked to participate in a teaching program. Private physicians who make teaching a part of their practice should inform their patients at the first patient visit that they are entering a teaching practice but that they have the right to refuse to be cared for by students and residents or by a given resident or student.

Patients should not be introduced to a student and then asked if they are willing to participate as teaching material. The patient should be asked first, out of the presence of the student. Most patients are willing to participate in teaching, but the physician must be prepared to honor the request of patients who do not want to participate. Ethically, the patient's decision to accept or refuse to participate in a teaching program should have no bearing on whether the physician will treat the patient. Linking the participation in the teaching program to access to medical care creates an improper coercive atmosphere. Legally, the physician must honor the patient's refusal but may refer the patient to another physician if the referral would otherwise be acceptable.

The physician should document the patient's wishes as to participating in teaching. Once general permission is obtained, simple consent is required before a specific medical student or resident may participate in a patient's care. This is obtained by introducing the student to the patient and asking the patient if the student may participate in the care. If the patient has concerns about privacy, the students and residents should be instructed to respect the patient's wishes. Some teaching programs generally ignore concerns with privacy of medical information as regards students and residents, but they are not excluded from either the state or federal laws that govern access to medical information.

Faculty Physicians

Physicians who are medical school faculty without private practices must balance the realities of their practices against patients' right to choose who delivers their medical care. This dilemma is exacerbated when the teaching program has assumed the obligation to care for classes of patients other than those who voluntarily choose to be treated at a teaching facility: emergency patients, indigent patients (when the teaching program has charge of an indigent care program), and patients with a contractual right to be treated, such as members of a managed care plan for which the medical school has contracted to provide care. Persons in these classes retain their right to refuse the care of students and residents.

Faculty physicians should obtain their patients' permission to be included in the teaching program in the same way that a private physician would. Except in emergencies when consent is not required, this permission should be obtained before the patient is seen by students or residents. In teaching programs with insufficient attending staff supervision that rely on students or residents for primary patient contact, the first person to see the patient should obtain the patient's consent. To lessen the implicit coercion in such a situation, the patients should be told that they have a right to refuse care from a resident or a medical student. Most patients consent to be treated by students and residents; the teaching program and the nursing personnel must respect the wishes of patients who refuse this care. The patient's right of privacy should not be violated for the convenience of the teaching staff.

Fraud

Medical students and residents who misrepresent themselves as fully licensed physicians or as specialists in some area of medicine defraud the patient and increase the probability of a malpractice lawsuit if the patient is injured by the care. If the patient understands that the person providing care is in training and if the trainee is properly supervised by a licensed physician, the patient may consent to care from a student or resident. The patient may not, however, waive the laws governing independent medical practice, and the providers may not subvert the patient's right to consent.

It is particularly important that consent and billing for surgical procedures be done appropriately. If a resident is going to be performing a surgical procedure, the patient must be aware of this and the attending surgeon must be scrubbed into the surgery and directly supervise the entire procedure. It is not good enough to be available if needed. In the first case, the attending surgeon is arguably doing the surgery through the resident.

In the second case, he or she is simply trying to collect a fee for services not rendered. If the patient has signed a consent for the attending surgeon to do the surgery, the absent surgeon is also perpetrating a fraud. Medical schools have paid more than $100 million in fines related to improper billing for medical student and resident care.

Medical Students, Residents, and Fellows

Academic medical centers are characterized by the variety of their graduate and postgraduate students. This can lead to confusion about who may do what to patients and who may supervise whom. In the extreme case, nonmedical personnel, such as graduate students in the basic sciences, may be confused with physician fellows and given clinical responsibilities. More generally, teaching programs are often lax in their supervision of unlicensed physicians and medical students, giving them authority beyond their legal scope of practice.[32] This creates medical malpractice liability for the attending physician when a patient is injured through the improper actions of a student or resident. Treatment by an unauthorized person can support a lawsuit for battery. Moreover, juries are unsympathetic to physicians who shirk the duty to care for patients personally.

Residents and Fellows

Legally, the most important question about residents and fellows is whether they are licensed to practice in the state where they are training. A resident who does not have either a personal license or an institutional license has no legal right to exercise independent medical judgment. This is often the case for first-year residents in states that require one year of postgraduate training for licensure. Since these residents are part of a properly supervised training program, there are seldom legal questions about their status.

The legal status of residents and fellows becomes an issue when an academic appointment is used to shelter the practice of an improperly trained or unlicensable individual: foreign medical graduates with questionable credentials, physicians with substance abuse problems, or physicians who have been disciplined by the board of medical examiners in another state. Juries and boards of medical examiners take a jaundiced view of subterfuges that allow unqualified physicians to practice on unsuspecting patients. Such personnel are not proper candidates for standard training programs. They should be accommodated in programs that explicitly recognize their disabilities and provide close supervision.

A physician receiving postgraduate training may be practicing under an institutional license, either formal or informal. Most states allow or tolerate limited medical practice by residents and fellows within a formal teaching system and under supervision. The terms of this institutional licensure are very limiting. The practice must be under genuine supervision and be limited to the institution. Institutional licensees frequently get into trouble by writing prescriptions for outpatients. Although state law may allow the physician to write medication orders on inpatients, this privilege seldom extends to outpatients. When such physicians work in a clinic, their prescription must be signed by a fully licensed physician with appropriate state and federal drug licenses.

Physicians and organizations outside the teaching institution should be careful to confirm that residents are practicing within the law before accepting them into a practice. If there is any question about the scope of the institutional licensure, practitioners should allow only independently licensed residents in their private practices and then only to the extent approved by their malpractice insurance carrier.

Besides externships, many residents accept short locum tenens, weekend call, or emergency room coverage to make extra money. Candidates for such jobs should be treated like any other physician seeking work. They must have an independent license to practice medicine and privileges that are extensive enough to cover foreseeable circumstances at any hospital at which they practice. The employing physician should ensure that they have adequate malpractice insurance coverage for the job. If a physician or hospital routinely uses moonlighting residents to provide emergency coverage, it is also a good idea to limit the amount of time the resident works in the combined programs. If the residents look upon the moonlighting as a paid rest, they are not going to be able to provide proper emergency coverage. Eventually, an overtired resident will face a major emergency with unfortunate results.

Medical Students

Medical students are often enthusiastic about new clinical opportunities, and it is tempting to let them try their hand at patient care, particularly if the problem seems simple. This situation can jeopardize a student's future. A medical student who is accused of practicing medicine without a license, even if it is at the instigation of a supervising physician, may not be allowed to complete his or her degree. Even if the school awards the student a degree, it may be difficult or impossible for the student to get a license, residency training, or malpractice insurance. Supervising physicians must protect themselves and their students from the temptation to delegate too much authority.

The practice of introducing a medical student to patients as "doctor," "young doctor," or a "student doctor" is fraud. A reasonable person introduced to a doctor in a medical setting assumes that this term denotes a licensed physician with a doctoral degree in medicine. Even holders of other doctoral degrees should not be introduced to patients as a doctor. A medical student who has a Ph.D. should not use the title in a medical setting in situations when it can lead to confusion. If a person with a Ph.D. is working in a medical setting, the difference should be explained to every patient. An example of a proper introduction might be introducing a clinical pharmacologist to a patient by saying the following: "This is Doctor Jones. Dr. Jones is a doctor of pharmacology who is trying to help us work out the problem with your medications." This tells the patient that Doctor Jones is not a medical doctor and why a pharmacologist is involved in the patient's care.

No matter how capable the student or how close to finishing training, medical students do not have the legal authority to practice medicine. Everything that a student does must be reviewed and checked by a licensed physician. The student should not be allowed even as much independence as a nurse or a paraprofessional. It may be permissible for a physician to delegate certain tasks to a nurse under protocol that should not be delegated to a medical student. The legal assumption is that the student is there to be taught. If the student knew the tasks well enough to be allowed to do them unsupervised, then he or she would not need to be doing them.

Under no circumstances should the student be used as a substitute for the physician in completing routine physician tasks. It is tempting to use medical students to do admission histories and physicals or to evaluate a patient without supervision, but it is very dangerous legally. If anything untoward happens to the patient, the physician will be responsible and will be in the position of having injured a patient by not fulfilling his or her medical duties. The attending physician must personally do the history and physical, not just cosign the work of a nonphysician.

The writing of orders and prescriptions is limited to physicians and other health care professionals who are properly licensed in the state. This may never be done by a medical student. A student may act as a transcriber of orders if it is the licensed physician who signs or approves them. Hospital and office staff should never act on an order from a medical student until it has been cosigned or otherwise endorsed by the attending physician. Even in an emergency, a nurse should follow established protocols and the orders of an appropriate physician, not the advice of a medical student.

It is particularly important to follow the laws of medical practice when prescribing or ordering drugs in a teaching situation. Most boards of medical examiners tend to be lenient toward physicians and medical students in the division of work. State and federal drug enforcement agencies are much less understanding. The rule is simple: only licensed persons may prescribe or dispense drugs. Those who violate this rule may be subjected to criminal prosecution and the punishments prescribed by law. The fact that the unlicensed prescriber is a student will only make prosecution politically easier.

Nursing and Other Students

The rules that apply to medical students apply to other types of students: their work must be supervised, and they may not do anything that requires licensure or certification.

As a practical matter, much of what other students do does not require licensure or is already supervised by a physician. For instance, an unlicensed individual may be authorized to draw blood or administer medication. A medical student or a nursing student also may be authorized to draw blood or give medicines. Caution must be used to make sure that these students are following specific orders and not using their own judgment. If there is an order from a physician saying that a blood glucose should be drawn at 8 A.M., a student may do the task. If the blood is being drawn under a protocol for registered nurses that says that the test should be done when the patient shows signs of hyperglycemia, a nurse's professional judgment is required; no student should assume responsibility for doing or not doing the test without supervision.

The Reality of Teaching Programs

The conflict between legal norms and medical practice is great in teaching programs. The improper supervision and delegation of work is a perennial problem in medical care delivery, and it is most troublesome in teaching programs. The medical-ethics and medical-legal literature contain elaborate theories of patient autonomy and student supervision that represent the expectations of the law. They bear little resemblance to medical training, however. The usual practice in teaching hospitals and medical schools has been to use medical students and residents for patient care with little or no attention to their legal status. Patients are implicitly (and sometimes explicitly) deceived about who is a licensed physician and about their right to refuse to participate in teaching programs.[33]

This conflict between legal expectations and medical practice has persisted for two reasons: (1) it is convenient for the physicians participating in the teaching programs, and (2) boards of medical examiners have had little interest in enforcing the provisions of the law that relate to patient autonomy and physician-endorsed unauthorized practice of medicine. Malpractice lawsuits become an issue only when a patient is severely injured. Even then, many programs are sheltered under various forms of governmental immunity, pushing the onus for paying the resulting claims onto any private physicians involved in the care of the injured patient.

Importance of the Law

Three themes in contemporary medical practice bode ill for physicians who continue to participate in illegally managed teaching programs. The first is the growing reluctance of medical malpractice insurers to continue to insure physicians who have preventable claims against them. If a physician's insurer pays off on a case involving an improperly supervised student, the physician may have difficulty in renewing the policy or in obtaining coverage from another insurer.

Second, with the demise of charitable immunity and the growth of formal risk management and quality assurance programs, hospitals are demanding that physicians supervise the care of their patients personally. Third, outside pressures are increasing the enforcement of the laws governing the supervision of nonphysician personnel. The driving force behind this enforcement has been the Medicare/Medicaid programs. Physicians who bill for work performed by students and residents violate the federal law against fraud and abuse. Private insurance companies are increasing their supervision of billing practices associated with teaching programs. The growing concern among politicians about the illicit use of drugs will result in more vigorous enforcement of the rules on who may write prescriptions and dispense drugs.

It is not necessary to deceive patients to persuade them to participate in teaching programs. Many patients enjoy having students involved in their care. The students generally have much more time to spend with an individual patient than do either the residents or the attending physician.

Medical schools that have been forced to adopt rigid policies of disclosure to patients have not seen the students driven from their hospitals.

In the past, properly supervising medical students and residents was more expensive than not supervising them. This is changing, however, as the federal government and third-party payers become more reluctant to pay for student work. An institution that is subject to an enforcement action for fraud can see its revenue stream from the federal government frozen for months or years. The physicians who are personally accused of fraud must expend tens of thousands of dollars of their own funds on defense lawyers because these actions are not covered under medical malpractice insurance. If the defense is not successful, the physician is subject to large fines, loss of licensure, and imprisonment.

Working with a Teaching Program

The critical legal issue in working with a teaching program is ensuring that the patient's care is always supervised by a properly trained and licensed physician. No matter how many residents, fellows, or medical students are participating in the care of a patient, it is the staff physician who is responsible. All the rules that apply to working with a consultant apply to staff physicians. If the patient is not referred to the teaching service for all care, then the original physician should be careful to supervise the patient's care personally.

When private physicians refer patients to a teaching hospital, they should make sure that the referral is to a fully licensed physician, not to a resident or a medical student. It may be a student who takes the telephone call, but the referral is to that student's supervising physician. If the referring physician is not certain who is taking the referral, then this should be determined or the patient should be referred elsewhere. If a physician refers a patient to a student or a resident without proper authority, and the supervising physician does not accept the patient, the referring physician has abandoned the patient and is liable for any problems that arise.

If a physician requests a consultation from a teaching service, both the physician and the patient should know who on the service will be primarily responsible for the work and who is the supervising staff physician. If problems arise during the consultation, these should be worked out between the attending physician and the supervising staff physician.

Maintaining Supervision

A staff physician should never turn over care of the patients on the service to an unsupervised resident. If the staff physician is unavailable to supervise the service, another equally qualified physician must assume this responsibility. Although residents and fellows may have independent licenses to practice medicine, they are viewed as students and therefore not appropriate substitutes for their teachers.

A physician who undertakes the education of students, whether in private practice or in the school, has a fundamental duty to supervise their activities. The most important part of this supervision is making sure that the student does not harm the patients or interfere with the physician–patient relationship. As a recent study illustrates, this is complicated by the tendency of residents to hide their mistakes from their attending physicians, as well as their patients.[34] This deception can have profound risk management consequences.[35] The students must understand the importance of reporting all problems to the attending physician. It must be clear that it is expected that students make mistakes.[36] It is covering up a mistake that is unacceptable. The physician also must ensure that the student does not violate the law or go beyond the allowable scope of practice.

Preventing harm to the patients requires close supervision of everything the student does to or for a patient. It is acceptable to have a student write orders if the nursing staff knows that the orders are only advisory and cannot be acted upon until reviewed and approved by the attending physician. If it is not possible to ensure that student orders will not be acted on, as is the case in most private hospitals, students should not write orders in the patient's chart. If a student is going to do a procedure on a patient, the attending physician

should personally assist the student to prevent wrong actions and to take over the procedure if the student has difficulty.

Maintaining the integrity of the physician–patient relationship is important to successful teaching within a private practice. Patients may choose whether they wish to participate in the teaching program. The student should understand that he or she must be as unobtrusive as possible. If the patient is uncomfortable with the situation, then compliance is likely to suffer and the quality of care will deteriorate. The attending physician's first duty is always to the patient.

The Physician–Student Relationship

The duty to teach students is sometimes contractual but usually only an ethical obligation. Faculty members who receive a salary for teaching must educate the students under their supervision. Physicians who accept staff privileges at a teaching hospital also may have a contractual duty to teach. If teaching is a requirement for staff membership, accepting the staff privileges means accepting the teaching responsibility. For most physicians, there is no formal contract that requires teaching, but there is an ethical duty to improve the practice of medicine and to educate new physicians. If the physician derives any benefit from the presence of students, this ethical duty becomes very strong.

In theory, a student should not be allowed to do anything to a patient that the supervising physician cannot legally authorize a layperson to do. The physician should verify everything the student does. For instance, if a medical student does a history and physical examination and dictates the findings, the physician must repeat the history and physical to determine their accuracy before signing the dictation. Otherwise, the physician would be illegally delegating the practice of medicine to the student.

If the person doing the history and physical is a resident in a teaching hospital, it may not be necessary for the attending physician to repeat all the work. The resident may have a limited license to practice medicine through his or her training institution. It is important to know the legal status of the student or resident. A student doing an intern-like rotation is still a student and may not do any medical practice. A resident who has no independent license is restricted to practicing within the limitations of whatever institutional license he or she may have. Even an independently licensed resident physician may be limited in the scope of practice by the residency policies. These may not carry the force of law, but they may affect malpractice insurance coverage.

Whether a physician has the right to refuse to treat a patient who will not participate in a teaching program depends on the circumstances of the physician's practice and the laws in that jurisdiction. A private practicing physician who chooses to act as a preceptor has the right to turn away patients who object to this, if the proper steps are taken to provide the patient with alternative care. Otherwise this might constitute abandonment. If the patient is entitled to care from the physician because of contractual arrangements, such as an HMO or because of emergency care laws, the physician does not have the right to force the patient to accept care from a student.

Fraud

It is Medicare/Medicaid fraud if the patient is billed for the student's or resident's services. Medical schools have paid substantial fines for billing Medicare for resident and student care, and the physicians who signed as providing the care could have been criminally prosecuted. All patients should be made aware of the status of all the people involved in their care and the identity of their attending physician. Federal programs and most state and private third-party payers will not pay for any service performed by a student or a physician in a training program. Payment can be expected if a student or resident performs the activity under the direct supervision of a licensed physician. If a medical student dictates a history and physical on a patient who is being admitted to the hospital and the attending physician cosigns this dictation and adds his or her own notes after doing a history and physical, the physician may bill for the service. A physician who cosigns the dictation without doing the work is not entitled to payment for a service he or she did not perform. The physician also may violate the terms of his or her hospital privileges or the laws on delegation of medical authority. Physicians must understand that every claim that is submitted to Medicare or Medicaid with their names on it implies that the physician personally ensures that every aspect of the bill and the care rendered is proper.

MEDICAL DIRECTOR'S LIABILITY

Physicians who also serve as medical directors in MCOs face special legal problems. Under ERISA, a medical director is a statutory fiduciary of the health plan because the ERISA defines a fiduciary as anyone who can allocate the plan's assets. Under state law, a medical director also has common law fiduciary responsibilities if the medical director makes decisions about the care of individual patients. This happens whenever the medical director looks at a patient's records or talks to a treating physician or an NPP about the patient and then makes any decision about that patient's care, including the decision that the care is fine and no changes need to be made.

Dual Capacity Doctrine

What may happen in MCOs is a variant on the dual capacity doctrine. The dual capacity doctrine evolved as an aspect of workers' compensation law. A worker who is injured by a fellow workers' negligence is usually limited to a worker's compensation recovery. Some courts created an exception to this rule if the negligent worker was a licensed professional who was expected to exercise independent judgment: "According to the dual-capacity doctrine, an employer who is generally immune from tort liability may become liable to his employee as a third-party tortfeasor; if he occupies, in addition to his capacity as employer, a second capacity that confers on him obligations independent of those imposed on him as an employer."[37] Physicians have been specific targets of this doctrine, based on their independent license and duties to the patient.[38]

The issue will not be a workers' compensation bar, but the unwillingness, or in the case of ERISA plans, inability of the courts to hold MCOs responsible for decisions to deny care. As plaintiffs search for additional defendants, especially those whom they can portray as concerned only with the bottom line, they will sue physician medical directors and other physician administrators in MCOs. The courts may hold as follows: "Once a physician, always a physician"—that is, every physician who reviews the patient's care or chart, or supervises those that do, or in any other way has the authority to affect care decisions, has independent liability for injuries to the patient. If the medical director's compensation includes any component tied to reduction in services, the medical director would be in a *Shea* conflict of interest position.

Such a judicial construct would be consistent with courts' ambivalence about medicine as "just another business." The physician's role in MCOs should be as a conscience, ensuring that patients are properly treated. It is also the best posture to assume in attempting to convince courts to reject employment terms in MCO contracts that prevent physicians from exercising independent medical judgment.

Medical Licensing Issues

The right to define and regulate medical practice is reserved to the states. Since ERISA has denied the states the right to regulate most private insurance plans, state legislatures and medical licensing boards are asserting their authority to regulate how physicians practice in MCOs. The central target of this regulation will be medical directors because they are the nexus between the plan and patient care. The two main risks will be improper supervision of NPPs and breach of the physician's fiduciary duty.

If an MCO does not ensure proper supervision of NPPs, the medical director could be held liable for facilitating the unauthorized practice of medicine. For example, many states require an NPP to be supervised by a specific physician, and limit the number of NPPs that any given physician can

supervise. These rules include the use of protocols approved by the supervising physician, and the ready availability of the supervising physician. If the MCO does not meet these requirements, such as by allowing the NPP and the supervising physician to work different shifts or in different locations, or by not following the letter of the law as regards the documentation required for proper supervision, the NPP will be engaged in the unauthorized practice of medicine. The medical director with the responsibility for supervising the medical personnel could then be charged with the crime of aiding in the unauthorized practice of medicine, or could lose his or her license to practice medicine in the state. Given the unpopularity of MCOs in many communities, it is not unreasonable to expect that a prosecutor would find such a prosecution politically attractive, especially if there were a well-publicized death or injury at the plan due to improper supervision, perhaps of a triage nurse.

As discussed earlier in this chapter, most states criminalize the bribery of physicians as a breach of the physician's fiduciary duty. A medical director engaged in any patient care–related decision making that violates those laws could be prosecuted under these laws, as could the plan administrators who set up the improper incentives. Since ERISA does not preempt state criminal law proceedings, this could be another attractive avenue for a prosecutor or medical licensing board attempting to meet a public call for action against overreaching MCOs.

BUSINESS RISKS IN DEALING WITH MCOS

MCOs pose many new business risks that most physicians are unaware of. Those who appreciate the risks generally do not have the tools to evaluate them. Physician contracts with MCOs, which frequently contain indemnification and capitation agreements, can make individual physicians liable for the managed care organization's medical malpractice costs and other litigation or regulatory risks.

Deselection from the MCO

An MCO's ultimate threat to a physician is deselection—being bounced from the plan. Legally, deselection is no different from being denied medical staff privileges at a hospital. The difference is the economic incentive. Traditionally, hospitals benefited from additional staff members. Each physician was a potential source of admissions to the hospital. Most of the cases involving improper termination of medical staff privileges arose from a group of physician competitors who captured the hospital's medical staff credentialing process.[39] While hospitals might deselect physicians to maintain the quality of medical care, they had no incentive to reduce their physician staff.[40]

In MCOs that employ physicians, each additional physician over the minimum needed to do the work is just more overhead. Even in MCOs that contract with individual physicians and pay only for services provided, additional physicians raise the overhead because they require additional case managers to oversee them.

MCOs are in a stronger bargaining position than physicians because the United States has an excess of physicians. Many specialties have more practitioners than can keep busy doing only specialty practice. Nongovernmental MCOs have only limited due process restrictions on their credentialing.[41] They may choose not to renew a physician's contract for any nondiscriminatory reason, including staff reductions to lower costs. If the MCO terminates the physician's contract for medical negligence–related conduct, most states will allow or require the MCO to report this to the State Board of Medical Examiners (BOME), who then report to the National Practitioner Data Bank (NPDB).[42] Physicians have a right to review their files, and to request corrections, but no right to force the Data Bank to make corrections. The NPDB allows hospitals and MCOs to query its files when they are hiring or granting staff privileges to a physician. An adverse report in the NPDB can make it impossible for a physician to obtain employment or medical staff privileges anywhere in the United States.

On balance, the NPDB is a good idea, but it poses several problems for physicians in MCOs. An unscrupulous plan can use threats of reports to the NPDB as coercion. This can be very effective if the physician is contesting a noncompete agreement, or does not want to follow the plan's rules. Arguably, federal law does not mandate reporting to the NPDB by MCOs, but it is difficult to contest the right of an MCO to make a report. Reporting entities have immunity unless it can be shown that the reporting entity knew the information in the report was false.[43] This is a difficult standard to meet. If the physician loses, and the contract with the plan has an indemnification agreement, then the physician may have to pay the plan's legal expenses.

For employee physicians the risk of deselection may be greater than just being fired. Many MCO employment contracts include noncompete clauses that can force the physician to leave the community. Some states strictly limit the enforcement of these clauses as being against public policy, and a few have outlawed them entirely.[44] However, in many states, these agreements are enforceable for reasonable limitations of time and distance. In at least one state, Missouri, the courts will enforce restrictions as long as two years, covering a 200-mile radius, and have failed to find any public policy rationale for treating physicians differently from other businesses or professionals. The deselected physician faces having to move, and perhaps getting licensed in another state. If physicians are deselected for not abiding by financial guidelines established by the plan, then it is unlikely that other plans will be interested in hiring them.

Physicians negotiating with an MCO should try to get a contract with very specific criteria for termination. This is increasingly difficult to do. In many communities, MCO contracts have become adhesion contracts because there are too many physicians willing to take positions on any terms. The physician should know at all times where he or she stands with the plan and what is necessary to meet the plan's objectives. These objectives should be spelled out in sufficient detail that the physician can determine if they can be achieved while preserving adequate quality of medical care. If possible, there should not be a provision for the annual termination of any given percentage of physicians, such as the 10% with the highest costs per capita. Such provisions can force physicians to reduce access to care below what is medically necessary.

Shifting Insurance Risks

The most significant financial risk to physicians in MCOs occurs when they assume some of the financial risks of either the operation of the MCO or the risk of insurance for the patients. The two main forms of risk shifting are capitation and indemnification agreements.

Capitation Agreements

In capitation agreements, the physician agrees to assume part or all of the cost of caring for a defined pool of patients. The risk arises because the cash flow through an MCO for the total cost of caring for a patient is much larger than the costs of physician services alone. Individual physicians and small group practices have very high overhead. This makes them very sensitive to even small reductions in patient volume or increased costs of caring for patients. Any agreements that put the physician at risk for the total cost of the patient's care, without fully compensating for that risk, can bankrupt all but the richest practices. The financial risk is dependent on the character of the patient pool and the number of lives covered. The risk is greatest when a few physicians contract for a portion of an MCO pool. Unless the physicians buy stop-loss insurance coverage on their share of the patient pool, an unexpected clustering of serious illnesses or major trauma could cost them millions in unanticipated medical care.

An inadvertent capitation situation can occur if the MCO becomes insolvent. A survey by the Solvency Working Group of the National Association of Insurance Commissions found that providers are owed an average of $2,005,000 at the time an HMO declares insolvency.[45] Further compli-cating the recovery of funds is whether the MCO is a debtor, in which case liquidation and reorganization proceeds pursuant to the Bankruptcy Code; or whether the MCO is an insurance company, which will proceed toward liquidation under the direction of the state insurance commissioner's office. Most states prohibit physicians from trying to collect payments directly from the MCO's patients because the patients already paid for the care when they paid their insurance premiums.

Indemnification Agreements

Indemnification agreements are simple contractual agreements requiring the physician to indemnify the MCO in certain circumstances. This can range from agreeing to reimburse the MCO for any costs related to the physician's malpractice to broad agreements to reimburse the MCO for any costs that result from any behavior by the physician. Even narrowly drawn, indemnification agreements can be troublesome. For example, many malpractice insurance policies will not cover a physician's indemnification agreement with an MCO. Even if the MCO does not have to pay any damages for the physician's negligence, it may have $500,000 in attorney's fees related to the case; for which the physician may be personally liable. More broadly drawn agreements can impose open-ended liability, including liability for administrative sanctions against the MCO for activities over which the physician was nominally in charge.

Indemnification agreements should be avoided if possible. Physicians who are forced to sign such an agreement should ensure that they have adequate umbrella insurance coverage, and that the insurer will pay indemnification claims. This may require a commercial insurance broker and a very high umbrella policy. It is especially important that physicians review all of their contracts with MCOs to identify any indemnification or other commercial risk clauses, and to do so when each contract is renewed. In many practices, the practice manager deals with MCOs and physicians just sign the papers placed in front of them. Many of these physicians do not know that they may have assumed significant uninsured financial risks.

Malpractice Insurance Considerations

Irrespective of whether they are independent contractors or employees, physicians remain liable for any torts they personally commit while delivering medical care. Physicians must ensure that they have adequate medical malpractice insurance and that they control the policy of insurance. This is no different from the responsibilities of a physician with medical staff privileges at a hospital. Physicians recognize that they have different interests from those of the hospital. In some cases, these interests are adverse, in that the physician may claim that it was the hospital's personnel who were negligent, or the hospital may claim that it was the physician's negligence that caused the injury.

As with hospitals, physicians must recognize that their interests and those of the managed care plan often will be adverse. If the physician has negotiated for an MCO to provide medical malpractice coverage, then the physician should ensure that he or she is the primary insured on the policy. This gives the physician enhanced control regarding whether or not a claim is defended or settled, and if settled, what the terms will be. Ideally, coverage will be provided in the manner to which the physician is accustomed, like independent private insurance, that is just paid for by the plan. More likely, however, physicians will be insured through a self-insurance trust funded by the plan. Again, referring to the experience with hospitals, some of these plans are less than scrupulous about protecting the interests of the physician. Hospitals have been known to treat the self-insurance fund like a piggybank from which it may defend the physician as a favor. Although this may violate conditions applicable to maintaining a self-insurance fund, there is little oversight of these funds, and less recourse for a physician caught in a conflict. A physician dealing with one of these funds, or any other insurer that may be captive of an adverse party, should hire his or her own counsel to monitor the defense attorney's work.

Antitrust Issues in Managed Care

MCO costs for physician services decrease as MCOs gain market power; that is, as the MCOs attain economies of scale. Once MCOs become established in a market, they become an almost irresistible force. In most markets, patient lives are divided between several managed care organizations. However, MCOs seldom compete in terms of the contracts they offer physicians. They may compete on the price they will pay for buying practices, but they hold the line on the contractual rights of the physicians delivering medical care services.

The cost of a practice is a one-time expenditure, but the costs and terms of physician contracts are long-term expenses that are key to the survival of MCOs. In many communities, physician contracts used by competing MCOs have identical terms. Although this might be parallel action based on similar needs, there also may be substantial collusion to ensure that no plan undermines the others by granting physicians substantially greater rights. In other businesses this would be an antitrust violation. MCOs are legally considered insurance companies, however, and they have McCarron-Ferguson immunity from federal antitrust laws.[46] They cannot be sued for most antitrust activities.

Unfortunately, physicians do not have the same immunity. Independent physician groups and local medical societies must be alert to potential antitrust violations. Independent contractor physicians who band together to resist cram-down contracts from MCOs can be held to have engaged in a group boycott or other violations of the Sherman Antitrust Act. Such groups have been prosecuted by the FTC. This limits collective action by physicians to those that are employees of an MCO. Physicians who are MCO employees can unionize by following National Labor Relations Board (NLRB) standards. Once in an NLRB-certified union, they can strike or take other actions. Independent contractor physicians cannot unionize to gain the protection of the NLRB. For independent contractor physicians, the only avenue for collective action is to petition their state legislatures and Congress for statutory protections. Such collective action to petition the government for redress is protected under the No-err-Pennington doctrine as a form of political speech.[47]

A major problem for physicians who are trying to band together to bargain more effectively with MCOs has been the lack of both common law and regulatory guidance. In 1996, the Department of Justice and the Federal Trade Commission issued guidelines on health care mergers and joint operating agreements.[48] Although some commentators have seen these as greatly expanding physician's right to take collective action, a close reading indicates no change from prevailing antitrust rules.

The only safety zones provided in the guidelines are for physician networks that involve significant shared financial risk and that do not have more than 20% of the market for exclusive arrangements, or 30% for nonexclusive arrangements. Although the guidelines say that it is possible to have complying networks without substantial shared financial risk, the criteria they use for evaluating these networks imply that it is unlikely many will pass. The guidelines make clear that informal associations of physicians that engage in anticompetitive activities, such as boycotts of MCOs or other bargaining activities, will be treated harshly:

> In contrast to integrated physician network joint ventures, such as these discussed above, there have been arrangements among physicians that have taken the form of networks, but which in purpose or effect were little more than efforts by their participants to prevent or impede competitive forces from operating in the market. These arrangements are not likely to produce significant procompetitive efficiencies. Such arrangements have been, and will continue to be, treated as unlawful conspiracies or cartels, whose price agreements are per se illegal.[49]

REFERENCES

1. Mars, S. The corporate practice of medicine: a call for action. *Health Matrix.* 1997;7:1,241–300.
2. *In re Co-operative Law Co.*, 92 N.E. 15, 16 (N.Y. 1910).
3. *American Med. Ass'n v. United States*, 317 U.S. 519 (1943).
4. 42 U.S.C. § 300e-10 (1973).
5. Medicare and Medicaid Programs, Requirements for Physician Incentive Plans in Prepaid Health Care Organizations, 61 Fed. Reg. 69,034 (Dec. 31, 1996).
6. Centers for Disease Control and Prevention. Rates of Cesarean delivery—United States, 1993. *MMWR Morb Mortal Wkly Rep.* 1995;44:303.
7. Blum, JD. The evolution of physician credentialing into managed care selective contracting. *Am J Law Med.* 1996;22:173, 189–192.
8. *Beach v. Wilton*, 91 N.E. 492, 495 (Ill. 1910).
9. *Witherell v. Weimer,* 421 N.E.2d 869 (Ill. 1981).
10. Model Penal Code, § 224.8, Commercial Bribery and Breach of Duty to Act Disinterestedly.
11. *Wickline v. State of California*, 228 Cal. Rptr. 661 (Cal. App. 1986).
12. *Wilson v. Blue Cross of So. Cal.*, 271 Cal. Rptr. 876, 833 (Cal. App. 1990).
13. *Fox v. Health Net of Cal.*, Cause No. 219692 (Cal. Super. Ct., Riverside Cty., Dec. 23, 1993).
14. Employee Retirement Income Security Act of 1974 (ERISA), 29 U.S.C. § 1001 (1996).
15. *Metropolitan Life Ins. Co. v. Taylor*, 481 U.S. 58 (1987).
16. *Katz v. Colonial Life Ins. Co. of Am.*, 951 F. Supp. 36 (S.D.N.Y. 1997).
17. Woodhandler S, Himmelstein DU. Extreme risk—the new corporate proposition for physicians. *N Engl J Med.* 1995;333:1706.
18. *Lancaster by Lancaster v. Kaiser Found. Health Plan*, 958 F. Supp. 1137 (E.D. Va. 1997).
19. *Id.* at 1150.
20. *Shea v. Esensten*, 107 F.3d 625 (8th Cir. 1997).
21. *Id.* at 628.
22. *Central States, Southeast & Southwest Areas Pension Fund v. Central Transp., Inc.*, 472 U.S. 559 (1985).
23. *Shea*, 107 F.3d at 628.
24. This term is used to denote physician's assistants, nurse practitioners, child health associates, public health nurses, and other personnel with medical care training who participate in the medical care delivery team.
25. Federal investigators report on clusters of infant deaths. July 25, 1985; *New York Times.* Investigators near end of inquiry into deaths of infants at hospital. April 11, 1984; *New York Times.*
26. *Sermchief v. Gonzales*, 660 S.W.2d 683 (Mo. 1983).

27. *People v. Varas*, 110 A.D.2d 646, 487 N.Y.S.2d 577 (N.Y.A.D. 2 Dept. 1985).
28. Hadorn DC, McCormick K, Diokno A. An annotated algorithm approach to clinical guideline development. *JAMA*. 1992;267:3311–3314.
29. Colford JM Jr, McPhee SJ. The ravelled sleeve of care: managing the stresses of residency training. *JAMA*. 1989;261:889–893.
30. Asch DM, Parker RM. The Libby Zion case: one step forward or two steps backward? *N Engl J Med*. 1988;318:771–775.
31. *Mozingo by Thomas v. Pitt County Mem'l. Hosp., Inc.*, 415 S.E.2d 341, 345 (N.C. 1992).
32. Gleicher N. Expansion of health care to the uninsured and underinsured has to be cost-neutral. *JAMA*. 1991;265:2388–2390.
33. Asch DM, Parker RM. The Libby Zion case: one step forward or two steps backward? *N Engl J Med*. 1988;318:771–775.
34. Wu AW, Folkman S, McPhee SJ, Lo B. Do house officers learn from their mistakes? *JAMA*. 1991;265:2089–2094.
35. Persson A. Letter concerning: do house officers learn from their mistakes? *JAMA*. 1991;266:512–513.
36. Bosk C. *Forgive and Remember: Managing Medical Failure*. Chicago: University of Chicago Press, 1979.
37. *Weber v. Armco, Inc.*, 663 P.2d 1221 (Okla. 1983).
38. Glenn. *Employer's Liability to Employee for Malpractice of Physician Supplied by Employer*, 16 A.L.R. 3d 564 (1968 & Supp. 1996).
39. *Patrick v. Burget*, 486 U.S. 94 (1988).
40. *Bryan v. James E. Holmes Reg'l Med. Ctr.*, 33 F.3d 1318 (11th Cir. 1994).
41. Liang, BA. Deselection under Harper v. Healthsource: a blow for maintaining patient–physician relationships in the era of managed care, *ND Law Rev*. 1997;72:799.
42. 42 U.S.C. §§ 11131, 11133, & 11134 (1996).
43. 42 U.S.C. § 1137(c) (1996).
44. Berg. Judicial enforcement of covenants not to compete between physicians: protecting doctors' interests at patients' expense. Rutgers Law Rev. 1992;45:1.
45. Howard, JM. The aftermath of HMO insolvency: consideration for provider. *Ann Health Law*. 1995;4:87, 89 (citing National Association of Commissioners 1989–1 NAIC Proc. 344, 362).
46. 15 U.S.C. § 1011 (1996).
47. *Eastern R.R. Presidents Conf. v. Noerr Motor Freight, Inc.*, 365 U.S. 127 (1961); *United Mine Workers v. Pennington*, 381 U.S. 657 (1965).
48. United States Department of Justice & Federal Trade Commission, Statements of Antitrust Enforcement Policy in Health Care sec. B1, Statement 8 (August 1996).
49. Id. at B(1).

SUGGESTED READINGS

Managed Care

Afflitto L. Managed care and its influence on physician–patient relationship—implications for collaborative practice. *Plast Surg Nurs*. 1997;17:217–218.

Appelbaum PS. Managed care and the next generation of mental health law. *New Directions Ment Health Serv*. 1996:65–69.

Barratt K. Reviewing gag clauses in managed care contracts. *Wisc Med J*. 1996;95:249–250.

Beinecke R, Pfeiffer R, Pfeiffer D, Soussou N. The evaluation of fee for service and managed care from the viewpoint of people with disabilities in the USA. *Disabil Rehabil*. 1997;19:513–522.

Bettman JW, Demorest BH, Craven ER. Risk management issues in the new managed care environment. *Survey Ophthalmol*. 1996;41:268–270.

Bitterman RA. Managed care authorization for emergency department services: a medical risk to patients, a legal risk for doctors and hospitals. *NC Med J*. 1997;58:260–263.

Boyd JW. The human toll of managed care. *Pharos*. 1997;60:32–34.

Brody BA. Ethical issues raised by managed care. *Tex Med*. 1997;93:43–45.

Brody H, Bonham VL Jr. Gag rules and trade secrets in managed care contracts: ethical and legal concerns. *Arch Int Med*. 1997;157:2037–2043.

Churchill LR. "Damaged humanity": the call for a patient-centered medical ethic in the managed care era. *Theor Med*. 1997;18:113–126.

Cohen RJ. Managed care and the physician–patient relationship: implications for peer review. Md Med J. 1997;46:91–93.

D'Ambrosia R. Managed care company's contract intolerable for physicians and patients. *Orthopedics*. 1998;21:20.

Danis M, Churchill L. The ethics of providing intensive care in managed care organizations. *New Horizons*. 1997;5:85–93.

De Ville K. Scapegoats for the organization? Physicians, managed care, and medical malpractice. *NC Med J*. 1997;58:340–344.

Ellis MS. Liability issues in managed care. *J La State Med Soc*. 1997;149:151–158.

Fiesta J. Understanding managed care law: key issues for nurse executives. *Aspens Adv Nurse Exec*. 1996;11:1–3.

Hall MA, Berenson RA. Ethical practice in managed care: a dose of realism. *Ann Int Med*. 1998;128:395–402.

Hall RC. Ethical and legal implications of managed care. *Gen Hosp Psychiatry*. 1997;19:200–208.

Halleland KJ, Galinson TL. Trends in managed care liability. *Minn Med*. 1998;81:49–50.

Hickson GB. Pediatric practice and liability risk in a managed care environment. *Pediatr Ann*. 1997;26:179–185.

Holleman WL, Holleman MC, Moy JG. Are ethics and managed care strange bedfellows or a marriage made in heaven? *Lancet*. 1997;349:350–351.

Ignagni K. Covering a breaking revolution: the media and managed care. *Health Affairs*. 1998;17:26–34.

Infante MC. The legal risks of managed care. *RN*. 1996;59:57–59.

Kolodinsky J. Gender differences in satisfaction with primary care physicians in a managed care health plan. *Women Health*. 1997;26:67–86.

Lansing AE, Lyons JS, Martens LC, O'Mahoney MT, Miller SI, Obolsky A. The treatment of dangerous patients in managed care: psychiatric hospital utilization and outcome. *Gen Hosp Psychiatry*. 1997;19:112–118.

Larkin GL, Adams JG, Derse AR, Iserson KV, Gotthold WE. Managed care ethics: an emergency? *Ann Emerg Med*. 1996;28:683–689.

Mang HJ Jr. Malpractice liability and managed care—a Hobson's choice? *J La State Med Soc*. 1996;148:341–343.

Maurer WJ. Organized medicine and managed care—a proposal for a new and better relationship. *Wis Med J*. 1997;96:20–22.

Miller TE. Managed care regulation: in the laboratory of the states. *JAMA*. 1997;278:1102–1109.

Moskowitz EH. Clinical responsibility and legal liability in managed care. *J Am Geriatr Soc*. 1998;46:373–377.

Murphy RN. Legal and practical impact of clinical practice guidelines on nursing and medical practice. *Nurse Pract*. 1997;22:138, 147–148.

Platt JB. Gatekeeper liability and managed care. *Minn Med*. 1996;79:25–27.

Plumeri PA. Managed care and risk management. *Gastroenterol Clin North Am*. 1997;26:895–910.

Retchin SM, Brown RS, Yeh SC, Chu D, Moreno L. Outcomes of stroke patients in Medicare fee for service and managed care. *JAMA*. 1997;278:119–124.

Rinn CC. ERISA and managed care: the impact of travelers. *Health Lawyer*. 1996;8:19.

Rodwin MA. Conflicts of interest and accountability in managed care: the aging of medical ethics. *J Am Geriatr Soc*. 1998;46:338–341.

Rosen L. Managed care and you, part II: managed care liability marketing claims. *Todays Surg Nurse*. 1997;19:43–44.

Rosen L. Managed care and you, part III: managed care liability—gatekeeper and cost-containment issues. *Todays Surg Nurse*. 1997;19:50–51.

Roth RL. Recent developments concerning the effect of ERISA preemption on tort claims against employers, insurers, health plan administrators, managed care entities, and utilization review agents. *Health Lawyer*. 1996;8:3.

Simon RI. Psychiatrists' duties in discharging sicker and potentially violent inpatients in the managed care era. *Psychiat Serv*. 1998;49:62–67.

Snyder L, Tooker J. Obligations and opportunities: the role of clinical societies in the ethics of managed care. *J Am Geriatr Soc*. 1998;46:378–380.

Stein HF. Euphemism in the language of managed care. *J Okla State Med Assoc*. 1997;90:243–247.

Stiffman MN, LeFevre ML. Are resident physicians serving as primary care providers for managed care patients? *Fam Med*. 1997;29:94–98.

Stoudemire A. Psychiatry in medical practice: implications for the education of primary care physicians in the era of managed care: part 2. *Psychosomatics*. 1997;38:1–9.

Tenery RM Jr. Patients need protection under managed care. *Tex Med*. 1998;94:44.

Thurber CF. Commentary: quality and managed care: where is the fit? *Am J Med Qual*. 1997;12:177–182.

Wachler AB, Avery PA. Physician incentive plan regulations: implications for managed care organizations and providers. *Health Lawyer*. 1996;8:1–5.

Weber RD. Managed care tort liability. *Mich Med*. 1997;96:8, 52.

Teaching And Supervision

Adams BL. Why must nurses risk their careers for safe care? *Am J Nurs*. 1997;97:80.

Barter M, Furmidge ML. Unlicensed assistive personnel. Issues relating to delegation and supervision. *J Nurs Adm*. 1994;24:36–40.

Berlin L. Liability of attending physicians when supervising residents. *AJR Am J Roentgenol*. 1998;171:295–299.

Berlin L. Liability of the moonlighting resident. *AJR Am J Roentgenol*. 1998;171:565–567.

Berlin L. Vicarious liability. *AJR Am J Roentgenol*. 1997;169:621–624.

Berliner MC. To fear or not to fear: hospital liability for teaching physician and resident billing issues. *J Health Care Finance*. 1996;23:86–87.

Booth D, Carruth AK. Violations of the nurse practice act: implications for nurse managers. *Nurs Manage*. 1998;29:35–39; quiz 40.

Butters JM, Strope JL. Legal standards of conduct for students and residents: implications for health professions educators. *Acad Med*. 1996;71:583–590.

Calfee BE. The legal consequences of practicing beneath your licensure status. *Revolution*. 1997;7:21.

Chiarella EM. Nurses' liability in doctor–nurse relationships. *Contemp Nurse*. 1993;2:6–10.

Collins SE. Supervision of and delegation to UAPs. *Fla Nurse*. 1997;45:8, 10.

Dewar MA. Medical law and ethics: from training to education. *J Fla Med Assoc*. 1994;81:11.

Falk JL. Medical direction of emergency medical service systems: a full-time commitment whose time has come. *Crit Care Med*. 1993;21:1259–1260.

Feldstein JH, Fishman CL. A hospital's liability for staffing its emergency room with an intern. *Leg Med*. 1990:179–188.

Fiesta J. Delegation, downsizing and liability. *Nurs Manage*. 1997;28:14.

George JE, Quattrone MS, Goldstone M. Nurse-physician

communication breakdown: is it a basis for nurse liability? *J Emerg Nurs.* 1996;22:144–145.

Grupp-Phelan J, Reynolds S, Lingl LL. Professional liability of residents in a children's hospital. *Arch Pediatr Adolesc Med.* 1996;150:87–90.

Hall SA. Potential liabilities of medical directors for actions of EMTs. *Prehosp Emerg Care.* 1998;2:76–80.

Hannah HW. Vicarious liability. *J Am Vet Med Assoc.* 1995;207:863–864.

Helms LB, Helms CM. Forty years of litigation involving residents and their training, II. malpractice issues. *Acad Med.* 1991;66:718–725.

Heylen R. The vicarious liability of a surgeon for a negligent anesthesiologist. *Acta Anaesthesiol Belg.* 1993;44:61–68.

Hirsh HL. Medico-legal considerations in the use of physician extenders. *Leg Med.* 1991;127–205.

Holliman CJ, Wuerz RC, Meador SA. Decrease in medical command errors with use of a "standing orders" protocol system. *Am J Emerg Med.* 1994;12:279–283.

Howard G. Vicarious liability of employers explained. *Occup Health (Lond).* 1991;43:266–267.

Jenkins SM. The myth of vicarious liability: impact on barriers to nurse-midwifery practice. *J Nurse Midwifery.* 1994;39:98–106.

Jerrold L, Jerrold R. Litigation, legislation, and ethics: vicarious liability: its importance in professional practices. *Am J Orthod Dentofacial Orthop.* 1998;114:114–116.

Keill SL. Moonlighting: why training programs should monitor residents' activities. *Hosp Community Psychiatry.* 1991;42:735–738.

Kollas CD. Exploring internal medicine chief residents' medicolegal knowledge. *J Leg Med.* 1997;18:47–61.

Kollas CD. Medicolegal program for resident physicians. *Pa Med.* 1997;100:28–29.

Larimore WL. Pregnancy care liability misperceptions among medical students in Florida. *Fam Med.* 1994;26:154–156.

Mannino MJ. Legal aspects of nurse anesthesia practice. *Nurs Clin North Am.* 1996;31:581–589.

McBride D. Who shoulders the risk? Liability and allied health providers. *Iowa Med.* 1996;86:201–202.

McMullen P, Philipsen N. An unsafe or unprofessional colleague: what's a nurse to do? *Nursingconnections.* 1993;6:46–47.

Murphy EK. Applications of the 'captain of the ship' doctrine. *AORN J.* 1990;52:863, 865–866.

O'Keeffe RM Jr, O'Keeffe CE. Becoming brother's keeper: legal responsibilities of those supervising care by residents. *NC Med J.* 1993;54:166–168.

O'Sullivan J. Healthcare changes bring increased liability risk for nurses. *Mo Nurse.* 1995;64:4.

Oehlert WH. Standard clinical protocols are important to your survival. *J Okla State Med Assoc.* 1996;89:131–134.

Pepe PE, Mattox KL, Duke JH, Fisher PB, Prentice FD. Effect of full-time, specialized physician supervision on the success of a large, urban emergency medical services system. *Crit Care Med.* 1993;21:1279–1286.

Plumeri PA. Endoscopic training directors: a few legal and ethical considerations. *Gastrointest Endosc Clin N Am.* 1995;5:447–455.

Purdom DT, Griffith RS, Weaver DL. A positive, systematic approach to improve inpatient medical record completion in a family practice residency program. *Fam Med.* 1996;28:411–414.

Reuter SR. Professional liability in postgraduate medical education: who is liable for resident negligence? *J Leg Med.* 1994;15:485–531.

Rhodes AM. Liability for unlicensed personnel, part II. *MCN Am J Matern Child Nurs.* 1997;22:327–328.

Sheehan JP. Safeguard your license: the disciplinary process. *RN.* 1997;60:53–55.

Tammelleo AD. Nurse's duty to guard against sexual predators on staff. *Regan Rep Nurs Law.* 1997;38:2.

Tekavec C. 'Vicarious' liability pinpoints weak staff management. *Dent Econ.* 1997;87:88.

Trott MC. Legal issues for nurse managers. *Nurs Manage.* 1998;29:38–41; quiz 42.

Wagner KD, Pollard R, Wagner RF Jr. Malpractice litigation against child and adolescent psychiatry residency programs, 1981–1991. *J Am Acad Child Adolesc Psychiatry.* 1993;32:462–465.

Weekley AS Jr. Vicarious malpractice liability. *J Fla Med Assoc.* 1991;78:498–501.

Wohlberg JW, Rosen D, Jorgenson LM. New developments in response to boundary violations: proceedings of the Harvard Residency Teaching Day. *Harv Rev Psychiatry.* 1997;5:28–35.

Disease-Specific Protocols

SAMPLE

A. Diagnostic Criteria:
1. Each diagnosis is defined by a set of signs, symptoms and tests results that must be taken together to establish the specific diagnosis.
2. There may be several pathways to a given diagnosis.*

B. Laboratory:
This states all the lab tests, X-rays, etc., that are required on a patient with this diagnosis. Some of the tests may be necessary to establish the diagnosis.

C. Treatment:
This contains specific instructions for treatment of patients with this diagnosis. These are standing orders and should be clear and complete written orders.

D. Follow-Up:
All patients should be given a return appointment and specific instructions for follow-up.

E. Epidemiology:
This authorizes treatment of contacts to the patient and specifies if the disease is reportable to the public health authority or the police.

F. When To Refer:
This states the severity of disease or the special circumstances that require referral to a different protocol, to the supervising physician, to the Emergency Room, or for other services. This defines the scope of practice for the nurse.

G. Notes:
This portion of the protocol is not binding on the providers. This is the place for clinical pearls and helpful hints.
*Differential diagnosis is not part of a strict protocol and should not be used.

STREP THROAT

A. Diagnostic Criteria:
1. Positive throat culture or Rapid Strep Test or
2. Sore throat and household contact to a patient with positive strep test.

B. Laboratory:
Rapid Strep Test

C. Treatment:
1. Amoxicillin 500 mg TID x 10 or
2. Erythromycin 250 mg QID x 10 (Use the dose protocol for children)

D. Follow-Up:
1. Return to clinic if not improved in 48 hours.
2. Dipstick urine for protein in 6 weeks.

E. Epidemiology:
1. Treat all symptomatic family members if anyone has a positive lab test for strep.
2. Scarlet fever must be reported to the health department.

F. When To Refer:
1. If Otitis Media is present, use that protocol.
2. Consult physician if scarlet fever rash is present or if the patient cannot take either antibiotic.
3. Refer to the ER any patient with airway compromise or peritosilar abscess.

G. Notes:
1. Office strep tests are only 50% to 70% sensitive.
2. There is no set of signs and symptoms that reliably distinguishes strep throat from viral pharyngitis.

CHAPTER 11

Peer Review and Deselection

HIGHLIGHTS

- Peer review is governed by state and federal law.
- Federal law provides protections for peer reviewers if the process meets federal standards.
- Improper peer review can result in civil and criminal liability.
- Adverse peer review decisions must be reported to the National Practitioner Data Bank.
- Physicians have few rights in managed care deselection procedures.

INTRODUCTION

In the 1980s, peer review of physicians for hospital medical staff privileges was the central legal battle ground for professional review. Physicians who were denied privileges or removed from hospital medical staffs sued, claiming unfair or illegal treatment. Physicians who conducted the reviews demanded legal protection because of the potential liability and costs associated with defending an action brought by a physician denied privileges. The federal government responded with sweeping immunity from damages in peer review–related lawsuits, effectively limiting the legal review of these decisions, if the peer review committee complied with the due process standards of the federal law. This has made peer review for hospital privileges less important as a legal issue, just as deselection by managed care organizations (MCOs) rises in importance.

Deselection is the process by which an MCO terminates a physician's contract to provide services. The term deselection is used, rather than peer review, because deselection is usually done for reasons that do not implicate preserving or improving the quality of medical care. This chapter reviews the law on traditional peer review, then discusses deselection and the laws that are applicable to deselection decisions.

PEER REVIEW

Hospitals conduct peer review to determine if a physician may be admitted to or can stay on the medical staff. MCOs conduct peer review, as opposed to deselection, when they hire a physician or terminate a physician because of problems with the quality of care the physician provides. These reviews share many characteristics of hospital privileges reviews. The hospital medical staff model for peer review is the best starting point for understanding the laws governing peer review.

The law grants the professions remarkable latitude in disciplining their own, a practice rooted in a historical context that is very different from current practice. This discretion was often abused. Historically, it was acceptable to discriminate against practitioners for racial, cultural, ethnic, gender, and anticompetitive reasons. The essence of peer review was to ensure that professionals were both technically qualified and socially acceptable, and in many cases social factors outweighed professional ones. Medical professional societies determined where and whether a physician could practice. Hospital medical staffs granted or denied the privilege to practice in a given hospital. In most parts of the United States, medical practice was completely segregated, and this segregation was enforced through the medical societies. Peer review as a method of social and racial segregation ended legally with the passage of the civil rights laws in 1964. (The federal immunity for peer review actions does not apply to claims made under the civil rights acts.)[1] With the enforcement of the civil rights laws, the stranglehold of local medical societies on medical practice was broken. Rulings that hospital privileges could not be predicated on medical society membership quickly followed.

Medical Staff Committees

Hospital medical staff committees, especially those involved in staff credentialing decisions, exist in a legal limbo. With the exception of some hospitals in small communities that are short of physicians, the members of a hospital's medical staff are competitors. Thus, medical staff committees are groups of independent small businesspersons making decisions that affect the ability of other small businesspersons to compete with them. This is facilitated by a larger business, the hospital, that controls essential facilities, delegating critical management decisions to this group of independent contractors.

Hospital administration based on decision making by independent committees of physicians can be traced to the Joint Commission on the Accreditation of Healthcare Organizations (Joint Commission). The Joint Commission was originally a joint endeavor by the American Hospital Association (AHA) and the American College of Surgeons (ACS). The AHA wanted to professionalize the management of hospitals but needed the support of the physicians. The ACS could see the benefit in the professionalism of hospital management

but did not want to concede to administrators the power to control the medical staff appointments process. Out of these needs and aspirations the Joint Commission was born. The surgeons agreed to support efforts to reform hospital management as long as the hospital administrators agreed not to interfere with the prerogatives of the medical staff. The result was an uneasy truce between administrators and physicians on the medical staff.

Because of its basic nature as a group of competitors conspiring to set the terms of the competition, the authority of a medical staff committee is legally suspect. This is the inverse of the prevailing opinion that medical staff committees are legally favored, except when they make biased decisions. It is important to understand the basis for turning this view on its head. If medical staff committees are legally favored unless they make biased decisions, then it should be relatively easy to establish criteria for making decisions that will avoid the biases that concern the courts. If, on the other hand, medical staff committees are inherently suspect, attempts to make their decisions legally supportable will result in ever more complicated rules and procedures, and these rules and procedures will be constantly under attack with the development of new legal theories. This has been the case, prompting the Congress to pass a law reducing legal attacks on peer review actions (see Chapter 11).

The Legal Status of Medical Staff Committees

A hospital medical staff is an unusual entity. It serves the interests of the hospital but is not part of the hospital corporation. Because most states place limits on the ability of physicians to work for hospitals directly, the hospital usually does not employ or control the actions of the members of the committee. The medical staff is legally separate from the constituent physicians' practices. They may engage in joint decision making for the hospital, but they are not a joint venture with the hospital. It is important to note that the courts have found that the members of a hospital medical staff are, by definition, a conspiracy.

This view was articulated in *Weiss v. York Hospital*,[2] an antitrust case. The plaintiff in *Weiss* had sued some of the individual physicians on the medical staff, but he had also sued the medical staff itself as an independent entity. The court found that the medical staff had no independent legal existence but accepted the plaintiff's allegation that the individual physicians were engaged in a conspiracy as defined in section 1 of the Sherman Antitrust Act:

> We agree with the Plaintiffs that, as a matter of law, the medical staff is a combination of individual doctors and therefore that any action taken by the medical staff satisfies the "contract, combination, or conspiracy" requirement of section 1.[3]

The key to this case is the distinction between the medical staff as an entity unto itself and the individual physicians who make up the medical staff. Although the trial court instructed the jury that the medical staff was an "unincorporated division" of the hospital and thus the two were a "single entity," incapable of conspiring, it was careful to distinguish the actions of the individual members of the medical staff:

> The Court also instructed the jury, however, that if they found that some or all of the individual Defendants took action against the Plaintiffs "in whole or in part in their individual capacities and motivated in whole or in part by independent personal economic interests, then such individual-named Defendants are, under the law, independent economic entities ... legally capable of conspiring with York Hospital or its Medical and Dental Staff."[4]

In the case of *Quinn v. Kent General Hospital,*[5] the court expanded on this distinction between the medical staff and the individual physicians:

> It is certainly true that, regardless of their specialty, the members of the Hospital's active medical staff have a financial interest in limiting the number of physicians admitted to active staff privileges at the Hospital, for all admitting staff members compete with each other.... The active staff cannot be regarded as a single economic unit, but must be viewed as a collection of independent economic actors who are capable of combining or conspiring with each other for purposes of the Sherman Act.[6]

The holdings of the *Weiss* and *Quinn* courts represent the view that medical staff committees satisfy the legal definition of a *conspiracy:* an informal relationship between independent parties to carry out joint action. Conspiracy is generally used as a pejorative term, but here it is presumed that the conspiracy is for good, not evil. Nonetheless, it means that medical staff committees that act improperly are subject to the same federal laws that govern traditional illegal conspiracies, including the antitrust laws and the Racketeering Influenced Corrupt Organizations Act (RICO).

LEGAL CLIMATE FOR PEER REVIEW

Although the law grants professionals substantial latitude in self-governance, under some circumstances their decisions are reviewable in court. If peer review decisions are based on fair criteria, fairly applied, they will be legally defensible. Legally defensible is not enough, however, because the cost of defending a peer review decision can be overwhelming for a small hospital or individual committee member. It is critical that peer review actions incorporate preventive law strategies to prevent lawsuits or reduce the cost of defending those that are brought.

Adverse peer review decisions damage and destroy careers. The termination of medical staff privileges can deprive a physician of the ability to continue to practice in his or her chosen community. More seriously, it can hamper his or her ability to obtain privileges at other hospitals. If professionals undertake private peer review activities (as opposed to state governmental activities), they should not be surprised when they are sued. There is a substantial penalty for being your brother's keeper.

The corporatization of medicine makes defensible peer review problematic. There is increasing pressure to expand peer review to include cost control matters. Hospitals and MCOs want to eliminate physicians who do not comply with managed care guidelines, a controversial legal issue because the legal authority to do peer review does not obviate the laws governing anticompetitive conduct. Traditionally, allegedly anticompetitive actions have been attacked as violations of the antitrust laws. Increasingly, however, they are being seen as potential violations of business fraud laws such as RICO. A peer review action that violates RICO will subject the medical staff committee members to individual liability for treble damages, attorney's fees, and potential jail time. It is not a crime to deny physicians medical staff privileges wrongfully, but it may be a crime if it is done as part of a conspiracy to eliminate competition or to compromise the rights of patients.

Although it is understandable that an aggrieved physician would sue after an adverse peer review decision, many physicians are baffled by the ready acceptance of these lawsuits by the courts and the public. This is easily explained. Average citizens (jurors) do not believe that there should be special legal protections for professionals. From a juror's perspective, peer review is obviously biased in favor of the medical establishment. It is only to be expected that established practitioners will use it against physicians they do not like or who pose a competitive threat.

Litigation arising out of peer review decisions is so dangerous because the potential damages are large. A physician wrongly deprived of his or her livelihood can sue for the cash value of that livelihood. Even if only his or her reputation is injured, the traditional rules for libel and slander place a high value on the reputation of a professional. High damages attract attorneys. If the physician has been in practice for a substantial period, he or she is usually willing and able to pay to defend that practice. If the physician is young, with good prospects, an attorney may be willing to take the case on a contingent basis. If either the conspiracy or the antitrust laws have been violated, the plaintiff may recover treble damages and attorney's fees. It is these multiplied damages that drive attorneys to sue for antitrust and RICO violations. This makes it critical that peer review be conducted so as to trigger the federal grant of immunity from damages.

State Law Violations

Many lawsuits contesting peer review decisions include state law claims, but these are usu-

ally secondary to federal actions. Most states have made it difficult for aggrieved physicians to contest peer review decisions under state law, due, in part, to state statutes immunizing peer review activities. In larger part, it is due to state discovery rules that block access to hospital records related to peer review. Plaintiffs cannot present their cases in court if they are denied access to the records that document their claims.

Defamation is harming a person's reputation through lies. Defamation may be slander—speaking the lies—or libel—writing them down. In either case, the statements must be not true. If the story is horrible but true, spreading it may invade the person's privacy, but it is not libel or slander. A physician may maintain that the fact that his or her medical staff privileges were terminated constitutes slander. More commonly, slander claims are based on specific comments about the physician. For example, if the chairperson of the peer review committee characterizes a surgeon as a butcher, this could result in a slander claim.

Most state laws prevent a physician from suing a member of a peer review committee for libel or slander for actions arising out of the peer review process. Unfortunately, many physicians forget that this protection does not extend beyond the formal peer review proceedings. Calling a colleague a ham-handed idiot may be protected in a peer review committee meeting; repeating the remark on the golf course is not protected. Physicians must restrict critical remarks to formal peer review proceedings.

A second state law action is *tortious interference* with the physician's business relationships. This is a special type of anticompetitive action but one that arises under the common law rather than the antitrust laws. The basis of this action is that legitimate competition is encouraged, but it is wrong to destroy a competitor's business with lies or improper interference. For example, assume that there are two surgeons on the medical staff of a hospital. Assume further that this is a small town with only one hospital. If surgeon Y starts a rumor that surgeon X is a drunk and is dangerous to his patients, this is slander. If surgeon Y starts this rumor to improve his or her practice by destroying surgeon X's practice, this is also tortious interference with surgeon X's business relationships.

Another form of tortious interference is to entice business associates not to honor their contractual obligations. For example, a physician group that tries to persuade a hospital to break its exclusive contract with a radiology group could be liable for tortious interference with a contractual relationship. In many states, tortious interference resembles invasion of privacy more than it does defamation. The truth of the accusation used to inflame the physician's business associates is not a defense. Even if the physician does cheat patients, it is improper to use this information to persuade the physician's business associates to change their allegiance. The proper course is to initiate appropriate disciplinary proceedings.

Federal Law Violations

Peer review actions are most commonly contested in federal court under federal laws. This allows the aggrieved physician to escape state law protections for peer review actions. More important, the federal courts do not recognize state laws that protect peer review committee minutes and related records from discovery. Some federal laws also provide for treble damages and attorney's fees if the plaintiff prevails. Without the possibility of this increased recovery, it would not make economic sense to contest most improper peer review actions. Laws that pay a bonus to a successful plaintiff are called *private attorney general laws*. These provisions are intended to encourage private enforcement of the law through civil litigation, saving the government the cost of prosecuting violators in the criminal justice system. Both the antitrust laws and RICO contain these private attorney general provisions.

Due Process Violations

Due process is legal shorthand for a set of notions regarding fairness. Daniel Webster defined this phrase to mean a law that "hears before it condemns, which proceeds on inquiry, and renders judgment only after trial." Courts divide their inquiry into the fairness of the law (substantive due process) and the fairness of the application of the law (procedural due process). Due process is a consideration in peer review in two situations: when the hospital or other entity carrying out the review is a governmental entity and if the review is governed by specific state or federal laws that impose due process requirements.

In governmental entities, such as a city or county hospital, the actions of the peer review committee are imputed to the state. Since the Constitution requires the states to deal fairly with citizens, these entities are required to provide some level of due process. The more severe the deprivation that might result from the state action, the more formal the required procedure. In the medical context, the criminal prosecution of a physician for violating the controlled substances act would require the most comprehensive protection of the physician's rights. If a due process hierarchy were established, it would be the following: (1) criminal law prosecutions, (2) state or federal civil law prosecutions, (3) private civil law actions, (4) actions involving the physician's license, (5) peer review actions at governmental entities, (6) private peer review regulated by state or federal law, (7) private peer review of independent contractors, and (8) private peer review of employee physicians.

With two exceptions, the due process requirements for peer review in private institutions are limited to the contractual provisions of the medical staff bylaws. This is sometimes extended by state law provision, but the major exception is the federal Health Care Quality Improvement Act (HCQIA) of 1986. This law does not set due process requirements. It encourages private institutions to provide due process protections by giving them conditional immunity from state and federal lawsuits over peer review activities if they provide due process described in the law.

What is usually called *due process* is more accurately called *procedural due process:* It refers to fair procedure. Procedural due process refers to the procedure used to conduct the peer review.

The procedure must be fair. Accused physicians must be allowed to present their case to an impartial decision maker. This may include examining the evidence, presenting and questioning witnesses, and appealing the decision to a neutral reviewer. It is not necessary to conduct the proceedings as if they are part of a court proceeding. The process may be informal, as long as it is consistent and the physicians subject to review know the rules.

Substantive due process is an old legal notion that more nearly approximates a lay idea of fairness. Courts use a substantive due process standard to invalidate rules or laws with which they disagree. A peer review example would be a medical staff rule banning osteopaths from the staff. A court might find that this rule, however fairly and uniformly applied, violates substantive due process. This would be an expression of the court's belief that the exclusion of osteopaths would not serve to enhance the quality of the medical care in the hospital. The court would be ruling on the substance of the rule rather than its fair application.

Substantive due process is a consideration in peer review only if the review criteria exclude classes of practitioners without evidence that this exclusion is reasonably related to the quality of medical care. An example of a current controversy is the blanket exclusion of podiatrists from many medical staffs. Podiatry is not a medical specialty, but its practitioners are licensed by the state to provide medical care. These state licensing laws also establish the scope of a professional's practice. In some states, hospital care is within the allowable practice of a podiatrist. In these states, a podiatrist could argue that a governmental hospital that excluded all podiatrists was violating their right to substantive due process. Whether the courts would agree is another question.

THE FEDERAL PEER REVIEW LAW

The HCQIA[8] was passed by Congress in response to the consumer demands for better control of the quality of medical care and lobbying by hospital and medical organizations who said that the potential damages from peer review–related litigation were chilling their ability to conduct proper peer review. At the same time, Congress was concerned with abuses of the peer review process, which were in the news with the district court decision in the *Patrick* case (see Chapter 3). The law they passed provided immunity for damages, but did not provide immunity from lawsuits. Thus an aggrieved physician with sufficient money to pay an attorney without relying on a contingent fee can file a lawsuit against a hospital and the peer review committee members, litigate it to a jury verdict, then let the judge throw out any damages the jury awards. This can be little consolation to the defendants who may have to spend a lot of money defending the lawsuit. (They cannot just ignore it because they have to make sure that the judge finds that they did comply with the act.) In reality, however, eliminating any potential recovery has limited this litigation and has encouraged medical malpractice insurers to include peer review under their policies.

The more important provision of the act may be the National Practitioner Data Bank. This is meant to be a clearinghouse for information on peer review actions, payments in medical malpractice cases, and other information bearing on the competence of physicians. The intent of the databank is to facilitate peer review and to prevent physicians from escaping disciplinary actions by moving to a different state. This information is available to malpractice plaintiffs in only very limited circumstances.

Provisions of the Act

The following are excerpts from the text of the act and explanatory materials. The act is divided into the following sections: Protection from Liability, Adequate Notice and Hearing, Reporting Malpractice Payments, Duty of Hospitals to Obtain Information, Definitions and Reports, and Attorney's Fees.

The need for this law was based on the following congressional findings:

1. The increasing occurrence of medical malpractice and the need to improve the quality of medical care have become nationwide

problems that warrant greater efforts than those that can be undertaken by any individual State.

2. There is a national need to restrict the ability of incompetent physicians to move from State to State without disclosure or discovery of the physician's previous damaging or incompetent performance.
3. This nationwide problem can be remedied through effective professional peer review.
4. The threat of private money damage liability under Federal laws, including treble damage liability under Federal antitrust law, unreasonably discourages physicians from participating in effective professional peer review.
5. There is an overriding national need to provide incentive and protection for physicians engaging in effective professional peer review. (sec. 11101)

Protection from Liability

If a professional review action (as defined in the Act) of a professional review body meets all the standards specified in the Act, then the professional review body, any person acting as a member or staff to the body, any person under a contract or other formal agreement with the body, and any person who participates with or assists the body with respect to the action, shall not be liable in damages under any law of the United States or of any State (or political subdivision thereof) with respect to the action.

This immunity does not extend to civil rights violations, nor does it apply to civil or criminal actions brought by the United States or any Attorney General of a State. There is no immunity for the peer review activities of an institution that does not comply with the reporting requirements of the Act. These protections apply to peer review actions taken on or after October 14, 1989, unless a state chooses, by legislation, to exempt itself from the protections of the Act. (sec. 11111)

Standards for Professional Review Actions

To qualify for immunity, a professional review action must be taken:

1. in the reasonable belief that the action was in the furtherance of quality health care,
2. after a reasonable effort to obtain the facts of the matter,
3. after adequate notice and hearing procedures are afforded to the physician involved or after such other procedures as are fair to the physician under the circumstances, and
4. in the reasonable belief that the action was warranted by the facts known after such reasonable effort to obtain facts and after required notice and hearing

A professional review action shall be presumed to have met the preceding standards unless this presumption is rebutted by a preponderance of the evidence. (sec. 11112)

Definition of Acceptable "Professional Review Action"

The term "professional review action" means an action or recommendation of a professional review body which is taken or made in the conduct of professional review activity, which is based on the competence or professional conduct of an individual physician (which conduct affects or could affect adversely the health or welfare of a patient or patients), and which affects (or may affect) adversely the clinical privileges, or membership in a professional society, of the physician. Such term includes a formal decision of a professional review body not to take an action or make a recommendation described in the previous sentence and also includes professional review activities relating to a professional review action. … [A]n action is not considered to be based on the competence or professional conduct of a physician if the action is primarily based on

(A.) the physician's association, or lack of association, with a professional society or association;

(B.) the physician's fees or the physician's advertising or engaging in other competitive acts intended to solicit or retain business;

(C.) the physician's participation in prepaid group health plans, salaried employment, or any other manner of delivering health services whether on a fee-for-service or other basis;

(D.) a physician's association with, supervision of, delegation of authority to, support for, training of, or participation in a private group practice with, a member or members of a particular class of health care practitioner or professional; or

(E.) any other matter that does not relate to the competence or professional conduct of a physician. (sec. 11151[9])

Limitations of the Act

Nothing in the Act shall be construed as requiring health care entities to provide clinical privileges to any or all classes or types of physicians or other licensed health care practitioners.

This Act only applies to physicians. It does not affect the activities of professional review bodies regarding nurses, other licensed health care practitioners, or other health professionals who are not physicians.

Nothing in this Act shall be construed as affecting in any manner the rights and remedies afforded patients under any provision of Federal or State law to seek redress for any harm or injury suffered as a result of negligent treatment or care by any physician, health care practitioner, or health care entity, or as limiting any defenses or immunities available to any physician, health care practitioner, or health care entity. (sec. 11115)

Adequate Notice and Hearing

A health care entity is deemed to have met the adequate notice and hearing requirement of the Act with respect to a physician if the following conditions are met (or are waived voluntarily by the physician). A professional review body's failure to meet the conditions for notice and hearing described in the Act shall not, in itself, constitute failure to meet the standards of the Act. (sec. 11112)

Notice of a Right to a Hearing

The physician has been given notice stating— that a professional review action has been proposed to be taken against the physician, the reasons for the proposed action, that the physician has the right to request a hearing on the proposed action, any time limit (of not less than 30 days) within which to request such a hearing, and a summary of the rights in the hearing. (sec. 11112)

Notice of the Nature of the Hearing

If a hearing is requested on a timely basis the physician involved must be given notice stating— the place, time, and date, of the hearing, which date shall not be less than 30 days after the date of the notice, and a list of the witnesses (if any) expected to testify at the hearing on behalf of the professional review body. The right to the hearing may be forfeited if the physician fails, without good cause, to appear. (sec. 11112)

Economic Competition

If a hearing is requested on a timely basis—the hearing shall be held (as determined by the health care entity) before an arbitrator mutually acceptable to the physician and the health care entity, before a hearing officer who is appointed by the entity and who is not in direct economic competition with the physician involved, or before a panel of individuals who are appointed by the entity and are not in direct economic competition with the physician involved. (sec. 11112)

Rights in the Hearing

In the hearing the physician involved has the right—to representation by an attorney or other person of the physician's choice, to have a record made of the proceedings, copies of which may be obtained by the physician upon payment of any reasonable charges associated with the preparation thereof, to call, examine, and cross-examine witnesses, to present evidence determined to be relevant by the hearing officer, regardless of its admissibility in a court of law, and to submit a written statement at the close of the hearing. (sec. 11112)

Rights at the Completion of the Hearing

Upon completion of the hearing, the physician involved has the right—to receive the written recommendation of the arbitrator, officer, or panel, including a statement of the basis for the recommendations, and to receive a written decision of the health care entity, including a statement of the basis for the decision. (sec. 11112)

Emergency Procedures

Nothing in the Act shall be construed as—requiring the notice and a hearing where there is no adverse professional review action taken; or in the case of a suspension or restriction of clinical privileges, for a period of not longer than 14 days, during which an investigation is being conducted to determine the need for a professional review action; or precluding an immediate suspension or restriction of clinical privileges, subject to subsequent notice and hearing or other adequate procedures, where the failure to take such an action may result in an imminent danger to the health of any individual. (sec. 11112)

Duty of Hospitals To Obtain Information

It is the duty of each hospital to request from the Secretary (or the agency designated by the Secretary), at the time a physician or licensed health care practitioner applies to be on the medical staff (courtesy or otherwise) of, or for clinical privileges at, the hospital, information reported under this Act concerning the physician or practitioner. Every two years the hospital shall request updated information concerning any physician or such practitioner who is on the medical staff (courtesy or otherwise) of, or has been granted clinical privileges at, the hospital. A hospital may request information at other times.

With respect to a medical malpractice action, a hospital which does not request information respecting a physician or practitioner as required by this Act is presumed to have knowledge of any information reported under this subchapter to the Secretary with respect to the physician or practitioner. Each hospital may rely upon information provided to the hospital under this Act and shall not be held liable for such reliance in the absence of the hospital's knowledge that the information provided was false. (sec. 11135)

Access to Information

The Secretary or the agency designated under the Act shall, upon request, provide information reported under the Act with respect to a physician or other licensed health care practitioner to State licensing boards, to hospitals, and to other health care entities (including Managed care organizations) that have entered (or may be entering) into an employment or affiliation relationship with the physician or practitioner or to which the physician or practitioner has applied for clinical privileges or appointment to the medical staff. (sec. 11137)

Disclosure and Correction of Information

With respect to the information reported to the Secretary (or the agency designated under the Act) respecting a physician or other licensed health care practitioner, the Secretary shall, by regulation, provide for—disclosure of the information, upon request, to the physician or practitioner, and procedures in the case of disputed accuracy of the information. (sec. 11136)

Confidentiality of Information

Information reported pursuant to the Act is considered confidential and shall not be disclosed (other than to the physician or practitioner involved) except with respect to professional review activity, as necessary to carry out the provisions of the Act or in accordance with regulations of the Secretary promulgated pursuant to the Act. Nothing in this subsection shall prevent the disclosure of such information by a party which is otherwise authorized, under applicable State law, to make such disclosure. Information that is in a form that does not permit the identification of any particular health care entity, physician, other health care practitioner, or patient shall not be considered confidential.

Any person who improperly discloses this information shall be subject to a civil money penalty of not more than $10,000 for each such violation involved. Information provided under the Act is intended to be used solely with respect to activities in the furtherance of the quality of health care. (sec. 11137)

National Practitioner Data Bank

Each entity (including an insurance company) which makes payment under a policy of insurance, self-insurance, or otherwise in settlement (or partial settlement) of, or in satisfaction of a judgment in, a medical malpractice action or claim shall report, in accordance with this Act [discussed below], information respecting the payment and circumstances thereof. (sec. 11131) In interpreting information reported under this subchapter [of the act], a payment in settlement of a medical malpractice action or claim shall not be construed as creating a presumption that medical malpractice has occurred. (sec. 11137)

The information to be reported under includes—the name of any physician or licensed health care practitioner for whose benefit the payment is made, the amount of the payment, the name (if known) of any hospital with which the physician or practitioner is affiliated or associated, a description of the acts or omissions and injuries or illnesses upon which the action or claim was based, and such other information as the Secretary determines is required for appropriate interpretation of information reported under this section.

Any entity that fails to report information on a payment required to be reported under this section shall be subject to a civil money penalty of not more than $10,000 for each such payment involved. (sec. 11131)

Reporting by Boards of Medical Examiners

Each Board of Medical Examiners which revokes or suspends (or otherwise restricts) a physician's license or censures, reprimands, or places on probation a physician, for reasons relating to the physician's professional competence or professional conduct, or to which a physician's license is surrendered, shall report, the name of the physician involved, a description of the acts or omissions or other reasons (if known) for the revocation, suspension, or surrender of license, and such other information respecting the circumstances of the action or surrender as the Secretary deems appropriate.

If, after notice of noncompliance and providing opportunity to correct noncompliance, the Secretary determines that a Board of Medical Examin-

ers has failed to report information in accordance with the Act, the Secretary shall designate another qualified entity for the reporting of the required information. (sec. 11132)

Reporting by Health Care Entities

Each health care entity which takes a professional review action that adversely affects the clinical privileges of a physician for a period longer than 30 days shall report to the Board of Medical Examiners. This duty also applies when the health care entity accepts the surrender of clinical privileges of a physician while the physician is under an investigation by the entity relating to possible incompetence or improper professional conduct, or in return for not conducting such an investigation or proceeding; or in the case of such an entity which is a professional society, takes a professional review action which adversely affects the membership of a physician in the society.

The information to be reported is—the name of the physician or practitioner involved, a description of the acts or omissions or other reasons for the action or, if known, for the surrender, and such other information respecting the circumstances of the action or surrender as the Secretary deems appropriate.

A health care entity that fails substantially to meet the reporting requirements of this Act shall lose the protections of section otherwise provided by the Act. This suspension of immunity does not become effective until the Secretary publishes the name of the entity as provided in the Act. (sec. 11133)

Form of Reporting

The information required to be reported under the Act shall be reported regularly (but not less often than monthly) and in such form and manner as the Secretary prescribes. Such information shall first be required to be reported on a date (not later than one year after November 14, 1986) specified by the Secretary. The information required to be reported under the Act shall be reported to the Secretary, or, in the Secretary's discretion, to an appropriate private or public agency which has made suitable arrangements with the

Secretary with respect to receipt, storage, protection of confidentiality, and dissemination of the information under this subchapter.

Information about malpractice lawsuit settlement payments or adverse verdicts shall also be reported to the appropriate State licensing board (or boards) in the State in which the medical malpractice claim arose. (sec. 11134)

Protection for Persons Providing Information

Notwithstanding any other provision of law, no person (whether as a witness or otherwise) providing information to a professional review body regarding the competence or professional conduct of a physician shall be held, by reason of having provided such information, to be liable in damages under any law of the United States or of any State (or political subdivision thereof) unless such information is false and the person providing it knew that such information was false. (sec. 11111)

Definitions and Reports (Sec. 11151)

1. *"adversely affecting"*—The term "adversely affecting" includes reducing, restricting, suspending, revoking, denying, or failing to renew clinical privileges or membership in a health care entity.
2. *"Board of Medical Examiners"*—The term "Board of Medical Examiners" includes a body comparable to such a Board (as determined by the State) with responsibility for the licensing of physicians and also includes a subdivision of such a Board or body.
3. *"clinical privileges"*—The term "clinical privileges" includes privileges, membership on the medical staff, and the other circumstances pertaining to the furnishing of medical care under which a physician or other licensed health care practitioner is permitted to furnish such care by a health care entity.
4. *"health care entity"*—The term "health care entity" means—a hospital that is licensed to provide health care services by the State in

which it is located, an entity (including a health maintenance organization or group medical practice) that provides health care services and that follows a formal peer review process for the purpose of furthering quality health care, a professional society (or committee thereof) of physicians or other licensed health care practitioners that follows a formal peer review process for the purpose of furthering quality health care. The term "health care entity" does not include a professional society (or committee thereof) if, within the previous 5 years, the society has been found by the Federal Trade Commission or any court to have engaged in any anti-competitive practice which had the effect of restricting the practice of licensed health care practitioners.
5. *"hospital"*—The term "hospital" means an institution which—is primarily engaged in providing, by or under the supervision of physicians, to inpatients (A) diagnostic services and therapeutic services for medical diagnosis, treatment, and care of injured, disabled, or sick persons, or (B) rehabilitation services for the rehabilitation of injured, disabled, or sick persons. In the case of an institution in any State in which State or applicable local law provides for the licensing of hospitals, (A) is licensed pursuant to such law or (B) is approved, by the agency of such State or locality responsible for licensing hospitals, as meeting the standards established for such licensing. (42 USCA sec. 1395x(e)(1)&(7))
6. *"licensed health care practitioner"*—The terms "licensed health care practitioner" and "practitioner" mean, with respect to a State, an individual (other than a physician) who is licensed or otherwise authorized by the State to provide health care services.
7. *"medical malpractice actions or claim"*—The term "medical malpractice action or claim" means a written claim or demand for payment based on a health care provider's furnishing (or failure to furnish) health care services, and includes the filing of a cause

of action, based on the law of tort, brought in any court of any State or the United States seeking monetary damages.

8. *"physician"*—The term "physician" means a doctor of medicine or osteopathy or a doctor of dental surgery or medical dentistry legally authorized to practice medicine and surgery or dentistry by a State (or any individual who, without authority holds himself or herself out to be so authorized).

9. *"professional review activity"*—The term "professional review activity" means an activity of a health care entity with respect to an individual physician—to determine whether the physician may have clinical privileges with respect to, or membership in, the entity, to determine the scope or conditions of such privileges or membership, or to change or modify such privileges or membership.

10. *"professional review body"*—The term "professional review body" means a health care entity and the governing body or any committee of a health care entity which conducts professional review activity, and includes any committee of the medical staff of such an entity when assisting the governing body in a professional review activity.

11. *"Secretary"*—The term "Secretary" means the Secretary of Health and Human Services.

12. *"State"*—The term "State" means the 50 States, the District of Columbia, Puerto Rico, the Virgin Islands, Guam, American Samoa, and the Northern Mariana Islands.

13. *"State Licensing Board"*—The term "State licensing board" means, with respect to a physician or health care provider in a State, the agency of the State which is primarily responsible for the licensing of the physician or provider to furnish health care services.

Attorney's Fees

In any suit brought against a defendant, if the court finds that the defendant has met the standards set forth in the Act, and the defendant substantially prevails, the court shall, at the conclusion of the action, award to the defendant the cost of the suit attributable to such claim, including a reasonable attorney's fee, if the claim, or the claimant's conduct during the litigation of the claim, was frivolous, unreasonable, without foundation, or in bad faith. A defendant shall not be considered to have substantially prevailed when the plaintiff obtains an award for damages or permanent injunctive or declaratory relief. (sec. 11113)

GOOD FAITH OR OBJECTIVE STANDARD?

There have been many cases construing the meaning of the HCQIA since its passage. There has been nothing surprising in these cases, the act is clearly written and has few ambiguities. The main issue has been the standard to judge the intent of the peer reviewers. Because the statutory title of the act is Chapter 117, Encouraging Good Faith Professional Review Activities, it was initially assumed only peer review done in good faith would be entitled to immunity under the act. The courts have found that the actual text of the act does not use a good faith standard, but an objective standard. This means that if the reviewing committee follows the procedures of the act, they are immune from damages even if they conducted the peer review in bad faith. Conversely, if the procedure is sufficiently flawed, it will not come under the act even if conducted in good faith.. The objective standard makes it much easier to know that a peer review process will be protected, even if some members of the committee have hidden motives.

The act's immunity is important if the jury finds that the peer review action was taken in the reasonable belief that it would further the quality of medical care but nonetheless violated a federal law. This might help when physicians on the peer review committee violate other laws but conduct the peer review properly. For example, assume that the physicians on the committee were engaged in anticompetitive activities that do not concern the practice of the physician they are reviewing. If they conduct a proper peer review activity, the act might prevent an aggrieved physician from alleging that the peer review action was tainted by the racketeering activities.

A more interesting question is whether the act would allow peer review activities designed to improve medical care by reducing competition. For example, specialty surgeons must get several cases of an unusual condition to keep their skills keen. If competition between two surgeons denies both the necessary level of cases to maintain their skills, this will adversely affect the quality of medical care in the community. It might be appropriate for a peer review committee to consider the adequacy of the patient base when granting or renewing a specialist's hospital privileges. The act, however, defines these considerations as per se improper:

"Action is not considered to be based on the competence or professional conduct of a physician if the action is primarily based on— ... [any] matter that does not relate to the competence or professional conduct of a physician."

Thus, if the specialty surgeons were still competent (before competition reduced their skills), the act seems to forbid peer review actions necessary to maintain that competence. Once the competition had reduced the surgeons' competence, the committee might be able to act to reduce competition. At this point, however, it might be impossible to justify penalizing one surgeon to the benefit of the other. This also may affect the general issue of the hospital's using medical staff privilege decisions to shape the package of services it offers.

Potential Adverse Impacts

One adverse impact of the act is that it is now very difficult to contest an improper peer review action. Unless the physician can assert grounds that are not covered by the act, such as sexual or racial discrimination, or can rebut the presumption that the review was proper if it the committee followed the proper procedures, there is little hope of winning damages in a peer review contest. Physicians are cautioned to keep medical staff privileges at more than one hospital so that they can continue practicing if one facility takes an improper peer review action against them. (Even this may not help—the report to the National Practitioner Data Bank can make it impossible to get privileges anywhere.)

Although physicians see the act as protecting them from lawsuits by the disgruntled victims of peer review, this may not be the act's major effect. The act shows the disparate agendas of its drafters. The central intent of Congress was to mandate a national clearinghouse for peer review actions and medical malpractice payments. This was the quid pro quo for granting the physicians' request that they get immunity for engaging in peer review. Unfortunately, many nonphysician groups, including nonscientific providers such as chiropractors, were successful in excluding from immunity the review of physicians who improperly delegate authority to nonphysician providers.

The act will make it more difficult to curb the inappropriate delegation of authority to nonphysician personnel as MCOs and hospitals attempt to use nonprofessional staff to care for patients.[10] This is an understandable, though not necessarily correct, response to cost containment. This will be harder to attack because the act defines as improper any peer review activities based on "a physician's association with, supervision of, delegation of authority to ... a member or members of a particular class of health care practitioner or professional." This provision will make it more difficult to discipline physicians who allow nurses, nonphysician practitioners, or others to practice medicine on their licenses. This practice can have a devastating effect on the quality of patient care, yet the act seems to preclude it as a ground for peer review if that peer review is to get federal immunity. This is aggravated in states that have uncritically incorporated the federal provisions into their own peer review laws.

The Problem of Bias

Until recently, the definition of a peer for peer review purpose was based on the historical notion of a peer. A "jury of one's peers" once meant a jury composed of persons who personally knew both the defendant and the community. These peers were assumed to be better able to determine the truth of the case than persons who did not know the participants and their history. The legal system gradually rejected the use of knowledgeable peers because of the problem of bias. The courts shifted their concern with the jurors' knowing the facts of the case to a concern that the jurors would let their prejudices for or against the defendant affect their ruling. Contemporary court rules allow the exclusion of jurors who know the parties or any facts of the case. Concern for bias is forcing peer review committees to make the same move to the uninvolved peer.

Bias has always been an issue in peer review. Until the Congress passed the Civil Rights and the Equal Employment Opportunity Acts, women and blacks were routinely excluded from medical staffs. It would be naive to assume that such forbidden criteria have been eliminated from all peer review decisions. Physicians with unconventional practice styles or uncollegial personalities pose a difficult problem of balance. Whereas it is unreasonable to expect every physician to behave in the same way, unconventional practice styles or personality problems may be evidence of substance abuse or psychological impairment. Peer review activities should not be conducted by physicians with outspoken biases against either the individual being reviewed or the aspects of the individual's practice that are being reviewed.

Peer review has always had an economic component. Hospital medical staffs tried to balance the needs of the community with the economic interests of the existing staff. Sometimes this meant preventing new physicians from starting practice in the community, but as often it resulted in efforts to encourage physicians in needed specialties to set up practice in the community. As physicians and hospitals have been forced into competition, economic biases have become a major confounding factor in peer review activities.

In most communities, physicians practicing the same specialty are either in business together or are competitors. In large cities, physicians and hospitals compete with their geographic neighbors. This competition is exacerbated by the blurring of specialty lines. As the number of physicians in a community increases, subspecialists often practice general medicine to supplement their incomes. General medicine physicians and others cross specialty lines to offer lucrative procedures such as liposuction. The act's requirement that hearing officers and panels must not be in "direct economic competition with the physician involved" seems to preclude traditional peer review committees composed of physicians in the same specialty or practice area who practice in the same community as the physician under review.

Conducting the Review

The act states that its notice and hearing requirements are not the only way to provide adequate due process for peer review. The courts, however, will tend to regard these statutory requirements as minimums. These requirements were developed in court cases against governmental health care institutions. The effect of the act is to require private institutions seeking immunity to comply with the same due process requirements as public institutions. Since most private hospitals already meet this standard, this should not require substantial changes in hospital procedures. It will require other health care entities, such as private clinics, to use formal, hospital-style proceedings rather than the informal procedures that are the norm in these environments.

The act only covers peer review activities carried out in a reasonable belief that they will improve the quality of medical care. The best evidence of a proper review decision is a written set of standards that explain what is expected of a physician practicing in the entity. These should be detailed and straightforward. They must be intelligible to jurors and physicians, as well as to attorneys. For hospitals, most of the relevant standards are already in force as part of the Joint Commission requirements. The problem is that few physicians are familiar with these requirements. These standards must be made available to members, and prospective members, of the medical staff. Adherence to these standards must be an explicit condition of medical staff privileges.

It is critical that the health care entity enforce all standards uniformly. There cannot be a double standard based on economic performance or personal relationships. If, for example, delinquent chart completion is used as a ground for the termination of staff privileges, then the hospital must ensure that all members of the medical staff complete their charts on time. Disparate enforcement of standards is less defensible than having no standards.

The only way to provide even-handed enforcement of standards is to shift from exception-oriented review to review based on statistical and population analysis. In some areas, such as completion of medical records, the hospital keeps data on every physician. The data can be compiled into profiles to establish the norm and standard deviations for chart completion. Physicians exceeding a set deviation would be flagged and counseled. If their performance did not improve, they would be terminated. In other areas, such as surgical complications, indirect measures are much less effective. These require that a random sample of charts from every physician be reviewed for problems.

DOCUMENTING THE PEER REVIEW PROCESS

The key to preventing litigation over peer review proceedings is careful documentation of a well-organized, exemplary process. It is not enough for an individual member to act properly. Every member of the committee must be above reproach because it is the committee that acts and will be sued. The hospital bylaws should require each committee member to disclose all personal and business dealings with members of the medical staff who might come before the committee. This information can be protected from general disclosure, but it should be available to the other committee members. The committee members should demand that the hospital or other institution indemnify them against any losses related to the peer review activities.

Defensible peer review depends on creating a clear record of the alleged deviations from standard practice. The record also should demonstrate that none of the reviewers was an economic competitor of the physician being reviewed. If it is impossible to assemble a review panel without financial conflicts, the committee should employ an outside reviewer or consulting service. Given the reality of medical business practices, it would seem necessary to use outside reviewers in all but the largest hospitals. Even in these facilities, subspecialty care will require outside review.

This record must be specific as to the facts of each incident, how these facts deviate from accepted practice, and the actual or potential harm resulting from this deviation from accepted standards. If there is no demonstrable harm or potential harm from the deviation, the deviation does not affect patient care and is not a proper basis for an adverse peer review action. The record should be objective and should be free of personal attacks on the physician in question. Copies of patient records should be attached and annotated as necessary to establish the validity of the facts in question. All complaints by patients and other health care providers should be investigated and incorporated into the record.

The record should demonstrate that the physician was warned about the deviations from standard practice and was given an opportunity to correct these deviations. These warnings should be communicated in writing, with the physician asked to respond in writing. If the nature of the deviation was such as to necessitate immediate suspension of medical staff privileges, this should be documented. The arrangements to care for the suspended physician's patients should be discussed, as should patients' reaction to their physician's suspension. Emergency suspensions are merited only when there has been little delay between the institution's learning of the problem and its taking action against the physician. It is impossible to defend an emergency action taken after months of discussion.

DESELECTION

Peer review and hospital privileges, at least in the past, had a critical check and balance—the hospital did need physicians to admit and care for patients, and in many communities the number of physicians was limited, relative to the number of hospitals. The federal antikickback laws, at least in theory, prevented the hospitals from just bribing physicians to admit to the hospital. Since the hospitals were competing for patients, the more physicians on staff the greater the chance that a given patient would be admitted to the hospital.

MCO Physician Market Strategy

MCOs face different incentives and a different market for physicians. Whereas hospitals have to compete for patients indirectly by persuading physicians to admit them, MCOs compete for patients directly by convincing employers to lock their employees into the MCOs plan. The MCO controls directly who can treat the patients and what can be done to them. The MCO needs some physicians to care for the patients, and many MCOs have obtained these physicians by buying their practices. Since MCOs reduce the care that patients receive, an MCO-dominated community needs relatively fewer physicians than it did when the patients had traditional health insurance. This ensures a surplus of physicians and limits the physicians' bargaining power (see Chapter 10). The objective of the MCO is to reduce the number of physicians to the minimum necessary to care for the patients, and to ensure that the physicians it retains deliver the most cost-effective/cheap care.[11]

The strategy is simple: hire or contract with more physicians than you need, then do not renew the contracts of the ones that spend the most resources on patient care. As long as the MCO–physician contracts are terminable at will, the physicians have no recourse. Any physicians who resist cost-cutting strategies that they believe compromise patient care are dropped from the plan. Their only protections are state laws such as the "any willing provider" law that forces MCOs to deal with all physicians in the community.

Due Process and HCQIA

Some physicians have sued plans for deselection, claiming their due process rights were denied because they were not given the same procedure as would be applicable in medical staff peer review proceedings. These cases failed because nongovernmental hospitals do not have to provide due process as a matter of right. They are only required to provide whatever due process they contract for in their medical staff bylaws. Hospitals provide extensive due process because they want to be able to claim immunity under HCQIA. MCOs, as insurers, are not subject to antitrust lawsuits, and are much harder to attack under the other theories used to attack peer review determinations. This means that they do not need the immunity provided by HCQIA so they have no need to provide the due process necessary to qualify for its protections. The courts also rejected claims that HCQIA itself created a cause of action for physicians denied due process, holding that it has no purpose beyond providing immunity for properly conducting peer review.

Public Policy Claims

Most states have some kind of doctrine to prevent employers from firing employees or terminating contractors when doing so would violate public policy. This includes any firings that would violate other statutes, such as the civil rights laws. It also includes situations where the employee was fired for trying to prevent the employer from breaking the law or endangering the public health. The protections are generally very limited and few employees can establish the facts necessary to use them. Some physicians have used this doctrine to attack deselection that is based on refusing to do cost-cutting that the physicians believe would injure patients, or when the plan just cuts the most expensive physicians, with no efforts to determine if their expenditures were valid.

To date, there has only been one successful case, *Harper v. Healthsource*.[12] Dr. Harper alleged that he was terminated because the plan resisted his efforts to provide proper patient care. The court found that New Hampshire did not allow terminations that violated public policy, and that various state regulations established that there was a policy protecting the health of MCO patients. The court held the following:

> Harper is entitled to proceed upon the merits of his claim that Healthsource's decision to terminate its relationship with him was made in bad faith or violated public policy. In his petition, he asserted that his efforts to correct errors made in patient records played a role in Healthsource's decision, and he argues on appeal that public policy should condemn "an insurance company which, upon receipt of a letter from a medical provider asking for assistance in correcting ... records of patient treatments, terminates the doctor's services."[13]

Subsequent courts have not adopted *Harper*, limiting it to the special circumstances of New Hampshire law.[14] In the absence of specific state laws or regulations, there are few limits on the rights of MCOs to terminate physicians' contracts without judicial review. At this time, a physician's only protection will have to be in the terms of the contract with the MCO and any due process that is provided as part of that contract. There are many legal challenges to the unfettered power of MCOs in progress, however it is likely that public concern with the quality of MCO care will force changes in this area.

REFERENCES

1. *LeMasters v. Christ Hosp.*, 791 F. Supp. 188 (S.D. Ohio 1991).
2. *Weiss v. York Hosp.*, 745 F.2d 786 (3d. Cir. 1984).
3. *Id.* at 815.
4. *Id.* at 813.
5. *Quinn v. Kent Gen'l Hosp.*, 716 F. Supp. 1226 (1985).
6. *Id.* at 1242.
7. *Trustees of Dartmouth College v. Woodward*, 17 U.S. 518 (1819).
8. 42 U.S.C.A. §§ 11101, et seq.
9. *Wayne v. Genesis Med. Ctr.*, 140 F.3d 1145 (8th Cir. [Iowa] 1998).
10. Adelman SH. Ways that hospitals control their physicians. *Am Med News*. 1991;34:26.
11. Blum JD. The evolution of physician credentialing into managed care selective contracting. *Am J Law Med*. 1996;22:173–203.
12. *Harper v. Healthsource N.H., Inc.*, 674 A.2d 962 (N.H. 1996).
13. *Id.* at 967.
14. *Sammarco v. Anthem Ins. Co.*, 1998 WL 804198 (Ohio App. 1 Dist. 1998).

SUGGESTED READINGS

Ankney RN, Coil JA. Residents' knowledge of the National Practitioner Data Bank. *Acad Med*. 1994;69:243.

Ankney RN, Coil JA, Kolff J, Esper E. NPDB: what physicians don't know can hurt them. *Pa Med*. 1994;97:10–14.

Ankney RN, Coil JA, Kolff J, Esper E. Physician understanding of the National Practitioner Data Bank. *South Med J*. 1995;88:200–203.

Bok S. Impaired physicians: what should patients know? *Camb Q Healthc Ethics*. 1993;2:331–340.

Brouillette JN. Bilateral deselection. *J Fla Med Assoc*. 1995;82:423.

Cohen RJ. Managed care and the physician–patient relationship: implications for peer review. *Md Med J*. 1997;46:91–93.

Corsino BV, Morrow DH, Wallace CJ. Quality improvement and substance abuse: rethinking impaired provider policies. *Am J Med Qual*. 1996;11:94–99.

Couch JB, Kauffman A, Merry M. The value of external peer review after the Health Care Quality Improvement Act and Patrick v. Burget. *Qual Assur Util Rev*. 1989;4:86–88.

Crespo RA. Physician deselection: what it means for you. *Wis Med J*. 1997;96:58–62.

Faunce TA, Rudge B. Deaths on the table: proposal for an international convention on the investigation and prevention of anaesthetic mortality. *Med Law*. 1998;17:31–54.

Freeman J. Peer review is critical to quality health care. *Iowa Med*. 1997;87:357.

Gilbert ML. The National Practitioner Data Bank: is big brother watching you? *J Colo Dent Assoc*. 1998;77:30–31.

Graddy B. Self-query and the National Practitioner Data Bank: issues of confidentiality. *Tex Med*. 1993;89:54–55.

Graddy B. TMA takes aim against deselection. *Tex Med*. 1994;90:14–17.

Granville RL, Flannery FT. The National Practitioner Data Bank: an overview for the emergency physician. *Emerg Med Clin North Am*. 1993;11:923–931.

Hay CR. Health Care Quality Improvement Act of 1986: what physicians need to know about the Act. *Kans Med*. 1989;90:239–240, 242, 244.

Heffernan M. The Health Care Quality Improvement Act of

1986 and the National Practitioner Data Bank: the controversy over practitioner privacy versus public access. *Bull Med Libr Assoc.* 1996;84:263–269.

Heim SW, Stevermer JJ. Do peer review organizations improve quality of care in AMI? *J Fam Pract.* 1998;47:95.

Horner SL. The Health Care Quality Improvement Act of 1986: its history, provisions, applications and implications. *Am J Law Med.* 1990;16:455–498.

Hotko B, Van Dyke D. Peer review: strengthening leadership skills. *Nurs Manage.* 1998;29:41, 44.

Kennedy KE. Peer review: federal and state protection. *Minn Med.* 1996;79:52–54.

King JY. Practice guidelines and medical malpractice litigation. *Med Law.* 1997;16:29–39.

Levine RD, Sugarman M, Schiller W, Weinshel S, Lehning EJ, Lagasse RS. The effect of group discussion on interrater reliability of structured peer review. *Anesthesiology.* 1998;89:507–515.

Liner RS. Physician deselection: the dynamics of a new threat to the physician– patient relationship. *Am J Law Med.* 1997;23:511–537.

Lingle EA, Frazier DS. Physician defamation: candor rarely results in liability. *J Leg Med.* 1997;18:521–538.

Maguire D. Ten commandments of peer review. *Neonatal Netw.* 1998;17:63–67.

Martz EW. Confidentiality and control. *Del Med J.* 1997;69:157–159.

Martz EW. National Practitioner Data Bank. *Del Med J.* 1995;67:492–493.

Meadow W, Bell A, Lantos J. Physicians' experience with allegations of medical malpractice in the neonatal intensive care unit. *Pediatrics.* 1997;99:E10.

Metter EJ, Granville RL, Kussman MJ. The effect of threshold amounts for reporting malpractice payments to the National Practitioner Data Bank: analysis using the closed claims data base of the Office of the Assistant Secretary of Defense (Health Affairs). *Mil Med.* 1997;162:257–261.

Montague J. Breaking the bank? MDs say NPDB needs screening. *Hosp Health Netw.* 1993;67:51.

Montague J. Should the public have access to the National Practitioner Data Bank? *Hosp Health Netw.* 1994;68:52, 54–56.

Neighbor WE, Baldwin LM, West PA, Hart LG. Rural hospitals' experience with the National Practitioner Data Bank. *Am J Public Health.* 1997;87:663–666.

Ortolon K. Deselection, round two: TMA takes due process fight with managed care organizations to US Congress. *Tex Med.* 1994;90:20–22.

Oshel RE, Croft T, Rodak J Jr. The National Practitioner Data Bank: the first 4 years. *Public Health Rep.* 1995;110:383–394.

Pallesen KS. The Health Care Quality Improvement Act of 1986: National Practitioner Data Bank. *Nebr Med J.* 1991;76:353–372.

Pugsley SC. Implementing the Health Care Quality Improvement Act. *Leg Med.* 1990:217–242.

Rifkin AM, Evans GE, Hall GD. Antitrust's recent attack on the peer review practitioner: is the Health Care Quality Improvement Act a viable remedy? *Md Med J.* 1990;39:21–32.

Ronai SE. Physician deselection by managed care plans: due process guidance for doctors terminated without cause. *Conn Med.* 1997;61:483–486.

Ronai SE, Meng ME. Civil liability of peer review participants: Patrick v. Burget and the Health Care Quality Improvement Act of 1986. *Conn Med.* 1988;52:537–540.

Sandrick K. Two years and running: the National Practitioner Data Bank begins to roll, but issues remain. *Hospitals.* 1993;67:44–45.

Scott C. Should physicians have a voice in insurer settlements of medical malpractice claims? *J Fla Med Assoc.* 1993;80:633–666.

Segall SE, Pearl W. Should due process be part of hospital peer review? *South Med J.* 1993;86:368–369.

Setness PA. What do you know about the NPDB? *Postgrad Med.* 1996;100:15–16, 21–22.

Sfikas PM. Peer review and antitrust. *J Am Dent Assoc.* 1997;128:496–498.

Sheets V. Why disciplinary databanks? Why the National Practitioner Data Bank (NPDB)? *Issues.* 1996;17:10–11.

Smart CM III. The peer review privilege: what documents are protected from discovery in litigation. *Mo Med.* 1998;95:205–206.

Smith MA, Atherly AJ, Kane RL, Pacala JT. Peer review of the quality of care: reliability and sources of variability for outcome and process assessments. *JAMA.* 1997;278:1573–1578.

Snelson E. Quality assurance implications of federal peer review laws: the Health Care Quality Improvement Act and the National Practitioner Data Bank. *Qual Assur Util Rev.* 1992;7:2–11.

Snelson EA. Peer review, hearing requirements, and antitrust: maximizing federal Health Care Quality Improvement Act compliance and immunity. *J Med Assoc Ga.* 1992;81:495–497.

Snelson EA. Physicians under surveillance: the National Practitioner Data Bank. *Minn Med.* 1993;76:31–33.

Stern DF. Handling clinical incidents. *Nurs Manage.* 1997;28:48B–48C, 48G–48H.

Todd JS. National Practitioner Data Bank: just numbers or knowledge? *Public Health Rep.* 1995;110:377–378.

Wolfe SM. Congress should open the National Practitioner Data Bank to all. *Public Health Rep.* 1995;110:378–379.

Wolfe SM. Questionable doctors—lots of them! *Revolution.* 1996;6:20–22, 85.

Wyden R. Transparency: a prescription against malpractice. *Public Health Rep.* 1995;110:380–381.

Yessian MR. Putting the controversy aside, how is the Data Bank doing? *Public Health Rep.* 1995;110:381–382.

CHAPTER 12

Public Health and Communicable Disease Control

HIGHLIGHTS

- The Constitution grants the states broad powers to protect the public health.
- Public health puts the safety of society above the rights of the individual.
- All health care practitioners have duties under the public health laws.
- Disease reporting is critical for controlling existing and emerging infectious diseases.
- Health care practitioners have many statutory reporting duties.

INTRODUCTION

From Pasteur's and Koch's discoveries in the 1800s through the conquering of polio in the 1950s, public health was one of the most prominent and powerful medical specialties. All physicians received training in basic public health and public health officers were respected members of the community. With the advent of magic bullets, effective vaccines, and widespread sanitation, public health fell into disrepute. When the National Institutes of Health studied the public health system in the United States, it found a system in chaos, with little consistent professional leadership.[1]

In retrospect, it is clear that the disorganized public health system hastened the spread of HIV/ AIDS in the United States. The advent of new emerging infectious diseases and the resurgence of old foes such as tuberculosis and foodborne illness has made public health newsworthy again. With the realization that bacterial and viral resistance is bringing the golden age of antimicrobials to an end, public health is again becoming a concern for every health care practitioner. The internist who diagnoses salmonellosis in a patient, the emergency room physician who suspects that a child may have been abused, and the family practitioner who signs a death certificate, wear the cloak of public health in these endeavors. Many health care practitioners are unaware of these public health responsibilities. This chapter introduces the basic legal and medical issues in public health that every health care practitioner should know.[2]

Source: Portions of this chapter adapted from E.P. Richards, The Jurisprudence of Prevention: Society's Right of Self-defense against Dangerous Individuals, *Hast Const L Q*, Vol. 16, p. 329 © 1989 E.P. Richards.

THE HISTORY OF PUBLIC HEALTH AUTHORITY

Sanitary laws were the first public health measures. An early record of these laws is in Leviticus 11:16. The Romans developed the discipline of sanitary engineering—building water works and sewers. The next advance in public health was the quarantine of disease-carrying ships and their passengers, instituted in Eurpope in response to the diseases brought back by the Crusaders. The word *quarantine* derives from *quadraginta,* meaning "forty." It was first used between 1377 and 1403 when Venice and the other chief maritime cities of the Mediterranean adopted and enforced a forty-day detention for all vessels entering their ports.[3]

The English statutory and common law recognized the right of the state to quarantine and limit the movement of plague carriers. Blackstone observed that disobeying quarantine orders merited severe punishments, including death. The American colonies adopted the English laws on the control of diseases. When the Constitution was written, public health power was left to the states, because it was considered fundamental to the state's police power:

> It is a well-recognized principle that it is one of the first duties of a state to take all necessary steps for the promotion and protection of the health and comfort of its inhabitants. The preservation of the public health is universally conceded to be one of the duties devolving upon the state as a sovereignty, and whatever reasonably tends to preserve the public health is a subject upon which the legislature, within its police power, may take action.[4]

Soon after the Constitution was ratified, the states were forced to exercise their police power to combat an epidemic of yellow fever that raged in New York and Philadelphia. The flavor of that period was later captured in an argument before the Supreme Court:

> For ten years prior, the yellow-fever had raged almost annually in the city, and annual laws were passed to resist it. The wit of man was exhausted, but in vain. Never did the pestilence rage more violently than in the summer of 1798. The State was in despair. The rising hopes of the metropolis began to fade. The opinion was gaining ground, that the cause of this annual disease was indigenous, and that all precautions against its importation were useless. But the leading spirits of that day were unwilling to give up the city without a final desperate effort. The havoc in the summer of 1798 is represented as terrific. The whole country was roused. A cordon sanitaire was thrown around the city. Governor Mifflin of Pennsylvania proclaimed a non-intercourse between New York and Philadelphia.[5]

The extreme nature of the actions, including isolating the federal government (sitting in Philadelphia at the time), was considered an appropriate response to the threat of yellow fever. The terrifying nature of these early epidemics predisposed the courts to grant public health authorities a free hand in their attempts to prevent the spread of disease:

> Every state has acknowledged power to pass, and enforce quarantine, health, and inspection laws, to prevent the introduction of disease, pestilence, or unwholesome provisions; such laws interfere with no powers of Congress or treaty stipulations; they relate to internal police, and are subjects of domestic regulation within each state, over which no authority can be exercised by any power under the Constitution, save by requiring the consent of Congress to the imposition of duties on exports and imports, and their payment into the treasury of the United States.[6]

Few cases have challenged the constitutionality of state actions taken to protect citizens from a communicable disease. The only successful attacks on such exercises of state police power have been based on federal preemption of state laws that restricted interstate commerce or on laws that were mere shams for racial discrimination. Yet even interference with interstate commerce is not always fatal to health regulations. If a state regulation is substantially related to health and safety, the Supreme Court will uphold it. This is true even if the regulation interferes with interstate commerce, such as would result from a cordon sanitaria in which all travel is forbidden. From vaccinations to quarantines, laws enacted to protect society have been upheld even when they force individuals to sacrifice liberty and privacy.

LEGAL STANDARDS FOR PUBLIC HEALTH AUTHORITY

As courts have reviewed the constitutionality of laws that ostensibly protect the public health and safety, they have developed consistent standards for defining an acceptable exercise of public health authority. The courts have allowed substantial restrictions on individual liberty as part of public health laws that seek to prevent future harm rather than to punish past actions. If a court finds that a law is directed at prevention rather than punishment, it will allow the state to do the following:

1. Rely on expert decision makers.
2. Provide for judicial review through habeas corpus proceedings rather than through prerestriction hearings.
3. Use a scientific, rather than a criminal law, standard of proof.

Although a state's power to protect the public health is broad, it is restricted to preventing future harm. The state may not punish a person under its public health police powers. Administrative deprivations of liberty are tolerated only if their purpose is not punitive. The distinction between allowable restrictions and forbidden punishment is sometimes finely drawn. For example, being put in the community pesthouse was seldom a pleasant prospect, and with the closing of pesthouses, public health restrictions have frequently been carried out in prisons and jails. In one such case, the court rejected the petitioner's claim that he was being punished without due process, concluding, "While it is true that physical facilities constituting part of the penitentiary equipment are utilized, interned persons are in no sense confined in the penitentiary, and are not subject to the peculiar obloquy which attends such confinement."[7]

Expert Decision Makers

Public health jurisprudence is based on a deference to scientific decision making. This deference may be expressed by incorporating scientific standards into legislation or by delegating the right to make public health decisions to boards of health or individual health officers who are skilled in the science of public health. This deference is illustrated in the best known of the traditional public health cases, *Jacobson v. Massachusetts*,[8] in which the scientific basis of a Massachusetts law requiring vaccination for smallpox was challenged.

Mr. Jacobson believed that the scientific basis for vaccination was unsound and that he would suffer if he was vaccinated. The Massachusetts Supreme Court found the statute consistent with the Massachusetts state constitution, and Jacobson appealed to the U.S. Supreme Court. The Court first ruled that being subject to vaccination was the price for living in society. The Court then considered Jacobson's right to contest the scientific basis of the Massachusetts vaccination requirement. Accepting that some reasonable people still questioned the efficacy of vaccination, the Court nonetheless found that it was within the legislature's prerogative to adopt one from many conflicting views on a scientific issue: "It is no part of the function of a court or a jury to determine which of two modes was likely to be most effective for the protection of the public against disease. That was for the legislative department to determine in the light of all the information it had or could obtain."

In a recent case upholding the closing of a bathhouse as a disease control measure, the court showed the same deference to discretionary orders by public health officers: "It is not for the courts to determine which scientific view is correct in ruling upon whether the police power has been properly exercised. The judicial function is exhausted with the discovery that the relation between means and ends is not wholly vain and fanciful, an illusory pretense."[9]

Reviewing Public Health Orders

Traditional public health laws do not require the health officer to obtain a court order before acting. Instead, the propriety of public health restrictions is determined by postrestriction habeas corpus proceedings brought on behalf of the restricted individual. Although courts have recognized that public health measures may involve grave intrusion into an individual's expectation of liberty, the control of communicable diseases and unsanitary conditions has been found to outweigh the individual privacy interest. Perhaps the clearest difference between public health detentions and criminal arrests is that public health detentions are not bailable: "to grant release on bail to persons isolated and detained on a quarantine order because they have a contagious disease which makes them dangerous to others, or to the public in general, would render quarantine laws and regulations nugatory and of no avail."[10]

The court's deference to public health authority finds further expression in rulings on the appropriate standard of proof for restricting an individual's liberty. When persons detained under the public health authority petition for habeas corpus relief, the courts use a *reasonable-belief* standard for determining the validity of the detention or testing orders. Reasonable belief may be based on individual specific information, such as a diagnosis of tuberculosis, which may be obtained through voluntary testing of individuals at risk. In modern public health practice, statutorily required disease reports usually provide the basis for the reasonable belief that an individual is infected and should be restricted to protect the public health:

> No patient can expect that if his malady is found to be of a dangerously contagious nature he can still require it to be kept secret from those to whom, if there was no disclosure, such disease would be transmitted. The information given to a physician by his patient, though confidential, must, it seems to us, be given and received subject to the qualification that if the patient's disease is found to be of a dangerous and so highly contagious or infectious a nature that it will necessarily be transmitted to others unless the danger of contagion is disclosed to them, then the physician should, in that event, if no other means of protection is possible, be privileged to make so much of a disclosure to such persons as is necessary to prevent the spread of the disease.[11]

Due Process and Privacy

Public health laws are often criticized as antiquated and thus unconstitutional. The argument is that traditional public health laws do not provide the privacy or due process protections required under modern constitutional law. It is true that standards for protecting privacy and for criminal due process protections were strengthened under the Earl Warren Court. None of these decisions, however, changed the traditional standards for public health practice. Rather than extend the protections of the Warren Court to public health matters, more recent Supreme Court cases clearly favor the state's right to control dangerous individuals. The recent case of *Hendricks v. Kansas*,[12] in which the Supreme Court upheld the preventive detention of a sexual predator, specifically endorsed traditional public health jurisprudence.

The more dangerous flaw in the argument that public health laws should provide extensive procedural protections is that it ignores the costs of those protections. Court proceedings take time and money. No health departments have sufficient legal staffs to have a court hearing before every enforcement action. This has been specifically recognized in several U.S. Supreme Court decisions.[13] The administrative costs of elaborate due process requirements prevent the enforcement of public health laws.

Some states have rewritten their communicable disease laws to provide more than the protections mandated by the Constitution. These protections often interfere with local health authorities' ability to deal with diseases such as drug-resistant tuberculosis. In many jurisdictions, health officers must bring their enforcement actions through the district attorney's office. These offices are so buried under crimes such as murder that it is impossible to get timely assistance with public health orders.

DISEASE CONTROL

The control of communicable disease, the essence of traditional public health, is not the same as the internal medicine subspecialty of infectious disease treatment. This subspecialty is concerned with the treatment of individual patients infected with viral and bacterial organisms, and the training is oriented to individual patients, not the community. In contrast, disease control is concerned with the prevention of the spread of diseases in the community rather than the treatment of individual patients.

Disease control was the core of public health until the last polio epidemics in the 1950s. With the development of antibiotics and effective immunizations, the public lost its fear of communicable diseases, undermining public support for disease control in the general populace and in schools of public health. Since the 1960s, public health has become a broad umbrella, encompassing every cause from nuclear war to controlling cholesterol levels. This loss of focus has weakened the disease control programs in most health departments. The diminished support for disease control is exacerbated by the burden of indigent health care. Although indigent health care is a critical community service, it is so expensive and demanding that it saps the resources of the much smaller preventive programs.

Disease Control and the Individual

The price of disease prevention in the group may be injury to an occasional individual. The fact that polio vaccine prevents thousands of cases of paralytic polio is little comfort to the rare individual who gets polio from the vaccine. Most mandatory immunization laws contain exceptions for individuals who have a high probability of being injured by an immunization. Many of these laws also exempt persons who have religious objections to immunization. The U.S. Constitution allows mandatory immunization of religious objectors, but most states do not take advantage of this power.

The effectiveness of the immunization laws depends on compliance by physicians and parents. If physicians give medical exemptions to a large percentage of their patients, the level of immunity in their school system might drop low enough to support a disease epidemic. The physician might be liable for the results of the disease in any child he or she exempted improperly. The physician also might be liable for injuries to children who are not the physician's patients who would not have been exposed to the disease but for the physician's improper behavior.

Epidemics and Plagues

The technical meaning of the word *epidemic* is an "excess of cases of a disease over the number expected in a given population." This is an important concept for a physician who may be required to report any unusual disease or group expression of disease to the health department. Influenza normally infects large numbers of people every winter. A few cases of influenza may herald the beginning of the season, but they are expected. Public health reports on the epidemic may even use the term "excess deaths." Only when a substantial number of people are ill and medical resources are strained does it become an epidemic. In contrast, one or two cases of a rare disease may constitute an epidemic. The occurrence of a few cases of diphtheria anywhere in the United States is an epidemic because we do not expect any cases of this disease.

To most people, the word *plague* brings to mind images of the decimation of Europe by the Black Death in the Middle Ages. *Plague* is not a technical term like *epidemic*. It is generally used to describe epidemic disease that is perceived as a disaster for a community or a specific group. A plague of locusts may be a disaster, but it is not an epidemic. The potential for disease epidemics that qualify as plagues is ever present. Many of these diseases appear and disappear without warning or in cycles that are poorly understood. The sudden appearance of HIV infection is not unusual for a plague. Bubonic plague goes through cycles that last about 400 years; on this cycle, we are due for another worldwide epidemic of bubonic plague. The population of rodents and fleas that is necessary to fuel such an epidemic is present, and the disease is endemic in most of the western United States. The question is not what would start such an epidemic but why it has not already started.

Public health procedures backed by strong laws are necessary to combat plagues. If disease control measures are postponed endlessly while policy is debated, the disease may spread so widely that no measure can contain it. More vigorous public health efforts, such as closing gay bathhouses as soon as it became obvious how HIV was spread, might have reduced the extent of the epidemic. Had the bathhouses been closed in the late 1970s when it became obvious that they were the vector for the spread of hepatitis B (HBV), HIV might have emerged slowly enough that gay men could have learned of its existence before infection became so widespread.

Carrier State

Typhoid Mary has become a general term for a person spreading a communicable disease. Typhoid Mary was an actual person, and typhoid carriers are not unusual. Most big cities have typhoid carriers who are registered with the health department, and they are living and working in the community. Because the carrier state cannot be cured with antibiotic treatment, the carriers must live with certain restrictions: they may not work as food handlers or as child care attendants. They can safely work in such establishments at other jobs—for example, as a restaurant accountant. This is an example of the restrictions on personal freedom that a health officer has the legal authority to impose on an individual as a disease control measure.

If a carrier is under orders to restrict activities and does not comply with the orders, the health officer may take stronger actions, including quarantine or incarceration. Typhoid Mary was a threat because she worked as a cook and refused to stop this work. Every time the health department located her, usually through a new outbreak of typhoid, she would move and change her name but not her occupation. She was finally placed under house arrest to keep her from cooking and infecting others. Typhoid Mary infected more than a hundred people, killing several of them, before the more restrictive measures were imposed.

A 1941 case involving a typhoid carrier is a good example of the court's view of the appropri-ateness of disease control measures. The case concerned whether the identity of typhoid carriers could be disclosed when necessary to prevent their handling food and thus exposing others to their disease:

> The Sanitary Code which has the force of law ... requires local health officers to keep the State Department of Health informed of the names, ages and addresses of known or suspected typhoid carriers, to furnish to the State Health Department necessary specimens for laboratory examination in such cases, to inform the carrier and members of his household of the situation and to exercise certain controls over the activities of the carriers, including a prohibition against any handling by the carrier of food which is to be consumed by persons other than members of his own household.... Why should the record of compliance by the County Health Officer with these salutary requirements be kept confidential? Hidden in the files of the health offices, it serves no public purpose except a bare statistical one. Made available to those with a legitimate ground for inquiry, it is effective to check the spread of the dread disease. It would be worse than useless to keep secret an order by a public officer that a certain typhoid carrier must not handle foods which are to be served to the public.[14]

Disease Control and the Physician–Patient Relationship

Basic to all public health is the reporting of communicable diseases and hazardous conditions to the public health officer. This information is used for tracking the course of epidemics and for intervening to protect the public health.

Reporting duties transcend the patient's right of privacy and the physician's obligation to protect the patient's confidential information. For some diseases, physicians are required to report only the number of cases they see. Other diseases and conditions require physicians to provide identifying information, such as name, address, occupation, or birth date of the patient, as well as information on the disease. For many diseases, the health department will contact the affected person and obtain information about additional persons who may have been exposed to the disease and will assist those persons in getting appropriate medical care.

The Centers for Disease Control and Prevention (CDC) in Atlanta, Georgia, is the federal agency responsible for accepting disease reports and participating in national and international disease control efforts. It is the U.S. agency that participates in the World Health Organization and the Pan-American Health Organization. CDC maintains many disease-specific programs, such as venereal disease control and tuberculosis control. It also stocks and distributes specialty drugs and biologicals that are not approved for distribution in the United States or that are needed too infrequently to justify commercial production. CDC maintains the Epidemic Investigation Service, which may be called in by a state health authority to assist with a difficult disease problem. Except for a few specific programs, the CDC does not accept disease reports directly. The programs work through state and territorial health departments.

All jurisdictions in the United States have laws that require the reporting of certain diseases to a local or state health officer.[15] The laws differ on which diseases are reportable, who must report, how the reports are made, and who accepts the reports, but the substance of the laws is the same. Reportable conditions are infectious diseases or toxic exposures that endanger the community. The courts have also imposed a duty on certain professionals to report potentially violent individuals. All states require that physicians report these diseases and conditions, and many extend this requirement to include nurses, dentists, veterinarians, laboratories, school officials, administrators of institutions, and police officials. Failure to report a reportable disease may constitute a criminal offense, and it creates civil liability if someone is hurt by it. Required reporting is exempt from confidentiality limitations and physician–patient privilege. The patient's right of privacy gives way to the societal need to prevent the spread of disease. However, physicians must not abuse this privilege and unnecessarily divulge a patient's medical information.

Reportable Diseases

Exhibit 12–1 lists diseases that are commonly reportable. Most of these are reportable in all jurisdictions; the remainder are of public health interest irrespective of their reportability in a given jurisdiction. They are divided into categories according to the mode of spread or the programs used to control them. This list is not comprehensive. State-specific information on what to report and to whom can be obtained from the state health department. Generally, if a disease is affecting an unusually large number of people or if it is a disease that may become epidemic, it should be reported. Except for HIV, most health departments accept reports for diseases that are not on the state list of reportable diseases. The health department may choose not to act on the reports, but physicians have no legal liability for making a report that is not required.

Complying with Reporting Duties

Irrespective of personal beliefs, physicians must comply with reporting laws. A physician should never withhold information or give false information to protect a patient's privacy. Although violators are seldom prosecuted, interfering with a public health investigation is a crime in most states. There is a much greater chance that a failure to comply with a reporting duty will result in a medical malpractice lawsuit. Failure to report an infectious person or a dangerous condition can make the physician liable for any harm to the patient or anyone else that compliance with the reporting duty would have prevented.

Legally required disease control reporting is not subject to informed consent; the patient has no right to veto the reporting. The reportability of a disease should not be part of the informed consent for laboratory tests. Information about the reportability of a disease might deter some patients from consenting to testing. Although this might protect the patient's autonomy, it can threaten the public's health. Also, the physician does not need a medical records release for disease reporting because neither the physician nor the patient has the right to refuse the release of information.

Physicians must never knowingly report false information to public health authorities. The physician is liable for any injuries occasioned by the false report. This does not mean that the physician must personally investigate the information that patients provide. It does mean that the physician must truthfully report what is known to him or her. The reality is that very few physicians do not know their patients' correct names and addresses. It is the rare patient who pays cash for medical care and never requires a prescription or other order that requires correct identity.

A physician who provides information in good faith is not liable if the information is incorrect. Conversely, a physician who intentionally provides false information may be liable for negli-

Exhibit 12–1 Commonly Reportable Diseases

DISEASE CATEGORIES	encephalitis (all types)	psittacosis
animal bites	pertussis syndrome (including parapertussis)	Q fever
any group expression of diseases	food poisoning	rabies
cancer	giardiasis	rat bite fever
congenital anomalies	gonorrhea	relapsing fever
food-borne diseases	granuloma inguinale	respiratory fungal infections
infestations	haemophilus influenzae infections	Reye's syndrome
occupational illness and injury	Hansen's disease (leprosy)	rheumatic fever
sexually transmitted diseases	hepatitis (all types)	Rocky Mountain spotted fever
toxic exposures	histoplasmosis	rubella
vector-borne diseases	HIV infection	rubella, congenital
zoonoses	HIV-related illness	salmonellosis
	influenza and flulike illness	scabies
SPECIFIC DISEASES	Kawasaki syndrome	schistosomiasis
	Lassa fever	shigellosis
AIDS	legionellosis	smallpox
amebiasis	leishmaniasis	streptococcal disease
animal bites	leprosy	syphilis
anthrax	leptospirosis	teniasis (tape worm)
ascariasis	listeriosis	tetanus
aspergillosis	Lyme disease	toxic shock syndrome
blastomycosis	lymphogranuloma venereum	toxoplasmosis
botulism (adult and infant)	malaria	trachoma
brucellosis	measles (rubeola)	trichinosis
campylobacter infection	meningitis—bacterial (all types)	tuberculosis
chancroid	meningococcal infections	tularemia
chicken pox	mumps	typhoid
chlamydia trachomatis infection	paratyphoid	typhus fever (epidemic, murine, and scrub)
cholera	pelvic inflammatory disease	vibrio infections
coccidioidomycosis	pinta	viral hemorrhagic fevers
Colorado tick fever	plague	visceral larva migrans
congenital infections (all types)	pneumonia	yaws
dengue fever	poliomyelitis	yellow fever
diphtheria		

Source: Reprinted from Case Definitions for Infectious Conditions under Public Health Surveillance, MMWR, Vol. 46, © 1997, Centers for Disease Control and Prevention.

gence per se. This means that the reporting statute establishes the proper standard of care and the physician is liable as a matter of law. Depending on the nature of the state's reporting laws, a physician's malpractice insurance may not cover damages due to knowingly breaking the law. Most states allow the board of medical examiners to restrict or revoke a physician's license for failing to comply with reporting laws.

Most state laws also require laboratories to report communicable diseases. The physician reports the clinical diagnosis, and the laboratory reports the results of tests that indicate the presence of a reportable disease. When the laboratory reports a disease, this does not obviate the physician's duty to report. Physicians who run laboratories in their offices may have to file duplicate reports if they perform the laboratory tests that establish the diagnosis.

Warning Third Parties

Any physician who diagnoses a contagious disease has a duty to counsel the patient about the communicability of the disease and to ensure that any other persons at risk are warned. This duty has been clear and explicit in the laws of this country since the nineteenth century. This duty can be discharged directly, by warning the exposed individuals, or indirectly, by reporting the disease to public health officials or by counseling the patient to warn persons at risk. The proper method of discharging this duty to warn is shaped by the applicable reporting and privacy laws. The patient's privacy is best protected by indirect warnings through the health department. This route may be ineffective, however, in jurisdictions where the health department declines to warn persons who are exposed to communicable diseases such as HIV. For example, a physician who treated a married man with syphilis would have to report the disease to the local health department, which would contact the man's wife. They would interview her to determine if there were other contacts who might require treatment. The physician would have discharged his or her duty to warn the wife and to report the disease. The health department also protects the patient's confidence. A dis-

ease investigator does not tell a contact to a communicable disease carrier who the carrier is—simply that there has been a contact.

In this case, if the wife has not had sexual relations with anyone except her husband, she will know who her contact was. It is important to keep in mind that the resulting family problems are not the fault of the reporting physician if the health department does the warning. Conversely, if a physician attempts to warn a person at risk and does so negligently, the physician may be liable for the ensuing marital disharmony.

In the classic Molien case, the physician negligently diagnosed syphilis in a married woman. The physician then told the woman to tell her husband that he might be infected and to come in for testing. The consequences of this negligent diagnosis and counseling were suspicion, disharmony, and divorce. The court found that the physician was responsible for this result and had to pay damages to the husband for negligent infliction of mental distress.[16] Had the physician reported the disease to the health department and relied on it to investigate the case and to warn the husband, the potential liability for marital distress would have been reduced or eliminated.

This case is especially interesting because the strategy of counseling patients to warn their own contacts is often recommended for HIV-infected persons. Under this court's analysis, instructing an infected plaintiff to warn others and ask them to come in for testing can leave the physician liable for any negligently inflicted mental distress suffered by the patient's contacts.

Such potential liability, coupled with the greater expertise of the health department disease investigators, means that physicians should rely on the health department to warn persons at risk. Some health departments, however, still refuse to trace and warn the contacts of HIV carriers. In such jurisdictions, physicians are in a difficult bind: they have a duty to warn but may be liable for consequences of negligent warnings, delivered by either the patient or the physician. If they warn without the patient's consent, they also may be liable for violating the patient's privacy. If the state law permits the physician to warn third persons without the patient's permission, the physician must be careful not to disclose the disease carrier's identity, even if the contact clearly knows the identity and asks the physician to confirm it. Laws allowing the physician to warn still leave the physician liable for the consequences of a negligent warning.

The problem of warning third parties is exacerbated if a contact is a patient of the physician, commonly the case for family physicians. Physicians who treat families can obviate the confidentiality problem by asking patients to authorize sharing necessary medical information with other family members. This should be done on the first patient visit to prevent the violation of state laws requiring the physician to protect each individual patient's confidential information. If the patient refuses, the physician must be careful not to violate his or her confidences. Even if the patient agrees, which she did in the *Molien* case, this is no protection against negligently inflicted harm.

Coercive Measures

State and federal public health laws provide the authority to restrict the liberty of individuals to protect the public health and safety. This includes the power to isolate individuals (quarantine), to force individuals to be immunized or treated, and to restrict the activities in which the individual may engage. Forced quarantine has fallen into disuse since antibiotics and the use of specific behavioral restrictions has made it possible to allow infected individuals more personal freedom without endangering others. However, quarantine is still used on some patients, such as tuberculosis carriers whose disease is resistant to all the antituberculosis drugs available. Mandatory immunization or incarceration for treatment is still used by public health officials.

Involuntary Testing

The least intrusive coercive public health measure is the involuntary testing of populations at risk for communicable disease. The most common example is testing for tuberculosis in high-risk populations. Involuntary testing has three benefits. First, it allows public health officials to learn the prevalence of a disease in the community. This is difficult to accomplish with voluntary testing because of the statistical problems associated with self-selected data sets. Second, it identifies infected individuals who may benefit from treatment. Third, it identifies individuals who may need to be restricted to protect the public health.

Involuntary testing for communicable diseases is legally different from testing for personal behavior such as drug use or the propensity to steal from an employer. The presence or absence of a communicable disease may be objectively determined, and the risk it poses is easily quantified. There are no criminal law consequences to the diagnosis of a communicable disease, so there is no need for protection against self-incrimination in disease screening. In many cases, treatment will eradicate the condition. Even when treatment is impossible, only rare circumstances demand more than minimal workplace restrictions to prevent the spread of the disease. When these restrictions are required, they are solely to protect others, not to punish the affected individual.

Contact Tracing

This is a method that has been used in the control of endemic contagious disease for decades.[17] A disease investigation begins when an individual is identified as having a communicable disease. An investigator interviews the patient, family members, physicians, nurses, and anyone else who may have knowledge of the primary patient's contacts, anyone who might have been exposed, and anyone who might have been the source of the disease. Then the contacts are screened to see if they have or have ever had the disease. The type of contact screened depends on the nature of the disease. A sexually transmitted disease will require interviewing only infected patients and screening only their sex partners. A disease that is spread by respiratory contact, such as tuberculosis, may require screening tens to hundreds of persons, such as other inmates in a prison.

Many persons object to contact tracing as an invasion of privacy. Since contact tracing is constitutionally permissible, these objections are often disguised as criticisms of the cost of contact tracing. Contact tracing is an expensive process but one that is cost-effective because it is highly efficient in finding infected persons.[18] This was best demonstrated in the campaign to eradicate smallpox.

Contrary to popular belief, smallpox was not controlled by immunizing every person on earth. It was controlled by extensive contact tracing to find infected individuals. Smallpox could be controlled only because the sores and scars prevented infected persons from escaping detection.[19] Fellow villagers and tribesmen were encouraged in various ways to identify infected persons. When a person with smallpox was identified, he or she was quarantined, and all the persons in the surrounding community or village were vaccinated. In this way smallpox was eventually reduced to isolated outbreaks and then eradicated.

Although many health departments have resisted contact tracing for HIV infection, the resurgence of infectious tuberculosis secondary to HIV-induced immunosuppression is forcing them to reexamine this policy.[20] Even gay groups traditionally opposed to HIV reporting and contact tracing are beginning to recognize its benefits. Recent outbreaks of drug-resistant tuberculosis have intensified the concern with contact tracing. Drug-resistant tuberculosis poses great public health problems because of its often fatal course and the inability to render the carriers noninfectious.[21]

Mandated Treatment

Implicit in the power to protect the public health is the power to treat disease carriers despite their objections. Since treatment is a less restrictive alternative to quarantine or isolation, it is favored as a disease control measure. A patient who refuses to accept treatment for a contagious disease may be ordered to accept the treatment by a health officer or, depending on the jurisdiction, a court. A common practice is to incarcerate a recalcitrant patient until the patient consents to the treatment. This coerced consent is not obtained as a sham on an informed consent but to obviate the need for physically subduing the patient. It also gives the patient an opportunity to contest the treatment through a habeas corpus proceeding.

Although coerced treatment for a communicable disease violates a person's autonomy, it is permissible under the U.S. Constitution. The alternative is to allow the infected person to threaten the health and life of others. With tuberculosis, failure to force a contagious homeless person to accept treatment may result in the infection of other persons with whom the person comes into contact in shelters. Since many of these contacts, especially the children, are poorly nourished or chronically ill, they will be susceptible to fast-spreading infection that is difficult to treat. This problem is already evident in the high rates of tuberculosis in homeless shelters.

Quarantine and Isolation

As a public health measure, quarantine has come to mean the restriction of disease carriers to an environment where their contact with outsiders is limited. Quarantine was widely used until the 1950s. For self-limited diseases such as measles, the infected person was required to stay home and not have visitors. For diseases such as infectious tuberculosis before antitubercular agents were available, the quarantine might be at a sanitarium with other tuberculosis patients.

Isolation, a special case of quarantine, is almost always used in an institutional setting. It may be reverse isolation, to protect the person being isolated. The most famous reverse isolation case was the "bubble baby," the child who was raised in an isolation chamber because he did not have a functioning immune system. The medical and psychological sequellae of indefinite length long-term protective isolation were sufficiently daunting to discourage its further use. Nevertheless, it is used routinely for short, controlled periods for patients undergoing certain types of chemotherapy and organ transplantation.

Isolation is used for diseases that are transmitted through casual contact or respiratory transmission. Strict isolation is used for highly infectious agents that may travel long distances through the air or be caught from cutaneous contact with sores or secretions. Strict isolation requires restriction to a private room with controlled air flow. Persons entering the room must wear gowns, gloves, and respirators capable of filtering out micron-level particles. Respiratory isolation is used for diseases such as tuberculosis that are spread through the inspiration of infected particles but have only limited spread through contact with wounds or secretions. Respiratory isolation requires the same precautions as strict isolation but without the extensive gowning and gloving. Contact isolation is for diseases that spread by direct contact and limited droplet spread. It requires personal protective measures but not a controlled air supply.[22]

Strict and respiratory isolation must be meticulously maintained to be effective. Patients may not leave the room without supervision to ensure that they do not remove their respirators. Staff must never break isolation, and visitors must be carefully monitored. The patient rooms must be at negative pressure to doors and hallways. The room air must be exhausted outside, preferably through high-efficiency air particulate air filters. Ultraviolet lights may also be used to reduce the spread of infectious particles. All treatment rooms must meet these isolation standards, including the control of personnel entering and leaving the room.[23] The CDC and the military maintain a few very high-level biohazard isolation and medical facilities for potential cases of unknown new agents or highly dangerous diseases such as the Marburg or Ebola viruses.

Using Isolation and Quarantine

When it became clear that AIDS was a communicable disease, there was discussion of quarantining persons with AIDS to prevent the spread of disease. Although this was never seriously considered, the resulting outcry made public health authorities reluctant to use or discuss quarantine and isolation in any circumstances. Some states even rewrote their disease control laws to make it difficult to restrict disease carriers. The repercussions of these policies are evident in the growing number of reports of the spread of tuberculosis and other diseases from known carriers to health care providers and members of the general community. These cases might have been prevented with the effective use of isolation.[24]

The transmittal of drug-resistant tuberculosis to health care workers remains a serious problem.[25] About 10% of otherwise healthy people who are infected develop acute disease, which is often impossible to cure and difficult to render noninfectious. A person with infectious tuberculosis must be put in respiratory isolation. This isolation lasts a short time for drug-sensitive tuberculosis, but it may last until the end of the patient's life for drug-resistant tuberculosis.

The biggest problem with quarantine and isolation is not the patient's civil rights but the logistics. Few city or county governments want to pay for feeding, housing, and caring for patients placed under isolation. The public health nurse may not consider doing grocery shopping and laundry for a quarantined patient as a proper part of nursing duties. Hospitals do not like to take in infectious patients who require extensive isolation precautions. The cost of these precautions is seldom reimbursed fully, and the patient cannot be discharged until noninfectious. This reticence to bear the responsibility of quarantine and isolation is often concealed behind a facade of concern for the individual's civil rights. The result in some jurisdictions is that people, including health care providers, continue to be exposed to carriers of easily communicated, deadly diseases such as drug-resistant tuberculosis.

IMMUNIZATIONS

Over the last thirty years, the American political system has handled immunization policy poorly. This reflects profound ignorance of disease control among elected officials and lawyers. These individuals see immunization as a personal health problem rather than a public health and safety issue. As a result of this narrow view of the role of immunization in protecting the community's health, litigation has been allowed to drive the cost of routine immunizations beyond the means of many families, and private individuals are encouraged in unfounded fears of the risks of immunization.

Herd Immunity and Community Health

Immunization protects community health in two ways. The more obvious is through protecting individuals from communicable diseases. The second is the promotion of herd immunity. If an immunization were 100% effective (an immunized person had a zero probability of becoming infected with the target disease), then immunizing every person in a community would eradicate the target disease in that community. In this situation, personal protection and community protection are the same.

If everyone in the community were immunized save one, that one unimmunized person would also be protected from infection. Assuming that the community is isolated from other, unimmunized communities, the single unimmunized individual is protected because the disease has been eradicated. The problem is that immunizations have risks, so every person wants to be the one unimmunized individual protected by the herd.

Herd immunity is critical to the control of immunizable diseases. It is difficult, however, to predict the precise level of community immunity that is necessary to prevent the spread of a disease. Herd immunity is dependent on the communicability of the disease, the nature of transmission, the effectiveness of the immunization, the duration of period that an infected person may communicate the disease, whether the disease is treatable, whether the disease has a silent period when it is communicable, the general health of the community, and the health of the infected individuals.

Herd immunity is also dependent on the dynamics of a given epidemic. What might be an acceptable level of immunity to prevent spread from random, single cases of the disease could be insufficient to stop a major inoculation such as the arrival of a planeload of infected refugees. Most critically, herd immunity depends on the unimmunized individuals' being randomly distributed in the community. If unimmunized persons cluster, then it is the percentage of immunization in the cluster that determines the spread of the disease. This is frequently the case with religious groups that refuse immunization. One hundred unimmunized persons in a large city will not be a problem until they all meet at church.

The inherent uncertainty in herd immunity limits its use as an explicit disease control strategy. A community must attempt to immunize every susceptible individual. Herd immunity will then cover the small number of susceptible persons who are inadvertently missed or who are not candidates for immunization. (Herd immunity is the only realistic defense for many immunocompromised individuals.) A community immunization plan must target the individuals who are weak links in a herd immunity system. The largest group is the poor, especially the medically indigent. These individuals are both less likely to be immunized and more susceptible to infection.

Compulsory Immunization

The more difficult problem is religious or cultural groups that oppose immunizations. These groups tend to cluster, reducing the effective immunization level in their neighborhoods, schools, and churches. In addition to endangering their own children, such groups pose a substantial risk to the larger community. By providing a reservoir of infection, a cluster of unimmunized persons can defeat the general herd immunity of a community. As these infected persons mix with members of the larger community, they will expose those who are susceptible to contagion.

Many physicians, lawyers, and judges believe that the constitutional protection for freedom of religion includes freedom from immunizations. This is not the law today, nor has it ever been the law in the United States. The U.S. Supreme Court, in *Jacobson v. Massachusetts*,[26] held that an individual could not refuse smallpox vaccination: "We are not prepared to hold that a minority, residing or remaining in any city or town where smallpox is prevalent, and enjoying the general protection afforded by an organized local government, may thus defy the will of its constituted authorities, acting in good faith for all, under the legislative sanction of the State."[27]

In the later case of *Prince v. Massachusetts*,[28] the U.S. Supreme Court spoke directly to the issue of religious objections to vaccination:

> But the family itself is not beyond regulation in the public interest, as against a claim of religious liberty. And neither rights of religion nor rights of parenthood are beyond limitation. Acting to guard the general interest in youth's well being, the state as parens patriae may restrict the parent's control by requiring school attendance, regulating or prohibiting the child's labor and in many other ways. Its authority is not nullified merely because the parent grounds his claim to control the child's course of conduct on religion or conscience. Thus, he cannot claim freedom from compulsory vaccination for the child more than for himself on religious grounds. The right to practice religion freely does not include liberty to expose the community or the child to communicable disease or the latter to ill health or death.

Despite the clear language of the U.S. Supreme Court, nearly all state immunization laws provide an exemption for persons with religious objections to immunization. This creates a large loophole because the Constitution will not allow laws that favor one religion over another. Christian Scientists are exempt if they choose to be, but so are individuals who have their own unique religious beliefs. If a state provides a religious exemption, the state may not question the validity of the religious beliefs of those who invoke the exception.

State compulsory immunization laws contain these exemptions because few legislators understand the public health and safety implications of immunization. No states exempt religious groups from child abuse laws or other criminal laws intended to protect either children or the general public. Physicians should make a concerted effort to educate their legislators to the risks of allowing children to remain unimmunized.

Consent for Immunizations

All states require that children be immunized for certain diseases before entering school. Since school attendance is mandatory, the law makes immunization mandatory. Philosophically, it is absurd to speak of informed consent to a mandatory treatment. Nonetheless, physicians are expected to obtain informed consent for these immunizations. There is only one acceptable way to obtain this consent: using the federally promulgated vaccine information pamphlets.[29] These are often referred to as the Important Information Forms because of their introductory header. They are available from the vaccine distributors, state health departments, and the CDC. The forms have a section to document the consent, including the manufacturer and lot number for the biological, and the date of the immunization. Although not part of the mandatory information, it is also useful to record the name of the person administering the immunization.

It is imperative that every patient or person authorizing the immunization (parent or guardian) be given the information in the federal form and a copy to keep. The consent can be further documented in a more conventional immunization record such as those provided by the World Health Organization. These formal immunization records are useful to show that the child's immunization status is current.

Medical Exemptions

All state immunization laws contain an exemption for individuals with medical contraindications to immunization. It is beyond the scope of this book to list all the contraindications to immunization. Every physician who cares for children or authorizes immunizations should have a current copy of the *Report of the Committee on Infectious Disease* published by the American Academy of Pediatrics (the "Red Book") and a copy of *Communicable Diseases Manual,* published by the American Public Health Association. These books are storehouses of invaluable information about immunizations and the management of communicable diseases. They set the legal standard of care for this branch of medical practice.

The general medical concern is that persons with suppressed immune systems should not be given live vaccine preparations. These include oral polio, oral typhoid, measles, mumps, rubella, and BCG vaccines. Persons with normal immune function develop antibodies to these agents and suffer a mild or subclinical infection. Persons with suppressed immune systems may develop full symptomatic disease, including adverse sequelae. Immunosuppressed persons, or patients who live with immunosuppressed persons, should receive live vaccines only under controlled circumstances.

Physicians must be careful to ensure that patients do not receive contraindicated immunizations. As discussed in the Red Book, there are several short-term contraindications to immunization, as well as the long-term contraindication of immunosuppression. All patients must be questioned or examined to identify the existence of medical contraindications. If these are present, they should be documented in the patient's medical record. Such patients should also be given a medical exemption form to allow them to enter school without the requisite immunizations. Unless required by state law, this exemption need not detail the patient's personal medical condition, only that the patient is not a candidate for immunization. If the exemption is based on a short-term contraindication, this should be reviewed on a subsequent visit and the child immunized as soon as medically advisable.

Physicians should never grant medical exemptions that are not based on objective medical findings. There are parents who are unwilling to claim a religious objection for their children but do not want their children immunized. A physician who grants such a child an exemption from immunization will be legally liable if the child contracts a disease that could be prevented through immunization. Physicians who exempt a child from immunization improperly may also be a party to child neglect. This could result in a legal prosecution if the child were to suffer a permanent injury from a preventable disease.

The Vaccine Compensation Act

Products liability losses by vaccine manufacturers have driven the cost of vaccines beyond the reach of indigent patients and many health departments. In an effort to control these losses, Congress passed the Vaccine Injury Compensation Act to compensate persons injured by vaccines (see Appendix 12–A). This compensation program is funded by a combination of tax revenues on vaccine sales and general tax revenues. This law has two major flaws. One is that the tax on vaccine sales is very high, amounting to several dollars a dose for some common vaccines. The more important is that it is not an exclusive remedy. Although the plaintiff is required to file a claim for review under the act, the plaintiff may reject the award offered under the act and sue the vaccine manufacturer. This is most likely to happen in cases involving brain-injured children. These are the cases that are sympathetic to jurors and thus are most likely to result in huge damage awards. Allowing these plaintiffs to opt out of the compensation system leaves further increases to vaccine costs.

Recording Duties

Section 300aa-25 of Title 42 of the U.S. Code requires the following:

Each health care provider who administers a vaccine set forth in the Vaccine Injury Table [see Appendix 12–A] to any person shall record, or ensure that there is recorded, in such person's permanent medical record (or in a permanent office log or file to which a legal representative shall have access upon request) with respect to each such vaccine—

1. the date of administration of the vaccine,

2. the vaccine manufacturer and lot number of the vaccine,

3. the name and address and, if appropriate, the title of the health care provider administering the vaccine, and

4. any other identifying information on the vaccine required pursuant to regulations promulgated by the Secretary.

Reporting Duties

Each health care provider and vaccine manufacturer shall report to the Secretary—

(A) the occurrence of any event set forth in the Vaccine Injury Table [see Appendix 12–A], including the events... which occur within 7 days of the administration of any vaccine set forth in the Table or within such longer period as is specified in the Table or section, [and]

(B) the occurrence of any contraindicating reaction to a vaccine which is specified in the manufacturer's package insert....

A report ... respecting a vaccine shall include the time periods after the administration of such vaccine within which vaccine-related illnesses, disabilities, injuries, or conditions, the symptoms and manifestations of such illnesses, disabilities, injuries, or conditions, or deaths occur, and the manufacturer and lot number of the vaccine.

Attorney's Duty

"It shall be the ethical obligation of any attorney who is consulted by an individual with respect to a vaccine-related injury or death to advise such individual that compensation may be available under the program for such injury or death."

Physicians probably have an ethical duty to counsel vaccine-injured patients about the availability of compensation under the Vaccine Compensation Act. If the physician assists the patient in obtaining compensation, the patient may be more likely to accept the award under the act and forgo a lawsuit. The problem is that the vaccine injury table (Appendix 12–A) and the vaccine package inserts list many events that have not been proven to be related to vaccine administration.[30] In addition to encouraging unfounded claims, the listing of these unproven risks fuels the myth that vaccines are dangerous.[31]

FOOD SANITATION

Community hygiene is an important part of public health that most physicians know little about, yet most physicians will have a case of food poisoning themselves at some time in their lives, besides treating cases in their patients. These cases usually involve food handled improperly in the home, such as tuna salad that was saved a little longer than it should have been. Generally, the physician need only make the report of a case of food poisoning to the local health department and remind the patient, "When in doubt throw it out."

Most community outbreaks of food poisoning arise from the same sources as individual cases. Potluck dinners and socials at churches and schools give more people food poisoning than any other source in the United States. The local health department usually has jurisdiction to deal with such outbreaks through local ordinances supported by state law. It is important that such outbreaks be reported to the health department because locating the problem and educating the leaders of the organization may avert future outbreaks.

Local health departments usually have jurisdiction over the preparation or sale of food in the community, although their control over schools and public institutions may be limited. Federal laws govern such matters as the handling of food in interstate commerce and special hazards such as seafood and meat processing. Physicians should try to cooperate with health authorities to protect the food supply. Recognizing and reporting cases of food poisoning is the first step. Powerful institutional providers may bring great pressure to bear on health officials and physicians to overlook deficiencies. A college physician may be encouraged to substitute a diagnosis of gastroenteritis for one of food poisoning if the presumed source of the problem is the college food service. This would violate professional ethics, reporting laws, and the physician's duty to patients. A better response is for the physician to work with public health authorities to correct the problems that are causing the food poisoning. A physician who did not make proper diagnoses and reports might be held liable for illness in subsequent patrons of the establishment.

There also will be times when food poisoning will result from food that is damaged before it reaches the retail level. Most people are familiar with the recall of canned food that appears to have been contaminated during manufacture. This is usually discovered by an attentive private physician who recognizes botulism or other unusual diseases. Food may also become unfit for consumption because of improper handling. If a carload of fish has lost refrigeration and spoiled, it may cause a local disease outbreak of considerable magnitude. A physician who recognizes and reports an early case may save many people from illness. The health department would have the opportunity to locate the problem and supervise the destruction of the contaminated food.

ENVIRONMENTAL HEALTH

Local health departments have a general responsibility for protecting the community from environmental hazards. These duties range from animal control to coordinating the cleanup of a toxic waste dump. Community physicians should cooperate with the health officials and report problem cases. This will help the public health physicians to draw on the many resources available through the public health system and national organizations such as chemical manufacturers.

A private physician should be cautious about making pronouncements on environmental hazards, either to patients or to the news media. An association between exposure and disease may seem obvious to a physician who has seen several cases, and yet be scientifically incorrect. A physician who publicly accuses a business of wrongdoing, rather than making a report to the health department, may be open to a suit for damages by the business. Public health officials are protected from such suits when they are acting as officers of the state. Their job is made more difficult by the publicity that often arises when individual physicians seek to publicize public health risks. It is better to discuss the problem with the health department personnel before attempting to publicize a risk that may not be significant. If, however, the health department is unresponsive, the physician might want to contact a state or national environmental protection group.

HIV/AIDS

HIV is given special consideration in this chapter because the epidemic has generated changes in

disease control, insurance, and patient privacy laws across the country. It has also had a profound effect on the functioning of public health departments. The epidemic has frightened the public, highlighted the flaws in our public health system, and exacerbated the inequities in the health insurance and indigent care systems. Many authors have stressed the special problems of AIDS and why traditional medical and public health practices are inappropriate for AIDS and HIV infection. In our view, AIDS poses no new and unique medical problems. It is unique only when the history of communicable disease control in this century is ignored.

History

Antibodies to HIV were found in blood and tissue samples as early as 1969. Retrospectively, it is believed that there may have been sporadic cases of the disease in the United States since 1965. The clinical syndrome of AIDS was first recognized among gay men in San Francisco and New York in 1981. The isolated cases of Kaposi's sarcoma and uncontrollable infections with normally nonpathogenic organisms were quickly recognized to be part of a single pathologic process. This identification was possible because the syndrome occurred in a subpopulation that was easily recognizable and well known to venereologists and infectious disease experts. Had an equally small number of cases been diluted in the general population, it might have taken several more years to recognize that AIDS was an epidemic infectious disease.

Hepatitis B in the Bathhouses

The emergence of a new disease, particularly if it affects a particular group, always suggests an infectious agent or a toxin of some type. In AIDS, the disease appeared in a subpopulation that was known to have significant risk for venereal infection and for illicit drug use: the small population of gays whose lifestyle included high-frequency, anonymous sex in bathhouses, frequently accompanied by the use of amphetamines and amyl nitrite.

The high-frequency, anonymous sex in the bathhouses made them ideal places to spread infections of all types. In addition to gonorrhea and syphilis, hepatitis B was spread widely through homosexual bathhouses. The epidemiology of this disease was studied intensively as part of the effort to develop a hepatitis B vaccine. It was evident that hepatitis B was spread by both sexual activity and by sharing needles when using intravenous drugs. By 1980 a high percentage of those who frequented bathhouses regularly were infected with hepatitis B.

The most interesting aspect of this hepatitis B epidemic was that few people in public health tried to stop it. Hepatitis B is a debilitating, sometimes fatal disease and the leading cause of cancer worldwide. Although only a small percentage of infected persons die of acute fulminate hepatitis, a substantial number of infected persons become chronic carriers, who may continue to spread the disease for years. These chronically infected persons develop liver cancer or cirrhosis at a much higher rate than the general population.

Despite the personal and public health costs of the disease, public health officials did not want to jeopardize their relationship with the gay community by closing the bathhouses, and they argued that this would compromise other disease control efforts. More fundamentally, it would have been political suicide. In New York City, San Francisco, Los Angeles, and Houston, gay men were a well-organized, powerful political lobby. Mayors did not want to risk offending them by supporting the control of a communicable disease with which their own community was not concerned. Thus, the rights of gay men were protected by denying them public health protections. This was the precedent for nonintervention that characterized the first several years of the AIDS epidemic.

How Infectious Diseases Emerge

AIDS is not the first disease that just appeared as if from nowhere. The classic example is syphilis. We often hear of the syphilization of Europe being attributed to Columbus's sailors bringing the disease back from the New World. However, since the disease was a major problem in the armies of both France and Naples in a war that broke out four months after the return of the explorer's ships to Spain, it is unlikely that a handful of sailors can be responsible. A spirochetal disease similar to yaws had been well known in northern Africa for centuries. It is probable that syphilis was a mutation of this disease. For the first 40 years that the disease existed, it was much more severe than syphilis is today. Secondary syphilis had a mortality rate of 20% to 40 % during this early time. The virulence of the disease then decreased to the level we know today.

Changing virulence is a common phenomenon in infectious diseases. The great plagues of the Middle Ages came and went in waves that had little to do with medical care, hygiene, or immunity in the general population. Today plague is endemic in Asia and the western United States. We have the necessary insect vectors, the animal reservoir of infection, and the potential human exposure yet there are only sporadic cases instead of epidemics. At the beginning of this century, streptococcal disease was dreaded. Even well-nourished and well-cared-for children died of strep throat and rheumatic fever. The severity of this disease has decreased so much that many states have removed it from the list of reportable diseases. Although this has been attributed to penicillin, the change occurred before the era of antibiotics and extends to children who have not received treatment. The cycle now is reversing as the severity of strep and the incidence of rheumatic fever increase.[32]

Initial Concentration in the Gay Community

Three factors were responsible for the original concentration of AIDS in the male homosexual population in the United States. First, it appears that AIDS originated in Africa as a mutation of an endemic virus and was carried from there to Haiti. Haiti was a popular vacation spot for homosexuals, and male prostitution was widespread among the impoverished Haitians. Irrespective of how the initial introduction of the disease occurred, the second factor was the existence of the bathhouses. These provided large numbers of sexual contacts and a high incidence of other sexually transmitted diseases. It is likely that genital lesions secondary to these other venereal diseases made the spread of HIV easier. The third factor was that the HIV subtype initially introduced into the United States is more difficult to spread heterosexuality.

Most important, the rate of spread of diseases is proportional to the frequency of contact with potentially infected individuals and the effectiveness of those contacts in spreading the disease. This becomes critical for diseases such as HIV with a low probability of transmission in a given sexual encounter. Some bathhouse patrons had more than 1000 sexual contacts a year. A very sexually active heterosexual man might have 100 contacts a year. Although HIV was probably introduced into the heterosexual population simultaneously as in the homosexual population, the spread would be less than one-tenth as fast. (Although female prostitutes do have large numbers of sexual contacts, women are less effective at infecting their sexual contacts than are men.)

Parallels with Other Diseases

HIV is not unique as an infectious agent. More than 60 infectious diseases are reportable in various states and are a common part of public health practice. HIV is less difficult to work with and control than many other diseases because it is less easily spread. Diseases that may be spread through casual respiratory contact, for example, can be much more difficult to prevent and control. Tuberculosis was controlled before it was treatable. Other diseases with carrier states must be managed without definitive therapy. Standard public health such as public education, screening, and contact tracing also are effective in the control of HIV.

Fear is both a problem and an opportunity in disease control. Public hysteria can make rational disease control measures impossible. Yet without some level of fear, it is impossible to keep the public and their elected representatives interested in disease control. During the polio epidemics of the 1930s and 1940s, people canceled group meetings of all kinds, threw away food because a fly

had lighted on it, and defied school attendance laws. The advent of Salk's vaccine brought the polio epidemics and the associated hysteria to an end. Less than 30 years later, it is difficult to maintain proper levels of immunization against measles because parents believe the disease is eradicated and do not have their children immunized.

Disease Control for HIV

The failure to institute traditional disease control measures for HIV infection indicates the disorganization of the American public health system. Even public health professionals became caught up in the rhetoric that since HIV is untreatable, there is no justification for using proved disease control techniques to control its spread. The rationale was that since carriers could not be cured and their contacts could not be immunized, there was no reason to report infected persons and to trace the contacts of these persons. This rationale ignores the success in controlling tuberculosis before it was treatable and the current efforts to control incurable viral illnesses.

Control of HIV has been unique in providing a common political ground for homosexual activists and the religious right. Homosexual activists fought efforts to control the spread of HIV because they did not want restrictions on their sexuality. The religious right fought disease control efforts because they saw AIDS as an expression of God's wrath about homosexual practices. The result was to paralyze the public health establishment for the critical first years of the epidemic. The same paralysis now extends to the conflict between Draconian laws against illicit drug use and public health measures to limit the spread of bloodborne pathogens among intravenous drug users.

VITAL STATISTICS

The keeping of good vital statistics is important to a society for several reasons. Infant mortality is generally considered the best indicator of the health of a population. Accurate records allow for allocation of health care funds to areas of greatest need. These records are of great historical value as well. On the individual level, the documentation of a birth certificate establishes the individual's legal existence and basic legal relationships like citizenship and parentage.

Vital statistics records are not uniform among the states. The forms, the information required, and the keeper of the records differ. Usually a county office houses these records. The records may be open to public view, access may be limited, or the records may be confidential. These records are always available to the person on whom they are kept or to a court. These records also fall under the full faith and credit clause of the Constitution. A state must honor the birth and death records of another state.

Historically, vital statistics records were kept in the locality where the event occurred rather than the place of current residence or a unified state office. A person born in Boston who moved to Los Angeles as an infant and lived there until he was killed in a Chicago plane crash would have a Massachusetts birth certificate and an Illinois death certificate. There would be no record of this person in the California vital statistics records. Another problem is that parents may not remember accurately where and when their children were born, making it impossible for these offspring to obtain their birth certificates. It also makes it difficult to match birth and death certificates to determine if a person has taken a false identity. Vital statistics records are becoming a more useful resource as states centralize their records and begin to correlate them with other states and the federal Social Security records.

Birth Certificates

Normally the law requires that the person who attended the birth or delivered the baby must file a birth certificate within a specified time of a few days. Although the health care practitioner is responsible for the accuracy of the medical information and the timely filing, most states allow the certificate to be completed and certified by someone other than the person who delivered the baby.

In most hospitals, someone from the medical records department obtains the necessary information from family members and prepares the certificate. The attending health care practitioner should ensure that it is completed fully and accurately.

Birth certificates also contain social information, such as the name of the baby's father. This should be completed accurately if the information is known, but the health care practitioner is allowed to rely on the family for the necessary information. There may be doubts about the accuracy of information such as parentage or citizenship, but this is not the health care practitioner's concern; there is no duty to investigate social information. On many certificates the source of this information is listed, and this person may be asked to sign the certificate.

It is important that the birth attendant file the birth certificate promptly. The certificate must be filed before a certified copy can be issued. The child cannot get a Social Security number without the certified copy of the birth certificate. This can be a problem it the family receives any type of public assistance. Federally funded assistance programs limit the amount of time that a child may be carried on the program without a Social Security number and case file.

Naming the Child

State laws on choosing children's surnames vary substantially. Some states allow the mother to choose any surname; others allow any surname except that of a putative but unacknowledged father; some require that the child be given the surname of a legally recognized relative. The highest federal court to consider this issue found that the parents' privacy interest did not supersede the state's interest in having children named for a legal parent. This case arose in Nebraska, which requires that a child be named for a legal relative. Two mothers challenged the law. One wanted to give her baby the surname of its father, which was different from her husband. The other mother just liked the name *McKenzie* and wanted to use it for her child's surname.[33]

Lower courts in two states had found a constitutional right to give children any desired name. This decision was based on the parents' right of privacy. The appeals court considering the Nebraska case agreed that the parents had a privacy right in naming their children, but it found that the state's right to orderly recordkeeping procedures and certainty of parentage outweighed the parents' privacy interest. Since the U.S. Supreme Court refused to review and overrule this case, it can be assumed that the state may restrict the allowable names for a child.

The name on the birth certificate does not establish the child's paternity. It may be evidence of paternity, if the named father agreed to the use of his name, but it does not affect the state's legal procedures for establishing paternity. State restrictions on choosing names on a child's birth certificate do not prevent the parents or the child from petitioning the court for a name change after the birth certificate proceeding.

Stillbirths

Some states use a separate form for filing a report of stillbirth. Other states require the birth attendant to file both a birth certificate and a death certificate.

The gestational age that constitutes a stillbirth differs from state to state but is usually around 20 weeks. In some cases, an induced abortion may require registration.

The stillbirth certificate may be the appropriate form even if the child is born alive. Separate birth and death certificates are required usually only if the child is potentially viable and lives for some period. If a fetus of any gestational age shows signs of life such as heartbeat or respiratory effort, it is best to file the appropriate certificates.

A reasonable attempt to determine the cause of death should be made for stillborn infants. Prematurity is usually a result of some underlying medical condition, not the cause itself. Prematurity is obviously not the cause of intrauterine death. Since some causes of stillbirth, such as infection or uterine abnormality, are treatable, the physician who does not establish the cause of a stillbirth

may be liable for similar problems in a subsequent pregnancy.

Death Certificates

The quality of death records in the United States is generally poor because physicians are not well trained in filing these reports. Death certificates are problematic for several reasons: unexpected deaths frequently occur outside the hospital; the cause of death may not be immediately obvious; there may be no one to provide information on the identity of the person who died; occasionally there may be a question of criminal activity having been involved in the death.

The cause of death is the most important information on a death certificate and is generally the most inadequate. Preferably the causes of death listed should be coded from the International Classification of Disease. But for many certificates, the actual cause of the death is not clear, let alone codable. "Cardiac arrest" is a result of death, not a cause. A death certificate that lists cardiac arrest as the cause of death and respiratory arrest following shock as the contributing causes may be for a patient who died of a gunshot wound or a terminal cancer patient or a patient with underlying heart disease. The cause of death should tell a reader what killed the patient—not what the terminal events were.

It is important that the death certificate contain the information that a death was caused or contributed to by infectious disease, cancer, toxic exposure, violent injury, or congenital defect. These causes may be reportable to the health department, child welfare, the police, or a state disease registry. An unusual number of deaths from a specific cause may lead to investigation of the problem and preventive measures.

An inaccurate death certificate may make it difficult for the survivors to collect benefits and insurance. If the death certificate lists septic shock and cardiac arrest as the cause of death in a patient who was involved in a motor vehicle accident without noting that they are secondary to an accident, the widow may have difficulty collecting on an insurance policy that pays only upon accidental death. Normally a certified copy of the death certificate must accompany every claim for death benefits.

Declaration of Death

Generally a physician must make the determination that a person is dead. The physician then makes a formal declaration of the death and a record of the time of death. In a hospital setting, the physician who declares the death may not be the one who signs the death certificate. A resident or the physician covering the emergency room may be asked to pronounce the death of a patient who was under another doctor's care. The attending physician would be expected to determine the cause of death and file the death certificate. The physician who pronounces the death must simply determine that the patient is dead and the time of death.

If the determination of death is difficult, a physician should consult with others and know the legal definition of death in the state. A patient may be legally dead because of lack of brain function but still have a heartbeat when on a mechanical ventilator. There is no point in ventilating a dead patient, but stopping the ventilator before the legal criteria for death have been met may involve the physician in both civil and criminal proceedings.

The legal time of death may be a long time after the death actually occurred. Many accident victims are obviously dead at the scene of the accident but are pronounced dead officially on arrival at a hospital because no physician was at the scene. When homicide is suspected or in large cities where the police handle large numbers of accidental deaths, a medical examiner may be on call to pronounce death at the scene and to determine the cause of death.

The time of death may be important because of survivorship clauses in wills. For example, a man may leave all his property to his wife unless she does not survive him by at least 30 days, in which case the property goes to a hospital fund. The wife might have a will that leaves everything to her son. If they are in a common disaster that kills him outright but leaves her comatose for 30 days, the determination of the time of brain death may well decide whether the hospital or the son receives the property. In such a case, a physician who had an interest in the hospital might be considered to have a conflict of interest in determining death.

Coroner Cases and Autopsies

A death is a coroner's case if it is unexpected or if there is any possibility that a law has been broken. Not every death that occurs outside a hospital is a coroner's case. If the deceased had a physician who is reasonably certain of the cause of death and is willing to sign a death certificate, further medical examination may not be required.

The coroner system in the United States is in difficulty. Only the largest cities have forensic pathologists to act as coroner and do the medical examinations. In small, rural counties, the coroner may be a physician who has no forensic training, or it may be the sheriff or the mortician. A physician who is asked to act as county coroner should try to learn something about forensic medicine and should be quick to ask for assistance from experts when it is needed. The time of death or the angle of gunfire may determine whether the person committed suicide or was murdered.

The percentage of deaths that are autopsied has been falling for many years. Autopsies benefit society by providing information about hidden pathologies and about the accuracy of medical diagnoses. But they do not benefit the patient, and they are sometimes opposed by physicians who do not want the accuracy of their diagnoses challenged. Because of these factors, there is little money available to pay for autopsies. Even when it is feasible to do an autopsy, many physicians do not know how to obtain consent. Physicians should be familiar with the state law in their jurisdictions governing the persons who may consent to an autopsy. If there is any question of criminal activity, the autopsy may be ordered by a court or the coroner.

Disease Registries

Disease registries are a special class of reporting laws. Since the objective is not to control a communicable disease, there is often no penalty for failing to report to a disease registry. Most disease registries are statewide and involve either cancer or occupational illness; some, such as the CDC registry of cases of toxic shock syndrome, are national. Reporting cases to the registry may be mandatory or voluntary, but it is always desirable to have a complete registry. These registries are used to determine the extent of certain problems in the community and to try to determine causes. If they are inaccurate, they may give false correlations and become useless for research and prevention.

Consider a cancer registry that contains only half the cases of a particular kind of cancer. If a local industry tries to determine whether its workers are exposed to something that causes the cancer, it will look at the rate among its exposed workers and the rate in the general population. If the company finds all the cases among its workers but the cancer registry has only half the cases in the general population, then an exposure that does not cause the cancer will look like it does by a factor of two. An epidemiologist may know that this is wrong, but the reporter from the local paper will not.

LAW ENFORCEMENT REPORTING

Every jurisdiction requires physicians to report certain types of injuries to law enforcement officials or protection agencies. Generally these laws require reporting of assaults, family violence, and criminal activity. The courts and codes of professional behavior have created a duty to report persons who are dangerous because of insanity. Physicians should avoid the tendency to investigate the crime before reporting it. Particularly in cases of family violence, the victim may have a plausible explanation of the injury and be anxious to avoid reporting. The injured person may fear reprisals or may be under investigation already. Proper reports should be made despite the victim's wishes. It will be up to the law enforcement agency to determine what use will be made of the report.

Child Abuse

Child abuse and neglect is a common problem in our society, prevalent in all races, religions, and socioeconomic groups. All states have laws requiring that physicians report suspected child abuse to a government agency in charge of protecting children. This is sometimes a frustrating experience for the physician. These agencies are overworked and have limited resources. All physicians who care for children should know which local agency enforces the child welfare laws in their state.

Child abuse is not a diagnosis; it is a legal determination. A physician who suspects that a child is abused or neglected or is in danger of being abused or neglected has a duty to report that suspicion. Physicians should not try to investigate the potential abuse on their own. This may endanger the child, confuse the legal issues, and subject the physician to prosecution for failing to report the suspected abuse. Many physicians are slow to report suspicions of child abuse because they are concerned that they may be making an unfounded judgment about the parents or the family. Physicians must also guard against parents' rationalizations about why their behavior should not be considered child abuse. The physician's obligation is to evaluate the effect of the behavior on the child. The child protection agency will investigate the parents' explanations before taking any legal action. Physicians must not second-guess the child protection agency or attempt private resolutions of possible abuse.

As with other reporting laws, neither the patient nor the parents nor the physician have the right to stop the reporting or to withhold information from the law enforcement agency. A parent may refuse to answer an investigator's questions under the Fifth Amendment protections against self-incrimination. This part of the process should not involve the physician. The physician should provide all the known information in as objective a manner as possible.

Child Neglect

Child abuse includes acts of omission as well as commission. Parents must provide a child with food, shelter, clothing, education, medical care, and reasonable emotional support within the limits of their ability. If a child appears to lack any of these necessities, the physician should be involved in finding out why. If the family is in crisis and lacks the resources to provide for the children, local social service agencies should be contacted to assist. A church food bank may be able to provide food until the family is eligible for food stamps, or a shelter for the homeless may be able to take them in until housing becomes available. Most public hospitals have social workers on staff who can help with such problems.

If the parents have the resources to care for a child properly but choose not to, they are neglecting that child. This includes parents who do not have adequate resources but refuse necessary social services for personal reasons. Parents who are disabled or emotionally disturbed may be incapable of caring for a child properly. In such situations, a report should be made to the child protection agency. If the parents have good intentions but difficulty coping, then protective services may be able to help them find the necessary community support. If the parents are not willing or able to meet the needs of the child, the protection agency may have to remove the child from the home.

Defending the Child

Because a parent or guardian is the one who consents to medical care for a child and pays for the care, it is easy to forget that the physician–patient relationship runs to the child rather than to the parents. Physicians who have reason to think that a child is in danger should pursue all avenues of protection for that child. Physicians should be prepared to testify in court proceedings and to work with protective services. If the child is returned to the custody of an abusive parent under a restrictive order, the child's physician should know the conditions and should contact protective services if there is any indication that the order is being violated.

If the child protection agency does not intend to pursue the case, a reporting physician should ask for a reasonable explanation of the injuries or conditions that led to the suspicion of child abuse. If the explanation is unsatisfactory or incomplete,

the physician should discuss this fully with the person in charge of the agency. Clearing up misunderstandings may save a child's life. The agency may also give more attention to a case in which a physician has serious concerns. Since the agency is not a court and must ask for court orders in serious cases, the support of the child's physician may help them to convince the judge that legal actions are needed.

Dangerousness Due to Mental Illness

In the landmark decision, *Tarasoff v. Regents of University of California*, the California court established the duty of medical professionals who know a patient is dangerous to prevent that person from harming third parties. In *Tarasoff*,[34] a patient told his psychologist that he planned to kill his girlfriend, Tatiana Tarasoff. The psychologist, who was a counselor at the University of California, believed the patient and notified the campus police. The campus police detained the patient, but let him go without a formal psychiatric evaluation. The psychologist was notified and did nothing further to stop the patient, who then killed Tarasoff. Tarasoff's family sued, and the court found that there was a duty to try and stop such a patient, including, under some circumstances, a duty to warn the intended victim.

Tarasoff is a peculiar case because it is unclear whether warning the victim is really the correct result. The information is of limited value to the victim because in most big cities such a threat will not trigger police protection. The better result in *Tarasoff* would have been for the psychologist to have initiated the proper proceeding for an involuntary civil commitment, as specified in the state's mental health code, rather than just calling the campus police. This would have been especially important after he learned that the campus police had released the patient. The advantage of properly invoking the mental health commitment procedures is that it does not violate the patient's confidence by involving the potential victim. Had the patient been properly evaluated by a forensic psychologist or psychiatrist before being released, it is very unlikely that the courts would have found a further duty to warn the intended victim.

The courts have found that *Tarasoff* is limited to situations where the health care practitioner is convinced that the patient is dangerous to a specific individual. General threats to kill everyone at the high school probably do not trigger a *Tarasoff* duty; however, if the health care practitioner suspects that the patient might attack the school, it would be better to act. Some states, such as Washington, have extended *Tarasoff* by passing laws requiring health care practitioners to report persons who are dangerous by reason of mental illness.

As with other reporting duties, a good faith report to the proper authorities should not subject the health care practitioner to legal liability for invasion of the patient's privacy and will generally fulfill the duty to warn. However, this does not mean just calling the police. The health care practitioner should find out the procedures that their state law provides for reporting and confining a person who is a danger to self or others. This usually involves some kind of affidavit attesting to the diagnosis and its factual basis, as well as identifying information about the patient. When the process is completed appropriately, the patient will be picked up and evaluated by a mental health expert, usually over a two- or three-day period. Only if this process fails, or is unavailable, should the health care practitioner start warning third parties.

Elder and Spousal Abuse

Most states now have laws requiring reporting of elder and/or spousal abuse. Just like with child abuse, health care professionals should make the reports and leave the investigation to the proper agency. Remember that the victim does not have to "press charges" for these crimes to be reportable. It is the state that brings criminal charges, even if the victim is an adult.

Violent Injuries

Generally physicians have a responsibility to report violent or suspicious injuries—all gunshot wounds, knifings, poisonings, serious motor vehicle injuries, and any other wounds that seem suspicious—to the local law enforcement agency. The legal assumption is that anyone who has knowledge that a crime may have been committed has a duty to report the possible crime to the police. If the patient is brought to the hospital in the custody of the police or from the scene of a police investigation, the physician may safely assume that the police have been notified. In all other cases, the physician should call the police and make the report.

Such injuries should be reported despite the wishes of the patient. The patient who has been shot escaping from the scene of a crime will be more interested in the wound's not being reported than the patient who is embarrassed about mishandling a gun while cleaning it. Some states have made domestic violence a reportable offense. In states where such reporting is not required, the physician should determine if battered spouses or partners may be reported under general violent injury laws. This is very important because of the high probability that the victim will be severely injured or killed eventually. In some cases, the couple will have made up by the time the stitches are in and the X rays are read. This should not stop the physician from reporting. In others, the victim will be too terrified to complain. If the woman who came in saying her husband cut her now claims she injured herself cooking, the injury must be reported nevertheless. Domestic violence is one of the most dangerous areas of police work, and the rate of repeat violence is very high. Health care providers should not try to handle these cases privately in emergency rooms.

Intoxications

Unlike child abuse or gunshot wounds, most jurisdictions do not have a law requiring physicians to report intoxications to police authorities. Without reporting laws that override the patient's rights of privacy, physicians should remember that they may not volunteer information about a patient without the patient's permission. As with other forms of medical care, physicians may not do testing without the patient's general consent. Physicians have the right and the duty to assert their patient's right of confidentiality when questioned by police officers about the patient's medical condition. If the physician's testimony is legally required, the court can order the physician to testify; the investigating officer cannot.

Although the consent of the patient is required for any type of medical care, physicians usually do not think about obtaining consent for routine laboratory procedures such as blood chemistry or urinalysis. It is assumed that the patient and the physician use the general consent to care for these. In addition, the patient may refuse to allow the drawing of the blood or to provide the urine for testing. This type of nonspecific consent should not be used when testing for intoxicants. The legal problems that may arise from positive tests make it necessary for the physician to obtain a valid, specific informed consent from the patient before doing the test when the law enforcement authorities are requesting the results of the test.

If this testing is being done for medical reasons, the rules of consent are like those for any other medical procedure. If a patient is brought into the emergency room unconscious, the emergency exception to consent will apply. This does not allow the substituting of consent from a third party, such as a spouse or a police officer. It simply relieves the physician of the necessity of obtaining consent for emergency care. If the normal medical evaluation of an unconscious patient includes a drug screen or a blood alcohol level, these tests should be done and recorded in the patient's medical records, just like a blood glucose or a skull X ray. They are part of the emergency medical care of the patient. Testing that is not necessary for the care of the patient may not be done under the emergency exception. If the physician does not normally do a blood alcohol level to evaluate an unconscious patient, then he or she should not include it at the request of a police officer.

If the patient is conscious and able to consent to medical care, then no matter how serious the medical condition may be, normal consent is necessary. A physician who wishes to do any testing for intoxicants must obtain the explicit consent of the patient if the testing is being done for law enforcement purposes. If the patient refuses to consent to such testing, the physician must respect the refusal even if it makes the care of the patient more difficult. A physician should never take a blood sample for a glucose level and do drug testing on the remainder to avoid the patient's refusal of consent. If the physician believes that the refusal to test threatens the patient's life, a court order may be sought for testing.

Physicians may order testing for intoxicants for purely legal purposes but should be cautious about doing so. Unlike having communicable diseases, substance abuse is both a public health threat and a criminal act. A physician has a duty to protect the patient's confidences in criminal matters. The physician must comply with state laws on testing and reporting drug abuse but should fully inform the patient before the specimen is taken. The patient should be aware that there is no medical indication for the test and that the physician cannot know what the results will be. If the patient has the right to refuse the test, the consent should be in writing, signed and witnessed, and it should contain the name and identifying information on the officer requesting the testing as well as the patient. If the physician has reason to think that the consent is being coerced improperly from the patient, then he or she should not accept the consent or do the testing.

Dealing with Peace Officers

There are two important questions that a physician should ask in dealing with a police officer in a medical care setting: Is the patient in custody? Is there a court order involving medical care? If the patient is not in custody, the police officer is a third party, with no right to information about the patient or the medical care. Medical information may become available to the officer later through a court action for the medical records, but that does not allow the officer to question the physician without the express permission of the patient. If the patient is unable or unwilling to give permission, the officer should be politely but firmly shown the door.

If the patient is in custody, the officer still has no right to consent to or know about the patient's medical care beyond the specific requirements of the state's laws. Being under arrest increases the importance of the patient's right of privacy. The physician must be careful not to interfere with the officer's duties, just as the physician should not allow the officer to interfere with the patient's medical care. If privacy is required for the medical examination, the patient's dignity should be protected as much as possible consistent with preventing the patient's escape. The physician should not interfere with actions that are necessary to maintain custody of a conscious and potentially dangerous prisoner.

Court-ordered medical care is different from care requested by a peace officer. A police officer does not have the right to overrule a patient's decisions on medical consent; a court does. A physician who is presented with a valid court order to do something to or for a patient may either honor the order or get a lawyer to fight the order. Physicians who are routinely involved with court-ordered care should be well versed in the procedures. The emergency physician in the county hospital may be routinely ordered to do drug testing on specific prisoners. This physician or the nurses who work there regularly may know the forms and the judges' names and have no problem with honoring the order. The physician in a private hospital who is presented with an unusual order should contact the hospital attorney or someone in the court system for a clarification of the order.

Some medical records are protected even from court orders, but these are usually in the custody of agencies that know the extent of their authority to withhold records. Venereal disease control programs frequently receive subpoenas for medical records that are protected from subpoena by state law. The judge in a divorce proceeding may not know about the law protecting these records or may have authorized that subpoena as one in a large group. The public health program will routinely request that the subpoena be quashed. A physician in public health or drug rehabilitation who deals regularly with protected records must view the possibility of spending some time in jail on a contempt citation as an occupational hazard. The physician who does not deal with these matters frequently should consult an attorney when presented with a court order.

REFERENCES

1. Institute of Medicine (U.S.). Committee for the Study of the Future of Public Health. *The Future of Public Health.* Washington, DC: National Academy Press; 1988.
2. Maxcy KF, Rosenau MJ, Wallace RB. *Public health and preventive medicine.* Stamford, CT: Appleton & Lange; 1998.
3. Bolduan CF, Bolduan NW. *Public Health and Hygiene: A Student's Manual.* 3rd, rev. ed. Philadelphia: W.B. Saunders; 1942.
4. *In re Halko,* 246 Cal. 2d 553, 556, 54 Cal. Rptr. 661, 663.
5. *Smith v. Turner,* 48 U.S. (7 How.) 283, 340–341.
6. *Holmes v. Jennison,* 39 U.S. (14 Pet.) 540, 616.
7. *Ex parte McGee,* 105 Kan. 574, 581, 185 P. 14, 16.
8. *Jacobson v. Massachusetts,* 197 U.S. 11.
9. *City of New York v. New Saint Mark's Baths,* 497 N.Y.S.2d 979, 983.
10. *Varholy v. Sweat,* 153 Fla. 571, 575, 15 So. 2d 267, 270 (Fla. 1943).
11. *Simonsen v. Swenson,* 104 Neb. 224, 228, 177 N.W. 831, 832 (Neb. 1920).
12. *Kansas v. Hendricks,* 521 U.S. 346 (1997).
13. *Camara v. Municipal Court of City and County of San Francisco,* 387 U.S. 523.
14. *Thomas v. Morris,* 286 N.Y. 266, 269, 36 N.E.2d 141, 142 (N.Y. 1941).
15. Chorba TL, Berkelman RL, Safford SK, Gibbs NP, Hull HF. Mandatory reporting of infectious diseases by clinicians. *JAMA.* 1989;262:3018–3026.
16. *Molien v. Kaiser Found. Hosp.,* 616 P.2d 813 (Cal. 1980).
17. Hethcote HW, Yorke JA. *Gonorrhea Transmission Dynamics and Control.* New York: Springer-Verlag; 1984.
18. Potterat JJ, Spencer NE, Woodhouse DE, Muth JB. Partner notification in the control of human immunodeficiency virus infection. *Am J Public Health.* 1989 July;79:874.
19. Carrell S, Zoler ML. Defiant diseases: hard-won gains erode. *Med World News.* 1990;31:12–20.
20. CDC. Transmission of multidrug-resistant tuberculosis from an HIV-positive client in a residential substance-abuse treatment facility—Michigan. *MMWR.* 1991;40:129.

21. CDC. Outbreak of multidrug-resistant tuberculosis—Texas, California, and Pennsylvania. *MMWR.* 1990;39:369.
22. Coleman D. The when and how of isolation. *RN.* 1987;34:50.
23. Drug-resistant TB outbreak highlights need for screening. *AIDS Alert.* 1991;6:96.
24. CDC. Outbreak of multidrug-resistant tuberculosis—Texas, California, and Pennsylvania. *MMWR.* 1990;39:369.
25. TB not limited to AIDS patients, can affect workers. *AIDS Alert.* 1991;6:9.
26. *Jacobson v. Massachusetts,* 197 U.S. 11.
27. *Id.* at p. 37.
28. *Prince v. Massachusetts,* 321 U.S. 158.
29. Goldsmith MF. Vaccine information pamphlets here but some physicians react strongly. *JAMA.* 1992;267:2005–2007.
30. Fulginiti VA. How safe are the pertussis and rubella vaccines? A commentary on the Institute of Medicine Report. *Pediatrics.* 1992;89:334–336.
31. Lynch TP. Vaccine myth and physician handouts. *Am J Dis Child.* 1991;145:426–427.
32. Carrell S, Zoler ML. Defiant diseases: hard-won gains erode. *Med World News.* 1990;31:20.
33. *Henne v. Wright,* 904 F.2d 1208 (CTA 8 1990).
34. *Tarasoff v. Regents of Univ. of Cal.,* 551 P.2d 334 (Cal. 1976)

SUGGESTED READINGS

Disease Control

Allos BM, Genshelmer KF, Bloch AB, et al. Management of an outbreak of tuberculosis in a small community. *Ann Intern Med.* 1996;125:114–117.
Balogun MA, Wall PG, Noone A. Undernotification of tuberculosis in patients with AIDS. *Int J STD AIDS.* 1996;7:58–60.
Behr MA, Hopewell PC, Paz EA, Kawamura LM, Schecter GF, Small PM. Predictive value of contact investigation for identifying recent transmission of Mycobacterium tuberculosis. *Am J Respir Crit Care Med.* 1998;158:465–469.
Braden CR. Infectiousness of a university student with laryngeal and cavitary tuberculosis: investigative team. *Clin Infect Dis.* 1995;21:565–570.
Braveman P, Pearl M, Egerter S, Marchi K, Williams R. Validity of insurance information on California birth certificates. *Am J Public Health.* 1998;88:813–816.
Chen RT, Rastogi SC, Mullen JR, et al. The Vaccine Adverse Event Reporting System (VAERS). *Vaccine.* 1994;12:542–550.
Clarke J. Contact tracing for chlamydia: data on effectiveness. *Int J STD AIDS.* 1998;9:187–191.
Clayton EW, Hickson GB. Compensation under the National Childhood Vaccine Injury Act. *J Pediatr.* 1990;116:508–513.
Dorsinville MS. Case management of tuberculosis in New York City. *Int J Tuberc Lung Dis.* 1998;2:S46–S52.
Drysdale SF. Knowledge of infectious disease reporting amongst military and civilian medical officers. *J R Army Med Corps.* 1994;140:125–126.
Edwards SK, White C. HIV seroconversion illness after orogenital contact with successful contact tracing. *Int J STD AIDS.* 1995;6:50–51.
Evans G. National Childhood Vaccine Injury Act: revision of the vaccine injury table. *Pediatrics.* 1996;98:1179–1181.
Faxelid E, Ndulo J, Ahlberg BM, Krantz I. Behaviour, knowledge and reactions concerning sexually transmitted diseases: implications for partner notification in Lusaka. *East Afr Med J.* 1994;71:118–121.
Fenton KA, Peterman TA. HIV partner notification: taking a new look. *AIDS.* 1997;11:1535–1546.
FitzGerald M, Bell G. Measuring the effectiveness of contact tracing. *Int J STD AIDS.* 1998;9:645–646.
Fourie PB, Becker PJ, Festenstein F, et al. Procedures for developing a simple scoring method based on unsophisticated criteria for screening children for tuberculosis. *Int J Tuberc Lung Dis.* 1998;2:116–123.
Gateley K. Communicable disease reporting: why? *J Tenn Med Assoc.* 1990;83:512–513.
Gaudino JA Jr, Blackmore-Prince C, Yip R, Rochat RW. Quality assessment of fetal death records in Georgia: a method for improvement. *Am J Public Health.* 1997;87:1323–1327.
Graves T. Communicable disease reporting. *J Okla State Med Assoc.* 1996;89:407–409.
Green DC, Moore JM, Adams MM, Berg CJ, Wilcox LS, McCarthy BJ. Are we underestimating rates of vaginal birth after previous cesarean birth? The validity of delivery methods from birth certificates. *Am J Epidemiol.* 1998;147:581–586.
Hall WN. A report on Michigan's new Lyme disease reporting requirement. *Mich Med.* 1990;89:45.
Herrick TA, Davison ZM. School contact tracing for tuberculosis using two-step Mantoux testing. *Can J Public Health.* 1995;86:321–324.
Hoffman RE, Spencer NE, Miller LA. Comparison of partner notification at anonymous and confidential HIV test sites in Colorado. *J Acquir Immune Defic Syndr Hum Retrovirol.* 1995;8:406–410.
Howell MR, Kassler WJ, Haddix A. Partner notification to prevent pelvic inflammatory disease in women: cost-effectiveness of two strategies. *Sex Transm Dis.* 1997;24:287–292.
Jordan WC, Tolbert L, Smith R. Partner notification and fo-

cused intervention as a means of identifying HIV-positive patients. *J Natl Med Assoc*. 1998;90:542–546.

Kassler WJ, Meriwether RA, Klimko TB, Peterman TA, Zaidi A. Eliminating access to anonymous HIV antibody testing in North Carolina: effects on HIV testing and partner notification. *J Acquir Immune Defic Syndr Hum Retrovirol*. 1997;14:281–289.

Kirby RS. The quality of vital perinatal statistics data, with special reference to prenatal care. *Paediatr Perinat Epidemiol*. 1997;11:122–128.

Kirsch T, Shesser R. A survey of emergency department communicable disease reporting practices. *J Emerg Med*. 1991;9:211–214.

Klovdahl AS, Potterat JJ, Woodhouse DE, Muth JB, Muth SQ, Darrow WW. Social networks and infectious disease: the Colorado Springs Study. *Soc Sci Med*. 1994;38:79–88.

Ktsanes VK, Lawrence DW, Kelso K, McFarland L. Survey of Louisiana physicians on communicable disease reporting. *J La State Med Soc*. 1991;143:27–28, 30–31.

Landwirth J. Medical-legal aspects of immunization: policy and practices. *Pediatr Clin North Am*. 1990;37:771–784.

Levy JA, Fox SE. The outreach-assisted model of partner notification with IDUs. *Public Health Rep*. 1998;113:160–169.

MacIntyre CR, Plant AJ. Preventability of incident cases of tuberculosis in recently exposed contacts. *Int J Tuberc Lung Dis*. 1998;2:56–61.

Mackay L. Evaluation is the key to success: a nurse-led tuberculosis contact tracing service. *Prof Nurse*. 1993;9:176–180.

Macke BA, Hennessy M, McFarlane MM, Bliss MJ. Partner notification in the real world: a four site time–allocation study. *Sex Transm Dis*. 1998;25:561–568.

Maudsley G, Williams EM. Inaccuracy in death certification—where are we now? *J Public Health Med*. 1996;18:59–66.

McDermott J, Drews C, Green D, Berg C. Evaluation of prenatal care information on birth certificates. *Paediatr Perinat Epidemiol*. 1997;11:105–121.

Menzies D. Issues in the management of contacts of patients with active pulmonary tuberculosis. *Can J Public Health*. 1997;88:197–201.

Norwood C. Mandated life versus mandatory death: New York's disgraceful partner notification record. *J Community Health*. 1995;20:161–170.

Oh MK, Boker JR, Genuardi FJ, Cloud GA, Reynolds J, Hodgens JB. Sexual contact tracing outcome in adolescent chlamydial and gonococcal cervicitis cases. *J Adolesc Health*. 1996;18:4–9.

Olsen CL, Polan AK, Cross PK. Case ascertainment for state-based birth defects registries: characteristics of unreported infants ascertained through birth certificates and their impact on registry statistics in New York state. *Paediatr Perinat Epidemiol*. 1996;10:161–174.

Oxman AD, Scott EA, Sellors JW, et al. Partner notification for sexually transmitted diseases: an overview of the evidence. *Can J Public Health*. 1994;85(suppl 1):S41–S47.

Oxman GL, Doyle L. A comparison of the case-finding effectiveness and average costs of screening and partner notification. *Sex Transm Dis*. 1996;23:51–57.

Peterson DC. Clinician responsibilities under the National Childhood Vaccine Injury Act. *Minn Med*. 1992;75:29–31.

Potterat JJ. Contact tracing's price is not its value. *Sex Transm Dis*. 1997;24:519–521.

Rahman M, Fukui T, Asai A. Cost-effectiveness analysis of partner notification program for human immunodeficiency virus infection in Japan. *J Epidemiol*. 1998;8:123–128.

Roberts DF. Disease reporting: the first step in surveillance. *SC Nurse*. 1996;3:16–17.

Robinson AJ, Greenhouse P. Prevention of recurrent pelvic infection by contact tracing: a commonsense approach. *Br J Obstet Gynaecol*. 1996;103:859–861.

Rodriguez EM, Steinbart S, Shaulis G, Bur S, Dwyer DM. Pulmonary tuberculosis in a high school student and a broad contact investigation: lessons relearned. *Md Med J*. 1996;45:1019–1022.

Rogers SJ, Tross S, Doino-Ingersol J, Weisfuse I. Partner notification with HIV-infected drug users: results of formative research. *AIDS Care*. 1998;10:415–429.

Rothenberg RB, Potterat JJ, Woodhouse DE. Personal risk taking and the spread of disease: beyond core groups. *J Infect Dis*. 1996;174:S144–S149.

Rothenberg RB, Sterk C, Toomey KE, et al. Using social network and ethnographic tools to evaluate syphilis transmission. *Sex Transm Dis*. 1998;25:154–160.

Rothenberg RB, Woodhouse DE, Potterat JJ, Muth SQ, Darrow WW, Klovdahl AS. Social networks in disease transmission: the Colorado Springs Study. *NIDA Res Monogr*. 1995;151:3–19.

Rothman LM, Dubeski G. School contact tracing following a cluster of tuberculosis cases in two Scarborough schools. *Can J Public Health*. 1993;84:297–302.

Ruben FL, Lynch DC. Tuberculosis control through contact investigation. *Pa Med*. 1996;99:22–23.

Salerno MC, Jackson MM. Clinical savvy: what does the National Childhood Vaccine Injury Act require of nurses? *Am J Nurs*. 1988;88:1019–1020.

Sepkowitz S. Perverse reactions to pertussis vaccine by government medical agencies. *J Okla State Med Assoc*. 1996;89:135–138.

Slabber CF, Davies JC. Reporting occupational disease. *S Afr Med J*. 1994;84:127–128.

Small PM, Hopewell PC, Singh SP, et al. The epidemiology of tuberculosis in San Francisco: a population-based study using conventional and molecular methods. *N Engl J Med*. 1994;330:1703–1709.

Starr P, Starr S. Reinventing vital statistics: the impact of changes in information technology, welfare policy, and health care. *Public Health Rep*. 1995;110:534–544.

Toomey KE, Peterman TA, Dicker LW, Zaidi AA, Wroten JE, Carolina J. Human immunodeficiency virus partner notification: cost and effectiveness data from an attempted randomized controlled trial. *Sex Transm Dis*. 1998;25:310–316.

Toreki W. Risk management...National Childhood Vaccine Injury Act of 1986. *Trends Health Care Law Ethics*. 1992;7:41–44.

Valway SE, Sanchez MP, Shinnick TF, et al. An outbreak involving extensive transmission of a virulent strain of Mycobacterium tuberculosis. *N Engl J Med*. 1998;338:633–639.

Watchi R, Kahlstrom E, Vachon LA, Barnes PF. Pediatric tuberculosis: clinical presentation and contact investigation at an urban medical center. *Respiration*. 1998;65:192–194.

West GR, Stark KA. Partner notification for HIV prevention: a critical reexamination. *AIDS Educ Prev*. 1997;9:68–78.

Woodhouse DE, Potterat JJ, Rothenberg RB, Darrow WW, Klovdahl AS, Muth SQ. Ethical and legal issues in social network research: the real and the ideal. *NIDA Res Monogr*. 1995;151:131–143.

Woodhouse DE, Rothenberg RB, Potterat JJ, et al. Mapping a social network of heterosexuals at high risk for HIV infection. *AIDS*. 1994;8:1331–1336.

Woolbright LA, Harshbarger DS. The revised standard certificate of live birth: analysis of medical risk factor data from birth certificates in Alabama, 1988–92. *Public Health Rep*. 1995;110:59–63.

Law Enforcement Reporting

Andronicus M, Oates RK, Peat J, Spalding S, Martin H. Non-accidental burns in children. *Burns*. 1998;24:552–558.

Archer PJ, Mallonee S, Schmidt AC, Ikeda RM. Oklahoma Firearm-Related Injury Surveillance. *Am J Prev Med*. 1998;15:83–91.

Atta HM, Walker ML. Penetrating neck trauma: lack of universal reporting guidelines. *Am Surg*. 1998;64:222–225.

Barber CW, Ozonoff VV, Schuster M, et al. Massachusetts Weapon-Related Injury Surveillance System. *Am J Prev Med*. 1998;15:57–66.

Budai P. Mandatory reporting of child abuse: is it in the best interest of the child? *Aust NZ J Psychiatry*. 1996;30:794–804.

Chiocca EM. Documenting suspected child abuse, part I. *Nursing*. 1998;28:17.

Chiocca EM. Documenting suspected child abuse, part II. *Nursing*. 1998;28:25.

Clark KD, Tepper D, Jenny C. Effect of a screening profile on the diagnosis of nonaccidental burns in children. *Pediatr Emerg Care*. 1997;13:259–261.

Clayton EW. Potential liability in cases of child abuse and neglect. *Pediatr Ann*. 1997;26:173–177.

Clift G, Dickerson M, Wosiski KS. Following up on child abuse suspicions. *Adv Nurse Pract*. 1997;5:12.

Coben JH, Dearwater SR, Garrison HG, Dixon BW. Evaluation of the emergency department logbook for population-based surveillance of firearm-related injury. *Ann Emerg Med*. 1996;28:188–193.

Committee on Child Abuse and Neglect. Shaken baby syndrome: inflicted cerebral trauma. 1993–1994. *Del Med J*. 1997;69:365–370.

David TJ, Wynne G, Kessel AS, Brazier M. Child sexual abuse: when a doctor's duty to report abuse conflicts with a duty of confidentiality to the victim. *BMJ*. 1998;316:55–57.

Davidhizar R, Newman-Giger J. Recognizing abuse. *Int Nurs Rev*. 1996;43:145–150.

Deisz R, Doueck HJ, George N. Reasonable cause: a qualitative study of mandated reporting. *Child Abuse Negl*. 1996;20:275–287.

Doyle JE. Firearms injury reporting system needed. *Wis Med J*. 1996;95:267.

Drake B, Zuravin S. Bias in child maltreatment reporting: revisiting the myth of classlessness. *Am J Orthopsychiatry*. 1998;68:295–304.

Erickson RA, Hart SJ. Domestic violence: legal, practice, and educational issues. *Medsurg Nurs*. 1998;7:142–147, 164.

Fox J, Stahlsmith L, Remington P, Tymus T, Hargarten S. The Wisconsin Firearm-Related Injury Surveillance System. *Am J Prev Med*. 1998;15:101–108.

Greipp ME. Ethical decision making and mandatory reporting in cases of suspected child abuse. *J Pediatr Health Care*. 1997;11:258–265.

Grossoehme DH. Child abuse reporting: clergy perceptions. *Child Abuse Negl*. 1998;22:743–747.

Hammond PV. Child abuse and neglect among school aged children: reporting weaknesses. *J Cult Divers*. 1994;1:19–20.

Hedegaard H, Wake M, Hoffman R. Firearm-related injury surveillance in Colorado. *Am J Prev Med*. 1998;15:38–45.

Hyman A. Domestic violence: legal issues for health care practitioners and institutions [published erratum appears in *J Am Med Womens Assoc*. 1996;August–October;51:132]. *J Am Med Womens Assoc*. 1996;51:101–105.

Jessee SA. Orofacial manifestations of child abuse and neglect. *Am Fam Physician*. 1995;52:1829–1834.

LeMier M, Cummings P, Keck D, Stehr-Green J, Ikeda R, Saltzman L. Washington State Gunshot-Wound Surveillance System. *Am J Prev Med*. 1998;15:92–100.

Lewin L. Child abuse: ethical and legal concerns for the nurse. *J Psychosoc Nurs Ment Health Serv*. 1994;32:15–18.

Martinez L. Child abuse and neglect investigative process. *J Tenn Dent Assoc*. 1995;75:27–29.

McDowell JD. Forensic dentistry: recognizing the signs and symptoms of domestic violence: a guide for dentists. *J Okla Dent Assoc*. 1997;88:21–28.

Mezey G, King M, MacClintock T. Victims of violence and the general practitioner. *Br J Gen Pract*. 1998;48:906–908.

Neiburger EJ. Detecting child abuse. *J Mass Dent Soc*. 1997;46:27–29.

Neiburger EJ. The false signs of child abuse. *CDS Rev.* 1997;90:10–11.

Paradise JE, Bass J, Forman SD, Berkowitz J, Greenberg DB, Mehta K. Minimum criteria for reporting child abuse from health care settings. *Del Med J.* 1997;69:357–363.

Resnick PJ, Scott CL. Legal issues in treating perpetrators and victims of violence. *Psychiatr Clin North Am.* 1997;20: 473–487.

Rhodes AM. Immunity for reporting child abuse. *MCN Am J Matern Child Nurs.* 1996;21:169.

Rodriguez MA, Craig AM, Mooney DR, Bauer HM. Patient attitudes about mandatory reporting of domestic violence: implications for health care professionals. *West J Med.* 1998;169:337–341.

Rosenblatt DE, Cho KH, Durance PW. Reporting mistreatment of older adults: the role of physicians. *J Am Geriatr Soc.* 1996;44:65–70.

Slovis TL. Child abuse: what one needs to know. *Acad Radiol.* 1995;2:728–729.

Spencer DE. Recognizing and reporting child abuse. *J Calif Dent Assoc.* 1996;24:43–49.

Steinberg KL, Levine M, Doueck HJ. Effects of legally mandated child-abuse reports on the therapeutic relationship: a survey of psychotherapists. *Am J Orthopsychiatry.* 1997; 67:112–122.

Tenney L. Child abuse: preventing, reporting, and responding. *Nurs Spectr (Wash DC).* 1995;5:8.

Teret SP. The firearm injury reporting system revisited. *JAMA.* 1996;275:70.

Teret SP, Wintemute GJ, Beilenson PL. The Firearm Fatality Reporting System: a proposal. *JAMA.* 1992;267:3073–3074.

Van Haeringen AR, Dadds M, Armstrong KL. The child abuse lottery–will the doctor suspect and report? Physician attitudes towards and reporting of suspected child abuse and neglect. *Child Abuse Negl.* 1998;22:159–169.

Wardinsky TD, Vizcarrondo FE, Cruz BK. The mistaken diagnosis of child abuse: a three-year USAF Medical Center analysis and literature review. *Mil Med.* 1995;160:15–20.

Weber RD. Adult and child abuse reporting requirements. *Mich Med.* 1998;98:8–9.

Weber RD. Reporting requirements for adult and child abuse. *J Mich Dent Assoc.* 1998;80:20, 48.

Woodall M. The fears and facts of reporting child abuse. *Penn Dent J (Phila).* 1995;62:11–16.

Appendix 12–A

National Vaccine Injury Compensation Program Vaccine Injury Table

Vaccine	Illness, disability, injury or condition covered	Time period for first symptom or manifestation of onset or of significant aggravation after vaccine administration
I. Vaccines containing tetanus toxoid (e.g., DTaP, DTP, DT; Td, or TT)	A.	4 hours
	B.	2–28 days
	C. Any acute complication (including death) of an illness, disability, injury, or condition referred to above which illness, disability, injury or condition arose within the time period prescribed	Not applicable
II. Vaccines containing whole-cell pertussis bacteria, extracted or partial cell pertussis bacteria, or specific pertussis antigen(s) (e.g., DtaP, DTP, P, DTP-HiB)	A.	4 hours
	B. (or encephalitis)	72 hours
	C. Any acute complication (including death) of an illness, disability, injury, or condition referred to above which illness, disability, injury or condition arose within the time period prescribed	Not applicable
III. Measles, mumps, and rubella vaccine or any of its components (e.g., MMR, MR, M, R)	A.	4 hours
	B. (or encephalitis)	5–15 days (not less than 5 days and not more than 15 days) for measles, mumps, rubella, or any vaccine containing any of the foregoing as a component
	C. Any acute complication (including death) of an illness, disability, injury, or condition referred to above which illness, disability, injury or condition arose within the time period prescribed	Not applicable
IV. Vaccines containing rubella virus (e.g., MMR, MR, R)	A.	7–42 days
	B. Any acute complication (including death) of an illness, disability, injury, or condition referred to above which illness, disability, injury, or condition arose within the time period prescribed	Not applicable

Note: Effective Date: March 24, 1997
Source: Data from Centers for Disease Control and Prevention.

Vaccine	Illness, disability, injury or condition covered	Time period for first symptom or manifestation of onset or of significant aggravation after vaccine administration
V. Vaccines containing measles virus (e.g., MMR, MR, M)	A.	7–30 days
	B. Vaccine-Strain Measles Viral Infection in an immunodeficient recipient	6 months
	C. Any acute complication (including death) of an illness, disability, injury, or condition referred to above which illness, disability, injury or condition arose within the time period prescribed	Not applicable
VI. Vaccines containing polio live virus (OPV)	A. Paralytic Polio	
	—in a non-immunodeficient recipient	30 days
	—in an immunodeficient recipient	6 months
	—in a vaccine-associated community case	Not applicable
	B.	
	—in a non-immunodeficient recipient	30 days
	—in an immunodeficient recipient	6 months
	—in a vaccine-associated community case	Not applicable
	C. Any acute complication (including death) of an illness, disability, injury, or condition referred to above which illness, disability, injury or condition arose within the time period prescribed	Not applicable
VII. Vaccines containing polio inactivated virus (e.g., IPV)	A.	4 hours
	B. Any acute complication (including death) of an illness, disability, injury, or condition referred to above which illness, disability, injury or condition arose within the time period prescribed	Not applicable
VIII. Hepatitis B. vaccines	A.	4 hours
	B. Any acute complication (including death) of an illness, disability, injury, or condition referred to above which illness, disability, injury or condition arose within the time period prescribed	Not applicable
IX. Hemophilus influenzae type b polysaccharide vaccines (unconjugated, PRP vaccines)	A.	7 days
	B. Any acute complication (including death) of an illness, disability, injury, or condition referred to above which illness, disability, injury or condition arose within the time period prescribed	Not applicable

Vaccine	Illness, disability, injury or condition covered	Time period for first symptom or manifestation of onset or of significant aggravation after vaccine administration
X. Hemophilus influenzae type b polysaccharide conjugate vaccines	No condition specified	Not applicable
XI. Varicella vaccine	No condition specified	Not applicable
XII. Any new vaccine recommended by the Centers for Disease Control and Prevention for routine administration to children, after publication by the Secretary of a notice of coverage	No condition specified	Not applicable

Qualifications and Aids to Interpretation

(1) Anaphylaxis and anaphylactic shock

Anaphylaxis and anaphylactic shock mean an acute, severe, and potentially lethal systemic allergic reaction. Most cases resolve without sequelae. Signs and symptoms begin minutes to a few hours after exposure. Death, if it occurs, usually results from airway obstruction caused by laryngeal edema or bronchospasm and may be associated with cardiovascular collapse. Other significant clinical signs and symptoms may include the following: Cyanosis, hypotension, bradycardia, tachycardia, arrhythmia, edema of the pharynx and/or trachea and/or larynx with stridor and dyspnea. Autopsy findings may include acute emphysema which results from lower respiratory tract obstruction, edema of the hypopharynx, epiglottis, larynx, or trachea and minimal findings of eosinophilia in the liver, spleen and lungs. When death occurs within minutes of exposure and without signs of respiratory distress, there may not be significant pathologic findings.

(2) Encephalopathy

For purposes of the Vaccine Injury Table, a vaccine recipient shall be considered to have suffered an encephalopathy only if such recipient manifests, within the applicable period, an injury meeting the description below of an acute encephalopathy, and then a chronic encephalopathy persists in such person for more than 6 months beyond the date of vaccination.

(I) An acute encephalopathy is one that is sufficiently severe so as to require hospitalization (whether or not hospitalization occurred).

(A) **For children less than 18 months of age** who present without an associated seizure event, an acute encephalopathy is indicated by a "significantly decreased level of consciousness" (see below) lasting for at least 24 hours. Those children less than 18 months of age who present following a seizure shall be viewed as having an acute encephalopathy if their significantly decreased level of consciousness persists beyond 24 hours and cannot be attributed to a postictal state (seizure) or medication.

(B) **For adults and children 18 months of age or older,** an acute encephalopathy is one that persists for at least 24 hours and characterized by at least two of the following:

(1) A significant change in mental status that is not medication related; specifically a confusional state, or a delirium, or a psychosis;

(2) A significantly decreased level of consciousness, which is independent of a seizure and cannot be attributed to the effects of medication; and

(3) A seizure associated with loss of consciousness.

(C) Increased intracranial pressure may be a clinical feature of acute encephalopathy in any age group.

(D) A "significantly decreased level of consciousness" is indicated by the presence of at least one of the following clinical signs for at least 24 hours or greater (see paragraphs of this section for applicable timeframes):

(1) Decreased or absent response to environment (responds, if at all, only to loud voice or painful stimuli);

(2) Decreased or absent eye contact (does not fix gaze upon family members or other individuals); or

(3) Inconsistent or absent responses to external stimuli (does not recognize familiar people or things).

(E) The following clinical features alone, or in combination, do not demonstrate an acute encephalopathy or a significant change in either mental status or level of consciousness as described above: Sleepiness, irritability (fussiness), high-pitched and unusual screaming, persistent inconsolable crying, and bulging fontanelle. Seizures in themselves are not sufficient to constitute a diagnosis of encephalopathy. In the absence of other evidence of an acute encephalopathy, seizures shall not be viewed as the first symptom or manifestation of the onset of an acute encephalopathy.

(ii) **Chronic encephalopathy** occurs when a change in mental or neurologic status, first manifested during the applicable time period, persists for a period of at least 6 months from the date of vaccination. Individuals who return to a normal neurologic state after the acute encephalopathy shall not be presumed to have suffered residual neurologic damage from that event; any subsequent chronic encephalopathy shall not be presumed to be a sequela of the acute encephalopathy. If a preponderance of the evidence indicates that a child's chronic encephalopathy is secondary to genetic, prenatal or perinatal factors, that chronic encephalopathy shall not be considered to be a condition set forth in the Table.

(iii) An encephalopathy shall not be considered to be a condition set forth in the Table if in a proceeding on a petition, it is shown by a preponderance of the evidence that the encephalopathy was caused by an infection, a toxin, a metabolic disturbance, a structural lesion, a genetic disorder or trauma (without regard to whether the cause of the infection, toxin, trauma, metabolic disturbance, structural lesion or genetic disorder is known). If at the time a decision is made on a petition filed under section 2111(b) of the Act for a vaccine-related injury or death, it is not possible to determine the cause by a preponderance of the evidence of an encephalopathy, the encephalopathy shall be considered to be a condition set forth in the Table.

(iv) In determining whether or not an encephalopathy is a condition set forth in the Table, the Court shall consider the entire medical record.

(3) Residual seizure disorder

A petitioner may be considered to have suffered a residual seizure disorder for purposes of the Vaccine Injury Table, if the first seizure or convulsion occurred 5–15 days (not less than 5 days and not more than 15 days) after administration of the vaccine and 2 or more additional distinct seizure or convulsion episodes occurred within 1 year after the administration of the vaccine which were unaccompanied by fever (defined as a rectal temperature equal to or greater than 101.0 degrees Fahrenheit or an oral temperature equal to or greater than 100.0 degrees Fahrenheit). A distinct seizure or convulsion episode is ordinarily defined as including all seizure or convulsive activity occurring within a 24-hour period, unless competent and qualified expert neurological testimony is presented to the contrary in a particular case.

For purposes of the Vaccine Injury Table, a petitioner shall not be considered to have suffered a residual seizure disorder, if the petitioner suffered a seizure or convulsion unaccompanied by fever (as defined above) before the fifth day after the administration of the vaccine involved.

(4) Seizure and convulsion

For purposes of paragraphs and of this section, the terms, "seizure" and "convulsion" include myoclonic, generalized tonic-clonic (grand mal), and simple and complex partial seizures. Absence (petit mal) seizures shall not be considered to be a condition set forth in the Table. Jerking movements or staring episodes alone are not necessarily an indication of seizure activity.

(5) Sequela

The term "sequela" means a condition or event which was actually caused by a condition listed in the Vaccine Injury Table.

(6) Chronic arthritis

For purposes of the Vaccine Injury Table, chronic arthritis may be found in a person with no history in the 3 years prior to vaccination of arthropathy (joint disease) on the basis of:

(A) Medical documentation, recorded within 30 days after the onset, or objective signs of acute arthritis (joint swelling) that occurred between 7 and 42 days after a rubella vaccination;
(B) Medical documentation (recorded within 3 years after the onset of acute arthritis) of the persistence of objective signs of intermittent or continuous arthritis for more than 6 months following vaccination;
(C) Medical documentation of an antibody response to the rubella virus.

For purposes of the Vaccine Injury Table, the following shall not be considered as chronic arthritis: Musculoskeletal disorders such as diffuse connective tissue diseases (including but not limited to rheumatoid arthritis, juvenile rheumatoid arthritis, systemic lupus erythematosus, systemic sclerosis, mixed connective tissue disease, polymyositis/dermatomyositis, fibromyalgia, necrotizing vasculitis and vasculopathies and Sjogren's syndrome), degenerative joint disease, infectious agents other than rubella (whether by direct invasion or as an immune reaction), metabolic and endocrine diseases, trauma, neoplasms, neuropathic disorders, bone and cartilage disorders and arthritis associated with ankylosing spondylitis, psoriasis, inflammatory bowel disease, Reiter's syndrome, or blood disorders.

Arthralgia (joint pain) or stiffness without joint swelling shall not be viewed as chronic arthritis for purposes of the Vaccine Injury Table.

(7) Brachial neuritis

Brachial neuritis is defined as dysfunction limited to the upper extremity nerve plexus (i.e., its trunks, divisions, or cords) without involvement of other peripheral (e.g., nerve roots or a single peripheral nerve) or central (e.g., spinal cord) nervous system structures. A deep, steady, often severe aching pain in the shoulder and upper arm usually heralds onset of the condition. The pain is followed in days or weeks by weakness and atrophy in upper extremity muscle groups. Sensory loss may accompany the motor deficits, but is generally a less notable clinical feature. The neuritis or plexopathy, may be present on the same side as or the opposite side of the injection; it is sometimes bilateral, affecting both upper extremities. Weakness is required before the diagnosis can be made. Motor, sensory, and reflex findings on physical examination and the results of nerve conduction and electromyographic studies must be consistent in confirming that dysfunction is attributable to the brachial plexus. The condition should thereby be distinguishable from conditions that may give rise to dysfunction of nerve roots (i.e., radiculopathies) and peripheral nerves (i.e., including multiple mononeuropathies), as well as other peripheral and central nervous system structures (e.g., cranial neuropathies and myelopathies).

(8) Thrombocytopenic purpura

Thrombocytopenic purpura is defined by a serum platelet count less than 50,000/mm^3. Thrombocytopenic purpura does not include cases of thrombocytopenia associated with other causes such as hypersplenism, autoimmune disorders (including alloantibodies from previous transfusions) myelodysplasias, lymphoproliferative disorders, congenital thrombocytopenia or hemolytic uremic syndrome. This does not include cases of immune (formerly called idiopathic) thrombocytopenic purpura (ITP) that are mediated, for example, by viral or fungal infections, toxins or drugs. Thrombocytopenic purpura does not include cases of thrombocytopenia associated with disseminated intravascular coagulation, as observed with bacterial and viral infections. Viral infections include, for example, those infections secondary to Epstein Barr virus, cytomegalovirus, hepatitis A and B, rhinovirus, human immunodeficiency virus (HIV), adenovirus, and dengue virus. An antecedent viral infection may be demonstrated by clinical signs and symptoms and need not be confirmed by culture or serologic testing. Bone marrow examination, if performed, must reveal a normal or an increased number of megakaryocytes in an otherwise normal marrow.

(9) Vaccine-strain measles viral infection

Vaccine-strain measles viral infection is defined as a disease caused by the vaccine-strain that should be determined by vaccine-specific monoclonal antibody or polymerase chain reaction tests.

(10) Vaccine-strain polio viral infection

Vaccine-strain polio viral infection is defined as a disease caused by poliovirus that is isolated from the affected tissue and should be determined to be the vaccine-strain by oligonucleotide or polymerase chain reaction. Isolation of poliovirus from the stool is not sufficient to establish a tissue specific infection or disease caused by vaccine-strain poliovirus.

(11) Early-onset Hib disease

Early-onset Hib disease is defined as invasive bacterial illness associated with the presence of Hib organism on culture of normally sterile body fluids or tissue, or clinical findings consistent with the diagnosis of epiglottitis. Hib pneumonia qualifies as invasive Hib disease when radiographic findings consistent with the diagnosis of pneumonitis are accompanied by a blood culture positive for the Hib organism. Otitis media, in the absence of the above findings, does not qualify as invasive bacterial disease. A child is considered to have suffered this injury only if the vaccine was the first Hib immunization received by the child.

For additional information call our public information line at 1-800-338-2382 or to send an e-mail inquiry.

Last updated 03/24/97

CHAPTER 13

Family Planning, Adoption, and Surrogacy

HIGHLIGHTS

- There are special constitutional protections for reproductive medicine.
- Family planning implicates the rights of fathers and mothers.
- Surrogacy has legal implications for all participants.
- Violation of adoption laws can result in criminal liability.
- Full disclosure and careful investigation is critical in adoption and surrogacy.

INTRODUCTION

Family planning issues have dominated medical law constitutional litigation for decades. Most precedent-setting litigation on the health care practitioner–patient relationship has arisen in the context of contraception first, then abortion, and now surrogacy because these are areas with no general political consensus on the proper reach of the law. Even the *Cruzan* right-to-die decision was based on a law passed as part of an antiabortion legislative package.

This chapter treats family planning and surrogacy together because of their interrelated legal status. Adoption is included because it is a necessary legal building block for many surrogacy issues: there cannot be a valid surrogacy transaction unless the state laws on adoption and parental rights are appropriately considered. The legal controversies over the topics transcend even abortion because they deal with most intimate relationships and must balance the rights of three parties—mother, father, and child. Since the interests

of these parties are often at odds, this will remain a controversial area of law.

ETHICAL DILEMMAS IN FAMILY PLANNING

Few other areas of medicine are as fraught with ethical and legal hazards as is reproductive care. Some health care practitioners see abortion and contraception as sins; some find it immoral that women who are not able to support their existing children are not prevented from having more children; most consider it unethical to deny women medical control over their own bodies. Charting a legally and ethically defensible path through this minefield is difficult. The fundamental principle that must underlie all medical care is that of honesty:

> The principle of autonomy requires that a patient be given complete and truthful information about her medical condition and any proposed treatment. Only with such information is she able to exercise her right to make choices about health

care. If complete information is not available, existing uncertainty should be shared with the patient. It is inappropriate for a health care practitioner to assume that he or she is better able to assess what the patient would want to know than is the patient herself. In general, a patient benefits from a full understanding of her medical condition, its prognosis, and the treatment available. The perception that a health care practitioner has concealed the truth or has engaged in deception will weaken the patient trust and undermine the health care practitioner–patient relationship. Thus the norm of honesty can be based on the principle of beneficence as well as on the principle of autonomy.[1]

Honest and ethical reproductive care should ensure (1) that patients are given full information about any restrictions on reproductive care provided by the health care practitioner; (2) that health care practitioners counsel patients about alternative care even if they do not provide the care; (3) that health care practitioners are not bound to provide elective care that is abhorrent to their religious beliefs; (4) that health care practitioners balance the medical necessity of sexual history taking with the patient's concern for privacy; and (5) that health care practitioners do not compromise a patient's health by refusing to provide needed care in an emergency, even if the health care practitioner could refuse to provide the same services on an elective basis.

Balancing the Health Care Practitioner's and the Patient's Rights

The tension between a health care practitioner's right to refuse to participate in certain types of medical care and a patient's right to receive care begins in medical school and residency training. The constitutional right to exercise one's religion freely has always been limited by the state's right to pass laws that apply equally to all citizens. Although the state has the right to specify the required training and specific factual knowledge of persons it licenses to practice medicine, this is usually left to the discretion of accreditation agencies for medical training programs. These agencies determine the extent to which a medical student or resident may avoid certain procedures and still be allowed to be certified.

Medical training programs must meet the requirements of their accrediting organizations if their students and residents are to be eligible for licensing or advanced certification after completing their training. The federal courts have recently upheld the right of the Accreditation Council for Graduate Medical Education (ACGME) to require residents in an ACGME-accredited program to receive training in abortion, sterilization, and contraception. The case in question arose when the ACGME rescinded the accreditation of a residency based in a Catholic hospital. Many Catholic hospitals prohibit residents from performing these procedures in the hospital itself. This program was unusual in forbidding the residents to perform the procedures in other hospitals, thus ensuring that the residents did not learn techniques for abortion and sterilization or have adequate training to provide information on contraception. The court found that the training requirement was not religiously motivated. Since the requirement did not advocate a religious doctrine and was nondiscrimatorily applied, it did not violate the First Amendment protections on free exercise of religion.[2]

Once they are in independent practice, health care practitioners must make any self-imposed limitations on the care they offer clear to their patients as early in the encounter as feasible. Ideally, patients will be asked what care they are seeking when making their initial appointment. If the patient is seeking care that the health care practitioner is unwilling to provide, the patient can be directed elsewhere at once. Under no circumstances should health care practitioners withhold their beliefs in an attempt to persuade the patient to change her mind. Implicitly or explicitly holding out the availability of services that are not in fact available is deception.

Putting the patient on notice of the health care practitioner's refusal to provide certain types of care does not obviate the health care practitioner's duty to inform the patient when this care is appropriate. For example, if the health care practitioner discovers that the patient has a medical condition that would make pregnancy difficult, the health care practitioner must counsel the patient on the availability of contraception and sterilization. The requirement that a health care practitioner refer a patient to an alternative source of care is the same whether the health care practitioner is unable to provide the care or the health care practitioner has personal objections to the care. A health care practitioner may not abandon a patient on religious grounds. The health care practitioner–patient relationship carries with it a duty to continue care until an alternative is provided.

Contractual Limitations on Refusing To Provide Care

Most health care practitioners today have signed contracts obligating themselves to care for various patients who are insured with a contracting third-party payer. It is unusual for these contracts to exempt the health care practitioner from providing care that is morally abhorrent to him or her. Without such a specific exemption, it is arguable that the health care practitioner is contractually obligated to provide all medically acceptable care that the patient requests.

Health care practitioners who work in emergency rooms or in locum tenens situations are also subject to a contractual obligation to provide all care that is not specifically exempted from the contract. Even if the health care practitioner has a contract that allows certain care to be avoided, a patient seeking care at the emergency room has the expectation that any appropriate care will be available. If there is a threat of immediate danger to the patient or there has been no provision for an alternative source of care for patients in an ambulatory care practice, the health care practitioner will have to provide the necessary care without regard for his or her personal beliefs. Even religious hospitals are constrained in the care that they must provide to emergency patients if the denial of care would result in preventable injury. A patient who presented in shock from an incomplete abortion should have an immediate uterine evacuation. It is an unacceptable standard of care to wait to see if the fetal heart had ceased to beat.

Consent for Reproductive Care

A mentally competent adult woman has the sole authority to consent to her medical care in all but very limited circumstances. A woman's husband has the right to veto care that will result in the conception of a child without his explicit or implied consent. This is limited to vetoing artificial insemination or embryo transplants. (If such a controversy arises, the health care practitioner may want to have his or her attorney review any agreements.) A husband has no veto or right to be informed of his wife's decisions on contraception, sterilization, or abortion. The state may also determine what care can be obtained or refused under its power to protect either the public health and safety or the best interests of an individual. Unless the state or federal government has passed a law governing consent or access to the care in question, the decision rests with the woman and her health care practitioner.

Health care practitioners should encourage women to discuss reproductive choices with their husbands or significant others, but it is improper to require the husband's consent. No court has allowed a husband to recover from a health care practitioner on the theory that the husband had a right to be consulted about his wife's medical care. Health care practitioners who obtain a husband's consent rather than the wife's (unless the husband is the legal guardian or has been delegated the right to consent in a durable power of attorney) can be liable for battery to the wife. A more subtle risk arises when the husband and wife are estranged or legally separated. In these cases, the wife's expectation of privacy is great, and a health care practitioner who consults her husband without her permission can be sued for breaching the confidential relationship. This becomes a serious medical risk if necessary care is denied or delayed because of a husband's wishes or because of a delay in finding the husband, or because the communication to the husband triggers abuse of the wife.

Health care practitioners should be very careful about interfering in marital relationships and about giving out patient information to spouses. If a patient does not want a spouse or family member to be informed about medical care, this wish must be honored. In one case, a woman who did not want more children was taking oral contraceptives without her husband's knowledge. When the husband asked the family doctor why the couple had not conceived, the doctor told the husband about the pills. The husband went home and severely beat his wife. In this case, the health care practitioner could be held liable for the beating because it was a foreseeable consequence of the health care practitioner's improper disclosure of private medical information.

TAKING A SEXUAL HISTORY

All reproductive care begins with a sexual history. Traditionally, health care practitioners avoided discussing sexual practices with their patients, due partly to mutual embarrassment and, more recently, a fear of seeming judgmental. This reticence has contributed to the epidemic spread of sexually transmitted diseases, including HIV. It has also encouraged the perpetuation of the stereotyping of patients, especially women, by the health care practitioner's assumptions about their sexual behavior. Sexually active females were not provided information because it was assumed they knew everything; those who were not obviously sexually active were assumed not to need the information. Patients were sometimes injured by health care practitioners who missed diagnosing sexually transmitted diseases because they assumed the patient was not sexually active.

Health care practitioners can ignore patient sexuality no longer. They must ask patients about high-risk behavior and counsel them in the risks of such behavior:

> Counseling and testing are recommended in any medical setting in which women at risk are encountered, including private practices and clinics offering services for gynecologic and prenatal care, family planning, and diagnosis and treatment of sexually transmitted diseases. Voluntary and confidential HIV antibody testing, with appropriate counseling and consent, should be offered to all women and encouraged for those who are at risk for acquiring the disease.

The risk factors for acquiring HIV infection apply to a woman or to her sexual partner and include the following:

- illicit drug abuse (especially intravenous drug use)
- current or previous multiple sexual partners or prostitution
- transfusion of blood or blood products before adequate screening began in the United States (between 1978–1985)
- bisexual activity
- origin in countries where the incidence of HIV is high
- symptoms of HIV-related illnesses
- history of or current sexually transmitted diseases

In addition, testing is recommended in the presence of tuberculosis or any illness for which a positive test result might affect the recommended diagnostic evaluation, treatment, or follow up.[3]

This sexual history must be documented as carefully as any other part of the medical history. The health care practitioner should ask every patient the same basic questions. Even if a woman is self-identified as homosexual, she should be counseled to ensure that she understands the options for contraception and reproductive health. These matters may not be of immediate concern to her, yet many male and female homosexuals do enter into heterosexual relationships to conceive children or as a variant on their usual sexual activity. It is also important to ask self-identifed heterosexuals about homosexual activity. This is especially important for prisoners who may engage in homosexual activities in prison but self-identify as heterosexuals and have only heterosexual relationships outside prison.

The health care practitioner's duty to ask about a patient's sexual activity must be balanced against the patient's right of privacy. If a patient denies sexual activity and there is no objective evidence to the contrary, the health care practitioner should treat this information like any other patient-reported information. As with other changeable behavior, however, the health care practitioner has a duty to re-explore the area on future visits. Given the general unreliability of self-reported information about behavior that the patient may wish to conceal, the health care practitioner should continue to consider pregnancy and venereal diseases when indicated by the patient's objective medical condition. This is especially important if the health care practitioner is considering prescribing a drug that is a known teratogen.

CONTRACEPTION

The contraceptive options for women in the United States have been unnecessarily limited by inappropriate litigation and pseudoscientific fear mongering by groups that believe contraception should be risk free. The benefit-to-risk ratio for oral contraceptives is among the highest for any pharmaceutical.[4] Even intrauterine devices (IUDs), which pose substantially greater risks than oral contraceptives, pose very low absolute risks.[5]

Contraception is medical therapy that is usually prescribed for healthy persons. As with childhood immunizations, the general populace have forgotten the risks of the alternative—be it unwanted pregnancy or pertussis. The very success of the drugs has contributed to the expectation that they should be risk free—not merely extremely safe.

The choice of a contraceptive is determined by physiological, behavioral, and psychological factors. Given that most women are physiologically able to tolerate oral contraceptives, IUDs, and barrier forms of contraception, behavioral and psychological factors have been most important. Until recently, these tended toward oral contraceptives. Women outside long-term relationships usually preferred the privacy and flexibility of IUDs or oral contraceptives. Because of the real and perceived risks of IUDs, the majority of these women choose oral contraceptives.

The standard of care for informed consent for oral contraceptives is set by contraceptive manufacturers, public health officials, and federal and state law. The standard for informed consent for IUDs is set by standard consent forms supplied by the IUD manufacturers.

The health care practitioner should inform a patient of risks and alternatives whether the contraceptives being used are prescription, over-the-counter, or so-called natural methods. It is important to consider the patient's life style and health behavior in tailoring informed consent to the patient. A patient who smokes is a poor candidate for birth control pills. However, if the patient has religious objections to abortion and intrauterine devices because she believes they are abortive, then pills may be the only acceptable alternative. The health care practitioner should explain the risks carefully and encourage the patient to stop smoking as an alternative method of reducing the risks.

Balancing the Risk of Pregnancy

Except for the growing threat of HIV infection, the risks posed by pregnancy are the most important consideration in choosing a method of contraception. For the patient with a disease condition that makes pregnancy dangerous, effectiveness may be the most important consideration. The patient with heart disease should realize that a barrier method that is only 70% effective is probably not adequate to her needs. For the patient who could not accept induced abortion in any form, the safety of the fetus in the event of conception may be paramount. It would be unwise to insert an IUD in a patient who would not allow its removal if she became pregnant with the device in place. The health care practitioner might be liable for an injury to the patient even if she refused to follow his or her advice when the pregnancy occurred.

Legally Mandated Warnings for Oral Contraceptives

Oral contraceptives are unusual in that Congress mandates that each patient receive a package insert with the pills to supplement the information provided by health care practitioners when obtaining informed consent to the use of these pills. Health care practitioners cannot rely on the patient's reading this package insert. Effective informed consent requires that the patient receive the information—not merely that the information be available. Since the patient will not receive the package insert until after the decision to take the pills has occurred, it is arguable that even a patient who reads the insert has already committed to the treatment.

Congress established a warning requirement for these pills because it believed that "the safe and effective use of oral contraceptive drug products requires that patients be fully informed of the benefits and the risks involved in their use." Although this law is aimed at persons dispensing and manufacturing oral contraceptives, it provides a useful benchmark for health care practitioners counseling patients. The federal law requires patients to be given the following information with a prescription for oral contraceptives:

Package Insert for Oral Contraceptives

- The name of the drug.

- A summary including a statement concerning the effectiveness of oral contraceptives in preventing pregnancy, the contraindications to the drug's use, and a statement of the risks and benefits associated with the drug's use.

- A statement comparing the effectiveness of oral contraceptives to other methods of contraception.

- A boxed warning concerning the increased risks associated with cigarette smoking and oral contraceptive use.

- A discussion of the contraindications to use, including information that the patient should provide to the prescriber before taking the drug.

- A statement of medical conditions that are not contraindications to use but deserve special consideration in connection with oral contraceptive use and about which the patient should inform the prescriber.

- A warning regarding the most serious side effects of oral contraceptives.

- A statement of other serious adverse reactions and potential safety hazards that may result from the use of oral contraceptives.

- A statement concerning common but less serious side effects which may help the patient

evaluate the benefits and risks from the use of oral contraceptives.

- Information on precautions the patients should observe while taking oral contraceptives, including the following:

  - A statement of risks to the mother and unborn child from the use of oral contraceptives before or during early pregnancy;

  - A statement concerning excretion of the drug in human milk and associated risks to the nursing infant;

  - A statement about laboratory tests that may be affected by oral contraceptives; and

  - A statement that identifies activities and drugs, foods, or other substances the patient should avoid because of their interactions with oral contraceptives.

- Information about how to take oral contraceptives properly, including information about what to do if the patient forgets to take the product, information about becoming pregnant after discontinuing use of the drug, a statement that the drug product has been prescribed for the use of the patient and should not be used for other conditions or given to others, and a statement that the patient's pharmacist or practitioner has a more technical leaflet about the drug product that the patient may ask to review.

- A statement of the possible benefits associated with oral contraceptive use. (21 CFR, sec. 310.501)

Health care practitioners should obtain the mandated package insert for each oral contraceptive that they prescribe and discuss the relevant insert with the patient as part of the informed consent for taking oral contraceptives. This is best done with a detailed consent form that follows the package insert for the oral contraceptives being prescribed. The health care practitioner should give the patient a copy of the insert irrespective of where she will obtain the pills. If the health care practitioner also gives the patient a starter pack or otherwise dispenses oral contraceptives, the law requires that the patient be given a package insert with the pills: "Each dispenser of an oral contraceptive drug product shall provide a patient package insert to each patient (or to an agent of the patient) to whom the product is dispensed, except that the dispenser may provide the insert to the parent or legal guardian of a legally incompetent patient (or to the agent of either)."

Implantable Contraceptives

There are two implantable contraceptives in general use in the United States: Norplant, a long-term, reversible contraceptive system; and Depo-Provera, an injectable contraceptive that lasts about 3 months as used in the United States. As with other high-maintenance implantables, health care practitioners have a duty to keep track of patients with implantable contraceptives. They should use the same tracking system for patients with implantable contraceptives as for patients with implanted devices such as pacemakers. The patient should be given written information about the importance of follow-up care and the symptoms that should prompt an immediate call to the health care practitioner.

The patient should be contacted before the date when the contraceptive is scheduled to lose effectiveness. If the patient cannot be contacted, the physician should send a certified letter to the patient's last known address and document that it was either received or returned. Patients with Norplant should be seen at least once a year for evaluation of potential side effects and must be seen at the end of five years to remove or replace the implants. Patients with Depo-Provera will be seen quarterly to renew the implant. When patients with either contraceptive are seen, they should be carefully checked for sexually transmitted diseases, especially HIV. Although implantable contraceptives do not facilitate pelvic infections as did IUDs, they do facilitate the spread of sexually transmitted diseases by giving the false sense that they provide protection during intercourse. Health care practitioners should be careful to educate patients that implantable contraceptives do nothing to protect against HIV and that patients must also use condoms if they are to be avoid sexually transmitted diseases. This should be fully documented in the consent form for implantable contraceptives.

Natural Family Planning

The rhythm method has been expanded to include several methods of determining the time of ovulation. Although most health care practitioners do not recognize rhythm as a medical matter, it is a form of contraception their patients may use or ask about. There are risks to this method, and these risks should be explained to patients.

The most obvious risk is pregnancy. This is an effective method if used properly in selected patients, but it requires training and good record keeping. In addition, the woman must consider the social problems of abstinence. One study of the effectiveness of rhythm was discontinued after several study subjects were beaten by their husbands for refusing intercourse. Another risk is the use of rhythm as an adjunct to barrier methods by a patient who is not trained. Many couples will not use barriers if the woman is menstruating in the mistaken belief that conception is not possible. This last risk should be discussed with patients who choose to use barrier contraceptives because it may increase the incidence of pregnancy.

HIV Infection and AIDS

HIV is already one of the most common venereal diseases. Its low infectivity has slowed its spread, but as an incurable disease with a long asymptomatic latency, its predicted equilibrium level is high. There is nothing unique about the problems posed by HIV as an STD (sexually transmitted disease). The widespread reliance on oral contraceptives and IUDs has contributed to the very high levels of other STDs such as gonorrhea and chlamydia. It is the catastrophic consequences of HIV, rather than its epidemiology, that commands our attention.

As HIV infection spreads in the United States, oral contraceptives, IUDs, and other nonbarrier contraceptives are no longer acceptable choices as the sole form of birth control for women outside long-term monogamous relationships. Although the known failure rates of condoms as birth control devices makes it dishonest to speak of "safe sex," it is clear that condoms, combined with certain spermicides, appear to provide substantial protection against infection with HIV. It has already become a standard of care to counsel about the risk of HIV infection whenever contraception is discussed with a patient:

> Historically, birth control and sexually transmitted disease control were closely linked. Abstinence and condoms were birth control options that also prevented the spread of sexually transmitted diseases. A changing attitude toward sex and improved contraceptive technology, however, has effectively severed the tie between birth control and control of sexually transmitted diseases. Users of intrauterine devices, birth control pills, and sterilization, though effectively protected from pregnancy, are still at risk of sexually transmitted diseases. AIDS has signaled the need to reintegrate these aspects of gynecologic care. When contraception is discussed, women should be informed about HIV transmission and how to lower the risk of sexual transmission.[6]

Every patient must be counseled about the risks of HIV infection. Patients in long-term, monogamous relationships should be given the surgeon general's AIDS information pamphlet and be informed that the disease is spreading in the population. These persons are not at risk if their relationship is monogamous, but studies repeatedly demonstrate that a significant percentage of apparently long-term, monogamous relationships are neither. Sexually active patients who have multiple partners over a period of years or those whose partners are not exclusive are at increasing risk of contracting HIV. These patients must be counseled that methods of birth control other than condoms subject them to a substantial risk of HIV infection. The patient may choose to accept this risk, but the health care practitioner must be able to prove that the risk was assumed knowingly. The health care practitioner must carefully document that the patient was counseled about the risk of HIV infection, that HIV infection leads to AIDS in both mother and child, and that HIV is increasingly a problem for heterosexuals.

An ethical question posed by HIV and contraceptive choice is the extent to which patient choice is swayed by health care practitioner rec-ommendations. Many patients rely on their health care practitioner to let them know what is medically dangerous. If the health care practitioner tells them to give up bacon and eggs forever because their cholesterol is elevated and the same health care practitioner continues to renew their oral contraceptive prescriptions, the implicit message is that HIV is less of a threat than a greasy breakfast. This does not mean that health care practitioners should refuse to prescribe oral contraceptives for women who are not in long-term, monogamous relationships. It does mean that the health care practitioner must take care that warnings about HIV are not lost in the general noise of good health tips and recommendations that are given each patient. Patients who engage in high-risk sexual activity must be helped to understand the seriousness of the threat of HIV infection. This information should be reiterated whenever contraception is discussed or a prescription for oral contraceptives is refilled.

Minors' Access to Contraception

Minors are constrained in their ability to consent to medical care. Ideally the minor and his or her parent will agree on the need for contraception, and the parent will authorize the medical care. However, many parents do not want their sons and daughters to use contraceptives because they believe that their availability will encourage sexual activity. Minors may purchase nonprescription contraceptives in all states, and many states explicitly allow mature minors to consent to prescription contraceptives without parental consent. Health care practitioners also may counsel minors about contraception without parental consent.

Some states do not explicitly allow minors to consent to prescription contraceptives, but no state prohibits minors from receiving prescription contraceptives. The federal family planning legislation (Title X) encourages medical care providers to make contraceptives available to minors. Although this legislation has a provision requiring the parents of minor patients to be notified after the minors receive care, the enforcement of this provision has been enjoined by the courts. Ethically, health care practitioners have a duty to respect the privacy of minors. Legally, however, many states allow health care practitioners to breach the health care practitioner–patient relationship and notify parents of medical care rendered to their minor children. Currently, no state requires parents to be notified when a minor is prescribed contraception. In general, health care practitioners should respect a minor's privacy, but there are situations when it is advisable to involve her parents—for example, ancillary conditions, such as suicidal tendencies, that are detected as part of the medical encounter. The mere fact of sexual activity does not justify breaching the minor's confidence although it may be grounds for suspecting abuse or neglect if the minor is younger than 14.

Medical Issues in Contraception for Minors

Contraceptives should be prescribed only if medically indicated and desired by the minor.[7] Most health care practitioners worry about the risks of giving minors prescription contraceptives without parental consent. Parental pressure to force contraceptives on an unwilling minor is a more subtle problem. A minor who is forced to use contraceptives by a parent or guardian cannot be said to have voluntarily assumed the risks. If this minor were to suffer a stroke or other serious side effect, the health care practitioner could be sued for failure of consent. The health care practitioner should talk to the minor alone and attempt to determine if she truly wants the contraceptive. If the minor is reluctant, the health care practitioner should refuse to prescribe a contraceptive for her.

Adolescents are at special risk for STDs:

> Adolescent contraceptive practices affect the risk of infections. Many adolescents never use a method or rely solely on the oral contraceptive. Whether or not oral contraceptives increase susceptibility to certain infections, they clearly reduce the impetus to use a barrier method or to involve males in prevention. Adolescents who decide or can be persuaded to use barrier methods

seldom use them consistently and often use them incorrectly. IUD are rarely advised for adolescents and should never be considered for those at high risk for infection or for poor compliance with close follow-up.[8]

Health care practitioners prescribing contraceptives should provide the minor with all the information that is usually provided to adult patients. If the contraceptives are prescribed without parental permission, then it is advised that additional information be considered and recorded in the medical record:

1. Inquiry should always be made as to the feasibility of parental consent.
2. A full case history, including preexisting sexual activity, should be obtained and maintained, and it should demonstrate that the health care practitioner has considered the "total situation" of the patient.
3. A record should be kept of the "emergency" need and a judgment by the health care practitioner that pregnancy would constitute a serious health hazard, one more serious than the possible disadvantages of the prescription.
4. The minor should be clearly aware of the problems presented and the nature and consequences of the procedures suggested, including very specific discussions of the side effects of contraceptive pills if those are to be prescribed. She should be required to sign a consent form so stating.
5. Where follow-up care is indicated, it should be insisted on.[9]

To this list and the consent form should be added a discussion of the risks of STD infection, with particular reference to HIV.

STERILIZATION

Legally, a health care practitioner is held to the same standards of informed consent for procedures affecting reproductive capacity as for any other type of procedure. Realistically, a health care practitioner should be particularly careful that the patient understands the procedure and its risks and limitations. It is also important to make sure that any patient undergoing treatment that will cause sterility or reproductive problems knows and understands this fact. A woman may freely consent to a hysterectomy for fibroid tumors without understanding that this will make her unable to bear a child. The level of knowledge of reproductive physiology in the general public is not high. The health care practitioner who performs the hysterectomy may incur considerable liability for rendering this woman sterile without her informed consent.

Informed consent for sterilization requires the disclosure of the risks and failures of the procedure involved and appropriate alternatives. A health care practitioner should be very careful not to overestimate the effectiveness of a particular procedure and not to oversell the patient. Most malpractice litigation arising from sterilizations concerns the reversibility of the procedure. Traditionally, patients sued health care practitioners when the procedure spontaneously reversed, resulting in an unwanted pregnancy. These complaints are now joined by lawsuits alleging that the health care practitioner indicated that the sterilization could be reversed, but the reversal has been unsuccessful. Both of these claims arising from reversibility can be prevented by obtaining proper consent for the sterilization.

Every patient undergoing a sterilization procedure should understand that the procedure could fail and allow conception. The patient should be told that such failures may occur immediately or years in the future. The health care practitioner must ensure that the woman is not already pregnant when the sterilization is performed.[10] The couple deciding on a procedure should also understand that it is possible to check the success of the procedure in a man but not in a woman. This may alter their decision on which procedure to choose. It is unwise to assume that any patient is in fact sterile. If there is any question of conception after a sterilization, the patient should be evaluated thoroughly. A health care practitioner who tells a vasectomy patient that he must be sterile, without proper medical tests, may precipitate a messy divorce and paternity actions as well as a lawsuit for malpractice.

Patients must understand the permanency of surgical sterilization. No one should undergo a sterilization procedure with the idea that it can be easily reversed with a change of mind. A patient may keep that idea whatever the health care practitioner may say, but the health care practitioner should not encourage the patient to think of sterilization as reversible. The health care practitioner who does surgical repairs of sterilizations should make sure that the patient who is being sterilized does not assume that this health care practitioner has some special ability to do temporary sterilizations.

Determining Which Partner To Sterilize

Informed consent to a sterilization should include information on the alternatives, among them the sterilization of the other partner. Many couples are not aware that tubal ligation on a woman is major surgery requiring general anesthesia, while vasectomy on a man is minor surgery that can be done under local anesthesia. A gynecologist should offer the alternative to a woman before doing a tubal ligation. Gynecologists who do not do vasectomies should refer the couple to a health care practitioner who can provide the service they desire. The limits of a particular health care practitioner are no excuse for limiting a patient's choices.

The Childless Patient

The childless patient who requests sterilization leads to a quandary for most health care practitioners because some of these patients may later wish they had not been sterilized. In most cases, health care practitioners have the right to refuse to perform the surgery. But too often the only reason for the refusal is the health care practitioner's imposing his own social values on the patient. Similarly, health care practitioners may be too quick to agree to sterilize a patient if the patient has a number of children. The patient who wants a vasectomy because his marriage is in trouble and he does not trust his wife to take prescribed oral contraceptives may regret the decision just as much in his next marriage as the bachelor who thought he would not want children.

A teaching obstetrician-gynecologist developed a system for sterilization procedures that is a useful model of how to provide these services. The patients had a full range of services available and the opportunity to make informed decisions. This health care practitioner first arranged to provide vasectomies through other members of his health care practitioner group so that he could offer couples the choice of who would be sterilized without having to refer to an outside health care practitioner. Second, he made it a policy that all patients who requested sterilization give him a written explanation of why they wanted to be sterilized. This allowed him to be sure that the patient had considered the procedure carefully.

The single man in his early twenties who wrote on the note pad, "My father has Huntington's Chorea," was scheduled for surgery immediately. But the single man who simply stated that he did not like children was also scheduled. The important point was that the patient was able to state reasons for making the decision. The reasons did not affect whether the patient would be operated on unless they were medically unsound. If a patient had unfounded fears of genetic disease, these could be discussed so the patient could reevaluate the decision in the light of accurate information. Many patients decided against sterilization when they were required to consider the decision carefully.

Sterilizing Minors and Incompetents

The sterilization of legal and mental incompetents is a legally risky endeavor because of a strong societal policy against forcing or coercing individuals to be sterilized. If a health care practitioner or other person uses the threat of withdrawal of federally funded services to coerce a person into agreeing to be sterilized, he or she commits a federal crime and is subject to imprisonment. The problem is that the courts tend to assume that coercion is involved whenever a minor or incompetent is sterilized. When a sterilization is otherwise medically and ethically indicated,[11] the health care practitioner should seek a court order approving the procedure. Under no circumstances should a minor be sterilized without the approval of the appropriate court in the state where the procedure is to take place.

Federal Law Requirements

Congress has passed specific, detailed laws governing consent to sterilizations performed under federal programs. With one exception, these laws are also a useful guide to the information that must be provided to all patients considering a sterilization procedure. The exception is that the federal law requires a 30-day waiting period between signing the consent to sterilization and the actual procedure. There is a waiver provision in cases of emergency abdominal surgery and premature delivery (as long as the form was signed more than 30 days before the estimated date of delivery), but these waivers require at least a 72-hour delay.

The waiting period and other federally mandated requirements must be followed by all health care practitioners who deliver services in "programs or projects for health services which are supported in whole or in part by Federal financial assistance, whether by grant or contract, administered by the Public Health Service." These health care practitioners must use the statutorily approved consent form and patient information brochures mandated in the federal law. These materials are available from the U.S. Public Health Service. The following is the summary of the information that must be provided and the structure of the consent form:

Informed Consent

Informed consent does not exist unless a consent form is completed voluntarily and in accordance with all the requirements of this [law].

A person who obtains informed consent for a sterilization procedure must offer to answer any questions the individual to be sterilized may have concerning the procedure, provide a copy of the consent form, and provide orally all of the following information or advice to the individual who is to be sterilized:

- Advice that the individual is free to withhold or withdraw consent to the procedure any time before the sterilization without affecting his or her right to future care or treatment and without loss or withdrawal of any federally funded program benefits to which the individual might be otherwise entitled;
- A description of available alternative methods of family planning and birth control;
- Advice that the sterilization procedure is considered to be irreversible;
- A thorough explanation of the specific sterilization procedure to be performed;
- A full description of the discomforts and risks that may accompany or follow the performing of the procedure, including an explanation of the type and possible effects of any anesthetic to be used;
- A full description of the benefits or advantages that may be expected as a result of the sterilization; and
- Advice that the sterilization will not be performed for at least 30 days except under the circumstances specified in sec. 50.203(d) of this subpart.

An interpreter must be provided to assist the individual to be sterilized if he or she does not understand the language used on the consent form or the language used by the person obtaining the consent.

Suitable arrangements must be made to insure that the information specified in paragraph (a) of this section is effectively communicated to any individual to be sterilized who is blind, deaf or otherwise handicapped.

A witness chosen by the individual to be sterilized may be present when consent is obtained.

Informed consent may not be obtained while the individual to be sterilized is:

- In labor or childbirth;
- Seeking to obtain or obtaining an abortion; or
- Under the influence of alcohol or other sub-

stances that affect the individual's state of awareness.

Any requirement of State and local law for obtaining consent, except one of spousal consent, must be followed. (42 CFR sec. 50.204)

Required Consent Form

The consent form appended to this subpart or another consent form approved by the Secretary must be used.

Required Signatures

The consent form must be signed and dated by:

- The individual to be sterilized; and
- The interpreter, if one is provided; and
- The person who obtains the consent; and
- The health care practitioner who will perform the sterilization procedure.

Required Certifications

The person obtaining the consent must certify by signing the consent form that:

- Before the individual to be sterilized signed the consent form, he or she advised the individual to be sterilized that no Federal benefits may be withdrawn because of the decision not to be sterilized,
- He or she explained orally the requirements for informed consent as set forth on the consent form, and
- To the best of his or her knowledge and belief, the individual to be sterilized appeared mentally competent and knowingly and voluntarily consented to be sterilized.

The health care practitioner performing the sterilization must certify by signing the consent form, that:

- Shortly before the performance of the sterilization, he or she advised the individual to be sterilized that no Federal benefits may be withdrawn because of the decision not to be sterilized,

- He or she explained orally the requirements for informed consent as set forth on the consent form, and
- To the best of his or her knowledge and belief, the individual to be sterilized appeared mentally competent and knowingly and voluntarily consented to be sterilized.

Except in the case of premature delivery or emergency abdominal surgery, the health care practitioner must further certify that at least 30 days have passed between the date of the individual's signature on the consent form and the date upon which the sterilization was performed.

If premature delivery occurs or emergency abdominal surgery is required within the 30-day period, the health care practitioner must certify that the sterilization was performed less than 30 days but not less than 72 hours after the date of the individual's signature on the consent form because of premature delivery or emergency abdominal surgery, as applicable. In the case of premature delivery, the health care practitioner must also state the expected date of delivery and that the consent was signed more than 30 days before the estimated date of delivery. In the case of emergency abdominal surgery, the health care practitioner must describe the emergency.

If an interpreter is provided, the interpreter must certify that he or she translated the information and advice presented orally, read the consent form and explained its contents and to the best of the interpreter's knowledge and belief, the individual to be sterilized understood what the interpreter told him or her. (42 CFR sec. 50.205)

ABORTION

Abortion is the most contentious issue in contemporary medical practice. It divides health care practitioner from patient and health care practitioner from health care practitioner; it submerges deep ethical problems such as the destruction of health care practitioners' duty of fidelity to their patients; and, perhaps most troubling, leads health care practitioners to support legal positions that are destructive of the privacy of the health care practitioner–patient relationship.

Abortion also poses medical malpractice risks because the courts do not give health care practitioners a right to veto a woman's decision to have an abortion. Even when the courts limit a woman's access to an abortion, they still leave the decision to the woman. This becomes a malpractice issue when a fetus potentially suffers from a genetic disease or congenital anomaly. If a woman is denied information about the availability of prenatal testing and abortion, the health care practitioner may be held liable for the costs of caring for the damaged infant.

The Politics of Abortion

The U.S. Supreme Court has never ruled that abortion is legal or, conversely, that it is illegal. Abortion itself is not a constitutional issue. The Supreme Court decisions that have shaped access to abortion have been based on the legal theory of privacy. The Court has been concerned with the extent to which legislatures may regulate the health care practitioner–patient relationship, not with abortion as a right independent of the health care practitioner–patient relationship. Legally, it matters little that the cases that are prosecuted concern abortion rather than orthopedic surgery. Politically, there is no strong lobby group pushing legislatures to regulate or deregulate access to orthopedic surgery. Concerned citizens do not seek injunctions to prevent strangers from having an arthroplasty.

Over the past several hundred years, the legality of abortion has changed with cultural norms. The antiabortion laws that were found to violate a woman's privacy unconstitutionally in *Roe v. Wade* had their roots in laws passed in the nineteenth century to protect women from the medical hazards of unsterile abortions. Abortion was legal when the Constitution was adopted but had been illegal in earlier periods. It is meaningless to argue that there is a historical justification for either banning abortion or making it universally available. Medieval societies banned abortion, but they also limited medical treatment in general. Societies that allowed abortion were frequently oppressive to women in other fundamental ways. Whatever legal course society chooses for abortion must be rooted in contemporary needs and values.

The Problem of Privacy

The recognition of personal privacy, as distinguished from privacy in one's possessions, is a relatively new legal concept. It is also a limited right. In the 1988 case of *Bowers v. Hardwick*,[12] the U.S. Supreme Court refused to extend the right of privacy to include homosexual activity between consenting adults. The Court reiterated that privacy considerations cannot be used to shelter socially unacceptable behavior such as drug use, possession of prohibited munitions, dangerous behavior, and behavior that offends deeply held societal norms. With this language, the Court shifted the balance between individual rights and societal stability toward community values.

In the 1989 *Webster v. Reproductive Health Services*[13] decision, the Court broadened the authority of states to regulate the availability of abortions. The Court found that there was no overriding privacy right that supersedes the states' traditional right to regulate medical practice to protect the public health and safety. Although this decision was heralded by antiabortion health care practitioners, it should give all medical practitioners pause. The extent to which the state may regulate the availability and performance of abortions is precisely the extent to which the state may regulate all other aspects of medical care delivery. A state that may condition practice in state facilities, or with state funds, on the banning of abortions could use these same powers to determine which patients health care practitioners may treat and what treatments will be allowed. The same authority that allows states to ban the routine treatment of addicts with controlled substances would allow the state to ban facelifts or any other medical treatment.

Protecting Personal Beliefs

The states and the federal government have passed laws that allow medical care professionals, with some exceptions, to refuse to participate in abortions. These laws are strictly the result of political compromises, not constitutional rights. Although most medical care providers who oppose abortion do so on religious grounds, this does not trigger the First Amendment's protection of the free exercise of religion. A law that regulated abortion or any other medical treatment on religious grounds would constitute an illegal establishment of religion.

These laws are limited in two respects. First, they apply to actions, not to patient counseling. A health care practitioner cannot appeal to a conscience law to defend a medical malpractice lawsuit based on failure to counsel a patient about the medical indications for abortion. Second, they have limited applicability in emergency situations. If a woman presents to the emergency room in extremis because of an incomplete abortion, the emergency room health care practitioner cannot hide behind a conscience law and allow the woman to die. Fortunately, almost all medical care providers treat saving a mother's life as of a higher ethical urgency than their personal religious beliefs.

Limiting Governmental Support

The most perverse aspect of abortion law in the United States is that it affects predominately poor women. The Supreme Court has ruled that it is not discriminatory for a governmental agency to refuse to pay for medical care that is otherwise available in the medical marketplace. Most states and the federal government will not allow the use of governmental funds to pay for abortions or abortion referral services. The restrictions on the federal Title X family planning grants are typical:

> Because Title X funds are intended only for family planning, once a client served by a Title X project is diagnosed as pregnant, she must be referred for appropriate prenatal and/or social services by furnishing a list of available providers that promote the welfare of mother and unborn child.... A Title X project may not use prenatal, social service or emergency medical or other referrals as an indirect means of encouraging or promoting abortion as a method of family planning,

such as by weighing the list of referrals in favor of health care providers which perform abortions, by including on the list of referral providers health care providers whose principal business is the provision of abortions, by excluding available providers who do not provide abortions, or by "steering" clients to providers who offer abortion as a method of family planning. (42 CFR sec. 59.8)

These restrictions were recently upheld by the U.S. Supreme Court, which found that the regulations did not interfere with health care practitioners' right of free speech. Referring to its previous decisions upholding the right of the government not to fund abortions, the Court reiterated the rule that refusing to fund the exercise of a right is not the same as prohibiting that right. As with other voluntary employment situations, the Court found that the employer has the right to restrict the workplace activities:

The same principles apply to petitioners' claim that the regulations abridge the free speech rights of the grantee's staff. Individuals who are voluntarily employed for a Title X project must perform their duties in accordance with the regulation's restrictions on abortion counseling and referral. The employees remain free, however, to pursue abortion related activities when they are not acting under the auspices of the Title X project. The regulations, which govern solely the scope of the Title X project's activities, do not in any way restrict the activities of those persons acting as private individuals. The employees' freedom of expression is limited during the time that they actually work for the project; but this limitation is a consequence of their decision to accept employment in a project, the scope of which is permissibly restricted by the funding authority.[14]

The Court found that the regulations were limited to a prohibition on abortion as a means of birth control. It specifically found that the personnel in Title X–funded facilities were free to discuss abortion and refer patients when the abortion was medically necessary:

On their face, the regulations cannot be read, as petitioners contend, to bar abortion referral or counseling where a woman's life is placed in imminent peril by her pregnancy, since it does not

seem that such counseling could be considered a "method of family planning" under sec. 1008, and since provisions of the regulations themselves contemplate that a Title X project could engage in otherwise prohibited abortion-related activities in such circumstances.[15]

The Court was careful to distinguish Title X regulations from a more general prohibition on abortion counseling:

Nor is the doctor–patient relationship established by the Title X program sufficiently all-encompassing so as to justify an expectation on the part of the patient of comprehensive medical advice. The program does not provide postconception medical care, and therefore a doctor's silence with regard to abortion cannot reasonably be thought to mislead a client into thinking that the doctor does not consider abortion an appropriate option for her. The doctor is always free to make clear that advice regarding abortion is simply beyond the scope of the program.

These restrictions have been suspended by executive order of the president.

Consent to Abortion

In 1992 the Supreme Court affirmed that a woman of adult years and sound mind has the same exclusive right to consent to an abortion as to any other medical care.[16] Putative fathers and husbands have no right to be informed or consulted about the woman's decision to have an abortion. The rights of minors are more limited. Although the U.S. Supreme Court has not allowed states to prevent minors from having abortions, states can require minors who do not have parental consent for an abortion to seek consent from a court and to demonstrate that the abortion is in their best interest. It is to be expected that the Supreme Court will allow further restrictions in the availability of abortions. Health care practitioners should keep informed on the current laws in their state of practice.

Health care practitioners should counsel their patients about the emotional consequences of an abortion and their need for social support. If the patient can discuss the matter with friends or family, that is preferable to keeping the decision to herself. But health care practitioners should never abuse their position of trust by coercing a patient into revealing confidential information or reversing her own decision. Health care practitioners who are personally unprepared to counsel their patients about abortion should refer them to another health care practitioner or a counselor trained in reproductive matters.

Informing the Patient

As with contraception, health care practitioners who do not perform abortions must fully inform all obstetrics patients of this restriction at the first patient visit, with this information documented in the patient chart. If a health care practitioner suspects that a pregnant patient may have a medical reason for terminating the pregnancy or may be carrying a defective fetus, the health care practitioner has a duty to inform the patient of the problem and the options available to her. If the patient decides to have an abortion, the health care practitioner is not obliged to perform the abortion but has a duty to refer the woman to a health care practitioner who will.

The information given to the patient should be complete and reasonably objective. A health care practitioner should never withhold information or downplay the seriousness of a problem in an attempt to guide a patient's decision. The essence of informed consent is that the patient has all the information necessary to make the decisions. A failure to inform the patient properly can create liability for the torts of wrongful life or wrongful birth.

Adoption Alternatives

A patient faced with a problem pregnancy may seek advice from her health care practitioner. If there is no medical reason for terminating the pregnancy, adoption should be discussed as an alternative to abortion. A health care practitioner should refer a patient to an approved adoption agency if the patient wants to place the child for adoption. The health care practitioner should be careful to avoid any conflict of interest in making this referral. No matter who pays the bills or arranges the

care, the health care practitioner's duties are to the patient, not the agency or adoptive parents.

Time Constraints

The Supreme Court decision that upheld a woman's right of privacy in deciding on abortion limited this right to the period when the fetus is not viable. As a purely medical matter, the safety and ease of induced abortion decrease as the pregnancy progresses. This puts a time restraint on the provision of abortion services. A patient must be provided necessary information and care in a time frame that maintains her options and safety.

When health care practitioners first see patients in the second trimester, they must make special efforts to get test results or referral appointments quickly. The health care practitioner who knows that time is short should personally ensure that the patient has access to timely care. A health care practitioner whose delay prevents the patient from aborting a damaged fetus can be liable for the consequences.

The Changing Nature of Abortion

Although abortion is still a surgical procedure in the United States, this may change as RU 486 and second-generation progesterone inhibitors become available. These drugs make it possible to perform 95% of first-trimester abortions as without surgical procedures. This is disturbing to anti-abortion activists because it does away with easily targeted abortion clinics. As states begin to restrict the availability of legal abortions, the demand for pharmaceutical abortions will increase. Since many of these agents also have value in the treatment of disorders such as progesterone-dependent cancer, it is anticipated that they will be licensed for cancer chemotherapy but not for abortions. This will allow health care practitioners to use them as an abortifacient because the use of prescription drugs is not limited to FDA-approved uses. (If drugs could be used only for FDA-approved uses, there would be very few drugs available for pregnant women.)

If the FDA refuses to license RU 486 or related compounds, they may become available on the black market either from supplies diverted from European clinics, or from those illegally manufactured in the United States. Given that an illegal abortion can cost several hundred dollars, the profit margin on a dose of RU 486 and a prostaglandin would be much higher than that on cocaine. Restrictive abortion laws probably will add RU 486 and its analogues to the profitable inventory of the illicit drug industry. This will pose a dilemma for health care practitioners who will be asked by patients to obtain RU 486 or to supervise the administration of patient-acquired RU 486. Although health care practitioners should not deal with illegally obtained drugs, ethical demands to help a patient otherwise unable to obtain an abortion will be strong.

ADOPTION AND PARENTAL RIGHTS

Medical technologies that disassociate sexual intercourse from reproduction plunge physicians into the age-old maelstrom surrounding legitimacy, fidelity, and heritage. Except for introducing ambiguity into maternity as well as paternity, medical technology has transformed old problems more than it has created new ones. The transformation has been to substitute medical technology for sexual intercourse. The medicalization of reproduction allows the participants to escape from the religious and social opprobrium that defined acceptable reproductive choices. This disassociation from traditional religious values and legal rules poses grave ethical and legal questions about the use of certain reproductive technologies. The problems of adoption are better understood, but they have also been complicated by reproductive technologies that confuse the problem of determining whose parental rights control the adoption. This section presents a basic legal framework for analyzing the issues arising from reproductive technologies.

Parental Rights

A legally recognized parent has the right to make decisions on a child's behalf and the responsibility to provide financial and emotional support for the child. Under the law in most jurisdictions, a child may have two parents (one father and one mother), one parent, or no parents. The identity of these parents can be determined by birth, marriage, legitimation, paternity proceedings, or through adoption. Since the rights and responsibilities attendant on parenthood are so encompassing, the law places certain restrictions on the rights of a woman to conceive a child without the permission of the man who will assume the legal duties of father to the child. The clearest restrictions are the requirements in artificial insemination statutes that a married woman have her husband's permission to be inseminated. Potential fathers have also asked courts to block the implantation of previously frozen embryos, although the absence of statutory guidance makes these cases more ambiguous. Outside of this right to veto certain reproductive procedures that will lead to the bearing of a child, fathers have no legal right to control the mother's medical care. Nor do they have the right to prevent or force a woman to have an abortion or to require that she use contraception.

It is important for a physician treating a child to know if the child has a legally identified father and whether the father has full parental rights. The rights of a legal father (not a merely biologic father) start at the child's birth and are coextensive with the mother's rights. This means that from the birth of the child on, a father and a mother have the same rights to determine the medical care their child will receive, where the child will live, and all the other decisions that parents normally make for their children. If the mother and father do not agree, it is the business of the family courts to decide who will care for the child.

The Presumption of Legitimacy

The law has always been concerned with paternity. Paternity was critical to the succession of monarchs and the inheritance of property. Paternity was a moral issue because of the church's insistence on fidelity in marriage and celibacy outside marriage. Infidelity could mean disgrace for a man and death for a woman. The moral taint was so strong that the law punished the child as well as the mother:

All the disabilities of bastardy are of feudal origin. With us it is of Saxon origin. The term bastard being derived from a Saxon word, importing a bad, or base, original. The disabilities of bastardy are the same under the civil as under the common law, and in all ages and nations. He has no ancestor; no name; can inherit to nobody, and nobody to him; can have no collaterals nor other relatives except those descended from him. He can have no surname, until gained by reputation.[17]

The stigma of bastardy lasted a lifetime and could blight the lives of the next generation, as witnessed by the heraldic bend (or bar) sinister on the family crest, designating bastardy. In addition to inheritance, a bastard was denied entrance into several callings and certain civil rights. These harsh laws persisted until relatively recent times in England and the United States. The stigma of bastardy was such that the common law developed legal presumptions in favor of legitimacy.

The presumption of legitimacy was a fundamental principle of the common law. Traditionally, that presumption could be rebutted only by proof that a husband was incapable of procreation or had had no access to his wife during the relevant period. As explained by Blackstone, nonaccess could only be proved "if the husband be out of the kingdom of England (or, as the law somewhat loosely phrases it, extra quatuor maria [beyond the four seas]) for above nine months...." And, under the common law both in England and here, "neither husband nor wife [could] be a witness to prove access or nonaccess." The primary policy rationale underlying the common law's severe restrictions on rebuttal of the presumption appears to have been an aversion to declaring children illegitimate, thereby depriving them of rights of inheritance and succession, and likely making them wards of the state. A secondary policy concern was the interest in promoting the "peace and tranquillity of States and families," a goal that is obviously impaired by facilitating suits against husband and wife asserting that their children are illegitimate. Even though, as bastardy laws became less harsh, "[j]udges in both [England and the United States] gradually widened the acceptable range of evidence that could be offered by spouses, and placed restraints on the 'four seas rule'...[,] the law retained a strong bias against ruling the children of married women illegitimate."[18]

The *Michael H.* case is a good, if unusual, example of this legal rule. Carole and Gerald were married. During this marriage, Carole had an adulterous affair with Michael. Sometime after this affair, the child Victoria was born. During a brief separation from her husband, Carole and Michael had blood tests performed to determine Victoria's paternity. The tests established, according to the evidence presented to the court, a 98% probability that Michael was Victoria's father. After a period of living with Michael and treating Victoria as Michael's daughter, Carole reconciled with Gerald. Michael, as probable biologic father of Victoria, sought visitation rights with Victoria.

The California law, which was more than a century old, held that "the issue of a wife cohabiting with her husband, who is not impotent or sterile, is conclusively presumed to be a child of the marriage." Subsequent revisions allowed this presumption to be "rebutted by blood tests, but only if a motion for such tests is made, within two years from the date of the child's birth, either by the husband or, if the natural father has filed an affidavit acknowledging paternity, by the wife."

Gerald had always acknowledged Victoria as his daughter. Carole, having reconciled with Gerald, also refused to request the court to examine Victoria's paternity. Michael, as the probable biologic father, argued that this law denied him a constitutional right to establish a parental relationship with his daughter. The U.S. Supreme Court upheld the California law as a valid exercise of the state's right to protect the family relationship. The Court made it clear that biologic parenthood did not supersede legal parenthood as defined by a state statute reflecting the common law tradition.

Biological Fathers and Legitimization

All states have legal procedures for establishing the paternity of children born out of wedlock, or when the husband is found to not be the child's father, pursuant to state law:

> The Commonwealth has an interest in its infant citizens having two parents to provide and care for them. There is a legitimate interest in not furnishing financial assistance for children who have a father capable of support. The Commonwealth is concerned in having a father responsible for a child born out of wedlock. This not only tends to reduce the welfare burden by keeping minor children, who have a financially able parent, off the rolls, but it also provides an identifiable father from whom potential recovery may be had of welfare payments which are paid to support the child born out of wedlock.[19]

If the mother is not married at the time of a child's birth, a father wishing to establish legal paternity must legally acknowledge the child as his own. In some states, this may be as simple as filing a form with the birth certificate. In other states, it may require a full court proceeding similar to an adoption. If the mother agrees that he is the father, a man seeking to acknowledge the child as his own usually does not have to prove that he is the biologic father to be declared the legal father of the child. If more than one man seeks to acknowledge the child or if the mother refuses to recognize the man as the father of the child, the courts in most states can order blood tests to determine paternity.

States also provide for the testing of potential fathers who do not voluntarily acknowledge their children. These lawsuits may be brought by the mother or by the state on behalf of the child. It is common for the state to require an unmarried woman seeking public assistance to identify the father (if known) of her children. Although a state is free to establish a stricter standard of proof, the U.S. Supreme Court has found that it is constitutional to establish paternity with a preponderance of the evidence standard. By allowing this less strict standard of proof than the standard required for termination of parental rights, the courts recognize the strong societal interest in the legitimation of children. Once the court rules that a man is the legal father of the child, the man has the same

rights and duties regarding the child as would the husband of the mother.

Termination of Parental Rights

Parental rights are not inalienable. Courts may terminate a parent's rights regarding a child if it is determined that the parent is unfit. In limited circumstances, a person may voluntarily relinquish his or her parental rights. The standards for proving a case for terminating a parent's rights are stricter than the standard for establishing those rights. Although a court may determine paternity based on a preponderance of the evidence, the state must prove a parent's unfitness by clear and convincing evidence because of the importance attached to a person's right to be a parent. Unfitness is also narrowly defined as a physical or psychological threat to the child. This is in contrast to the "best interests of the child" standard used to decide which parent gets custody of the child in a divorce. It is not enough for the state to show that the child would be better off if a parent's rights were terminated. The state must show some fault on the part of the parent.

Since a parent's duty to support a child ends with a termination of that parent's rights, the states generally allow parents to waive their parental rights voluntarily only when they are putting a child up for adoption. Parents may waive their parental rights implicitly by abandoning the child. This is most commonly done by the fathers of illegitimate children, but it is increasingly common among mothers with HIV or who are addicted to drugs. The state must still bring a formal termination proceeding, but it has a lower burden of proof than in a termination based on unfitness:

> When an unwed father demonstrates a full commitment to the responsibilities of parenthood by "com[ing] forward to participate in the rearing of his child," his interest in personal contact with his child acquires substantial protection under the due process clause. At that point it may be said that he "act[s] as a father toward his children." But the mere existence of a biological link does not merit equivalent constitutional protection. The actions of judges neither create nor sever genetic bonds. "[T]he importance of the familial re-

lationship, to the individuals involved and to the society, stems from the emotional attachments that derive from the intimacy of daily association, and from the role it plays in 'promot[ing] a way of life' through the instruction of children as well as from the fact of blood relationship."[20]

The implications of this holding extend beyond the termination of the rights of an absent father. By emphasizing the importance of the familial rather than the genetic relationship, the court also provides a hint about how it might analyze a contest between a birth mother and an embryo donor. A bias in favor of the birth mother would be consistent with the Supreme Court's determination later in this case that the law at issue did not violate the equal protection clause. The father argued that the law gave the mother's rights more protection than it did those of a putative father. The Court found that the statute protected all parents with a real, custodial relationship with the child. The mother's interests were protected because she gave birth to the child and took care of her after birth, not because she was the biological mother.

When a court grants a divorce, it also determines who gets custody of the children. States differ in the extent of the parental rights remaining to the noncustodial parent. This can pose problems when getting consent for the child's medical care. Even states that generally allow the noncustodial parent to consent to medical care for the child allow the court to deny the noncustodial parent the right to make decisions for the child.

Physicians should find out the applicable rules for their state. If the state does not allow the noncustodial parent to consent to or direct the child's medical care, the physician should ask custodial parents their wishes. If the custodial parent wants the noncustodial parent to be able to obtain medical care for the child and there is no court order to the contrary, the custodial parent should sign a delegation of authority to consent to the child's medical care (see Chapter 11). In all states, the physician should ask the custodial parent if there are any court-ordered limitations on the rights of the noncustodial parent. If a pregnant woman is divorced during the course of the pregnancy, the courts will sometimes make a determination of paternity as well as custody of the child. A physician should handle this the same way as any other child of divorce.

Adoption

Adoptions are proceedings that vest parental rights in a person who was not the child's legal parent before the proceeding. Adoption involves the termination of the existing legal parent's parental rights and the determination that the potential adoptive parent is fit. All conflicting parental rights must be terminated before an adoption is final. If a parent marries a person who is not the child's legal parent, this stepparent does not have full parental rights unless he or she formally adopts the child. Such an adoption will require the rights of the previous parent, if known and still living, to be terminated. If a married couple, neither of them parents of the child, or a single adult seeks to adopt a child, the rights of both of the child's existing parents must be terminated. Parents may voluntarily relinquish their parental rights in an adoption proceeding, but most states protect the parent (usually the mother) from precipitous decisions concerning termination of parental rights. These protections may include a ban on agreements signed before the baby is born and a waiting period after birth during which the parent may revoke the decision to give up parental rights.

In most states it is illegal to pay parents to induce them to terminate their parental rights. It would be legal to give the mother almost anything as long as she did not give up her baby. It is only when she gives up the baby that coercion becomes an issue. It is acceptable to pay for the mother's medical expenses and support during the pregnancy, but this cannot be conditioned on a waiver of parental rights. Although the courts realize that this payment is an incentive, they treat it as a gift. Payments made after the birth of the baby are suspect because they have no relationship to providing for the mother's and baby's welfare during the pregnancy. Payments to husbands are impossible to characterize as anything other than bribes to terminate their parental relationship. Although it is acceptable for physicians to receive their routine fees from an agency or prospective parent, any payment in excess of the fees charged in other situations could subject the physician to prosecution for receiving money in connection with an adoption.

In addition to bans on paying parents, the courts are sensitive to efforts to coerce parents into relinquishing their parental rights. This concern with coercion, combined with the fiduciary nature of the physician–patient relationship, makes it improper for physicians to participate in obtaining a waiver of parental rights from their patients. The physician's legal and ethical duty is to protect the patient's best interests, consistent with public health and safety. If the physician has doubts about the mother's fitness to care for the baby, they should be reported to the child welfare department. Such beliefs are not an excuse for helping the patient by participating in obtaining her waiver of parental rights so the baby can find a good home. Improper participation by physicians is grounds for setting aside the termination of parental rights. This imperils whatever good a physician seeks to do by expediting the child's placement in an adoptive home.

Risks to Health Care Practitioners

In most areas of medical practice, adult patients are entitled to make their own medical decisions. The state may limit these decisions, and the patient must make the decisions in consultation with a physician, but other private persons have no right to interfere with the patient's decisions. In reproductive medicine, however, a woman's partner has the right to veto her medical decisions that would lead to the conception of a child. Once the child is born, the legal parents have responsibility for the child's care and well-being. The legal parents, however, are not always the biological parents. Some of the most bitter ethical and legal disputes in reproductive medicine center on the determination of legal parentage and the subsequent right to custody of the child.

New reproductive technologies exacerbate the problem of determining parental rights rather than creating unique new problems. Although rela-

tively few physicians are involved in providing high-technology reproductive services, most physicians who deal with families face the traditional problems raised by parental rights determinations. These include investigations of child abuse, examination of children and parents to determine medical and psychological fitness before termination of parental rights or adoption proceedings, and questions about the privacy of adoption records. Additionally, physicians are faced with questionable private placement adoptions and attempts to use reproductive technologies to avoid state restrictions on adoptions. These creative alternatives to state-regulated adoptions have been driven by the declining pool of infants available for adoption. If physicians involved with such practices violate the state laws governing adoption proceedings, they may be prosecuted for baby selling and be subject to discipline by the board of medical examiners and to adverse publicity:

Petitioner, a physician licensed to practice in New York, is an obstetrician/gynecologist with a subspecialty in infertility. In May 1988, petitioner was arrested and charged with the unclassified misdemeanor of unlawfully placing a child for adoption in violation of Social Services Law sec. 374(2) and sec. 389. Petitioner pleaded guilty to the charge admitting that he had, in June 1986, arranged for the placement of a baby boy, now known as Travis Smigiel, for adoption by Joel Steinberg and Hedda Nussbaum without complying with the appropriate provisions of the Social Services Law.

The mother of the baby boy, Nicole Smigiel, was an unwed teenager whose mother became suspicious of the pregnancy only a few days prior to the infant's birth.... Petitioner was contacted and he agreed to deliver the child and to cooperate with the adoption plans in secrecy. He insisted that the child be placed with Steinberg, his attorney and business associate. Petitioner had been treating Steinberg and Nussbaum for infertility for some time.... Petitioner did not seek or receive a fee for delivering or placing the boy and this was the only time he had ever participated in arrangements for an adoption. Petitioner told Smigiel that Steinberg and Nussbaum were a "wonderful couple" and the baby would be well taken care of. Petitioner learned otherwise when Steinberg was arrested and ultimately convicted of manslaughter in connection with the death of Steinberg's other illegally adopted child, Lisa....

In connection with the criminal charge against petitioner, Criminal Court of the City of New York sentenced petitioner, an individual with no criminal history, to three years of probation, 100 hours of community service and a $1,000 fine. In its decision, the court noted that, although many physicians in New York were unfamiliar with Social Services Law sec. 374(2) and sec. 389 and may have unwittingly violated these provisions, "ignorance of the law is no excuse." Based on this criminal conviction, the Office of Professional Medical Conduct initiated a disciplinary proceeding against petitioner charging him with professional misconduct for having been convicted of an act constituting a crime.... The report by the Regents Review Committee...recommended...that petitioner's license to practice medicine be suspended for three years, with the last 30 months of said suspension to be stayed at which time petitioner would be placed on probation for 30 months.[21]

The Board of Regents (the medical licensing board in New York State) went beyond the committee's recommendation. Taking "a more serious view of petitioner's misconduct," it revoked the physician's license to practice medicine. The physician appealed this sanction, and the court found that the revocation was unnecessarily harsh, given the criminal sentence and adverse publicity that the physician had already endured. The court reiterated, however, that the defendant's good intentions and lack of knowledge of the technical requirements of the law were no defense to the charges. They served only to mitigate the physician's punishment.

Matchmaking

In most states, the adoption laws provide that potential adoptive parents must be screened to determine if they will be fit parents. Unlike parental rights, which arise in the common law's overriding concern with the preservation of families, adoption has no common law heritage to give rise to special protections for the rights of potential adoptive parents. The states are free to establish strict criteria for evaluating prospective parents. Whereas these criteria must not violate constitutional protections or federal law, persons may be denied the right to adopt for reasons that would not support terminating their parental rights were they already legal parents. This process has been criticized for giving babies to the highest income couple whose religion and politics agree with those of the baby's case worker.

As the physician in the *Sarosi* case discovered, physicians should not second-guess this procedure by trying to set up matches between prospective parents and pregnant women. Physicians have neither the resources nor the authority to investigate prospective parents properly. No physician wants to face the nightmare of finding that the couple he or she recommended became child killers. It is to be expected, however, that some couples will seek private placement because they would be found unsuitable in a parental fitness evaluation. As with the physician's participation in obtaining a patient's waiver of parental rights, such matchmaking raises ethical questions about the coercion implicit in the physician–patient relationship. A patient may feel coerced into complying with the physician's recommendation on placement. As in the *Sarosi* case, this matchmaking can violate state adoption laws.

Physicians should be cautious about participating in adoptions that are arranged outside the state welfare system or recognized nonprofit agencies. Termination of parental rights and adoption are also implicated in fertility procedures that involve the transfer of a baby from the birth mother or her husband to the family contracting for her services. If the birth mother is profiting from the adoption, if the attorneys or physicians are being paid excessive fees, or if there is a broker, the transaction will violate the baby-selling laws in some states. In states that do not allow private nonagency placements, any involvement with private parties who are seeking to arrange or facilitate adoptions can be illegal. The physician should be especially cautious about participating in adoptions that cross state lines. If the transaction is illegal in either state, there can be prosecutions for kidnapping when the baby is moved across the state line.

Physicians who assist private placements should always retain their own attorney to advise them on the legality of each transaction.

Evaluating Potential Adoptive Children

The publicity about crack babies and babies infected with HIV has made potential adoptive parents very concerned with the health of the baby in question. Less well publicized is the high level of tuberculosis in adoptive children from Third World countries. Physicians examining babies for adoption are subject to malpractice lawsuits if they fail to diagnose conditions, within the standard of care for pediatrics, that would be grounds for not adopting the baby. In some states, physicians may be sued for fraud if they withhold information about the baby that would influence the adoption decision. Since such information may involve the mother's behavior, the physician must have a written authorization from the mother or a court order before transmitting such information to the adoption agency or prospective parents. There may be a conflict with the physician–patient relationship for family practitioners and others who are treating both the mother and the baby. Evaluating the infant for adoption may put the physician in conflict with the mother if the physician's determination is at odds with the mother's wishes.

In addressing the specific problem of HIV testing for children to be placed in foster care or adoptive homes, the American Academy of Pediatrics' Task Force on Pediatric AIDS[22] found the following:

In response to the legitimate need for preplacement HIV testing of the infant or child in areas of high prevalence of HIV infection in childbearing women, procedures should be established by foster care and adoption agencies in collaboration with health care facilities, to accomplish the following.

1. Develop the expertise to provide prospective foster care or adoptive families with comprehensive and up-to-date information regarding all aspects of pediatric HIV infection.

2. Establish a process that would accomplish, with the appropriate consent of the infant's legal guardian, the preplacement HIV testing of infants or children, initiated either (a) at the request of the prospective adopting or foster care parents through the physician who is responsible for that child's care, or (b) through the request of the infant's physician in response to his or her judgment that the mother is at high risk for HIV infection and that the infant's health supervision and/or placement may be affected by knowing the infant's antibody status.

3. Provide comprehensive and up-to-date interpretation of the meaning of test results, taking into account the age and health status of the child and the reliability of the test.

4. Establish a record-keeping system to contain information regarding the child's test results with access to such information strictly limited to those who need to know, but specifically including the informed adoptive or foster care family and the physician responsible for the infant's medical care.

5. Establish a procedure whereby all infants who have positive results on HIV antibody tests are retested on a regular basis to distinguish between passively transmitted antibody and true HIV infection in the infant.

Access to Adoption-Related Records

One of the lingering controversies surrounding adoption is whether the process should be confidential. Irrespective of the physician's personal beliefs on the matter, the state law must be followed. A physician should not disclose information in violation of confidentiality provisions, but neither should persons be denied information that they are entitled to under state law. This question often arises when adopted children approach the physician who attended their delivery and request a copy of their birth record. (Most states leave the physician's and/or the hospital's name on the adoptee's birth certificate.) Unless the state has a specific provision in its access to medical records law, adult adoptees are entitled to read or copy any medical records that contain information about their own birth or pediatric care.

As with all other medical records, the physician is advised not to alter or mutilate the records to disguise the birth mother's name. If the physician is concerned about the child's access to the records, the state agency regulating adoptions should be contacted for advice. It may be able to provide medical information to the child without violating anyone's privacy. Most states also have a registry system whereby former parents can express their wish to contact or provide medical information to the children they relinquished for adoption. If the parent has notified the state of such a wish, the registry can direct the child to the parent without violating the laws governing adoption. A physician treating a person who has given up a child for adoption should inform the patient of any information about genetic diseases or other conditions (such as DES exposure, birth injuries, and congenital infections) that might be necessary medical information for the child.

SURROGATE PARENTHOOD

These issues are addressed within the traditional context of adoption and parental rights determinations. This leads to a conservative approach based on the stricter state laws in each area. Although this provides a more generally applicable legal and ethical approach to reproductive technologies, physicians in less restrictive states may choose to be more aggressive in their use of these technologies, consistent with appropriate legal and ethical guidelines. Since legitimacy determinations and adoption laws differ dramatically from state to state, it is important for physicians to ensure that they comply with applicable state laws. Procedures that are legal and acceptable in one state may subject the physician to criminal prosecution and imprisonment in a different state.

Most of the legal disputes involving reproductive technologies have centered on the disputes over traditional parental rights to the resulting child or fertilized ova. Some cases, usually denominated as baby selling, are criminal prosecutions for failing to comply with the applicable adoptions laws. The most highly publicized cases have been custody disputes such as the *Baby M*

case in New Jersey and the *Davis* divorce case in Tennessee. The *Davis* case, while involving more sophisticated technology, had a simpler legal solution. The only technology involved in the *Baby M* case was artificial insemination, but it had a much more complex legal result. In a thoughtful and articulate opinion, the New Jersey court discussed the legal problems posed by so-called surrogacy agreements and, implicitly, the general policy considerations in heterogeneous parentage situations. The following discussion includes quotation from the legal opinions themselves to convey the attitude of the courts as well as the legal rules in the cases. The holdings of these cases are limited to their respective states, but the attitude of the courts are representative of courts in other jurisdictions.

Davis v. Davis—The Tennessee Appeals Court Decision[23]

In this divorce action, the sole issue on appeal is essentially who is entitled to control seven of Mary Sue's ova fertilized by Junior's sperm through the in vitro fertilization process. The fertilized ova are cryopreserved at the Fertility Center of East Tennessee in Knoxville.

The trial judge awarded "custody" of the fertilized ova to Mary Sue and directed that she "be permitted the opportunity to bring these children to term through implantation."

At the outset, it should be emphasized no pregnancy is involved. Both Mary Sue and Junior are now married to other spouses; moreover, neither wants a child with the other as parent.

There are significant scientific distinctions between fertilized ova that have not been implanted and an embryo in the mother's womb. The fertilized ova at issue are between 4 and 8 cells. Genetically each cell is identical. Approximately three days after fertilization the cells begin to differentiate into an outer layer that will become the placenta and an inner layer that will become the embryo. This "blastocyst" can adhere to the uterine wall, the hallmark of pregnancy. Once adherence occurs, the inner embryonic layer reorganizes to form a rudimentary "axis" along which major or-

gans and structures of the body will be differentiated. It is important to remember when these ova
were fertilized through mechanical manipulation,
their development was limited to the 8 cell stage.
At this juncture there is no development of the
nervous system, the circulatory system, or the pulmonary system and it is thus possible for embryonic development to be indefinitely arrested at
this stage by cryopreservation or "freezing."

Treating infertility by in vitro fertilization
[IVF] results in a low success rate. As one writer
has observed:

> In IVF programs the embryo will be transferred to
> a uterus when it reaches the four-, six-, or eight-
> cell stage, some 48 to 72 hours after conception. It
> is also at this stage that the embryo would be cry-
> opreserved for later use.... In vitro culture until
> the blastocyst stage may be possible, but beyond
> that it has not occurred. Finally, only one in ten
> pre-embryos at this stage goes on to initiate a suc-
> cessful pregnancy.

Moreover, cryopreservation poses risks to the
fertilized ova, which have only a 70% rate of via-
bility after having been frozen.

The parties, after concluding a normal pregnancy was unlikely, jointly decided to attempt to
have a child by in vitro fertilization and, after several attempts, nine of Mary Sue's ova were successfully fertilized in December of 1988. For the
first time, their doctors advised that freezing was
an option and would enable them to avoid all but
the implantation phase of in vitro fertilization if
later attempts were undertaken. The couple
agreed to attempt implantation of two of the fertilized ova and to preserve the others. There was no
discussion between them or their doctors about
the consequences of preservation should the
Davises divorce while the fertilized ova were
stored. Mary Sue testified she had no idea that a
divorce might be imminent and she would not
have undergone the in vitro fertilization procedure
had she contemplated divorce. Junior testified he
believed the marriage was foundering but believed that having a child would improve the marriage and did not anticipate a divorce at the time
of the in vitro fertilization procedure.

Davis v. Davis—The Tennessee Supreme Court Decision[24]

Resolving disputes over conflicting interests of
constitutional import is a task familiar to the
courts. One way of resolving these disputes is to
consider the positions of the parties, the significance of their interests, and the relative burdens
that will be imposed by differing resolutions. In
this case, the issue centers on the two aspects of
procreational autonomy—the right to procreate
and the right to avoid procreation. We start by
considering the burdens imposed on the parties by
solutions that would have the effect of disallowing the exercise of individual procreational autonomy with respect to these particular preembryos.

Beginning with the burden imposed on Junior
Davis, we note that the consequences are obvious.
Any disposition which results in the gestation of
the preembryos would impose unwanted parenthood on him, with all of its possible financial and
psychological consequences. The impact that this
unwanted parenthood would have on Junior Davis
can only be understood by considering his particular circumstances, as revealed in the record.

Junior Davis testified that he was the fifth
youngest of six children. When he was five years
old, his parents divorced, his mother had a nervous break-down, and he and three of his brothers
went to live at a home for boys run by the Lutheran Church. Another brother was taken in by an
aunt, and his sister stayed with their mother. From
that day forward, he had monthly visits with his
mother but saw his father only three more times
before he died in 1976. Junior Davis testified that,
as a boy, he had severe problems caused by separation from his parents. He said that it was especially hard to leave his mother after each monthly
visit. He clearly feels that he has suffered because
of his lack of opportunity to establish a relationship with his parents and particularly because of
the absence of his father.

In light of his boyhood experiences, Junior
Davis is vehemently opposed to fathering a child
that would not live with both parents. Regardless
of whether he or Mary Sue had custody, he feels
that the child's bond with the non-custodial parent

would not be satisfactory. He testified very clearly that his concern was for the psychological obstacles a child in such a situation would face, as well as the burdens it would impose on him. Likewise, he is opposed to donation because the recipient couple might divorce, leaving the child (which he definitely would consider his own) in a single-parent setting.

Balanced against Junior Davis's interest in avoiding parenthood is Mary Sue Davis's interest in donating the preembryos to another couple for implantation. Refusal to permit donation of the preembryos would impose on her the burden of knowing that the lengthy IVF procedures she underwent were futile, and that the preembryos to which she contributed genetic material would never become children. While this is not an insubstantial emotional burden, we can only conclude that Mary Sue Davis's interest in donation is not as significant as the interest Junior Davis has in avoiding parenthood. If she were allowed to donate these preembryos, he would face a lifetime of either wondering about his parental status or knowing about his parental status but having no control over it. He testified quite clearly that if these preembryos were brought to term he would fight for custody of his child or children. Donation, if a child came of it, would rob him twice—his procreational autonomy would be defeated and his relationship with his offspring would be prohibited.

The case would be closer if Mary Sue Davis were seeking to use the preembryos herself, but only if she could not achieve parenthood by any other reasonable means. We recognize the trauma that Mary Sue has already experienced and the additional discomfort to which she would be subjected if she opts to attempt IVF again. Still, she would have a reasonable opportunity, through IVF, to try once again to achieve parenthood in all its aspects—genetic, gestational, bearing, and rearing.

Further, we note that if Mary Sue Davis were unable to undergo another round of IVF, or opted not to try, she could still achieve the child-rearing aspects of parenthood through adoption. The fact that she and Junior Davis pursued adoption indicates that, at least at one time, she was willing to

forgo genetic parenthood and would have been satisfied by the child-rearing aspects of parenthood alone.

Conclusion

In summary, we hold that disputes involving the disposition of preembryos produced by in vitro fertilization should be resolved, first, by looking to the preferences of the progenitors. If their wishes cannot be ascertained, or if there is dispute, then their prior agreement concerning disposition should be carried out. If no prior agreement exists, then the relative interests of the parties in using or not using the preembryos must be weighed. Ordinarily, the party wishing to avoid procreation should prevail, assuming that the other party has a reasonable possibility of achieving parenthood by means other than use of the preembryos in question. If no other reasonable alternatives exist, then the argument in favor of using the preembryos to achieve pregnancy should be considered. However, if the party seeking control of the preembryos intends merely to donate them to another couple, the objecting party obviously has the greater interest and should prevail.

But the rule does not contemplate the creation of an automatic veto, and in affirming the judgment of the Court of Appeals, we would not wish to be interpreted as so holding.

For the reasons set out above, the judgment of the Court of Appeals is affirmed, in the appellee's favor. This ruling means that the Knoxville Fertility Clinic is free to follow its normal procedure in dealing with unused preembryos, as long as that procedure is not in conflict with this opinion.

In the Matter of Baby M[25]

Facts

In this matter the Court is asked to determine the validity of a contract that purports to provide a new way of bringing children into a family. For a fee of $10,000, a woman agrees to be artificially inseminated with the semen of another woman's husband; she is to conceive a child, carry it to term, and after its birth surrender it to the natural father and his wife. The intent of the contract is that the child's natural mother will thereafter be forever separated from her child. The wife is to adopt the child, and she and the natural father are to be regarded as its parents for all purposes. The contract providing for this is called a "surrogacy contract," the natural mother inappropriately called the "surrogate" mother.

In February 1985, William Stern and Mary Beth Whitehead entered into a surrogacy contract. It recited that Stern's wife, Elizabeth, was infertile, that they wanted a child, and that Mrs. Whitehead was willing to provide that child as the mother with Mr. Stern as the father.

The contract provided that through artificial insemination using Mr. Stern's sperm, Mrs. Whitehead would become pregnant, carry the child to term, bear it, deliver it to the Sterns, and thereafter do whatever was necessary to terminate her maternal rights so that Mrs. Stern could thereafter adopt the child. Mrs. Whitehead's husband, Richard, was also a party to the contract; Mrs. Stern was not. Mr. Whitehead promised to do all acts necessary to rebut the presumption of paternity under the Parentage Act. Although Mrs. Stern was not a party to the surrogacy agreement, the contract gave her sole custody of the child in the event of Mr. Stern's death. Mrs. Stern's status as a nonparty to the surrogate parenting agreement presumably was to avoid the application of the baby-selling statute to this arrangement.

Mr. Stern, on his part, agreed to attempt the artificial insemination and to pay Mrs. Whitehead $10,000 after the child's birth, on its delivery to him. In a separate contract, Mr. Stern agreed to pay $7,500 to the Infertility Center of New York ("ICNY"). The Center's advertising campaigns solicit surrogate mothers and encourage infertile couples to consider surrogacy. ICNY arranged for the surrogacy contract by bringing the parties together, explaining the process to them, furnishing the contractual form, and providing legal counsel.

Invalidity and Unenforceability of Surrogacy Contract

We have concluded that this surrogacy contract is invalid. Our conclusion has two bases: direct conflict with existing statutes and conflict with the public policies of this State, as expressed in its statutory and decisional law.

One of the surrogacy contract's basic purposes, to achieve the adoption of a child through private placement, though permitted in New Jersey "is very much disfavored." Its use of money for this purpose—and we have no doubt whatsoever that the money is being paid to obtain an adoption and not, as the Sterns argue, for the personal services of Mary Beth Whitehead—is illegal and perhaps criminal. In addition to the inducement of money, there is the coercion of contract: the natural mother's irrevocable agreement, prior to birth, even prior to conception, to surrender the child to the adoptive couple. Such an agreement is totally unenforceable in private placement adoption. Even where the adoption is through an approved agency, the formal agreement to surrender occurs only after birth, and then, by regulation, only after the birth mother has been offered counseling. Integral to these invalid provisions of the surrogacy contract is the related agreement, equally invalid, on the part of the natural mother to cooperate with, and not to contest, proceedings to terminate her parental rights, as well as her contractual concession, in aid of the adoption, that the child's best interests would be served by awarding custody to the natural father and his wife—all of this before she has even conceived, and, in some cases, before she has the slightest idea of what the natural father and adoptive mother are like.

The foregoing provisions not only directly conflict with New Jersey statutes, but also offend long-established State policies. These critical terms, which are at the heart of the contract, are invalid and unenforceable; the conclusion therefore follows, without more, that the entire contract is unenforceable.

A. Conflict with Statutory Provisions

The surrogacy contract conflicts with: (1) laws prohibiting the use of money in connection with adoptions; (2) laws requiring proof of parental unfitness or abandonment before termination of parental rights is ordered or an adoption is granted; and (3) laws that make surrender of custody and consent to adoption revocable in private placement adoptions.

(1) Our law prohibits paying or accepting money in connection with any placement of a child for adoption. Violation is a high misdemeanor. Excepted are fees of an approved agency (which must be a non-profit entity), and certain expenses in connection with childbirth.

Considerable care was taken in this case to structure the surrogacy arrangement so as not to violate this prohibition. The arrangement was structured as follows: the adopting parent, Mrs. Stern, was not a party to the surrogacy contract; the money paid to Mrs. Whitehead was stated to be for her services—not for the adoption; the sole purpose of the contract was stated as being that "of giving a child to William Stern, its natural and biological father"; the money was purported to be "compensation for services and expenses and in no way… a fee for termination of parental rights or a payment in exchange for consent to surrender a child for adoption"; the fee to the Infertility Center ($7,500) was stated to be for legal representation, advice, administrative work, and other "services." Nevertheless, it seems clear that the money was paid and accepted in connection with an adoption.

Mr. Stern knew he was paying for the adoption of a child; Mrs. Whitehead knew she was accepting money so that a child might be adopted; the Infertility Center knew that it was being paid for assisting in the adoption of a child. The actions of all three worked to frustrate the goals of the statute. It strains credulity to claim that these arrangements, touted by those in the surrogacy business as an attractive alternative to the usual route leading to an adoption, really amount to something other than a private placement adoption for money.

The evils inherent in baby-bartering are loathsome for a myriad of reasons. The child is sold without regard for whether the purchasers will be suitable parents. The natural mother does not receive the benefit of counseling and guidance to assist her in making a decision that may affect her for a lifetime. In fact, the monetary incentive to sell her child may, depending on her financial circumstances, make her decision less voluntary.

Furthermore, the adoptive parents may not be fully informed of the natural parents' medical history.

The negative consequences of baby-buying are potentially present in the surrogacy context, especially the potential for placing and adopting a child without regard to the interest of the child or the natural mother.

(2) The termination of Mrs. Whitehead's parental rights, called for by the surrogacy contract and actually ordered by the court, fails to comply with the stringent requirements of New Jersey law. Our law, recognizing the finality of any termination of parental rights, provides for such termination only where there has been a voluntary surrender of a child to an approved agency or to the Division of Youth and Family Services ("DYFS") accompanied by a formal document acknowledging termination of parental rights, or where there has been a showing of parental abandonment or unfitness.

Such an action, whether or not in conjunction with a pending adoption, may proceed on proof of written surrender, "forsaken parental obligation," or other specific grounds such as death or insanity. Where the parent has not executed a formal consent, termination requires a showing of "forsaken parental obligation," i.e., "willful and continuous neglect or failure to perform the natural and regular obligations of care and support of a child."

In this case a termination of parental rights was obtained not by proving the statutory prerequisites but by claiming the benefit of contractual provisions. From all that has been stated above, it is clear that a contractual agreement to abandon one's parental rights, or not to contest a termination action, will not be enforced in our courts. The Legislature would not have so carefully, so consistently, and so substantially restricted termination of parental rights if it had intended to allow termination to be achieved by one short sentence in a contract.

These strict prerequisites to irrevocability constitute a recognition of the most serious consequences that flow from such consents: termination of parental rights, the permanent separation of parent from child, and the ultimate adoption of the child.

The provision in the surrogacy contract, agreed to before conception, requiring the natural mother to surrender custody of the child without any right of revocation is one more indication of the essential nature of this transaction: the creation of a contractual system of termination and adoption designed to circumvent our statutes.

B. Public Policy Considerations

The contract's basic premise, that the natural parents can decide in advance of birth which one is to have custody of the child, bears no relationship to the settled law that the child's best interests shall determine custody.

The surrogacy contract guarantees permanent separation of the child from one of its natural parents. Our policy, however, has long been that to the extent possible, children should remain with and be brought up by both of their natural parents. The impact of failure to follow that policy is nowhere better shown than in the results of this surrogacy contract. A child, instead of starting off its life with as much peace and security as possible, finds itself immediately in a tug-of-war between contending mother and father. And the impact on the natural parents, Mr. Stern and Mrs. Whitehead, is severe and dramatic.

The depth of their conflict about Baby M, about custody, visitation, about the goodness or badness of each of them, comes through in their telephone conversations, in which each tried to persuade the other to give up the child. The potential adverse consequences of surrogacy are poignantly captured here—Mrs. Whitehead threatening to kill herself and the baby, Mr. Stern begging her not to, each blaming the other. The dashed hopes of the Sterns, the agony of Mrs. Whitehead, their suffering, their hatred—all were caused by the unraveling of this arrangement.

The surrogacy contract violates the policy of this State that the rights of natural parents are equal concerning their child, the father's right no greater than the mother's. The whole purpose and effect of the surrogacy contract was to give the father the exclusive right to the child by destroying the rights of the mother.

Here there is no counseling, independent or otherwise, of the natural mother, no evaluation, no warning. Under the contract, the natural mother is irrevocably committed before she knows the strength of her bond with her child. She never makes a totally voluntary, informed decision, for quite clearly any decision prior to the baby's birth is, in the most important sense, uninformed, and any decision after that, compelled by a pre-existing contractual commitment, the threat of a lawsuit, and the inducement of a $10,000 payment, is less than totally voluntary. Her interests are of little concern to those who controlled this transaction.

Worst of all, however, is the contract's total disregard of the best interests of the child. There is not the slightest suggestion that any inquiry will be made at any time to determine the fitness of the Sterns as custodial parents, of Mrs. Stern as an adoptive parent, their superiority to Mrs. Whitehead, or the effect on the child of not living with her natural mother. This is the sale of a child, or, at the very least, the sale of a mother's right to her child, the only mitigating factor being that one of the purchasers is the father. Almost every evil that prompted the prohibition on the payment of money in connection with adoptions exists here.

The differences between an adoption and a surrogacy contract should be noted, since it is asserted that the use of money in connection with surrogacy does not pose the risks found where money buys an adoption.

First, and perhaps most important, all parties concede that it is unlikely that surrogacy will survive without money. Despite the alleged selfless motivation of surrogate mothers, if there is no payment, there will be no surrogates, or very few. That conclusion contrasts with adoption; for obvious reasons, there remains a steady supply, albeit insufficient, despite the prohibitions against payment. The adoption itself, relieving the natural mother of the financial burden of supporting an infant, is in some sense the equivalent of payment.

Second, the use of money in adoptions does not produce the problem—conception occurs, and usually the birth itself, before illicit funds are offered. With surrogacy, the "problem," if one views it as such, consisting of the purchase of a woman's procreative capacity, at the risk of her life, is caused by and originates with the offer of money.

Third, with the law prohibiting the use of money in connection with adoptions, the built-in financial pressure of the unwanted pregnancy and the consequent support obligation do not lead the mother to the highest paying, ill-suited, adoptive parents. She is just as well-off surrendering the child to an approved agency. In surrogacy, the highest bidders will presumably become the adoptive parents regardless of suitability, so long as payment of money is permitted.

Fourth, the mother's consent to surrender her child in adoptions is revocable, even after surrender of the child, unless it be to an approved agency, where by regulation there are protections against an ill-advised surrender. In surrogacy, consent occurs so early that no amount of advice would satisfy the potential mother's need, yet the consent is irrevocable.

In the scheme contemplated by the surrogacy contract in this case, a middle man, propelled by profit, promotes the sale. Whatever idealism may have motivated any of the participants, the profit motive predominates, permeates, and ultimately governs the transaction. The demand for children is great and the supply small. The availability of contraception, abortion, and the greater willingness of single mothers to bring up their children has led to a shortage of babies offered for adoption.

The point is made that Mrs. Whitehead agreed to the surrogacy arrangement, supposedly fully understanding the consequences. Putting aside the issue of how compelling her need for money may have been, and how significant her understanding of the consequences, we suggest that her consent is irrelevant.

There are, in a civilized society, some things that money cannot buy. In America, we decided long ago that merely because conduct purchased by money was "voluntary" did not mean that it was good or beyond regulation and prohibition.

The long-term effects of surrogacy contracts are not known, but feared—the impact on the child who learns her life was bought, that she is the offspring of someone who gave birth to her only to obtain money; the impact on the natural mother as the full weight of her isolation is felt along with the full reality of the sale of her body and her child; the impact on the natural father and adoptive mother once they realize the consequences of their conduct. Literature in related areas suggests these are substantial considerations, although, given the newness of surrogacy, there is little information.

The surrogacy contract is based on principles that are directly contrary to the objectives of our laws. It guarantees the separation of a child from its mother; it looks to adoption regardless of suitability; it totally ignores the child; it takes the child from the mother regardless of her wishes and her maternal fitness; and it does all of this, it accomplishes all of its goals, through the use of money.

A sperm donor simply cannot be equated with a surrogate mother. The State has more than a sufficient basis to distinguish the two situations—even if the only difference is between the time it takes to provide sperm for artificial insemination and the time invested in a 9-month pregnancy—so as to justify automatically divesting the sperm donor of his parental rights without automatically divesting a surrogate mother.

This case affords some insight into a new reproductive arrangement: the artificial insemination of a surrogate mother. The unfortunate events that have unfolded illustrate that its unregulated use can bring suffering to all involved. Potential victims include the surrogate mother and her family, the natural father and his wife, and most importantly, the child. Although surrogacy has apparently provided positive results for some infertile couples, it can also, as this case demonstrates, cause suffering to participants, here essentially innocent and well-intended.

REFERENCES

1. ACOG Committee Opinion 63, *Sterilization of Women Who Are Mentally Handicapped.* September 1988.
2. *St. Agnes Hosp. v. Riddick*, 748 F. Supp. 319 (1990).
3. ACOG Technical Bulletin 169. *Human Immune Deficiency Virus Infections.* June 1992.
4. ACOG Technical Bulletin 106. *Oral Contraception.* July 1987.
5. ACOG Technical Bulletin 104. *The IUD.* May 1987.
6. ACOG Technical Bulletin 136. *Ethical Decision-Making in Obstetrics and Gynecology.* Nov 1989.
7. ACOG Technical Bulletin 145. *The Adolescent Obstetric-Gyncologic Patient.* September 1990.
8. Berman SM, Hein K. Adolescents and STDs. In Holmes, KK, et al, eds. *Sexually Transmitted Diseases.* 3rd ed. New York: McGraw-Hill Professional Publishing; 1998:117–128.
9. Holder AR. *Legal Issues in Pediatrics and Adolescent Medicine.* 2nd ed. New Haven, CT: Yale University Press; 1985.
10. ACOG Technical Bulletin 113. *Sterilization.* February 1988.
11. ACOG Committee Opinion 63. *Sterilization of Women Who Are Mentally Handicapped.* September 1988.
12. *Bowers v. Hardwick*, 478 U.S. 186 (1986).
13. *Webster v. Reproductive Health Serv.*, 492 U.S. 490 (1989).
14. *Rust v. Sullivan*, 500 U.S. 173 (1991).
15. *Id.* at 175.
16. *Planned Parenthood v. Casey*, 505 U.S. 833 (1992).
17. *Stevesons's Heirs v. Sullivant*, 18 U.S. 207 (1820).
18. *Michael H. & Victoria D., Appellants v. Gerald D.*, 491 U.S. 110 (1989).
19. *Rivera v. Minnich*, 506 A.2d 879 (Pa. 1986).
20. *Lehr v. Robertson*, 463 U.S. 248 (1982).
21. *Sarosi v. Sobol*, 155 A.D.2d 125, 553 N.Y.S.2d 517 (N.Y.A.D. 3 Dept. 1990).
22. American Academy of Pediatrics Task Force on Pediatric AIDS. Perinatal human immunodeficiency virus (HIV) testing. *Pediatrics.* 1992;89:791–794.
23. *Davis v. Davis*, 1990 WL 130807 (Tenn. Ct. App. 1990).
24. *Davis v. Davis*, 842 S.W.2d 588 (Tenn. 1992).
25. *In re* Baby M, 537 A.2d 1227 (N.J. 1988).

SUGGESTED READINGS

Adoption

American Academy of Pediatrics Committee on Early Childhood, Adoption, and Dependent Care. Issues of confidentiality in adoption: the role of the pediatrician [published erratum appears in *Pediatrics* 1994 October;94(4 pt 1):523]. *Pediatrics.* 1994;93:339–341.

ACOG Committee Opinion Number 194, November 1997. Obstetrician-gynecologists' ethical responsibilities, concerns, and risks pertaining to adoption. Committee on Ethics, American College of Obstetricians and Gynecologists. *Int J Gynaecol Obstet.* 1998;61:87–90.

Blanton TL, Deschner J. Biological mothers' grief: the postadoptive experience in open versus confidential adoption. *Child Welfare.* 1990;69:525–535.

Curtin LL. Of confidentiality, co-workers and adoption. *Nurs Manage.* 1994;25:22, 24–25, 28.

Demartis F. Mass pre-embryo adoption. *Camb Q Healthc Ethics.* 1998;7:101–103.

DuRocher R. Balancing competing interests in post-placement adoption custody disputes: how do the scales of justice weigh the rights of biological parents, adoptive parents, and children? *J Leg Med.* 1994;15:305–343.

Freundlich MD. The case against preadoption genetic testing. *Child Welfare.* 1998;77:663–679.

Friedland B. Physician-patient confidentiality: time to re-examine a venerable concept in light of contemporary society and advances in medicine. *J Leg Med.* 1994;15:249–277.

Garfinkel FL, Goldsmith LS. Child welfare agencies: possible bases of liability for placement of children with AIDS in adoptive or foster homes. *J Leg Med.* 1989;10:143–154.

Grotevant HD, McRoy RG, Elde CL, Fravel DL. Adoptive family system dynamics: variations by level of openness in the adoption. *Fam Process.* 1994;33:125–146.

Hollinger JH. The Uniform Adoption Act. *Future Child.* 1995;5:205–211.

Horsley MR. A family for Josue: pediatric practitioner Maureen Horsley faces a transcultural ethical dilemma. *J Christ Nurs.* 1996;13:24–27.

Kaunitz AM, Grimes DA, Kaunitz KK. A physician's guide to adoption. *JAMA.* 1987;258:3537–3541.

Krigel SP, Rosenberg KS. The adoption choice. *Mo Med.* 1997;94:690–692.

Lamport AT. The genetics of secrecy in adoption, artificial insemination, and in vitro fertilization. *Am J Law Med.* 1988;14:109–124.

Lauderdale JL, Boyle JS. Infant relinquishment through adoption. *Image J Nurs Sch.* 1994;26:213–217.

Lobar SL, Phillips S, Simunek LA. Legal issues in nonrelated infant adoption: nursing implications. *J Soc Pediatr Nurs.* 1997;2:116–124; quiz 125–126.

MacIntyre JCD, Donavan DM. Resolved: children should be told of their adoption before they ask. *J Am Acad Child Adolesc Psychiatry.* 1990;29:828–833.

Mander R. Seeking approval for research access: the gatekeeper's role in facilitating a study of the care of the relinquishing mother. *J Adv Nurs.* 1992;17:1460–1464.

Morris M, Tyler A, Harper PS. Adoption and genetic prediction for Huntington's disease. *Lancet*. 1988;2:1069–1070.

Post SG. Reflections on adoption ethics. *Camb Q Healthc Ethics*. 1996;5:430–437; discussion 437–439.

Rhodes AM. Adoption: an overview. *MCN Am J Matern Child Nurs*. 1995;20:7.

Sachdev P. Achieving openness in adoption: some critical issues in policy formulation. *Am J Orthopsychiatry*. 1991;61:241–249.

Silverstein DR, Demick J. Toward an organizational-relational model of open adoption. *Fam Process*. 1994;33:111–124.

Smit EM. Unique issues of the adopted child: helping parents talk openly and honestly with their child and the community. *J Psychosoc Nurs Ment Health Serv*. 1996;34:29–36.

Steinbock B. Surrogate motherhood as prenatal adoption. *Law Med Health Care*. 1988;16:44–50.

Steinglass P. Taking a stand on open adoption. *Fam Process*. 1994;33:109–110.

Tourse P, Gundersen L. Adopting and fostering children with AIDS: policies and progress. *Child Today*. 1988;17:15–19.

Turnpenny PD, Simpson SA, McWhinnie AM. Adoption, genetic disease, and DNA. *Arch Dis Child*. 1993;69:411–413.

Wrobel GM, Ayers-Lopez S, Grotevant HD, McRoy RG, Friedrick M. Openness in adoption and the level of child participation. *Child Dev*. 1996;67:2358–2374.

Family Planning and Abortion

American Academy of Pediatrics, Committee on Adolescence. The adolescent's right to confidential care when considering abortion. *Pediatrics*. 1996;97:746–751.

Annas GJ. The Supreme Court, liberty, and abortion. *N Engl J Med*. 1992;327:651–654.

Benagiano G, Cottingham J. Contraceptive methods: potential for abuse. *Int J Gynaecol Obstet*. 1997;56:39–46.

Callahan D. The abortion debate: can this chronic public illness be cured? *Clin Obstet Gynecol*. 1992;35:783–791.

Charo RA. Mandatory contraception. *Lancet*. 1992;339:1104–1105.

Cohen LS, Greer A, Appelbaum PS. Abortion, pregnancy, and mental illness: treatment, legal competence, and therapeutic interventions. *Harv Rev Psychiatry*. 1993;1:118–122.

Council on Ethical and Judicial Affairs, American Medical Association. Mandatory parental consent to abortion. *JAMA*. 1993;269:82–86.

Crosby MC, English A. Mandatory parental involvement/judicial bypass laws: do they promote adolescents' health? *J Adolesc Health*. 1991;12:143–147.

Curtin LL. Abortion: a tangle of rights. *Nurs Manage*. 1993;24:26, 28, 30–31.

Devine M. Care and secrets. *Nurs Times*. 1997;93:30.

Dresser R. Long-term contraceptives in the criminal justice system. *Hastings Cent Rep*. 1995;25:S15–S18.

Egan TM, Siegert RJ, Fairley NA. Use of hormonal contraceptives in an institutional setting: reasons for use, consent and safety in women with psychiatric and intellectual disabilities. *N Z Med J*. 1993;106:338–341.

Frost JJ, Kaeser L. Adolescent use of Norplant implants: clinic services, policies and barriers to use. *J Adolesc Health*. 1995;16:367–372.

Greenberger MD, Connor K. Parental notice and consent for abortion: out of step with family law principles and policies. *Fam Plann Perspect*. 1991;23:31–35.

Gupta S, Bewley S. Medicolegal issues in fertility regulation. *Br J Obstet Gynaecol*. 1998;105:818–826.

Henry PF. Overview of Norplant litigation. *Nurse Pract Forum*. 1995;6:58–59.

Henshaw SK. The impact of requirements for parental consent on minors' abortions in Mississippi. *Fam Plann Perspect*. 1995;27:120–122.

Johannsen L. Adolescent abortion and mandated parental involvement. *Pediatr Nurs*. 1995;21:82–84.

Keywood K. Hobson's choice: reproductive choices for women with learning disabilities. *Med Law*. 1998;17:149–165.

Krowchuk DP, Satterwhite W, Moore BC. How North Carolina laws affect the care of adolescents: issues of confidentiality and consent. *NC Med J*. 1994;55:520–524.

Lommel LL, Taylor D. Adolescent use of contraceptives. *NAACOGS Clin Issu Perinat Womens Health Nurs*. 1992;3:199–208.

Martin J. Contraception and the under-16s: the legal issues. *Nurs Stand*. 1996;10:46–48.

May JW. Legal issues in pediatric gynecology. *Clin Obstet Gynecol*. 1997;40:241–253.

Meier KJ, Haider-Markel DP, Stanislawski AJ, McFarlane DR. The impact of state-level restrictions on abortion. *Demography*. 1996;33:307–312.

Modungwa T. Contraceptives and informed consent. *Nurs RSA*. 1993;8:17–18.

Moskowitz EH, Jennings B, Callahan D. Long-acting contraceptives: ethical guidance for policymakers and health care providers. *Hastings Cent Rep*. 1995;25:S1–S8.

Nelson HL, Nelson JL. Feminism, social policy, and long-acting contraception. *Hastings Cent Rep*. 1995;25:S30–S32.

O'Donnell LN, Duran RH, San Doval A, Breslin MJ, Juhn GM, Stueve A. Obtaining written parent permission for school-based health surveys of urban young adolescents. *J Adolesc Health*. 1997;21:376–383.

Pierson VH. Missouri's parental consent law and teen pregnancy outcomes. *Women Health*. 1995;22:47–58.

Randall T. United States loses lead in contraceptive choices, R&D; changes in tort liability, FDA review urged. *JAMA*. 1992;268:176, 178–179.

Rauh JL. The pediatrician's role in assisting teenagers to avoid the consequences of adolescent pregnancy. *Pediatr Ann*. 1993;22:90–91, 95–98.

Resnick MD, Bearinger LH, Stark P, Blum RW. Patterns of consultation among adolescent minors obtaining an abortion. *Am J Orthopsychiatry*. 1994;64:310–316.

Scally G. Confidentiality, contraception, and young people. *BMJ*. 1993;307:1157–1158.

Smith J. Abortion—a debate. *S Afr Med J.* 1995;85:137–139.

Soderberg H, Andersson C, Janzon L, Sjoberg NO. Continued pregnancy among abortion applications: a study of women having a change of mind. *Acta Obstet Gynecol Scand.* 1997;76:942–947.

Stephenson JN. Pregnancy testing and counseling. *Pediatr Clin North Am.* 1989;36:681–696.

Wardle LD. Protecting the rights of conscience of health care providers. *J Leg Med.* 1993;14:177–230.

Weber RD. Minors: Consent to treatment and informing parents. *Mich Med.* 1998;97:8–9.

Wertz DC, Fletcher JC. Feminist criticism of prenatal diagnosis: a response. *Clin Obstet Gynecol.* 1993;36:541–567.

Worthington EL Jr, Larson DB, Lyons JS, et al. Mandatory parental involvement prior to adolescent abortion. *J Adolesc Health.* 1991;12:138–142.

Yussman SM. Minor's abortion: is the requirement for parental consent ethically justified? *Pharos.* 1996;59:2–6.

Surrogacy

American College of Obstetricians and Gynecologists. Ethical issues in surrogate motherhood. *Womens Health Issues.* 1991;1:129–134.

Berner LS. Legal contracts in oocyte donation and surrogacy: don't put all your eggs in one basket! *J Womens Health.* 1997;6:605–607.

Brahams D. Designating parents in surrogate pregnancies. *Lancet.* 1998;351:8.

Bromham DR. Surrogacy: ethical, legal, and social aspects. *J Assist Reprod Genet.* 1995;12:509–516.

Bulfin MJ. Surrogate motherhood. *Womens Health Issues.* 1991;1:140–142.

Capron AM, Radin MJ. Choosing family law over contract law as a paradigm for surrogate motherhood. *Law Med Health Care.* 1988;16:34–43.

Chervenak FA, McCullough LB. Respect for the autonomy of the pregnant woman in surrogacy agreements: an elaboration of a fundamental ethical concern. *Womens Health Issues.* 1991;1:143–144.

Craft I. Surrogacy. *Br J Hosp Med.* 1992;47:728–730.

Dimond B. Responsibility for the surrogate mother. *Mod Midwife.* 1995;5:34–35.

English ME, Mechanick-Braverman A, Corson SL. Semantics and science: the distinction between gestational carrier and traditional surrogacy options. *Womens Health Issues.* 1991;1:155–157.

Erlen JA, Holzman IR. Evolving issues in surrogate motherhood. *Health Care Women Int.* 1990;11:319–329.

Fischer S, Gillman I. Surrogate motherhood: attachment, attitudes and social support. *Psychiatry.* 1991;54:13–20.

Grodin MA. Surrogate motherhood and the best interests of the child. *Womens Health Issues.* 1991;1:135–137.

Harrison M. Financial incentives for surrogacy. *Womens Health Issues.* 1991;1:145–147.

Jessee SS. Infertility, surrogacy and the new reproductive techniques: psychoanalytic perspectives. *Int J Psychoanal.* 1996;77:129–133.

Jones HW Jr. Commentary on ACOG Committee Opinion Number 88, November 1990—"Ethical issues in surrogate motherhood." *Womens Health Issues.* 1991;1:138–139.

Klock SC. The controversy surrounding privacy or disclosure among donor gamete recipients. *J Assist Reprod Genet.* 1997;14:378–380.

Lawrence RA. The medico-legal, social and ethical implications of surrogate parenthood. *Med Law.* 1992;11:661–668.

Macklin R. Commentary: ethical issues in surrogate motherhood. *Womens Health Issues.* 1991;1:148–150.

Macnaughton M. Ethical issues in surrogate motherhood. *Hum Reprod.* 1997;12:93–94.

Macnaughton M. Surrogacy. *J Assist Reprod Genet.* 1992;9:179–180.

Marrs RP, Ringler GE, Stein AL, Vargyas JM, Stone BA. The use of surrogate gestational carriers for assisted reproductive technologies. *Am J Obstet Gynecol.* 1993;168(6 pt 1):1858–1861; discussion 1861–1863.

McLachlan HV. Defending commercial surrogate motherhood against Van Niekerk and Van Zyl. *J Med Ethics.* 1997;23:344–348.

Platt EF. Whose child is it anyway? *Med Leg J.* 1994;62(pt 4):180–197.

Reame NE, Parker PJ. Surrogate pregnancy: clinical features of forty-four cases. *Am J Obstet Gynecol.* 1990;162:1220–1225.

Robertson JA. Ethical and legal issues in human embryo donation. *Fertil Steril.* 1995;64:885–894.

Rothenberg KH. Gestational surrogacy and the health care provider: put part of the "IVF genie" back into the bottle. *Law Med Health Care.* 1990;18:345–352.

Shuster E. When genes determine motherhood: problems in gestational surrogacy. *Hum Reprod.* 1992;7:1029–1033.

Snowdon C. What makes a mother? Interviews with women involved in egg donation and surrogacy. *Birth.* 1994;21:77–84.

Sureau C. From surrogacy to parenthood. *Hum Reprod.* 1997;12:410–411.

The Ethics Committee of the American Academy of Otolaryngology-Head and Neck Surgery. Patient rights and surrogacy. *Otolaryngol Head Neck Surg.* 1996;115:186–190.

Thomas AK. Human embryo experimentation and surrogacy. *Med J Aust.* 1990;153:369–371.

van Niekerk A, van Zyl L. Commercial surrogacy and the commodification of children: an ethical perspective. *Med Law.* 1995;14:163–170.

van Niekerk A, van Zyl L. The ethics of surrogacy: women's reproductive labour. *J Med Ethics.* 1995;21:345–349.

Wasserman D, Wachbroit R. The technology, law, and ethics of in vitro fertilization, gamete donation, and surrogate motherhood. *Clin Lab Med.* 1992;12:429–448.

CHAPTER 14

Obstetrics

HIGHLIGHTS

- Obstetrics is legally risky because of potential conflicts between the mother and baby.
- Genetic counseling is legally complex.
- Birth injury litigation can be greatly reduced with structured obstetrics records.
- A birth plan can reduce legal conflicts.
- Drug use and alcoholism put obstetric patients and health care practitioners in conflict.

INTRODUCTION

Obstetrics has the most critical medical malpractice problems. Routine prenatal care and delivery are the cornerstones of community health. These are imperiled by fears, both real and imagined, of litigation. Physicians in rural areas find it increasingly difficult to obtain affordable malpractice insurance coverage. Urban physicians turn away indigent patients in a mistaken belief that they pose an elevated risk of malpractice litigation. Under federal antidumping regulations, physicians will face these same patients as emergency admissions late in labor, when they may present a greater legal risk.

It is not possible to prevent every birth-related lawsuit. It is possible to limit systems failures and attendant negligent injuries, to correct patient and attorney misapprehensions about birth injuries, and to document better the nonnegligent basis of most birth injuries. Such strategies will greatly reduce the incidence of birth-related lawsuits while providing excellent, cost-effective medical care.

GENETIC COUNSELING

Three factors are combining to complicate the ethics and the law of genetic counseling. The first is the tightening of restrictions on abortion. Great advances have been made in postconception genetic testing, but the objective of most of these determinations is to allow the patient to make an informed choice of an abortion. The second is the publicity surrounding the human genome project. Although this project only extends existing work on mapping and identifying the chromosomal basis for hereditary traits and diseases, it has gotten extensive publicity. This is partly because the federal research grant funding this project allocates several million dollars a year for legal and ethical research. This money has created an industry of conferences and articles on the potential societal problems of doing genetic research and has fueled both unreasonable fears and expectations.[1]

The third factor is a backlash to the medicalization of pregnancy. A primary manifestation of this backlash is the willingness of women to sue their physicians if their baby is born with a defect. Many women interpret the marketing of obstetric services as a guarantee of a healthy baby, and physicians reinforce this message by implying that women who do not follow their recommendations have a greater chance of having a defective baby than women who do what their physicians recommend. This factor is complicated for genetic counseling because society is ambivalent about the proper goals of such counseling. In one author's view, there are three overlapping and conflicting models for genetic counseling: "1) as an assembly line approach to the products of conception, separating out those products we wish to develop from those we wish to discontinue; 2) as a way to give women control over their pregnancies, respecting (increasing) their autonomy to choose the kinds of children they will bear; or 3) as a means of reassuring women that enhances their experience of pregnancy."[2]

Conflicts over genetic counseling and obstetric care span the political spectrum. Conservative religious groups object to abortion, whereas some radical feminist groups decry high-technology obstetric care as a conspiracy against women. The stakes are high. Few states provide high-quality community care to reduce the burden on families with mentally handicapped children. Financial necessity requires that both parents work outside the home in most families, complicating the care of disabled children. The chance of children with mental disabilities finding productive work and some level of independence becomes more problematic as American society shifts from a labor-based economy to an information-based economy, although this can help individuals with physical disabilities.

These factors combine to pressure women to strive for the perfect baby, while at the same time creating a sense of guilt for not treating pregnancy as a natural, nonmedical condition. This conflict can take the form of denial and the refusal of indicated testing or a hypersensitivity to risk and the aborting of fetuses with a fair probability of normal development. Physicians must be sensitive to both of these reactions, while carefully documenting the information provided and raising the issue

at more than one encounter so that the woman has an opportunity to reconsider her decisions.

Medical Risks

All physicians who care for pregnant women or patients with genetic diseases have a duty to counsel their patients about the nature of the diseases, their probability of being passed on to children, and the diagnostic options available. A physician who does not offer genetic screening because he or she is opposed to abortion, or for any other reason, has a duty to refer the patient to another physician who can carry out the necessary counseling and testing. The physician has a duty to provide full information to the patient. There is no therapeutic exception to informing patients about potential risks to their unborn children.

In some cases it may be necessary to give a patient medical information about another person. It is not possible to counsel the children of a patient with Huntington's disease without letting the children know about the parent's disease. Often the information will have been obtained with a release from the affected parent. If not, every effort should be made to protect the privacy of the other patient. Names and other identifying information should not be used, although it is probable that the patients can determine who is affected. There may also be situations in which the courts can help persons obtain necessary medical information about genetic diseases. In most states, adoption records are sealed, but the court that granted the adoption can order the records opened if there is a compelling reason for doing so (see Chapter 13).

Screening for Neural Tube Defects as a Model

The available tests and medical standards for detecting specific genetic diseases are changing rapidly. Rather than attempting to discuss each test and disease, this chapter identifies commonalities in counseling and testing through a discussion of a small number of diseases. Currently, maternal serum alpha-fetoprotein (MSAFP) is the only screening test for genetic diseases recommended for all women.[3] It provides a good model for genetic counseling because it is a disease with both a hereditary component and a random component that defies easy separations into risk groups. Neural tube defects are common, occurring in 1 or 2 per 1000 births among couples with no history. With one affected parent, the risk rises to 5% of births, rising further to 6% to 10% if the couple has two previous affected children. Despite this genetic link, 90% to 95% of the cases are in families with no previous history, prompting the recommendation that the screening test be offered to all pregnant women.

When first made, this recommendation was controversial because the test for MSAFP is quite sensitive but not very specific. There was concern that women would be frightened into aborting fetuses on the basis of the preliminary screening test. This led to specific standards of practice that stress the importance of the entire process of counseling and testing:

> The successful implementation of a screening program for MSAFP should include patient education, accurate and prompt laboratory testing, competent counseling and support services, access to consultants for sonography, and complex prenatal diagnosis, as well as available options for pregnancy termination. Success is further dependent on the proper coordination of these components, all of which must function within a relatively short time span from screening to decision-making. Missing components or malfunctions could result in unnecessary anxiety for the patients, as well as improper diagnoses that could lead to unnecessary termination of pregnancy or other serious errors in judgment.[4]

The coordination of the various components is critical because it is recommended that the test not be performed until 16 weeks of gestation. If the test indicates a sufficiently increased level of MSAFP, the patient should be offered a second test a week or two later, if time permits. Otherwise ultrasound should be used to correct the gestational age, check for multiple gestation, and, if possible, identify a neural tube defect. Among patients with two high MSAFP levels (or one low one) slightly over half will have a singleton fetus at the appropriate gestational age without an apparent anomaly. These patients should be offered amniocentesis. Of the patients undergoing amniocentesis, one to two will have significantly increased amniotic fluid AFP that indicates a high probability of a fetus with a serious abnormality.[5]

At this point further tests can be done to identify the specific defect, but this will be impossible in some cases. If a defect is confirmed, the patient must decide whether she wants an abortion. Many patients choose to abort the fetus. Some may be willing to accept a child with spina bifida but be unwilling to carry a fetus with anencephaly. The woman with an elevated amnionic AFP but no identifiable defect has the more difficult decision. She should be given full information and an opportunity to seek in-depth counseling before making her decision. Once the process of recommending the initial test begins, every following step must be planned carefully and executed. It is critical that the patient be carefully tracked to ensure that there are no delays that can push the abortion into the third trimester, with the attendant medical and legal complications.

MSAFP and Down Syndrome

The first widely available postconception test was for Down syndrome. This condition becomes more common with increasing age of the pregnant woman, reaching a level of 1 per 11 births at a maternal age of 48. Because testing for Down syndrome requires amniocentesis, with its attendant costs and risks, in women without specific risk factors the test is recommended only for those over 34 years of age. This is an arbitrary figure, however, because the risk rises relatively smoothly from the age of 21. As a result, approximately 80% of cases of Down syndrome occur in babies born to women under age 35. Once most pregnant women were being screened for MSAFP, it was found that an abnormally low level of MSAFP indicates an increased probability of Down syndrome. This information can be used to identify women under age 35 who should be offered amniocentesis for potential Down syndrome.[6]

The Genetic History

The indications for testing for MSAFP and Down syndrome depend more on epidemiologic information than patient-specific information. The proper management of other genetic diseases begins with a genetic history. Given that a significant number of children will be born with unanticipated genetic diseases, this history should be carefully recorded and the significance of the questions explained to the patient. In a recent case, a couple sued when they gave birth to a child with Tay-Sachs disease. This couple had received genetic counseling, but no mention was made of testing for this disease because neither member of the couple met the traditional profile for persons at high risk for Tay-Sachs. After the birth of the child and the diagnosis of the disease, an exhaustive review of the parents' genealogy was done. The mother was found to be descended from a small, closed community of French Canadians who were at increased risk for Tay-Sachs.

The judge found that the physicians had asked the appropriate questions and that the plaintiffs had not given the physicians any information that would have indicated that either was at high risk for Tay-Sachs disease. The judge rejected the plaintiff's argument that they should have been offered testing for Tay-Sachs irrespective of the probability of their carrying the disease. In rejecting this claim, the judge noted that there were more than 70 tests that physicians would have had to offer to every patient to meet the plaintiff's requirements.[7]

The American College of Obstetrics and Gynecology (ACOG) has established recommended procedures for taking genetic histories and diagnosing genetic diseases.[8] These are the starting point for all physicians providing general medical or obstetric care. The objective of this genetic history is to determine which women are at elevated risk for genetic disease. Once these women are identified, they can be referred to specialists in genetic diseases or managed by the treating physician if he or she has the necessary expertise.

Information about Specific Diseases

Physicians have an ethical duty to avoid reinforcing the belief of many women that all children with genetic disease are doomed to marginal lives. Legally, it is tempting to encourage a woman to abort. Even if she regrets the decision later, she cannot sue her physician for discussing too many risks. Women should be given enough information about the impact of the disease on an affected child to make an informed choice. The nature of the disease is important to most patients in making decisions about screening, conception, and abortion. The woman who has uncles, brothers, and sons who are healthy hemophiliacs may have no interest in prenatal diagnosis. The woman who has lost a child to Tay-Sachs disease may choose to avoid conception altogether or use donor sperm to avoid a recurrence.

An informed decision about genetic screening requires that the patient understand the treatment options available for the disease and whether they are curative or palliative. The prospect of having a child with a cleft lip that can be surgically corrected is not nearly so daunting as the prospect of a child with a biochemical defect that will result in a short life of illness and disability.

Knowing the likelihood of a particular fetus's having a genetic defect is also important for the patient's decision. A woman in her forties may find a 1 in 40 chance of Down syndrome an acceptable risk, particularly if she has amniocentesis and abortion as an option. A woman who has one child with Down syndrome and a chromosome attachment that gives her a 1 in 2 chance of conceiving another affected child may not be willing to accept the risk even if she has the same options for prenatal diagnosis.

Patient Characteristics

The personal concerns of the patient must be taken into consideration. A woman who has conceived and aborted several fetuses because of a genetic defect may decide not to try again even if her theoretical chances of bearing a healthy child are good. A defect that might seem difficult to one family may seem minor to another. There are many cases of women giving birth to child after child affected with the same genetic problem without creating family problems. There are also cases of women institutionalizing or relinquishing children with relatively minor problems because they were psychologically unprepared to cope with the child's needs. Patients receiving genetic counseling should be encouraged to consider their personal feelings about the anticipated disabilities the child could suffer.

Risks of the Diagnostic Procedures

There are risks to most of the prenatal diagnostic procedures, and these risks should be fully explained to patients considering this type of testing. The risk of the test causing a miscarriage may be greater than the risk that the fetus is affected. This does not necessarily mean that the test should not be done. A 35-year-old woman who has finally conceived after three years of fertility treatment may feel that she would rather have a child with Down syndrome than no child at all. On the other hand, this woman may feel that it is morally reprehensible knowingly to bring a retarded child into the world. These decisions must be made by the patient. A physician who is asked for an opinion on what should be done should be sure that the patient understands what is medical opinion and what is personal belief.

Reliability of Testing

The reliability of various tests will also affect a patient's decision about genetic testing and abortion. The physician should try to give the patient a realistic understanding of what test results mean. No test is without false positives and false negatives. It is never wise to tell a patient that the amniocentesis was normal and therefore the fetus is normal. If the baby is born with a defect that was not detected on the amniocentesis, the family may have more trouble dealing with the problem and may be very angry with the physician who indicated the baby was healthy. On the other hand, a woman who appears to be carrying a defective fetus must understand that many tests are uncertain and there is some possibility that there is no de-

fect. It is difficult to tell a patient this without raising unreasonable hopes. If the decision to abort is made, patients should not be encouraged to ask for testing on the abortus unless this will provide useful medical information for future pregnancies. There is little to be gained from second-guessing an irrevocable decision.

Time Limitations

With prenatal diagnostic testing, there is a duty to schedule tests in a timely manner so that a patient is not deprived of choice by delays. If the only available abortion facility will not perform an abortion after 20 weeks, then amniocentesis cannot be scheduled for 17 weeks if the results may take 6 weeks to come back. The results must be available in time for the patient to abort a defective fetus if she chooses. A physician who refers patients out for such testing has the responsibility to ensure that the test results are available in a timely manner. There should be a system of flagging the calendar so that results that have not come back in time are investigated. If the results are lost or the specimen destroyed, the physician must have left enough time to try again. The physician may have to work to find a laboratory that can handle a rush job or to arrange a late abortion. It is the physician's duty to do everything possible to preserve the patient's options. If a screening program routinely schedules such tests toward the end of the window of opportunity, the physicians should get this corrected or refer to another program. If the time is cut close on all the patients, eventually there will be a mistake in dates or a laboratory failure that will push a patient beyond the limit. The fact that the system endangered other patients in the same way will be a poor defense in a lawsuit.

Social Considerations

Some very tough questions arise in the process of genetic counseling or evaluation. The following is an attempt to guide physicians in answering these questions in ways that preserve the patients' rights without embroiling the physician in too many legal and social problems.

Am I the Baby's Father?

Legally, a child's father is the mother's husband or a man who has been assigned paternity in a court proceeding. Biologic paternity is virtually irrelevant without legal recognition. Courts may choose to transfer legal paternity from one man to another, but they endeavor not to disturb paternity when it will render an otherwise legitimate child a bastard. Physicians should also avoid casting doubts on paternity when a family is already in crisis. Although physicians should not lie to patients, there is enough uncertainty about paternity determinations to allow room for differing interpretations. Even tissue typing can be confused by mutation, the presence of related males among the candidates, or laboratory error.

It is best to avoid questions of paternity unless they are directly relevant to the patient's medical condition or care. If the father is concerned about possible genetic disease in his child, the information gathering should be directed to the disease, not the paternity. Physicians should decline to test a child to determine paternity unless it is a medical necessity. (This is usually an issue only for certain rare genetic diseases and as a side issue in tissue typing for organ transplantation.) If a court orders paternity testing, the physician must honor the order. But the physician acting as an expert witness in such a case should inform the court of the limitations of the tests and avoid making any unequivocal pronouncements of paternity.

While modern DNA testing techniques make paternity testing much more certain, they do little for the social consequences flowing from such tests. DNA testing is now available and marketed directly to the public. If the reasons for testing are social, not medical, physicians should advise patients to seek this information outside the medical setting. If the issue is legal paternity or child support, the state child welfare agency should be involved.

Can I Have a Healthy Baby with Someone Else?

This is a very difficult question because the answer is so often yes. A woman who asks this question should be warned that choosing a father at random may be as risky as conceiving with her husband. Artificial insemination is a standard option that allows the woman to avoid genetic disease. But most programs will not inseminate a woman unless she is married and her husband consents. If the woman does not want her husband to know that he is not the genetic father, then she will have to seek help outside the traditional medical care system.

A physician who suspects that a patient is considering such private selection should be sure that she understands the risks. If she is the carrier, she must understand that another father will not alter the risk. If the problem is a recessive disease with a high gene prevalence, such as sickle cell disease or cystic fibrosis, she may have the bad luck to pick a father who is also a carrier. On the other hand, if her husband is the carrier and she is not, her idea is medically sound, if socially questionable. Although it is reasonable to try to talk a woman out of seeking a surrogate father without telling her husband, it would violate her privacy to tell her husband. A physician who is uncomfortable with the situation should withdraw from the case. He or she should not try to control the actions of an independent adult.

Should We Get Married?

Although this is not a medical question, it is one that a physician doing genetic counseling may be asked. The answer for a particular couple will depend on many things: How much do they want children? How great is their risk of genetic disease? How severe is the disease? What are their feelings about prenatal diagnosis and abortion? The birth of a handicapped child is a strain on any marriage and often contributes to divorce. If there are other potential problems, such as family objections or teenage partners, then the risk of divorce is fairly high.

Should We Get Divorced?

The general understanding of genetic disease is not great. There are people who believe that there is a moral duty to dissolve a marriage if the parties are even distantly related or if there is genetic disease involved. One of the most widely publicized cases involved a biologic brother and sister who were adopted by different families as small children. They met in adulthood, married, and had three healthy children. Another person who knew of their earlier relationship tried to force them to divorce. They quite rightly refused.

Couples should understand the genetic problem they face and the likelihood that children will be affected. Once they understand their options, the parties to the marriage will have to make their own choices. Whatever a physician may advise, strong marriages will tend to survive; weak ones may not, and genetic compatibility is often only a small part of the equation.

What Should I Tell My Family?

The best answer to this one is "nothing." If a couple is considering alternative methods of conceiving a healthy child, such as artificial insemination, or if the couple is going to have prenatal diagnosis and abortion of a defective fetus, they are well advised to tell as few people as possible. If enough people are told, there is certain to be someone who will disagree with the decision out of ignorance or moral outrage. The child may also face ostracism in the family. A grandparent who has a number of biologic grandchildren may not care about a child of artificial insemination. The couple should be counseled to choose their confidants wisely.

If there are other members of the family who may be at risk or are concerned for themselves, they should be encouraged to come to the genetic counselor for their information. Even patients who understand their own problems fairly well can be a mine of misinformation for others. The birth of a child with a congenital defect can stop whole extended families from having children, a tragedy when these other couples may not be at risk.

Recordkeeping for Genetic Counseling

Genetic counseling should be done before conception. This is impossible for women who first seek medical care after conception but is simple for women who specifically seek preconception care. Physicians providing primary care for women with childbearing potential should discuss the importance of preconception counseling when they discuss contraception with their patients. Physicians should also consider obtaining a basic genetic disease history as part of the initial history when the woman begins her care. If this initial history demonstrates any risk factors, these can be discussed at the first patient visit. Bringing up a genetic disease history at the first visit also gives patients an opportunity to obtain information about their families' genetic history, if warranted.

It is critical to document the information given to the patient about her own specific risk factors: advanced maternal age, a history of genetic illness in her family, or an ancestor in a high-risk group for genetic illness. The physician must ensure that these risks are not lost in the boilerplate information that is provided to every patient. Patient information sheets on specific, identified risks should be differentiated from general information sheets. For example, they could have a place at the top to write in the patient's name and note that she has a special risk for the condition.

As with other medically indicated testing, it is as important to document the patient's informed refusal as to document the patient's informed consent to the test. Unless the test is hazardous, it is much more likely that a poorly documented refusal will result in litigation than will an equally poorly documented consent. The physician should periodically review the original recommendation with the patient to reinforce the importance of the test and to allow the woman to reevaluate her decision to refuse it. It is not unusual for a woman's attitude toward testing for congenital disease to change as her personal situation and attitude toward pregnancy change with time.

FERTILITY TREATMENT

Infertility is a condition with unique and profound psychological and emotional impacts. Infertility is experienced by most couples as a life crisis in which they feel isolated and powerless. Feelings of frustration, anger, depression, grief, guilt, and anxiety are common and should be anticipated and dealt with appropriately.[9]

The treatment of infertility poses many controversial issues, ranging from religious objections to questions of fraudulent inducement by unscrupulous fertility clinics that misrepresent their actual success rate. Infertility treatment has become a big business as the number of couples defined as infertile has increased. Some of this increase is related to the increased age at which many women attempt to conceive their first child. This delay shortens the period available to have children. Women who might have conceived by age 35 if they had begun trying to have children at age 20 are out of time if they start trying to conceive at age 35. Modern birth control methods allow women to be sexually active without becoming pregnant. This increases the probability that the woman will suffer complications of a sexually transmitted disease (STD) that will impair her fertility. Perhaps the greatest increase in infertile couples has come from a more liberal definition of infertility.

Current statistics indicate that more than 14% of couples who desire a child are unable to conceive within a year.[10] It is recommended that fertility treatment not be started (in the absence of a specific problem) until the couple have tried to conceive without using birth control for one year.[11] This is considered a conservative time period and was recommended because some fertility clinics were beginning treatment only a few months after a couple had begun to try to conceive. In earlier periods, however, a couple would not see themselves as having a medical problem until they had tried to conceive for several years. It is impossible to know how many of the 14% who did not conceive in a year would eventually conceive without intervention. Thus, it is impossible to determine what component of the infertility epidemic represents changed expectations and the ready availability of fertility services for those able to pay for them.

Patient Privacy

When genetic counseling a pregnant or potentially pregnant woman, the physician should include her husband or other family members only at her request. Violating the patient's privacy can have devastating results. Legal and social paternity do not necessarily imply biologic paternity. Although it would be proper to discuss these matters with the patient, this type of information should not be disclosed to others.

If the patient is a child, the situation is somewhat different. A father and mother who are married to each other have equal authority over their children. If the legal father does not question his biologic paternity, there is usually no problem. If a father asks whether he is the child's biological father, a physician should be cautious. Both mutation and test variability can confound any genetic test of paternity. It is better to address the question of whether the child has a genetic disease than whether the disease came from the man asking the question.

Fitness

Although treating infertility is undoubtedly a medical benefit in many cases, there are women who for physical or psychological reasons should not carry a pregnancy. For these woman, pregnancy becomes a threat to their own health and subjects the fetus to great risk of permanent injury or death. Fertility technology itself becomes a risk when it increases the probability of multiple births. Most fertility specialists are conscientious in counseling their patients about the risks and limitations of fertility treatment, but these physicians are reticent to deny a woman treatment if she is willing to assume the risks of the treatment.

The legal problems arise because a woman does not have an unfettered right to waive her injured baby's cause of action against the physician. The informed consent to fertility treatment must be complete and specific. Just reciting the risks is insufficient. The consequences of risks such as multiple births must be described in detail. Telling a woman that her baby may be premature does not give her the necessary information that a frequent complication of severe prematurity is brain damage. Although it may be improper to deny women the right to risk their lives and the health of their potential offspring for the sake of becoming pregnant, they must be told exactly what risks they are assuming.

Medical Fitness

The first question that should be asked is whether the woman is medically fit to carry a pregnancy. There are many protective mechanisms within the body that reduce fertility if the woman is in poor condition to conceive. Hormone therapies can often overcome these protective mechanisms without correcting the underlying problem and increasing the risk that there will be a poor outcome for mother or baby. An obese woman who has ceased to ovulate may not want to hear that she must lose weight to become pregnant. It is much easier to give her pills to stimulate ovulation. This apparently simple solution can lead to respiratory compromise and weeks of hospitalization for which the physician may be held liable. The physician should exercise the same caution in recommending fertility treatment as any other hazardous procedure.

Studies on the products of spontaneous abortions point to a higher than normal rate of genetic problems. Given that the human body eliminates fetuses with genetic diseases in many cases, women who have had several unsuccessful pregnancies should be considered at risk for genetic disease. This is another situation in which medical science can sometimes overcome natural protective mechanisms. The couple who is disappointed at their lack of children may not realize that there could be a genetic problem with the babies. They should have a careful evaluation to rule out the presence of a genetic disease that might be complicating their efforts to carry a fetus to term.

Psychiatric Problems

It is important to rule out infertility caused by compulsive behavior that undermines a woman's health. A woman who cannot conceive because she has an eating disorder should not be helped to conceive by artificial means. The risk of turning a mild chronic psychiatric problem into an acute problem is substantial. If the woman continues to try to maintain a physiologically unreasonably low weight, the fetus may suffer substantial damage. Given the psychiatric basis of the problem, an informed consent to accept the risk of pregnancy is problematic. If the woman had control of her behavior, she would have been able to conceive by gaining weight. The patient should be referred for psychological evaluation before any risky therapies are instituted.

Prospects for Successful Treatment

In spite of all the advances in infertility treatment, not every couple will be able to conceive and bear a child. Any couple asking for infertility treatment should be given a realistic idea of their chances. Adoption is a long process in the United States today, and there are age limits placed on adoptive parents. A physician who is treating an infertile couple should be sure that they are not offered false hope that limits or excludes the possibility of adoption. Patients should be reminded that they should preserve their options while the various therapies are tried.

Dealing with Multiple Gestation

Some fertility drugs substantially increase the probability of multiple births.[12] In vitro fertilization techniques can also result in multiple gestations if more than one embryo is introduced, with a rate of twins of 15% to 18% and of triplets of 1% to 2% with four preembryos.[13] Multiple gestation poses grave risks to both the fetuses and the mother.[14] These risks should be explained in detail. The woman must understand that the risk is not that she will have twins or triplets (or more) but that one or more of the babies may be severely disabled and that she may suffer medical complications. The physician should also discuss the possibility of pregnancy reduction and selective fetal termination. A woman with multiple gestation must be informed of her options:

1. Abort all fetuses
2. Attempt to carry all fetuses to term
3. Terminate some of the fetuses[15]

The introduction of multiple preembryos is intended to increase the success rate of in vitro fertilization. This benefits the patients by reducing the cost and medical risks of multiple procedures, but it is also critical to the success of the fertility center's marketing. Few persons would be willing to undergo the risk and expense of in vitro fertilization if the success rate were only 3% to 4%. Physicians have a duty to ensure that patients understand this trade-off between success and the attendant risk of multiple births.

The physician should also discuss the possibility of amniocentesis on the individual fetuses and the termination of those with genetic diseases. This is a dangerous process, however, because it is usually done later in the term, and retained fetal tissue can cause disseminated intravascular coagulation, with fatal consequences for the mother.[16]

Artificial Insemination

Artificial insemination has been widely practiced for decades, so many of the legal problems have been worked out. The issues of child custody are often covered by statute. There may be questions of malpractice involving either genetic disease or infection. There is also a societal problem because artificial insemination usually involves the rights of four people: the wife, the husband, the sperm donor, and the resulting child. Physicians should know and understand the laws of their states and the standard of care before working in this area.

As in any other area of medical practice, patients should not be given guarantees about the outcome of attempts at artificial insemination. If an unknown donor is used, the patient should understand that the donors are screened for disease, not for social desirability. Reasonable effort is made to ensure that the donor does not carry HIV or Huntington's chorea; no effort can ensure that the child will be smart or beautiful. Accepting artificial insemination carries most of the same risks as picking out a spouse.

Consent

This is a rare area of medical care in which the consent of the patient is not sufficient. The consent of the husband should be obtained before a married woman is impregnated by artificial insemination. Legal questions can arise when a married woman is artificially inseminated with donor sperm. In most states, this child is legally defined as legitimate to the husband. This presumption can be defeated if the physician fails to follow the statutory requirements. If the statute requires the permission of husband and wife, failing to obtain the husband's permission could allow him to deny paternity. Unconsented artificial insemination can have the same legal consequences as adultery. Although the courts might view this as strictly between the husband and wife, they might honor a suit against the physician for any mental pain and suffering the unconsented insemination caused the husband.

Choosing a Donor

Choosing a sperm donor can be legally and medically risky. Even if the laws of the state cut off parental rights for a sperm donor, the donor might make a legal challenge if he knows who his biologic child is. These challenges can be very disruptive for the child and the legal parents. Friendships and family relationships are easily strained by conflicts that arise over custody and the raising of children. Artificial insemination may also be medically risky if the sperm donor is not rigorously screened for both genetic and communicable diseases. If the physician procures the sperm, it will be difficult to avoid liability if the mother or the child is harmed by a discoverable condition.

The Husband as Donor

If the husband is the source of the sperm, there are few legal problems. Custody and paternity are not at issue because the biologic father and the legal father are the same man. There may be problems if reasonable caution is not exercised in screening the couple for underlying problems. If there is genetic disease that is making it difficult for the woman to carry a pregnancy, this should be determined before steps are taken that might improve the chance of carrying a defective fetus.

Related Donors

Using the sperm of a relative of an infertile man may seem to be a good solution; the child will be genetically related to the legal father and will look like a member of the family. There are, however, some serious drawbacks. If a genetic problem is involved in the infertility, then the closer the relationship is to the father, the greater is the chance that the donor is also affected. Even if state law severs parental rights for a sperm donor, it will not sever the other relationship. If a brother is used as a donor, he is still the child's legal uncle. If the extended family is aware of the arrangement, they may treat the child as though the biologic father were the legal or social father. In case of divorce of the legal parents and/or infertility in the marriage of the donor, there may be a battle for custody of the child. An uncle has the right to go to court and challenge the fitness of a parent. If the uncle is also the biologic father of the child, this relationship may strengthen his case before the judge whatever the law on sperm donation may be.

The use of a relative of the mother carries the same legal risks plus the medical risks of consanguinity. In most cases, the risks of recessive genetic disease are not high, but using a maternal relative as donor carries a higher risk than using an unrelated donor. In addition, if custody questions do arise, the mother may face undue prejudice because of the cultural abhorrence of incest. Although artificial insemination with her brother's sperm is not the same as marrying her brother, the distinction may be irrelevant to a judge or a jury in a custody case.

Unrelated Donors

Physicians should be cautious about participating in fertility treatments or conceptions that involve anyone but the couple under treatment. Many states have specific laws on artificial insemination that specify that the donor father has no legal rights. However, if a couple wants to choose their own donor or to arrange a contract pregnancy, the laws are not as clear. Custody fights and criminal charges of baby selling are known problems with these arrangements. The control of infectious and genetic diseases must also be considered. The use of any tissue from a third party requires that the physician have a complete genetic history and that the donor be tested for infectious diseases as would an anonymous donor.

The presence of contracts or sperm donation laws may not prevent the parties from ending up in a court case or a custody battle. Even without legal entanglements, the social dislocations may be considerable. A man may believe that he can be indifferent when the child is only a theoretical possibility and find that he cannot keep away from the child when he or she is born. The mother and her husband may also have ambivalent feelings. It is very difficult to accept paternity as an abstraction or as a legal concept when all the people involved know one another well.

The use of banked sperm from an unidentified donor is legally safer than using a chosen donor. The anonymous donor has been screened for disease and has relinquished any right to the child conceived. The donor is unlikely to know who his biologic children are, and in general he is barred from making any legal claim to them. Conversely, the child is cut off from important information about the biologic parent's medical and psychiatric history.

Genetic Disease

Standard of care requires reasonable screening of any prospective sperm donor for genetic disease. This is true whether accepting donations to a sperm bank or accepting a donation for a specific woman. This screening should include testing when indicated. The availability of easy, inexpensive testing for sickle cell trait, for instance, makes this test mandatory for all prospective donors who are Black. The fact that the woman has chosen the donor does not relieve the physician of the responsibility for using reasonable care. Many people are unaware of any genetic disease they may carry. The patient and the donor have a right to expect that proper precautions are taken.

Infection Control

The increase in severe sexually transmitted disease in the general population has made this a paramount consideration in artificial insemination. Virtually any venereal disease can be transmitted by fresh or processed semen. There have been cases of infection with HIV through artificial insemination. In such a case, there could be costly suits on behalf of the infected woman and on behalf of the baby if it is also infected.

There are medical standards for screening donors and treating specimens to prevent the spread of disease, and these should be followed carefully. The current recommendation on HIV control requires that the donor be tested for HIV when the semen is collected. The semen is then frozen for six months. The donor is tested again at the end of the six months. Only after this second test is negative can the semen be used.[17]

Unmarried Couples

There is an ethical debate over whether fertility technology should be available to unmarried couples. This is not an issue for techniques that correct physiological or psychological conditions that impair fertility, when the patient then conceives through intercourse with a self-selected partner. Although the physician may not approve of the behavior, just as he or she might disapprove of premarital sex in general, the physician has no right to impose his or her values on the patient. It does become an issue when physicians are asked to do procedures such as in vitro fertilization or artificial insemination.

Although many physicians believe that marriage should not be a precondition to artificial insemination or in vitro fertilization, there is a societal policy, expressed through various laws, against having children outside of marriage. Most state laws on artificial insemination by donor (AID), which is the usual request, are written in terms of a married couple. It is not clear whether any of these laws forbids the artificial insemination of an unmarried woman. They do, however, leave a child born of AI outside of marriage in a legal limbo.

In some states, specific statutory authorization was necessary to permit AID. Without the statutory authorization, AID contravened state laws on adultery or fornication. If an authorizing law is written solely in terms of a married couple, then AID of an unmarried woman might violate fornication or adultery laws. Given that laws against fornication and adultery are constitutional, the constitutional right of reproductive freedom may not extend to unmarried couples. State civil rights laws requiring married and unmarried persons to be treated in the same way might imply that an unmarried person is entitled to AID or in vitro fertilization. Conversely, since in most states a married woman cannot be artificially inseminated without her husband's permission, equal treatment might also mean that AID is not available without a husband.

Physicians who choose to offer AID and in vitro fertilization to unmarried persons should seek legal advice to ensure that they do not violate any state laws. They should be meticulous in both infectious and genetic disease investigation. This is a controversial area. Physicians may be involved in highly publicized lawsuits if the couple decides to break up and the donor contests paternity.

A STRUCTURED APPROACH TO OBSTETRIC CARE

Most obstetric malpractice is due to medical system failures rather than intentionally made, incorrect decisions. System failures (more informally called "slipping through the cracks") occur when a patient receives, or fails to receive, needed care due to inadvertence. Patients are at the greatest risk for system failures when they have nonserious conditions that are routinely managed without ongoing evaluation. System failures usually involve overlooking unexpected data. This might be ignoring the third call back by the mother of a child with an infected throat, which should have triggered a reevaluation of the patient's treatment.

This is not usually a problem because most children with infected throats have no major problem. It is the child with meningitis injured when the physician inadvertently continues routine treatment whose injuries lead to litigation.

In obstetrics, common system failures include failing to diagnose existing systemic diseases, failing to offer screening tests at the appropriate time, failing to act on positive test results, and failing to respond quickly to threats to fetal or maternal health. System failures pose the major risk in obstetric care because most pregnant women are healthy and most pregnancies end in the birth of a healthy baby.

Since the medical component of prenatal care is a screening program, failures in the prenatal care system are irrelevant to most women because they do not have any of the conditions for which the screening is performed. As with the child with an infected throat, the system failure harms only the patient who does not have the usual condition. In obstetrics, the failure of the prenatal system does not matter for most women; it does matter for a woman who has a medical condition that requires nonroutine treatment to protect her health or the health of the baby.

To use the MSAFP example (see Chapter 13) assume the physician has all abnormal laboratory reports put on the front of the chart for review. The file clerk loses 2% of all laboratory reports. Since the physician depends on abnormal results being flagged, no flag is taken to be a normal result.

Assuming a rate of 1 neural tube defect per 500 births, the probability of a missed diagnosis is .02 × .002, or 1 per 25,000 births. The odds are that this practice could go on for years before resulting in an injury in any given physician's practice. That injury can be very expensive. A $1 million award would not be unusual in such a case. Assume further that an average obstetrician delivers 50 babies a year. (This is a low number for a full-time obstetrician but is used to include family practitioners who deliver babies and physicians with substantial gynecology practices.) Then 25,000 births represent 500 obstetrician-years, for a risk of $2,000 per obstetrician-year.

From a management perspective, delivering routine obstetrical services is more like flying an airliner than like treating an acute illness: small things matter, and mistakes are infrequent but costly. As with flying the airliner, most of the things that matter are not done by the person in charge. The pilot does not service the engines, and most prenatal care is done by persons other than the supervising physician.

Zero-Defects Management

Zero-defects management is based on the premise that it is better to detect problems before they cause accidents or product defects. Airlines must use a zero-defects approach to maintaining and flying their planes. Everything is done and recorded by written protocol designed to identify problems before they become threats. Parts are replaced when they are worn but still safe rather than being allowed to fail. Judgment and art are critical in flying, but the objective is to recognize when they are necessary before it is too late for them to help. Medicine has the same problem. An obstetrician's skill in managing a complication of pregnancy can be exercised only if the complication is detected while still treatable.

The foundation for a zero-defects approach in obstetric practice is a highly structured medical record integrated with standardized patient education materials. This record system should be self-prompting and self-documenting. The simplest way to achieve this is with a preprinted medical record form. This form tracks the patient's care through time, with entries for every test and issue to be discussed with the patient. Most important, the patient educational materials are keyed to the protocol. For example, early in the pregnancy the patient receives information about the tests that will be performed during the pregnancy, including when they should be performed.

At 16 weeks, the record indicates that it is time for the MSAFP sample to be drawn, and a handout given to the patient. Even if the provider forgets to discuss the test and draw the sample, there is a high probability that the patient will remember the test and ask about it. The structured record both prompts the care provider and allows the patient to participate in the quality control for her own care.

Legal and Ethical Benefits of Structured Care

In a carefully designed structured prenatal care system, there are no second-class patients. Every woman is offered all appropriate care and is fully informed about the process of prenatal care. This does not resolve issues about who will pay for such care, but it is ethically preferable to rationing care by having different standards of prenatal care for different socioeconomic groups. To the extent that a substantial number of physicians use structured systems with the same core of services, these systems define the acceptable level of care. Such evidence of a standard of care should aid physicians in disputes with third-party payers over what is reimbursable care.

There have been no large-scale controlled studies of the legal benefits of structured prenatal care systems. Preliminary data and our experience with one of these systems in the malpractice insurance context are very suggestive. Physicians have used this system (Pre-Natal Care—A Systems Approach, developed by Arnold Greensher and his colleagues in Colorado Springs) for more than 550,000 births over 18 years. During this time there have been approximately five lawsuits involving births using the system, and total payouts of less than $500,000.

The observed number of medical malpractice claims is much lower than would be expected for this number of deliveries. Analysis of the data is confounded by several potential biases

1. Are high-risk or difficult births excluded from the system? This does not appear to be the case. Physicians who use the system generally use it for all deliveries.
2. Is there a bias in the selection of physicians using the system? This raises an intriguing question. If it is not the prenatal care system that protects these physicians from litigation, then what other physician characteristics correlate with an extremely low rate of birth injury claims? (Experience with com-

munities where all the physicians use the system seem to mitigate physician selection as the sole basis for the system's effectiveness.)

Thinking Like a Plaintiff's Attorney

These systems prevent litigation for three reasons. The first is that they prevent the systems failures that result in prenatal care–related injuries. The second is that they reduce the patient's incentive to sue. By making her a partner in her care and by providing full information about potential problems, the patient is less likely to be angry and surprised by things that happen in her care. Third, they present an unambiguous record of the care provided, the information given each woman, and the woman's choices based on that information. In this regard, the patient education handouts are as important as the record. Without the patient education component of the system, structured records are less credible because they are easy to alter. If the patient receives a handout, it helps prove the care was rendered. Perhaps most important for the psychology of litigation, they present this information in a well-organized, graphically attractive form. This is in stark contrast to the illegible notes or stream of consciousness dictations that make up many medical records. Physicians and their attorneys see so many medical records that they do not appreciate that most laypersons assume that medical records are an important measure of a physician's skills. A skillful plaintiff's attorney can easily convince a juror that sloppy, incomplete medical records equate to sloppy incomplete care.

The combination of extensive patient handouts and a complete and well-structured record creates the impression that the physician was careful and competent. This makes the case much less attractive to a plaintiff's attorney whose strategy is to win on jury sympathy rather than on a showing of clear and unambiguous negligence. Conversely, a highly structured record used improperly is a litigation disaster. If the records are completed haphazardly and the patients are not given the proper information, the record is no longer self-auditing and will no longer prevent systems failures. Its elegant structure turns against the physician, making the record the plaintiff's best evidence of the physician's negligence. This has led some defense attorneys to recommend against the use of structured records, based on the correct analysis that physicians who do not use the system properly will be hard to defend. It ignores the probability that most physicians will use the system properly and thus not be sued.

THE BIRTH PLAN

Beyond a structured prenatal care system, physicians delivering babies should use birth plans to reduce conflicts and misunderstandings surrounding the delivery. Avoiding such conflicts can reduce the likelihood of litigation and improve the quality of medical care. The best way to reduce conflict is to make agreements in advance about what will be done in a normal delivery and what will be necessary if an emergency arises. A written birth plan provides a vehicle for exploring the expectations of patients who are either reticent to state their preferences or who have not yet considered the issues attendant upon delivery. The exercise of preparing the plan gives the physician an opportunity to determine the patient's level of sophistication and to educate her about the childbearing process. This avoids misunderstandings about which items are a matter of convenience or comfort and which are medically necessary.

Purpose of a Birth Plan

The birth plan serves three purposes. First, it structures the discussion between the physician and the patient. This ensures that all important issues are addressed with each patient. Second, it provides a framework for resolving inconsistencies between the patient's expectations and the risks of her particular pregnancy. Finally, it serves as documentation of the agreement between the physician and the patient. This will obviate questions about the information given the patient and any promises by the physician as to the management of the delivery. Legally most important, it will document the risks of pregnancy and the specific risks attendant on the delivery strategy chosen by the patient. This will not relieve the physician of liability for negligence. It will, however, bolster the physician's claim that certain injuries were foreseeable risks of pregnancy and not iatrogenic birth injuries.

Contraindications

The birth plan should detail all aspects of the individual patient's health that influence decisions about the management of the pregnancy: maternal diseases, habits such as smoking and drug use, medications that the woman must continue taking during pregnancy, and any other factors that might influence the course of the pregnancy. Discussing these factors with the patient will help her understand that her pregnancy must be managed differently from those of her friends. It will also help the physician remember that the patient has special needs. This can help avoid giving a patient medications that she cannot tolerate, or performing contraindicated procedures in the haste of an emergency delivery.

Authority To Consent

Except for certain fertility treatments, the patient has sole authority to make the decisions about her care. Paternalism in obstetric care is legally dangerous. An obstetrician who tells a patient not to worry because everything will be fine is making a guarantee on the outcome of a pregnancy with almost no ability to influence that outcome. Consent is a simple problem made complicated by misinformation. A pregnant woman is the only person who may consent to her medical care. This is always true for adults, and in most states a pregnant minor has the right to consent to her medical care. Neither husbands, lovers, prospective grandparents, prospective adoptive parents, nor adoption agencies have a right to consent to, or interfere in, the medical care of the pregnant woman. Any discussion of the woman's medical care with such third parties is a violation of the patient's rights unless she has given her explicit permission.

Participation of Others

Although the pregnant woman has the right to exclude all third parties from consultation about her medical care, most women want to involve other persons in their decisions. The birth plan should include the names of any persons the patient designates to receive information about her pregnancy. The patient may also want to sign a durable power of attorney to delegate the right to consent to care to a third party if she becomes medically incompetent to consent to her own care. If the patient wants her husband or other person in the delivery room, this should be stated in the birth plan. The plan should discuss any restrictions on the presence of this third person (special training, a hospital orientation tour, etc.) and under what circumstances the person will be excluded. It is recommended that the husband or other person mentioned in the plan also be requested to read and sign the relevant portions of the plan.

Risk-Benefit Analysis

Although it is the patient who must consent to medical intervention, it is the physician who must provide the information necessary to make the decisions. Risk-benefit analysis in obstetrics is complicated because there are two patients and many social factors involved. The starting point for risk analysis in pregnancy is the risks of pregnancy itself. A woman must be warned that women die in childbirth, that 6% of children have some congenital abnormality, that things may happen in her pregnancy that will adversely affect the baby, and that some babies are inadvertently born injured. The woman must be warned about geographic risks such as high altitude and the limitation of local birth and emergency facilities.

The purpose of this background information is to establish the baseline risks of pregnancy. Understanding these risks is necessary to understanding the risks and benefits of various medical interventions. This is especially important for women who have been exposed to misinformation about the birth process. Some women believe that modern medicine is a conspiracy to subjugate women. Although obstetric care could be made much more responsive to the needs of pregnant women, dispensing with medical attendance is not a proper response to this problem.

The Patient's Interests

The physician should learn as much as possible about social factors that affect a patient's decisions. The patient must consider the risks of losing the baby, the risks of a damaged infant, and the risks that she is willing to assume to carry the baby. The decisions of a married woman in her thirties who has taken years to conceive are likely to be very different from the decisions of a single woman in her teens who is considering adoption. A patient who does not tell her physician about her desires and expectations should be asked about them. Most women have a personal image of childbirth that the physician must understand. The further this image is from reality, the greater is the likelihood of conflict.

The physician should work to avoid exercising undue influence on the patient's decisions. If there are strong medical reasons for making a certain decision, the physician should make these reasons clear. The physician should realize that the social reasons may outweigh the medical reasons for a particular patient. The choices of a married male physician in his forties with six healthy children at home are not likely to match the decisions of either of our hypothetical patients.

Risks to the Baby

Although pregnant women have great latitude in assuming the risk of various medical care options, they do not have an unlimited right to assume risks for the baby. Physicians should be careful not to agree to medical care that unnecessarily increases the risk to the baby. For example, a physician may not want to accept a patient who refuses consent to a Cesarean section under all circumstances. The physician should not humor the patient with the intention of forcing care on her when an emergency arises. Physicians should be wary of situations that limit their options in an emergency. Conversely, physicians must tell their patients of the risks that are imposed by their practice styles. Physicians who practice at high altitudes or in facilities that cannot provide proper emergency services must document that the patient understands that she and her baby are at substantial additional risk because of these factors.

Emergencies

It is particularly important that the physician and patient discuss what will be done if an emergency arises or something does not work out as hoped. A woman who wants a large family may be very upset if a Cesarean section becomes necessary during her first delivery. If she has not been prepared for the possibility, she may become angry with the physician who is doing the surgery. If the reason for the Cesarean section leads to a birth injury, this family is primed to sue. In contrast, if the woman understands that Cesarean delivery is necessary if the fetus is in trouble and that it does not necessarily lead to repeat surgery and limited family size, then she is better prepared for the surgery and the possible adverse outcome in the baby.

The physician should document how the birth plan will be modified for different emergencies to obviate the emotional turmoil that occurs when the patient's expectations are suddenly disappointed. This gives the patient time to consider and consent to different emergency options. Although the patient retains her right to change her mind after the birth plan has been signed, the process of preparing and negotiating the plan should reduce the probability that she will become dissatisfied with her decisions.

Availability of Facilities and Personnel

The patient must be warned if there is a possibility that the hospital may not be able to supply expected facilities. For example, the birthing room may not be available if there is a cluster of births on the day the patient delivers. It is imperative that the patient be warned if the hospital cannot provide essential services such as an emergency Cesarean section within a short period. If the patient is being delivered in a nonhospital-based birthing center, then provisions for emergency transfer and its risks must be documented. The patient must be informed of the potential consequences of such deficiencies and given the opportunity to seek care elsewhere.

The physician should explain the call system, identify who will attend the patient if her primary physician is not available, and give the patient an opportunity to meet the substitute physician. If the primary physician is a member of a multiphysician call system, the physician should make it clear to the patient that she may be seen by any member of the group. It is critical that every member of the group be aware of the existence of the patient's birth plan. A substitute physician should not be allowed to abandon the plan unless it is necessary because of unexpected medical complications. Any substitute physician who disagrees with the way the primary physician manages deliveries should not be in the same call system.

Custom versus Fashion

Both obstetricians and their patients are subject to fads and fashion. Although there are no properly controlled studies indicating benefits for natural childbirth, LeBoyer deliveries, Lamaze, and other current fashions, there is also no evidence that they are harmful. The physician should accommodate the patient's wishes as much as possible without endangering the health of the mother or baby. Conversely, if the physician believes that certain procedures are medically necessary, they should not be bargainable issues. Physicians should be cautious, however, and consider whether the procedure or medication is medically necessary or just their usual practice.

EVALUATING THE MOTHER'S MEDICAL CONDITION

Several tests are required by law or medical standards for every pregnant woman. It is important that any physician who cares for a pregnant woman know the results of these tests and act upon them if necessary.

The first and most important test is for pregnancy. Any woman of childbearing age should be considered pregnant unless there is evidence to the contrary if any medical treatment might affect the pregnancy or the fetus. Most radiology departments are covered in signs that ask women if they might be pregnant. Many internists, however, do not ask a woman about pregnancy and contraception before prescribing a drug that is not accepted for use in pregnancy. The risks, both medical and legal, are much greater for some drugs than they are for a chest X ray.

On the other hand, there is no laboratory test that can establish pregnancy beyond doubt. A physician should never tell a woman that she is or is not pregnant on the basis of a laboratory test alone. A history and physical examination are as necessary to making this diagnosis as any other. A patient who is assured that she is not pregnant may expose herself to agents that can harm her fetus. Even if there are no expected problems, failure to diagnose the pregnancy can interfere with the patient's receiving proper prenatal care and will reduce her options about abortion or prenatal diagnosis.

Maternal Disease

Pregnant women should be tested for diseases that directly affect their health and thus secondarily affect the outcome of the pregnancy. Some of these tests are mandated by law or public health regulation. Others are widely accepted as the standard of care. Failing to diagnose or manage maternal illness properly is a major source of liability in obstetrics. The problem arises because most pregnant women are healthy. This makes it easy to attribute what would otherwise be symptomatic illness to the normal effects of pregnancy.

Once the tests are done, the physician must be very careful to evaluate the results in every patient and take action when necessary. In caring for a pregnant woman, a few days can make a tremendous difference in the outcome, so a physician should pay particular attention to the timely evaluation of test results. If a result has not been received, it should be treated as bad news until the result is available. If the syphilis serology or the blood type has been lost, it should be repeated promptly. The only true negative screening test is the one that has been reported by the laboratory and evaluated by the physician.

Tests should never be ordered simply as a defensive measure. It is legally more dangerous not to act on a test that indicates maternal illness than not to do the test. For example, if a patient has a negative rubella titer, her physician should be concerned if she develops a rash. What may be dismissed as an allergy in an immune patient should be worked up in a woman who may have rubella. In addition, this patient should be immunized as soon as she delivers. The obstetrician who failed to immunize a patient after her first pregnancy may be liable for a congenital rubella baby from her second pregnancy.

Legally Mandated Testing

Although congenital rubella has almost been conquered, the risk of congenital infection with herpes, hepatitis, syphilis, or HIV is increasing.[18] The laws requiring the reporting of such infections should be carefully followed to allow the health department to investigate the source of the disease. It does not help to treat a woman for syphilis in her first trimester if her consort remains infectious. If she contracts the disease again in the third trimester, the risk of fetal infection is greater than it was before. If the patient or the child is injured by the failure to comply with testing and reporting laws, the physician can be held liable for negligence per se.

It is imperative to consider the possibility of HIV infection in every pregnant woman.[19] Ideally, women should be counseled and tested before becoming pregnant.[20] It is important to counsel and offer testing to every pregnant woman. In some urban centers, more than 1% of pregnant women are already HIV infected, and the rate appears to be increasing.[21] As HIV becomes more prevalent, it is anticipated that states will require prenatal testing for HIV. Until this happens, it is critical that physicians stress the medical necessity of knowing a patient's HIV status when managing maternal and child health problems. If the patient refuses testing, this should be carefully documented.

MEDICAL INTERVENTIONS

There is evidence that induction of labor and Cesarean sections have been overused in the United States. This overuse has been driven by nonmedical factors such as fear of legal liability, physician and patient convenience, and reimbursement policies that encourage medical procedures. Unlike most other forms of defensive medicine, however, there is a rational basis for the perception that performing a Cesarean section makes it easier to defend a potential birth injury case. It is easier for a plaintiff's attorney to attack a physician's decision to do nothing or to operate too late than it is to prove technical errors in the performance of the Cesarean section.

More fundamentally, whereas a medically unnecessary Cesarean section subjects the mother to operative risks and increased morbidity, these risks are inherent in the procedure. If a proper informed consent is obtained or the jury does not believe that the patient would have refused the operation had she been properly informed, it is difficult to convince a jury that a patient should recover for the consequences of a properly performed but unnecessary operation. Paradoxically, efforts to reduce unnecessary medical interventions may exacerbate this problem.

As patients become more reticent to consent to Cesarean sections and induction of labor, and insurance companies increase financial incentives not to perform these interventions, the probability increases that necessary interventions will be delayed or omitted. There is no evidence, however, that juries will accept cost containment as a defense. Juries are also skeptical about a patient's refusal to consent to needed treatment. When the question is refusal of necessary care, juries tend to believe that physicians ultimately can convince patients to consent. These factors require that de-

cisions not to use medical interventions be well documented and the patient carefully educated.

Past-Term Pregnancies

Education about potential medical interventions should start at the first patient encounter and should be part of the birth plan. It is important to determine, at the earliest possible time, if the patient has unreasonable fears or expectations. The patient must understand that whereas induction of labor is medically necessary in many situations, it should not be done as a matter of physician or patient convenience. Patients should be discouraged from seeing induction of labor as a benign process, but they also must appreciate its usefulness in appropriate circumstances.

A patient's birth plan should detail the indications and risks of induced labor. These should include the medical reasons for what might otherwise appear to be an induction done merely for convenience. If the mother lives in a secluded area where emergency services are nonexistent, then induction at near term may be safer than risking an unattended home delivery in a snowbound mountain cabin. If a mother is likely to need special care for herself or the infant and the entire area is under a hurricane warning, it may be better to deliver her than to leave her to compete for attention in a hospital on disaster status. These are valid indications for inducing labor and should be documented in the chart. This documentation will be important if the snow does not fall or the hurricane hits elsewhere and the delivery has an unfortunate outcome.

The patient should understand that babies that are well past dates may need to be delivered by induction or section. Physicians should enlist the aid of the woman in ensuring that the progress of the pregnancy is appreciated. If the physician is suspicious about the patient's reported dates, this should be investigated before the patient is grossly past term. The problem of past-dates babies has been exacerbated by the fragmentation of the medical care delivery system. It is easy for a woman to get lost in a group practice where all the prenatal care is delivered by nonphysician personnel. If no one physician is responsible for her care, there may be no one to notice if she misses an appointment or is several weeks overdue.

As changing health insurance plans force patients to move to new physicians, it is difficult for a physician to know if the patient has left the practice or is just not coming in for her appointments. Physicians must have tracking systems for pregnant patients. If the patient has been lost to follow-up as her due date approaches, the physician should attempt to contact her. If she is under the care of another physician, refuses to come in for an appointment, or cannot be located, this information should be documented in the chart.

Cesarean Sections

The possibility of a Cesarean section should be discussed with every patient as part of the patient's birth plan, with contingent consent for a Cesarean section obtained early in the woman's pregnancy. The woman must sign the consent form herself; her husband should not be asked to sign it. At the time the Cesarean section becomes necessary, the woman should be asked to re-sign the original consent form, indicating that the conditions for needing a Cesarean section have now occurred. The fact that the mother may have had some pain-relieving drugs does not render her legally incompetent to acknowledge the need for the procedure. Her husband has no authority to sign the consent to her surgery unless she has given him this right in a power of attorney. If the mother is medically unable to consent because she is mentally incompetent, the surgery may go forward based on the consent signed as part of the birth plan.

The standard of care for pregnant women who have had a previous Cesarean section has changed rapidly in the last few years. Many obstetricians encourage women to attempt labor if the reason for the original operation is not likely to be repeated. On the other hand, some highly respected obstetricians believe that vaginal delivery should never be attempted by these patients. Physicians should be careful to inform the patient of all her options. The consent to surgical delivery or to

vaginal delivery must be well informed. If the patient wants a trial of labor and the physician does not believe that it is advisable, he or she should help the patient find another doctor who will accept her decision. The consent to a trial of labor should be discussed as part of the patient's birth plan.

Disagreements over the advisability of a trial of labor are different from a refusal of a Cesarean section in all circumstances. A woman has a right to refuse surgical delivery without regard for the risk to the fetus. She may refuse a Cesarean section for reasons that have no medical basis, even if her decision endangers the life or health of her fetus. Neither the pregnant woman's husband nor her physician has the right to force her compliance by physical force or chemical restraint. The only way to challenge a woman's refusal of a Cesarean section is to obtain a court order. General medical-ethical thinking opposes the involuntary treatment of pregnant women who make a knowing decision to refuse medical care.

The strongest case for seeking to overturn a competent woman's decision is when the care is necessary for her own survival rather than the survival of the fetus. In analogous cases involving nonpregnant patients, the courts have expressed reluctance to allow an otherwise healthy person to refuse acute lifesaving care. The physician's ethical duty is difficult to determine in such situations. Ethicists who hold autonomy as the highest value argue that the patient should be allowed to die without attempts at legal intervention. Those who stress beneficence and the right of the state to act as parens patria for its citizens argue that the physician has an ethical duty to seek a judicial determination.

If this refusal is made during the first patient encounter, it presents the physician with the dilemma of whether to continue treating the woman. Most of the ethical debates have centered on the right of the state to force women to undergo unwanted medical care for the sake of the fetus. There has been much less attention to the right of the physician to refuse to treat a patient who prospectively refuses potentially lifesaving care. Many physicians ignore the refusal on the basis that the woman will change her mind if the section becomes necessary or in the hope that a section will not be required. This is a dangerous approach if an emergency section becomes necessary. Since there will be no time to obtain a court order, the physician must choose between respecting the woman's wishes or operating against her consent. Irrespective of the patient's expressed wishes, it will be difficult to defend allowing the patient and baby to die. The best that can be expected is a verdict based on the court's requiring the enforcement of a rigorously documented informed refusal of care. Conversely, operating against a patient's express refusal, without judicial authorization, is legally and ethically unacceptable.

HOME DELIVERIES

There is little legal experience with home deliveries because very few home deliveries in the United States are attended or supervised by physicians. Although there is a small, visible group of middle-class and affluent women seeking home deliveries, most women delivered at home are poor and would prefer to be delivered in a hospital by a physician. Once these women are in labor, they can be brought into the hospital under the antidumping provisions of the Medicare/Medicaid laws, but they will still be responsible for their medical bills. These poor women pose a dilemma for physicians because of the conflict between their desire to help the woman avoid the hospital costs and the ethical and legal problems in engaging in potentially substandard care.

The Politics of Home Deliveries

Women who choose home deliveries because of political beliefs or involvement in quasi-religious antimedical groups are problematic because they usually have high expectations. Many believe that by avoiding the medicalization of birth, they will have a unique experience and a perfect baby. Physicians who might otherwise consider supervising a home delivery should be very cautious when working with a patient who has such unrealistic beliefs. The greatest threats posed by

such patients are the refusal of necessary hospitalization should an emergency arise and the delay in getting hospital care once the patient agrees.

Even if the physician has discussed this possibility and documented the patient's agreement to hospitalization in the birth plan, the patient retains the right to refuse a transfer to the hospital. This can put the physician in the ethical and legal bind of a patient's refusing emergency medical care that is necessary to preserve her and her baby's health. There is no time for a court order for care, and, unlike the usual situation where the patient is in the emergency room, the patient must be transported against her will to make the care possible.

Participating in Home Deliveries

As long as a home delivery is successful, the physician is not at any special legal risk. If the mother or the baby is injured because of a complication that could have been successfully managed in the hospital, the physician must convince a jury that home deliveries constitute proper medical care. At this point the woman's attorney will pose the argument that the physician endorsed the safety of home deliveries by consenting to perform one. The woman's assumption of risk will evaporate if the jury agrees. Very few jurors are sympathetic to physicians who claim that the patient bullied them into agreeing to provide unsafe care. The defense that the woman could not afford to go to the hospital can be countered with the availability of emergency admissions. If the woman is in active labor and the physician is willing to fight with the hospital administrator, the woman will be admitted because of the laws governing emergency care of women in labor. The hospital may punish the physician for holding it to its legal duty, but that is not the pregnant woman's problem.

Legally, there is little to recommend participation in home deliveries. Analogies to the successful use of home deliveries in Europe have limited persuasion. The European countries have a structurally different medical and legal system that does not encourage a patient to sue her physician for any complications of a home birth. The ethics of home deliveries are more ambiguous. A woman in good health, without risk factors for birth complications, and with realistic expectations could reasonably consent to a home delivery. Although the physician's legal risk might be great if any complications arose, it would not be unethical to participate in such a delivery.

Ethical problems arise when any of these preconditions is not met. If there are medical contraindications to a home delivery, the physician should hesitate before implicitly minimizing those risks by agreeing to deliver the woman at home. If the woman has unreasonable expectations, the physician should consider the possibility of not being able to render needed care in a crisis. A woman has a legal right to refuse necessary care, but physicians have an ethical duty not to encourage or support unreasonable medical care decisions. Physicians who choose to participate in home deliveries should carefully document the circumstances that make a home delivery necessary or appropriate. The informed consent must recite the added risks of the home delivery and why delivery in a hospital is undesirable or impossible.

WORKING WITH MIDWIVES

One of the most difficult areas in referral and consultation is the relationship between obstetricians and midwives in states that allow the independent practice of midwifery. Some states allow midwives to practice only under a physician's supervision. In these states, the relationship between physicians and midwives is governed by the principles discussed in Chapter 10. Midwives pose unique problems because of the view that pregnancy is a natural function that does not require sophisticated medical attendance.

The level of maternal and fetal morbidity and mortality is unacceptable for any woman accustomed to modern medicine. An effective midwifery system depends on the patients of independently practicing midwives being ensured of access to necessary medical and surgical care. European midwifery practice is often touted as a model of such a system, but the model is not directly applicable to the United States because of profound differences in the underlying health care systems.

Except for women having contractions, there is no guaranteed access to medical care for pregnant women in the United States. In many states, there is little regulation of the training and competence of lay midwives. The underlying morbidity and mortality of the population generally, and pregnant women in specific, is higher than in Europe, and it is dramatically higher in many low-income areas. These factors increase the percentage of women who will need physician-directed care during pregnancy or delivery. Most problematically, women who choose midwives because they believe that the perfect baby results from a natural pregnancy will be especially intolerant of pregnancy-related morbidity or neonatal mortality. The anger, and litigation, will be directed at the obstetrician because the midwife will usually transfer the patient before the disaster.

These factors contribute to, and reflect, the lack of a rational system for midwifery practice in the United States. This makes it legally risky for obstetricians to work with independently practicing midwives. Midwives also pose ethical problems for the physicians who are called on to treat their patients. It is not unusual for lay midwives in states with weak regulations to avoid physician referrals until there is a crisis, and then to refer the patient to the emergency room. Many obstetricians want to help the patients of such midwives but do not want to be seen as endorsing their practices.

Financial issues complicate the relationship between obstetricians and midwives. Some obstetricians oppose midwife practice as unwanted competition, whereas others employ midwives to increase their patient base. In smaller communities that can support only one or two obstetricians, extensive midwifery practice drains off the routine deliveries that are the financial base for obstetric practice. This increases the pressure on the obstetricians to shift to gynecology-only practices or to leave the community, compromising the availability of surgical deliveries and other medical interventions for all pregnant women in the community.

Classes of Midwives

Referral and consultation practices vary with the class of midwife. Nurse-midwives are registered nurses with specialty training in midwifery. All laws governing nursing licensure and practice apply to nurse-midwives. As a consequence, nurse-midwife practice is usually well regulated and reliable even in states that do not otherwise regulate midwives. Although there are special considerations in working with independently practicing nurses, referral and consultation with nurse-midwives does not pose the ethical and legal problems of working with lay midwives.

The training of lay midwives varies enormously. Some have been through extensive training and apprenticeship programs; some may be physicians or nurses who are not licensed in the United States; others are self-taught from books or experience; and some have virtually no training or skills. A state may license and regulate lay midwives as extensively as nurses or physicians, but few do. There are contradictory reasons for allowing lay midwifery. Some groups argue for lay midwives because of their opposition to the medicalization of pregnancy. Others believe that lay midwifery compromises the health and safety of pregnant women. They point to the lack of lay cardiologists and urologists as evidence that lay practice on women is tolerated only because of the low status of women in the legal system.

Physicians must be wary about practicing with lay midwives. If they are inadequately trained, they are much more likely to delay physician referrals until the patient is in grave danger. The most dangerous situation is lay midwives who practice under the umbrella of an antimedical religious group. Some states specifically exempt religious healers from state laws forbidding the practice of medicine without a license. Even states that forbid or regulate independent midwifery may allow religious practitioners to practice without supervision.

States that regulate the practice of midwifery are often lax in enforcing these regulations. A physician who knows that an individual is practicing midwifery in violation of the law must report such practice to the proper authorities—the board of medical examiners, the board of nursing examiners, or the police—and not practice with such an individual under any circumstances. However, the physician should assist a patient who is in danger, even if that means taking over the patient from the illegal midwife. Reporting the illegal practice establishes that the physician was not condoning or participating in the practice.

Referrals and Consultations

Consulting and referrals with midwives are complicated because the tort law generally assumes that physicians are in charge whenever they work with nonphysician personnel in medical settings. A physician who consults on a case for a midwife is in a very different legal position than if the consultation were for another physician. If the consulting physician determines that physician procedures or prescription medications are necessary, carrying out these recommendations is the responsibility of the attending physician. With no attending physician, the responsibility remains with the consultant because the midwife cannot deliver the necessary care. The physician must ensure that the patient appreciates the limitations of the midwife's authority and understands the necessity for the recommended care and that it can be delivered only by a physician. Since a consultation, even for limited tasks such as ordering screening blood tests, creates a physician–patient relationship, the physician may have a duty to render the needed treatment if requested by the patient.

Referrals from midwives are less problematic than consultations because the physician will assume responsibility for the patient's ongoing care. There must be a good working relationship that ensures that referrals are made before the patient's medical condition deteriorates. In the ideal medical arrangement, the midwife and the physician discuss each new patient to evaluate future medical needs. The midwife then confers with the physician whenever something unusual develops in the patient's condition. Legally, such close cooperation would result in the physician's being found liable for negligent medical care. If the physician is confident of the midwife's skills and judgment, assuming liability for the care is preferable to not being involved in the prereferral care.

BEHAVIORAL RISKS IN PREGNANCY

Many physiologic conditions make pregnancy dangerous to the mother and the baby. Most of these, such as diabetes, are intrinsic and, except for compliance issues, beyond the control of the woman. Some, such as alcoholism or cocaine use, are behavioral problems with substantial voluntary components. An unfortunate nexus of the medical efforts to improve prenatal health and the political debate on whether the fetus is a person deserving independent protection is the pregnant woman who engages in activities that might harm her fetus. Such women have been subjected to forced medical care, including Cesarean sections, and to incarceration in prison.

Debates over the legality and even the usefulness of coercive policies aimed at pregnant women have obscured the issues in managing high-risk pregnancies. There is vast gulf between a physician seeking to have a woman treated against her will and the much more common problem of helping a patient understand the risks and benefits of various behaviors and medical care alternatives. In general, physicians providing personal health services should not attempt to force unwanted medical care on their pregnant patients. The American Medical Association's (AMA's) position is illustrative.

The American Medical Association Policy Statement[22]

The AMA Board of Trustees recommends adoption of the following statement:

1. Judicial intervention is inappropriate when a woman has made an informed refusal of a medical treatment designed to benefit her fetus. If an exceptional circumstance could be found in which a medical treatment poses an insignificant or no health risk to the woman, entails a minimal invasion of her bodily integrity, and would clearly prevent substantial and irreversible harm to her fetus, it might be appropriate for a physician to seek judicial intervention. However, the fundamental principle against compelled medical procedures should control in all cases that do not present such exceptional circumstances.
2. The physician's duty is to provide appropriate information, such that the pregnant woman may make an informed and thoughtful decision, not to dictate the woman's decision.
3. A physician should not be liable for honoring a pregnant woman's informed refusal of medical treatment designed to benefit the fetus.
4. Criminal sanctions or civil liability for harmful behavior by the pregnant woman toward her fetus are inappropriate.
5. Pregnant substance abusers should be provided with rehabilitative treatment appropriate to their specific physiological and psychological needs.
6. To minimize the risk of legal action by a pregnant patient or an injured child or fetus, the physician should document medical recommendations made including the consequences of failure to comply with the physician's recommendations.

Implications of the AMA Policy

The use of judicial process to force medical care on an unwilling patient has a long and checkered history. It is a power that has been abused in the past and will continue to be abused in the future. It is also a necessary power in the management of persons who are not able to make rational decisions about medical treatment. Most of these are chronically mentally ill, although some are suffering from acute toxic or psychiatric conditions that render them temporarily incompetent. The forced care of pregnant women is controversial because it is being applied to women who are mentally competent. These women may have made self-destructive decisions, but they are rational decisions. The forced care is rationalized on the need to protect the fetus, not the health of a woman who is unable to make rational medical care decisions.

The AMA policy emphasizes that the duty of private physicians is to inform and educate their patients, not to make their decisions for them. (The duty of certain public health and mental health physicians is to protect the public, even at the derogation of an individual's right to determine his or her own medical care.) It is important to note that this presumes an informed refusal of medical care. Patients who are not able to make rational decisions are not able to make an informed refusal of medical care. In these cases, it is proper for the court to intervene and ensure that the person receives proper medical care. Physicians have the same duty to seek appropriate judicial intervention for a mentally incompetent pregnant woman as for a mentally incompetent diabetic man. They do not have the right to intervene to protect the health of the fetus if the woman is otherwise competent to make her own health decisions.

Consent in High-Risk Pregnancies

The physician's duty to inform and educate is the same whether the factor complicating the pregnancy is intrinsic or behavioral. This duty is complicated by the legal dilemma that the woman is the proper arbitrator of her medical care, but she is not the only person who can sue the physician for the consequences of that care. The patient's husband or surviving children can sue the physician if the patient dies or is gravely injured. If the woman knowingly assumes the risk of the pregnancy and her medical decisions, then she can waive her right to sue. This waiver will bar others who might sue on her behalf or on their own behalf because of their suffering occasioned by her injuries.

The patient's assumption of risk (or informed consent) is effective only if it is carefully obtained and documented. The risks to the patient and to the baby must be fully explained and the explanation documented. This is best done with a structured prenatal care system, tailored to the patient's special needs. Dilemmas arise because the law is ambiguous about a woman's right to assume the risk of injury for her fetus. Although it is expected that the courts will not hold a physician liable when a woman clearly refuses care, the burden will be on the physician to convince the jury that the refusal was both knowing and unshakable. Juries assume that patients are rational and refuse care only if they are insufficiently informed of the risks. Juries will have a stronger prejudice that a pregnant woman would not knowingly have put her baby at risk. Although it may be easy to convince a jury that a woman who uses crack does not care about her baby's well-being, it will be much harder to convince them that refusing medical care evidences the same level of disregard.

The Self-Destructive Pregnant Woman

Self-destructive behavior poses different legal and ethical problems depending on whether it is legal behavior, such as alcoholism, or illegal behavior, such as cocaine use. The AMA policy statement suggests that the physician should provide information and document consent. Beyond this, physicians must decide how far they are willing to accommodate a patient who is unwilling to modify medically destructive behavior. Is there a point where the physician's continued treatment of complications of self-destructive behavior becomes an impediment to the patient's commitment to changing the behavior? Is refusing to continue to treat the patient ethically justifiable if the patient does not have access to appropriate treatment programs? Should the physician's role differ for illegal activities such as cocaine use?

Every self-destructive patient poses these questions. They are more urgent when the patient is pregnant and her behavior threatens to injure her fetus. Absent a state law requiring the reporting of the behavior in question, the physician has no duty to report a patient's illegal drug use to the police or public health authorities. If the state offers only jail to illegal drug users, it is difficult to argue that reporting such a patient is in the patient's interest. A physician's ethical duty is more difficult to determine if the state offers appropriate rehabilitation services. Given the current knowledge of addictive behavior and the effects of drugs such as cocaine, it is difficult to speak of a knowing and voluntary refusal of care by an addicted patient. If the patient cannot make an informed choice, the physician's duty may be to seek judicial intervention to determine the patient's best interests.

OBSTETRICS RISK MANAGEMENT

When a baby is born with a severe genetic disease or intrauterine injury, the parents often blame themselves for the injury. If there is any indication that the physician might have been at fault, this guilt can rapidly turn to anger and a lawsuit. These lawsuits often can be particularly acrimonious because the parents may be driven by an emotional need to shift the guilt as much as by the potential monetary recovery.

There are two potential injured parties when a defective child is born: the parents or guardian and the child. The parents' lawsuit, which can be for negligence or for *wrongful birth,* will claim for the extra cost of the medical and other services required to treat their child's condition. The traditional component of this claim is for these expenses during the child's minority, or the child's lifetime, if the child will be permanently incompetent (see Chapter 4). The more controversial claim is for the mental anguish of having to observe the child's suffering and for the disruption in family life. The courts are suspicious of such claims, recognizing that even injured children provide an emotional benefit to most parents.

The value of the parents' claim for mental anguish will be based on the court's perception of the set-off of having the child. This set-off is greatest in the failure-of-sterilization cases. Assuming that there was no medical injury to the mother or the baby, the courts have generally found that the benefit of a healthy baby exceeds the detriment of having an unwanted child. Conversely, parents are most likely to recover when

the child is badly damaged; an extreme case would be the birth, through the failure of genetic counseling, of a child with Tay-Sachs disease.

The courts have been much more hostile to lawsuits brought by injured children. If the child states a specific damage claim for an expense necessitated by the injury that is not covered by the parents' claim, then some courts will allow for this expense to be recovered. These claims are seen as related to the cases in which the child is affirmatively injured, such as the Rh sensitization cases. The controversy arises over what are termed *wrongful life claims.* A wrongful life claim asserts that the child would have been better off not having been born. The set-off and public policy issues are very strongly against recovery on such claims:

> Ultimately, the infant's complaint is that he would be better off not to have been born. Man, who knows nothing of death or nothingness, cannot possibly know whether that is so. We must remember that the choice is not between being born with health or being born without it; it is not claimed that the defendants failed to do something to prevent or reduce the ravages of rubella. Rather the choice is between a worldly existence and none at all.... To recognize a right not to be born is to enter an area in which no one could find his way.[23]

Preconception versus Postconception Remedies

Abortion creates a critical ethical and legal distinction between pre- and postconception care. Abortion is ethically abhorrent to a substantial minority of persons in the United States. (Some antiabortion groups also oppose the use of contraception, but contraception has become so widely accepted that its use generates no moral outrage comparable to abortion.) Even persons who support a woman's right to choose to terminate an unwanted pregnancy are not necessarily proabortion but see it as a necessary evil. As a matter of public policy and individual patient welfare, it is preferable that reproductive decisions be made before conception.

In a failure of preconception counseling, the parents must prove that had they been properly informed of the risk of having an injured child, they would have chosen not to conceive the child. In contrast, when the information is sought after conception, the parents must convince the jury that they would have aborted the fetus had they known of the risk. Juries are clearly more sympathetic to decisions not to conceive than to decisions to abort. As a result, they are willing to believe that a couple would choose not to conceive based on the risk of minor conditions such as congenital deafness. Conversely, it is be much more difficult to convince a jury that the same condition, discovered postconception, would justify an abortion.

Patients' Views about Abortion

A patient's personal beliefs about abortion change the risk–benefit determinations for genetic counseling and, to a lesser extent, for fertility treatment. Physicians must not assume, however, that a patient who is opposed to abortion in the abstract will not consider abortion if she is personally faced with a high probability of giving birth to a child with a severe defect. All women, even those who are opposed to abortion, should be offered all appropriate testing and counseling. This does not mean that a physician should advocate abortion. Ideally, a patient should receive the necessary information about genetic diseases and the risks of fertility treatment without reference to either her or her physician's views about abortion. The woman's personal views about abortion should shape the risks that she is willing to assume of conceiving a child with a genetic disease, the prenatal testing to which she will consent, and under which circumstances, if any, she will terminate a pregnancy.

Physicians who do not perform abortions because of personal ethical beliefs should ensure that their beliefs do not compromise their patients' right to choose an abortion. In addition to providing every patient full information, the physician should arrange an easy referral system so that a patient who chooses an abortion can obtain it without unnecessary delay or expense. Con-

versely, physicians who support abortion as a valid therapeutic technique must not force their views on their patients. They must be prepared to respect the wishes of a woman who, after being fully informed of the risks and benefits of pre- or postconception testing, chooses to bear her child without regard to potential genetic diseases.

Creating Unreasonable Expectations

Marketing has a strong influence on obstetric services today. Many hospitals offer special facilities and services to compete for the lucrative market in delivering well-insured obstetrics patients. This is seen as a particularly attractive market because of the many ancillary services to be sold to affluent patients. These marketing strategies have varying impacts on patients' medical care. Providing comfortable waiting rooms or champagne for the family may attract patients, but it does not ensure quality medical care. Offering birthing rooms and informal settings can be beneficial to the patient but requires changing the practice habits of obstetricians and pediatricians.

Marketing obstetrics services becomes a legal problem when it reinforces the illusion that childbirth is a risk-free, enjoyable experience. Advertisements with pictures of healthy babies and smiling mothers may be accurate for most deliveries but not for all. For those who are not so lucky, those advertisements fuel the resentment and bitterness that lead to medical malpractice lawsuits. Obstetricians should be especially careful about associating with physician referral services that are coupled with public advertisements. These referral services often make explicit and implicit promises about the physician services, promises that can complicate the physician–patient relationship.

Both physicians and hospitals should be careful that their advertisements do not constitute a guarantee that patients will be delivered in whatever way they wish. The special facilities may not be available if there is a clustering of births on one day. In some cases, birthing chairs or natural childbirth may not be appropriate for a given patient. An obstetrician should know what the hospital offers and what his or her patients want. If the hospital has special programs that the physician does not participate in, every patient should be told of the nonparticipation. These matters must be addressed in the first prenatal visit. Seven months into the pregnancy is too late to find out that the patient has reserved the birthing room and the physician will not use it. This will anger the patient and could raise the issue of consumer fraud if the hospital's advertisements promise services that are not available.

The Birth-Injured Infant

The first priority with a potential birth injury is to manage the infant's medical condition. Under no circumstances should concerns about possible litigation be allowed to interfere with the infant's medical care. The second priority is to make a definitive diagnosis. Determining what caused the problem may guide the treatment of the child and may help avoid similar problems in future children. It is also critical to the defense of any subsequent litigation.

The careless use of diagnoses such as cerebral palsy or anoxic birth injury has exacerbated the problem of obstetric malpractice litigation.[24] The pediatrician and the obstetrician should work together to obtain a good etiologic diagnosis for the child. There is a general assumption among laypersons and plaintiffs' attorneys that all nonspecific central nervous system damage is due to birth hypoxia and is therefore the physician's fault. Obstetricians have fostered this belief by failing to investigate the underlying causes of seeming birth injuries.

One example has been the development of placental analysis. Historically physicians have either discarded placentas or sold them to drug companies. Only recently have obstetricians realized that the placenta is an invaluable research tool and forensic pathology specimen. Placental research is documenting chronic placental insufficiency diseases that may account for 50% of what have traditionally been termed birth injuries. Placental pathology studies showing placental insufficiency have been used to defend physicians from charges of negligently injuring a child at birth.

In cases of suspected birth injury, the entire placenta and umbilical cord should be weighed and appropriately preserved. The placenta may be stored until it is determined that the baby does not have any residual damage. If the baby is injured, the placenta should be examined by a pathologist who is skilled in placental pathology. This is not a routine skill and must be specifically sought out. If an unskilled pathologist records that the placenta looks normal, this opinion will only bolster the plaintiff's case. Since these examinations are expensive and usually cannot be billed to the patient, physicians and their malpractice insurance companies must cooperate to pay for the pathologist's services.

REFERENCES

1. Beckwith J. The human genome initiative: genetics' lightning rod. *Am J Law Med.* 1991;17:1.
2. Lippman A. Prenatal genetic testing and screening: Constructing needs and reinforcing inequities. *Am J Law Med.* 1991;17:15.
3. ACOG Technical Bulletin 154. *Prenatal Detection of Neural Tube Defects.* April 1991.
4. ACOG Technical Bulletin 154. *Prenatal Detection of Neural Tube Defects.* April 1991.
5. ACOG Technical Bulletin 154. *Prenatal Detection of Neural Tube Defects.* April 1991.
6. ACOG Technical Bulletin 154. *Prenatal Detection of Neural Rube Defects.* April 1991.
7. *Munro v. Regents of Univ. of Cal.*, 215 Cal. App.3d 977, 263 Cal. Rptr. 878 (Cal. App. 2d Dist. 1989).
8. ACOG Technical Bulletin 108. *Antenatal Diagnosis of Genetic Disorders.* September 1987.
9. ACOG Technical Bulletin 125. *Infertility.* February 1989.
10. ACOG Technical Bulletin 120. *Medical Induction of Ovulation.* September 1988.
11. ACOG Technical Bulletin 142. *Male Infertility.* June 1990.
12. ACOG Technical Bulletin 120. *Medical Induction of Ovulation.* September 1988.
13. ACOG Technical Bulletin 140. *New Reproductive Technologies.* March 1990.

14. ACOG Technical Bulletin 120. *Medical Induction of Ovulation.* September 1988.

15. ACOG Committee on Ethics, Committee Opinion 94. *Multifetal Pregnancy Reduction and Selective Fetal Termination.* April 1991.

16. Novick LF, et al. New York State HIV Seroprevalence Project, Chapter II Newborn Seroprevalence study: methods and results. *Am J Pub Health Supp.* 1991;81:15–21.

17. ACOG Committee Opinion 109. *Maximizing Pregnancy Rates Resulting from Donor Insemination with Frozen Semen.* April 1992.

18. ACOG Technical Bulletin 114. *Perinatal Viral and Parasitic Infections.* March 1988.

19. ACOG Committee Opinion 85. *Human Immunodeficiency Virus Infection: Physicians' Responsibilities.* Committee on Ethics, September 1990.

20. ACOG Technical Bulletin 169. *Human Immune Deficiency Virus Infections.* December 1988.

21. Novick LF, et al. New York State HIV Seroprevelance Project, Chapter II Newborn Seroprevalence study: methods and results. *Am J Pub Health Supp.* 1991;81:15–21.

22. AMA Board of Trustees Report. Legal interventions during pregnancy: court-ordered medical treatments and legal penalties for potentially harmful behavior by pregnant women. *JAMA.* 1990; 264:2663–2670.

23. *Gleitman v. Cosgrove,* 227 A.2d 689, 711.

24. ACOG Technical Bulletin 163. *Fetal and Neonatal Neurologic Injury.* January 1992.

SUGGESTED READINGS

Fertility Treatment

Ahuja KK, Mamiso J, Emmerson G, Bowen-Simpkins P, Seaton A, Simons EG. Pregnancy following intracytoplasmic sperm injection treatment with dead husband's spermatozoa: ethical and policy considerations. *Hum Reprod.* 1997;12:1360–1363.

Annas GJ. The shadowlands—secrets, lies, and assisted reproduction. *N Engl J Med.* 1998;339:935–939.

Appleton T. Ethical issues in assisted reproductive medicine: a pragmatic approach. *Br J Urol.* 1995;76(suppl 2):85–92.

Baird P. Proceed with care: new reproductive technologies and the need for boundaries. *J Assist Reprod Genet.* 1995;12:491–498.

Baird PA. Ethical issues of fertility and reproduction. *Annu Rev Med.* 1996;47:107–116.

Benshushan A, Schenker JG. The right to an heir in the era of assisted reproduction. *Hum Reprod.* 1998;13:1407–1410.

Brahams D. Ethics and the law: the law and assisted human conception. *Br Med Bull.* 1990;46:850–859.

Braverman AM, English ME. Creating brave new families with advanced reproductive technologies. *NAACOGS Clin Issu Perinat Womens Health Nurs.* 1992;3:353–363.

Bromham DR, Lilford RJ. Autonomy and its limitations in artificial reproduction. *Baillieres Clin Obstet Gynaecol.* 1991;5:529–550.

Craft I. Assisted conception. *Med Leg J.* 1990;58(pt 1):7–15; discussion 15–7.

Daniels K. The controversy regarding privacy versus disclosure among patients using donor gametes in assisted reproductive technology. *J Assist Reprod Genet.* 1997;14:373–375.

Davis DS. Legal trends in bioethics. *J Clin Ethics.* 1997;8:204–207.

Dawson K, Singer P. Should fertile people have access to in vitro fertilisation? *BMJ.* 1990;300:167–170.

Ethics Committee of the American Fertility Society. Ethical considerations of the new reproductive technologies. *Fertil Steril.* 1990;53:1S–104S.

Garcia SA. Reproductive technology for procreation, experimentation, and profit: protecting rights and setting limits. *J Leg Med.* 1990;11:1–57.

Garcia SA. Sociocultural and legal implications of creating and sustaining life through biomedical technology. *J Leg Med.* 1996;17:469–525.

Gazvani MR, Wood SJ, Kingsland CR. Assisted conception: current techniques and outcome. *Br J Hosp Med.* 1997;58:268–271.

Harvey JC. Ethical issues and controversies in assisted reproductive technologies. *Curr Opin Obstet Gynecol.* 1992;4:750–755.

ISLAT (Institute for Science Law, and Technology) Working Group. Art into science: regulation of fertility techniques. *Science.* 1998;281:651–652.

Johnson MH. Genetics, the free market and reproductive medicine. *Hum Reprod.* 1997;12:408–410.

Jones HW Jr. Assisted reproduction. *Clin Obstet Gynecol.* 1992;35:749–757.

Keifer WS. Preparing for obstetrics in the twenty-first century: Quo Vadis? *Am J Obstet Gynecol.* 1993;168:1787–1790.

Kim MH. Current trends in human IVF and other assisted reproductive technologies. *Yonsei Med J.* 1990;31:91–97.

Kopfensteiner TR. Ethical aspects of in vitro fertilization and embryo transfer. *Biomed Pharmacother.* 1998;52:204–207.

Lowy FH, Paterson MA, De Martis F, Klotzko AJ, Friedl B. Immortality through the fertility clinic. *Camb Q Healthc Ethics.* 1995;4:375–386.

Lupton ML. Artificial reproduction and the family of the future. *Med Law.* 1998;17:93–111.

Macnaughton M. Ethics and reproduction. *Am J Obstet Gynecol.* 1990;162:879–882.

Marshall BM. Ethical issues in assisted reproduction. *Ann Acad Med Singapore.* 1992;21:582–588.

Maun AR, Williams RS, Graber B, Myers WG. The passage of Florida's Statute on Assisted Reproductive Technology. *Obstet Gynecol*. 1994;84:889–893.

Meirow D, Schenker JG. The current status of sperm donation in assisted reproduction technology: ethical and legal considerations. *J Assist Reprod Genet*. 1997;14:133–138.

Meniru GI, Craft I. In vitro fertilization and embryo cryopreservation prior to hysterectomy for cervical cancer. *Int J Gynaecol Obstet*. 1997;56:69–70.

Robertson JA. Ethical and legal issues in human embryo donation. *Fertil Steril*. 1995;64:885–894.

Robertson JA. Innovations in infertility treatment and the rush to market. *Womens Health Issues*. 1997;7:162–166.

Rothman BK. Ideology and technology: the social context of procreative technology. *Mt Sinai J Med*. 1998;65:201–209; discussion 215–223.

Schenker JG. Religious views regarding treatment of infertility by assisted reproductive technologies. *J Assist Reprod Genet*. 1992;9:3–8.

Shenfield E. Privacy versus disclosure in gamete donation: a clash of interest, of duties, or an exercise in responsibility? *J Assist Reprod Genet*. 1997;14:371–373.

Shenfield F. Filiation is assisted reproduction: potential conflicts and legal implications. *Hum Reprod*. 1994;9:1348–1354.

Shenfield F, Steele SJ. A gift is a gift is a gift, or why gamete donors should not be paid. *Hum Reprod*. 1995;10:253–255.

Tyson JE. Moral and ethical issues in reproductive medicine: a crisis of conscience. *Curr Opin Obstet Gynecol*. 1990;2:869–876.

Veeck LL. Frozen preimplantation embryos: parental responsibility versus laboratory liability. *Hum Reprod*. 1997;12:1121–1124.

Wallach EE. Medicolegal and ethical problems of assisted conception. *Curr Opin Obstet Gynecol*. 1990;2:726–731.

Weil E. Privacy and disclosure: the psychological impact on gamete donors and recipients in assisted reproduction. *J Assist Reprod Genet*. 1997;14:369–371.

Wendland CL, Burn F, Hill C. Donor insemination: a comparison of lesbian couples, heterosexual couples and single women. *Fertil Steril*. 1996;65:764–770.

Yoon M. The Uniform Status of Children of Assisted Conception Act: does it protect the best interests of the child in a surrogate arrangement? *Am J Law Med*. 1990;16:525–553.

GENETIC COUNSELING

Andrews LB. Legal aspects of genetic information. *Yale J Biol Med*. 1991;64:29–40.

Atkin K, Ahmad WI. Genetic screening and haemoglobinopathies: ethics, politics and practice. *Soc Sci Med*. 1998;46:445–458.

Ayme S, Macquart-Moulin G, Julian-Reynier C, Chabal F, Giraud F. Diffusion of information about genetic risk within families. *Neuromuscul Disord*. 1993;3:571–574.

Bondy M, Mastromarino C. Ethical issues of genetic testing and their implications in epidemiologic studies. *Ann Epidemiol*. 1997;7:363–366.

Briard ML, Mattei JF. Cystic fibrosis: preimplantation diagnosis, prenatal diagnosis and medical ethics, a successful combination. *Pediatr Pulmonol Suppl*. 1997;16:65.

Burgess MM, Laberge CM, Knoppers BM. Bioethics for clinicians, 14: ethics and genetics in medicine. *CMAJ*. 1998;158:1309–1313.

Chadwick RF. What counts as success in genetic counseling? *J Med Ethics*. 1993;19:43–46; discussion 47–49.

Clarke A, Parsons E, Williams A. Outcomes and process in genetic counseling. *Clin Genet*. 1996;50:462–469.

Dailey JV, Pagnotto MA, Fontana-Bitton S, Brewster SJ. Role of the genetic counselor: an overview. *J Perinat Neonatal Nurs*. 1995;9:32–44.

Danks DM. Germ-line gene therapy: no place in treatment of genetic disease. *Hum Gene Ther*. 1994;5:151–152.

Davis JG. Predictive genetic tests: problems and pitfalls. *Ann NY Acad Sci*. 1997;833:42–46.

Dickens BM. Legal issues in predictive genetic testing programs. *Alzheimer Dis Assoc Disord*. 1994;8:94–101.

Dickenson D. Carriers of genetic disorder and the right to have children. *Acta Genet Med Gemellol*. 1995;44:75–80.

Donley J. The perfect child mirage. *Midwifery Today Childbirth Educ*. 1994:20–21.

Elkins TE, Brown D. Ethical concerns and future directions in maternal screening for Down syndrome. *Womens Health Issues*. 1995;5:15–20.

Fletcher JC, Evans MI. Ethics in reproductive genetics. *Clin Obstet Gynecol*. 1992;35:763–782.

Glover NM, Glover SJ. Ethical and legal issues regarding selective abortion of fetuses with Down syndrome. *Ment Retard*. 1996;34:207–214.

Grantham JJ. Ethical issues and genetic counseling. *Contrib Nephrol*. 1995;115:39–43.

Greely HT. Genetic testing for cancer susceptibility: challenges for creators of practice guidelines. *Oncology (Huntingt)*. 1997;11:171–176.

Henn W. Predictive diagnosis and genetic screening: manipulation of fate? *Perspect Biol Med*. 1998;41:282–289.

Kennedy M. Genetic testing: harbinger of hope or landmine in the medical landscape? *Wis Med J*. 1998;97:30–3, 37.

Lupton ML. The impact of genetics on society: the law's response. *Med Law*. 1991;10:55–76.

McAbee GN, Sherman J, Davidoff-Feldman B. Physician's duty to warn third parties about the risk of genetic diseases. *Pediatrics*. 1998;102:140–142.

McGee G, Arruda M. A crossroads in genetic counseling and ethics. *Camb Q Healthc Ethics*. 1998;7:97–100.

McKinnon WC, Baty BJ, Bennett RL, et al. Predisposition genetic testing for late-onset disorders in adults. A position paper of the National Society of Genetic Counselors. *JAMA*. 1997;278:1217–1220.

Milunsky JM, Milunsky A. Genetic counseling in perinatal medicine. *Obstet Gynecol Clin North Am*. 1997;24:1–17.

Modell B. The ethics of prenatal diagnosis and genetic counseling. *World Health Forum.* 1990;11:179–186.

Pelias MZ. Duty to disclose in medical genetics: a legal perspective. *Am J Med Genet.* 1991;39:347–354.

Pembrey ME. In the light of preimplantation genetic diagnosis: some ethical issues in medical genetics revisited. *Eur J Hum Genet.* 1998;6:4–11.

Pueschel SM. Ethical considerations relating to prenatal diagnosis of fetuses with Down syndrome. *Ment Retard.* 1991;29:185–190.

Reilly P. Physician responsibility in conducting genetic testing. *J Natl Cancer Inst Monogr.* 1995;17:59–61.

Report of a WHO Scientific Group. Control of hereditary diseases. *World Health Organ Tech Rep Ser.* 1996;865:1–84.

Rhodes R. Genetic links, family ties, and social bonds: rights and responsibilities in the face of genetic knowledge. *J Med Philos.* 1998;23:10–30.

Roberts SF. Prenatal diagnosis: chances, choices. *J Fla Med Assoc.* 1997;84:374–378.

Schaap T. Confidentiality in counseling for X-linked conditions. *Clin Genet.* 1995;47:155–157.

Schutzer PJ. Genetics and ethics. *Pharos.* 1995;58:26–31.

Scourfield J, Soldan J, Gray J, Houlihan G, Harper PS. Huntington's disease: psychiatric practice in molecular genetic prediction and diagnosis. *Br J Psychiatry.* 1997;170:146–149.

Smith MS. Problems of confidentiality in genetic counseling. *J R Nav Med Serv.* 1994;80:95–99.

Sosnowski JR. Genetic screening and counseling: ethical considerations. *J SC Med Assoc.* 1995;91:73–78.

te Meerman GJ, Dankert-Roelse JE. Pros and cons of neonatal screening for cystic fibrosis. *Adv Exp Med Biol.* 1991;290:83–92.

Trippitelli CL, Jamison KR, Folstein MF, Bartko JJ, DePaulo JR. Pilot study on patients' and spouses' attitudes toward potential genetic testing for bipolar disorder. *Am J Psychiatry.* 1998;155:899–904.

Turnpenny PD, Simpson SA, McWhinnie AM. Adoption, genetic disease, and DNA. *Arch Dis Child.* 1993;69:411–413.

Walker B, Berry A, Ross S. A fiancee seeking genetic advice. *Practitioner.* 1996;240:353–356, 358, 360.

Wertz DC. Ethical and legal implications of the new genetics: Issues for discussion. *Soc Sci Med.* 1992;35:495–505.

Wertz DC. Society and the not-so-new genetics: what are we afraid of? Some future predictions from a social scientist. *J Contemp Health Law Policy.* 1997;13:299–345.

Wertz DC, Fletcher JC. Ethical and social issues in prenatal sex selection: a survey of geneticists in 37 nations. *Soc Sci Med.* 1998;46:255–273.

Wertz DC, Fletcher JC. Feminist criticism of prenatal diagnosis: a response. *Clin Obstet Gynecol.* 1993;36:541–567.

White MT. Decision-making through dialogue: reconfiguring autonomy in genetic counseling. *Theor Med Bioeth.* 1998;19:5–19.

Wilcke JT. Late onset genetic disease: where ignorance is bliss, is it folly to inform relatives? *BMJ.* 1998;317:744–747.

Yagel S, Anteby E. A rational approach to prenatal screening and intervention. *Hum Reprod.* 1998;13:1126–1128.

Zidovska J. Ethical aspects of genetic counseling. *Funct Dev Morphol.* 1992;2:127–128.

GENERAL OBSTETRICS

Abrams FR. Commentary on ACOG Committee Opinion #108 May 1992, ethical dimensions of informed consent. *Womens Health Issues.* 1993;3:27–28.

Adamson TE, Baldwin DC Jr, Sheehan TJ, Oppenberg AA. Characteristics of surgeons with high and low malpractice claims rates. *West J Med.* 1997;166:37–44.

Altshuler G. Some placental considerations in alleged obstetrical and neonatology malpractice. *Leg Med.* 1993:27–47.

American College of Obstetricians and Gynecologists. Ethical dimensions of informed consent. *Womens Health Issues.* 1993;3:1–10.

Annas GJ, Elias S. Confusing law and ethics: why the Committee's report on informed consent should be reconsidered. *Womens Health Issues.* 1993;3:25–26.

Baldwin LM, Greer T, Wu R, Hart G, Lloyd M, Rosenblatt RA. Differences in the obstetric malpractice claims filed by Medicaid and non-Medicaid patients. *J Am Board Fam Pract.* 1992;5:623–627.

Baldwin LM, Hart LG, Lloyd M, Fordyce M, Rosenblatt RA. Defensive medicine and obstetrics. *JAMA.* 1995;274:1606–1610.

Baldwin LM, Larson EH, Hart LG, Greer T, Lloyd M, Rosenblatt RA. Characteristics of physicians with obstetric malpractice claims experience. *Obstet Gynecol.* 1991;78:1050–1054.

Boehm FH. Medicolegal climate for obstetrician-gynecologists. *Obstet Gynecol Surv.* 1993;48:715–716.

Brown D, Elkins TE. Ethical issues in obstetric cases involving prematurity. *Clin Perinatol.* 1992;19:469–481.

C BL, Coker A, Dua JA. A clinical analysis of 500 medicolegal claims evaluating the causes and assessing the potential benefit of alternative dispute resolution. *Br J Obstet Gynaecol.* 1996;103:1236–1242.

Cardwell MS. Interhospital transfers of obstetric patients under the Emergency Medical Treatment and Active Labor Act. *J Leg Med.* 1995;16:357–372.

Clements RV. Litigation in obstetrics and gynaecology. *Br J Obstet Gynaecol.* 1991;98:423–426.

Committee on Ethics, American College of Obstetricians and Gynecologists. Ethical guidance for patient testing: Number 159—October 1995. *Int J Gynaecol Obstet.* 1996;52:87–89.

Committee on Ethics, American College of Obstetricians and Gynecologists. Ethical dimensions of informed consent; ACOG committee opinion: Number 108—May 1992. *Int J Gynaecol Obstet.* 1992;39:346–355.

Committee on Professional Liability, American College of

Obstetricians and Gynecologists. Coping with the stress of malpractice litigation; ACOG committee opinion: Number 150—December 1994. *Int J Gynaecol Obstet.* 1995; 49:83–84.

Davidson EC Jr, Gibbs CE, Chapin J. The challenge of care for the poor and underserved in the United States: an American College of Obstetricians and Gynecologists perspective on access to care for underserved women. *Am J Dis Child.* 1991;145:546–549.

Eitel DR, Yankowitz J, Ely JW. Legal implications of birth videos. *J Fam Pract.* 1998;46:251–256.

Elkins TE, Brown D. Informed consent: commentary on the ACOG Ethics Committee statement. *Womens Health Issues.* 1993;3:31–33.

Entman SS, Glass CA, Hickson GB, Githens PB, Whetten-Goldstein K, Sloan FA. The relationship between malpractice claims history and subsequent obstetric care. *JAMA.* 1994;272:1588–1591.

Fiesta J. Obstetrical liability update—part II. Nurs Manage. 1995;26:22, 25.

Finnerty JJ, Pinkerton JA. Ethical issues in managed care for the obstetrician and gynecologist. *Am J Obstet Gynecol.* 1998;179:308–315.

Freeman JM, Freeman AD. Cerebral palsy and the 'bad baby' malpractice crisis: New York State shines light toward the end of the tunnel. *Am J Dis Child.* 1992;146:725–727.

Glassman PA, Rolph JE, Petersen LP, Bradley MA, Kravitz RL. Physicians' personal malpractice experiences are not related to defensive clinical practices. *J Health Polit Policy Law.* 1996;21:219–241.

Gupta S, Bewley S. Medicolegal issues in fertility regulation. *Br J Obstet Gynaecol.* 1998;105:818–826.

Heland KV. Ethics versus law: a lawyer's road map to the Ethics Committee opinion on informed consent. *Womens Health Issues.* 1993;3:22–24.

Heland KV. Failure to diagnose breast cancer malpractice claims: a new threat to obstetrics and gynecology? *Womens Health Issues.* 1991;1:96–101.

Hensleigh PA. Undocumented history of maternal genital herpes followed by neonatal herpes meningitis. *J Perinatol.* 1994;14:216–218.

Hirsh HL. Phantom of the delivery room: the no-show obstetrician. *Leg Med.* 1993:1–26.

Jacobson HN, Richter AM, Mahan CS, Boisvert PT. Physician attitudes toward nurse-midwives: results of 1993 survey. *J Fla Med Assoc.* 1994;81:825–829.

Keifer WS. Preparing for obstetrics in the twenty-first century: Quo Vadis? *Am J Obstet Gynecol.* 1993;168:1787–1790.

King NM. Informed consent and the practicing obstetrician-gynecologist. *Obstet Gynecol Surv.* 1994;49:295–296.

Klingman D, Localio AR, Sugarman J, et al. Measuring defensive medicine using clinical scenario surveys. *J Health Polit Policy Law.* 1996;21:185–217.

Koska MT. Malpractice risk the same for female and male ob/gyns. *Hospitals.* 1992;66:50.

Langton PA. Obstetricians' resistance to independent, private practice by nurse-midwives in Washington, D.C., hospitals. *Women Health.* 1994;22:27–48.

Larimore WL. Pregnancy care liability misperceptions among medical students in Florida. *Fam Med.* 1994;26:154–156.

Larimore WL, Sapolsky BS. Maternity care in family medicine: economics and malpractice. *J Fam Pract.* 1995;40: 153–160.

Localio AR, Lawthers AG, Bengtson JM, et al. Relationship between malpractice claims and cesarean delivery. *JAMA.* 1993;269:366–373.

Ludlam JE. Using malpractice claims data to successfully attack the problem of infant brain damage. *Leg Med.* 1991:227–244.

Meire HB. Ultrasound-related litigation in obstetrics and gynecology: the need for defensive scanning. *Ultrasound Obstet Gynecol.* 1996;7:233–235.

Michael CA. Obstetric litigation—what are the problems. *Ann Acad Med Singapore.* 1993;22:212–214.

Mitnick JS, Vazquez MF, Plesser KP, Roses DF. Breast cancer malpractice litigation in New York State. *Radiology.* 1993;189:673–676.

Nesbitt TS, Tanji JL, Scherger JE, Kahn NB. Obstetric care, Medicaid, and family physicians: how policy changes affect physicians' attitudes. *West J Med.* 1991;155:653–657.

Norton SA. The malpractice premium costs of obstetrics. *Inquiry.* 1997;34:62–69.

Phelan JP. Ambulatory obstetrical care: strategies to reduce telephone liability. *Clin Obstet Gynecol.* 1998;41:640–646.

Reame NE. The surrogate mother as a high-risk obstetric patient. *Womens Health Issues.* 1991;1:151–154.

Richards BC, Thomasson G. Closed liability claims analysis and the medical record. *Obstet Gynecol.* 1992;80:313–316.

Richards BC, Thomasson GO. Medical records figure prominently in malpractice cases: a closed liability claims analysis. *Colo Med.* 1992;89:398–401.

Roberts DK. Medical-legal aspects of placental examination. *Obstet Gynecol Surv.* 1993;48:777–778.

Rommal C. Risk management issues in the perinatal setting. *J Perinat Neonatal Nurs.* 1996;10:1–31.

Sanders RC. Legal problems related to obstetrical ultrasound. *Ann NY Acad Sci.* 1998;847:220–227.

Schifrin BS. Medicolegal ramifications of electronic fetal monitoring during labor. *Clin Perinatol.* 1995;22:837–854.

Sloan FA, Whetten-Goldstein K, Githens PB, Entman SS. Effects of the threat of medical malpractice litigation and other factors on birth outcomes. *Med Care.* 1995;33:700–714.

Sloan FA, Whetten-Goldstein K, Stout EM, Entman SS, Hickson GB. No-fault system of compensation for obstetric injury: winners and losers. *Obstet Gynecol.* 1998;91:437–443.

Smith DH. How to be a good doctor in the 1990s: stand and deliver. *Am J Obstet Gynecol.* 1994;170:1724–1728.

Stanley F. Cerebral palsy: the courts catch up with sad realities. *Med J Aust.* 1994;161:236.

Stratton WT. Birth-related neurological injury compensation programs [published erratum appears in *Kans Med.* 1995 Spring;96:9]. *Kans Med.* 1994;95:266–267.

Sureau C. Ethical problems in gynaecology and obstetrics. *Eur J Obstet Gynecol Reprod Biol.* 1992;44:27–30.

Symonds EM. Fetal monitoring: medical and legal implications for the practitioner. *Curr Opin Obstet Gynecol.* 1994;6:430–433.

Taylor DH Jr, Ricketts TCd, Berman JL, Kolimaga JT. One state's response to the malpractice insurance crisis: North Carolina's Rural Obstetrical Care Incentive Program. *Public Health Rep.* 1992;107:523–529.

Tussing AD, Wojtowycz MA. Malpractice, defensive medicine, and obstetric behavior. *Med Care.* 1997;35:172–191.

Vincent C. The causes of obstetric accidents. *Nurs Times.* 1991;87:56.

Walker R, Rollins L, Husain M, Kahler V, Powell W, Porta AM. Do obstetrical charts present a liability risk? *Tex Med.* 1991;87:82–86.

Wall EM. Family physicians performing obstetrics: is malpractice liability the only obstacle? *J Am Board Fam Pract.* 1992;5:440–444.

Watts RW, Marley JE, Beilby JJ, MacKinnon RP, Doughty S. Training, skills and approach to high-risk obstetrics in rural GP obstetricians. *Aust NZ J Obstet Gynaecol.* 1997;37:424–426.

CHAPTER 15

Occupational Medicine and Disability Law

INTRODUCTION

Occupational medicine is characterized by conflicts between the employee's interests and those of the employer. These conflicts arise from the employer's obligation to pay for workplace injuries and disabilities, and potential regulatory sanctions against employers who have disproportionate numbers of OSHA (Occupational Safety and Health Administration) reportable events. It is to the employer's benefit to minimize injuries and to attribute them to off the job activities or personal illness. Conversely, in today's marketplace, many employees have limited or no personal health benefits. This gives the employee an incentive to claim that personal medical problems are workplace related so that they must be paid for by the employer.

State and federal law recognizes that the physician–patient relationship is different in occupational medicine, and that there are situations where physicians make medical evaluations of patients without forming a legal physician–patient relationship. Conversely, the law expects occupational medicine practitioners of all types to be honest with their patients and to respect their autonomy and their right to consent to, and be informed about, their medical care.

This chapter discusses the basic state and federal laws governing occupational medical practice, special legal problems such as communicable disease control in the workplace, and occupational medical services in general health care settings. Occupational medicine is a recognized medical specialty, and nonspecialist physicians who are not experts in occupational medicine can incur substantial legal risks. Unlike most other areas of medical practice, providers of occupational medical services must comply with very intrusive federal regulations on access to and retention of medical records, including the right of OSHA and others to enter the practitioner's office and go through all the occupational medical records.

LEGAL AND ETHICAL PROBLEMS IN OCCUPATIONAL MEDICINE

Occupational medicine is one of the three sub-specialties certified by the Board of Preventive Medicine. It is a subspecialty of preventive medicine because occupational medicine physicians must practice primary prevention, evaluating the short-term and long-term hazards of the workplace as they relate to people and disease. In the 40-year history of the board, only a few thousand physicians have become board certified in occupational medicine. This certification assumes competence in general medicine and minor emergency care, toxicology, environmental medicine (heat, physical stress, etc.), ergonomics, and job fitness evaluations.

In general, it is ethically questionable for physicians to offer services they are not properly qualified to perform. Occupational medicine poses a particular problem because the employee usually has no right to refuse the physician's services or seek alternative care. There is a special duty to protect patients who are in coercive environments. Employees are peculiarly dependent on the occupational medicine physician's expertise for protection them from workplace hazards. It is anticipated that occupational medicine physicians will seek information about hazards, even if that information involves a trade secret. Independent contractor physicians with limited access to the workplace and no detailed knowledge of workplace environment cannot effectively protect their employee patients from hazards and toxic exposures.

In several specific situations, state or federal regulations mandate special training or certification for physicians performing a regulated activity. The most widely known are the Department of Transportation regulations on who may do physical examinations of licensed pilots. Only a Federal Aviation Administration–approved flight sur-

geon is allow to perform these exams. Yet even simple activities such as reading routine X rays of industrial employees may require a special certification. Physicians who read chest X rays on workers exposed to asbestos must be certified for the readings to satisfy OSHA surveillance requirements. In some instances, the OSHA regulations require occupational medicine physicians to refer workers to specialists. If the white blood cell count on a benzene-exposed worker falls below a certain level, the occupational medicine physician must refer the patient to a hematologist for further evaluation.

Despite the special nature of occupational medicine practice, most ambulatory care centers, minor emergency clinics, and group practices hold themselves out as offering occupational medicine services. Until recently this meant preemployment physical examinations and treatment for acute workplace injuries. Increasingly, however, these entities are contracting with employers to provide services that are expected to be professionally comparable to in-house occupational medical services provided by experienced occupational medicine professionals. These contracts subject such providers to the full panoply of state and federal regulations.

Outside occupational medicine providers are handicapped by their isolation from the workplace. They are generally limited to second-hand, fragmented information about working conditions and workplace exposures, yet determining job fitness requires detailed information about both the job and the workplace. If they also provide the employee's general medical care, they are faced with significant questions about the segregation of job-related and personal medical information. Moreover, the checks and balances inherent in having general medical care rendered by a physician who is independent of the company are lost in these hybrid practices. This raises ethical issues when the physician is asked to determine whether an injury, such as a heart attack, is work related, triggering workers' compensation coverage, or not work related, perhaps denying the employee compensation but reducing costs for the employer. These conflicts are greatly exacerbated when the employee lacks insurance for general health problems.

Outside occupational medicine providers are subject to medical malpractice litigation for the services they provide to employees. Whereas corporate employee physicians may also be sued for malpractice under the dual-capacity doctrine, employers usually indemnify their physicians for any losses that result from actions within the course and scope of their employment. (The dual capacity doctrine discussed in Chapter 10 allows employees to sue fellow employees with independent professional licenses, on the theory that the company does not control a licensed professional.) Unless contractually indemnified by the employer, physicians are also liable for the cost of complying with state and regulatory agency actions. Such actions can be very expensive in terms of legal costs and lost time for the providers involved. Unlike lawsuits that allege medical negligence, these costs will not be paid by the physician's malpractice insurer. In contrast, if the occupational medicine provider is an employee of the company, these actions will be brought against the employer rather than the physician. Even if the physician is individually joined, the company will remain liable for the incurred costs. Physicians who contract with employers to deliver occupational medical services must ensure that their contracts require the employer to pay for the costs of agency enforcement actions that arise from treating its employees. Private physicians without special training or experience in occupational medicine should consult an attorney about their allowable scope of practice and legal obligations before agreeing to provide occupational medical services.

Return to Work Certifications

All physicians engaged in clinical practice face the problem of certifying that a patient was legitimately absent from work because of an acute illness or injury. Most employees who are covered by the Americans with Disabilities Act (ADA) because of long-term disabilities have periods of acute illness. Acute problems are not covered by

the ADA. The same medical standards for work fitness apply to disabled employees covered by the ADA as to other employees. It is not certain, however, whether the ADA's limitations on information to be provided to employers prevents the employer from inquiring into the cause of a disabled employee's absence.

Return-to-work evaluations fall into two classes, depending on whether the employee is seeking to avoid returning or wishes to return to work. Situations in which the patient wishes to return to work pose fewer ethical problems because the patient and the employer generally have the same interest. Nevertheless, the physician must still determine the employee's medical fitness to return to prevent possible injuries to the employee and potential legal liability for the physician. Except for company-employed occupational medicine physicians, the decision about return to work will usually involve both the physician and the employer. The physician can describe the medical limitations on the worker, but without special knowledge (of OSHA rules, the nature of certain jobs, etc.), he or she cannot decide that a patient can do the job adequately and safely. When evaluating patients' ability to return to work, the environment in which they work must be given careful consideration. A painter with a broken leg may be able to paint walls while wearing a cast but could not work on scaffolding high above the ground. Cardiac patients who want to go back to work may tell their physicians that they sit at a desk or walk around slowly for the entire workday. What the physician may not know is that the patient works in an area of the plant with an ambient temperature of 120 degrees. On the other hand, the section foreman is not likely to be able to judge how much weight a postoperative patient may lift without danger. These questions should be worked out cooperatively among the worker, the employer, and the physician.

Physicians should be cautious about accepting the patient's evaluation of the work environment. Patients may not know company policies on limited work or the availability of special positions for temporarily disabled employees. Private physicians should get their patients' permission to talk to their supervisors for an accurate description of the work available for the patient and the environmental conditions under which the work is to be done. In many cases, the only way to determine if patients are fit to return to work is to allow them to try, but with instructions to both the patient and the supervisor to watch for signs of fatigue or reoccurrence of the medical problem.

The important thing for the physician to remember is that the medical decision is what limitations the worker has. Statements such as "able to return to work" or "light duty only" are not appropriate. The physician should provide explicit limitations such as "no reaching overhead, no lifting greater that ten pounds, and no exposure to extremes of heat." With this information, the employer is the one to decide if there is a job for this worker that fits the restrictions. Ultimately, it is the employer who must consider the information available and decide whether to allow the employee back in the workplace.

Release from Work Certifications

Employees seeking off-work slips pose more difficult ethical problems. Although most have legitimate illness, some do not. There are also employees with valid reasons for missing work, such as caring for a sick child, who seek medical excuses for missing work because personal illness is the only approved reason for paid absence from their workplace. Employers argue that unnecessary absences hurt all employees by reducing the productivity of the company. This can result in reduced benefits for employees with legitimate medical needs and in lost jobs or even bankruptcy. Disputes over time off from work are a recurring dilemma in occupational medical practice: How are physicians to resolve the conflict between the patient's interests and the employer's interests?

This conflict is greatest when the patient sees the physician after recovering from the putative illness, requesting an excuse for time already taken. Assuming that there is no objective evidence to corroborate the patient's claims, the physician is put in the position of being an investigator for the employer. Some physicians believe that employees do not have a duty to tell the truth to a physician who is acting in this investigatory role.[1] These physicians may accept the patient's assertions unquestioningly because they see their role as one of patient advocate. This may benefit the patient, but it misrepresents the physician's role to the employer. In extreme circumstances, it may even constitute a fraud against the employer. It is also detrimental to the physician's professional reputation. Physicians who become known as an easy source of time off will find that they have the same unsavory reputation as those who dispense drugs too freely.

Another approach is to refuse to participate in off-work certifications. This position harms the employee because many employers punish unexcused absences. The best approach may be to limit off-work certifications to patients whom the physician has treated or diagnosed with an injury or illness. This does not put the physician into the position of an investigator, while still allowing legitimately ill employees to be excused from work. As a work policy matter, this may unnecessarily increase health care costs by forcing employees to see a physician for every minor illness. It also fails to deal with problems such as the illness of other family members for whom the employee must care.

Many employers are adopting no-fault absence plans. Employees are given a certain number of personal days that can be used for illness, vacations, or other personal business. This eliminates the incentive to fake illness to get time off from work. It has benefits in dealing with ADA-covered disabled employees because it does not require the employer to inquire into the employee's reason for missing work. Such plans have disadvantages too. If employees do not need to see a physician to get a back-to-work slip, they may return to work before it is medically wise. Treating all absences alike may also put the employer in conflict with the ADA. Although the ADA does not require disabled employees to be given more sick days than those who are not disabled, the rules interpreting the ADA indicate that part-time work unpaid leave may be part of a reasonable accommodation to the employee's disability.

WORKERS' COMPENSATION

Workers' compensation is a state program whose rules vary substantially by state. The basic structure of these programs guarantees compensation for work-related injuries and illness without the need to prove fault on the employer's part. The amount of compensation is fixed for each injury, and the employee has a very limited right to sue the employer for additional compensation. Because this compensation is much lower than the employee might recover in the courts, workers' compensation laws are often criticized for not creating a sufficient incentive to protect workers. The courts have allowed this limitation of liability because all injured workers receive medical care and some compensation. In contrast, private civil litigation is generally not available.

All physicians who treat work-related injuries and illnesses should understand their state workers' compensation system. Failing to comply with reporting requirements and claims filing procedures can deny the patient needed care and delay payment of physician charges. Physicians should be prepared to provide reports to workers' compensation hearing examiners. They should also realize that workers' compensation laws have not eliminated litigation over workplace injuries. Employees must still litigate whether their injury was workplace related and the extent of their incapacitation. Physicians should contact the agency that regulates workers' compensation in their state for specific information about complying with its claims procedures.

The Payment System

The most important difference in state workers' compensation systems is who chooses the treating physician. In general, workers' compensation costs are lower is states where the company chooses the medical care providers, and higher where the patient has the choice. Although it is tempting to infer sinister reasons for this, the difference is similar in personal health care insurance. When the company chooses the providers, the workers' compensation system tends to resemble managed care or health maintenance organizations (HMOs). A limited number of providers are used by the employer or its insurance company. These providers are generally chosen because they are convenient and cooperative. They may be asked to sign provider contracts to accept reduced fees. If the outcomes are not good, if the employees are not getting well and quickly returning to regular work, the provider will be dropped from the program.

If the employee chooses the physician, the system works more like indemnification insurance. There are no negotiated discounts to reduce the fee-for-service costs. The patients tend to "doctor shop" until they find a physician who agrees with their opinions. And the employee may be given more time off for rest and recovery. Most states have a system for excluding specific physicians from providing workers' compensation care if they are clearly biased, but the situations are usually extreme. The independent medical examiner who did not find a single permanent injury in 20 years of exams, and the orthopedist who took the employee off all work for six months for a sprained finger are equally unacceptable to the state administrators. They are not exercising good medical judgment, they are selling paper.

Any physician who is providing care for a work-related injury should base the decisions about care on his or her best medical judgment. As with any other payment system, it is not legal or ethical to withhold necessary care because it may not be covered by the insurance. On the other hand, providing care that is not indicated or giving employees time off that is not justified borders on fraud. One practice must be avoided because it is fraud: employees may ask their personal physician to treat them for a work-related injury and bill the charges to their personal health insurance. Their motives may be as benign as preferring the doctor they know and trust. However, their motives may be more complicated. The employee may be dissatisfied with the amount of treatment or time off they can obtain through the workers' compensation system. The company may have policies or incentives that encourage employees to say that a work injury is not work related. Or the employee may simply not understand that it is illegal to lie about whether an injury occurred at work.

Health care providers should be very careful about treating work injuries as though they were personal. If the patient is already being treated when the physician learns that this may be work related, the physician should contact the employer immediately. Treating a workers' compensation injury as personal just to be sure you get paid is clearly fraud against the health insurer and may be a specific crime under the state's insurance laws.

Work Relatedness

A physician does not have to investigate whether an injury or illness was caused by the work environment. The doctor's role is to provide good medical care. The workers' compensation system will decide whether the problem is work related. The doctor should keep good records that include information about underlying medical problems and that differentiate between what the patient said and what were objective findings.

If either the doctor or the patient thinks the problem may be work related, the doctor should contact the employer. The employer can provide information about the work environment and the availability of work accommodations. This is good business as well as good medicine. Large employers are constantly looking for physicians in the community who are acceptable to the employees and cooperative with the company. In some cases the company may remove the patient from care, but they may also send the doctor more business.

There are also situations where the employee may firmly believe that their problem is work related when it clearly is not. The patient with asthma may be convinced that he was exposed to chemical fumes at work. A call to the employer may provide the information that the work environment is continuously monitored for toxins and that the only exposure was to the air-freshener in the bathroom.

Talk to the appropriate people at the company if there are questions about whether the problem is work related. "It seems reasonable" is not a good reason for accusing a company of wrongdoing. One inappropriate public remark can cost a business millions of dollars and defamation is not covered by your medical malpractice insurance.

Emergency Treatment

Even in states where the employer has the sole right to choose health care providers under workers' compensation, there is an exception for emergency care. If a patient presents to an emergency room or a doctor's office with an injury or illness that may threaten life or limb, that person should be treated appropriately. Most hospitals and emergency room personnel are well aware of the penalties under federal law for turning away such a case. However, this is not an excuse for ignoring the state's laws on choosing workers' compensation care providers.

It is common practice for the hospital to contact the insurance company to get permission to treat a patient, so that the insurance will cover the bill. In real emergencies this is done after the treatment is started. For the patients with an earache or a cough, it is usually done first. Particularly in managed care plans, the insurer may direct the patient to another hospital or to an office the next day. If there is no medical reason why the patient cannot wait, this is legal and acceptable practice. The patient may choose to pay cash and receive treatment there or they may go where their insurance will pay the bill.

Work-related injuries should be treated the same way in an emergency room. Federal law requires medical triage. If the illness or injury is a true emergency, treatment should be rendered immediately and the employer contacted later. If the hospital has a formal or informal agreement with the specific employer to provide workers' compensation care, then this should be adequate. If the patient does not have a life- or limb-threatening emergency and the hospital does not have an agreement with the employer, then the employer should be contacted before care is given, subject to the requirements of EMTALA as discussed in Chapter 4. In any state, the patient may choose to pay cash for the visit and argue it out with the workers' compensation insurance system later. And, in some states, it is unwise to ignore the requirement to notify the employer unless you are thoroughly familiar with the state and federal laws.

In a doctor's office when providing routine care, there is no justification for ignoring the employer. If the employee is claiming a work-related injury and he or she wants workers' compensation to pay for it, the employer has a legal right to the employee's relevant medical information. The doctor should be prepared to work with both the patient and the employer or should not be practicing occupational medicine.

Reporting

Many states require reporting of certain types of occupational illnesses and injuries to the health department just like communicable diseases. As with other public health reports, the health care provider has a personal duty to make the report regardless of who else may be reporting. Generally, OSHA reporting by a physician or hospital is optional. However, OSHA may be the best source of information for patient care and they may be the most appropriate agency to do an investigation.

RECORDS

Providers who care for work-related injuries must know the laws on recordkeeping in their state. These records are not always confidential like personal medical records. There is a long list of people who have statutory access to workers' compensation or OSHA records. At a minimum, the patient, the employer, and the workers' compensation insurance company have access to the records on the specific injury. In some states, the health department or other state agency also has statutory access. In some circumstances, the union may have a right to the information even if the patient is not a member. And, OSHA generally has access if it is a regulated workplace or a specific type of injury.

If you practice occupational medicine, make sure your medical records people know the rules and release information appropriately. Do not insist that the patient sign a release before complying with statutory requirements. If the patient is willing to sign a release, fine. If not, simply inform the patient that you must comply with the law and release the records.

If the patient wants to keep the records closed and not inform the company, then the patient must pay for the care out of his or her own pocket. They may not charge the care to their personal health insurance. Even the patient's paying does not prevent access by state agencies and OSHA if they have a statutory right to see the records. In some states, this may not prevent access by others as well, particularly the employer. Also, public health reporting requirements apply regardless of who pays the bills.

Most states have very specific reporting forms for work-related injuries. Typically there are specific sections for the employer, the employee, and the physician. Copies of routine medical records may be acceptable from the physician or they may not. Most occupational medicine physicians prepare these forms as part of their regular medical recordkeeping. In addition, there may be specific OSHA records required. Do not do workers' compensation care if you cannot comply with the recordkeeping requirements.

OSHA recordability and records retention requirements are a major consideration in occupational medicine practice and are discussed in detail later in the chapter.

DEALING WITH OSHA

Occupational medicine physicians face a conflict between the interests of the patient and those of the employer. The physician's ethical duty to the patient has always been primary, but corporate pressures have sometimes prevailed over patient interests. This leads employees and unions to distrust occupational medicine physicians. In highly regulated industries such as transportation, employers and employees may jointly pressure occupational medicine physicians to ignore individual health conditions even though they might endanger the public safety. These conflicts have resulted in the extensive regulation of occupational medicine practice by state and federal agencies to ensure that both employee health and the public's interests are properly protected.

The Occupational Safety and Health Administration (OSHA) is the basic source of regulations governing workplace safety and occupational medicine practice. OSHA regulations are supplemented by the ADA and specific workplace rules from other agencies, such as the U.S. Department of Transportation (DOT). Most states have their own regulations that complement the federal regulations and, in some cases, substantially extend their requirements. These regulations were originally targeted at large employers with internal occupational medicine departments and corporate legal counsel. As small employers have been pressured to comply with the rules, and as large employers contract out occupational medicine services, many private physicians and clinics are providing regulated occupational medical services. These providers are predominantly family physicians and general internists without specialty certification in occupational medicine. This section discusses the OSHA rules that company and contract physicians must follow in their occupational medicine practice.

Employee Medical Information

In 1980 OSHA promulgated rules governing access to and maintenance of employee medical records (29 C.F.R. sec. 1910.20, Access to employee exposure and medical records). (The following discussion omits citations to specific statutory language.) Although directed at managing medical information, these regulations define the scope of occupational medicine practice through their expansive definition of workplace-related medical information. These rules were written for records maintained in a company-based occupational medicine department, but they specifically include nonemployee physicians and clinics that provide occupational medical services. Any physician who treats workplace-related injuries or ill-

nesses or does preplacement or work fitness evaluations is subject to these regulations.

OSHA promulgated the rules to:

1. Ensure employees, their representatives, and OSHA access to the employees' medical records.
2. Require employers to supply medical care providers sufficient information about toxic exposures to allow the treatment and long-term evaluation of exposed employees.
3. Create a way for medical care providers to report potential hazardous exposures to OSHA without violating the employer's trade secrets.
4. Ensure that employee medical records are maintained for a sufficient period (30 years after the termination of employment) to allow the monitoring of conditions with long latency.

These rules are directed at employers rather than medical care providers. The employer is expected to see that the medical care personnel follow the rules, and it is the employer that is subject to administrative sanctions if the rules are not followed. Physicians employed in a company occupational medicine department that does not comply with the rules may be subject to sanctions as company representatives. Nonemployee physicians may be subject to sanctions if they contractually accept the responsibility for maintaining employee medical information. This can become a problem if the employer goes out of business without arranging for an orderly transition in responsibility for the employees' medical information. An abrupt termination of business may leave the physician with the duty and financial responsibility to maintain the records or transfer them properly.

OSHA clearly intended these rules to supplement, rather than replace, traditional practices: "Except as expressly provided, the rules do not affect existing legal and ethical obligations concerning the maintenance and confidentiality of employee medical information, the duty to disclose information to a patient/employee or any other aspect of the medical-care relationship, or affect existing legal obligations concerning the protection of trade secret information." The rules do not pose any ethical problems beyond those already inherent in occupational medicine practice. In the case of providing access to trade secret information, they help resolve an existing ethical dilemma.

Defining OSHA-Regulated Occupational Medicine

The OSHA regulations indirectly define occupational medical practice by establishing what constitutes OSHA occupational medical information. By inference, physicians generating such regulated medical information are practicing occupational medicine as regulated by OSHA. The regulations apply to any employer "who makes, maintains, contracts for, or has access to employee ... medical records ... pertaining to employees exposed to toxic substances or harmful physical agents." The rules include all medical records maintained on a covered employee—not just those mandated by "specific occupational safety and health standards." The rules specifically include records maintained by physicians who are not employees of the covered employer but provide medical services on a contractual or fee-for-service basis. There are additional regulations that require monitoring of exposure to specific toxic substances. These regulations prevent employers from avoiding the rules on employee medical records by ignoring employee health entirely.

It is the definitions of exposure and toxic agents that account for the broad reach of these rules:

- "Exposure" or "exposed" means that an employee is subjected to a toxic substance or harmful physical agent in the course of employment through any route of entry (inhalation, ingestion, skin contact or absorption, etc.), and includes past exposure and potential (e.g., accidental or possible) exposure.

- "Toxic substance or harmful physical agent" means any chemical substance, biological agent (bacteria, virus, fungus, etc.), or physical stress (noise, heat, cold, vibration, repetitive motion,

ionizing and non-ionizing radiation, hypo- or hyperbaric pressure, etc.) which (i) Is listed in the latest printed edition of the National Institute for Occupational Safety and Health (NIOSH) Registry of Toxic Effects of Chemical Substances (RTECS); (ii) Has yielded positive evidence of an acute or chronic health hazard in testing conducted by, or known to, the employer; or (iii) Is the subject of a material safety data sheet kept by or known to the employer indicating that the material may pose a hazard to human health.

Given that the current edition of the RTECS contains over 45,000 chemicals, it is hard to imagine an industrial employee who is not covered by these regulations. The addition of biological agents expands coverage to most health care workers. The inclusion of repetitive motion and nonionizing radiation adds every office worker who touches or sits near a computer. There are exceptions for situations where the employer can "demonstrate that the toxic substance or harmful physical agent is not used, handled, stored, generated, or present in the workplace in any manner different from typical non-occupational situations," but these exceptions are construed strictly, which means there are very few exceptions.

Employee Medical Records

The OSHA rules govern information rather than just traditional paper records and they govern several types of records in addition to medical records. For the purposes of these rules, a record includes "any item, collection, or grouping of information regardless of the form or process by which it is maintained (e.g., paper document, microfiche, microfilm, X-ray film, or automated data processing)." A medical record means "a record concerning the health status of an employee which is made or maintained by a physician, nurse, or other health care personnel or technician," including:

- Medical and employment questionnaires or histories (including job description and occupational exposures).

- The results of medical examinations (preemployment, preassignment, periodic, or episodic) and laboratory tests, including chest and other X-ray examinations taken for the purposes of establishing a baseline or detecting occupational illness, and all biological monitoring not defined as an "employee exposure record." (Under the ADA, information obtained from preplacement physicals may need to be kept separate from the remainder of the employee medical record.)
- Medical opinions, diagnoses, progress notes, and recommendations.
- First-aid records.
- Descriptions of treatments and prescriptions.
- Employee medical complaints.

Information that is not covered by these rules (and thus not subject to the access and retention provisions) includes the following:

- Physical specimens (e.g., blood or urine samples) that are routinely discarded as a part of normal medical practice
- Records concerning health insurance claims if maintained separately from the employer's medical program and its records and not accessible to the employer by employee name or other direct personal identifier (e.g., Social Security number, payroll number)
- Records created solely in preparation for litigation, which are privileged from discovery under the applicable rules of procedure or evidence
- Records concerning voluntary employee assistance programs (alcohol, drug abuse, or personal counseling programs) if maintained separately from the employer's medical program and its records

It would seem that records of employee assistance programs that are mandated for employees with identified problems would be subject to the rules. It is usually argued, however, that these programs are voluntary in that the employee can always choose to lose his or her job.

In all cases, information will be subject to the provisions of these rules if it is maintained in the same record as covered information. Even information prepared for litigation would lose its privilege if kept in the patient's medical record. This is a general rule of evidence and is not specific to the OSHA-regulated information. Given the potentially broad access to covered records, it is especially important that information on voluntary employee assistance programs be kept separate from covered medical information. Ideally this means separate folders in separate filing systems. This level of physical separation is not legally mandated, but whatever system is used must prevent the inadvertent release of information when OSHA or the union inspects a large number of records.

Authorization To Release Covered Records

The OSHA rules provide that employees, their designated representatives, and OSHA will have access to covered employee medical records. Access means the right to examine and copy the records. If the employee is dead or legally incapacitated, the employee's legal representative may exercise all the employee's rights under the rules. A designated representative is any individual or organization to whom the employee gives written authorization for access to his or her medical records. A recognized or certified collective bargaining agent is automatically treated as a designated representative without requiring written employee authorization for access to some regulated records. This implied authorization does not extend to employee medical records.

A designated representative must have the employee's specific written consent to have access to the employee's medical records. This written authorization must include the following:

- The name and signature of the employee authorizing the release of medical information
- The date of the written authorization
- The name of the individual or organization that is authorized to release the medical information
- The name of the designated representative (individual or organization) that is authorized to receive the released information

- A general description of the medical information that is authorized to be released
- A general description of the purpose for the release of the medical information
- A date or condition upon which the written authorization will expire (if less than one year)

A written authorization (Exhibit 15–1) does not authorize the release of medical information not in existence on the date of the written authorization, unless the release of future information is expressly authorized. A written authorization is not valid for more than one year from the date on the authorization. A written authorization may be revoked in writing at any time.

Although OSHA has the right to have access to employee medical information without the employee's written permission, the employer must notify its employees when OSHA seeks access to their medical records:

> Each employer shall, upon request, and without derogation of any rights under the Constitution or the Occupational Safety and Health Act of 1970, 29 U.S.C. 651 et seq., that the employer chooses to exercise, assure the prompt access of representatives of the Assistant Secretary of Labor for Occupational Safety and Health to employee exposure and medical records and to analyses using exposure or medical records.... Whenever OSHA seeks access to personally identifiable employee medical information ... the employer shall prominently post a copy of the written access order and

Exhibit 15–1 Sample Authorization Letter for the Release of Employee Medical Record Information to a Designated Representative

I, _____ (full name of worker/patient), hereby authorize (individual or organization holding the medical records) to release to (individual or organization authorized to receive the medical information), the following medical information from my personal medical records.
(Describe generally the information desired to be released)

I give my permission for this medical information to be used for the following purpose:

But I do not give permission for any other use or redisclosure of this information.

(Note: several extra lines are provided below so that you can place additional restrictions on this authorization letter if you want to. You may, however, leave these lines blank. On the other hand, you may want to (1) specify a particular expiration date for this letter (if less than one year); (2) describe medical information to be created in the future that you intend to be covered by this authorization letter; or (3) describe portions of the medical information in your records which you do not intend to be released as a result of this letter).

_____ Full name of Employee or Legal Representative

_____ Signature of Employee or Legal Representative

its accompanying cover letter for at least fifteen (15) working days.

Physical Access to Records

The OSHA rules provide that employees and their designated representatives have access to their medical records and the allowable conditions on that access. Although these rules were drafted for employer-based medical departments, they also apply to private physicians' offices and clinics. The rules can be problematic for private physicians and clinics, since some of their requirements differ from customary private medical practice. The most fundamental of these differences is that OSHA grants the employee or representative the right to examine the original medical record.

This right differs from the usual practice of limiting the patient to a copy of his or her original medical record. This practice reflects state laws that are concerned with ensuring patients access to their medical information rather than the record itself. The state laws assume that physicians maintain records in a proper manner. The OSHA rule allowing inspection of the original record arises from the suspicion that company physicians may try to cover up occupationally related health conditions. OSHA does allow the medical records custodian to "delete from requested medical records the identity of a family member, personal friend, or fellow employee who has provided confidential information concerning an employee's health status." In the absence of specific authorization by the patient, however, this provision does not give medical care providers the right to discuss the patient's medical condition with third parties.

A demand to examine the original record should not disrupt office routines in the individual case, but it can become a problem when a designated representative requests access to the records of all the employees of a company. The physician or clinic is required to provide proper facilities for reviewing the records, which can take weeks or months, or to loan the records to the requesting organization. In either case, the physician or clinic may find it necessary to make and retain a copy of the records to provide ongoing care for the employees during the period when the records are unavailable. This can be very expensive and should be addressed in the contract between a company and a contract provider of occupational medical services.

Whenever an employee or designated representative requests a copy of a record, the employer (or contracting occupational medicine provider) must provide a copy of the record without charge, provide free access to a copying machine, or loan the record to the requesting employee or representative for a reasonable period of time to allow copying. "In the case of an original X-ray, the employer may restrict access to on-site examination or make other suitable arrangements for the temporary loan of the X-ray." If the record has been previously provided without cost to an employee or designated representative, the employer may charge reasonable, nondiscriminatory administrative costs (search and copying expenses but not including overhead expenses) for additional copies of the record. The employer shall not charge for an initial request for a copy of information that has been added to a record since it was previously provided.

Limitations on Access to Medical Records

When an employee requests access to his or her medical records, the physician may recommend that the employee discuss the records with the physician, accept a summary of material facts and opinions in lieu of the records requested, or accept release of the requested records only to a physician or other designated representative. If the employee persists in his or her request to see the complete record, the rules provide that release may be made to a designated representative rather than to the employee:

> Whenever an employee requests access to his or her employee medical records, and a physician representing the employer believes that direct employee access to information contained in the records regarding a specific diagnosis of a terminal illness or a psychiatric condition could be detrimental to the employee's health, the employer may inform the employee that access will only be

provided to a designated representative of the employee having specific written consent, and deny the employee's request for direct access to this information only. Where a designated representative with specific written consent requests access to information so withheld, the employer shall assure the access of the designated representative to this information, even when it is known that the designated representative will give the information to the employee. (29 CFR sec. 1910.20)

This provision presupposes that an employee's medical records may contain information that has not been provided to the employee. Case law, and related OSHA regulations on informing employees of medically significant information, would seem to mitigate against the right of an occupational medicine physician to withhold information from a patient. Whereas some state laws allow withholding potentially damaging information from patients, OSHA allows the physician only to impede, not prevent, a patient's access to his or her records. Ethical questions aside, requiring a patient to get his or her records indirectly and then having those records contain an unpleasant surprise would certainly increase the chance that the patient will see an attorney.

This section discusses the requirements for keeping and disclosing OSHA-regulated records only. Many of these medical records are for work-related illnesses or injuries and are covered under the workers' compensation laws of the state. These laws differ from state to state, but typically they allow access to injury records to a much larger group of people. This is discussed further in the Workers' Compensation section of this chapter.

Preservation of Records

OSHA regulations on preservation of records are very specific and require much longer retention than ordinary medical records, which is a very good reason for not mixing records for personal illnesses with occupational records. Few general medical offices are prepared to keep records for 60 years (30 years after the employee quits, retires, dies, or is fired).

Unless a specific occupational safety and health standard provides a different period of time,

... the medical record for each employee shall be preserved and maintained for at least the duration of employment plus 30 years. This requirement does not apply to health insurance claims records maintained separately and to first aid records (not including medical histories) of one-time treatment and subsequent observation... if made on-site by a nonphysician and if maintained separately from the employer's medical program and its records.

The medical records of employees who have worked for less than (1) year for the employer need not be retained beyond the term of employment if they are provided to the employee upon the termination of employment.

Nothing in this section is intended to mandate the form, manner, or process by which an employer preserves a record as long as the information contained in the record is preserved and retrievable, except that chest X-ray films shall be preserved in their original state.

The OSHA rules also provide for the maintenance of records on employees whose employer is no longer in business. If an employer goes out of business, its employee's medical records shall be transferred to the successor employer, who must receive and maintain the records. This can pose problems if the successor employer chooses to sever the relationship with the private physician or clinic and take possession of the records. The records must be surrendered, but it is important, as much as possible, to comply with state laws governing the transfer or release of medical information. It may be advisable to notify the employees that their records will be transferred and that they should contact the new employer if they have questions or objections. Since the successor employer has the right to the records of all previous employees, not just those whom it rehires, there may be employees who would want the physician to retain a copy of the records and continue providing medical care. The physician or clinic may also want to retain copies of the records for medical-legal concerns.

When there is no successor employer, the employees must be notified of their rights of access to the records at least three months prior to the cessation of the employer's business. The employer must also transfer "the records to the Director of the National Institute for Occupational Safety and Health (NIOSH) if so required by a specific occupational safety and health standard" or "notify the Director of NIOSH in writing of the impending disposal of records at least three (3) months prior to the disposal of the records." The physician or clinic maintaining the records should ensure that these obligations have been carried out before disposing of any records.

OSHA 200 Log

The OSHA 200 log is a record of illnesses and injuries that arise from exposures in the work environment. The log is kept by an employer for the use of the Bureau of Labor Statistics. The Occupational Safety and Health Act of 1970 is very extensive and covers most private employers in the United States. (OSHA does not apply to state government.) However, the keeping of an OSHA 200 log has been limited by regulations, to permit OSHA to concentrate its safety efforts on high-risk industries.

The OSHA act itself exempts religious establishments and employers of household workers. These are very limited exemptions. A church is not covered under OSHA if it employs only individuals who perform religious services; employees who carry out secular duties are covered under OSHA. A large church may not have to consider the ministers under OSHA regulations, but the secretaries and maintenance workers are covered. Household workers are the maids and babysitters that work in an individual home. Cleaning services and home health nurses do not fall under the exemption.

Even if the employer is regulated by OSHA, it may not be required to keep an OSHA 200 log. Small employers and employers in low-hazard industries are not required to keep the log. Small employers are defined as those who had no more than 10 employees at any time during the previous calendar year. This is an absolute limit of 10 employees, not an average or a full-time equivalent. An employer who has eight part-time employees who are with him all year and three employees who only last a month has eleven employees for the year and is not exempt.

Low-hazard industries are generally retail trade and service industries. This includes such activities as sales of cars, clothes, and furniture; financial or legal service industries, such as banking, insurance, and real estate; and eating establishments. It does not include sales and service industries with a moderate or high rate of injuries such as garden supplies, food stores, hotels and motels, repair services, amusement and recreation, or health services industries.

It is noteworthy that hospitals, clinics, nursing homes, and other health care service industires are not exempt from OSHA regulation or the OSHA 200 log. This is true whether they are for-profit, not-for-profit, or owned by a church.

The keeping of the OSHA 200 log is the responsibility of the employer. A separate log is kept for each establishment or business location and the manager determines what entries are made. There are fines up to $70,000 for false entries in an OSHA log and it is just as bad to make too many entries as too few. The entries are simple and straightforward and they are expected to be correct.

The following information is required in an OSHA 200 log:

- Case or file number
- Date of injury or onset of illness
- Employee's name
- Occupation
- Department
- Description of injury or illness
- Extent or outcome of injury or type, extent of, and outcome of illness

The extent of injury or illness is defined by whether there were lost work days, whether these days involved restricted work activity or days away from work and whether the injury or illness was fatal. For illnesses, the log must note which of seven categories of occupational illness is involved.

Recordable Injuries

Anyone who practices occupational medicine or nursing needs to know what injuries and illnesses must be recorded on an OSHA 200 log and what makes them recordable (Exhibit 15–2). Many large employers use the OSHA 200 log as a measure of safety and/or quality of medical care. It is common for managers to be evaluated on the injury rate in their plant and bonuses often depend on this rate. Employees may also have a financial stake in not getting hurt. There are often incentives for groups of workers that do not have any serious injuries during a specific time period.

This does not mean that physicians should collude with employees or the company to conceal the severity of an injury. The first duty of the physician is to provide all necessary and appropriate care to the injured worker. However, the physician should be cautious about providing care beyond what is necessary, particularly if it is only done to appease an angry patient.

The OSHA act requires that all work-related deaths and illnesses be recorded on the OSHA 200 log, but it limits the recording of injuries to specific types of cases. The act states that all injuries must be recorded unless they are "minor injuries requiring only first aid treatment, and which do

Exhibit 15–2 First Aid Procedures Recordable and Not Recordable on an OSHA 200 Log

First Aid Procedures—*Not Recordable*
1. First degree burns
2. Application of bandages
3. Application of elastic bandages at the first visit
4. Simple removal of foreign body from eye
5. Simple removal of foreign body from wound
6. Use of nonprescription medications or one dose of prescription medication.
7. Soaking a wound on the first visit
8. Application of heat or cold on the first visit
9. Application of ointments
10. Whirlpool therapy on the first visit
11. Negative X rays
12. Observation of an injury

Medical Procedures—*Recordable*
1. Treatment of infection or application of antiseptics at a subsequent visit
2. Second or third degree burns
3. Suturing or use of butterfly closures or steristrips in lieu of sutures
4. Removal of embedded foreign body in the eye
5. Removal of embedded foreign body or surgical debridement of a wound
6. Use of prescription medicines
7. Soaking therapy on a subsequent visit
8. Application of cold or heat on a subsequent visit
9. Whirlpool therapy on a subsequent visit
10. Positive X ray diagnosis from the injury (fractures)
11. Admission to a hospital for treatment

Source: Reprinted from Occupational Safety and Health Act.

not involve medical treatment, loss of consciousness, restriction of work or motion, or transfer to another job." In other words, an injury must involve at least one of these four conditions to be recordable.

Two of the four triggers are beyond the control of the medical care provider. If the worker lost consciousness from the injury it is recordable, even if no medical treatment is required. Also, if the employer chooses to move the worker to another job because of the injury or the treatment, that is their decision. It is the need for medical treatment and the restriction of work or motion that the treating nurse or physician can control.

The simplest condition for the physician to evaluate is the need for restriction of work or motion, but it is also the most contentious. Years of careful research by the National Institutes of Occupational Safety and Health have shown clearly that rest and/or splinting is not appropriate treatment for mild to moderate sprains, strains, or tendinitis. The appropriate treatment is antiinflammatory drugs and exercise. Unfortunately, the average worker thinks that the best thing for a sore back is a few days sitting in front of the television. Physicians should limit the use of rest, restrictions, or splinting to injuries that have clear signs (not just symptoms) of moderate to severe injury. This is good medicine not just good politics.

All restrictions should be very specific about the limits on activity and the time these limits will be in effect. A physician doing occupational medicine should never say, "Mr. Smith is on light duty." The restrictions should say such limits as "no lifting over 20 pounds," or "no typing," or "no use of the left arm."

The last trigger for recordability is that the injury requires medical treatment, not just first aid. This does not mean that seeing a doctor triggers recordability. It is the nature of the treatment, not who gives it, that makes an injury recordable. Because the distinction between first aid and medical treatment is vague, OSHA has established some specific guidelines.

The list is long, but there are some general rules that make sense. Second and third degree burns, fractures, and wounds that become infected or re-

quire surgical treatment such as sutures or debridement are severe enough that they should be recorded. In addition, sprains and strains that require physical therapy or repeated treatments past the first visit are requiring medical treatment, not just first aid.

Prescription medications are also clearly medical treatment. A worker can take over-the-counter ibuprofen without a prescription. This is not considered medical treatment even if he or she takes 800 mg three times a day. If a doctor writes a prescription for 800mg ibuprofen, the injury is recordable.

Physicians who do occupational injury care only occasionally should be careful about overtreating simple injuries and making them recordable. Prescription nonsteroidal anti-infalammatory drugs (NSAIDs), narcotics, antibiotics, and physical therapy should be reserved for injuries that are severe enough to warrant such treatment. If the physician gives a prescription just to appease a troublesome patient, the physician should note in the chart that the injury was not severe, but the medication or therapy was given for patient comfort. But remember, if the physician would not be comfortable explaining a narcotic prescription to the Drug Enforcement Administration (DEA) then it shouldn't be given at all.

It is clear from this discussion of what makes an injury recordable that not all workers' compensation injuries are recordable. The reverse is also true. Not all recordable injuries are covered under workers' compensation. Many states do not require payment under workers' compensation until an injury has limited the worker's activity or required care for a specific number of days. A laceration that is sutured by the plant doctor is a recordable injury, but there may not be a workers' compensation claim filed. In contrast, a worker with a strained back may be treated in an emergency room and given heat treatment, massage, Advil, and exercise instruction. This would be billed to the workers' compensation insurance but it would not be recordable.

In summary, there are very specific rules about what injuries and illnesses should be listed on the OSHA 200 log. Physicians and nurses who frequently treat work-related injuries should be familiar with these rules. The U.S. Department of Labor publishes *Recordkeeping Guidelines for Occupational Injuries and Illnesses* (O.M.B. No. 1218–0176), which answers most of the questions that arise.

Material Safety Data Sheets

Workers in modern industrial workplaces are exposed to myriad toxic chemicals. In an effort to inform employees and persons in the community about the risks of toxic chemicals in the workplace, OSHA requires that employers make material safety data sheets (MSDSs) available to employees, health care providers, local fire departments, and other community organizations with an interest in toxic exposures. Physicians who practice occupational medicine or emergency medicine should be familiar with the MSDS and how to use it.

MSDSs are the starting point for determining if an employee has been exposed to a toxic substance. Occupational medicine physicians should obtain appropriate MSDSs from each employer for whom they provide occupational medical services. MSDSs can also be useful for general medicine physicians who suspect that a patient is suffering from an occupational exposure. The regulations require that the MSDS be in English, that it contain specific information on the contents and hazards of the product, that it provide information on emergency treatment, and that it list information for contacting the manufacturer.

There are several important limitations that may make the data on MSDS misleading. Within certain limitations, the manufacturer is not required to perform toxicity testing on the mixture or its constituents. The MSDS need only be based on a review of the literature. Even this review is subject to question because there are no standards to define an adequate search or to resolve conflicting research reports. It is not unusual to find manufacturers of the same chemical list different health risks on their MSDS. In addition, manufacturers sometimes ignore chemicals that they use as vehicles but do not manufacture themselves.

Although these are generically described as inert ingredients, they sometimes include highly toxic aromatic hydrocarbons or complex organic resins.

If the MSDS does not provide enough information, either because trade secret information has been left out or because the physician suspects that an ingredient is toxic, the physician can obtain more detailed information directly from the manufacturer identified on the MSDS. This may require several inquiries, however, because only the original manufacturer of the substance is responsible for keeping full information on health hazards. Thus the physician may need to call the manufacturer of each substance that has been mixed into a product.

Trade Secrets

Although keeping track of exposures to known chemicals can be a daunting problem, the exact constituents in some chemical processes are trade secrets. These are defined as "Any confidential formula, pattern, process, device, or information or compilation of information that is used in an employer's business and that gives the employer an opportunity to obtain an advantage over competitors who do not know or use it." With certain exceptions, employers and manufacturers of chemicals are allowed to withhold trade secret information if they warn the health care provider, employee, or designated representative that the information has been deleted. When information is withheld, the employer or manufacturer must provide an MSDS with "all other available information on the properties and effects of the toxic substance."

There are circumstances when medical care providers need to know the specific chemical and concentration to which an employee has been exposed. If there is a medical emergency and the "specific chemical identity of a toxic substance is necessary for emergency or first-aid treatment," the employer or manufacturer must provide the needed information. The medical care providers obtaining this information must not disclose it except as necessary to provide the needed medical care. The employer or manufacturer may not withhold the information in an emergency but may require that the medical providers sign a confidentiality agreement as soon as circumstances permit. Irrespective of the existence of such a written agreement, disclosing such information is illegal in most states and can subject the violator to substantial civil damages.

The OSHA rules also allow access to trade secret information in nonemergency situations if the request is in writing and describes with reasonable detail one or more of seven specific occupational health needs for the information.

The request must explain in detail why the disclosure of the specific chemical identity is essential. The request should also describe the procedures for maintaining the confidentiality of the disclosed information. If the employer or manufacturer refuses to disclose the requested information, the requesting person may ask OSHA to force the employer to disclose the needed information.

Irrespective of the contents of any confidentiality agreements, trade secret information may be disclosed to OSHA if the person receiving the information believes that such a disclosure is necessary to workplace safety.

Physicians in occupational medicine practice have a duty to inquire into the cause of toxic symptoms observed in their patients. Such physicians must also respect the employer's need to protect its trade secrets. Many chemical processes are not patented, either because the disclosures necessary to obtain a patent would give away the company's competitive edge or because the process is not sufficiently different from known processes to qualify for patent protection. In most cases, this is not a problem because it is not the identity of the chemicals that matters as much as the way they are used. In some circumstances, however, the identity of the chemical itself would be enough to allow competitors to copy the process. An occupational medicine physician should inquire about potential trade secret problems before agreeing to provide services to an employer. Any necessary confidentiality agreements should be part of the contract between the physician and the employer. This will avoid misunderstandings if the physician should inadvertently identify a

chemical that the employer considers a trade secret. Such an agreement should make clear that the employer understands that under some circumstances the physician may be required to disclose trade secret information to OSHA.

DRUG TESTING

Drug testing has become a big part of occupational medicine in recent years. Many employers have started drug-free workplace programs, either by choice or because of government regulation. Drug testing is often used for preemployment screening because it is not considered a medical exam and so it is permissible under the Americans with Disabilities Act.

Procedures and regulations differ according to the specimen being tested. The most important legal distinction is whether the test is regulated by the U.S. Department of Transportation (DOT). DOT has been the leading agency for drug testing. There are elaborate rules governing how the test is done and how the results are used. The very large volumes of tests done every year allow the DOT to discover and respond to legal and technical problems quickly. The simplest and best way to operate a drug testing program is to follow DOT procedures for unregulated as well as regulated testing.

It is wise to use DOT-certified laboratories for all testing as well. These laboratories do large volumes of drug tests so they can be quite inexpensive. They are carefully regulated and the system is designed to prevent false positives: this means that any equivocal results are interpreted in favor of the person being tested. Despite the fact that they do millions of tests per year, any documented false positive drug test is carefully investigated by federal agents.

Hospital labs and those that do general clinical work do very poorly by comparison. Drug testing is an evidence-gathering procedure, not a medical test. It is the chain-of-custody and evidentiary procedures that favor the regulated labs, not their medical expertise.

Urine testing is the most common sampling technique and is the backbone of the DOT system.

There is a 23-step system for gathering the sample that deals with acceptable techniques for ensuring that the specimen is not tampered with by the donor or the collector. It has been said that only the federal government could require 23 steps to tell someone to pee in a jar. However, this elaborate system ensures that the specimen may be used as legal evidence without being an undue invasion of the individual donor's privacy. There are also provisions for other types of testing if the individual is medically unable to provide a urine specimen.

Blood testing is the preferred method for medical management of drug problems. Most emergency rooms have access to rapid screening for drugs when treating a known overdose or a coma of unknown etiology. Blood levels are used for setting medication doses in order to keep within therapeutic range. Blood tests are sometimes used as evidence for making medical care decisions: "Is the Alzheimer patient taking his digoxin?"

Unless it is being done at the patient's request or under a specific court order, blood testing for drugs can be legally problematic. It is more invasive than sampling urine, breath, or hair. Most people resist having blood drawn purely for evidence and most doctors are hesitant to force the issue. If there is a clear legal process, such as an agreement that the county hospital emergency room (ER) will draw blood alcohols on all drivers who are taken into custody, then the physician should follow the procedure. If there is not an established legal procedure, then the doctor is wise to do only those blood tests that are medically necessary.

Evidentiary breath testing is the preferred method of testing for alcohol where it is available. This is not the old Breathalyzer test. It is a new technology that is very accurate. It is just as reliable as blood alcohol testing, but it is noninvasive so legal refusal is more difficult.

The evidentiary breath tests are also DOT regulated. This is the system used for screening truckers, pilots, etc. for illegal alcohol use or intoxication. There are a limited number of brands of machines that are authorized for this program, and the technicians doing the tests must have specific training. Because of these safeguards, the evidentiary breath test is accepted as accurate medical evidence in court.

Hair testing is the new technique for drug screening. It is new and relatively untried. The technical procedures are designed to remove contaminants, such as hair dye and shampoo, and environmental contamination, such as passive smoke, from the hair before it is tested for drugs. The biggest disadvantage of hair testing is that many people find it hard to believe that such contaminants can be removed. The other disadvantage is that many people object to having hair pulled from their bodies, leaving a small bald spot.

The greatest advantage to hair testing is that it detects drug use for the last several months instead of a few hours or days, like urine testing. Some large corporations have gone to hair testing for preemployment screening because it is more effective. A regular drug user may be able to abstain for a few days or a week in order to get a good job. Few drug addicts can stay clean for three to six months just to pass a hair test.

For-cause drug testing is a special issue, regardless of what specimen is being tested. Most screening tests only cover the five federally prohibited drugs: cocaine, marijuana, heroin, amphetamines, and PCP. If the employee is acting intoxicated, it may be necessary to test for legal drugs and alcohol as well. In addition, the physician or nurse may have a duty to evaluate the patient for life-threatening conditions, such as severe head trauma and diabetic ketoacidosis. Most law enforcement personnel assume that the smell of ketones on the breath means alcohol intoxication. A medical professional should realize that diabetes and starvation can cause the same odor and that trauma, seizures, and heart attacks can easily occur when someone is drinking.

OCCUPATIONAL MEDICINE FOR HEALTH CARE ORGANIZATIONS

The OSHA regulations on treatment and reporting of work-related injuries and on surveillance for toxic workplace exposures apply to hospitals, nursing homes, and most clinics. In recent years, with privatization and management contracts, even many county hospitals no longer fall under the local government exemption from OSHA regulation. Yet few hospitals have adequate occupational medicine programs and most have very poor compliance with OSHA regulations.

Hospitals must learn to do OSHA compliance and recordkeeping properly. As hospitals have moved from being government or religious charitable institutions to being privately owned or managed, federal and state prosecutors have demonstrated their willingness to treat hospitals like any other business. Health care is a dangerous business by almost any standard. Nurses have one of the highest rates of back injuries of any occupation. The risk of death from infectious disease exposures has always been a part of medical practice, and health care workers have some of the worst toxic exposures. Hydrocarbon exposures in manufacturing industries are nothing compared to the risk to the pharmacist who is handling chemotherapeutics that are themselves carcinogenic and which may have an LD50 measured in grams. Exposure to X rays, ultraviolet light, and other forms of radiation is an everyday fact of life in a hospital. This very familiarity can cause damaging carelessness.

Hospitals are also the natural home of curbside consults. Busy nurses and physicians find it easier to ask for help or information informally than to make an appointment and go to the office. It also allows everyone to avoid insurance forms and co-pays. The problem is that it also avoids proper recordkeeping. Providing medical care informally without records is usually a poor idea. If it involves a work-related injury, it is probably illegal.

As with other businesses, hospitals should have a well-planned system for dealing with occupational injuries and exposures. There should be one place or person that takes care of all the occupational medicine for the institution, and it must be available all hours the business is open. If the work injuries are handled in the emergency room, there must be proper forms and procedures in place. Staff should not be sent to the ER when they are hurt because it is the easiest place to find their own bandages. The employee should be

checked in and all care should be documented in the medical record. Even first aid for an injury that is not severe enough to be OSHA recordable should be in a medical record. The injury or exposure may also be reportable under state laws even if it is not OSHA recordable. Doing care off the record to avoid OSHA recordability or workers' compensation filings is illegal and carries hefty fines. Once proper care has been given, all the applicable forms must be completed. A workers' compensation claim must be filed and, if applicable, an OSHA 200 log entry made. Even if the hospital does not have to make specific payments to the doctor or the profit center where care was rendered, most workers' compensation programs require that the value of the care be on record.

Control of workplace exposures to communicable disease is a major consideration in health care occupational medicine.[2] Most hospitals are aware of federal bloodborne pathogen regulations and make an attempt to comply. Far fewer understand and follow the rules on the control of tuberculosis. These regulations are discussed at length later in the chapter. The important thing to remember is that there are extensive regulations on how these problems are to be handled and they are mandatory requirements, not guidelines.

Hospitals should also keep in mind that their responsibilities as employers are not limited to people on their payroll. Volunteers, physicians, professional students, and employees of contractors such as laundry or food service may be the hospital's legal responsibility when it comes to prevention of illness or injury from work in the hospital. Both the medical care providers and the hospital administration should know the federal and state rules and should follow them carefully.

THE AMERICANS WITH DISABILITIES ACT

The ADA attempts a comprehensive solution to discrimination against the disabled. This section examines only the provisions dealing with the hiring and retention of disabled employees. The ADA covers all workplaces with 15 or more employees. Unlike OSHA, which excludes governmental entities, the ADA covers both government and private businesses. The best statement of the broad reach of the ADA is from the congressional findings in the statute itself.

Findings and Purpose

(a) Findings

The Congress finds that

(1) some 43,000,000 Americans have one or more physical or mental disabilities, and this number is increasing as the population as a whole is growing older;

(2) historically, society has tended to isolate and segregate individuals with disabilities, and, despite some improvements, such forms of discrimination against individuals with disabilities continue to be a serious and pervasive social problem;

(3) discrimination against individuals with disabilities persists in such critical areas as employment, housing, public accommodations, education, transportation, communication, recreation, institutionalization, health services, voting, and access to public services;

(4) unlike individuals who have experienced discrimination on the basis of race, color, sex, national origin, religion, or age, individuals who have experienced discrimination on the basis of disability have often had no legal recourse to redress such discrimination;

(5) individuals with disabilities continually encounter various forms of discrimination, including outright intentional exclusion, the discriminatory effects of architectural, transportation, and communication barriers, overprotective rules and policies, failure to make modifications to existing facilities and practices, exclusionary qualification standards and criteria, segregation, and relegation to lesser services, programs, activities, benefits, jobs, or other opportunities;

(6) census data, national polls, and other studies have documented that people with disabilities, as a group, occupy an inferior status in our society, and are severely disadvantaged socially, vocationally, economically, and educationally;

(7) individuals with disabilities are a discrete and insular minority who have been faced with restrictions and limitations, subjected to a history of purposeful unequal treatment, and relegated to a position of political powerlessness in our society, based on characteristics that are beyond the control of such individuals and resulting from stereotypic assumptions not truly indicative of the individual ability of such individuals to participate in, and contribute to, society;

(8) the Nation's proper goals regarding individuals with disabilities are to assure equality of opportunity, full participation, independent living, and economic self-sufficiency for such individuals; and

(9) the continuing existence of unfair and unnecessary discrimination and prejudice denies people with disabilities the opportunity to compete on an equal basis and to pursue those opportunities for which our free society is justifiably famous, and costs the United States billions of dollars in unnecessary expenses resulting from dependency and nonproductivity.

(b) Purpose

It is the purpose of this chapter—

(1) to provide a clear and comprehensive national mandate for the elimination of discrimination against individuals with disabilities;

(2) to provide clear, strong, consistent, enforceable standards addressing discrimination against individuals with disabilities;

(3) to ensure that the Federal Government plays a central role in enforcing the standards established in this chapter on behalf of individuals with disabilities; and

(4) to invoke the sweep of congressional authority, including the power to enforce the fourteenth amendment and to regulate commerce, in order to address the major areas of discrimination faced day-to-day by people with disabilities.[3]

Predecessor Legislation

The employment provisions of the ADA mirror the requirements of section 504 of the Rehabilitation Act of 1973.[4] The ADA covers more employers, however, because section 504 was limited to employers who did business with the government.

Although these included most large employers—universities, medical institutions, and governmental entities themselves—many small businesses were exempt. Section 504 of the Rehabilitation Act remains good law. In disability litigation the plaintiff usually pleads the Rehabilitation Act along with an ADA claim, if the defendant is covered by the Rehabilitation Act.[5]

Section 504 was a remedial statute that provided standards to judge whether a given individual was the victim of discrimination. It allowed employers to use medical examinations and inquiries to determine the status of a potential or current employee's medical condition, including disabilities. The ADA presumes that employers will discriminate against disabled individuals. It seeks to prevent discrimination by limiting the employer's access to information, as well as providing legal remedies for victims of discrimination. It is this shift from nondiscrimination to noninquiry into disability that changes traditional occupational medicine practice.

ADA-DEFINED DISABILITY

Disability, as used in the ADA, is much more expansive than the accepted medical usage. In the congressional findings supporting the ADA, it was estimated that approximately 43 million persons were disabled by the standards of the ADA. Although traditional definitions of disability would hardly include one fifth of the population, the ADA defines disability, with respect to an individual, as the following:

1. a physical or mental impairment that substantially limits one or more of the major life activities of such individual;
2. a record of such an impairment;
3. or being regarded as having such an impairment.

Exemptions

The ADA covers only long-term disabilities, not those from acute illnesses or injuries that affect the worker for less than six months. The ADA specifically exempts illegal drug use, drunkenness, sexual preference (homosexuality, bisexuality, and transvestism), and pregnancy from the definition of disability. Beyond these specific exemptions, it provides that the employee's physical or mental condition cannot be considered except as directly relevant to job performance. This follows the existing law that limits educational testing to qualifications that are directly related to job performance. Employers may not use a calculus test to screen applicants for janitorial jobs,[6] and they may not use blood sugar testing to screen potential secretaries.

What Is a Major Life Activity?

Many of the federal courts do not like the broad reach of the ADA and have attempted to limit it by a restricted reading of what constitutes a major life activity. The regulations to the Rehabilitation Act, which also govern this aspect of the ADA, are ambiguous: "Major life activities" means functions such as caring for one's self, performing manual tasks, walking, seeing, hearing, speaking, breathing, learning, and working.[7] Some courts take this literally, finding that activities that are not on the list, such as reproduction, are not major life activities.[8]

The U.S. Supreme Court ruled on the definition of major life activity in a case involving a patient who claimed she was discriminated against by a health care practitioner because she had HIV.[9] The defendant claimed that HIV was not a disability because the patient was asymptomatic and thus there was no affect on any of her major life activities.

The Majority Opinion

The Court first considered whether the plaintiff was disabled as defined in the ADA. The relevant section is 12102(2)(A) "a physical or mental impairment that substantially limits one or more of the major life activities of such individual." Before discussing whether the plaintiff met this test, the Court indirectly addressed the lower courts' attempts to narrow the ADA by over restrictive readings of its provisions. The Court noted that when Congress uses well-established terms, it intends that they be construed in accordance with established interpretations, and that this is explicit in the ADA: "Except as otherwise provided in this chapter, nothing in this chapter shall be construed to apply a lesser standard than the standards applied under title V of the Rehabilitation Act of 1973 (29 U.S.C. § 790 et seq.) or the regulations issued by Federal agencies pursuant to such title."

The Court found that the plaintiff had to show three things: (1) that HIV was a physical impairment; (2) that it affected some major life activity; and (3) that this limitation be substantial. All of the judges' opinions accepted that HIV infection, irrespective of the symptoms, is a physical impairment as contemplated by the ADA. The Court's opinion goes into unnecessary length on the technical details of HIV infection. (Although these are not necessary to its conclusions, most courts cannot resist the temptation to lift scientific jargon from the briefs before them, irrespective of whether it is relevant or even in evidence.)

The Court's analysis is complicated by the politics of HIV-related disability litigation. The position of AIDS rights organizations is that asymptomatic HIV infection has no effect on the infected person's ability to carry on day-to-day life activities. This position is incompatible with the requirements of the ADA—if there is no effect on a major life activity, then the physical impairment is not a covered disability. However, conceding that asymptomatic HIV infection does have an effect on major life activities means that employers and others might have a right to know HIV status if its effect on major life activities might endanger others. Plaintiff finessed this by focusing on her ability to bear children.

Defendant argued that reproduction, as the court termed it, was not a major life activity as contemplated by the ADA. Defendant's theory was that the ADA required that the life function affected be of a public, economic, or daily character. (Although not put in these terms, this essentially means that the disability be related to the claimed discrimination.) In what may be the most significant part of the opinion, the Court found that a major life activity need not be economic,

public, or recurrent, that the key word was major, and that reproduction was a major life activity. This analysis potentially overrules many circuit cases that used a very narrow definition of major life activity.

The third prong of the ADA definition is whether the impairment affects the major life activity. Plaintiff argued that the chance of infecting a partner and passing the infection on to her children affected the major life activity of reproduction. The Court could find no guidance on this issue, but agreed that these factors certainly affected a person's decision to have children. The Court held that this satisfied the ADA requirements, making her HIV infection a covered disability.

The Dissent on Major Life Activity

The Chief Justice's opinion attacked this conclusion by focusing on the language in the ADA that demands that the determinations of disability and accommodation be individualized. This language was put into the ADA to prevent employers from excluding disabled workers based on stereotypes of what persons with a specific disability can do. The employer must give the employee a chance to do the job, rather than have blanket exclusions based on laundry lists of disabilities. The Chief Justice argued that this standard of individualized determination of disability should also be applied to the plaintiff. The plaintiff rejected this individualized determination and denied that she, personally, suffered any impairment to a major life function:

> There is absolutely no evidence that, absent the HIV, respondent would have had or was even considering having children. Indeed, when asked during her deposition whether her HIV infection had in any way impaired her ability to carry out any of her life functions, respondent answered "No." It is further telling that in the course of her entire brief to this Court, respondent studiously avoids asserting even once that reproduction is a major life activity to her. To the contrary, she argues that the "major life activity" inquiry should not turn on a particularized assessment of the circumstances of this or any other case.

Unanswered Questions

Unfortunately, the Court's opinion ignored the issue of whether the determination of effect on a major life activity must be specific to the plaintiff. Instead, the court presented a barrage of information about what a bad disease HIV is and how it is clear that HIV-infected persons are impaired. It is clear that HIV infection does affect several major life activities and that this case is correctly decided. However, the Chief Justice's concern with individualized determinations is well founded. Not every disability is so clear-cut as to its effects on the major life activities. Many diseases have a spectrum of effects, ranging from minor alterations in diagnostic tests with little chance of progression, to full-blown disease with major illness and death. This is especially problematic in mental illnesses, with their highly variable course. In these cases, the question of whether the individual plaintiff need show an effect of the disease is very relevant. The Court gives no guidance on this very difficult issue. (Although not discussed by any judge, the converse problem is also possible: if the standard is a generic one, what happens to a plaintiff who is personally disabled by a condition that usually does not disable others.)

PREEMPLOYMENT MEDICAL EXAMINATIONS

The ADA bifurcates the hiring process into the preoffer stage and the postoffer stage when there has been an offer of employment. At the preoffer stage, with certain exceptions for mandated affirmative action recordkeeping, "It is unlawful for a covered entity to conduct a medical examination of an applicant or to make inquiries as to whether an applicant is an individual with a disability or as to the nature or severity of such disability" (sec. 1630.13(a)).

The employer may ask the applicant if he or she is able to do the job and may require job-oriented skills tests. The employer must provide any reasonable accommodations that the applicant requires to complete these tests.

Allowable Examinations

A covered entity may require a medical examination after an offer of employment has been made to an applicant and prior to the commencement of the employment duties of such applicant, and may condition an offer of employment on the results of such examination, if

1. all entering employees are subjected to such an examination regardless of disability;
2. information obtained regarding the medical condition or history of the applicant is collected and maintained on separate forms and in separate medical files and is treated as a confidential medical record.

Preemployment Examination Records

Maintaining employee medical examination records as separate, confidential medical records is a fundamental change from the practices in most workplaces. This appears to preempt directly the OSHA requirement that medical information from preemployment evaluations be maintained with the occupational medical record. The employer and its agents have only limited access to such information:

- supervisors and managers may be informed regarding necessary restrictions on the work or duties of the employee and necessary accommodations;
- first aid and safety personnel may be informed, when appropriate, if the disability might require emergency treatment;
- government officials investigating compliance with this Act shall be provided relevant information on request.

State workers' compensation laws are not preempted by the ADA. Consequently, employers or other covered entities may submit information to state workers' compensation offices or second injury funds in accordance with state workers' compensation laws without violating this part.

These restrictions also apply to routine medical examinations of employees made in the regular course of their employment, which creates a dilemma for employers who process employee medical examination data through their personnel department. The intent of the ADA is to deny information about disabilities to persons involved in employee hiring and retention. This would seem to require that the occupational medicine department, or the examining physician, maintain and disperse this information in accordance with restrictions in the ADA and its regulations.

New Duties for Occupational Medicine Physicians

Shifting the burden of compliance with the ADA medical examination restrictions to the medical department or the examining physicians creates new risks for the medical providers. The physician now has the burden of determining employee fitness, with the attendant risk of error. The greatest risk is that the physician improperly withholds information that results in the employee's being injured. However, if the employee's confidential medical information is available to unauthorized persons, there will be a presumption that any disciplinary action against the employee was due to his or her disability. If the physician is an independent contractor, there can be substantial liability for improperly releasing medical information to an employer.[10]

The best way to deal with this dilemma is to obtain the patient's authorization to release information to persons outside the medical department. This should not be a blanket authorization to release all medical information. The employee should be given a copy of the report the physician proposes to send to the supervisors and first-aid personnel authorized to receive such information. If the examinee refuses to authorize the release of the information, the physician should give the examinee a written description of the potential risks to the patient's health from withholding the information. If an incomplete report may mislead the employer, then the physician may be ethically bound to refuse to provide any report on the examinee.

The ADA is not intended to affect group and individual health insurance plans, even if the restrictions of these plans on matters such as sick leave and coverage of preexisting conditions have an adverse impact on disabled persons. Although not clearly defined in the proposed rules, an employer may offer "voluntary medical examinations, including voluntary medical histories, which are part of an employee health program available to employees at that work site." It is assumed that these include various wellness programs, as well as group medical insurance plans.

Persons with Known Disabilities

The ADA allows employers to hold all employees to the same workplace productivity standards, as long as these standards are a fair measure of the core functions of the job. Employers are prohibited from discriminating against qualified individuals with a disability:

> The term "qualified individual with a disability" means an individual with a disability who, with or without reasonable accommodation, can perform the essential functions of the employment position that such individual holds or desires.... Consideration shall be given to the employer's judgment as to what functions of a job are essential, and if an employer has prepared a written description before advertising or interviewing applicants for the job, this description shall be considered evidence of the essential functions of the job.

The term "reasonable accommodation" may include the following:

- making existing facilities used by employees readily accessible to and usable by individuals with disabilities; and
- job restructuring, part-time or modified work schedules, reassignment to a vacant position, acquisition or modification of equipment or devices, appropriate adjustment or modifications of examinations, training materials or policies, the provision of qualified readers or interpreters, and other similar accommodations for individuals with disabilities.

The occupational medicine physician, in consultation with appropriate experts and the employee, determines the appropriate accommodation. The employer must then decide if the person is otherwise qualified. Can the employee do the job with the accommodation, and is the accommodation reasonable? These decisions are legally contentious because they reflect economic and policy questions about the workplace. For example, is it reasonable to employ a sign-language interpreter for a manual laborer when the cost of the interpreter may double the cost of employing the laborer? Although the employer may consult with the occupational medicine physician about the accommodation, the physician should avoid making the determination of reasonability. Making such decisions will impair the neutrality that the ADA seeks to preserve for the examining physician.

Collective Bargaining and the ADA

The courts have decided that the Rehabilitation Act and the ADA do not overrule seniority systems or collective bargaining agreements. In major industries with strong unions, job placement is often based on union rules rather than employer choice. The employer makes the decision to hire an individual into a broad job category, but it is the shop rules that determine which specific job the individual is assigned. (The EEOC has announced that it believes the ADA should preempt collective bargaining agreements and that the court decisions to the contrary are incorrect, so this area of the law is subject to change.)

If this individual is disabled according to the ADA, the employer may be required to provide accommodations, but this does not include assigning the individual another job if that would violate union seniority rules. For example, the employer may be required to prevent smoking by team members if the individual is allergic to smoke. The employer is not required to move the employee to another team that has no smokers if this violates seniority or shop rules.

Although this seems unreasonable at times, there are sound reasons for maintaining a seniority system. As workers grow older, they tend to acquire arthritis, heart and lung disease, and a history of injuries, along with their seniority. These workers can use their seniority to bid into jobs that are less demanding physically. If ADA enforcement allowed new workers to bump workers with high seniority, these workers would have to declare their disabilities to keep the less stressful jobs. The result would be more aggravation for the established workers, but no more jobs for the individuals with disabilities.

Direct Threats to Health and Safety

The ADA does allow an employer to refuse to hire persons whose employment in the proposed job would pose a direct threat to others. This recognizes the existing rule that employers may choose to protect employees from harm and protect themselves from workers' compensation claims. The primary difference under the ADA is a greatly strengthened presumption that the employee is fit for work.

Direct threat means a significant risk of substantial harm to the health or safety of others that cannot be eliminated or reduced by reasonable accommodation. The determination that an individual poses a "direct threat" shall be based on an individualized assessment of the individual's present ability to perform the essential functions of the job safely. This assessment shall be based on a reasonable medical judgment that relies on the most current medical knowledge and/or on the best available objective evidence. In determining whether an individual would pose a direct threat, the factors to be considered include the following:

1. The duration of the risk;
2. The nature and severity of the potential harm;
3. The likelihood that the potential harm will occur; and
4. The imminence of the potential harm.

Most critically, the determination must be made on a case-by-case basis. Employers must be prepared to prove a "high probability, of substantial harm; a speculative or remote risk is insufficient." For example, if the threat is due to a behavioral disorder, the employer must identify the specific behavior that would pose a threat and the likelihood of occurrence. If the behavior is quasi-voluntary, such as sexual assault, an assurance by the employee that he is reformed would probably defeat the employer's attempt to prove him unfit. Compliance with the ADA provides no defense, however, if the employee assaults a customer. The injured customer may sue the employer for negligently hiring a known rapist. Although the ADA requires that accommodations be reasonable, it often seems to employers that the law itself is unreasonable.

Interestingly, there are only two U.S. Supreme Court decisions on the meaning of "direct threat" and both deal with communicable disease. The first arose under the Rehabilitation Act and involved a teacher who was infected with tuberculosis.[11] The school district wanted to remove her from the classroom because it feared that the children would be infected. The teacher had an expert from the public health department who certified that she was not infectious at the time. The Court found that she did not pose a direct threat and could not be excluded from the workplace. However, the Court stated forcefully that if she became infectious to others, she would pose a direct threat and would have to be excluded from the workplace. (This case is discussed more fully later in this chapter.)

The second case is the dentist case discussed earlier in this chapter. The dentist refused to do dental work, including drilling, on an HIV–infected person in his office. The dentist claimed that he was concerned that he could not do adequate infection control in his office and offered to do the work at no extra charge at the hospital. (There was no discussion of whether there would be a charge by the hospital, but it is assumed there would be.) The patient refused and sued, alleging that the dentist violated the ADA. The dentist asserted the direct threat defense. He lost in the lower courts, but the U.S. Supreme Court ruled that he should be allowed to present evidence that HIV posed a threat to him or others unless he did the procedure at the hospital. This is an important precedent, although not necessarily the best facts. The case was remanded for trial and at the time of publication it was not determined if the jury accepted his defense.

THE LEGAL RISKS OF THE ADA

Although not specifically addressed in the law, the presumption that it is improper for employers to inquire into potential and current employees' disability status could be used in litigation against occupational medicine physicians. Prior to the ADA, the employer could not discriminate based on disability status, but it was proper for the examining physician to provide the employer with such information. Under the ADA, the inquiry itself is suspect. Even when such inquiries are permitted, the employer has only limited access to the information. The courts may find that the occupational medicine physician has a duty to refuse to make improper inquiries and examinations. This policy of noninquiry poses new ethical problems for occupational medicine physicians.

The problem posed by the ADA is that it encourages employees and employers to make decisions without information, rather than to make informed choices about the risks of employment. This can create ethical conflicts for physicians, whose usual role is to ensure that patients have enough information to make an informed choice. Concomitant with that duty to provide full information is the duty to evaluate the patient's full medical status. Legally, the ADA does not provide any immunity for certifying physicians or employers. Employers remain strictly liable under workers' compensation for any injuries the employee suffers due to workplace conditions. If the occupational medicine physician is an independent contractor (or in states that recognize the dual capacity doctrine), the injured employee may also sue the examining physician for malpractice for improperly certifying the employee as fit for the job. These legal and ethical problems make it questionable to agree to undertake pre-employment and job placement examinations that do not fully explore the examinee's medical condition.

The provisions of the ADA do not preempt specific federal laws and regulations on evaluating persons in certain public safety positions such as aviation and transportation. However, the regulations do make it difficult for an employer to disqualify a person based on a threat of harm to themselves or to others. This conflicts with the increasing pressure on employers to protect fellow employees and the public from dangerous employees. The ADA's limitations on preemployment inquiries on behavioral problems also conflict with efforts to encourage employers in businesses such as child care and delivery services to protect the public by screening for sexual offenders and other dangerous individuals. The ADA does not give employers immunity for liability for injuries caused by a dangerous employee.

Drug and Alcohol Testing under the ADA

Congress intended the ADA to be neutral on testing for substance abuse. Persons using drugs or alcohol are specifically exempted from the coverage of the ADA, and tests for substance abuse are not regulated by the ADA. This means that employers can do preemployment drug screening and refuse to hire persons testing positive (as allowed by other laws and union agreements) without violating the ADA. Persons in the workplace may also be screened and disciplined without violating the ADA. However, the ADA does apply to a person who has "successfully completed a supervised drug rehabilitation program and is no longer engaging in the illegal use of drugs, or has otherwise been rehabilitated successfully and is no longer engaging in such use" or "is participating in a supervised rehabilitation program and is no longer engaging in such use."

The employer may adopt policies, including periodic drug testing, to ensure that such persons are not engaging in substance abuse. The employer may prohibit the use of alcohol and illegal drugs at the workplace, may require that employees not be under the influence of illegal drugs or alcohol while at work, and may hold "an employee who engages in the illegal use of drugs or

who is an alcoholic to the same qualification standards for employment or job performance and behavior that such entity holds other employees, even if any unsatisfactory performance or behavior is related to the drug use or alcoholism of such employee." The employer may also regulate or ban smoking in the workplace without violating the ADA.

Physicians involved in drug and alcohol screening programs should appreciate that alcohol remains the most serious drug problem in most workplaces. It is medically (though perhaps not legally) unjustifiable to screen for illegal drug use and not screen for alcohol use. Although the legislatures and the courts are increasingly allowing and encouraging random drug testing, there are arguments that such policies are unnecessarily intrusive. They present ethical problems for the supervising physician who is put in an adversary position with the employee. Moreover, the evidence is not conclusive that such programs substantially improve workplace safety or productivity. Physicians advising on such programs should consider behavior-related testing as an alternative to random screening. Behavior-related testing is less intrusive to innocent workers. Most important, it may identify workers with dangerous personality problems who are not drug users but need medical or psychiatric attention.

Pregnant Workers under the ADA

The ADA does not apply to pregnant women. Workplace discrimination against pregnant women is prohibited by Title VII of the Civil Rights Act of 1964, as amended by the Pregnancy Discrimination Act (PDA). This law was construed by the U.S. Supreme Court in the landmark case of *International Union v. Johnson Controls*.[12] The decision held that fetal protection policies are against federal law. More generally, the Court found that employers cannot treat women differently because they may become pregnant, nor may they treat pregnant women differently solely because of their pregnancy. Under federal law, pregnancy must be handled like any other illness or disability. This applies to medical and disability insurance, leave policies, and fitness-for-work decisions. As with the ADA, the employer's only appropriate criterion is whether the pregnancy affects the woman's ability to do the job.

The *Johnson Controls* case was highly controversial because it pitted the job rights of the pregnant worker against the health of the fetus. Irrespective of an employer's emotional or religious views on protecting a fetus, injuring a fetus can be catastrophically expensive. Under current law, a fetus is a third person for workers' compensation purposes. This means that there is no cap on the damages that may be recovered from the employer. A woman may not absolve the employer of this liability by signing a waiver because the right to compensation belongs to the baby, not to the mother. The most difficult problem is that many women do not realize that they are pregnant quickly enough to prevent exposure during the critical first trimester. This led employers to deny women with reproductive capacity the right to work in certain jobs, although there has been little objective evidence of work-related fetal injuries.

The *Johnson Controls* case found that the employer had no independent right to protect the fetus. If a woman chooses to expose her fetus to workplace toxins, the employer cannot interfere. The majority opinion asserted that federal workplace safety laws might prevent lawsuits against the employer if the fetus was injured in such a situation, but this has not been the case for other workplace safety problems. The Court also reiterated the popular misconception that workplace toxins pose the same reproductive risks to men as to women. This ignores the issue that most of the known risks are due to in utero exposure.

Companies who employ women in positions that might endanger a fetus must warn women of the risk and provide alternative employment opportunities if the woman becomes pregnant. A physician who believes that a patient might be endangering her fetus by the work she does has the responsibility to warn her. This belief must be based on scientific evidence. Physicians who care for women in their childbearing years should realize that not all chemicals are dangerous to a fetus. The current tendency to worry pregnant women

with potential but minimal risks has the effect of discrediting warnings of serious risks such as smoking. Although there are occupational exposures that endanger a fetus, the more common risk is to the mother because of her reduced agility and shifting center of gravity.

A woman may be put on leave or alternative duties if the pregnancy makes her physically unable to fulfill her regular duties or if the work might endanger her health or the public safety. An airline was allowed to limit flights by pregnant women because their condition impaired their ability to function effectively in an emergency. Such decisions must be made on sound medical and workplace safety grounds. In the rare circumstances where such restrictions would be appropriate, employers should find alternative employment when possible. A pregnant telephone company employee may not be able to climb poles safely by the time she is 15 weeks pregnant, but she can do indoor installations safely until she goes into labor.

Physicians involved in obstetric care of women in the work force should make a clear distinction between social issues and medical decisions. A healthy woman with an uncomplicated pregnancy may want a maternity leave that extends for three months after the baby is born. Her company may offer a six-week leave. It is generally accepted that the normal physical disability associated with pregnancy and delivery should resolve by six weeks. It would not be legitimate to give this woman a medical excuse from work for the second six weeks postpartum unless she had a specific medical indication for such leave. No matter how strongly a physician feels about issues like bonding and breast-feeding, these are social issues that do not bear on the woman's physical fitness for work.

DISABILITY INSURANCE EVALUATIONS

Disability evaluation and qualification for various public and private disability programs is becoming increasingly important in general medical practice. Evaluation of impairments is no longer limited to neurologists, orthopedists, and physical medicine physicians. The laws have expanded and so have the types of problems that are considered disabilities. Every health care practitioner must deal with patients who are considered disabled under the Americans with Diabilities Act (ADA) and most will have patients who qualify, or want to qualify, for disability compensation under Social Security or private insurance.

Social Security Disability

The Social Security Administration (SSA) has responsibility for two disability programs. Title II is the Social Security Disability Insurance program, which is an insurance program for those who have worked and paid into the system. This is comparable to private disability insurance. Title XVI is the Supplemental Security Income program (SSI) that provides for individuals (including children under 18) who are disabled and have limited income and resources. Many individuals who have worked in the past but are now disabled qualify for payments from both programs.

The process for qualifying for Social Security Disability and for SSI are the same. Once an individual has applied for benefits there will be a medical determination made. If the medical evidence shows that the person is disabled, then the income and payment history will determine whether the person qualifies for either or both of the programs. Although it is not part of the medical evaluation, physicians who care for disabled patients can be very helpful in qualifying for benefits.

SSA Disability or SSI

SSA Disability is an insurance program. To qualify, an individual must have paid the premiums, which are Federal Insurance Contributors Act (FICA) or self-employment taxes. If the individual has not worked for an employer who paid and withheld FICA and has not filed and paid self-employment taxes, then this individual has not paid the premiums and is not insured.

Unlike most private insurance, one does not lose coverage as soon as the premiums stop being paid. An individual is insured under SSA Disability if they have paid into the system for a certain number of quarters in the last five to ten years. The calculations are complicated, but there is a simple principle to follow. Any worker who has become disabled should file with the SSA as soon as possible. Someone who has worked steadily for five years or more will be insured for five years after they stop working. If the person has a less consistent work history, or has periods of work where FICA was not paid, then the "date last insured" may come sooner than five years.

SSI is the program for the poor. Eligibility for this program does not run out because the patient has not been working. However, these benefits are available to individuals who are also receiving SSA Disability if they have little other income. Since neither program is particularly generous, it is not good to allow the insurance to lapse just because SSI is available.

How To Qualify

When a person applies for disability benefits under the SSA programs, they must state what medical problems they have that are disabling and who has been treating them for these. They are also required to give their work history and discuss how the medical problems have affected their functioning.

The initial application is made to the State Disability Determination Services (DDS) in the state where the claimant resides. The DDS investigates the claim by obtaining copies of medical records and by verifying work history and FICA payments. If the claimant does not have a doctor or if there is not an adequate evaluation in the records, then DDS must arrange for a medical exam at DDS expense. Usually, the DDS has a group of physicians in various specialties who know the requirements of the program and who regularly do consultative exams for the program.

Once the medical evidence (records) is received, it is given to a physician to evaluate. This physician is an employee or contractor of the DDS who only sees the records. If the physician knows the claimant or has cared for him or her in the past, then this physician does not process the case.

Listing of Impairments

The Social Security Administration has a Listing of Impairments that is used to judge the severity of the disability. This can be found in SSA Publication No. 64-039, *Disability Evaluation Under Social Security*. This booklet should be in the office of every physician who does disability evaluations of any kind. The system is not complicated, but it is nit-picking. Leaving one finding out of a report can cost a patient his or her benefits. The "Listing of Impairments" is divided into fourteen body systems or groups of disorders. Within each group, there are specific diseases or disabilities. For each disability there are specific problems that must be present for the claimant to "meet listing."

An example of a commonly used disability listing is 1.05 Disorders of the Spine:

1.05C. Other vertebrogenic disorders (e.g., herniated nucleus pulposus, spinal stenosis) with the following persisting for at least 3 months despite prescribed therapy and expected to last 12 months. With both 1 and 2:

1. Pain, muscle spasm, and significant limitation of motion in the spine; and

2. Appropriate radicular distribution of significant motor loss with muscle weakness and sensory and reflex loss.

Notice that all the sentences use "and." In order to meet the listing, and automatically get disability, the records must show that the claimant has all the problems described. Most doctors who have documented the nerve damage described in number 2 don't bother to note muscle spasm in the records. But without that notation, the patient has more difficulty getting benefits.

Residual Functional Capacity

If the claim does not meet listing, then the DDS doctor determines whether there are multiple conditions that will "equal" a listing. This is most common in claims for disability from a multisystem disease such as diabetes. The claimant may not have eye disease or peripheral neuropathy that qualifies on its own. But, if they can't walk without tripping because they can't feel their feet and they can't see the floor, then the two problems together equal the listing for diabetes with peripheral neuropathy, and the claimant is disabled.

If the claims do not meet or equal one of the listings, then the DDS doctor must form an opinion about the claimant's "Residual Functional Capacity." This is how most SSA disability claims are decided. DDS determines whether the claimant is able to do a job in the national economy. Unlike many private insurance systems, this is not based on whether the person can go back to his or her previous job. The question is whether the person can do any job.

Taking all the medical problems and allegations into consideration, the DDS doctor rates impairments on a specific form. The ratings include how much weight can be lifted, how far and how long can the person walk, how long can they sit, can they operate foot pedals and hand controls, can they climb, can they crawl, can they squat, etc. It also requires rating of impairments in use of the hands and arms, vision, communication (both hearing and speech), and environmental limitations such as heat, cold, or dust. This list of limitations is then compared to the work the person has done in the past and any related work the person might do. If they are so limited that they can't do any regular job, then they qualify for disability.

This is the area where the personal physician can be of the most help to disabled patients. Too many doctors write letters that say, "John Doe has spinal stenosis and is totally and permanently disabled." The diagnosis is clear but the rest of the statement will be ignored by DDS. Under the law, it is the Commissioner of the Social Security Administration who decides whether the person is disabled.

On the other hand, if the treating source opinion (the attending physician's notes) gives specific limitations, these must be given careful consideration. The statement that "John Doe has spinal stenosis and cannot lift more than 10 pounds or walk more than 100 feet or sit for more than 20 minutes without changing position" will probably get Mr. Doe his SSA disability benefits promptly.

Other Program Requirements

There are some additional components to qualifying for SSA Disability or SSI. First, there must be objective medical evidence of a severe injury or illness. For musculoskeletal problems this means an X ray, MRI, or CT scan that shows a disease or injury. For other types of disease, there must be a positive lab test or an objective physical finding. This might be a positive ANA or a typical malar rash to document systemic lupus erythematosus. For diabetic neuropathy, an elevated blood sugar and an absent reflex would usually be enough. This requirement is simply intended to weed out the disability claims that are based solely on pain or disability when there is no underlying disease causing it. A diagnosis alone is not enough. The diagnosed disease must cause some impairment. The diabetic who has normal eyes and kidneys and no peripheral neuropathy has a disease but not an impairment.

Regardless of how severe the impairment is, it must last or be expected to last 12 months to qualify for disability payments under Social Security. The person who is in a coma for a month after a head injury is clearly severely disabled for that month. However, if they have full use of their arms and legs, can see and hear, and come out of the coma with cognitive function intact, then they do not qualify for SSA Disability. On the other hand, the impairment does not have to have existed for 12 months before disability is granted. If the coma patient also has a crushed spinal cord and is going to be paraplegic, then the patient's guardian can apply for disability immediately. If the physician supports the prognosis that the disability will last for more than 12 months, the patient may be on SSA Disability and/or SSI before he or she regains consciousness.

Social Factors

The person's age and education are also factors in whether they qualify for disability. Individuals who are less than fifty years old must be more severely disabled to qualify than those who are older. The principle is that young people with a good basic education should be able to learn new skills and go back to work. If the claimant is over 55 and has limited education, the program acknowledges that retraining or changing careers is not a reasonable option. Age fifty to fifty-five is a gray area where some will qualify and some will not.

The other important consideration is credibility. The claimant is asked to tell the DDS how their functioning is limited by their disease and by their pain. The level of pain and how it affects their life is often very important in determining disability. Regardless of how bad the degenerative disc disease appears on X ray, if the claimant can go deer hunting, he can obviously walk more than 100 feet. On the other hand, someone whose X rays don't look too bad may have such severe pain that he has given up all social activities, and cannot sit long enough to watch a TV program. A claimant who can do things that he or she likes but can't do work is not very credible.

Medicare and Medicaid

Individuals who are on Social Security Disability or SSI may also qualify for the government health insurance programs. As with disability, income and resources determine which programs apply. If the patient is on SSD, then he or she may apply for Medicare after two years. This is a big hole in the system since an employer only has to allow continuation of private health insurance under COBRA for 18 months.

In contrast, the individual who has SSI, with or without SSD, probably qualifies for Medicaid immediately. Although most people think of Medicaid as a program for poor women and children, more than three quarters of all Medicaid benefits go to the disabled.

Private Disability Insurance

In contrast to the public programs like the Social Security Administration, private disability insurance tends to be fairly straightforward. There is an insurance contract that spells out the benefits and qualifications. There may also be a benefits coordinator for the patient's employer who can be very helpful.

This doesn't necessarily mean that getting benefits is easy. There will be specific forms to be completed by the attending physician for each insurance company. They may also require copies of medical records. The company may want an independent medical exam or functional capacity evaluation done. The attending physician and other medical care providers should cooperate fully with the process.

Clearly it is in a patient's best interest to receive disability benefits if the patient qualifies for them and is disabled. Part of a physician's duty to a patient is making and keeping adequate medical records. The physician should not hinder the process because he or she does not like dealing with insurance systems. On the other hand, the physician should be cautious about being too sympathetic with the patient. Like any other medical opinion, disability statements should be based on a specific diagnosis and objective medical evidence. They should not be a recitation of the patient's complaints or allegations. If the patient drives himself to the doctor's office, walks in unassisted, and waits for thirty minutes, then he clearly is able to walk fifty feet and sit for thirty minutes. Statements that defy common sense are not likely to carry weight with the insurance company.

DETERMINING DISABILITY: WORKERS' COMPENSATION VERSUS ADA

The ADA blurs the traditional distinction between the medical determination of a functional impairment and the legal determination of the disability resulting from that impairment. In addition to disability determinations under the ADA, physicians are routinely asked to make functional impairment determinations for workers' compensation claims and for civil litigation arising from nonworkplace injuries. The physician's role is to determine the patient's loss of function in the affected organ system. The insurance company, court, or administrative agency providing the compensation decides how much of a disability this limitation of function constitutes. A disability may be caused by either illness or injury. The etiology of the illness or injury may determine how the patient will be compensated for the disability but is not important to the evaluation of the extent of the disability. For the purpose of the medical evaluation, it does not matter whether the patient is injured on the job or playing football on the weekend.

For instance, a physician may determine that a patient has lost 20% of the range of motion in his right hand. This determination is unrelated to the patient's occupation. The extent of disability caused by a functional impairment is a job-specific determination. For a manual laborer or an attorney, this loss of range of motion may not constitute a disability. The patient is able to pursue his usual occupation with little or no difficulty, and there is no substantial limitation on household tasks. If the patient is a concert pianist or a surgeon, this 20% loss of range of motion may constitute a total disability from his chosen work.

The severity of the workplace disability is not directly related to the extent of functional impairment or disability in personal living. A telephone operator who is blinded is severely disabled in his or her personal life but may not be occupationally disabled. A stevedore with a back injury may have little handicap in day-to-day living but be totally and permanently disabled regarding this work. In an evaluation of disability under the ADA or Social Security, the focus is on alternative related employment. The proposed rules discuss the example of a surgeon with a mild palsy. Although the surgeon may be disqualified from performing surgery, he or she may be employed in other medical activities and is thus not disabled. This is consistent with a policy that encourages full employment. Conflicts arise because a person making a tort or workers' compensation claim wants to be found maximally disabled, whereas a person claiming under ADA does not want to be found to be unqualified for a given job.

COMMUNICABLE DISEASES IN THE WORKPLACE

The HIV epidemic and the reemergence of other infectious diseases have lead to increased interest in communicable disease control in the workplace. Concern with discrimination against the disabled and HIV-infected persons led Congress to pass the Americans with Disabilities Act (ADA) in 1990. The ADA reduces employers' right to ask about a potential employee's health. It also limits the right of employers to refuse to hire persons who are at increased risk of injury in the workplace or who may pose a risk to others.

These limitations come as the courts and legislatures are expanding employers' duty to protect workers and the public. With diseases such as tuberculosis on the rise, employers need comprehensive plans to manage communicable diseases in the workplace. With the ADA's stress on the individual evaluation of employees, physicians must play the central role in these communicable disease plans. This requires assessing the risk posed by individual infected employees and developing legally sound protocols for balancing the risk of contagion against the employee's right to continued employment. The ADA and its administrative regulations provide little guidance because they are silent on all communicable diseases except for those that are foodborne. This section presents a general approach to communicable diseases in the workplace. Medical care workplaces are treated as a special case of the general communicable disease plan.

The Increase of Communicable Diseases in the Workplace

The morbidity and mortality from communicable diseases is increasing in the United States. Although much of this is secondary to the HIV epidemic, traditional threats such as tuberculosis are also increasing. HIV has also overshadowed new epidemic diseases, such as Lyme disease. Paradoxically, the legal risks of communicable diseases are increasing because the diseases themselves are still relatively rare. If an epidemic afflicts most of the population, it is difficult to link an individual case to a workplace exposure. However, if outbreaks of the disease are infrequent, it will be obvious when an employee's exposure occurred at work.

Immunizations and Antibiotic Misuse

The root cause of the increase of immunizable diseases in the United States is public complacency. After one or more generations of a successful immunization program, the targeted disease becomes rare and no longer frightening. Once the public is no longer concerned about a disease, the financial and political support for disease control measures such as mass immunizations disappears. This creates cohorts of susceptible adults who were neither immunized nor exposed as children, a dangerous situation for employers because many childhood diseases are much more serious in adults. For example, before mumps immunizations, epidemics of mumps would pass through a community regularly, and most of the susceptible population would become immune through having the disease. Complications in these susceptible children were rare, and most children had the disease before reaching puberty. Now, through vaccine failure, lack of exposure to disease or vaccine, and waning immunity, workplace epidemics of mumps can occur. These adult epidemics are dangerous because adults are prone to severe sequelae, with attendant high workers' compensation costs.

Controlling communicable diseases is complicated by the rise of drug resistance secondary to the misuse of antibiotics. Overprescription by physicians, sharing prescriptions by patients, the use of massive amounts of antibiotics in animal husbandry, and the absence of international controls on antibiotics leads to the evolution of antibiotic-resistant strains of common diseases. Tuberculosis is the best example of the problem. The tuberculosis bacillus is hard to kill and prone to developing drug resistance. The repeated exposure of tuberculosis carriers to ineffective doses of antitubercular drugs dramatically increases the incidence of drug-resistant tuberculosis. There are only a few effective antitubercular drugs. These are all prescription drugs in the United States, but some are available in over-the-counter cough syrup in Mexico. Thus, the incidence of drug-resistant tuberculosis increases closer to the Mexican border.

Immunosuppression

The wide use of immunosuppressive drugs and HIV infection have resulted in a large number of workers with suppressed immune systems who are more susceptible to infectious diseases in the workplace. They also may spread diseases such as tuberculosis to others. Until recently, significant immunosuppression was not a workplace issue because it occurred only secondary to severe illness. Because otherwise healthy immunosuppressed workers are a new phenomenon in the workplace, their legal status is not well defined.

Immunosuppressed individuals are disabled under the federal law and are entitled to work if they meet the other requirements of the law. If a secondary infection such as active tuberculosis threatens other workers or third parties, the infected person may be removed from the workplace. The difficult question is whether immunosuppressed persons may be denied employment to protect them from workplace-acquired infections. It is argued that the worker has the right to accept the risk of infection. Workers' compensation laws, however, do not allow the worker to accept the financial risk of workplace injury. The employer must pay for the costs of treatment or disability if the immunosuppressed worker becomes infected in the workplace, irrespective of the employee's assumption of the risk of infection.

The Legal Risks of Communicable Diseases

Communicable diseases in the workplace pose three classes of risk: (1) workers' compensation liability, (2) third-party liability, and (3) productivity losses. All three are potentially very expensive, yet have been accorded scant attention from employers or employees. The HIV epidemic has sensitized employees and employers to the problems of workplace-acquired infections. As declining health insurance coverage forces more per-

sons to seek compensation through the courts for illness, workers' compensation claims for workplace-acquired infections will increase.

Workers' compensation laws are not limited to accidents or occupational illnesses; they cover all illnesses and injuries acquired in the workplace, including communicable diseases and intentional injuries such as rape. The employee is entitled to the cost of medical care, disability, and lost time for work. In return, the law prevents the employee from suing the employer for the more extensive damages available in tort litigation. This exemption is important because some usually mild diseases can cause serious injuries in adults. Mumps can cause sterility, measles sometimes kills, chicken pox can cause brain injury, and tuberculosis can require long-term treatment.

Earlier in this century, it was common for employees to claim compensation for communicable diseases such as typhoid caught from the company water supply. As the public awareness of communicable diseases diminished, claims for workplace-acquired infections decreased. Even health care workers, who have a high rate of morbidity from workplace infections, have tended to rely on group health coverage for workplace-acquired infections rather than workers' compensation. Progressive reductions in group health coverage and reduced job security are causing workers to seek workers' compensation for illnesses that in the past would not have resulted in compensation claims. This will require physicians to be more sensitive to the epidemiology of workplace-acquired infections.

Third-Party Liability

Employers are liable to nonemployees, called third parties, who are injured by negligent employees. These third parties can sue the employer for all the damages allowed in tort litigation. Although the workers' compensation costs of a communicable disease cannot be ignored, they pale before the costs of third-party liability. Hiring a truck driver with severe heart disease or an alcoholic physician would be negligent, making the company liable to anyone the employee injured. Allowing an employee with infectious tuberculosis to work in a day care center or a demented HIV carrier to be an airplane pilot poses the same risks.

The risk of third-party infections is greatest for foodborne illnesses and highly contagious diseases such as measles that are spread by contact or respiratory transmission. Less infectious respiratory illnesses such as tuberculosis require close or prolonged contact with the infected person. These pose the greatest threat in service industries such as day care centers, where there is close contact between the employees and the customers. Blood-borne illnesses such as hepatitis B virus (HBV) and HIV pose a threat to customers only when there is a chance of exposure to contaminated blood. This is usually thought to be limited to medical care but can happen in any activity where a customer's skin is pierced. Tattooing, for example, has been implicated in HBV transmission and could transmit HIV.

The most likely third-party victims of workplace-acquired infections are the family members or the unborn children of the worker. When a worker infects a family member with a workplace-acquired infection, the family member may sue the employer. The most serious risks to third parties are those to unborn children. A pregnant worker cannot be excluded from the workplace to protect her fetus. But under current law, if that fetus is injured by a workplace exposure, perhaps to rubella, the employer could be liable for the resulting injuries.

Immunosuppressed family members or other third parties pose difficult legal problems. There is no simple legal rule for determining when a company should be liable for a workplace-related infection to an immunosuppressed worker or third party. Traditional tort law holds that negligent persons take their plaintiffs as they find them: if an employer negligently allows a chicken pox–infected employee to stay in the workplace, the employer would be liable if an immunosuppressed customer contracts chicken pox encephalitis from the employee. Conversely, the doctrine of foreseeability acts as a brake on unlimited liability: if a customer catches a cold from an employee, and then falls off a cliff while sneezing, the employer would not be liable for the fall. However, it is dif-

ficult to reconcile jurors' tendency to hold employers liable for injuries to third parties with the ADA's strict limitations on the employer's right to exclude infected workers from the workplace.

Productivity

A workplace epidemic can bring the operations of the business to a halt. If the mail clerk comes to work with the flu and gives it to every secretary, three days later most of the secretarial force may call in sick. If the doughnut vendor gives everyone hepatitis A, the onset of the disease will not be simultaneous, but the disease will last long enough that at some point many workers will be absent. In years past, it was common to close the elementary school for an epidemic of a childhood disease. High-technology service industries that are dependent on skilled personnel are particularly vulnerable: "Between August 18 and December 25, 1987, 116 employees at the three futures exchanges in Chicago developed clinically diagnosed mumps. Three cases subsequently occurred in household contacts of affected exchange employees. Twenty-one persons developed complications; nine were hospitalized."[13] The direct medical costs were over $56,000, with the total work loss probably in excess of 700 days. The potential tort liability was significant: the mumps virus induced premature labor in a pregnant employee. Fortunately, the labor was arrested, preventing a premature birth with the attendant liability for possible injury to the infant. The report of this epidemic does not discuss whether any of the infected men were rendered sterile. This corporate epidemic was costly and completely preventable. Yet like most other employers, the futures exchange did not recognize communicable diseases as a workplace issue.

Communicable Diseases as a Handicap or Disability

The ADA incorporates and expands existing protections provided in section 504 of the Rehabilitation Act. In cases decided under this predecessor act, the U.S. Supreme Court held that a person with a communicable disease (tuberculosis) was handicapped under the definitions of the law.[14] This case involved a school teacher with a history of recurrent activation of her tuberculosis who was fired after becoming sputum positive. Although acknowledging that Arline was covered under the provisions of the act, the Court was left with the question of whether she was otherwise qualified to be a school teacher:

> The remaining question is whether Arline is otherwise qualified for the job of elementary school teacher. To answer this question in most cases, the District Court will need to conduct an individualized inquiry and make appropriate findings of fact. Such an inquiry is essential if sec. 504 is to achieve its goal of protecting handicapped individuals from deprivations based on prejudice, stereotypes, or unfounded fear, while giving appropriate weight to such legitimate concerns of grantees as avoiding exposing others to significant health and safety risks. The basic factors to be considered in conducting this inquiry are well established. In the context of the employment of a person handicapped with a contagious disease, we agree with amicus American Medical Association that this inquiry should include "[findings of] facts, based on reasonable medical judgments given the state of medical knowledge, about (a) the nature of the risk (how the disease is transmitted), (b) the duration of the risk (how long is the carrier infectious), (c) the severity of the risk (what is the potential harm to third parties) and (d) the probabilities the disease will be transmitted and will cause varying degrees of harm."

In making these findings, courts normally should defer to the reasonable medical judgments of public health officials. The next step in the "otherwise-qualified" inquiry is for the court to evaluate, in light of these medical findings, whether the employer could reasonably accommodate the employee under the established standards for that inquiry.[15]

The Supreme Court did not decide if Arline was otherwise qualified. The case was remanded to allow the trial court to obtain evidence on whether, after appropriate accommodations, Arline posed a threat of infection to the students. The evidence presented to the trial court established that Ar-

line's tuberculosis was under control to the satisfaction of the public health authorities. Since she did not pose a threat of infection, she was reinstated and given back pay.

Additional Requirements of the ADA

The ADA and its administrative regulations (29 C.F.R. 1630, July 16, 1991) introduced the concepts of direct threat and significant risk of substantial harm. These narrow the traditional right of an employer to exclude workers who might be injured or injure others. The following regulations must be combined with the requirements of *Arline* to determine the proper balance between employee rights and the duty to protect the employee and the public when developing a communicable disease policy:

> Direct Threat means a significant risk of substantial harm to the health or safety of the individual or others that cannot be eliminated or reduced by reasonable accommodation. The determination that an individual poses a "direct threat" shall be based on an individualized assessment of the individual's present ability to safely perform the essential functions of the job. This assessment shall be based on a reasonable medical judgment that relies on the most current medical knowledge and/or on the best available objective evidence. In determining whether an individual would pose a direct threat, the factors to be considered include
>
> (1) The duration of the risk;
>
> (2) The nature and severity of the potential harm;
>
> (3) The likelihood that the potential harm will occur; and
>
> (4) The imminence of the potential harm.
>
> Determining whether an individual poses a significant risk of substantial harm to others must be made on a case by case basis. The employer should identify the specific risk posed by the individual. For individuals with mental or emotional disabilities, the employer must identify the specific behavior on the part of the individual that would pose the direct threat. For individuals with

physical disabilities, the employer must identify the aspect of the disability that would pose the direct threat. The employer should then consider the four factors listed in part 1630:

(1) The duration of the risk;

(2) The nature and severity of the potential harm;

(3) The likelihood that the potential harm will occur; and

(4) The imminence of the potential harm.

Such consideration must rely on objective, factual evidence—not on subjective perceptions, irrational fears, patronizing attitudes, or stereotypes—about the nature or effect of a particular disability, or of disability generally.... Relevant evidence may include input from the individual with a disability, the experience of the individual with a disability in previous similar positions, and opinions of medical doctors, rehabilitation counselors, or physical therapists who have expertise in the disability involved and/or direct knowledge of the individual with the disability.

An employer is also permitted to require that an individual not pose a direct threat of harm to his or her own safety or health. If performing the particular functions of a job would result in a high probability of substantial harm to the individual, the employer could reject or discharge the individual unless a reasonable accommodation that would not cause an undue hardship would avert the harm.

The assessment that there exists a high probability of substantial harm to the individual, like the assessment that there exists a high probability of substantial harm to others, must be strictly based on valid medical analyses and/or on other objective evidence. This determination must be based on individualized factual data, using the factors discussed above, rather than on stereotypic or patronizing assumptions and must consider potential reasonable accommodations. Generalized fears about risks from the employment environment, such as exacerbation of the disability caused by stress, cannot be used by an employer to disqualify an individual with a disability. (29 CFR1630, Appendix at 1630.2(r))

THE ELEMENTS OF A COMMUNICABLE DISEASE POLICY

Paradoxically, the more the law stresses individual evaluation, the more the employer must rely on carefully drafted written policies. Individualized evaluation makes it easier for the employee to contest the employer's standards. Although the employer may ultimately prevail in court, careful adherence to written guidelines can discourage attorneys from difficult-to-win lawsuits. If this policy is to be credible, it must be developed before the business is embroiled in controversy over potentially discriminatory actions against disease carriers.

Following is a framework for a disease control plan based on the analysis suggested in the Supreme Court decision in *Arline*. A completed disease control plan must detail the actual circumstances of the company and diseases that pose a risk in that environment. There are guidelines for control of tuberculosis (TB) and of bloodborne pathogens, but other communicable diseases should be considered as well. The medical information should be based on CDC (Centers for Disease Control and Prevention) recommendations and the American Public Health Association publication, *Communicable Diseases in Man*. The workplace-specific parts of the plan are more difficult. Although many large companies have a corporate policy on AIDS, these plans are usually equal employment guidelines with no reference to other diseases.

Nature of the Risk

Nature of the risk is the Supreme Court's term for the method of spreading the disease. Airborne transmission poses the greatest risk and sexual transmission the smallest risk in the workplace. When analyzing communicability, the most important question is whether the mode of transmission for the disease in question occurs in the workplace. Airborne transmission occurs in all situations, whereas sexual transmission is usually not a workplace risk. Foodborne illnesses are a problem for food handlers in the employee cafeteria but do not pose a threat from assembly line or sales personnel.

Methods of Transmission

Airborne

These are diseases that may be spread through the air from the infected person to a healthy person. This may be direct spread, as when a disease carrier coughs near another person, or indirect spread, when the disease organisms spread through the air ducts in a building. Indirect spread can infect workers several floors away from the disease carrier.

Fomites

A fomite is an inanimate object that is contaminated with disease-causing microorganisms. Fomites may be too small to see, or they may be large objects such as contaminated clothing or safety equipment. Although not as dangerous as airborne transmission, fomite transmission, including fecal-oral transmission, can be a particular problem in child care and nursing situations.

Foodborne

Foodborne illnesses are a risk only if the disease carrier prepares or serves the food. Typhoid is the classic foodborne illness. Casual contact with a typhoid carrier will not spread the disease. Typhoid is spread when the carrier prepares food on which the typhoid organisms can grow. The typhoid carrier infects the food, which infects the person who eats it.

Insect Vectors

Many diseases are spread by insects. These are generally not a problem for office workers but can be a significant risk to persons working with animals, raw animal products, or in the outdoors. Insectborne diseases that may be workplace problems include Rocky Mountain spotted fever, Lyme disease, and encephalitis.

Sexually Transmitted Diseases

Outside of a few brothels in Nevada, sexually transmitted diseases are not usually thought of as workplace hazards. They may, however, create a risk in health care or laboratory settings where personnel can come in direct contact with infected specimens or body fluids. It should be noted, however, that there may be liability if an employer is on notice of sexual relations between employees and customers and does not prevent them. This can be a problem in sex-oriented businesses or at resorts where personnel may supplement their income through prostitution.

Bloodborne

Few diseases are strictly bloodborne. Most, like hepatitis B and HIV, are also transmitted through intimate contact. Bloodborne diseases are a risk only in workplaces where workers can come into contact with blood or other bodily fluids—most common in medical care delivery and laboratory work. It is also a consideration for employees who provide first aid to other employees or customers. Employers should be careful of hidden blood exposures. Ear piercing in a department store can effectively spread HBV between customers if the instruments are reused without sterilization.

Direct Contact

Some diseases and parasites are spread by direct contact between individuals or their personal items such as clothing. These include scabies, lice, and ringworm. These can be a substantial problem where employees share living quarters or coat closets. Other than inconvenience, however, infestations seldom pose any serious health risk.

Duration of the Risk

Duration of the risk is the Court's term for the period the carrier remains infectious. This period may be self-limited for diseases such as measles, limited by antibiotic treatment for diseases such as strep throat, or unlimited, such as for HIV and the carrier states of typhoid and HBV. Employees remain disabled under the law after the disease is no longer infectious because the law also includes persons who are perceived to be disabled.

Severity

The Court was rightly concerned with the severity of the disease. This would be judged as a function of the morbidity of the disease, the duration of the disease, and whether the disease has permanent sequelae. It is important to note when the characteristics of the organism and the patient can increase the severity of the disease. Diseases such as influenza are mildly incapacitating in healthy workers but could be dangerous to the residents of a nursing home.

Probability of Transmission and Complications

This is the final element in the Court's analysis, although it is more a synthesis of the first three elements. The probability of transmission depends on the mode of transmission and the infectivity of the diseases. This is sometimes called *contact effectiveness*. The higher the contact effectiveness is, the higher is the probability that a person coming into proper contact with a disease carrier will contract the disease. For example, HIV is a disease with a low contact effectiveness; a sexual encounter has a less than 5% chance of spreading the disease. There is no possibility of spreading HIV by casual contact such as coughing. Conversely, measles is a disease with a high contact effectiveness. A single exposure to a coughing person infected with measles usually results in infection among susceptible persons.

If the usual mode of transmission does not occur in the workplace, then there is a very low probability of transmission. This is the usual case for sexually transmitted diseases that are not otherwise bloodborne. If the mode of transmission occurs in the workplace but the contact efficiency is very low, there is also a low probability of transmission. This would be the case for a disease such as leprosy that is spread by physical contact but the contact efficiency is so low that it poses a risk only to intimate family members. Conversely, active tuberculosis, an airborne disease with a medium contact efficiency, poses a threat to anyone with whom the infected person has frequent contact.

The Court did not specifically address the problem of persons with special susceptibility to communicable diseases—primarily immunosuppressed persons and pregnant women. The court has ruled that fertile women as a class cannot be excluded from workplaces where there is exposure to teratogens. It is likely that current law prevents pregnant women from being excluded from workplaces where there is only a possibility of infection with a disease that adversely affects the fetus. If there is a high probability of exposure, as on a hospital service caring for persons infected with the disease, the court might allow some restrictions on pregnant workers. The limited set of infections that pose a risk to the fetus and the fixed length of pregnancy would make pregnancy-related restrictions unusual outside certain medical care workplaces.

Federal and State Requirements

The communicable disease plan should identify all applicable federal and state disease control laws and administrative regulations. These may include statutory reporting duties that apply to the company physician or laboratory, sanitation rules that govern the company cafeteria, or OSHA regulations. OSHA has already issued regulations with detailed specifications on the management of bloodborne infections in the workplace. There are also specific requirements for TB control in health care organizations. Any relevant CDC recommendations should be incorporated in the plan, as should standard-setting documents from private professional groups and accrediting agencies.

Identifying Employees at Risk or Who Pose Risks

Employees who are inadequately immunized against diseases such as measles and mumps are susceptible to the workplace spread of these diseases. Medical care workers who are not properly immunized may become infected and spread these diseases to patients. Medical care workers who are not immunized against hepatitis B may contract the disease in the workplace. Farm workers may acquire tetanus if they have not been immunized within the past ten years. Animal control workers should be immunized against rabies. Employers should know the immunization status of all employees and ensure that all employees are adequately immunized. OSHA requires that HBV vaccine be provided free of charge to employees at risk of infection. Whereas other immunizations may not be covered by OSHA requirements, the employer should provide them at no cost. The employer may require employees to be immunized as a condition of employment.

Screening for contagious disease may be done on employees, clients, or both. Screening has a bad reputation among health care professionals because many of the old screening programs included diseases that were not spread in the workplace. The health card system for food handlers is a good example. Until recently, most states and cities required that restaurant workers get a health card, obtained after tests for syphilis and tuberculosis. The tuberculosis test was a holdover from earlier times when it posed a general workplace risk; syphilis, however, has never been associated with food handling.

In contrast, requiring an annual test for tuberculosis on medical care and social services personnel does protect clients and the employee from the risks of tuberculosis. A worker who smokes and has hay fever may have a highly contagious cough for months before realizing that it is due to tuberculosis. If an employee is found to have infectious tuberculosis or another communicable disease, the health department should be contacted at once. The health department, in cooperation with the corporate medical department if one is available, should screen coworkers as necessary to prevent further spread at the worksite. This screening is mandatory, and the employer should ensure that the health department's recommendations are fully implemented.

The Special Problems of Immunosuppression

Immunosuppressed workers pose a double-edged problem: they are more susceptible to workplace-acquired infections, and they may harbor infectious diseases such as tuberculosis that pose a threat to other workers. The conventional legal wisdom is that immunosuppressed workers do not need special protections in the workplace. This is predicated on *Pneumocystis carinii* pneumonia as the model secondary infection. *Pneumocystis carinii* is a ubiquitous organism that is acquired from the environment rather than from personal spread. The person's risk of infection is not increased by being at work. More important, there is no way to prove that the organism was acquired at a workplace, so it is impossible for an infected person to claim for either workers' compensation or third-party tort damages.

The problems arise when the immunosuppressed person is infected with an agent that is traceable to the workplace. This could be a common communicable disease such as chicken pox, or an unusual infection that is acquired because of the immunosuppression. Most employees are in workplaces that do not pose an increased risk of infection. The ADA prevents immunosuppressed workers from being excluded from such workplaces because of their general increased risk of infection. The employer must protect such employees from known risks posed by fellow employees or customers, but this protection must interfere as little as possible with the employee's opportunities in the company.

The employee might be removed from the workplace to avoid a specific customer with a known infectious disease. In general, however, the employer's duty will be to identify other employees with communicable diseases. If these employees pose a threat to other workers, they must be removed from the workplace while they are infectious. If these employees pose a threat only to the immunosuppressed employee, the infected employee may be moved away from the immunosuppressed employee during the infectious period.

Many workplaces pose an increased risk of infection: hospitals, medical offices, day care centers, and other workplaces that render personal services to populations that regularly include customers with communicable diseases. The Supreme Court's test from *Arline* was intended for judging the risk that an infected employee poses to others. If the court uses the same analysis to judge the risk to the employee, the employer must demonstrate substantial risk of harm before the employee can be excluded from the workplace. An infectious disease service in a large hospital might properly refuse to hire an immunosuppressed nurse or ward clerk. A plastic surgeon whose practice is limited to elective cosmetic surgery would not be able to refuse to hire an immunosuppressed person.

As the spread of tuberculosis secondary to HIV-induced immunosuppression demonstrates, immunosuppressed persons can bring communicable diseases into the workplace. This is a significant problem for workplaces such as day care centers or hospitals whose customers are at special risk of infection. Such persons should have special counseling about the risks of secondary infections and undergo periodic screening for tuberculosis and other diseases that are demonstrated to pose special problems. This is controversial, however, because it requires screening for HIV-infected employees.

Bloodborne Pathogens

All workplaces are required to have procedures for dealing with bloodborne pathogens. These regulations were developed in response to the fears raised by the HIV epidemic, but they serve to protect employees from a variety of illnesses, particularly viral hepatitis.

A workplace that does not provide medical service and has no other significant exposures to body fluids can make do with a very simple program for cleaning up blood. Obviously, there is always a risk of blood exposure in a workplace. Any employee can have a nose bleed or a cut that spreads blood in the environment. There must be a written procedure for cleaning up the blood without coming into contact with it and then sanitizing the environment with a cleaning solution that kills bloodborne pathogens. Rubber gloves, paper towels, and a spray bottle of bleach solution are the only equipment needed in most workplaces.

Health Care Organizations

For health care organizations and other high-risk occupations the requirements are much more extensive. In 1991, OSHA issues its final rules on "Occupational exposure to bloodborne pathogens." These rules are based on CDC recommendations that were issued earlier that year. The rules encompass primary and secondary prevention in three categories of protection.

The primary prevention required is immunization for hepatitis B. In 1991, many organizations required employees and volunteers to pay for their own immunizations. For many, the expense was prohibitive. Under the OSHA rules, the employer must now provide the immunization free of charge to all employees who may be exposed to blood or body fluids. And, most employees of a hospital, laboratory or nursing home would be considered at risk. Other immunizations were not included in the requirement or were not available in 1991. However, given the legal and medical risks of disease transmission, the immunization program should include Tetanus/diphtheria, measles/mumps/rubella, hepatitis A, chicken pox, and rabies if animal exposure is a consideration.

The second and most expensive requirement is universal precautions. This protection requires barriers to exposure in all situations where a worker is or might be exposed to blood, body fluids or other tissue. As with any industrial exposure, engineering controls such as vent hoods and administrative controls, such as limiting the number of people exposed should take precedence over personal protective equipment. However, there is very little that can be done by engineering or administration. All employees who are at risk of exposure must be given eye protection, disposable gloves, masks, and clothing as needed. This must be appropriate for each individual and readily available.

The disposal of contaminated materials is also carefully regulated. Sharps containers must be available wherever needles or cutting instruments are used. Labeled containers for not-sharp trash and soiled laundry must also be available. All of these containers must be changed regularly to prevent overfilling and disposed of properly.

The third type of prevention included in the rules is care of the individual who has been exposed to bloodborne pathogens. Needle stick is still the most common type of exposure, but blood on a cut or mucous membrane exposure is still a serious problem. Employees with exposure must be provided with an evaluation by a physician and a written discussion of the medical recommendations and options. This medical care should include testing, immunization and/or antiviral drugs as appropriate. The system must be set up in advance of the need. It is not possible in most health care institutions, to produce a knowledgeable physician and all the necessary immunizations and drugs in the few hours of opportunity that are critical to preventing infection with HIV or hepatitis.

The regulations also require that all employees be given training in prevention of bloodborne pathogen exposure. This requirement can be quite easy to meet. Several commercial training programs can provide all the necessary training materials and forms for recordkeeping.

The Reach of the Regulations

The bloodborne pathogen regulations of OSHA have a very broad reach. Unlike most OSHA regulations, employees of units of local and state governments are not exempt. Since many ambulance systems and hospitals are part of city or county government services, this would exempt too many high risk employees from these important protections. In addition, many people are covered who are not normally considered employees. Hospital volunteers and physicians on the staff are also the responsibility of the hospital.

From a legal liability standpoint, hospitals should make sure that anyone who works in their system is in compliance with all the bloodborne pathogen requirements. If they are not employees they are probably not covered by workers' compensation. These individuals could sue the hospital as third parties if they contracted an infectious disease while working in the hospital. If the hospital can be shown to have allowed this infection because they were saving themselves a few dollars an immunizations or protective equipment, then the jury is likely to make a very large award.

Tuberculosis Control

The OSHA regulations on occupational exposure to tuberculosis are less well known than the bloodborne pathogen rules but they affect a much broader set of businesses.[16] The following is a list of the groups, industries, and work settings that are covered by the standard. Basically, this includes all types of health care, social work, and law enforcement agencies and personnel:

- hospitals
- nursing homes
- correctional facilities
- immigration detainment facilities
- law enforcement facilities
- hospices
- substance abuse treatment centers
- homeless shelters
- medical examiners' offices
- home health care providers
- emergency medical services
- research and clinical laboratories handling TB
- Contract work on ventilation systems or areas of buildings that may contain aerosolized M. tuberculosis
- physicians performing certain high-hazard procedures
- social service workers providing services to individuals identified as having suspected or confirmed infectious TB
- personnel service agencies when providing workers to covered facilities
- attorneys visiting known or suspected infectious TB patients

The CDC guidelines on TB control recommend that a facility does risk assessment to determine the level of TB exposure risk for the facility as a whole and for specific work areas and occupational groups. The CDC defines five levels of risk based on the number of clients with active TB, the rate and pattern of PPD skin test conversions, and whether there is evidence of person-to-person transmission of TB. OSHA has chosen a simpler approach. Employers are required to determine which employees have occupational exposure to TB. OSHA then specifies that measures must be taken to protect these exposed employees

Institutions that have no internal TB exposure and that are in communities with little or no active TB are exempt from some of the OSHA requirements. However, some actions are required of all covered institutions:

- There must be a written exposure control plan.
- Baseline PPD skin testing and medical history must be obtained on all employees who are identified as having occupational exposure.
- Medical management and follow-up must be provided after exposure incidents.
- Infectious employees must be removed from the workplace until noninfectious.
- There must be acceptable employee training and recordkeeping.

The OSHA regulations require PPD retesting every three to twelve months depending on the level of risk and exposure history of a given employee. Employees with a low risk of exposure may be retested yearly. Those with higher risk must be retested every six months. The latter include those who (1) enter AFB isolation rooms, (2) perform high-hazard procedures, (3) transport TB patients in an enclosed vehicle, or (4) work in intake areas in an institution with a high number of TB patients (6 in 12 months). If there has been a direct exposure, the employee must be retested immediately and again in three months.

The OSHA regulations do allow for the limitations of the PPD skin test as a screening test. Anyone who has not had a TB skin test in the last 12 months, must have a two-step baseline test. This involves doing the test and then repeating it in two weeks if it is negative or equivocal. This allows them to distinguish true conversions from the booster effect. A true conversion occurs when the patient becomes infected with TB between two tests. The booster effect occurs when a patient has

been infected in the past but does not have high levels of antibody. The first test boosts the antibody levels so that the repeat in two weeks will give a true reading. Contrary to popular myth, you cannot develop a positive PPD skin test by having too many tests.

If the employee already has a documented positive PPD skin test, then it does not have to be repeated. The employer may rely on careful history and chest X ray when indicated to follow these employees. Routine chest X rays are not required or recommended. In addition to regular screening of individual employees, regulated establishments must watch for clusters of disease or skin test conversion. These may indicate areas where active TB has gone unnoticed or where administrative or engineering controls have broken down.

When an employee has become infected with TB, whether they have active disease or silent infection detected on skin testing, the employer must provide medical care and follow-up. Some states recognize such infection as a compensable injury under workers' compensation. Other do not. However, under OSHA regulation, proper care and treatment must be provided.

An employee who is found to have infectious TB must be put on medical exclusion from work until they are no longer infectious and do not pose a risk to others. This means that a health care professional cannot practice until they are noncontagious. The nurse who is on medical exclusion from the hospital may not do immunization clinics or home health visits.

An important consideration about TB control in the work environment is that it must fit with the control of this disease in the larger community. The OSHA regulations and recordkeeping do not negate the state public health laws. TB is a reportable disease in every state and territory of the United States. There is a large federal TB control program administered at the local health department level. In addition, charity hospitals, homeless shelters, and jails have a large number of clients in common. Patients receive better care and workers have a safer work environment when there is coordination of TB control efforts by local public health officials.

REFERENCES

1. Holleman WL, Holleman MC. School and work release evaluations. *JAMA*. 1988;260:3629–3640.
2. Bolyard EA, Tablan OC, Williams WW, Pearson ML, Shapiro CN, Deitchmann SD. Hospital Infection Control Practices Advisory Committee: guideline for infection control in healthcare personnel, 1998. *Infect Control Hosp Epidemiol*. 1998;19:407–463.
3. 42 U.S.C.A. §§ 12101, *et seq.*
4. 29 U.S.C. § 706 (1988 ed.).
5. *Bartlett v. New York State Bd. of Law Examrs,* 156 F.3d 321 (2d Cir. 1998).
6. *Griggs v. Duke Power Co.*, 401 U.S. 424 (1971).
7. 45 C.F.R. § 84.3(j) (ii).
8. *Krauel v. Iowa Methodist Med. Ctr.*, 95 F.3d 674 (8th Cir. 1996).
9. *Bragdon v. Abbott*, 118 S. Ct. 2196, 141 L. Ed. 2d 540 (1998).
10. *Pettus v. Cole*, 49 Cal. App. 4th 402, 57 Cal. Rptr. 2d 46 (Cal. App. 1 Dist. 1996).
11. *School Bd. of Nassau County, Fla. v. Arline*, 480 U.S. 273 (1987).
12. *International Union v. Johnson Controls*, 499 U.S. 187 (1991).
13. Mumps in the workplace—Chicago. *MMWR*. 1988;37:533–538.
14. *School Bd. of Nassau County v. Arline,* 107 S.Ct. 1123 (1987).
15. *Id.* at 1130–1131.
16. Proposed Rules Department of Labor Occupational Safety and Health Administration. 29 C.F.R. part 1910, Occupational Exposure to Tuberculosis, Friday, October 17, 1997, 62 Fed. Reg. 54160–01 (1997).

SUGGESTED READINGS

Health Care Organizations

Agerton TB, Mahoney FJ, Polish LB, Shapiro CN. Impact of the bloodborne pathogens standard on vaccination of healthcare workers with hepatitis B vaccine. *Infect Control Hosp Epidemiol*. 1995;16:287–291.

Alty CT. A historical look at infection control. *RDH*. 1994;14:32–33, 34.

Alty CT. Select protective gear carefully. *RDH*. 1994;14:25–27.

Breathnach AS, de Ruiter A, Holdsworth GM, et al. An outbreak of multi-drug-resistant tuberculosis in a London teaching hospital. *J Hosp Infect*. 1998;39:111–117.

Bryan CS, Brenner ER. Utility of the hospital tuberculosis registry. *Infect Control Hosp Epidemiol*. 1994;15:536–539.

Centers for Disease Control. Immunization of health-care workers: recommendations of the Advisory Committee on Immunization Practices (ACIP) and the Hospital Infection Control Practices Advisory Committee (HICPAC). *MMWR Morb Mortal Wkly Rep*. 1997;46:1–42.

DeJoy DM, Gershon RR, Murphy LR, Wilson MG. A work-systems analysis of compliance with universal precautions among health care workers. *Health Educ Q*. 1996;23:159–174.

Feldman M, Bramson J. What is the cost of office compliance? An ADA survey on OSHA regulations, dentistry. *Dent Teamwork*. 1994;7:26–29.

French AL, Welbel SF, Dietrich SE, et al. Use of DNA fingerprinting to assess tuberculosis infection control. *Ann Intern Med*. 1998;129:856–861.

Garner JS. Guideline for isolation precautions in hospitals, I. evolution of isolation practices, Hospital Infection Control Practices Advisory Committee. *Am J Infect Control*. 1996;24:24–31.

Gittelman EL. An office OSHA inspection—up close and personal. *J NJ Dent Assoc*. 1996;67:26–31.

Grimm EJ, Robinson JF. Biomedical waste rules: their intent, scope, and difference. *J Fla Med Assoc*. 1993;80:541–542.

Hunter S. Your infection control program. *Occup Health Saf*. 1998;67:76–80.

Jarvis WR, Bolyard EA, Bozzi CJ, et al. Respirators, recommendations, and regulations: the controversy surrounding protection of health care workers from tuberculosis. *Ann Intern Med*. 1995;122:142–146.

Kerr CM, Savage GT. Managing exposure to tuberculosis in the PACU: CDC guidelines and cost analysis. *J Perianesth Nurs*. 1996;11:143–146.

Kessler ER. Vaccine-preventable diseases in health care. *Occup Med*. 1997;12:731–739.

Lanphear BP. Transmission and control of bloodborne viral hepatitis in health care workers. *Occup Med*. 1997;12:717–730.

Lerner CJ. Health care worker protection: it is more than HIV. *Urol Nurs*. 1994;14:48–51.

McDiarmid M, Gamponia MJ, Ryan MA, Hirshon JM, Gillen NA, Cox M. Tuberculosis in the workplace: OSHA's compliance experience. *Infect Control Hosp Epidemiol*. 1996;17:159–164.

McDiarmid MA, Gillen NA, Hathon L. Regulatory considerations of occupational tuberculosis control. *Occup Med*. 1994;9:671–679.

McGowan JE Jr. Success, failures and costs of implementing standards in the USA—lessons for infection control. *J Hosp Infect*. 1995;30 (suppl):76–87.

McRae AT, 3rd, Stephens JL. Hepatitis B virus vaccination of medical students: a call for rigorous standards. *JAMA*. 1995;274:1081.

Miller C. CDC immunization policy advocates broad, preventive measures for dental staffs. *RDH*. 1998;18:44–46, 68.

Miller MA, Valway S, Onorato IM. Tuberculosis risk after exposure on airplanes. *Tuber Lung Dis*. 1996;77:414–419.

Muraskin WA. The role of organized labor in combating the hepatitis B and AIDS epidemics: the fight for an OSHA bloodborne pathogens standard. *Int J Health Serv*. 1995; 25:129–152.

Murphy DC, Younai FS. Obstacles encountered in application of the Centers for Disease Control and Prevention guidelines for control of tuberculosis in a large dental center. *Am J Infect Control*. 1997;25:275–282.

Pugliese G, Tapper ML. Tuberculosis control in health care. *Infect Control Hosp Epidemiol*. 1996;17:819–827.

Purtilo RB. Ethical issues in the handling of bloodborne pathogens: evaluating the Occupational Safety & Health Administration Bloodborne Pathogen Standard. *J Intraven Nurs*. 1995;18:S38–S42.

Ramsey PW, McConnell P, Palmer BH, Glenn LL. Nurses' compliance with universal precautions before and after implementation of OSHA regulations. *Clin Nurse Spec*. 1996;10:234–239.

Riley M, Loughrey CM, Wilkinson P, Patterson CC, Varghese G. Tuberculosis in health service employees in Northern Ireland. *Respir Med*. 1997;91:546–550.

Rinnert KJ. A review of infection control practices, risk reduction, and legislative regulations for blood-borne disease: applications for emergency medical services. *Prehosp Emerg Care*. 1998;2:70–75.

Rodrigo T, Cayla JA, Garcia de Olalla P, et al. Characteristics of tuberculosis patients who generate secondary cases. *Int J Tuberc Lung Dis*. 1997;1:352–357.

Runnells R. The downside of infection-control recommendations, guidelines and requirements: legal exposure. *CDS Rev*. 1994;87:31–33.

Sanborn SK. Legal and ethical implications for physicians who treat their own employees. *Mo Med*. 1998;95:127–128.

Semes L. The OSHA bloodborne pathogens standard: implications for optometric practice. *Optom Vis Sci*. 1995;72: 296–298.

Sprouls LS. Developing an infection control training program. *Dent Teamwork*. 1994;7:13–16.

Sullivan JP. Infection control: it doesn't cost, it pays. *CDS Rev*. 1994;87:8–9.

Tereskerz PM, Pearson RD, Jagger J. Occupational exposure to blood among medical students. *N Engl J Med*. 1996;335:1150–1153.

Walls C. Implementing tuberculosis control guidelines in a hospital environment. *NZ Med J*. 1996;109:12–13.

Williams HF. Integrating the Occupational Safety & Health Administration mandates on bloodborne pathogens in the practice setting. *J Intraven Nurs*. 1995;18:S9–S16.

Wiseman GR. The impact of the Occupational Safety & Health Administration regulations on management decision-making strategies. *J Intraven Nurs*. 1995;18:S3–S8.

Yusuf HR, Braden CR, Greenberg AJ, Weltman AC, Onorato IM, Valway SE. Tuberculosis transmission among five school bus drivers and students in two New York counties. *Pediatrics*. 1997;100:E9.

Zaza S, Beck-Sague CM, Jarvis WR. Tracing patients exposed to health care workers with tuberculosis. *Public Health Rep*. 1997;112:153–157.

Americans with Disabilities Act

Aristeiguieta CA. Substance abuse, mental illness, and medical students: the role of the Americans with Disabilities Act. *JAMA*. 1998;279:80.

Bachelder JM, Hilton CL. Implications of the Americans with Disabilities Act of 1990 for elderly persons. *Am J Occup Ther*. 1994;48:73–81.

Blanck PD. Implementing the Americans with Disabilities Act: 1996 follow-up report on Sears, Roebuck and Co. *Spine*. 1996;21:1602–1608.

Blanck PD. Resolving disputes under the Americans with Disabilities Act: a case example of an employee with a back impairment. *Spine*. 1995;20:853–859.

Blanck PD, Butkowski CR. Pregnancy-related impairments and the Americans with Disabilities Act. *Obstet Gynecol Clin North Am*. 1998;25:435–445.

Calfee BE. Health care workers with mental illness: what does the Americans with Disabilities Act offer? *AAOHN J*. 1998;46:221–222.

Carlson B. Americans with Disabilities Act: are you in compliance? *Indiana Med*. 1994;87:276–282.

Dolin LH. How to marshal the power of the Americans with Disabilities Act to minimize your company's exposure to liability to individuals seeking accommodations for "multiple chemical sensitivity disabilities." *Regul Toxicol Pharmacol*. 1996;24:S168–S181.

Eash C. The interview and hiring process according to the Americans with Disabilities Act and the Equal Employment Opportunities Commission, part I. *Am J Orthod Dentofacial Orthop*. 1996;109:570–571.

Egan LW. Americans with Disabilities Act: what the Act mandates for medicine. *Mt Sinai J Med*. 1995;62:85–88; discussion 116–123.

Essex-Sorlie D. The Americans with Disabilities Act, I: history, summary, and key components. *Acad Med*. 1994;69:519–524.

Essex-Sorlie D. The Americans with Disabilities Act, II: implications and suggestions for compliance for medical schools. *Acad Med*. 1994;69:525–534.

Fersh D. Complying with the Americans with Disabilities Act. *J Am Pharm Assoc (Wash)*. 1996;NS36:189–194.

Gloeckler LC. The spirit and intent of the Americans with Disabilities Act. *Optom Vis Sci*. 1995;72:328–331.

Harber P, Fedoruk MJ. Work placement and worker fitness: implications of the Americans with Disabilities Act for pulmonary medicine. *Chest*. 1994;105:1564–1571.

Harber P, Hsu P, Fedoruk MJ. Personal risk assessment under the Americans with Disabilities Act: a decision analysis approach. *J Occup Med*. 1993;35:1000–1010.

Johns RE Jr, Bloswick DS, Elegante JM, Colledge AL. Chronic, recurrent low back pain: a methodology for analyzing fitness for duty and managing risk under the Americans with Disabilities Act. *J Occup Med*. 1994;36:537–547.

Kopelman LM. Ethical assumptions and ambiguities in the Americans with Disabilities Act. *J Med Philos*. 1996;21:187–208.

Kosinski M. The Americans with Disabilities Act: importance to occupational health. *AAOHN J*. 1994;42:8–9.

Kuss CL. Absolving a deadly sin: a medical and legal argument for including obesity as a disability under the Americans with Disabilities Act. *J Contemp Health Law Policy*. 1996;12:563–605.

McRae JC, Yorker B. Update on the Americans with Disabilities Act for occupational health nurses. *AAOHN J*. 1993;41:250–257.

Mechanic D. Cultural and organizational aspects of application of the Americans with Disabilities Act to persons with psychiatric disabilities. *Milbank Q*. 1998;76:5–23.

Mital A, Shrey DE. Cardiac rehabilitation: potential for ergonomic interventions with special reference to return to work and the Americans with Disabilities Act. *Disabil Rehabil*. 1996;18:149–158.

Nethercott JR. Fitness to work with skin disease and the Americans with Disabilities Act of 1990. *Occup Med*. 1994;9:11–18.

Nichols AW. Sports medicine and the Americans with Disabilities Act. *Clin J Sport Med*. 1996;6:190–195.

Parmet WE, Daynard RA, Gottlieb MA. The physician's role in helping smoke-sensitive patients to use the Americans with Disabilities Act to secure smoke-free workplaces and public spaces. *JAMA*. 1996;276:909–913.

Rischitelli DG. Avoiding discriminatory drug testing practices under the Americans with Disabilities Act. *J Leg Med*. 1993;14:597–615.

Scheid TL. The Americans with Disabilities Act, mental disability, and employment practices. *J Behav Health Serv Res*. 1998;25:312–324.

Sfikas PM. What's a 'disability' under the Americans with Disabilities Act? *J Am Dent Assoc*. 1996;127:1406–1408.

Smith JJ, Gay SB. Disabled residency candidates and federal law: implications of the Americans with Disabilities Act. *Acad Radiol*. 1998;5:207–210.

Struthers MS, Raphan M. The impact of the Americans with Disabilities Act on medical licensing and credentialing. *Minn Med*. 1997;80:47–49.

Thompson DL, Thomas KR, Fernandez MS. The Americans with Disabilities Act: social policy and worldwide implications for practice. *Int J Rehabil Res*. 1994;17:109–121.

Weiss L. Compliance by physical medicine and rehabilitation residency applications with the Americans with Disabilities Act, the Civil Rights Act of 1964, and the Rehabilitation Act of 1973: a commentary. *Am J Phys Med Rehabil*. 1997;76:433–434.

General Occupational Medicine

Adams RM. The dermatologist and workers' compensation: theory and practice. *Dermatol Clin*. 1994;12:583–589.

Bellamy R. Compensation neurosis: financial reward for illness as nocebo. *Clin Orthop*. 1997:94–106.

Boden LI. Workers' compensation in the United States: high costs, low benefits. *Annu Rev Public Health*. 1995;16:189–218.

Bondi D. Spotting red flags in workers' compensation cases. *Natl Med Leg J*. 1997;8:6.

Boynton B. Independent medical examinations: analyzing IME reports for workers compensation cases. *Natl Med Leg J*. 1996;7:1, 6–7.

Brooks A, Ward FG. Assessment of disability under the Social Security Industrial Injuries Benefit Scheme. *Occup Med (Oxf)*. 1997;47:112–116.

Brooks A. Occupational disease and injury and state compensation. *J R Soc Health*. 1997;117:123–126.

Calfee BE. Workers' compensation litigation review, part I. *AAOHN J*. 1997;45:609–611.

Calfee BE. Workers' compensation litigation review, part II. *AAOHN J*. 1998;46:45–46.

Cameron SJ. Workers' compensation—what role the doctor? *Med J Aust*. 1996;164:26–27.

Carey TS. Chronic back pain: behavioral interventions and outcomes in a changing healthcare environment. *Behav Med*. 1994;20:113–117.

Carr JD. Workers' compensation systems: purpose and mandate. *Occup Med*. 1998;13:417–422.

Chibnall JT, Tait RC. The Pain Disability Index: factor structure and normative data. *Arch Phys Med Rehabil*. 1994;75:1082–1086.

Choi BC. Recording, notification, compilation, and classification of statistics of occupational accidents and diseases: the Thai experience. *J Occup Environ Med*. 1996;38:1151–1160.

Dembe AE, Himmelstein JS, Stevens BA, Beachler MP. Improving workers' compensation health care. *Health Aff (Millwood)*. 1997;16:253–257.

Engelberg AL. Disability and workers' compensation. *Prim Care*. 1994;21:275–289.

Evans W. Occupational asthma—a lawyer's view. *J R Soc Health*. 1996;116:229–230.

Feinberg JS, Kelley CR. Pregnant workers: a physician's guide to assessing safe employment. *West J Med*. 1998;168:86–92.

Fisher EL, Fuortes LJ, Field RW. Occupational exposure of water-plant operators to high concentrations of radon-222 gas. *J Occup Environ Med*. 1996;38:759–764.

Fox DD, Gerson A, Lees-Haley PR. Interrelationship of MMPI-2 validity scales in personal injury claims. *J Clin Psychol*. 1995;51:42–47.

Gaw DW, Emerson T. Use and misuse of the AMA guides in assessing impairment. *J Tenn Med Assoc.* 1996;89:77–78.

Gots RE. Multiple chemical sensitivities—public policy. *J Toxicol Clin Toxicol.* 1995;33:111–113.

Groves FB, Gallagher LA. What the hand surgeon should know about workers' compensation. *Hand Clin.* 1993;9:369–372.

Harte D, Smith DA. Workers' compensation appeals systems in Canada and the United States. *Occup Med.* 1998;13:423–427.

Hartman DE. Missed diagnoses and misdiagnoses of environmental toxicant exposure: the psychiatry of toxic exposure and multiple chemical sensitivity. *Psychiatr Clin North Am.* 1998;21:659–670, vii.

Hoyt K. Workers' compensation for illness and injury. *J Emerg Nurs.* 1997;23:164.

Hughson WG. Work related disabilities. *Med Sect Proc.* 1994:53–65.

Jarvis KB, Phillips RB, Danielson C. Managed care preapproval and its effect on the cost of Utah worker compensation claims. *J Manipulative Physiol Ther.* 1997;20:372–376.

Johnson WG, Baldwin ML, Burton JF Jr. Why is the treatment of work-related injuries so costly? New evidence from California. *Inquiry.* 1996;33:53–65.

Kasdan ML, Vender MI, Lewis K, Stallings SP, Melhorn JM. Carpal tunnel syndrome: effects of litigation on utilization of health care and physician workload. *J Ky Med Assoc.* 1996;94:287–290.

Katz RT, Rondinelli RD. Impairment and disability rating in low back pain. *Occup Med.* 1998;13:213–230.

Klekamp J, McCarty E, Spengler DM. Results of elective lumbar discectomy for patients involved in the workers' compensation system. *J Spinal Disord.* 1998;11:277–282.

Langworthy JR. Evaluation of impairment related to low back pain. *J Med Syst.* 1993;17:253–256.

Leamon TB, Murphy PL. Occupational slips and falls: more than a trivial problem. *Ergonomics.* 1995;38:487–498.

Lee JR. Medical monitoring damages: issues concerning the administration of medical monitoring programs. *Am J Law Med.* 1994;20:251–275.

Long AB, Brown RS Jr. Workers' compensation introduction for physicians. *Va Med Q.* 1995;122:108–111.

Mah DR. Reducing workers' compensation fraud: a deterrent approach. *Occup Med.* 1998;13:429–438.

Menard MR, Hoens AM. Objective evaluation of functional capacity: medical, occupational, and legal settings. *J Orthop Sports Phys Ther.* 1994;19:249–260.

Michaels D. Fraud in the workers' compensation system: origin and magnitude. *Occup Med.* 1998;13:439–442.

Morrison DL, Wood GA, MacDonald S. Factors influencing mode of claims settlement in workers' compensation cases. *Int J Rehabil Res.* 1995;18:1–18.

Muir DC. Cause of occupational disease. *Occup Environ Med.* 1995;52:289–293.

Muir DC. Compensating occupational diseases: a medical and legal dilemma. *CMAJ.* 1993;148:1903–1905.

National Association of School Nurses, Inc. New position statement: regulations on bloodborne pathogens in the school setting. *Nasnewsletter.* 1997;12:12.

Needleman C. Worker notification: lessons from the past. *Am J Ind Med.* 1993;23:11–23.

Nelson WJ Jr. Disability trends in the United States: a national and regional perspective. *Soc Secur Bull.* 1994;57:27–41.

Nevitt C, Daniell W, Rosenstock L. Workers' compensation for nonmalignant asbestos-related lung disease. *Am J Ind Med.* 1994;26:821–830.

Norris CR. Understanding workers' compensation law. *Hand Clin.* 1993;9:231–239.

Oleinick A, Gluck JV, Guire K. Factors affecting first return to work following a compensable occupational back injury. *Am J Ind Med.* 1996;30:540–555.

Plumb JM, Cowell JW. An overview of workers' compensation. *Occup Med.* 1998;13:241–272.

Pollack R. Update on TB, waterlines, ventilation and ergonomics. *Dent Today.* 1995;14:102–104.

Rainville J, Sobel JB, Hartigan C, Wright A. The effect of compensation involvement on the reporting of pain and disability by patients referred for rehabilitation of chronic low back pain. *Spine.* 1997;22:2016–2024.

Rey P, Bousquet A. Compensation for occupational injuries and diseases: its effect upon prevention at the workplace. *Ergonomics.* 1995;38:475–486.

Robinson JP, Rondinelli RD, Scheer SJ, Weinstein SM. Industrial rehabilitation medicine, 1: why is industrial rehabilitation medicine unique? *Arch Phys Med Rehabil.* 1997;78:S3–S9.

Rudd R. Coal miners' respiratory disease litigation. *Thorax.* 1998;53:337–340.

Sbordone RJ, Seyranian GD, Ruff RM. Are the subjective complaints of traumatically brain injured patients reliable? *Brain Inj.* 1998;12:505–515.

Shinozaki T, Yano E. Results of pneumoconiosis examination—different trends among industries. *Ind Health.* 1995;33:23–27.

Slabber CF, Davies JC. Reporting occupational disease. *S Afr Med J.* 1994;84:127–128.

Stout NC. Do workers' compensation laws protect industrial hygienists from lawsuits by injured workers? *Am Ind Hyg Assoc J.* 1993;54:701–704.

Tammelleo AD. Does workers' compensation cover on the job heart attack? *Regan Rep Nurs Law.* 1997;38:4.

Valat JP, Goupille P, Vedere V. Low back pain: risk factors for chronicity. *Rev Rhum Engl Ed.* 1997;64:189–194.

Voiss DV. Occupational injury: fact, fantasy, or fraud? *Neurol Clin.* 1995;13:431–446.

Wyman ET, Cats-Baril WL. Working it out: recommendations from a multidisciplinary national consensus panel on medical problems in workers' compensation. Committee on Occupational Health, American Academy of Orthopedic Surgeons. *J Occup Med.* 1994;36:144–154.

Yorker B. Workers' compensation law: an overview. *AAOHN J.* 1994;42:420–424.

CHAPTER 16

Institutional Medicine

HIGHLIGHTS

- Health care practitioners treating prisoners must respect their patient's autonomy, within the bounds of prison regulations.
- Prisoners have the right to consent to and refuse medical care, but these rights are limited.
- Team physicians must always put the interests of the player first.
- Team and school physicians must be aware of the special duties involved in treating minors.
- School physicians must respect their patient's privacy and the parents' right to oversee their children's care.

INTRODUCTION

Institutional practitioners are health care practitioners who work for an entity whose interests are sometimes adverse to their patients' interests. The most common institutional practice is occupational medicine, which is reviewed in Chapter 15. This chapter discusses prisons, sports teams, and schools. These represent a continuum, with prisons having the greatest conflict between the institution and the patients, and schools having the least. When health care practitioners practicing in these environments balance their duty to the patient against their duty to the institution and the community, they must not confuse public safety issues with institutional convenience. For example, prison health care practitioners should not drug patients just to keep them quiet, but must not hesitate in diagnosing and treating communicable diseases that may spread in the prison setting. School physicians face the same dilemma when requested to recommend Ritalin to quiet an unruly student.

The team and school physicians share the conflict between institutional obligations and the fiduciary duty to the individual patient. This conflict is exacerbated because many patients are unable to make knowing choices of treatment. Often the patients are minors. In others, the coercive atmosphere of team sports makes it difficult for individual athletes to resist the pressure to compete when it is medically inadvisable. School and team physicians must be careful to protect their adult patients' autonomy. When the patient is a minor, the physician may have to intercede to protect the child from the pressure of overly competitive parents and coaches.

THE PRISON DOCTOR

Over the last 30 years, the role of prison physicians has changed dramatically. Being the doctor for the county jail used to be a relatively easy job. The position was frequently filled by a physician who had retired from private practice. Prisoners were viewed as having little right to medical care, and there was not much concern about its quality. Even incompetent physicians were usually immunc from suits for medical malpractice because, as governmental employees, they enjoyed immunity for many of their actions.

Prisons are now highly regulated. (This chapter will use *prison* as a generic term for all correctional and detention facilities.) State and federal court cases, combined with legislation, set minimum standards for medical care in prisons and jails. The first effect of these standards was to end most medical experiments on prisoners. In addition, the standards ensure that inmates receive adequate medical care and make it easier to sue physicians and others involved in improperly run prison medical programs. Despite these regulations, prison conditions are deteriorating in many parts of the country. Prisons are overcrowded, and inmates are increasingly HIV infected secondary to the drug abuse that may have led to their incarceration.

Prison Medical Care

Our most fundamental constitutional right is that no person may be deprived of life, liberty, or property without due process of law. When an individual is deprived of liberty by the state, the state assumes the responsibility for caring for the basic needs of that individual. A prisoner is unable to go out and get food and water, so the state must provide it. If the state did not provide it, the prisoner would be deprived of life. This is also the basis for a prisoner's right to medical care: a prisoner deprived of necessary medical care may be deprived of life or health. It is the extent of this constitutional right to care that is at issue.

The legal standard for judging the adequacy of prison medical care delivered by state employees is whether there is a deliberate indifference to the prisoners' welfare. (Health care practitioners who work for private contractors are liable for ordinary malpractice.) The prisoner need not show that the prison officials intend harm through inadequate or improper medical care. A mere showing of malpractice is not enough, however. The legal standard for prison medical care is much lower than the standard for free persons. This poses an ethical dilemma for prison health care practitioners: when is it ethically permissible to provide lower-quality medical care for prisoners? Although the easy answer is "never," there are few prisons that will fund community standard medical care for prisoners. Is it unethical for physicians to work for these institutions, or is it better to provide the care that is possible under the limited circumstances?

Physician–Prisoner Relationship

The physician–prisoner relationship is different from the traditional physician–patient relationship. The physician–prisoner relationship is not a fiduciary relationship. Legally, it most closely resembles the relationship between a public health physician and a patient. In both cases, the physician's first duty is to the health and safety of the community rather than to the patient. Prison officials have broad discretion to preserve order in the prison. Prisoners lose most of their rights to privacy along with their liberty. Prison officials have a right to any information a physician may obtain that would affect the health and safety of the prison community.

Although prisoners have little expectation of privacy, they do have an expectation that their physician will exercise independent medical judgment regarding the diagnosis and treatment of their medical conditions. The correctional staff should not be in the position of dictating medical care decisions. Under no circumstances should access to proper medical care be used as a disciplinary tool. The prison officials do have the right to ensure that prisoners do not use untreated illness to avoid prison discipline and that prisoners' medical conditions do not interfere with prison order.

Right To Refuse Medical Care

Prisoners have a liberty interest, protected by the Fourteenth Amendment, in not being treated against their will. The extent of this liberty interest was defined in *Washington v. Harper*,[1] a case arising from a prisoner's objection to being given antipsychotic medications. The Washington prison system provided elaborate administrative protections before an inmate could be medicated against his will. The Washington Supreme Court rejected these administrative protections as inadequate and required that an inmate be given a full adversarial hearing before being treated against his will:

> The [Washington Supreme] Court concluded that the "highly intrusive nature" of treatment with antipsychotic medications warranted greater procedural protections.... It held that, under the Due Process Clause, the State could administer antipsychotic medication to a competent, nonconsenting inmate only if, in a judicial hearing at which the inmate had the full panoply of adversarial procedural protections, the State proved by "clear, cogent, and convincing" evidence that the administration of antipsychotic medication was both necessary and effective for furthering a compelling state interest.[2]

Mr. Harper, the prisoner who brought this action, claimed that the prison authorities could not medicate him unless he was found to be mentally incompetent in an adversarial hearing. He further alleged that even if he was found to be incompetent, he could be medicated only if the fact finder determined that he would have consented to the medication had he been competent. The U.S. Supreme Court rejected these claims, finding that the prison's policy was constitutionally adequate. The Court's rationale for endorsing the prison's policy is relevant to the general problem of prison health because it accepts expert decision making as a substitute for adversarial decision making.

The Court reviewed the Washington Supreme Court's decision to determine what facts would support a decision to force antipsychotic medication on a prisoner and what procedural protections were necessary to determine those facts. It agreed that Harper had a liberty interest in not being medicated against his will. However, the Court held that this liberty interest was sufficiently protected by the prison's administrative proceeding, which required that a psychiatrist certify the treatment's appropriateness.

The Court's acceptance of expert decision making as a substitute for an adversary hearing seems to be rooted in the limited autonomy granted to prisoners. The Court found that a prisoner's right to refuse antipsychotic medication was limited by the conditions of his confinement. In particular, the Court found that the purpose of the prison's medication policy was "to diagnose and treat convicted felons, with the desired goal being that they will recover to the point where they can function in a normal prison environment."

The Court in *Harper* balanced the prisoner's best interests against the prison's interest in returning him to the general prisoner population and his punishment. The role of the expert decision maker, the prison psychiatrist, was to ensure that the prisoner was mentally ill and dangerous and that medication was appropriate to remedying these conditions. The protection of the prisoner's interests was left to the integrity of the prison psychiatrist. The Court's finding that expert decision making satisfied the prisoner's due process interests reflects the Court's general reticence to interfere in matters of prison safety and security.

Prisoners retain some right to refuse medical care after *Harper,* but this is severely circumscribed as compared with the rights of a nonprisoner patient. Prisoners may not refuse testing or treatment for a condition that would threaten the health and safety of the prison community, these including communicable diseases and treatable psychiatric conditions. Prisoners may also be forced to accept treatment that is necessary to protect their health from permanent injury. Prisoners with religious objections to medical treatment may be treated against these objections if the treatment is necessary to preserve prison discipline.

For prisoners in Federal Bureau of Prisons facilities, there are specific regulations governing care provided without or against the prisoner's informed consent. These regulations deal with a specific judicial process for such care involving infectious diseases or mental illness. There are also provisions for emergency care. Although these regulations may not apply in other facilities, they set a medical and a legal standard for handling such cases that state and local correctional facilities would be wise to adopt or adapt to their specific situations.

Emergency Medical Care

The weakest part of most jail medical programs, especially small programs without full-time physician supervision, is the evaluation and treatment of acute injuries and illnesses. These are most common in the drunk tank: a large room where those who are intoxicated and other prisoners are held until they post bond. The drunk tank is an ongoing source of unnecessary deaths and accompanying liability suits against local governments and physicians. Neither police officers nor physicians can visually distinguish an intoxicated prisoner with a mild bump on his head from a severe head injury patient who has had a couple of drinks. Diabetic coma and a drunken stupor look and smell very much alike. Most physicians know this; most police officers do not.

Considering the extent to which alcohol is involved in traffic accidents and crimes of violence, it is hard to think of any profession with more experience with drunkenness than law enforcement. The vast majority of those who are intoxicated have no acute medical problems, so it is not reasonable to expect police officers to learn to do a medical evaluation on every intoxicated person they arrest. No one, however, should be locked up without such an evaluation. This means that every prisoner who appears intoxicated at the time of arrest should be taken to the jail physician or practitioner on duty before being put in a cell. The jail physician should review the protocols for treating intoxication frequently and should be sure that they are being followed carefully. Evaluating a lot of prisoners is the price for preventing jail cell deaths from diabetes, and picking up the head injuries early may protect the officers from accusations of brutality in the jails.

Experimentation

For most purposes, the use of healthy prisoners as medical research subjects has stopped in this country. The reason is that a prisoner cannot freely consent to being a research subject. The situation is coercive by its nature. If prisoners are good research subjects for a particular experiment, they will assume that participating will bring favors from the jailers and refusing to participate will bring retribution. Research on prisoners is highly regulated by the Department of Health and Human Services. At the very least, prisoners should never be used as research subjects without careful appropriate institutional review board approval.

Public Health and Safety in Prisons

Prisons pose unique public and mental health problems. Many prisoners are poorly educated, of limited intelligence, behaviorally impaired, and often drug addicted. They are crowded together in communal facilities with marginal provisions for sanitation. In some systems, nearly 20% of newly incarcerated prisoners are HIV infected, posing a direct risk to other prisoners through sexual assault. Indirectly, HIV infection poses a risk through its suppression of normal immune system function, increasing the chance of infection with diseases such as tuberculosis that are easily spread to others. More critically, providing humane care for HIV-infected prisoners is outstripping the prison health resources in the states with substantial HIV-infected prisoner populations.

Disease Control in Prisons

Every prisoner who will be incarcerated for longer than a few hours should be screened for communicable diseases, including tuberculosis and sexually transmitted diseases (STDs), because transmission is common in prison populations. The prison population is predominantly young, single males who have a high prevalence of venereal infections. These infections should be identified and treated to protect the health of the infected prisoner and to prevent the spread of disease in the prison. Prisoners should also be screened for HIV and hepatitis because of the high infection rates among drug addicts.

Beyond these common diseases, prison physicians should work with local health authorities to determine which other communicable diseases are prevalent in their prison population. Ideally, prisoners with inadequate immunization histories would be immunized against tetanus, measles, and other childhood diseases. An admission physical should also screen for chronic diseases or conditions that might cause problems if they remain untreated. Since work will be part of prison life in most cases, the prison physician should look for any disabling conditions that might require special consideration. Just as prisoners are entitled to expect reasonable care for acute problems, they are entitled to expect that their prison work will not endanger their health.

It is wise for any jail or prison to have comprehensive policies for control of certain communicable diseases, particularly tuberculosis, hepatitis, and HIV. Without formal policies, decisions tend to be made in the heat of the moment on nonmedical grounds. This ad hoc disease control is usually ineffective and can be expensive. For instance, if there is no policy for immunizing staff against hepatitis and no determination of who is at risk for contracting hepatitis, then there is likely to be a large demand for gamma globulin shots every time a prisoner develops jaundice. In addition to the cost of the shots, the institution that perpetuates the myth that hepatitis can be spread by casual contact may find itself paying for every case of community-acquired hepatitis among its employees as a workers' compensation claim.

Prison communicable disease policies should be developed in conjunction with state and local public health authorities. In most instances, the prison physician is not exempt from the communicable disease control laws of the state, including reporting laws. Telling the county sheriff that there is tuberculosis in the jail is not the same as telling the county health officer. As a practical matter, the prisoner and his or her disease is probably well known to the local public health clinics. Getting current records can save a lot of time, effort, and money.

Communicable disease control policies must protect inmates from infection while not unduly interfering with the rights of the infected prisoners. HIV-infected prisoners must be identified to ensure that they receive proper preventive medical care, but there are no disease control justifications for isolating them unless they pose a risk of sexual assault to other prisoners. In contrast to HIV, tuberculosis is a severe problem in prisons and demands both aggressive investigation of outbreaks and the isolation of infectious prisoners. The federal courts have found that failing to protect prisoners from tuberculosis violates the requirements of the U.S. Constitution. The National Center for Prevention Services of the Centers for Disease Control and Prevention has prepared a monograph "Controlling TB in Correctional Facilities," which should be part of every correctional medicine program.

The Physician's Obligations to the Jailers

As with other institutional settings, physicians should request a written description of their duties before accepting a position. For example, some jurisdictions have specific arrangements in the jail health system or with the county hospital system to take blood samples and other specimens from criminal suspects. Physicians accepting a position in prison health should know whether they will be called upon to obtain such biologic evidence and to provide court-ordered medical testing and involuntary treatment.

Independent contractor physicians do not enjoy governmental immunity from suit in the way that governmental employee prison officials do. Such physicians should be particularly careful not to compromise their professional standards when caring for prisoners. Care that would be protected from suit if performed by an employee of the prison system may be actionable if performed by an independent physician. Contract physicians should also ask the prison authorities to indemnify them for legal expenses and lost time if they are named as parties in civil rights litigation against the prison medical care system. Such actions may not be covered by medical malpractice insurance. Without such an agreement, a private physician may have to spend tens of thousands of dollars and hundreds of hours of uncompensated time defending actions taken on behalf of the prison.

THE TEAM DOCTOR

Sports medicine was once the province of a few physicians serving professional sports teams. It has spread as a specialty through the professionalization of college and high school athletics and through the popularization of high-performance athletics for personal fitness. The sports medicine physician must balance the issues of long-term health with short-term performance. This compromise is not new to sports medicine, but it has become controversial as questionable practices such as the use of steroids, local anesthetics, and various forms of doping have come to the attention of the public. Sports medicine poses substantial legal problems, particularly when it is practiced on children.

The team physician has a more ambiguous role than the sports medicine physician who treats individual athletes but has no involvement with organized sports teams. The team physician's job has become more difficult as the notion of amateur athletics has been displaced by professionalism in all but name. College football is run as a farm club for professional teams. In large high schools, the coach who in the past might have been an ex-football player and taught in the school system has been replaced by highly specialized coaching staffs with trainers and big budgets. The responsibilities of the team doctor have changed from being available to treat injuries at the weekly game to an ongoing responsibility for the development and care of the athletes. These coaches train their players for professional-style play and expect team physicians to minister to them as if they were professional athletes. This situation creates a conflict of interest for the physician when the athletes are legally and physiologically children.

The Physician–Player Relationship

Team physicians' duties are to their patients as individuals, not to the team or to the school. The physician must have proper consent to provide medical care and must respect patient confidentiality. No matter how interested the coach may be in a star athlete, he or she has no right to participate in the medical care of the athlete without the patient's permission. Medical decisions must be made on medical grounds by the physician responsible for the care.

The most difficult decision in sports medicine is determining when to allow injured athletes to play. The football player with a sprained ankle may miss the entire season if his activities are limited for as long as is usual in nonathletes. If he is allowed to play too soon, he has a greater chance of reinjuring the ankle and being disabled for a longer time. Blanket prohibitions on play for an extended period may encourage the athlete to ignore the physician's advice altogether. If the athlete is an adult who can understand the risks of playing while injured, the physician may only need to provide accurate information on the risks of continued play. If the athlete is a child, the situation is more complicated. The parents must be involved in the decision and must be given full information about the risks.

When sports medicine physicians are dealing with athletes with less information and support than are available to professionals, they should be more conservative in balancing the need to get back to play against the probability of impairing permanent healing. For example, if a sprain can be adequately supported by tape, the athlete should be taught to tape and be allowed to play. If an injury would heal without surgery but surgery will speed the process, the athlete may choose to be operated on. Although a physician may aid a professional athlete in a calculated decision to compromise future healing for short-term gain, this should not be done for college and high school players. Using pain killers or steroids to get the player back on the field when this endangers permanent recovery is bad medicine and legally risky. The promising player who wants to be in the game when the pro scout is there will not be grateful if that game is his last because his injury becomes permanent.

Team versus Player

Team physicians face the ethical problem of determining when it is appropriate to compromise an athlete's long-term health for short-term performance. Informed consent is at the heart of this problem. A physician must be sure that the athlete understands the long-term consequences of the recommended medical treatment or lack of treatment. Physicians who do not tell patients the risks of treatments that allow an athlete to compete when it is medically contraindicated face substantial malpractice liability. If there is evidence that the coach encouraged the physician to withhold information about the risks of treatment, the physician may face punitive damages for fraud.

An equally difficult problem is the degree to which players exercise the free choice that is necessary for an informed consent. There is pressure to maintain team performance, irrespective of the risk to the individual. Players who will not take risks for the team do not last long in the starting lineup. It is arguable whether consent given out of the fear of ending one's career is coerced. Conversely, physicians are limited in their right to impose their values on patients. The decision to risk disability by continuing play is the reasoned choice of some athletes.

Athletes in highly competitive, commercialized sports such as football are under constant pressure to play when injured and to submit to risky surgery rather than prolonged convalescence. The risks posed by these actions are much the same for all athletes. The benefits, however, are vastly different, depending on the athlete's status. A veteran professional football player is protected by a pension system and extensive knowledge of the consequences of various injuries. Such a player is paid very well to accept the risk of permanent injury.

Moving back in the athletic hierarchy to college teams, players have little protection if their injuries are permanently disabling. The college athlete faces the pressure to play but with limited benefit as compared with the risk. This is a special problem for athletes who are able to attend college only because of athletics. If they aggravate an injury and are unable to play, few will stay in college as regular students even if they can continue their scholarship. Since the probability of a given college athlete's entering professional athletics is small, it is

difficult to justify the risk of aggravating an injury to play an extra few games in a season.

The Child Athlete

College and high school athletes pose additional problems. Persons under the age of 18 are legally able to make their own medical decisions only in certain situations established by state law. Most states allow minors to consent to treatment for substance abuse, communicable diseases, pregnancy, and other conditions that pose a threat to persons other than the minor. No state specifically authorizes minors to consent to treatment for sports injuries. Sports medicine may not be practiced on minors without parental consent and this parental consent is constrained by the child welfare laws.

Parents may consent only to medical care that is in the child's best interest. If a physician believes that a medical regime chosen by the parents is not in the child's best interest, the physician must report this to the child welfare authorities. Children themselves are unable to balance the desire to get back in the game against the risk of permanent injury. A child who is later unable to continue in athletics or is otherwise disabled may sue the physician for malpractice. Physicians should not allow the enthusiasm of child athletes or their parents to weigh in medical decisions that will affect the long-term health of the child. Most parents will not persist if they are fully informed as to the risks of continued participation by an injured child. If the parents continue to pressure the child to engage in unsafe activity, then this becomes a matter of child abuse.

Supervision of Nonphysician Personnel

In most cases, the physician is not a full-time employee of the team. Most routine first aid and training programs are carried out by nonphysician personnel. This creates the same liability issues as supervision of nonphysician personnel in other medical settings.

Trainers were once a luxury reserved for professional athletes and world-class amateurs. Today large high schools often employ trainers on their coaching staffs, and professional coaches are also taught these skills. The trainer is both an athletic coach and a medical assistant. Treating minor injuries, doing physical therapy, and overseeing such preventive measures as taping and reconditioning are all part of the trainer's job. Consequently, the team physician must oversee the activities of the trainer in the same way that the physician would supervise a nurse or a physical therapist. This is a politically sensitive issue because trainers are usually given a free hand in both diagnosing and treating medical conditions. That trainers violate the medical practice act in many states is usually ignored by the state boards of medical examiners. When a physician is involved, however, infractions by the trainer are grounds to discipline the supervising physician, and they subject the physician to medical malpractice liability. Physicians must ensure that trainers comply with applicable scope-of-practice laws.

The team physician may not delegate control of prescription medications to a nonphysician. Providing the trainer with a bottle of codeine tablets to use when someone gets hurt is illegal. As with other drug law violations, there is a high probability that the physician will face criminal charges if the practice is discovered. Although narcotics are the most likely to lead to trouble, there is increasing scrutiny of prescriptions for other drugs, particularly steroids. Prescriptions can be written for direct use only by the affected individual. If a physician wishes to stock and dispense medication, it must be done in compliance with the pharmacy laws of the state. Writing a prescription for office use and letting the trainer dispense the drugs is no longer acceptable practice, nor is allowing nonphysicians to distribute samples of prescription drugs.

Performance Enhancement

The most controversial issue in sports medicine is performance enhancement beyond what can be achieved by proper nutrition and general conditioning. The publicity has focused on drugs: first

amphetamines, now steroids, next human growth hormone and other genetic engineering products. The problems are not limited to drugs. Biomechanics and the use of direct muscle stimulation tools are changing the nature of training and allowing the selective overdevelopment of muscle groups. Improperly used, these techniques can increase the probability of injury and disability.

Taking drugs to improve athletic performance has been publicly deplored but privately practiced for years. It has become a risky practice for both the athlete and the physician. Most competitive athletic organizations have rules against any use of drugs or doping to enhance performance. Urine testing has become cheap, quick, and easy. The athlete who gets caught is likely to be excluded from participation for some time. Blood doping is less easily detected but may be more dangerous. Even the use of the patient's own blood can be risky. Physicians should remember that it is unethical and usually illegal to prescribe for nontherapeutic purposes. As drug enforcement programs adopt zero-tolerance policies, physicians with questionable prescribing habits can expect to face investigation and prosecution.

Engineering People

Medicine has a history of bad therapies that failed because they tried to subvert the natural human growth or healing processes. We are appalled by the practices of societies that produce physical deformity for a perceived social good. We would not allow the castrating of young boys who sing well so that they can continue to sing soprano. We would not allow parents to bind the feet of infant girls to produce a lotus foot. Yet it is not clear how far this society will go to prevent the use of medical and hormonal techniques to alter normal development to produce a better athlete.

Physicians who practice sports medicine on children should be very careful about interfering with natural development. Modern training techniques and machines have made it possible to alter the balance of muscle function in a way that natural exercise cannot. Drugs and hormones can be used to change the very processes of growth.

These changes can have unexpected and undesirable side effects. What seems reasonable during training or performance may appear unreasonable in later years if it results in permanent deformity or disability. The engineering of people to improve athletic performance may appear to the adult athlete or the jury as abhorrent as castrating boy sopranos. Physicians should be cautious about recommending any nontherapeutic interventions in athletes who are not fully grown.

SCREENING FOR PARTICIPATION

The other area of sports medicine that has received a lot of attention is screening for health conditions that might endanger the young athlete. In recent years there have been several highly publicized cases of athletes dropping dead during sports activities. In hindsight, some of these deaths would have been prevented if the medical management of a heart condition had taken precedence over the pressure to play. Most states require that public school athletes have some medical screening before athletic participation. Unfortunately, few states have adequate requirements for the content of the screening and/or for who is allowed to do the screening.

Thirty years ago we lost many student athletes to heat stroke every year, particularly in the South and Southwest. A concerted effort to educate coaches and trainers about prevention and treatment has made heat stroke among athletes an uncommon occurrence today. Today, most sudden deaths during athletic participation are cardiac deaths. Many of the athletes who die have warning signs or symptoms that could be detected on a proper screening exam. The American Heart Association publishes consensus guidelines for athletic screening. Every physician who does routine screening for athletic participation should follow these guidelines and the recommendations of the American Academy of Pediatrics. Doing the minimum required by the school is not acceptable medical practice. The physician should keep in mind that signing that school physical is saying that the child is healthy enough to participate in the athletic activities without endangering life or health. The national medical standards are what the physician will be judged by if the child is injured by inadequate screening.

THE SCHOOL DOCTOR

There are two distinct types of school medicine practice. The more common is practiced in nonresidential elementary and secondary schools. This practice is a combination of pediatrics, emergency medicine, and public health. Large school districts usually employ a physician to direct the school health programs and oversee the nursing staff. Smaller districts rely on physicians in the community to provide these services as paid consultants or as unpaid volunteers. The second practice type is school medicine programs in residential schools—usually in colleges but in some elementary and secondary boarding schools. The basic problems are the same in both settings, but the physician's responsibilities are greater in the residential settings.

Supervisory Responsibilities

Only the largest school health programs employ physicians to deliver direct patient care. In most programs, the primary role of the school physician is to supervise nonphysician personnel: school nurses, dietitians, coaches, and trainers. In some smaller districts, the school physician also may need to oversee food sanitation in the lunch room and zoonosis problems in vocational agriculture classes.

Most states require nurses, child health associates, physicians' assistants, and other such personnel to be supervised by a physician. If the school employs personnel (or uses volunteers) who may not practice without physician supervision, the duty to supervise these personnel will flow to any physician who is nearby. The legal theory for this responsibility by proximity is called *ostensible agency*. This means that if it appears to the patient that the physician is supervising the personnel, the law will hold that physician responsible. Since ostensible agency is judged from the patient's perspective, a contract between the physician and the school to exclude such supervision will not obviate the physician's responsibility. Explicitly declining to supervise a given activity may not be enough. The physician must not become involved with the activity in such a way as to appear to supervise it. For this reason, all school physicians should have their supervisory responsibilities listed and described in a contract. The contracts should provide for the supervision of all personnel who may require it under state law to protect both the physician and the other personnel.

The school physician has a duty to ensure that all the medical professionals that he or she supervises are competent, adequately trained, and practicing within the limits of the law. Disciplining a nurse may be difficult if the nurse reports to a nursing supervisor or other administrator who is not responsible to the physician. If a supervising physician has reason to believe that a nurse is practicing in an incompetent or illegal manner, the physician must stop the practices or resign. The physician cannot defend improper supervision by blaming nonphysician administrators.

School Clinics

Increasingly, acute care clinics, which provide preventive services and care for minor illnesses, are being placed in nonresidential school facilities. Unlike the nurse's office, where students are sent so the nurse can call home, these clinics establish a provider–patient relationship with the students. The physicians and nurses in the clinic have the same legal responsibilities that they would have in a private office. If the clinic is part of the school health program, it is the school doctor's responsibility. If the clinic is a separate entity, it must have its own supervising physician.

Physicians overseeing a school clinic should ensure that there are proper protocols, policies, and procedures for the staff of the clinic just as they would for any other outreach clinic or physician extender. There should be formal agreements on the scope of practice within the clinic and provision for appropriate follow up for problems that go beyond this scope of practice. The physician

should not lose sight of the fact that he or she is assuming all the responsibilities of the physician–patient relationship for the patients who use the clinic. This includes the duties of continued treatment and proper referral.

Consent to Care

The general rules of consent to care for minors apply to school children. The emergency exception, legally mandated care, proxy consent, and prior consent of parents all apply in various school situations.

Parents may sign a proxy consent for medical care if it is required when the child is at school. These often ask for information on preferred physicians and hospitals. All residential schools with students under the age of 18 should require that a proxy consent be part of the student's admission materials. The extent to which the proxy consent should be relied upon depends on the circumstances and the difficulty of contacting the parents. A physician treating children in a neighborhood public school should rely on proxy consent only to deliver urgent care until the children's parents can be contacted. (This type of care is usually sheltered under the emergency exception anyway.) If the children are in a residential school and their parents are out of the country, the proxy consent will have to cover all routine and emergency medical care. Such extensive consent is best documented by a power of attorney to consent to the child's medical care.

If a child is seriously ill or injured, the emergency exception to the need for consent generally applies. Reasonable attempts should be made to contact the child's parents and to follow their wishes in selecting caregivers, but these should not interfere with getting the child prompt emergency care. The school system should have a formal policy, and preferably a written contract, for ambulance services for children who are seriously ill or injured. Schools need not wait for parental permission to call an ambulance. Paying the ambulance fee is much less expensive than settling the claim on the broken neck that became a spinal cord injury when the teacher carried the child into the office.

Medicines at School

School health programs should be cautious about inserting themselves between a physician and a patient or between a parent and a child when providing medical care for children. It has become common practice to take medicines away from school children and insist that the child come to the office or the nurse for treatment. If the school is prepared to take responsibility for administering the medicine properly and on time and if the teacher or nurse can be sure that the child leaves with the medicine so that nighttime doses can be given, the school may not increase its legal risks by doing this. It also does not reduce its risks.

This policy can lead to major problems for the school in two situations. If the school nurse or physician does not agree with the prescriptions of the attending physician and prevents the child from following the physician's orders, then the school personnel would be liable for any harm that came to the child because of the lack of medical care. A school nurse or doctor who substituted other medical care for that prescribed by the attending physician would be liable for rendering care without legal consent. It is wise to remember that for a physician or a nurse, telling a patient not to do something is an act of medical judgment.

The other serious problem involves situations when it is medically important that the patient control his or her own medications. The asthmatic child cannot use inhalers on demand if the inhalers are in the nurse's office. The attack that could have been aborted by the inhaler in the pocket may require emergency care in the time it takes to find the person with the key to the medicine locker.

If responsibility is a central issue in the patient's care, then no amount of planning by the school nurse can make up for the harm done by removing medications. Adolescents with diabetes are typically very hard to maintain in control. They shift from denial to dependence very quickly. They must cooperate with their physicians and their parents and a host of others. If the school officials are not active participants in this child's care program, they should not interject themselves into the care.

Athletics

The information elsewhere in this chapter about being a team doctor applies whether the physician takes on the team separately or as part of the work of the school doctor. Physicians who are considering accepting a position as a school physician should find out whether they are expected to care for athletes. If the school engages in any form of athletic activity and does not have a separate sports medicine system, the school health physician will be assumed to be supervising the sports medicine program.

Medical and Public Health Responsibilities

The federal and state governments use schools as the vehicle to enforce various public health laws directed at children. States have customarily required proof of immunization for childhood diseases for school admission. Some states are mandating that schools screen children for personal health problems. State laws also provide schools with the authority to screen and exclude students to prevent the spread of communicable diseases. The controversies over school children with HIV have sensitized the public to communicable diseases in schools. This has forced school physicians to become a front line force in community disease control.

All states require that physicians report communicable diseases to the public health department. Most also require reporting of outbreaks of any disease that may be caused by infection, infestation, or environmental hazards, particularly if they occur in a school. School physicians have personal responsibility for seeing that the reports are made. Normally, the school nurses will do the actual tallying and reporting of routine cases such as influenza or chicken pox. They should report unusual disease problems to the school physician immediately.

Every school needs a detailed, written policy on the management of students with communicable diseases. Schools have the right and duty to screen and restrict students infected with diseases that pose a risk to other students, but they cannot use this power to remove students who pose a political problem rather than a communicable disease problem. For example, a student with asymptomatic HIV infection does not pose a risk to other students. This student must be allowed to stay in school without restrictions unless the student is violent due to dementia or has a secondary disease, such as infectious tuberculosis.

Screening

A variety of screening programs are carried out in schools. Some of these, such as scoliosis screening, are of questionable medical importance. Others, such as vision and hearing testing, are very important but overinclusive. These programs must be combined with reliable follow-up systems for all positive findings. The follow-up examination may be done by the school physician, but it is preferable to refer the child to a personal physician or clinic that can oversee treatment and continued evaluation.

Physicians who receive these referrals should make a careful evaluation of any abnormalities detected on screening and notify the school of the disposition of the referral unless the child's parents object. School physicians must ensure that the child keeps the referral appointment and is properly evaluated.

Handicapped Children

Handicapped children have special rights under federal law. School physicians are often caught between the needs of the handicapped child and the limited resources of the school district. Special education programs and facilities for the handicapped are expensive. If the school district employs only one speech therapist, the physician will be pressured to limit the diagnosis of significant speech defect to the number of children this therapist can treat. Since handicapped children are protected by federal law and seldom pose a threat to other students, the school physician's duty is clearly to the student rather than to the school. The diagnosis of articulation defect must be based on

an objective evaluation of the speech performance of the individual child, not on the willingness of the school to provide services.

Physicians must not compare one child with another to determine which will be referred for special help or care. If both children require therapy, that should be the physician's recommendation. If there are not sufficient resources to provide for all the handicapped children, then it is the duty of the school district to find the resources. The physician cannot legally or morally withhold a diagnosis in order to withhold special care. Irrespective of state law immunity for schools, a physician who did so as a matter of routine might be sued under the federal civil rights act for violating the child's rights.

College Health Programs

College students face many of the same health problems as younger students, but the legal problems are more complicated. The college student is often away from home and without the usual support system in times of illness. Dormitories do not provide chicken broth and dry toast to every student with the flu. They may even be the source of food poisoning, measles, epidemic respiratory disease.

As in other school settings, the physician's duty is to the patient, not the institution. If the college food service is a frequent source of food poisoning, the college physician should insist that something be done to correct the problem. Physicians must not change the diagnosis from food poisoning to gastroenteritis of unknown origin to avoid political problems. They should work with the college administration to address particular health problems, but medical judgments should not be compromised for administrative convenience.

Issues of consent and confidentiality do not change when the patient is a college student. All residential schools should have a power of attorney to consent to medical care for students who are still minors. It is risky to assume that they will all stay healthy until they reach their majority. This is especially important for minors who are far from home, particularly international students.

It is also useful for students who are not minors to consider a power of attorney to consent to medical care if their parents are not readily available or if they do not want their parents involved in their medical care decisions.

College physicians must respect the students' confidentiality. The fact that a parent may be paying the tuition or medical bills does not give the parent the right to medical information about a child who is not a minor. At the same time, the parents of a college student have the reasonable expectation that they will be contacted if the student is in trouble or requires significant medical care. The university should require students to sign a waiver that allows it to contact the student's parents in such circumstances. (The university should allow exceptions for students who are estranged from their parents.) For certain kinds of care, such as treatment for drug abuse or venereal disease, the information should be protected unless the student requests that parents be notified. However, students must understand that they may have to pay for the care if they want to keep it confidential. The physician should explain to students who ask that something not appear on a bill that few parents and no insurance company will pay for unspecified services.

Comprehensive Care

Many college physicians are caught in a dilemma between the medical needs and the financial problems of students. With rising tuition and fees for education, many administrators are loath to require all students to show that they are covered by health insurance. The expectation of both students and administrators is that the student health service will take care of most health problems. The student's failure to buy insurance does not relieve the physician of responsibility for providing quality medical care. The student health service and the individual physicians should set policies for dealing with students who are unable to pay for necessary medical care.

For residential students with major medical problems, physicians must consider whether the student can stay in school. If the student is hospitalized or otherwise completely unable to attend school, the decision is obvious. The issue becomes one of where and when to transfer the patient for ongoing care.

For students with less severe problems, the decision is more difficult. Most people do not choose a school based on the availability of medical care. However, if the student has a major disease requiring care that is unavailable at or near the school, the potential for crisis is great. Student health physicians should be cautious about accepting responsibility for caring for students with problems that they would consider beyond their skills in another setting. The presence of such disease in a student constitutes a federally protected handicap. The school must make proper accommodation for the student's handicap, including arrangements for medical care, or justify why providing that care is impossible.

REFERENCES

1. *Washington v. Harper,* 110 S. Ct. 1028 (1990).

2. *Id.* at 1035.

SUGGESTED READINGS

Schools

Bradford BJ, Benedum KJ, Heald PA, Petrie SE. Immunization status of children on school entry: area analysis and recommendations 1991. *Clin Pediatr (Phila.).* 1996;35:237–242.

Cheng TL, Savageau JA, Sattler AL, DeWitt TG. Confidentiality in health care: a survey of knowledge, perceptions, and attitudes among high school students. *JAMA.* 1993;269:1404–1407.

Donovan P. School-based sexuality education: the issues and challenges. *Fam Plann Perspect.* 1998;30:188–193.

Dorman SM. Assistive technology benefits for students with disabilities. *J Sch Health.* 1998;68:120–122.

Fothergill K, Ballard E. The school-linked health center: a promising model of community-based care for adolescents. *J Adolesc Health*. 1998;23:29–38.

Graff JC, Ault MM. Guidelines for working with students having special health care needs. *J Sch Health*. 1993;63:335–338.

Gratz RR. School injuries: what we know, what we need. *J Pediatr Health Care*. 1992;6:256–262.

Greene S. Occupational therapy intervention with children in school systems. *Hosp Community Psychiatry*. 1993;44:429–431.

Gross EJ, Larkin MH. The child with HIV in day care and school. *Nurs Clin North Am*. 1996;31:231–241.

Harrison BS, Faircloth JW, Yaryan L. The impact of legislation and litigation on the role of the school nurse. *Nurs Outlook*. 1995;43:57–61.

Henry PM, Mills WA, Holtan NR, et al. Screening for tuberculosis infection among secondary school students in Minneapolis-St. Paul: policy implications. *Minn Med*. 1996;79:43–49.

Henshelwood J, Polnay L. Facilities for the school health team. *Arch Dis Child*. 1994;70:542–543.

Mahler K. Condom availability in the schools: Lessons from the courtroom [published erratum appears in *Fam Plann Perspect*. 1996;May–June;28:134]. *Fam Plann Perspect*. 1996;28:75–77.

Ortolon K. It takes teamwork. *Tex Med*. 1996;92:30–34.

Passarelli C. School nursing: trends for the future. *J Sch Health*. 1994;64:141–149.

Rienzo BA, Button J, Wald KD. The politics of school-based programs which address sexual orientation. *J Sch Health*. 1996;66:33–40.

Santelli J, Kouzis A, Newcomer S. Student attitudes toward school-based health centers. *J Adolesc Health*. 1996;18:349–356.

Stryker J, Samuels SE, Smith MD. Condom availability in schools: the need for improved program evaluations. *Am J Public Health*. 1994;84:1901–1906.

Vessey JA. School services for children with chronic conditions. *Pediatr Nurs*. 1997;23:507–510.

Wolk LI. School-based health centers. *Colo Med*. 1994;91:321–322.

Yates SR. The school nurse's role: early intervention with preschool children. *J Sch Nurs*. 1992;8:30–36.

Teams

Albrecht RR, Anderson WA, McGrew CA, McKeag DB, Hough DO. NCAA institutionally based drug testing: do our athletes know the rules of this game? *Med Sci Sports Exerc*. 1992;24:242–246.

Albrecht RR, Anderson WA, McKeag DB. Drug testing of college athletes: the issues. *Sports Med*. 1992;14:349–352.

American Medical Society for Sports Medicine (AMSSM) and the American Academy of Sports Medicine (AASM). Human immunodeficiency virus (HIV) and other blood-borne pathogens in sports. Joint position statement. *Am J Sports Med*. 1995;23:510–514.

Boudreau F, Konzak B. Ben Johnson and the use of steroids in sport: sociological and ethical considerations. *Can J Sport Sci*. 1991;16:88–98.

Brodie DA, Stopani K. Experimental ethics in sports medicine research. *Sports Med*. 1990;9:143–150.

Christophersen AS, Morland J. Drug analysis for control purposes in forensic toxicology, workplace testing, sports medicine and related areas. *Pharmacol Toxicol*. 1994;74:202–210.

Classe JG. Legal aspects of sports vision. *Optom Clin*. 1993;3:27–32.

Ghosh A. Sports medicine is dead: long live sports medicine! *J Indian Med Assoc*. 1991;89:29–30.

Levine BD, Stray-Gundersen J. The medical care of competitive athletes: the role of the physician and individual assumption of risk. *Med Sci Sports Exerc*. 1994;26:1190–1192.

Maron BJ, Brown RW, McGrew CA, Mitten MJ, Caplan AL, Hutter AM Jr. Ethical, legal and practical considerations affecting medical decision-making in competitive athletes. *J Am Coll Cardiol*. 1994;24:854–860.

McConnell AA, Mackay GM. Consent in medicine and sport. *J R Coll Surg Edinb*. 1995;40.

McConnell AA, MacKay MG. Medical confidentiality in sport and the public interest. *Med Sci Law*. 1995;35:45–47.

Mitten MJ, Mitten RJ. Legal considerations in treating the injured athlete. *J Orthop Sports Phys Ther*. 1995;21:38–43.

Patterson PH, Dyment PG. Being a team physician. *Pediatr Ann*. 1997;26:13–16, 18.

Pipe AL. J. B. Wolffe Memorial Lecture. Sport, science, and society: ethics in sports medicine. *Med Sci Sports Exerc*. 1993;25:888–900.

Pollack BR. Legal considerations in sports dentistry. *Dent Clin North Am*. 1991;35:809–829.

Polsky S. Winning medicine: professional sports team doctors' conflicts of interest. *J Contemp Health Law Policy*. 1998;14:503–529.

Pope HG Jr, Katz DL. Homicide and near-homicide by anabolic steroid users. *J Clin Psychiatry*. 1990;51:28–31.

Press JM, Akau CK, Bowyer BL. Sports medicine, 5: the physiatrist as team physician. *Arch Phys Med Rehabil*. 1993;74:S447–S449.

Randolph C. The free running athletic screening test. *Ann Allergy Asthma Immunol*. 1998;81:275a–275g.

Silberstein CE. The professional sports team physician. *Md Med J*. 1996;45:683–685.

Sim J. Sports medicine: some ethical issues. *Br J Sports Med*. 1993;27:95–100.

Spillane DM. Dentists, mouthguards, and the law. *J Mass Dent Soc*. 1994;43:21–24, 65.

Prisons

Aiyebusi A. Forensic nursing. *Nurs Times*. 1998;94:51.

Albrecht LJ. Cell block doc: medical practice inside the walls of the Texas prison system. *Tex Med.* 1993;89:38–44.

American Society of Health-System Pharmacists. ASHP guidelines on pharmaceutical services in correctional facilities. *Am J Health Syst Pharm.* 1995;52:1810–1813.

Blank S, McDonnell DD, Rubin SR, et al. New approaches to syphilis control: finding opportunities for syphilis treatment and congenital syphilis prevention in a women's correctional setting. *Sex Transm Dis.* 1997;24:218–226.

Case P, Meehan T, Jones TS. Arrests and incarceration of injection drug users for syringe possession in Massachusetts: implications for HIV prevention. *J Acquir Immune Defic Syndr Hum Retrovirol.* 1998;18:S71–S75.

Castledine G. Prison services are in need of urgent reform. *Br J Nurs.* 1998;7:616.

Cline P. Correctional nursing: an insider's view. *Pa Nurse.* 1997;52:13.

Conklin TJ, Lincoln T, Flanigan TP. A public health model to connect correctional health care with communities. *Am J Public Health.* 1998;88:1249–1250.

Danto BL. Suicide litigation as an agent of change in jail and prison: an initial report. *Behav Sci Law.* 1997;15:415–425.

Davis-Barron S. Psychopathic patients pose dilemma for physicians and society. *CMAJ.* 1995;152:1314–1317.

Dollard MF, Winefield AH. A test of the demand-control/support model of work stress in correctional officers. *J Occup Health Psychol.* 1998;3:243–264.

Drake VK. Process, perils, and pitfalls of research in prison. *Issues Ment Health Nurs.* 1998;19:41–52.

Drobniewski F. Tuberculosis in prisons—forgotten plague. *Lancet.* 1995;346:948–949.

Droes NS. Correctional nursing practice. *J Community Health Nurs.* 1994;11:201–210.

Edens JF, Peters RH, Hills HA. Treating prison inmates with co-occurring disorders: an integrative review of existing programs. *Behav Sci Law.* 1997;15:439–457.

Elliott RL. Evaluating the quality of correctional mental health services: an approach to surveying a correctional mental health system. *Behav Sci Law.* 1997;15:427–438.

Feinstein RA, Lampkin A, Lorish CD, Klerman LV, Maisiak R, Oh MK. Medical status of adolescents at time of admission to a juvenile detention center. *J Adolesc Health.* 1998;22:190–196.

Hayden JW, Laney C, Kellermann AL. Medical devices made into weapons by prisoners: an unrecognized risk. *Ann Emerg Med.* 1995;26:739–742.

Hayes LM. Controversial issues in jail suicide prevention, II: Use of inmates to conduct suicide watch. *Crisis.* 1995;16:151–153.

Hayes ML. Controversial issues in jail suicide prevention. *Crisis.* 1995;16:107–110.

Jochem K, Tannenbaum TN, Menzies D. Prevalence of tuberculin skin test reactions among prison workers. *Can J Public Health.* 1997;88:202–206.

Kendig N. Tuberculosis control in prisons. *Int J Tuberc Lung Dis.* 1998;2:S57–S63.

Klein MD. The prison patient. *Ann Intern Med.* 1997;127: 648–649.

Kohli HS. HIV and prisons. *Natl Med J India.* 1995;8:180–181.

Lee CT, Davies M, Stevenson JH. Burns in prisoners: an assessment of problems in handling prisoners in a burns unit. *Burns.* 1996;22:546–548.

Metzner JL. An introduction to correctional psychiatry, part II. *J Am Acad Psychiatry Law.* 1997;25:571–579.

Metzner JL. An introduction to correctional psychiatry, part III. *J Am Acad Psychiatry Law.* 1998;26:107–115.

Miller D, Trapani C, Fejes-Mendoza K, Eggleston C, Dwiggins D. Adolescent female offenders: unique considerations. *Adolescence.* 1995;30:429–435.

Mutter RC, Grimes RM, Labarthe D. Evidence of intraprison spread of HIV infection. *Arch Intern Med.* 1994;154:793–795.

Norris MP, May MC. Screening for malingering in a correctional setting. *Law Hum Behav.* 1998;22:315–323.

Nurco DN, Hanlon TE, Bateman RW, Kinlock TW. Drug abuse treatment in the context of correctional surveillance. *J Subst Abuse Treat.* 1995;12:19–27.

Parker D, Lawrence D. Prison health: a matter of priority. *J Med Assoc Ga.* 1998;87:202–205.

Perera J, Dias N, Amarasiri A. Health-care and housing for prisoners. *Ceylon Med J.* 1998;43:43–45.

Robey A. Stone walls do not a prison psychiatrist make. *J Am Acad Psychiatry Law.* 1998;26:101–105.

Skolnick AA. Critics denounce staffing jails and prisons with physicians convicted of misconduct. *JAMA.* 1998;280: 1391–1392.

Skolnick AA. Prison deaths spotlight how boards handle impaired, disciplined physicians. *JAMA.* 1998;280:1387–1390.

Smith R. Health services for prisoners: lost in ambiguities. *Clio Med.* 1995;34:134–145.

Solomon P, Draine J. Issues in serving the forensic client. *Soc Work.* 1995;40:25–33.

Spaulding AC. The role of correctional facilities in public health: the example of sexually transmitted diseases. *Med Health RI.* 1998;81:204–206.

Thorburn KM. Conditions in prisons. *Lancet.* 1998;351:1003–1004.

Thorburn KM. Health care in correctional facilities. *West J Med.* 1995;163:560–564.

Tulsky JP, White MC, Dawson C, Hoynes TM, Goldenson J, Schecter G. Screening for tuberculosis in jail and clinic follow-up after release. *Am J Public Health.* 1998;88:223–226.

Vaughn MS. Civil liability against prison officials for prescribing and dispensing medication and drugs to prison inmates. *J Leg Med.* 1997;18:315–344.

Vaughn MS. Section 1983 civil liability of prison officials for denying and delaying medication and drugs to prison inmates. *Issues Law Med.* 1995;11:47–76.

Ward K. AIDS. HIV in prison: the importance of prevention. *Nurs Stand.* 1996;11:51–52.

Glossary

Note: **Bold** terms are referenced in other parts of the glossary.

Abandonment	As a general legal term, abandonment is the surrender, relinquishment, disclaimer, or cession of property or rights. In medical law, abandonment is the physician's unilateral refusal to continue treating a patient with whom the physician has a physician–patient relationship.
Action	A civil or criminal proceeding in a court of law, a lawsuit.
ACOG	American College of Obstetrics and Gynecology.
ADA	The Americans with Disabilities Act of 1990.
Adjudication	A decision by a court of law or an administrative law judge.
Ad litem	(Usually attorney or guardian ad litem.) A person, usually an attorney, appointed to protect the rights of a minor or an incompetent who is involved in a legal proceeding. An attorney or guardian ad litem's duty is limited to issues that arise in the legal proceeding. The usual role of the attorney or guardian ad litem is to ensure that the parents or legal **guardian** do not put their interests before the child or incompetent. See Guardian.
Administrative Agency	An executive branch department of the state or federal government arm which administers or carries out legislation. The **FDA, DHHS, HCFA,** and state **BOME**s are administrative agencies.
Admissible	Facts or testimony that the judge in a lawsuit allows the jury to consider. For example, the judge in a medical malpractice lawsuit must decide if the **expert witnesses** presented by the plaintiff are properly qualified to give evidence to the jury. If they are not, the judge can declare their testimony to be inadmissible and they cannot testify to the jury.
ADR	Alternate Dispute Resolution. The resolution of conflicts using means other than litigation; chiefly by **arbitration, mediation,** or facilitated settlement conferences.
Affiant	A person who makes an **affidavit.**

Affidavit	A voluntary, sworn statement of facts or a declaration in writing made before a person with the authority to administer an oath. These are usually prepared by an attorney in consultation with the affiant, then signed before a **notary public.**
Affirmative Defenses	Arguments raised by a defendant in a civil lawsuit that indicate extenuating circumstances that negate the plaintiff's claim. A physician sued for failure to attend a patient in a hospital could plead the affirmative defense that he or she had not admitted the patient, previously treated the patient during the hospital admission, or been consulted by the patient's admitting physician. If the judge accepts this evidence as true, then the plaintiff's case would be dismissed.
Affirmed	Action of an appellate court in which it declares that a judgment, decree, or order of a lower court is valid and correct and must stand.
Agency	The legal term for the relationship in which one person either acts for or represents another. The person acting is the agent and the person for whom the agent acts is called the principal. Lawyers act as agents for their clients when they negotiate leases and other contracts with a **third-party** for their client. Physicians act as agents for their patients when they order medical tests for which a patient is legally obliged to pay a hospital.
AI	Artificial Insemination. (Confusion sometimes arises because in medical computing AI means artificial intelligence.)
AID	Artificial Insemination by Donor.
Amicus Curiae	"A friend of the court." A person who has no right to appear in a suit (no **standing**), but is allowed, at the court's discretion, to present legal arguments or evidence to the judge. Medical professional organizations often file **briefs** as amicus curiae in cases such as *Cruzan v. Director, Missouri Dept. of Health* (1990) that affect medical practice.
Answer	The defendant's response to the plaintiff's **complaint** or **original petition.**
Antitrust Laws	State and federal laws intended to prevent businesses from using their market power to injure their competitors.
Appeal	A complaint to a superior court to reverse or correct an alleged error committed by a lower court.
Appellant	The party who appeals the decision of a lower court to a higher, appellate court.
Appellate Court	A court which has the power to review the actions and decisions of a lower court. The U.S. Supreme Court has final appellate jurisdiction over all the courts in the United States.
Appellee	The party against whom an appeal to a higher court is taken.

Arbitration	A private, nonjudicial proceeding in which two or more parties agree to allow one or more arbitrators to decide disputed issues. This agreement may be made before there is a dispute, as when patients insured by an **MCO** agree to arbitrate medical malpractice disputes. Arbitration is binding if the parties agree that neither can bring a legal action on the same facts that are subject to the arbitration agreement. Arbitrators are persons who have no interest in the dispute. They may be attorneys, but are often lay specialists in the area being arbitrated. Each party chooses one or more arbitrators. The parties often agree to abide by the American Arbitration Association (AAA) established rules for arbitration. They may also agree to choose arbitrators from a list of persons certified by the AAA.
Assault	Legally, an assault is the act of putting a person in apprehension of immediate harm. (Battery is actually inflicting the threatened harm.) In general usage, and even in many legal proceedings, assault is used to denote both the threat and the action. Threatening a person with a gun is an assault, and an unwanted sexual touching is also an assault. Since assault is a threat of immediate action, upsetting a person by threatening to do something in the future is **intentional infliction of mental distress** rather than assault.
Assignment	The transfer of rights or property to another. This is commonly done by physicians when assigning their delinquent accounts to a collection agency.
Assumption of Duty	The process of agreeing to accept legal obligations. A physician has the legal right in most circumstances to drive by a roadside accident without stopping to render aid. A physician who does stop to render aid assumes certain obligations to care for the patient in a professional manner.
Assumption of Risk	An important legal doctrine whereby a person agrees to accept the consequences of certain behavior. Assumption of risk is effective only if the person makes a free, uncoerced choice and understands the risk being assumed. Informed consent is the assumption of the risks of the medical treatment that the patient agrees to undergo.
Attestation	Signing a written statement that a document is correct or that you have witnessed the document being signed. The witnesses to a living will may attest that the patient making the will was of sound mind and made the will of his or her own volition.
Award	The amount of money a court orders a party in a legal proceeding to pay.
Battery	An unconsented, harmful, or offensive touching. A patient who is restrained without permission, or properly documented medical indications, could bring an action for battery. A patient who is sexually assaulted will bring a legal action for battery, with the sexual touching

being the offensive contact. Since a battery is considered an injury to the person's dignity as well as to their person, the court can find large **damages** even if the person suffered no physical harm.

Best Evidence Rule

A legal doctrine that requires the primary evidence of a fact should be found, or its absence explained, before a copy or oral evidence on the same matter can be introduced. This is often at issue in medical records. A physician may not testify about the contents of medical records unless the record is in evidence. If the defendant can show that the medical record was lost in a fire, then the court will allow the testimony. If, however, a party intentionally destroys a record, the court may not allow that party to testify about the contents of that record.

Boilerplate

A disparaging term for generic paragraphs that are inserted in legal documents without reference to the specific subject of the contract. A common example is the endless pages of fine print that fills commercial leases. A certain amount of boilerplate is necessary in most legal documents to establish the assumptions underlying the agreement. Boilerplate becomes a problem when it is inserted as a matter of course without determining its effect on the document. This is a special problem for physicians because of the special laws that govern medical practice. A standard commercial lease often has terms that base part of the rent on the tenant's net sales. While acceptable for a clothing store, such terms violate the medical practice acts of many states when applied to a physician's office.

BOME

Board of Medical Examiners.

Bona Fide

In good faith; openly, honestly, or innocently; without knowledge of fraud; without fraudulent intent.

Borrowed Servant

An employee temporarily under the control of another. The temporary employer of the borrowed servant will be held responsible for the negligent acts of the borrowed servant. Hospital employees were once considered to be the physician's borrowed employees for all medical care. See **Captain-of-the-Ship Doctrine.**

Breach of Contract

Failing to comply with the terms of a contract. A breach can occur through failing to comply at all, through incomplete compliance, or through untimely compliance. A breach can be excused if the court finds that either the contract contained an applicable exclusion, such as a physician not being able to fulfill an employment contract requiring a medical license because he lost his license, or that the contract was breached because of the occurrence of an event, such as an act of war, beyond the control of the contracting parties.

Briefs

Written arguments on questions of law or facts to assist the judge in making a decision. May be filed by the parties to the lawsuit or by **amicus curiae.**

Captain-of-the-Ship Doctrine	A legal doctrine holding a surgeon liable for the acts of the entire operating room personnel. This is an old doctrine, predating physician anesthesiologists and nurses with independent duties to the hospital. It has been overruled in most jurisdictions, at least as regards the actions of other physicians.
Causation	The legal test for whether a given action lead to the plaintiff's claimed injury. It is not enough to be negligent: the negligence must cause the injury. Causation is often at issue in claims of malpractice associated with the treatment of severe illness. In most states, plaintiffs must prove they had a more than 50% probability of recovering from their medical condition before they can sue a physician for allegedly reducing their change of recovery.
Cause of Action	A set of facts or legal circumstances that can support a claim for relief in the courts.
CCU	Critical Care Unit.
CDC	The Centers for Disease Control and Prevention.
Certification	A designation by a private or governmental body that a person or entity has satisfied a preestablished set of standards or requirements. In medicine, it is common for governmental agencies to defer to certifications by private, voluntary organizations such as the **Joint Commission.**
Certiorari	A legal order directing a lower court to transmit the record of a proceeding to an appellate court for review.
CFR	Code of Federal Regulations. A listing of federal regulations arranged by subject matter into fifty different titles.
Charge	The final address by a judge to the jury in which the judge instructs the jury how to apply the law to the facts in the case before them. Since the slant of the jury charge has a great impact on the jury's final decision, many appeals cases are based on the errors in the charge.
Charitable Immunity	A disappearing legal doctrine that gives a charitable hospital immunity from the negligent acts of its employees.
Civil Law	In the United States, legal actions that cannot result in a person being punished by imprisonment. In most of Europe, and Louisiana, civil law refers to a system of law based on statutes rather than court decisions. See **Common Law.**
Claim	A demand for compensation, benefits or relief.
COBRA	Congressional Omnibus Budget Reconciliation Act. The massive bill passed at the end of a term of Congress that approves the spending for all areas not previously authorized in specific bills.

Common Law	Law made by judges in the context of particular cases, and based on decisions made in previous cases involving related facts and laws. In the United States, the Constitution provides a limit on the reach of judges making common law. (Most of constitutional law, however, deals with disputes over the extent of these limits.) The United States has a combination of common and **civil law** because the legislatures can overturn the common law made by judges.
Comparative Negligence	The legal theory that allows the jury to consider the plaintiff's negligence in determining whether the defendant's actions caused the plaintiff's injuries. In most states, negligent plaintiffs can still recover, provided that they were not more than 50% negligent. See **Contributory Negligence.**
Compensatory Damages	Money paid to an injured or wronged plaintiff based on their proven losses.
Complaint	The written statement in a civil case setting forth the plaintiff's claims and the legal basis for the lawsuit.
CON	Certificate of Need.
Confidential Communication	Communications between persons in fiduciary or confidential relationships. The right of confidentiality belongs to the client or patient, not to the fiduciary. A patient can freely discuss his physician's advice, but the physician cannot freely discuss the patient's condition or the advice given the patient.
Consent	A voluntary choice based on appropriate information. Informed consent to medical treatment is a special case of the general laws governing consent. The legal effect of consent is the **assumption of the risks** of the acts consented to.
Contingent Fee	When attorneys base their fees on a percentage of their client's recovery. This allows clients to secure representation without having to pay the costs of the litigation. Most medical malpractice litigation is done on a contingent fee, as is some medical business litigation.
Contributory Negligence	A legal theory that prevented plaintiffs from recovering damages if they were even 1% at fault. This has been supplanted in most states by **comparative negligence.**
Conversion	Any unauthorized interference in a person's or legal entity's right to goods or personal possessions, usually the conversion of those goods to another's use or possession. Keeping an insurance payment intended for a patient but mistakenly sent to the physician's office would be conversion.
Coroner's Jury	A special jury called by the coroner to determine whether a person died because of criminal action.

Corporate Practice of Medicine   When physicians are employees of nonphysician corporations that are in the business of providing medical services.

CPT Code   Current Procedural Terminology code. A standard system for describing medical procedures.

Criminal Law   Laws dealing with individuals and society as defined by acts that are prohibited by statute or regulation and punishable by fine or imprisonment.

CRNA   Certified Registered Nurse Anesthetist.

Cross-Examination   Witnesses who testify in a legal proceeding may be questioned by the opposing counsel to test the truth and credibility of their character and testimony.

Damages   The amount of money necessary to compensate a plaintiff for injuries caused by the defendant's conduct.

Declaratory Judgment   A court decision that interprets a law without a trial on the merits of a particular dispute. In some states, the State Supreme Court can give declaratory judgments about the constitutionality of proposed state laws.

De Facto   A right or obligation that is recognized because of existing custom, rather than by a statute or court decision. Many physicians believed that joint ventures in health businesses were de facto legal because they were so widely practiced. See **de jure.**

Defamation   The injury of a person's reputation or character by untrue statements made (published) to a third person. Defamation includes both **libel** and **slander.**

Defendant   The person accused of committing a crime in a criminal case; or the party against whom suit is brought seeking either damages or relief in a civil case.

Defense   The defendant's answer to the **plaintiff's complaint.** A defense may contest the truth of the plaintiff's allegations, or claim a legal **privilege** to commit the act complained of.

De Jure   Status of a right or obligation that exists by an act of law. See **De Facto.**

Depositions   Oral or written testimony taken under oath but outside of a courtroom. A verbatim transcript is made and can be used as evidence in a trial.

Dicta   The writings of a judge in an opinion that do not specifically affect the resolution or determination of the case and are not part of the common law resulting from the decision. Dicta are important when used to indicate how the court might rule in future cases with related facts.

Directed Verdict   When a trial judge decides that the evidence or law is so clearly in favor of one party that it is pointless for the trial to proceed, the judge may direct the jury to return a verdict for that party.

Discovery	The pretrial investigation by an attorney to determine the relevant facts of a case.
Discovery Rule	A rule **tolling** the **statute of limitations** until the plaintiff knew or should have known of the injury. This is important for conditions such as cancer due to a toxic exposure that take years to become manifest.
DHHS	United States Department of Health and Human Services.
Doe or Roe	Fictitious names used in test cases brought on behalf of many parties by representative plaintiffs who, although they may also have a personal interest and standing to bring to the case, prefer to remain unnamed. The best known example is *Roe v. Wade,* where Roe was a pseudonym and Wade was the District Attorney in Dallas, Texas.
DOJ	United States Department of Justice.
Donee	One who receives a gift.
Donor	One who makes a gift.
DRG	Diagnosis-Related Groups. A prospective payment system based on diagnoses rather than on the medical services provided to the patient.
Due Care	The degree of care that would or should be exercised by an ordinary person in the same position.
Due Process	*Procedural Due Process*: The ensurance of fundamental fairness in the legal procedure used. A physician who has his or her hospital privileges terminated has a right to a hearing before an impartial party to ensure the fairness of the termination proceeding. *Substantive Due Process*: The ensurance of fundamental fairness in the result reached. Terminating a physician's hospital privileges because of his or her religious beliefs (independent of actions taken to further those beliefs) would be unfair, irrespective of the procedural due process afforded him or her.
Durable Power of Attorney	The written authorization of one person to act for another should he or she become disabled. A recent variation would be living wills or termination of care provisions.
ELISA	Enzyme Linked Immunosorbent Assay. This acronym is commonly used to refer to the screening test for HIV infection.
Emancipated Minor	A person who, although not having reached the statutory age of majority, is granted the legal status of an adult. This may be done through a legal proceeding where the minor proves that he or she is not living with his or her parents and is self-supporting. Marriage and joining the military also convey adult status in most states.
Equity	A historic term for courts dealing with situations where there was no specific legal remedy.

Evidentiary Standards	The level of evidence required by a court to reach a finding differs depending on the nature of the claim. Criminal actions must be proven beyond a reasonable doubt, while civil actions must only be proven by a preponderance of the evidence. The legal question in the *Cruzan* right to die case was whether Missouri could require an incompetent patient's wishes to be proven by clear and convincing evidence, a standard more strict than a preponderance of the evidence.
Exculpatory	Tending to disprove or excuse a charge of fault or guilt.
Execute	To sign, seal, and deliver a written legal instrument.
Expert Witness	One who has special training, experience, skill, and knowledge in a relevant area, and is allowed to offer his or her personal opinion as testimony in court.
Express	Manifestation using direct, clear language, either spoken or written.
FDA	Food and Drug Administration.
Federal Question	Legal question involving the U.S. Constitution or a statute enacted by Congress.
Federal Register	A daily journal (running to hundreds of pages) that contains all the official announcements by federal agencies. Agency regulations must be published in the *Federal Register* before they are accepted as legally binding.
Felony	A serious crime usually punishable by imprisonment for a period of more than one year, or death.
Fiduciary Duty	A class of legal duties that arise when one party in a legal relationship has greater power than the person seeking the party's aid. The attorney–client relationship is a fiduciary relationship, as is the relationship of trustee to the beneficiary of a trust. Most states hold that the physician–patient relationship is a fiduciary relationship. A fiduciary is bound to act in the client/patient's best interests even if it is against the fiduciary's interests. Most important, the fiduciary must avoid conflicts of interest. The **safe harbor regulations,** while viewed as overly restrictive by some physicians, merely reflect traditional fiduciary law.
First Impression	A case that presents issues in controversy for which there is no prior judicial precedent.
Forensic	The investigation, preparation, preservation, and presentation of medical evidence and opinion in court.

Foreseeability	The degree to which a reasonable person would expect a given injury to follow from a specific action. While defendants are liable for unexpectedly severe injuries (**thin skull rule**), they are not necessarily liable for injuries that are too remote from the negligent action. The classic example is the physician who saves the life of a baby who later becomes a bank robber. While it is logically correct that, had the physician not saved the baby's life, there would have not been a bank robbery, the physician is not liable for the bank robbery.
Fraudulent Concealment	Hiding or suppressing a material fact or circumstance that the party is legally or morally bound to disclose.
Fungible	Items that are so similar to one another that a consumer does not care if they are interchanged. Most produce is fungible; personal computers are becoming fungible. Many health insurance plans assume that physicians are fungible.
Good Faith	Honesty in intentional acts toward others. Part of a physician's fiduciary duty is to act in good faith to further the interests and well-being of the patient.
Good Samaritan Laws	Laws designed to protect those who stop to render aid in an emergency. These laws generally provide immunity for specified persons from any civil suit arising out of care rendered at the scene of an emergency, provided that the one rendering assistance has not done so in a grossly negligent manner.
Guardian	A person appointed by the court to protect the interests of a **ward:** a minor or legal incompetent. The guardian has the rights of a parent for minors. A guardian may have full powers over an incompetent, or the court may limit the guardian's powers to a specific task such as managing the finances of the incompetent. A guardian has a right to full informed consent before making medical decisions for a ward.
Habeas Corpus	Literally, bring me the body. A petition to the court requesting the release of an individual who claims to be unjustly or illegally confined. The traditional remedy for a person who claims to have been improperly quarantined is to seek habeas corpus.
HBV	Hepatitis B Virus.
HCFA	Health Care Financing Administration.
Hearsay Rule	Testimony of what another person witnessed or said is inadmissible in a trial as being hearsay. A nurse who was present in an examining room could not testify as to what the physician told a patient during diagnosis. He or she can testify as to whether the physician's testimony reflects what he or she remembers.
Health Care Practitioner	An individual who directly provides health care services.
Health Care Provider	An individual or an institution who provides health care services.

HEPA	A high-efficiency particulate filter that can remove bacteria and some virus from air.
HMO	Health Maintenance Organization.
Iatrogenic Injury	Injury or sickness caused by medical treatment.
Immunity	Society has decided that certain endeavors or institutions provide such a vital service that they should be protected from attack in the courts should injuries result from the providing of the service. Some types of immunity are codified as law. Governmental or sovereign immunity protects governmental units from some types of lawsuits. At one time hospitals were granted immunity because they were charities serving the public good.
Incident Reports	Reports, usually filed by nurses, describing any unexpected events. These are used to identify quality of care and potential legal problems.
Indemnity	A contractual agreement in which one party agrees to reimburse another for losses of a particular type. Many insurance policies have indemnity clauses that allow them to recover money paid to an insured who later recovers damages in court for the same injury.
Independent Contractors	Persons with special expertise hired for a specific job. Independent contractors control the details of their own work. The person or entity contracting for the work of the independent contract is not legally responsible for the negligent actions of the contractor. The contracting party can be liable if the independent contractor was negligently chosen or retained. The medical staff members of a hospital are independent contractors. The hospital is only liable for their actions if it was negligent in giving or continuing their medical staff privileges.
Indictment	A formal written accusation of crime brought by the prosecuting attorney against a person charged with criminal conduct.
Informed Consent	A physician cannot perform any procedure upon a patient without ensuring that the patient understands the purpose of the procedure, including its potential benefits and dangers. The physician must make certain the patient has all the information needed to make a knowledgeable decision to accept or reject a given treatment or to choose an alternative treatment. See **Assumption of Risk** and **Consent.**
Injunction	A court order preventing a person or entity from performing a certain act. A preliminary injunction is temporary and awarded prior to a trial on the merits of the case. A permanent injunction is awarded after the trial and is a final order.
In Loco Parentis	Literally, in the place of the parents. At one time, colleges and universities acted as the parents of their students, but this ended in the 1960s. The state has the right to act in loco parentis in child welfare cases. See **Parens Patria.**

Intentional	The law punishes intentional acts more severely than negligent acts. A physician who negligently fails to obtain an informed consent may be sued only if an injured patient can establish that he or she would have refused the surgery had he or she been given sufficient information. A physician who intentionally deceives a patient about surgery can be sued for battery even if the surgery is a success.
Intentional Infliction of Mental Distress	A cause of action for intentionally causing emotional suffering. The defendant must intend to cause the suffering, the defendant's conduct must be outrageous, and the suffering must be more than just the ordinary distress of daily living.
Interrogatory	Written questions used to investigate a lawsuit or establish facts for a trial. These are answered in writing and under oath. The most common interrogatories are those that are used to establish that a copy of a medical record is complete and that the original record was properly created and maintained.
IRB	Institutional Review Board.
IVDU	Intervenous Drug User.
JNOV	Judgment Non Obstante Veredicto (not withstanding the verdict). A judgment entered by order of the court in favor of one party, notwithstanding the verdict by the jury in favor of the other party. A court only orders a JNOV when the jury's findings contradict the clear evidence in the case.
Joint and Several Liability	When several persons share responsibility for another's injury, they are each liable for the full amount of the damages, irrespective of their percentage of fault. This becomes a problem when one or more of the defendants are underinsured or are insolvent. Many states have abolished joint and several liability in medical malpractice lawsuits. This increases the pressure on plaintiffs to sue everyone who had any part in the patient's care.
Joint Commission	Joint Commission on Accreditation of Healthcare Organizations.
Judgment	The court's official decision in a legal case. The judgment in a case establishes what damages, if any, must be paid, and the legal responsibilities of all the parties in the lawsuit.
Jurisdiction	Jurisdiction over the subject matter of a claim is the power of a court to hear the case and bind the parties. There are monetary, geographic, and political limits on jurisdiction.
Laches	A defense in which the defendant claims that the plaintiff waited so long in bringing the complaint that it would be unjust to allow the case to go to trial. The laches defense is important in claims that have no clear **statute of limitations.**

Learned Intermediary	This is a doctrine that modifies the **strict liability (products liability)** that usually accompanies injuries due to dangerous products such as drugs. In general, the manufacturer of a product has a duty to warn the consumer about the dangers posed by the product. Since patients cannot purchase prescription drugs without a physician's order, the law holds the drug manufacturer must warn the physician. If the physician is provided proper warnings, the drug company is not liable if the patient is injured because the physician improperly prescribed the drug.
Liability	A legally enforceable obligation.
Libel	**Defamation** by written or printed materials, including pictures.
Litigation	Trial of a dispute in a court of law or other legal forum to determine factual and legal issues, rights, and duties between the parties.
Living Wills	A legal document that outlines the patient's wishes for refusing or discontinuing lifesaving medical treatment if the patient becomes incompetent.
MCO	Managed Care Organization.
Malpractice	Professional negligence resulting from improper discharge of professional duties or failure to meet the standard of care of a professional, resulting in harm to another.
Mandamus	A court order compelling public officers to do their legally mandated duties.
Mediation	A process in which the parties to a dispute ask a neutral person to help them come to a mutually beneficial settlement.
Medicare	A federal health insurance program for the aged and the disabled.
Medicaid	A federal health insurance program for the poor.
Misdemeanor	An unlawful act of a less serious nature than a felony, usually punishable by fine or imprisonment for a term of less than one year.
MSAFP	Maternal Serum Alpha-Fetoprotein. Used in the prenatal diagnosis of neural tube defects and Down syndrome.
MSDS	Material Safety Data Sheet.
National Practitioner Data Bank	A national clearing house for data about physician disciplinary actions, including adverse peer review finds and payments in medical malpractice litigation.
Negligence	The failure to exercise the degree of diligence and care that a reasonable and ordinarily prudent person would exercise under the same or similar circumstances.

Negligence Per Se	Violation of a law or statute that leads to an injury. The law or statute provides the proof of the proper standard of care. The harm complained of must be the kind the statute was intended to prevent, and the plaintiff must be in the class of persons that the law was intended to protect. If a person catches a communicable disease because the physician does not comply with a state disease reporting law, then the physician can be liable for negligence per se.
Nonfeasance	Failure to do an act that should have been done.
Notary Public	Historically, a notary was a powerful public official who approved the filing of all official documents. In the United States (outside of Louisiana) a notary, or notary public, is a public officer, usually bonded, who may attest to the signing of legal documents. In most states the notary must affix a seal or stamp to the document and must keep a record book of all witnessed documents. Since the notary only attests that he or she saw the document signed, not the content of the document, notarization adds little but pomp to a legal document.
Notice	Knowledge of the existence of a fact by a party such that they can be held accountable for any ramifications resulting from the receipt of that knowledge. Notice may be either actual or constructive. If a hospital administrator knows that a physician has a drinking problem, the hospital has actual notice that the physician is impaired even if the medical staff committee never disciplines the physician. The hospital will then be liable for negligent continuation of medical staff privileges. If the National Practitioner Data Bank of the Department of Health and Human Services contains the information that the physician is an alcoholic, the hospital is charged with knowledge of this information even if it never checks the database. This is constructive notice.
Nuncupative Will	Oral statement intended as a last will made in anticipation of death.
OIG	The Office of the Inspector General. While most federal agencies have an OIG, in health care this usually refers to the OIG of the Department of Health and Human Services.
Opinion	The judicial reasons given for an appellate court's decision.
Ordinance	A law passed by a municipal legislative body such as a city council.
Original Petition	The **pleading** that begins a lawsuit. Also called the **complaint.**
OSHA	The Occupational Safety and Health Administration.
OSHA 200 Log	A specific log of occupational injuries and illnesses that must be kept by businesses with high risk.
Parens Patria	The power of the state to act as parent to protect an individual for the individual's own good. This is different from the **police power,** in that the individual is protected because of the state's interest in not having to bear the burden of injured citizens. Motorcycle helmet laws are enacted under parens patria.

Parol Evidence   Oral evidence rather than written evidence. The parol evidence rule says that a written contract is presumed to be the final expression of agreement between the parties and other oral testimony cannot be used to vary the terms of the contract.

Party   Any direct, named litigant in a legal proceeding.

Patient Dumping   The slang term for transferring a patient because the patient is unable to pay for the needed care.

Peer Review   The process whereby a group of physicians determines the medical competence and general professionalism of a physician.

Per Curiam   A court opinion made by all members of the court.

Perjury   The willful act of giving false testimony under oath.

Nonphysician practitioners   Nonphysician personnel who are limited to practicing under the direction and supervision of the attending physician. Physicians are personally liable for the actions of such personnel.

Plaintiff   The party to a civil suit who brings the suit seeking damages or other legal relief.

Pleadings   A formal statement made to the court setting out a party's claims. The plaintiff initiates a lawsuit by a pleading called a "**complaint.**" The defendant responds to the plaintiff's complaint by filing an "**answer.**"

Police Power   The power of the state to protect the health, safety, morals, and general welfare of the people. The police power is the power to restrict the liberty of individuals to protect other individuals. Communicable disease laws are enacted under the police power.

Prima Facie   When all the necessary elements of a valid cause of action are alleged to exist. Once the plaintiff has established a prima facie case, the defendant will lose unless he or she can rebut one or more elements of the case.

Privilege   A special legal status that prevents the privileged actor from being held legally liable for actions that would otherwise trigger liability. The state and federal governments are privileged to do actions, such as exposing a population to atomic radiation, that would be torts if done by a private individual. The physician–patient relationship is privileged in most states, allowing the physician to refuse most requests for information about the patient's medical condition.

Privileges   Business relationship between a physician and a health care facility, in which the physician remains an independent contractor but has the right to be part of the medical staff and to admit and treat patients in the facility, in return for meeting certain standards set by the facility.

Probate   The judicial proceeding that determines the existence and validity of a will in the Probate Court.

Production	To bring (produce) documents or physical objects during the **discovery** phase of a lawsuit.
Products Liability	Manufacturers are liable for injuries caused by their products, regardless of whether they were negligent in designing or manufacturing the product. This **strict liability** is based on the policy that the manufacturer is better able to bear the cost of injuries, and that strict liability for injuries will encourage the manufacturers to be more careful in product manufacture and design. There is an exception for inherently dangerous products such as guns and tobacco, and for products such as drugs that are controlled by a **learned intermediary.**
Punitive Damages	Money awarded to a plaintiff to punish a defendant for intentional or grossly negligent conduct.
Reasonable-Person Standard	The vaguest of all legal terms of art. Typically used to describe an objective standard of behavior, for example, one that is based on what a reasonable person would have done, had that reasonable person been in the defendant's position. For physicians, this is a reasonable physician familiar with the standards of practice that would apply to the defendant physician.
Rebuttal	Answering the allegations of an adverse party in a legal proceeding. If a charge is not rebutted, the court must accept it as true.
Regulation	A standard published by a governmental administrative agency under legal authority delegated to it by the legislature. Regulations have the force of law in both civil and criminal proceedings. Much of medical practice is governed by regulations rather than by statutes.
Regulatory Agency	An executive branch department such as the FDA or HCFA that enforces legislation regulating an act or activity in a particular area.
Reliance	The legal requirement that persons making claims based on representations made to them prove that they actually relied on the representations. In cases alleging failure of **informed consent,** patients must show that they relied on the physician's representations, for example, that they would not have undergone the treatment had they been given correct information.
Remand	When an appellate court reverses the decision of a lower court and sends the case back to the lower court for retrial or other action in accordance with the appellate court's ruling in the case.
Remedies	The means by which a court will enforce a party's rights or redress a wrong. These include payment of damages, injunctions, and ordering the parties to carry out specific actions.
Remittitur	A judge may decrease the amount of a jury award if the amount is clearly unjust. Many of the large jury verdicts reported in the news and in jury verdict reports are reduced, often substantially. The plaintiff may either accept the reduced award or retry the case.

Res Ipsa Loquitur	A legal presumption against a defendant who had exclusive control of the instrument causing the harm when the harm suffered would not ordinarily occur without negligence. Res ipsa loquitur allows a plaintiff to make a claim when no one knows how the injury occurred. A surgery patient who wakes up with a dislocated shoulder can claim that although no one knows how the injury occurred, it must have been due to someone's negligence. Many states have limited the use of res ipsa loquitur in medical malpractice litigation.
Res Judicata	A rule that a final judgment on the merits of a case precludes any further litigation on the issues decided.
Respondeat Superior	An employer or supervisor of a person who is not an **independent contractor** is liable for the actions of that person. In some cases this **vicarious liability** extends to intentional acts such as sexual assault.
Respondent	The party who argues against a petition or appeal.
Restraining Order	A court order forbidding a threatened or imminent act until a hearing on the proposed act can be held.
RICO	The common abbreviation for state or federal racketeering laws.
Safe Harbor Regulations	The legal regulations governing the involvement of physicians in medical businesses. They are termed "safe harbor regulations" because they describe what practices are legal under laws prohibiting **self-referral** arrangements.
Self-Referral	The practice of sending patients to a medical business because the physician referring the patient has an interest in the business or is given a benefit by the business for patient referrals. Self-referrals create a conflict of interest, violating the physician's **fiduciary duty** to the patient. Self-referrals are also criminal conduct under federal and some state laws.
Service of Process	Notification to persons named as defendants in a lawsuit that a suit has been filed against them. Made by an agent of the court, either in person or by mail.
Slander	**Defamation** by spoken words.
SSI	Supplemental Security Income. A disability program for the poor managed by the Social Security Administration.
Standing	The required status, based on a party having a personal stake in the outcome of a suit, to raise a particular issue in court. The critical issue in many constitutional law cases is who has standing to bring an issue before the court. Standing is always at issue when physicians bring lawsuits over issues such as Medicare funding where patients are the intended beneficiary of the litigation.

Stare Decisis	"Let the decision stand." The legal doctrine stating that courts should follow previous decisions and apply them to subsequent cases involving similar facts and questions.
Statute of Frauds	The requirement that contracts governing certain transactions be in writing. This is intended to prevent fraudulent lawsuits based on allegations that the parties had entered into an oral contract.
Statute of Limitation	A statutory deadline for filing lawsuits. Unless the statute is **tolled,** the plaintiff cannot bring an action after the statute of limitation has run. The statute of limitation is typically two to four years for medical malpractice actions. See **Discovery Rule.**
STD	Sexually Transmitted Disease.
Stipulate	Where the parties to a lawsuit agree to a particular statement of facts and dispense with the need to produce evidence to formally prove those facts.
Strict Liability	Liability without fault. Traditionally, strict liability has been limited to ultrahazardous activities such as blasting. **Products liability** is a modified form of strict liability, as is **vicarious liability.**
Subpoena	A command to an individual by a court that the individual must obey or face discipline from the court. A *subpoena ad testificandum* is a command to appear at a certain time and place to testify on a matter. A *subpoena duces tecum* is a command to produce specific documents needed in a trial or court proceeding.
Suit	Civil court proceeding where one person seeks damages or other legal remedies from another.
Summary Judgment	A judgment that decides a case based on affidavits or depositions. Requests for summary judgment are made before trial. A summary judgment is desirable because it saves the time and expense of a trial.
Survivor Action	A legal cause of action brought on behalf of a dead person to recover losses sustained by the deceased during his or her lifetime.
Survivorship Clause	A contractual agreement between joint owners of property that, should one of the owners die, the surviving owner is entitled to the decedent's ownership rights in the property.
Testimony	Statements made at a hearing or trial by a witness under oath.
"Thin Skull Rule"	The legal principle that a defendant must take the plaintiff as he finds him. For example, the defendant cannot complain that the plaintiff's injuries were unusually severe because the plaintiff has an unusual physical condition. The term comes from an apocryphal case involving a plaintiff with a thin skull who suffers a serious head injury in a very minor accident.

Third Party	A third party, sometimes abbreviated TP, is a person who is not a party to a legal relationship or transaction, but is affected by the transaction.
Third-Party Liability	A defendant in a civil case can compel a third party to join the suit as their codefendant and share in the liability if the third party is also liable to the plaintiff. A surgeon who is named in a wrongful death suit may implead an anesthetist who is partially or completely at fault.
Toll	Under some circumstances the **statute of limitations** is suspended, allowing an action to be brought after the usual deadline. These include the plaintiff's minority, which tolls the statute until the plaintiff reaches eighteen, and periods when the defendant is out of the United States and thus unavailable for service of process. The **discovery rule** also gives a plaintiff additional time to file a lawsuit.
Tort	A civil wrong done to an individual by a private individual or private legal entity. Torts usually involve personal injuries. A criminal wrong done to an individual becomes a matter of state interest with prosecution and punishment being handled by the state on behalf of the people of the state. Accidentally injuring someone in a car crash is a civil matter; attempted murder using a car is a criminal matter.
Tortfeasor	A person who commits a tort.
Uniform Act	A model act concerning a particular area of the law created by a nongovernmental body in the hopes that it will be enacted in all states to achieve uniformity in that area of the law.
USCA	United States Code, Annotated. A collection of all the federal laws, arranged by topic under fifty broad headings and cross-referenced to specific case law that has arisen concerning the law in question.
Utilization Review	The review of the medical care rendered a patient to determine its medical and financial appropriateness.
Vacate	When a court sets aside a previously entered order or judgment.
Verdict	The formal declaration of the jury of its findings of fact.
Vicarious Liability	Liability for the actions of another. This is a special case of **strict liability.** Vicarious liability arises from a special legal relationship between the parties. This may be the employer–employee relationship, parent–child relationship, or relationships created by licensing and certification laws, such as the medical licensing laws. The **borrowed-servant** rule made physicians vicariously liable for the actions of nurses taking care of their patient, even though the nurses were employees of a hospital. See **Respondeat Superior.**
Waiver	The voluntary, informed relinquishment of a legal claim or right.
Ward	A minor or legal incompetent who has a legally appointed guardian.

Work Product	Attorneys preparing for litigation enjoy protection from **discovery** for their work product, for example, their writings, documents, and impressions of the case. This is a limited immunity. A physician's confidential interview with his or her attorney concerning pending malpractice litigation is protected. Giving otherwise discoverable materials such as personal diaries to one's attorney will not protect them from discovery. The privilege applies only to the attorney's own work. A court may order the **production** of work product if it is the only way to obtain critical facts.
Written Authorization	Consent given in writing specifically empowering someone to do or assume a duty for another.
Wrongful Birth	A legal cause of action by the parents for the extra medical costs of raising a baby with birth defects. The legal claim is a form of failure of informed consent: had the physician properly informed the parents about the risk of a defective baby, the woman would either have not become pregnant or would have aborted the fetus. A wrongful birth claim is different than a claim that the physician's actions injured the baby.
Wrongful Death	A legal cause of action brought by the relatives of a person who has died to recover the relatives' losses, such as the loss of economic support.
Wrongful Life	A legal cause of action brought on behalf of a child with birth defects claiming damages for being alive. Since the essence of these claims is that the child would have been better off dead, most courts reject wrongful life claims.

Table of Cases

FEDERAL CASES

Abbott v. Bragdon, 163 F.3d 87 (1st Cir. 1998) 202

Addington v. Texas, 441 U.S. 418 (1979) 248

American Med. Ass'n v. United States, 317 U.S. 519 (1943) 286

American Soc'y of Mechanical Engin'rs v. Hydrolevel, 456 U.S. 556 (1982) 61

Bartlett v. New York State Bd. of Law Examrs, 156 F.3d 321 (2d Cir. 1998) 455

Bell v. Wolfish, 441 U.S. 520 (1979) 60

Bowers v. Hardwick, 478 U.S. 186 (1986) 375

Brady v. Maryland, 373 U.S. 83 (1963) 131

Bragdon v. Abbott, 118 S. Ct. 2196, 141 L. Ed. 2d 540 (1998) 455

Bryan v. James E. Holmes Reg'l Med. Ctr., 33 F.3d 1318 (11th Cir. 1994) 287

Camara v. Municipal Ct. of San Francisco, 387 U.S. 523 (1967) 60, 335

Carpenter v. United States, 484 U.S. 19 (1987) 61

Central States, Southeast & Southwest Areas Pension Fund v. Central Transp., Inc.,
    472 U.S. 559, (1985) 286

City of New York v. New Saint Mark's Baths, 497 N.Y.S.2d 979, 983 (1986) 335

Cruzan by Cruzan v. Director, Mo. Dept. of Health, 497 U.S. 261 (1990) 11, 248

Daubert v. Merrell Dow Pharm., Inc., 509 U.S. 579 (1993) 131

Day v. Woodworth, 54 U.S. (13 How.) 363, 371, 14 L. Ed. 181 (1851) 36

Eastern R.R. Presidents Conf. v. Noerr Motor Freight, Inc., 365 U.S. 127 (1961) 287

Fletcher v. Peck, 6 Cranch 87 (1810) 60

Frye v. United States, 293 F. 1013 (App. D.C. Dec 03, 1923) 131

Gideon v. Wainwright, 372 U.S. 335 (1963) 60

Goldberg v. Kelly, 397 U.S. 254 (1970) 76

Goldfarb v. Virginia State Bar, 421 U.S. 733 (1975) 61

Gregory v. United States, 253 F.2d 104, 109 (5th Cir. 1958) 61

Griggs v. Duke Power Co., 401 U.S. 424 (1971) 455

H.J. Inc. v. Northwestern Bell Tel. Co., 492 U.S. 229 (1989) 61

Henne v. Wright, 904 F.2d 1208 (CTA 8 1990) 336

Hinsdale Women's Clinic, S.C. v. Women's Health Care of Hinsdale, 690 F. Supp. 658
    (N.D. Ill., Jun. 20, 1988) 61

Holmes v. Jennison, 39 U.S. (14 Pet.) 540, 616 (1840) 335

In re Search Warrant (Sealed), 810 F.2d 67 (3d Cir. 1987) 171

International Union v. Johnson Controls, 499 U.S. 187 (1991) 455

Jacobson v. Massachusetts, 197 U.S. 11 (1905) 76, 335, 336

Jefferson Parish Hosp. Dist. No. 2 v. Hyde, 466 U.S. 2 (1984). 61

Kansas v. Hendricks, 521 U.S. 346 (1997) 335

Katz v. Colonial Life Ins. Co. of Am., 951 F. Supp. 36 (S.D.N.Y. 1997). 286

Krauel v. Iowa Methodist Med. Ctr., 95 F.3d 674 (8th Cir. 1996) 455

Lancaster by Lancaster v. Kaiser Found. Health Plan, 958 F. Supp. 1137 (E.D. Va. 1997) 286

Lehr v. Robertson, 463 U.S. 248 (1982) 375

LeMasters v. Christ Hosp., 791 F. Supp. 188 (S.D. Ohio 1991) 307

Mazur v. Merck & Co., Inc., 964 F.2d 1348 (3d Cir. [Pa.] 1992) 202

Metropolitan Life Ins. Co. v. Taylor, 481 U.S. 58 (1987) 286

Michael H. & Victoria D., Appellants v. Gerald D., 491 U.S. 110 (1989) 375

Miranda v. Arizona, 384 U.S. 436, 16 L. Ed. 2d 694, 86 S. Ct. 1602 (1966) 60

Moore v. Ashland Chemical Inc., 151 F.3d 269 (5th Cir. [Tex.] 1998). 131

North Am. Cold Storage Co. v. City of Chicago, 211 U.S. 306 (1908) 76

Ohio v. Akron Ctr. for Reproductive Health, 110 S. Ct. 2972 (1990) 248

Parker v. Brown, 317 U.S. 341 (1943). 61

Patrick v. Burget, 486 U.S. 94 (1988) 287

Planned Parenthood v. Casey, 505 U.S. 833 (1992) 375

Prince v. Massachusetts, 321 U.S. 158 (1944) 336

Public Citizen v. Heckler, 653 F. Supp. 1229 (D.D.C. Dec. 31, 1986) 76

Purviance v. Angus, 1 U.S. 180 (1786) 61

Quinn v. Kent Gen'l Hosp., 716 F. Supp. 1226 (1985) 307

Reynolds v. McNichols, 488 F.2d 1378 (10th Cir. 1973). 247

Roberts v. Galen of Va., Inc., 119 S. Ct. 685 (1999) 202

Rust v. Sullivan, 500 U.S. 173 (1991) 375

Santosky v. Kramer, 455 U.S. 745, 755 (1982) 248

Schachar v. American Academy of Ophthalmology, Inc., 870 F.2d 397 (7th Cir. 1989). 248

School Bd. of Nassau County, Fla. v. Arline, 480 U.S. 273 (1987). 455

Sedima, S.P.R.L. v. Imrex Co., 473 U.S. 479, (1985) 61

Shea v. Esensten, 107 F.3d 625 (8th Cir. 1997). 286

Shoemaker v. Shirtliffe, 1 U.S. 127 (1785). 61

Smith v. Turner, 48 U.S. (7 How.) 283, 340–341 (1849). 335

St. Agnes Hospital v. Riddick, 748 F. Supp. 319 (1990) 375

Stevesons's Heirs v. Sullivant, 18 U.S. 207 (1820) 375

The T.J. Hooper, 60 F.2d 737 (C.C.A.2 1932). 131

Trustees of Dartmouth College v. Woodward, 17 U.S. 518 (1819) 307

United Mine Workers v. Pennington, 381 U.S. 657 (1965) 287

United States v. Bachynsky, 934 F.2d 1349 (5th Cir. 1991) 61, 248

United States v. Bay State Ambulance & Hosp. Rental Serv., Inc., 874 F.2d 20
 (1st Cir. 1989) 61

United States v. Greber, 760 F.2d 68 (3d Cir. 1985). 61

United States v. Kats, 871 F.2d 105 (9th Cir. 1989) 61

United States v. Bagley, 473 U.S. 667, 682 (1985) 131

United States v. Bornstein, 423 U.S. 303 (1976). 61

United States v. Clark, 928 F.2d 733, 738 (6th Cir. 1991) 131

United States v. Lorenzo, 768 F. Supp. 1127 (E.D. Pa. 1991). 61

United States v. Salerno, 481 U.S. 739 (1987) 131

United States v. Westinghouse Elec. Corp., 638 F.2d 570, 578 (3d Cir. 1980). 171

Upjohn Co. v. United States, 449 U.S. 383 (1981) 155
Vacco v. Quill, 521 U.S. 793, 117 S.Ct. 2293 (1997) 248
Washington v. Glucksberg, 521 U.S. 702 (1997) 248
Washington v. Harper, 110 S. Ct. 1028 (1990). 471
Wayne v. Genesis Med. Ctr., 140 F.3d 1145 (8th Cir. [Iowa] 1998). 307
Webster v. Reproductive Health Serv., 492 U.S. 490 (1989) 375
Weiss v. York Hospital, 745 F.2d 786 (3d Cir. 1984) 307

STATE CASES

Alberts v. Devine, 479 N.E.2d 113, 121 (Mass. 1985) 171
Beach v. Wilton, 91 N.E. 492, 495 (Ill. 1910). 286
Biddle v. Warren Gen'l Hosp., 1998 WL 156997 (Ohio App. 11 Dist. Mar. 27, 1998) 171
Bouvia v. Superior Ct., 179 Cal. App. 3d 1127, 225 Cal. Rptr. 297 (Cal. App. 2 Dist. 1986) 203
Bovara v. St. Francis Hosp., 700 N.E.2d 143 (Ill. App. 1 Dist. 1998) 202
Carr v. Strode, 904 P.2d 489 (Haw. 1995) 247
Collins v. Thakkart, 552 N.E.2d 507 (1990) 36
Cruzan v. Harmon, 760 S.W.2d 408 (Mo., 1988). 248
Davis v. Davis, 1990 WL 130807 (Tenn. Ct. App. 1990). 375
Davis v. Davis, 842 S.W.2d 588 (Tenn. 1992) 375
Doe v. Noe, 690 N.E.2d 1012 (Ill. App. 1 Dist. 1997) 248
Ex parte McGee, 105 Kan. 574, 581, 185 P. 14, 16 (1919) 335
Faya v. Almaraz, 438, 620 A.2d 327 (1993). 248
Fosmire v. Nicoleau, 551 N.E.2d 77 (N.Y. 1990). 248
Fox v. Health Net of Cal., Cause No. 219692 (Cal. Super. Ct., Riverside Cty., Dec. 23, 1993) 286
Gaither v. City Hosp., Inc., 487 S.E.2d 901 (W.Va. 1997). 131
Gleitman v. Cosgrove, 227 A.2d 689, 711 (1967). 406
Harper v. Healthsource N.H., Inc., 674 A.2d 962 (N.H. 1996) 307
In re Conservatorship of Foster, 547 N.W.2d 81 (Minn. 1996). 247
In re Co-operative Law Co., 92 N.E. 15, 16 (N.Y. 1910). 286
In re Halko, 246 Cal. 2d 553, 556, 54 Cal. Rptr. 661, 663 (1966) 335
In re Baby M, 537 A.2d 1227 (N.J. 1988). 375
Jardel Co. v. Kathleen Hughes, 523 A.2d 518, 529–530 (1987) 36
McVey v. Englewood Hosp. Ass'n, 216 N.J. Super. 502, 524 A.2d 450
 (N.J. Super. A.D. 1987). 248
Mero v. Sadoff, 31 Cal. App. 4th 1466, 37 Cal. Rptr. 2d 769 (Cal. App. 2 Dist. 1995) 202
Merriman v. Toothaker, 515 P.2d 509 (Wash. App. Div. 2 1973) 202
Miller v. Rhode Island Hosp., 625 A.2d 778 (R.I. 1993) 247
Molien v. Kaiser Found. Hosp., 616 P.2d 813 (Cal. 1980). 335
Moore v. Regents of Univ. of Cal., 793 P.2d 479 (Cal. 1990). 248
Mozingo by Thomas v. Pitt County Mem'l Hosp., Inc., 415 S.E.2d 341, 345 (N.C. 1992) 287
Munro v. Regents of Univ. of Cal., 215 Cal. App. 3d 977, 263 Cal. Rptr. 878
 (Cal. App. 2 Dist. 1989) 405
Nishi v. Hartwell, 473 P.2d 116 (Haw. 1970). 247
Payton v. Weaver, 131 Cal, App. 3d 38, 182 Cal. Rptr. 225 (Cal. App. 1 Dist. 1982). 203
Pettus v. Cole, 49 Cal. App. 4th 402, 57 Cal. Rptr. 2d 46 (Cal. App. 1 Dist. 1996). 455
Phillips v. Good Samaritan Hosp., 416 N.E.2d 646 (Ohio App. 2 Dist. 1979) 202

Reynolds v. Decatur Mem'l Hosp., 660 N.E.2d 235 (Ill. App. 4 Dist. 1996) 202
Rivera v. Minnich, 506 A.2d 879 (Pa. 1986) 375
Sammarco v. Anthem Ins. Co., 1998 WL 804198 (Ohio App. 1 Dist. 1998) 307
Sarosi v. Sobol, 155 A.D.2d 125, 553 N.Y.S.2d 517 (N.Y.A.D. 3 Dept. 1990) 375
Schoendorff v. Society of New York Hosp., 105 N.E. 92, 93 (N.Y. 1914) 247
Sermchief v. Gonzales, 660 S.W.2d 683 (Mo. 1983) 286
Simonsen v. Swenson, 104 Neb. 224, 228, 177 N.W. 831, 832 (Neb. 1920) 335
Tarasoff v. Regents of Univ. of Cal., 551 P.2d 334 (Cal. 1976) 336
Texaco, Inc. v. Pennzoil Co., 729 S.W.2d 768, 822
 (Tex.App.—Houston [1st Dist.] 1987, *writ ref'd* n.r.e.) 131
Thomas v. Morris, 286 N.Y. 266, 269, 36 N.E. 2d 141, 142 (N.Y. 1941) 335
Townsend v. Turk, 218 Cal. App. 3d 278, 266 Cal. Rptr. 821 (Cal. App. 4 Dist. 1990) 202
Truman v. Thomas, 611 P.2d 902 (Cal. 1980) 202
Tumblin v. Ball-Incon Glass Packaging Corp., 478 S.E.2d 81 (S.C.App. 1996) 202
Varholy v. Sweat, 153 Fla, 571, 575, 15 So. 2d 267, 270 (Fla. 1943) 335
Ward v. Lutheran Hosp. & Homes Soc'y of Am., Inc., 963 P.2d 1031 (Alaska 1998) 247
Weber v. Armco, Inc., 663 P.2d 1221 (Okla. 1983) 287
Wickline v. State of California, 228 Cal. Rptr. 661 (Cal. App. 1986) 286
Wilson v. Blue Cross of So. Cal., 271 Cal. Rptr. 876 (Cal. App. 1990) 286
Witherell v. Weimer, 421 N.E.2d 869 (Ill. 1981) 286

FEDERAL STATUTES

15 U.S.C. § 1011 (1996) 287
29 U.S.C. § 706 (1988 ed.) 455
31 U.S.C. §§ 3729, et seq. (1997) 61
31 U.S.C. § 3730(d)(1) 61
42 U.S.C. § 300e-10 (1973) 286
42 U.S.C. § 1395nn 60
42 U.S.C. §§ 11131, 11133, & 11134 (1996) 287
42 U.S.C. § 1137(c) (1996) 287
42 U.S.C.A. § 290dd-2 171
42 U.S.C.A. §§ 12101, et seq. 455
42 U.S.C.A. §§ 11101, et seq. 307
42 U.S.C.A. § 1320a-7b. (1998) 61
Employee Retirement Income Security Act of 1974 (ERISA), 29 U.S.C. § 1001 (1996) 286

Index

A

Abandonment
  of child, 363
  of patient, 195, 276
Abortion, 18, 236, 357
  adoption alternatives to, 360
  consent to, 359
  controversies about, 357, 360
  counseling on, 359, 404
  government support of, 358
  minors and, 244
  parental information on, 359
  personal beliefs and, 358, 404
  politics of, 357
  privacy rights and, 357
  RU 486 and changes to, 360
Academy of Pediatrics, 54
Accidents, 177, 237, 330, 462
Accreditation Council for Graduate Medical Education
  (ACGME), 346
Acquired immunodeficiency syndrome (AIDS), 351
Acute illness observation scale, 169
Administrative agencies, 67
Administrative law, 66, 67
  administrative law judges, role of, 71
  agency expertise, 70
  civil penalties, 74
  Congressional casework, 68
  criminal law, parallels with, 38
  delegation, 67
  enabling legislation, 67
  enforcement, 73
  Food and Drug Administration, 67
  formal agency actions, 70

Goldberg rights, 71
  independent agencies, 68
  injunctions and seizures, 74
  licenses, 73
  permits, 73
  political control, 68
  political control by Congress, 68
  political control by the President, 68
  registrations, 73
  rulemaking, 72
  separation of powers, 69
  The Jungle, 67
Administrative orders, 74
Adoption, 364
  as abortion alternative, 360
  Baby M surrogacy case and, 370
  evaluating children for, 367
  fertility procedures and, 366
  matchmaking in, 366
  parental rights and, 361, 364
  payments in, 364
  private placement in, 365, 366
  proceedings in, 363, 365
  records in, 367
  state restrictions in, 368
Advertising, 217, 258, 404
Affidavit, 114
Affirmative defense, 113
Alcoholism, 401, 438
Alternative dispute resolution (ADR), 9
  American Arbitration Association, 10
  arbitration, 10
  mediation, 10
  mini-trials, 10
Ambulance services, 468

Ambulatory care centers, 194, 412
American Academy of Pediatrics, 322, 367
American Arbitration Association, 10
American College of Obstetrics and Gynecology
    (ACOG), 381
American Medical Association (AMA), 244, 401
Americans with Disabilities Act (ADA), 67, 193, 430
    collective bargaining, 436
    communicable diseases in workplace and, 444, 446,
        451
    direct threat, 436
    legal risks of, 437
    occupational health and, 414, 430
    physician's duty to treat, 193
    return to work certification and, 413
    union seniority rules, 436
Amniocentesis, 380, 382, 387
Antitrust, 3, 52
    Federal Trade Commission, 285
    Justice Department Guidelines, 286
    managed care organizations and, 285
    per se violation, 52
    physicians collective bargaining, 285
Antitrust laws, 52
Appellate process, 3, 8, 126
Appointments
    abandonment of patient and, 195
    delegation of authority to staff to make, 267
    follow-up after missing, 195, 197
    physician-patient relationship and, 174, 193
Arbitration, 10
Arline, 437
Articles of Confederation, 1
Artificial insemination (AI), 387
    choosing donor in, 383, 387
    consent in, 387
    infection control in, 389
    restrictions on, 361
    surrogacy and, 370
Athletics, 370
Attending physicians, 189, 265, 400
Attorney fees, 126
    caps on, 128
    contingency and, 23, 128
    malpractice litigation and, 118
    plaintiff's attorney's fees, 127
    structured settlements and, 29
Attorneys
    as witnesses, 153
    attorney client communications, 151
    attorney work product, 151
    autonomy and clients of, 141
    being an effective client of, 149
    billing practices, 147
    billing, effect practice styles of, 148
    business ventures between physician and, 145
    choosing, 142
    conflict of cultures between physician and, 140
    conflicts of interest, 144
    delegation of work to others by, 142
    fees, padding of, 149
    highlights concerning, 137
    identification with clients, 144
    importance of independence, 151
    in-house counsel, 146, 151
    limited engagement doctrine and, 141
    physician refusal to treat, 192
    physician-patient relationship, differences with, 140
    preparing for trial and, 6, 130
    preventive law audit by, 150
    structure of legal work and, 146
    working with, 139
Audit, preventive law, 150
Automobile accidents, 177, 237, 330, 462
Autopsies, 330

B

Baby M case, 368, 370
Baby-selling, and adoption, 364
Backup coverage, 194
Bankruptcy, 126
Basic life support, 179
Bastardy, 361
Battery
    legal standard for, 17, 205
Bendectin, 124
Beyond a reasonable doubt standard, 44
Birth certificates
    filing of, 328
    information on, 328
    naming child on, 328
    public health statistics and, 327
Birth control, 349
Birth plan, 392, 396
Birth records, 328, 329, 367
Birthing room, 394, 404
Birth-injured infants
    malpractice litigation over, 403
    pregnancy risks and, 393, 405
Blood doping, and sports, 466

Blood tests, and paternity, 363
Blood transfusions, refusal of, 222
Boards of medical examiners, 52, 66, 266, 276, 316, 365, 400
Boards of nursing examiners, 400
Boards of pharmacy, 270
Borrowed-servant doctrine, 265
Brady Request, 117
Breach of contract, 18
Business records
    evidence, 120
    hearsay rule exception for, 120, 162
Business ventures
    medical research and, 223
    physician-attorney partnership in, 145
    RICO litigation over failure of, 56

C

Capitation agreements
    managed care organizations and, 284
    risks to physicians, 284
Captain-of-the-ship doctrine, 265
Cardiology, 181, 183, 190
Cardiopulmonary resuscitation (CPR), 177, 243
Carrier state
    disease control and, 314
    HIV infection, 314
Causation, 25, 118
Cause of death, 329
CCU, 31
Centers for Disease Control and Prevention (CDC), 314, 322, 330, 448, 450
Certification
    basic life support and, 179
    occupational medicine and, 418
Cesarean section, 396
    consent in, 397
    emergency care with, 33, 393
Charts, 268
Child abuse
    as legal finding, 332
    investigation of, 365
    pediatric care and, 331
    reporting of, 188, 220, 331, 365
    treatment for, 221
Child custody
    document in medical record, 162
Child welfare agency, 220, 365
Children, 467

abandonment of, 363
conflict between parents and, 221
custody after divorce and, 220, 364
development and hormonal techniques for, 466
guardianship and, 232
HIV infection in, 367
informed consent and emergency care for, 207
litigation over injuries to, 404
parental refusal of medical care to, 233
school doctor and, 467
Civil law, 12
    administrative regulations and, 66
    nonmonetary remedies in, 22
    peacekeeping function of, 12
Civil penalties, 74
Civil rights legislation, 1, 14, 389
Civil rights movement
    quarantine and, 320
Clayton Act, 52
Clear-and-convincing-evidence standard, 238
COBRA (see Emergency Medical Treatment and Actice Labor Act), 192
Cocaine abuse
    pregnancy and, 401, 402
Code of Federal Regulations (CFR), 72
Collateral source rule, 28
College students, 465
    health programs for, 470
    sports and, 465
Commercial bribery, 258
Common law, 310, 361
    Democratic traditions and, 1
    English, 5
    evolution of precedent, 8
    legitimacy of children under, 361
    physician-patient relationship in, 138
    pleading under, 112
    precedent, importance of, 7
    public health authority under, 310
Communicable diseases, 444
    Americans with Disabilities Act (ADA) concerning, 446
    as disabilities, 446
    direct threat, 446
    direct threat from, 447
    direct threat to others, 436
    duration of risk, 449
    fear of, 327
    immunosuppression and, 445, 451
    legal risks of, 445
    nature of the risk, 449

of minors, 221
origin of, 326
policy regarding, 448
prison doctor and, 462
reporting of, 221, 312, 315, 469
school doctor and, 470
significant risk from, 447
Supreme Court case, 449
third-party liability in, 445
transmission methods for, 449
treatment of, 221
workplace and, 444
Community
    immunization programs and, 320
    respect for physicians in, 130
Company doctor (see Occupational Medicine)
    competition, 138
    professional standards and, 21
Compliance plans, 58
    as preventive law, 150
Compliance, and termination of care, 196
Computers, and medical records, 163
Condoms, and birth control, 351
Confidentiality
    adoption records and, 367
    college health programs and, 470
    disease control reporting and, 314
    medical records and, 168
    occupational medicine and, 427
    preemployment medical examination and, 434
Conflicts of interest, 253
    attorneys and, 144
    hospital ownership and, 218
    incentive plans and, 55
    informed consent and, 217
    laboratory ownership and, 218
    medical research and, 223
    physician-patient relationship and criminal activity,
        44
    proxy consent and, 231
    sexual relationships with patients and, 218
    team doctor and, 464
    treating family members and, 218
Congress, 323, 444
    contraception and, 349
    Medicare/Medicaid regulation by, 54
Congressional casework, 68
Consent, 219
    defining, 206
    documenting, 219, 230
    for autopsy, 330

guardianship and, 220, 232, 233
intoxication testing and, 334
minors and, 219
proxy, 219, 230
right to refuse treatment, 207
Consortium, 27
    Constitution, 241, 319
    public health authority and, 310, 311, 313
Constitution
    commerce clause, 4
    criminal law, 39
    limits on federal power, 5
    police power, 4
    preemption of state laws, 5
    sovereignty determination under, 3
Constitutional protections, 40
    bail, 41
    double jeopardy, 44
    ex post facto laws, 41
    grand jury indictments, 41
    habeas corpus, 40
    just compensation for takings, 41
    rights of the accused, 41
    searches and seizures, 41, 43
    self-incrimination, 42
    trial by jury, 41
Consultations, 180
    child abuse seen in, 188
    documentation of, 182
    function of, 180
    informal, 177, 181
    information on patient provided in, 187
    institutional, 188
    physician's duty to choose, 182
    recordkeeping in, 188
    referrals differentiated from, 180
    tests and procedures and, 187
Consulting physicians, 180
    duty to inform patient, 188
    duty to inform treating physician, 188
Contact effectiveness, 450
Contact tracing, 318
Contingent fees, 126, 127, 180
Continuing care, 185
Contraception, 349, 353
    balancing health care practitioner's and patients'
        rights in, 352
    choice in, 349
    HIV infection and, 351
    implantable contraceptives and, 351
    minor's access to, 221, 352

natural family planning and, 351
risk of pregnancy and, 349, 384
sterilization and, 353
Contracts, 18
artificial insemination and, 388
between hospitals and physicians, 192
breach of, 18
civil law covering, 23
managed care organizations and, 193
medical research and, 223
occupational medicine physicians and, 412, 418
preferred provider organizations (PPOs) and, 193
preventive law audit of, 150
school doctor and, 468
surrogacy and, 368, 370
Uniform Commercial Code (UCC), 13
Copayments
waiving as fraud, 50
Coroner cases, 330
Corporate practice of medicine
attorneys as model, 254
interference with professional judgment, 254
physicians, limited to, 255
prohibition of, 254
Costs
trial, 126
Court costs
lawyers' fees and, 23, 30
Court system
administrative agencies, deference to, 75
administrative regulations enforced by, 74
appellate process in, 8, 126
definition of death by, 239
guardianship in, 207
life support system termination and, 241
litigation bias in, 9
role of judges in, 7
treatment mandated by, 207, 319, 335
Criminal law, 7, 39
administrative law, parallels with, 38
citizen's duty under, 45
decision to prosecute under, 44
medical research and, 223
Miranda rights, 42
physician-patient relationship protection under, 45
punishment, 40
reporting duties under, 331
right to counsel, 42
vague laws, attacking, 41
Critical care unit (CCU)
fetal monitors in, 31

legal risks with safety devices in, 31
products liability in, 30
pulse oximetry, 33
Cross-examination, 120
Cruzan case, 237
Custody
medical treatment of children and, 220

D

Damages, 15, 23
civil law mandating, 12
collateral source rule and, 28
costs of litigation and, 23
direct economic, 23
emotional distress, 27
future earning capacity, 24
indirect economic, 26
lost wages, 24
lump sum damage payments, 29
medical expenses, future, 25
medical expenses, past, 25
pain and suffering, 27
paying, 29
punitive, 28
structured settlements, 29
Daubert, 124
Davis v. Davis (custody of embryos), 368
Death
a legal definition of, 239
public health records on, 327
Death certificates, 329
Decision making
Declaration of Helsinki, 223
in contraception, sterilization, and abortion, 345
public health authority and, 311
Declaration of Geneva, 224
Defensive medicine, 34
Delegation of authority
classes of medical tasks in, 266
explicit, 267
implicit, 267
issues to consider in, 266
limitations on, 266
midwives and, 400
physician's orders and, 271
protocols and, 270
supervision with, 268
Dementia
children in school and, 469

Denial of care
    ERISA, 260
    physician's duty and, 259
    Wickline, 259
Denver Development Screening Test, 170
Department of Health and Human Services (DHHS), 223
Department of Justice, 39, 56
    health care criminal prosecutions, 39
Department of Transportation, 412, 418
Deposition, 113
Development of child
    birth injuries in, 405
    hormonal techniques for altering, 466
    medical records on, 169
Diagnosis
    differential diagnosis list for, 271
    protocols for, 270, 273
Diagnosis-related groups (DRGs), 241
Dilatory practice, 149
Direct orders, 272
Direct threat, 436
Disabled persons (see Americans with Disabilities Act)
    Americans with Disabilities Act (ADA) definition
        of, 432
    communicable diseases and, 446
    damage award for expenses of, 25
    immunosuppression and, 445
    workers' compensation and, 443
Discovery, 113
    Brady Request, 117
    contesting orders for, 117
    cross-examination for, 115
    definition of, 113
    forms of, 113
    in criminal cases, 117
    latitude for, 117
    medical records and, 114, 115
Discrimination
    HIV carrier state, 314
Disease registries, 330
Divorce
    embryo custody after, 368
    genetic counseling and, 383
    medical treatment of children, 219, 363
    parental rights in, 363
    pregnancy and, 364
Domestic violence, 333
Down syndrome, 380
Drug abuse, 438
    college students and, 471

preemployment medical examination and, 438
    prisoners and, 462
    rehabilitation program for, 438
Drug Enforcement Administration (DEA), 270
Drugs
    laws covering, 270
    prescription of, 270
    samples of, 270
    testing of, 333
Dual capacity doctrine, 281
Due process
    prison doctor and, 460
    public health and, 311
Durable power of attorney, 231, 238, 240, 393

E

Electrocardiograms (EKGs), 190
Electronic medical records, 170
    authentication, 170
    backup, 164
    privacy, 170
    theft, 171
Emancipated minor, 222
Embryo transplantation, 363
    divorce and custody of, 368
    donors in, 363
Emergency care
    abortion, sterilization, and contraception counseling
        and, 347
    adults who refuse, 207, 233
    death certificates, 330
    definition of, 207
    Good Samaritan laws on, 178
    guardianship and, 233
    guardianship for, 207, 233
    informed consent and, 206
    intoxication and, 334
    living wills and, 243
    medical office and, 179
    midwives and, 399
    prison doctor and, 462
    prisoner care in, 335
    school doctor and, 467
Emergency Medical Treatment and Active Labor Act
        (EMTALA), 76
    certification for transfer, 79
    definition of emergency medical condition, 80
    definition of stabilize, 81
    delays to check insurance, 81

duty to treat, 192
enforcement, 79
fines under, 79
medical screening, 78, 192
Medicare hospitals, special duties, 82
negligence per se, 17
physician duties, 192
physician liability, 192
private cause of action, 80
refusal to consent to transfer, 78
refusal to consent to treatment, 78
stabilization, 78
statutory cause of action, 14
whistleblower protections, 81
women in labor, 80
Emerging infectious diseases, 309
Emotional distress, 27
Employees, 139
Employers, physician as, 139
Enabling legislation, 67
agency enforcement, 73
agency interpretation of law, 75
Americans with Disabilities Act, 67
delegation of Congressional power, 67
EMTALA, 76
executive orders, 68
rulemaking, 72
English common law, 310
Environmental health, 325
Epidemics, 310, 313, 321, 326
Epidemiology, protocols for, 274
Equal Employment Opportunity Commission (EEOC),
14
ERISA, 260
MCOs and, 260
premption of state laws regulating MCOs, 261
purpose of, 260
Evidence
admission of, 119
Daubert case, 124
Daubert rule, 124
Frye rule, 123
general acceptance, 123
hearsay rule, 120
lie detector, 123
prison doctor and, 463
scientific, 123
standards for, 44
Examination of patient
standard of care on, 18
Exclusionary rule, 43

Executive orders, 68
Exemplary damages, 28
Experiments, 209
Expert witnesses
locality rule, 20
malpractice litigation and, 19
paternity testing, 383
product liability and, 30
qualifying, 125
specialty qualifications of, 19
standard of care and, 16, 125
trial and, 130
witnesses, expert, 122

F

Fact witnesses, 122
False Claims Act, 14, 45
enforcement, 48
history, 49
penalties, 49
risk management, 49
Families
artificial insemination and, 361, 387
disease control reporting and, 317, 318
fertility treatment and, 384
guardianship and, 232
life support system termination and, 8, 236, 239, 242,
244
obstetric care and, 378
of physician, and treatment decisions, 218
parental rights in, 368
pediatrics and, 219
power of attorney to consent to medical care and, 231
substituted consent and conflicts in, 244
surrogacy and, 368
workplace acquired infection and, 445
Family planning
federal policy and, 352, 357
Family practitioners, 190
Fathers
adoption and, 364
artificial insemination, and choice of, 383, 387, 388
assuming legitimacy of children and, 361
determination of legitimacy for, 361, 368
genetic counseling and, 383
medical care of mothers and, 361
Federal court system, 3
administrative regulations enforced in, 66
appellate process in, 3, 8

district courts, 3
  medical malpractice in, 3
  sovereignty of, 3
Federal laws
  abortion and, 345, 359
  communicable disease plan and, 450
  family planning and, 352, 358
  handicapped children and, 470
  immunization programs and, 322
  informed consent under, 213
  occupational medicine and, 412
  patient dumping under, 184
  sterilization and, 355
Federal preemption, 5
Federal Sentencing Guidelines, 57
  compliance plans, 58
  fiduciary duty, 57
  health care practitioners and, 60
  Office of Inspector General, 58
  sexual assault of patient, 57
  white collar crime, 57
Federal taxes, 264
Federal Trade Commission (FTC), 21, 53, 258
Federalist system, 1
  checks and balances, 2
  executive branch, 2
  judicial branch, 3
  legislative branch, 2
Fertility treatment, 385, 389
  adoption and, 366
  embryo custody after divorce and, 368
  fitness issues in, 385
  multiple gestation in, 386
  unmarried couples and, 389
Fetal monitors, 32
Fiduciary duty, 257
  commercial bribery, 258
  duty to disclose incentives, 263
  federal laws, 258
  incentive plans and, 55
  informed consent, 259
  institutional practice and, 459
  managed care, 173
  market factors in choice of provider and, 258
  medical research and, 217
  physician-patient relationship, 173, 253, 258
  physicians, 257
  RICO fraud and, 55
  state laws, 257
Fifth Amendment, 42
First Amendment, 358

Follow-up care
  medical records and, 164
  missed appointments and, 195
  protocols for, 273
Fomites, 449
Food and Drug Administration, 67, 164, 351, 360
Food sanitation, 324, 467
Football, 464, 465
Fourteenth Amendment, 460
Fourth Amendment, 43
Fraud, 38
  advertising medical services and, 404
  failure to disclose a risk as, 211, 213
  Mail and wire, under RICO, 54
  medical students and residents and, 276
Free speech rights, 359
Frye rule (see Expert witnesses), 123

G

General denial, 113
Genetic counseling
  abortion views and, 404
  choice of father and, 383
  consent in, 384
  genetic history in, 381
  screening in, 379
  time limitations in, 382
  torts and, 403
Goldberg rights, 71
Good Samaritan laws
  emergencies and, 178
Group health insurance
  subrogation agreement and, 29
Growth hormone deficiency, 222
Guardianship, 232
  document in medical record, 162
  emergency and, 233
  establishing, 232
  informed consent and, 207, 219
  judicial determinations, 13
  release of medical records and, 166
  wards, 232
Gunshot wounds, 333

H

Habeas corpus, 40
Handicapped persons
  communicable diseases and, 446
  school doctor and, 470

Health Care Financing Administration (HCFA), 66
Health Care Quality Improvement Act of 1986, 53
Health departments, 313, 317, 320
Health Insurance Portability and Accountability Act of 1996 (HIPAA), 51
   private insurance fraud, 160
Health maintenance organizations, 253
Health officer
   disease control and, 314, 325
Hearsay rule, 120, 162
   evidence, 120
Hepatitis B (HBV), 325, 446, 449, 450, 462
Herd immunity, 321
High school athletics, 464, 465
High-technology
   informed consent and, 209
High-technology medicine
   life support under, 235
   malpractice and, 34
   medicalization of reproduction and, 361
Hippocratic oath, 235
HMOs (see Managed care organizations), 10, 253
Home deliveries, 398
Hospital
   prison doctor and, 463
Hospital records, 158
Hospitals
   abortion, sterilization, and contraception counseling and, 346
   charitable immunity, 265
   consultations within, 188
   disease control in, 320
   guardianship authority and, 232
   liability of physician for employees of, 265
   life support system termination and, 236, 241
   medical records in, 165, 170
   obstetric care in, 396, 404
   ownership by physicians of, 218
   parental consent for minor care and, 220, 233
   patient dumping practices and, 184
   physician's legal relationship with, 139, 192
   referrals to, 184, 185
   refusal of care by patient and, 241
   staff privileges in, 185
Human growth hormone, 222, 466
Human immunodeficiency virus (HIV) infection, 320, 325, 348, 444, 449
   children with, 367
   contraception counseling and, 351
   disease control for, 327, 389
   environmental health and, 325

   epidemics and plagues and, 313
   fear of, 327
   food sanitation and, 324
   historical overview of, 325
   immunization laws and, 320
   immunosuppression and, 445
   in the workplace, 437
   informed consent by infected physician, 215
   medical records in, 166
   mothers with, 363
   obstetric care and, 395
   physician-patient relationship and, 314
   prison doctor and, 463
   prisoner, doctor and, 461
   quarantine and, 320
   school doctor and, 469
   screening for, 389
   testing for, 348
   warning third parties in, 317
   workplace infection with, 446, 450
Husbands
   as artificial insemination donor, 387
   power of attorney to consent to medical care and, 231
   reproductive counseling for wives and, 387, 392
Hydration, termination of, 237

I

Immunization, 219, 318
   compulsory, 321
   consent for, 322
   disease control programs with, 313, 444
   medical exemptions for, 322
   political factors in, 320
   prison doctor and, 462
   reportable events following, 324
   Vaccine Compensation Act on, 323
Immunosuppression, 322, 445, 450, 451
Implants
   medical records for, 164
In vitro fertilization (IVF), 389
   embryo custody after divorce and, 369
   unmarried couples and, 389
Inadvertent abandonment, 195
Incentive plans, 196, 261
Indemnification agreements, 284
Independent contractor physician
   occupational medicine and, 412
   prisons and, 463
Indirect economic damages, 26

Induction of labor, 396
Infectious disease (see Communicable diseases), 326
Informed consent, 9, 206, 209
    abortion and, 360
    alternative treatments and, 212
    artificial insemination and, 387
    cesarean section and, 397
    conflicts of interest on, 217
    consultations and referrals with, 180
    contraception and, 349, 351, 354
    disease control reporting and, 317
    documentation of, 228
    emergency care exception to, 206
    forms for, 228
    genetic counseling and, 384
    illiterate patients and, 229
    immunizations and, 322
    individual liberty issue, 210
    knowable and unknowable risks and, 213
    legal standards for, 210
    legally mandated treatment and, 207
    medical records on, 228
    medical research, 217, 225
    medical value of, 216
    medically unnecessary procedures and, 215
    non-English speakers and translation in, 229
    obstetric care with, 401
    oral, 230
    paternalism of physician and, 210
    patient's expectations and, 216
    physician with HIV, 215
    physician-patient relationship and, 138, 140
    school doctor and, 469, 470
    sports and injuries and, 465
    sterilization and, 353
    surrogacy contract and, 374
    teaching programs and, 280
    telemedicine, 202
    therapeutic exception to, 208
    voluntariness of, 214
    what must the plaintiff prove, 216
    withheld information and, 208
In-house counsel, 146
    conflicts of interest, 146
    criminal representation, 146
    legal privilege, 146
Injunctions, 22
Injunctions and seizures, 74
Institutional practice, 459, 464
    consultations within, 188
    physician's legal relationship with, 139

    proxy consent for, 184, 220
    school doctor and, 467
    teams and, 464
Institutional review boards (IRBs), 226
Insurance companies, 29
    abandonment of patient and, 195
    attorney fees and, 127, 149
    collateral source rule and, 28
    college students and, 471
    damages payment by, 29
    incentive schemes from, 196, 253
    obstetric care and, 396
    pediatric care and, 21
    physician-patient relationship and contracts with, 193
    referrals and, 184
    rehabilitation expenses and, 26
    subrogation provision and, 29
Intensive care medicine, 236
Intentional torts, 17, 265
Internal Revenue Service (IRS), 264
International classification of disease, revision 9 (ICD-9), 329
International codes on medical research, 223
Internet medicine, 197
Interrogatories, 113
Intoxication
    reporting of, 333
Intrauterine devices (IUDs), 349
Invoking the rule, 119
IPA, 256
Isolation, in disease control, 318, 319

J

Joint Commission on Accreditation of Healthcare Organizations (Joint Commission), 121, 170
    ambulatory care standards, 161
    medical records standards, 157, 160
    physicians office records and, 161
Joint research agreements, 223
Joint ventures, 223
Judges, role of, 7
Judgment in trial, 126
Justice Department, 56

K

Kaposi's sarcoma, 325
Kennedy-Kassebaum bill (see Health Insurance Portability and Accountability Act of 1996), 51

Kickbacks, 51
Kidnapping, and adoption, 366

L

Labor
  fetal monitors during, 31
  induction of, 396
Laboratories
  ownership by physicians of, 218
  protocols for, 273
  research in, 273
Law, 140
  difference between finding and making, 7
  professional paradigm for, 140
Law enforcement
  blood alcohol testing, 207
  involuntary testing of prisoners, 207
  reporting of violent injuries, 331
Lawyers, 444
Lay midwives, 399
Legal audit, 150
Legal education, 141
Legal privilege, 151
  attorney–client communications, 151, 152
  attorney workproduct, 151, 152
  spousal privilege, 152
Legal standards, 122
  importance of, 21
  products liability and, 30
  proving malpractice in, 122
Legal system, 140
  appellate process, 8
  federal court system and, 3
  litigation bias in, 9
  relationships within, 138
  role of judges in, 7
  sovereignty determination, 3
  state court system, 5
Legitimacy
  assumption of, 361
  determination of, 361, 363, 383
Letter of termination, 197
Levonorgestrel implants, 351
Liability
  communicable diseases, 445
  disease reporting and, 317
  emergency care and, 178
  hospital employees and, 265
  hospital ownership, 218

referrals and, 185
  vicarious, 264
Licensing, 73
  acupuncture, 199
  adoption and, 366
  disease control reporting and, 316
  emergency care and, 178
  enforcement issues, 199
  history, 198
  nonphysician practitioners (NPPs), 268
  reproductive medicine counseling and, 346
  residents and, 276, 279
  state law, 198
  trade regulations, 199
Life support system termination, 236
  clear-and-convincing-evidence standard in, 238
  Cruzan case and, 237, 244
  duty to counsel in, 240
  ethical issues regarding, 234
  families and, 8, 236, 239, 244
  hospitals and, 236
  judicial intervention in, 23, 242
  legal aspects of, 9
  patient's wishes in, 238, 240, 241, 244
  persistent vegetative state and, 239
  physician's advisory role in, 140
  right to, 234
  society's interests in, 236
Limited engagement doctrine, 141
Litigation, 140
  alternative dispute resolution (ADR) instead of, 9
  cost of, 126
  discovery in, 113
  informed consent requirements and, 213
  legal system bias toward, 9, 140
  making a claim in, 112
  medical records in, 159
Living wills
  emergency rooms and, 243
  medical record, file in, 162
  proxy consent using, 230, 238, 239, 241
Locality rule, 20
Lost wages, 24

M

Managed care organizations (MCOs), 253
  alternative dispute resolution (ADR) and, 10
  business of, 282
  capitation agreements, 284
  closed-panel, 193

contractual arrangements between physicians and, 193
controlling entity, 256
cost control, 257
deselection of physicians, 283
duty to disclose incentives, 263
false claims act and, 49
history, 255
HMO Act of 1973, 255
incentive plans under, 55
informed consent, 217
market factors in choice of, 258
medical records in, 162
National Practitioner Data Bank, 283
physician consultants and, 186
physician incentive plans, 261
physician-patient relationship and contracts in, 193
physician-patient relationship in, 174
protocol for medical services in, 270
protocols in, 271
relationship to physicians, 256
structure of, 256
supervision of nonphysician practitioners, 268
Market share
    choice of provider and, 258
    peer review and, 52
Marketing, and obstetric care, 404
Marriage, 354
    domestic violence reporting in, 333
    fertility treatment and, 389
    genetic counseling and, 383
    sterilization of partner in, 354
Master-servant relationship, 264
Maternal serum alpha-fetoprotein (MSAFP), 379, 390
Mediation, 10
Medicaid fraud, 38
Medical business, 253
Medical care costs
    standard of care and, 21
Medical devices, and products liability, 30
Medical directors
    commercial bribery of, 282
    criminal prosecution of, 282
    dual capacity doctrine, 281
    ERISA and, 282
    liability, 281
    managed care organizations, 281
    medical license issues, 282
    unauthorized practice of medicine, 282
Medical education
    teaching medical law, 141

Medical insurance, 196
Medical licensing, fiduciary duty and, 258
Medical malpractice, 218
    alternative dispute resolution (ADR) in, 9
    artificial insemination and, 387
    breach of contract and, 16, 18
    court system and, 3, 12
    defensive medicine and, 34
    disease control reporting and, 316
    duty of physician, 16, 184
    litigation bias and, 9
    obstetric care, 378, 391
    occupational medicine, 413
    prima facie case in, 112
    prison doctor, 459
    proving, 15
    referrals, 184
    sexual assault and, 18, 218
    specialty focus and, 36
Medical malpractice insurance
    attorney conflict of interest in, 145
    conflicts between defendants, 145
    damages paid by, 129
    laboratory ownership by physician and, 218
    managed care organizations and, 285
    occupational medicine and, 412
    self-insurance trusts, 145
    teaching programs and, 278
    trial costs and, 126, 145
Medical malpractice insurance companies
    alternative dispute resolution (ADR) and, 10
    rates set by, 22
    sexual assault claims paid by, 18
    unfair claims practices, 18
Medical malpractice litigation
    adoption and, 367
    as civil litigation, 13
    attorney fees in, 118, 147
    costs of, 23, 126
    damage awards in, 25, 26, 129
    depositions in, 114
    discovery in, 113
    emotional distress claims in, 27
    expert witnesses in, 19, 122
    medical expenses in, 25, 26
    medical records in, 159
    patient's expectations and, 216
    pediatric care and, 21
    preexisting illness and, 25
    prima facie case in, 15
    punitive damages in, 28

Medical malpractice prevention
  medical records in, 161
Medical practice
  as a business, 253
  corporate practice of medicine, 254
  history, 254
  legal relationships in, 138
  protocols in, 270
  quality assurance program for, 269
  regulation of, 266
  teaching programs and, 278
Medical records, 315
  access by government, 43
  administrative agency review, 160
  alterations for, 163
  as defensive record, 159
  as legal document, 158, 159
  basic information in, 161
  consistency of, 163
  consultations documented in, 182, 188
  contraception counseling for minors and, 352
  criminal prosecutions and, 160
  critical care unit and, 32
  destruction of, 165
  development and growth of a child on, 169
  discovery process before trial and, 114
  electronic, 164, 170
  family information in, 162
  historical perspective on, 157
  hospital records, 158, 170
  informal consultations documented in, 177
  informed consent documented in, 228
  legal information in, 162
  legal requirements covering, 121
  living wills in, 162
  maintaining, 162
  malpractice litigation and, 159
  managed care and office records, 158
  Medicare fraud, as basis for, 161
  nonphysician practitioners (NPPs) and, 269
  obstetric care, 390
  occupational health and, 419
  of minors, 166, 353
  off-chart records, 32, 166
  office records as, 161
  ownership, 43
  pediatric care and, 168
  physician's orders in, 271
  police access to, 334
  preemployment medical examination and, 434
  primary uses for, 158
  protection of, 163, 422
  readability of, 163
  refusal of care, 240
  release of, 166, 420
  retention of, 164, 165, 419, 434
  search warrants, 160
  selling or transfer of, 167, 196
  statutory requirements affection, 165
  subpoena of, 116
  telephone calls documented in, 165, 175, 176, 177
  termination of care documented in, 196
  test evaluations in, 268
  tracking implants, 164
Medical research, 223
  contracts covering, 23
  controversial nature of, 223
  disease registries and, 330
  HHS regulation on, 226
  informed consent for, 225
  international codes covering, 223
  prisoners and, 462
Medical students, 277
  fraud and, 276
  legal status and, 277
  supervision of, 279
Medical supervision
  documented in medical records, 162
Medical tests
  defensive medicine against malpractice and, 35
  multiple test panels used in, 35
Medicare fraud, 38
  improper charges, 47
  kickbacks, 45
  kickbacks as, 51
  medical records, 161
  professional courtesy, 50
  Stark laws, 51
Medicare/Medicaid laws, 3
  Health Care Financing Administration (HCFA)
    regulations and, 66
  obstetric care under, 398
Medicare/Medicaid programs
  life support under, 235
  medical records retention under, 165
  teaching programs and, 279
Mental illness
  reporting dangerous individuals, 332
  Tarasoff, 332
Mental impairment
  sterilization and, 355
Midlevel practitioners, 139

Midwife
    classes of, 400
    consultations and referrals with, 399
Mini-trials, 10
Minors, 221
    abortion, birth control, and pregnancy information
        for, 221, 222, 245, 352, 359, 385
    communicable disease treatment for, 221
    consent issues for, 207, 219
    emancipated, 222
    family circumstances and decision making
        regarding, 220
    guardianship for, 220
    institutional practice and, 459
    legal status of, 219, 221
    obstetric care for, 392
    parental conflict regarding, 220
    parents' legal rights over decisions regarding, 219
    release of medical records and, 166
    statutory right to treat, 221
    sterilization of, 355
    substance and drug abuse treatment for, 221
Missed appointments, 197
Mothers, 370
    addiction of, 363
    adoption and, 364
    artificial insemination and, 361
    diseases of, 395
    embryo donors and, 364
    fathers and medical decisions of, 361
    surrogacy contracts and, 368, 370
Motion for production, 115

N

National Institute for Occupational Safety and Health
    (NIOSH), 419, 423
Natural family planning, 351
Neglect of child, 221, 331
Negligence
    causation and, 18
    per se, 17
    preventive law audit for, 150
    prima facie case of, 112
    product liability and, 30
    res ipsa loquitur, 16
Neural tube defects, screening for, 379, 390
Neuromuscular development, 170
Nonphysician personnel, 465
    sports staff and, 465

Nonphysician practitioners (NPPs)
    delegation of authority to, 267
    documentation of work, 269
    drug prescription by, 270
    nursing diagnosis and, 269
    referrals to, 183
    supervision of, 266
    unauthorized practice of medicine, 282
    use of term, 263
Norplant, 164
Nuremberg Code, 209, 223
Nuremberg Doctrine, 209
Nurse-midwives (see Midwife), 400
Nurses
    attending physician and, 265
    medical records and, 158, 166
    physician's legal relationship with, 139
    public health and, 320
    school doctor and, 467, 469
    teaching institutions and, 277
Nutrition, termination of, 466

O

Obstetric care, 378
    behavioral risks in pregnancy and, 401
    birth plan in, 392
    birth-injured infant and, 405
    evaluation of mother's medical condition in, 394
    home deliveries and, 398
    malpractice and, 378, 391
    marketing of, 404
    medical interventions in, 396
    refusal to treat by, 177
    structured approach to, 389
    zero-defects management in, 390
Occupational medicine, 411, 412, 417, 459
    Americans with Disabilities Act (ADA) and, 430
    communicable diseases in the workplace and, 450
    medical record information in, 418, 419
    medical records retention and, 165, 418, 423
    occupational medicine and, 411, 413, 417
    return to work certification and, 413
    trade secrets and, 427
    workers' compensation and, 443
Office, medical records, 161
Operating room, surgeon's authority in, 265
Oral contraceptives
    informed consent for, 349
Oral deposition, 113

Oral informed consent, 229
Orders
  delegation of authority with, 268
  direct, 272
  preprinted, 271
  public health, 311
  standing, 271
Ownership
  of hospitals, 218
  of laboratories, 218

P

Pacemakers, 164
Pain, damage awards for, 25
Pan-American Health Organization, 315
Parental rights, 361, 364
  adoption and, 364
  baby-selling and, 367
  child abuse and, 331
  immunization programs and, 322
  legal aspects of, 365
  legitimacy determination and, 362, 368
  medical treatment of children and, 219, 364
  presumption of legitimacy in, 361
  surrogacy and, 368
  termination of, 363
  unfitness and, 363
Parents, 128
  college health programs and, 471
  conflict between children and, 221
  conflict over treatment decisions by, 220
  contraception counseling for minors and, 352, 359
  custody arrangements and, 220
  drug abuse treatment and, 221
  guardianships and, 220, 232
  refusal of medical care for children, 233
  sports and injuries and, 465
  suspicion of child abuse and, 220
Parker v. Brown immunity (see Antitrust), 52
Paternity
  assuming legitimacy of children and, 361
  determination of, 368
  genetic counseling and, 383
Pathologists, 188, 189, 405
  duty to inform patient, 188
  duty to inform treating physician, 188
Patient dumping, 17, 184
Patient Self-Determination Act of 1990, 240
Patients, 138, 173

ability to pay fees, 21, 195, 275, 281
  as consumers, 216
  physician right to refuse, 174
Patients' rights, 138
  to choose medical care, 209, 275, 404
  to choose physician, 181, 275
  to refuse treatment, 195, 207, 234
Pediatric care, 219
  child abuse seen in, 331
  consent in, 219
  immunizations and, 320
  interests of child versus parents in, 222
  malpractice litigation and, 21
  records in, 168
  school doctor and, 467
  statutes of limitations in, 22
  telephone calls in, 168
  unique legal aspects of, 219
Peer review
  Health Care Quality Improvement Act on, 53
  managed care organizations and, 283
  RICO litigation covering, 56
  standard of care and, 21
Performance enhancement drugs, 466
Permits, 73
Personal knowledge test for business records, 121, 162
Physician assistants (see Nonphysician practitioners),
  139
Physician's fees
  patient's inability to pay, 177, 195
Physician's orders, 271
Physician-employee relationship
  as legal relationship, 139
  borrowed-servant doctrine in, 265
  captain-of-the-ship doctrine in, 266
  contracts and, 23
  control in, 264
  employment criteria set out in, 265
  method of payment and, 264
  scope of employment and, 264
  vicarious liability and, 264
Physician-patient relationship
  abandonment of patient in, 194, 276
  as legal relationship, 173
  backup coverage and, 194
  consultations and, 186
  criminal activity and, 45
  disease control and, 314
  duty of physician in, 16, 59, 174, 192, 195
  duty to disclose incentives, 263
  emergency care and, 192

establishment of, 174
expectation of treatment in, 194
fiduciary relationship in, 257
follow-up on missed appointments in, 195, 197
independent medical judgment in, 174
informal consultations and, 177
informed consent and, 244
managed care, 173
midlevel practitioners, 138
occupational medicine and, 191
paternalistic aspect of, 140
pediatric care and, 331
physician as medical director, 281
referrals in, 190, 191
refusal of care and, 174
romantic attachments in, 218
specialists and, 188, 190
teaching programs and, 280
telemedicine, 201
telephone calls and, 165, 175
terminal illness and, 245
termination by patient, 194, 196
termination of physician in, 196
treatment recommendations and, 174
walk-in patients and, 176
Physician-player relationship, 464
Plagues, 313
Pleading, 112
Pneumocytis carinii pneumonia, 451
Police power, 4
criminal law, 39
public health and safety, 4
Police, and reporting, 331
Polio, 313
Political factors
abortion and, 357
immunization programs and, 320
Power of attorney, 470
Practitioner-patient relationship
as legal relationship, 138
Precedent case, 7
Predicate act (see Racketeering Influenced Corrupt
Organizations Act), 54
Preembryos, custody of, 368
Preemployment medical examination, 434
Preferred provider organizations (PPOs), 256
incentive plans under, 55
peer review in, 56
Pregnancy, 18
divorce during, 364
duty to counsel in, 378

high-risk, 402
midwives and, 399
minors and information on, 222
past-term, 396
refusal of care during, 242, 398
risk analysis in, 393
self-destructive behavior during, 401
testing for, 394
workplace acquired infection and, 446, 450
workplace discrimination against, 438
Prenatal care, 160
diagnostic procedures during, 382
screening programs in, 390
structure medical records in, 160
Preponderance of the evidence standard, 44
Prescription practices
development and hormonal techniques and, 466
medical students and, 278
performance enhancements in sports and, 466
state regulation of, 218, 270
telephone calls and, 175
treatment of family members and, 218
Preventive law audit, 150
Prima facie case
negligence, 15
pleading, 112
Prisons
adequacy of care in, 460
disease control in, 462
emergency care in, 462
medical research in, 462
physician in, 459
privacy and medical information in, 335
public health and, 462
Privacy of patient
abortion and, 357
consultations and, 181
contraception, sterilization, and abortion decisions
and, 345
disease control and, 314, 317, 318
police access to records and, 334
prison doctor and, 460
public health and, 311
sexual history taking and, 348
Privileges, hospital staff as creating a duty to treat, 185
Process server, 112
Product liability, 30, 323
Professional courtesy (see Medicare fraud), 50
Proof, standard of
civil law, 44
criminal law, 44

Prosecutorial discretion, 44
Protocols
    delegation of authority with, 267
    medical students and writing of, 271
    sample text for, 272
    telephone calls in pediatric care and, 168
    use of term, 270
Proxy consent, 219, 230
Psychiatrists
    medical records and, 166
    physician-patient relationship for, 45
    sexual relationships between patients and, 218
Public health, 309
    AIDS and, 325
    communicable diseases in the workplace and, 444
    costs of due process, 312
    disease control and, 312
    historical view of, 310
    Institute of Medicine study, 69
    law enforcement reporting and, 331
    legal standards for, 311
    prison doctor and, 461
    reasonable-belief standard in, 312
    school doctor and, 467, 469
    state and health care practitioners and, 138
    vital statistics in, 327
Public health laws
    coercive measures for disease control under, 318
    mandated treatment under, 207, 319
    prison doctor and, 462
Public Health Service (PHS), 223, 355
Public policy
    informed consent and, 214
    surrogacy and, 373
Pulse oximetry, 31
Punitive damages, 28, 213

Q

Quality assurance programs, 21, 269, 279
Quarantine
    disease control with, 318, 319
    precedents for, 310
    public health and, 310

R

Racketeering Influenced Corrupt Organizations Act
    (RICO), 3, 54

breach of fiduciary duty, 54
    business failure under, 57
    incentive plans under, 55
    mail and wire fraud under, 54
    patterns of racketeering under, 56
    peer review under, 56
    predicate acts, 54
    prosecution of claim under, 56
Radiologists, 188
    direct patient care, 189
    duty to inform patient, 188
    duty to inform treating physician, 188
Reasonable-belief standard (see Public health), 312
Recordkeeping, 158
    adoption and, 367
    consultations and, 188
    preventive law audit of, 150
    statutory requirements affecting, 164
Red Book, American Academy of Pediatrics, 322
Referrals, 183
    consultations differentiated from, 180
    continuing care and, 185
    duty of physician regarding, 183
    liability for, 185
    obstetric care and, 404
    patient refusal of, 185
    protocols for, 274
    school doctor and, 470
    specialists and, 190
    to institutions, 184
    to nonphysician, 183
Refusal of medical care, 242
    blood transfusions and, 222
    by adult, 233
    by parent for child, 233
    by physician, 281
    pregnancy and, 242, 398
    prisoners and, 460
    referrals and, 185
    religious grounds for, 222
    teaching institution and, 276
    termination of life-support cases and, 242
Registrations, 73
Registries
    adoption records, 367
    communicable diseases, 330
    toxic effects of chemical substances, 419
Regular course of business test for business records,
    120, 162
Regulations
    administrative law and, 66

courts enforcing, 67
federal and state laws covering, 1
licenses under, 264
medical research and, 226
prison care and, 460
Rehabilitation
and damage awards, 26
Rehabilitation Act (see Americans with Disabilities Act), 431, 446
Relationships in law, 138, 174
Release from work certification, 414
Release of medical records
authorization for, 166
occupational medicine and, 421
refusal of, 167
Religious beliefs
abortion, sterilization, and contraception counseling and, 346, 358, 379
care for minors and, 222, 233
immunization programs and, 321
refusal of medical care and, 234, 242
Remitted judgment, 126
Reporting laws
child abuse and neglect and, 188, 220, 331
consultation, 188
disease control and, 221, 311, 314, 315, 330, 460, 463, 469
law enforcement and, 331
midwives and, 400
substance abuse and, 402
violent injuries and, 333
Reports
consultation, 188
Reproduction, 368
balancing health care practitioner's and patient's rights in, 346
ethical dilemmas in, 345
medicalization of, 361
parental rights and, 365
sexual history taking and, 348
surrogacy and, 368
Requests for admissions, 114
Requests for production, 115
Res ipsa loquitur (see Negligence), 16
Residents, 274, 276
death certificates and, 330
fraud and, 276
licensing of, 276, 279
Respectable minority rule, 16
Respondeat superior, 264
Restatement of Torts 402a (see Products liability), 30

Retraining
damage awards and need for, 26
Return to work certification, 413
Review of court judgment, 126
Right to counsel, 15
Risks
birth-injured infants and, 393, 405
communicable diseases in the workplace and, 447, 450
contraception and pregnancy and, 349
factors influencing patient's tolerance of, 217
genetic counseling for, 404
HIV infection and, 352
informed consent regarding, 207, 210, 213
knowable and unknowable, 213
nature of, 448
pregnancy and, 392, 402
preventive law audit for, 150
teaching programs and management of, 278, 279
withheld information concerning, 208
RU 486 pill, 360
Rubella, 395
Rulemaking (see Administrative law), 72

S

Safe harbor regulations, 59
Scheduling system, 195
School doctor, 467
college students and, 470
comprehensive care and, 471
consent and, 468, 470
duty to patient in, 469
handicapped children and, 470
medicines at, 469
public health and, 469
school clinics and, 468
screening programs in, 470
School nurse, 466, 469
Screening
artificial insemination and, 388
neural tube defects and, 379, 390
neuromuscular development on, 170
obstetric care with, 390
preemployment medical examination and, 438
prison doctor and, 462
school doctor and, 469
tuberculosis and, 451
Searches and seizures
electronic surveillance, 43
email, 43

medical records, 43
testimony, 43
Securities law
medical research, 223
Securities and Exchange Commission, 68
Self-incrimination, 122
Service of process, 112
Severity of communicable diseases, 450
Sexual abuse, reporting of, 333
Sexual assault, 18
Sexual history, 348
Sexually transmitted diseases (STDs), 449
college students and, 471
minors and contraception counseling, 353
of minors, 221
reporting of, 221
risks for, 353
treatment of, 221, 335
Sherman Antitrust Act (see Antitrust), 52
Sickle cell trait, 388
Significant risk of substantial harm (see Americans
with Disabilities Act), 447
Smallpox, 311, 318
Society
life support system termination and, 236, 243
physician's role defined in, 138
Special education programs, 470
Specialists
emergency care and, 179
expert witness qualifications, 19
informed consent and, 212
locality rule and, 20
malpractice litigation and, 36
physician-patient relationship, 176, 190
referrals to, 183, 190
technology-oriented medicine, 34
Sperm banks, 388
Spontaneous abortions, 386
Sports medicine, 464
Spousal privilege, 152
Staff, 23
Standard of care, 16
competition and, 21
distinctions among schools concerning, 20
establishing, 19
expert witness and, 16, 21
intentional torts and, 17
legal definition of, 16
locality rule on, 20
negligence per se, 17
patient examinations and, 18

res ipsa loquitur, 16
sexual assault by health care practitioner, 18
Standard of proof, 15
civil litigation, 15
Standing orders, 271
Stark laws, 51
State courts, 3, 5
administrative regulations enforced, 74
appeals process, 6
appellate process in, 3, 8
definition of death by, 239
sovereignty of, 3
State laws, 8, 138
ability to pay and right to care under, 275
abortion and, 345
adoption and, 364, 368
autopsies under, 330
caps on lawyers' fees under, 128
collateral source rule, 29
emancipated minor under, 222
emergency care under, 17, 177, 221, 233
immunization programs and, 322, 469
informed consent under, 210, 244
legitimacy determination in, 362, 368
licensing under, 178, 268
life support system termination and, 236, 240
locality rule in, 20
medical care for minors under, 219, 220, 233
medical practice under, 266
medical records under, 165, 167
midwives under, 399
occupational medicine and, 413
parental rights and, 363, 365
physician-patient relationship, 138
power of attorney to consent to medical care under,
230, 231
prescription regulation under, 218, 270, 466
public health authority under, 311, 318
refusal of care under, 241
religious beliefs and medical care under, 233
sports and athletics under, 465
state attorneys general, 39
status of health care practitioners created by, 138
substance abuse and, 402
trial judgments under, 126
vital health statistics under, 328
worker's compensation in, 415
State taxes, 264
State, health care practitioner's relationship with, 138
Sterilization, 345, 353
federal law requirements on, 355

informed consent for, 353
minors and mentally impaired patients and, 355
Steroids, and sports, 466
Stock fraud, and medical research, 223
Strict liability (see Products liability), 30
Structured settlement of damage awards, 29
Students, 147
Subjects in medical research, 226
HHS regulations covering, 226
Subpoena, 116
subpoena duces tecum, 113, 116
Subrogation, 29
Substance abuse
medical records of treatment of, 165
minors and, 221
preemployment medical examination and, 438
pregnancy and, 401, 402
testing and reporting of, 335
Substituted consent
definition of, 234
drawbacks of, 244
Supervision, 258
consultation and, 189
of nonphysician practitioners (NPPs), 266, 268
physician-physician legal relationship in, 138
school doctor and, 467
sports and athletics and, 465
teaching institutions and, 275, 277, 279
Supreme Court, 7, 222, 230, 321, 460
abortion and, 345, 357, 359
disabilities legislation and, 446, 448, 451
federal court system, 3
parental rights and, 362, 364
peer review and, 52, 53
public health and, 310
right to counsel, 42
terminal illness and treatment and, 234, 237, 238, 244
Surgery
operation room team and, 266
Surrogate parenthood, 368
Baby M case and, 370
divorce and preembryos in, 368
parental rights and, 368
Syphilis, 326, 395

T

Take nothing judgment, 126
Tarasoff
duty to report dangerous individuals, 332

Taxation, and method of employee payment, 264
Tay-Sachs disease, 381
Teaching institutions, 275
conflicts between legal norms and medical practice in, 278
faculty physicians in, 275
medical students, residents, and fellows in, 276
patients' rights and, 275
personal knowledge test for medical records and, 121
physician-student relationship in, 280
supervision in, 274, 275
teaching protocols in, 271
Team care, 263
medical records in, 162
Team doctor, 464
children as athletes and, 465, 469
performance enhancement and, 466
physician-player relationship in, 464
role of, 464
Technology-oriented medicine, 34
Telemedicine, 197
First Amendment issues, 200
informed consent to, 202
interstate licensing, 199
physician–patient relationship, 201
practicing telemedicine, 200
telephone consultations as, 198
unethical practices, 199
Telephone calls
across state lines, 198
pediatric care and, 168
physician-patient relationship and, 175
treatment recommendations and, 175, 177
Temporary injunctions, 22
Terminal illnesses
autonomy of patients with, 245
refusal to accept treatment for, 234
withheld information about, 210
Termination of life support system, 60
Testimony
at trial, 119
laboratory ownership by physician and, 218
Testing
artificial insemination and, 388
consultations for evaluation of, 181, 186
delegation of authority to evaluate, 268
disease control and, 315, 318
for drug use, 334
for pregnancy, 394
genetic counseling with, 382, 385
HIV infection and, 348, 367

intoxication and, 333
paternity and, 363
performance enhancement drugs and, 466
specialist evaluation and, 188
The Jungle, 67
Therapeutic exception (see Informed consent), 208
Third-party payers, 138
abortion, sterilization, and contraception counseling and, 347
consultations and, 182, 186
life support system termination and, 236, 244
physician-patient relationship and, 138
teaching programs and, 279, 281
Timely entry test for business records, 121, 161
Torts
alternative dispute resolution (ADR) for, 9
intentional, 17, 265
midwives and, 400
workplace infection and, 446
Trade secrets, 427
Training, 346
midwives and, 399
occupational medicine and, 412
right to practice medicine, 258
Transcription of patient notes, 121, 163
Transmission of communicable diseases, 448
Treatment decisions, 141
alternative treatments in, 212
by physician of own family, 218
court-mandated, 207, 319, 335
fraud regulations covering, 213
incentive plans and conflicts in, 55
paternalism of physician and, 209
patient's right to refuse recommendations in, 195
physician's advisory role in, 141
protocols for, 272
telephone calls and, 168, 175
withheld information concerning, 208
Trial court
surviving, 130
Trials
adversarial system, 6
attacking defendant or plaintiff in, 130
costs of, 126
cross-examination in, 120
delays and progress of, 118, 130
discovery before, 113
focus on people in, 129
inquisitorial system, 6
judgment rendered in, 126
pleadings in, 112
preparing for, 15, 130
procedures after, 126
protecting the jury, 119
witnesses in, 122
Tuberculosis, 319
carriers of, 318
drug-resistant, 312, 320, 444
HIV infection risks in, 452
in the workplace, 437
prison doctor and, 462
screening for, 451
workplace infection with, 445, 450, 451
Twins, and fertility treatment, 386
Typhoid, 318, 445
Typhoid Mary, 314

U

Unfitness of parents, 363
Uniform Commercial Code (UCC), 13
Union rules
Americans with Disabilities Act (ADA), 436
Universities
medical research in, 223
student health programs in, 470
Upjohn case, 152
Urine testing for drugs, 466

V

Vaccinations
public health and, 311
smallpox and, 311
Vaccine Compensation Act, 323
Vasectomy, 354
Venereal disease (see Sexually transmitted diseases), 326
Vicarious liability, 264
Videotape deposition, 115
Violent injuries, reporting of, 333
Vital statistics, 327
Volunteers, and school doctor, 467

W

Waiver
college health programs and, 471
informed consent requirements and, 213
of parental rights in adoption, 364
Wards, 232
Washington Manual of Medical Therapeutics, 271

Weight loss clinics, 213
Wickline case, 259
Wire fraud, 54
Witnesses, 113, 122
    criminal defendants as, 122
    cross-examination of, 120
    establishing qualifications of, 122
    evaluating expert, 123
    expert as fact witness, 122
    expert witnesses, 122
    fact witnesses, 122
    Frye rule, 123
    hearsay rule, 120
    informed consent documented by, 230
    invoking the rule and, 119
    self-incrimination, 122

Wives
    power of attorney to consent to medical care and, 231
Workers' compensation insurance, 264
    disabled workers and, 443, 445
    occupational medicine physician and, 412, 415
    subrogation provision in, 29
Workplace (see Occupational medicine)
    communicable diseases in, 444
    disease transmission modes in, 449
    immunosuppressed workers and, 451
    screening tests in, 451
World Health Organization, 315, 322
World Medical Association, 223, 224
Wrongful birth action, 403
Wrongful life claim, 403